MAHĀMUDRĀ

The Nine Stages of Tranquility

MAHĀMUDRĀ

The Quintessence of Mind and Meditation

TAKPO TASHI NAMGYAL

Translated and annotated by
Lobsang P. Lhalungpa

Foreword by Chögyam Trungpa

MOTILAL BANARSIDASS PUBLISHERS
PRIVATE LIMITED • DELHI

First Indian Edition: Delhi, 1993
Reprint Edition : Delhi, 2001

ISBN: 81-208-1064-3 (Cloth)
ISBN: 81-208-1074-0 (Paper)

Also available at:
MOTILAL BANARSIDASS
236, 9th Main III Block, Jayanagar, Bangalore 560 011
41 U.A. Bungalow Road, Jawahar Nagar, Delhi 110 007
8 Mahalaxmi Chamber, Warden Road, Mumbai 400 026
120 Royapettah High Road, Mylapore, Chennai 600 004
Sanas Plaza, 1302 Baji Rao Road, Pune 411 002
8 Camac Street, Kolkata 700 017
Ashok Rajpath, Patna 800 004
Chowk, Varanasi 221 001

FOR SALE IN INDIA ONLY

Printed in India
BY JAINENDRA PRAKASH JAIN AT SHRI JAINENDRA PRESS,
A-45 NARAINA, PHASE-I, NEW DELHI 110 028
AND PUBLISHED BY NARENDRA PRAKASH JAIN FOR
MOTILAL BANARSIDASS PUBLISHERS PRIVATE LIMITED,
BUNGALOW ROAD, DELHI 110 007

Contents

Foreword

I am so delighted that this text is being published in the English language. It will greatly benefit English-speaking students of Buddhism. I myself have used this text in working with my students, and I have always found that it communicates, clearly and simply, the mahāmudrā teachings of the Practice Lineage. I am very pleased that now English-speaking students can read and study this book in their own language.

The term *mahāmudrā* in Sanskrit or *chaggya chenpo* (phyag rgya chen po) in Tibetan literally means "the great symbol." Mahāmudrā refers to an actual experience of realization that we ourselves might have. As this text makes very clear, the ground of mahāmudrā is experienced in the sitting practice of meditation. So although mahāmudrā is very deep and profound, it can only be realized through the direct and simple practice of śamatha and vipaśyanā meditation.

The precision and accuracy of meditation allow us to rest in our natural state of being, and out of that we are able to realize that hopes and fears and emotions of all kinds no longer need be regarded as obstacles or highlights. In meditation practice, there is always some sense of going and not going, some process of thinking and not thinking taking place. Nonetheless, beyond that process of thinking and not thinking, there is some basis of nonthought, nonconceptualization. No matter how confused we might be, there is a dancing ground of experience that is common to everyone. Another way of saying this is that, although the nature of saṃsāra is like a water wheel that turns around and around, constantly creating actions that produce later effects, nonetheless there is a basic state of mind that is clear and pure and natural. The realization of that basic state of mind is what is known as mahāmudrā.

The English edition of this text is titled simply *Mahāmudrā*. In Tibetan this work is usually referred to as *Moonbeams of Mahāmudrā* (*Chakchen dawai özer*). The moon is the brightest source of light at night, and it is the light from the moon that illuminates the darkness. We are so grateful to Dagpo Tashi Namgyal for having written this book to illuminate the darkness of beings suffering in saṃsāra. We are also thankful to the translator and the publisher for bringing this light of wisdom into the Western world. May it benefit countless multitudes of beings.

With blessings,

Vidyādhara the Venerable Chögyam Trungpa, Rinpoche
Boulder, Colorado
7 March 1986

Preface

Mahāmudrā: The Quintessence of Mind and Meditation was translated from 1976 to 1977. The finalization was done in stages, from 1981 to 1983, in between my other work. I paid special attention to the careful checking of the entire translation and editorial work, to the preparation of footnotes, to the bibliography of the Sanskrit and Tibetan titles of the Tibetan texts quoted in this treatise, and to the index.

For many years I have devoted myself to the translation of Tibetan literature—both secular and religious—into English, but have delayed publishing my translations of Buddhist texts in order to ensure their complete accuracy. None of us in the tradition has any illusions about being able to achieve the same high standard of writing and translating as that of the learned and enlightened Lama-Lotsavas of ancient Tibet, who translated Buddhist works from many other languages. Besides, the conditions for serious translators are not favorable in these modern times. Yet a series of significant events in my life finally brought about the translation of this great esoteric text.

Since 1959, when many thousands of Tibetans escaped to India and other neighboring countries, I had been asked to translate Buddhist texts by the highest authority within our tradition and by many of my Lamas. In 1969 the late Venerable Dukchen Thuksay Rinpoche, renowned master of the Drukpa Kagyü Order, presented me with a xylographed print of a Tibetan text during an assembly at Sangngak Chöling Monastery in Darjeeling (India). While blessing me, Rinpoche, in his gentle voice, said: "This is the most important sacred text! I urge you to translate it." When I opened the book and read the title, I was deeply moved. Here was the *Mahāmudrā* text, one of the great Buddhist classics that I had already been studying.

A few years later, His Holiness Karmapa Rigpe Dorje, the Sixteenth Karmapa, presented me with seven great commentaries on the sutric and tantric teachings. He also handed me a certificate bearing his seal that assigned me the task of translating these texts. On the list of titles this *Mahāmudrā* text was especially marked for translation.

Finally, during a visit to New York in 1975, Dr. C. T. Shen, president of the Institute for Advanced Studies of World Religions at Stonybrook, offered me a contract for translating the same *Mahāmudrā* text. Dr. Shen also invited the Venerable Dezhung Rinpoche to be adviser for this project.

In addition to his generous financial support, Dr. Shen provided us with a lovely, quiet residence on his Long Island estate of Bodhifield. Throughout our two-year stay there, both Dr. and Mrs. Shen extended to us every possible courtesy and assistance. I personally and all of us in the Dharma are indeed deeply indebted to Dr. Shen, especially since his sponsorship represents only one of his many invaluable projects for the advancement of Buddhism. I here also express my deep respect and appreciation to the Venerable Dezhung Rinpoche, a great eclectic Lama and a teacher of the Sakyapa Order, for his advice and explanations of the difficult passages found in this text and in the many other texts I read.

My sincere appreciation and thanks are due to my family for their encouragement and support: to my wife, Gisela Minke, for having enthusiastically and tirelessly typed and checked the English; to my son Samphe Dorje for his invaluable help in editing the first part of the translation; and to my younger son, Nawang Tenzin, for providing me with much practical help.

I wish to acknowledge with deep appreciation the advice and assistance given by a number of individuals: first and foremost my dear friends Mary Ann and Lawrence Tucker, who have consistently encouraged and supported me; my friend Ani Tsering Chodon (Martha Hamilton) for checking and typing the bilingual bibliography of the titles quoted in *Mahāmudrā*; the Venerable Chögyam Trungpa, Rinpoche, Dr. Herbert V. Guenther, and Dr. Garma C. C. Chang for reading my list of Buddhist technical terms in English and Tibetan; and as my friends Gene Smith, Hannah Robinson, Dr. Gloria Count–van Manen, and Elizabeth Dale for having read parts of the translation and for having encouraged me.

My sincere appreciation and thanks also go to the staff of the Institute for Advanced Studies of World Religions at Stonybrook, Long Island, for making available to me many Tibetan texts and for allowing me to use the facilities of the institute.

I want to express special thanks to those institutions and individuals who have provided me with some of the funds required for the finalization. The major part of this expense and much voluntary assistance came from my own family. I am very grateful to Buddhayana Foundation in Massachusetts, to the Marsden Foundation in New York, and to Mr. Michael Wurmbrand for providing me with part of the funding.

Last but not least, I am very grateful indeed to my publisher, Mr. Samuel Bercholz, who took a personal interest in this publication.

The xylographed text of *Mahāmudrā* used in this translation was printed on handmade Tibetan paper from carved woodblocks that had been preserved at Sri Neuthang of Gyal, in Dingri, western Tibet, until the "cultural revolution." The folio numbers of this text appear in the left-hand margins of the English translation.

Since this text is an original Tibetan composition and contains numerous terms of distinct Tibetan character, I have included a limited list of Sanskrit equivalents.

The Tibetan script (which was adapted from an ancient Indian script) employs many silent letters. The recent practice of literally transcribing Tibetan words seems only to confuse foreign readers. I myself was surprised and amused when I first read my name in English as "bLobzang Phunt-shogs." In this text I have deliberately adhered to the more practical phonetic rendering, which facilitates smooth reading.

Unfortunately, owing to certain pressures, a bilingual index could not be included at this time. And if the terms *Bodhisattvas*, *Arahats*, and *Buddhas* (not referring to the historical Buddha) are not capitalized in the text, this is according to the wishes of the publisher.

Despite my dedicated efforts, there could still be errors and inaccuracies in this translation. If so, I sincerely apologize for these shortcomings.

I must confess that in both the translation and in my introduction I have addressed myself mainly to practicing Buddhists and only partly to the general readership. It is my sincere wish that this great text may serve practicing Buddhists as an illuminating guide while conveying the Buddha's message of universal enlightenment, thus fulfilling the noble goal of the sponsor and of all others directly involved with this effort.

May this translation also be regarded as one of the worthy memorials in honor of over one million Tibetan Buddhists killed in Tibet during the last three decades.

Lobsang P. Lhalungpa
McLean, Virginia
May 1986

Translator's Introduction

Mahāmudrā: The Quintessence of Mind and Meditation represents the advanced doctrine and practice as understood and realized by the Kagyüpa Order of Tibetan Buddhism.

The original Tibetan title of this sixteenth-century text is *Ngedon chakgya chenpoi gomrim seyvarjepai lekshey dawaiozer*, which reads literally as "Moonlight: An Excellent Elucidation of the Meditational Stages of the Ultimate Great Seal." The term "great seal" (mahāmudrā) contains many different meanings. Here it stands for the ultimate nature of mind and reality. Just as a royal seal wields unchallengeable authority, so the all-encompassing voidness of the ultimate reality prevails upon the cosmic phenomena. It also stands for the path of self-realization, which integrates authentic vision, contemplation, and action into one perfect insight.

This extraordinary treatise provides not only a wealth of knowledge but also methods for realizing enlightenment. In writing this work the great Tibetan teacher Tashi Namgyal (1512–1587) made known many of the ancient secret oral teachings and published them as xylographic prints. Among other well-known treatises by the author are *The Resplendent Jewel: An Elucidation of the Buddhist Tantra* and *The Sunlight: An Elucidation of Hevajra-tantra.* In the course of his extensive studies and training Tashi Namgyal studied with some Sakyapa teachers and even acted as the abbot of Nālandā Sakyapa Monastery, north of Lhasa. During his later years he functioned as Gampopa's regent and as chief abbot of the monastery of Dakla Gampo, in South Tibet.

The *Mahāmudrā* is neither a students' manual nor a self-explanatory book. Like other great Buddhist treatises it is studied under the guidance of a chosen teacher. The need for a tutor becomes apparent when one considers the magnitude of this very esoteric work, the profundity of the subject, its complex structure, its conceptual subtlety, and its technical intricacy. Among the problems untutored students would encounter are a certain (deliberate) vagueness, enigmatic quotations, allusions, and even some apparent contradictions.

This great Tibetan classic, which is widely recognized as an outstanding original work, reveals profound wisdom. The text draws systematically on the vital knowledge and the practical methods of the Buddhist sciences that form the major part of the monastic syllabus. From the sacred law (vinaya) comes the tenet of self-control, the conquest and transformation of the mind. From the essential aspects of logic (pramāṇa) come the methods of determining the nature of reality. From the psychological branch of the sublime doctrine (abhidharma) come the methods of identifying and eliminating the root of self-delusion. From the tenets of the Buddha's transcendental wisdom (prajñāpāramitā) come the ways of achieving insight into the universal voidness (sarvadharma-śūnyatā) as the ultimate state. From the Mahāyāna system of self-realization comes the essential practice known as (the twin principles of) transcendental wisdom and infinite compassion. From this ideal emanate the psychological methods for reorienting self-centeredness to a definite concern and compassion for others. From the Buddhist tantric doctrine come the methods of transforming inner delusion and its manifestations into aspects of transcendental wisdom. The distinct mahāmudrā meditation will then reveal the ways of achieving instantaneous insight into the innate perfection of every perception or thought.

The entire text is divided into two parts. The first part contains the principles and practices of tranquility and insight meditation according to the Hīnayāna (Little Vehicle) and Mahāyāna (Great Vehicle) systems. The second part contains the advanced meditational system according to Mahāyāna followed by the higher system of mahāmudrā (the great seal).

The intricate structure of this text is divided into many segments, which may appear confusing to those outside the Tibetan tradition, but it does not obscure the textual sequence or the thematic coherence. The divisions are designed to help teachers explain the text systematically and to enable the students to comprehend the complex doctrine and practice.

The elucidation is written in classical Tibetan prose and is illustrated by innumerable quotations, all drawn from the Buddha's sūtras and tantras, from the exegetical treatises (śāstras) of the ancient Buddhist masters, and their mystical poems (dohās).

Before the actual text begins, there is the traditional homage by the author, Tashi Namgyal, to the lineage of the mahāmudrā transmission: to his personal guru (without name), to the Indestructible Mind (vajramana), and to the Buddha in his ultimate state (dharmakāya) and in his earthly manifestation (nirmāṇakāya). The principal masters duly venerated here are Saraha, Nāgārjuna, Marpa, Milarepa, and Gampopa (all of the Kagyüpa order). The author especially honors Gampopa as the second buddha and the expounder of this unique mahāmudrā system.

The text begins with a description of the two distinct insights and approaches originating from the Buddha's teachings of the sūtras and tantras, that is, the common path of gradual self-realization and the uncommon path of instantaneous self-realization. The stages of the mahāmudrā meditation embody these two paths systematically and coherently. The fundamental and advanced sutric meditations on tranquility and insight represent the gradual path, while the actual mahamudric tradition represents the instantaneous path. The sutric meditations on the gradual path form the foundation, while the mahāmudrā meditation represents the nonmystical, direct approach. However, mahāmudrā meditation does not employ tantric methods per se. Even though the Buddhist tantra is looked upon as the rapid path of self-realization, it is generally considered to be an essential element of the gradual path.

THE FOUNDATION OF BUDDHIST STUDIES

I am here incorporating a description of the fundamental religious training required of trainees before they start the mahāmudrā meditation, in order to provide a complete panorama of Tibetan Buddhist practice. Such training generally consists of the study of both the fundamental and advanced sūtras and tantras. This can be achieved by taking either a comprehensive or a selective course in such traditional subjects as the moral canon (vinaya), logic (pramāṇa), the central philosophy (madhyamaka), the sciences of mind and materiality (abhidharma), and transcendental wisdom (prajñāpāramitā). Some of the Tibetan orders such as the Kagyüpa prefer to specify these courses in terms of thirteen main treatises. These texts are studied and tested daily in the form of debates. Individual students alternately take the role of challenger and defender. Each defender is questioned by a number of challengers on a one-by-one basis. Instructors, scholars, and abbots witness the debates, especially during the major and minor public examinations. Among the topics chosen by individuals outside their formal courses could be Sanskritic semantics, linguistics, and philology, the Tibetan poetics and prose composition, astrology, astronomy, holistic medicine, arts, architecture, and crafts.

One who cannot devote years to such comprehensive studies might take a condensed course. This could be done by studying either the broad outlines of certain texts or abridged versions of them. For every Buddhist order there is a popular and practical text that explains, in simpler language, the general teachings and which is studied by every meditator, student, and scholar. For the Kagyüpa practitioners there is Gampopa's renowned text *The Jewel Ornament of Liberation*.

The selective course consists of texts on sutric and tantric doctrines. Here individuals may choose some of the concise doctrinal treatises and meditational guides.

Buddhist studies represent a complete process of human and intellectual development as illustrated by the following maxim: "Self-control, wisdom, and compassion are achieved only through listening, examining, and meditating." The test of the training should be an immediate spiritual maturity resulting from the taming of the worldly mind through the elimination of some basic malaise like selfishness, greed, or hatred; a deepening insight into the true reality; and a growing concern for the well-being of others.

In the Buddhist tradition, scholarship is only a means to an end. Buddhism combines rationality and faith, knowledge and inner awakening, as a way to spiritual attainment. Knowledge is acquired through years of Buddhist textual studies and debates, awakening through consistent meditational practices.

A trainee will begin by seeking the oral transmission of a chosen text from a teacher. This is regarded as a significant event, as the teacher bestows on him the energy-stream of the sacred words, along with the blessings of the lineage, both of which he himself received from his teachers. This empowers the student for tutorial studies. He will then receive the oral elucidation of the text, which may take weeks or months. There are various forms of explaining the texts: a simple literal explanation (tsigtri), a full (interpretative) explanation (dontri), and an experiential elucidation (nyamtri or martri) based on the teacher's personal experience. The most important of all is the elucidation on each successive stage, which requires the student to meditate for a period of time and to then relate his experience to the teacher. This leads to regular discussions with the teacher in respect to the practice, its problems, and its progress. All the various orders of Tibetan Buddhism practice these oral transmissions.

This text presupposes that the trainee already has a good understanding of the gradual path to enlightenment as the essential religious foundation.

The Contemplative Foundation

The following will show how the student completes the entire contemplative course according to the tradition of the gradual path. The whole course is divided into three practices for "three types of spiritual aspirants": primary, average, and advanced. In the course of these practices the student develops a right view, right contemplation, and right actions. These practical principles represent wisdom, tranquility, and discipline. He learns how to harmonize his contemplative experience with his active life—how, for instance, to inspire and invigorate his daily life with contemplative insight and tranquility.

The student starts out by emulating a model of a "lesser spiritual aspirant." He appraises life with all its innate miseries. By examining the potential of his body and mind, he then recognizes them to be precious vehicles for reaching an ever-higher spiritual attainment. Next, he focuses on life's impermanence and fragility and resolves that the selfish pursuit of material goals creates continuous negative karma with all its inevitable consequences for the here and hereafter.

He takes control over his own destiny by reorienting his life toward more meaningful pursuits and nobler goals and commitments, following the Buddha's words: "Spiritual sons, I have shown you the way to liberation. Understand that its achievement will depend on you!"

Devoting himself to right thought, speech, action, and livelihood, he consciously avoids violence of any kind. He looks upon the Three Precious Jewels as the refuge from existential miseries. This means that in his daily practice he reverentially invokes the blessings of Buddha, as the teacher; the sacred doctrine, as the path to liberation; and the enlightened lineage, as inspiration and support.

As a result of this practice the student should accomplish the level of refinement, discrimination, and faith (in causality) of a "lesser aspirant."

The student now moves on to the second level of training, that of an "average aspirant." Here he inculcates the spiritual motivation to achieve personal liberation (prātimokṣa) from the turbulent ocean of samsāra. He contemplates the Four Noble Truths: all existence is misery; the cause of misery is self-delusion; the elimination of these is possible; it is accomplished through the Path. The student devotes himself to the practical application of these by cultivating superior morality, contemplation, and wisdom in order to eliminate his existential miseries and their psychological causes. By developing a yearning for personal enlightenment, he conducts himself in accordance with a complex code of ethics. Then, with ever-present mindfulness and vigilance, he shields his whole stream-consciousness from selfish worldly ambitions and harmful thoughts and emotions, while at the same time developing faith, honesty, tolerance, forbearance, and kindness. The moral purity achieved through this effort is a dependable foundation for contemplation. It is said that a person of enduring mindfulness and self-control will make a good meditator. The main purpose of this fundamental spiritual training is the taming of the mind and all its forces. Therefore, the test of the student's immediate attainment must necessarily be seen in his morality, calmness, sensitivity, and insight. This inner transformation is marked by a new awakening into the "voidness" (nonselfhood) of his stream of consciousness.

Having familiarized himself with the principles, techniques, and procedures, as well as with the oral instructions, the student now devotes himself to the mastery of the superior contemplation. He first works toward a concentrated tranquility and then toward a deeper insight. He will discover that such a state with its wonderful ease, ecstasy, clarity, and nonduality effectively pacifies all inner disquiet and afflictions. Yet the tranquility by itself does not completely eliminate the hidden psychological causes. Like a clear mirror, contemplative tranquility offers a perfect condition for penetrating analysis—one of the vital factors in insight meditation. Only perfect insight (in meditation) can bring about an awakened wisdom that perceives the falsity of the centralized self (or ego-entity) and at the same time the truth of the nonselfhood of personality as being the valid nature of man's stream-consciousness.

The main purpose of this training is the development of superior wisdom. Liberation from inner delusions and their resulting miseries is achieved only by means of transcendental wisdom. This transcendental wisdom comes about through the perfection of insight meditation. Whereas listening, reading, and absorbing bring about the conceptual knowledge, critical examination produces a determined vision of reality. And even though this discrimination contains inherent limitations, such "worldly" wisdom nonetheless serves as an avenue to deeper insight. The great Buddhist master Nāgārjuna expressed it in these words: "One cannot realize the ultimate reality without relying on conceptual knowledge; one cannot realize nirvanic enlightenment without realizing the ultimate reality."

The student is now prepared to embark upon the third level of training, that of the advanced aspirant, by accepting the bodhisattva precept known as bodhicitta (enlightened attitude) from a chosen master who embodies the essence of this unique spiritual discipline. The bodhicitta encompasses all aspects of the Mahāyāna path from a perfect motivation and endeavor for universal enlightenment to a development of compassion and wisdom and finally to enlightenment (which is the ultimate bodhicitta).

The practical bodhicitta requires the mastery of the twin principles of enlightenment (skillful means and discerning wisdom). The devotee as an aspiring bodhisattva inculcates kindness and compassion and in the process practices generosity, altruism, tolerance, striving, and inner quiet. In order to complete the enlightenment process he develops his intellectual power to its transcendental level, for wisdom opens up a revolutionary insight into the ultimate state (voidness) of mind and reality, on the one hand, and encompasses the wider dimension of reality—i.e. the imperceptible unity of the material and mental phenomena and, indeed, the inseparability of existence and enlightenment (saṃsāra and nirvāṇa).

The significance of the all-encompassing bodhicitta must be clearly understood: one cannot achieve enlightenment without bodhicitta! This path—from the progressive nurturing of bodhicitta to its realization—is the path of the bodhisattva, popularly called in Tibetan "the way of the warrior," since a practicing bodhisattva conquers formidable enemies—his egoistic delusion and all its forces—and then seeks to liberate others enslaved by similar adversaries. The test for such a practitioner lies simply in his character and capacity to embody the wisdom/compassion ideal and to manifest it in all his thoughts and actions. This religious training will be greatly strengthened if the student, as practicing bodhisattva, pursues the Diamond Vehicle of the Buddhist tantra.

In summary: all students are required to apply the Buddha's middle path in their life, that is, in their ethical conduct. This means avoiding the two extreme modes of living: uncontrolled sensuality and self-abnegation. In their metaphysical orientation it means steering clear of the two conflicting views of reality: the absolute substance (or self) and materialistic nihilism. In terms of meditation the middle path means elimination of the two extreme defects: dullness and sensory incitement.

TRANQUILITY AND INSIGHT: THE BASIC STAGE OF MAHĀMUDRĀ MEDITATION

Building the aforementioned foundation will qualify a trainee for the meditational stages of mahāmudrā. I shall give a short description of the meditation on tranquility and insight. (If my comments seem repetitive it is because the text deals with the subject of tranquility and insight in both Part I and Part II, but in different contexts.) The trainee usually begins with the common sutric meditation on tranquility and insight, which forms the basis for the mahāmudrā meditation. Only the mastery of these two distinct aspects of the sutric meditation will enable a regular meditator to fully experience and appreciate the mahāmudrā meditation. They are first mastered separately and then jointly so that the meditator can then practice the contemplative absorption, also called "tranquil equipoise," which represents the true meditation. Tranquility and insight encompass all forms of the Buddhist meditation. Even though tranquility is naturally quietening and insight analytical, the two not only complement each other but also blend harmoniously during each session, eventually culminating in the abovementioned state. The significance of the two was emphasized by Buddha when he said: "All meditators should consistently dwell in tranquility and insight, because all forms of meditation are embodied in these."

This text first provides detailed guidelines on how to master the concentrated tranquility. They deal with the fostering of the right attitude, the right motivation, the application of the principles and methods. The text elucidates the ways of maintaining the concentration—detecting, differentiating, and eliminating the defects, and enhancing the progress toward self-realization. Good results are achieved by developing a universal perspective, a skillful approach, and consistent application. The meditator's self-appraisal of his progress or deterioration is an integral part of his training.

His rational view of life and reality, inculcated through these studies, is examined, tested, and then absorbed into a contemplative equipoise. Also, his meditative calmness and clarity are integrated into his daily life. The meditator will experience a progressive dawning of enlightenment in proportion to his elimination of the psychological causes of the existential miseries and to his achieving the transcendental qualities that constitute a perfect enlightenment (sambodhi).

The practical elements that are designed to direct his meditation as well as his life are called the Three Excellences. The first, the "excellence in the beginning" (of the meditation), refers to an engendering of an attitude motivated by the yearning for the well-being and enlightenment of others. The second, the "excellence in the middle," means the reorienting of one's meditational state to its transcendental aspect by transmuting the meditation into a nonconceptual awareness. The third, the "excellence at the end," refers to the sharing of the meditator's spiritual merits with others through a genuine dedication.

Meditation on Tranquility

Enlightenment is achieved by means of transcendental wisdom (prajñā), which in turn arises from the joint mastery of tranquility (śamatha) and insight (vipaśyanā). "Insight" here means two interdependent aspects: the process and the result. The process is the analysis, while the result is a deeper vision of reality. Yet it must be pointed out that such insight cannot emerge without the essential support of inner purity, calmness, and clarity, all of which are intimately connected with the meditation on tranquility. "Tranquility" means a quietude of body and mind. A special quality that this tranquility contains is "perfect ease," which turns body and mind into a tractable and efficient spiritual vehicle. The other terms currently used in the English language for meditative tranquility are "concentration," "one-pointedness," "quietude," and "calm abiding." Like every self-realization process, this tranquility also has several levels of its own—a worldly, a superworldly, and a transcendental level—all of which can be reached by meditators.

The basic level, known as "approximate tranquility," represents the human "plane of desire" (kāma-dhātu). This can be reached through the "nine levels of (worldly) tranquility." Tranquility on the superworldly level refers to the "eight contemplative absorptions," which correspond to the celestial "plane of fine form" and the "formless plane" (rūpa-dhātu and arūpa-dhātu). Tranquility on the transcendental level is realized in the preparatory stage of "arhathood."

A beginner should first learn how to practice and maintain the tranquility representing the worldly level. He can start by concentrating on a chosen object, either concrete or visualized. This is a mental state of calmness. To a meditator, "tranquility" should mean a perfectly concentrated state. It contains two intrinsic qualities: stability and clarity. The two are present in what the tradition calls "one-pointed mental focus." While concentrating in this manner, one relies upon the vital force of "mindfulness." Such concentrated tranquility is aptly described by the incomparable Tsongkhapa (1357–1415), the founder of the Gelukpa order of Tibetan Buddhism: "Concentration is a king who commands the mind. If settled, it remains immobile, like Mount Sumeru; if projected, it permeates all images of virtue. It creates a perfect ease, which makes body and mind tractable."

The Role of Mindfulness

There can be no concentration without mindfulness, for mindfulness infuses the concentrated state with the vital energy. Supported by self-control, mindfulness will then command all aspects of one's life, both contemplative and active. If the meditator concentrates one-pointedly in his tranquil meditation, he is bound to achieve calmness, for this concentration integrates the fragmented inner forces in a natural way. The success or failure of the meditation is largely caused by the presence or absence of mindfulness.

Mindfulness is by nature a neutral force, and as such it can be turned into either a positive or a negative element. The meditator must therefore know how to manage and direct it. In his daily life he must turn its neutral or negative aspect into a positive one.

During the early stage one may find that the concentration is weak because one's mindfulness is unsteady as a consequence of the restless mind. With the help of self-control and dedication, one's mindfulness will become more steady and will act as "guardian" of the concentrated state. It will then instantly detect and determine any emerging distraction. This process can be compared to that of an experienced fisherman whose watchfulness and unalertness help him detect a fish instantly. The mindfulness itself will undergo transformation until it finally becomes the transcendental awareness.

The Periodical Vigilance

The act of detecting and removing a distraction is called sheyzhin (vigilance). The text spells out suitable remedies for distractions. The latter are grouped into two separate categories: senses and thoughts (either good, bad, or neutral) represent the "ebullient distractions," while sullenness, lethargy, drowsiness, and torpor are classified as diverse forms of "creeping distractions." An ebullient distraction is caused by one's indulgence in sensuality or passion, by excitement, hatred, nervous tension, or stress. A creeping distraction is brought on by physical weakness, overrelaxation, laziness, insolence, stupidity, or frustration. A subtle dullness may emerge almost imperceptibly through a sensation of ecstasy. This problem crops up during a stable concentration. It produces sensations of ease and ecstasy, which in turn relax the mind and dull the clarity of the concentration. It is like getting intoxicated and losing the sharpness of the senses.

In addition to prescribing suitable remedies for any major or minor distraction, the text enumerates sets of methods for removing these obstacles and enhancing each meditational state. These are categorized as the eight points of progress, the six powerful methods, the four mental applications, and the nine stages of tranquility.

The Nine Stages of Tranquility

The study of a painted scroll or sketch depicting the nine stages of tranquility will vivify the intricate process of mastering this concentrated tranquility. The frontispiece of this book illustrates step by step how the problems are resolved, how a meditator's mindfulness is stabilized and vivified and his concentration strengthened until eventually he achieves the ideal tranquility (in the ninth stage).

The temple in the thangka painting indicates the need, at least during the early training, for serene solitude. The monk represents the meditator and symbolizes his detachment from worldly pursuits. The winding path signifies the nine stages of tranquility.

The first and lowest stage is symbolized by the monk trailing an elephant and a monkey. At this stage the meditator usually finds it hard to concentrate on a chosen image. He discovers that his inner world is overcome by the restless senses, thoughts, or passive dullness. These three powerful distractions continuously toss off his concentration like a little boat in a turbulent river and obscure it like a path shrouded in darkness. The gray monkey represents the restless mind and the gray elephant the heavy dullness. These conditions are typical of worldly minds. The image of the monk holding an ax and a rope indicates the need for self-control and mindfulness in the early stages of settling the mind. The flame along the first six stages represents vigilance. This is the dynamic aspect of mindfulness. While mindfulness watches attentively over the mental focus of the concentration, its vigilance detects any emergence of distraction—in either its crude or subtle forms—with agility and sharpness.

The second stage shows some progress in the monk's endeavor to concentrate, as indicated by the white patch on both the monkey and the elephant. This limited progress means that the meditator is now able to achieve a concentrated focus every few moments to be interrupted again by a forceful distraction. This condition is like that of a flag that alternately flutters and stops, depending on the movement of the air.

The third and fourth levels show the monk making slow but steady progress by clearing the restlessness and dullness that alternately interfere with his concentration. The image of the monk roping the animals indicates his steady mindfulness and vigilance at these stages. But the sudden appearance of a gray rabbit on the elephant's back indicates the emergence of a "subtle dullness." This is a mixed blessing. While the concentrated tranquility gradually stabilizes itself, it also produces an inner ease and ecstasy. This natural sensation imperceptibly lures the mind into a sullen state, robbing the mindfulness of its sharp focus. However, the white patch on the rabbit indicates the steadiness of the concentrated tranquility. This means fewer restless events at these stages.

The fifth and sixth stages show the monk achieving greater tranquility, as indicated by the animals' widening white spots. The sixth and seventh stage show the monk achieving even greater—and irreversible—progress in perfecting his tranquility and removing distractions, as illustrated by the rapidly whitening bodies of the animals. The eighth stage shows the near-perfect tranquility, as symbolized by the virtually white elephant and monkey.

The ninth stage shows the monk in solitude, absorbed in the "approximate tranquility," as indicated by the equally restful white elephant. The approximate tranquility represents the serenity associated with the "human plane of desire." Mastery of the approximate tranquility will lead to the next stages, the superworldly and transcendental states.

The top of the thangka shows two monks riding on white elephants on two bands of multicolored rays of light, representing the two higher contemplative, superworldly levels. One of the levels, with its four states, corresponds to the natural consciousness on the refined plane of form, while the other, with its four states, corresponds to the formless plane (i.e., the two planes are within the existential realm). The sword in the monk's hand symbolizes the sword of ultimate knowledge, which cuts through self-delusion. The monk soaring through the sky represents the preparatory and actual meditative absorption achieved by seekers of personal enlightenment (arhats).

The test of a meditator's immediate achievement should be discernible through his ability to maintain the concentrated tranquility unperturbed for any given time.

MEDITATION ON INSIGHT (INTO THE TRUE REALITY)

The text covers various aspects of the meditation on insight ranging from its definition, categories, nature, role, and purpose to the doctrinal concepts of mind and reality, the interpretations, methods of investigation, the contemplative absorption, and the progressive realization of transcendental insight.

The insight meditation consists of three aspects: dynamic analysis, contemplative absorption, and the postabsorptive views of the illusory reality. Insight meditation basically means analytical investigation that provides the key to understanding the true nature of reality. This is why the Tibetan tradition calls it the "superior seeing." The early phase of the insight meditation consists of the intellectual investigation of what constitutes the true or false reality. The "insight" as dynamic analysis cannot be meaningful without a stable inner tranquility. The reestablishing of tranquility before an insightful analysis will pacify not merely any residual disquiet but will effectively guard the concentrated investigation against any distractions. Besides, an analysis conducted without the essential calmness and clarity will activate an inner disquiet. Without this exhaustive process, the mere analytical determination of one's psychoneurotic problems can neither touch the root nor bring about a reliable solution.

To understand the insight meditation, one has to look at the nature and level of wisdom. Insight, as the authentic vision of reality, deepens in proportion to the expansion of wisdom. Insight and wisdom are thus inseparable, like a mirror and its reflecting clarity. Indeed, "insight" in the Buddhist tradition means the wisdom's vision or the way of seeing things.

If one cannot achieve an insight into the nature of reality without first developing wisdom, what role does wisdom play in bringing about true insight? Wisdom plays an indispensable and consistent role throughout the training and the stages of enlightenment. Wisdom as a discriminating faculty guides the meditator on his path to the highest reality. As a powerful psychological weapon, it destroys the inner delusions; as a supreme vision, it uncovers the hidden mystery of reality; and as a voice of truth, it affirms the inherent unity of all things. As the incomparable Tsongkhapa said:

> Wisdom is the eye that looks at the profound nature of reality;
> It is the means to cut the root of saṃsāra.
> An inexhaustible source of qualities praised in the scriptures,
> It is renowned as the brilliant light that illuminates the darkness of delusion.

A meditator's immediate purpose is to develop transcendental wisdom progressively through the rational and contemplative processes. He will first develop a "rational intellect," which the tradition refers to as "intellectual wisdom" (thopai sherab). This is done through the study of the Buddhist doctrine, under some highly attained teachers, and the understanding of definitive terms and conceptual meanings. He will then seek a refined intellect referred to as "discriminating wisdom" (sampai sherab) by examining—among others—the doctrinal views of existence, its causes, the ways of resolving the fundamental problems, and the realization of inner freedom. Again the close guidance of the teacher and his vital oral instructions play an important role. The combination of intellectual and discriminating wisdom represents the "worldly wisdom."

This worldly wisdom can also arise through the basic sutric meditation. The four concentrated states bring forth the insight into the refined nature of the psychophysical realm as manifested in the sensations of joy, bliss, lucidity, and the even state. The other contemplative source of worldly wisdom is that of the "four equalizing quietudes," in which an ever-subtler vision of one's stream-consciousness arises. This vision perceives the consciousness as being first an infinite space, then an infinite consciousness, then as nonexistent, and finally as neither existent nor nonexistent.

These worldly wisdoms cannot, however, penetrate the imperceptible aspect of reality, since the latter's inconceivable nature remains hidden behind the deceptive appearance. Therefore, these wisdoms are incapable of eradicating the psychological root of life's miseries and misconceptions.

Only the "contemplative wisdom" can penetrate the hidden mystery of the ultimate reality, for it contains a revolutionary vision that exposes the false nature of the perceived reality and leads to the vision of nondualism. Such nondualism may generally be characterized as "relative" or "interdependent" reality, which contains the inherent union of its imperceptible simplicity (voidness) and dynamic appearance. The false nature is understood to be "merely an illusory appearance," completely devoid of an inherent substance. Yet its intriguing dynamism springs from the creative interaction between its natural causes and conditions.

Once the meditator masters the insight meditation and then harmonizes its determinate awareness with the tranquil equipoise (samādhi), he will make steady progress toward contemplative wisdom. His extraordinary experience of directly perceiving the true nature of nondual reality still remains on the level of worldly achievements. However, the moment he achieves the "dawning of the first stage of enlightenment," his contemplative wisdom reaches its transcendental state.

At this stage the meditator is capable of perceiving the intimate link between the two aspects of reality, despite the apparent contradictions they contain. Such a contemplative wisdom, nurtured through tranquil equipoise and the postequipoisal discernment, will lead to the eventual realization of transcendental wisdom (prajñāpāramitā). Transcendental wisdom is the completion of the intellectual expansion that, in the Buddhist tradition, is often compared to the full moon.

Every meditator follows a specific approach to his investigation of the mind and reality, as elucidated and interpreted by a particular school. A Kagyüpa meditator follows the School of Valid Empiricism (svatantra madhyamika), while others, notably the Gelukpa meditators, follow the School of Rational Reductionism (prasangika madhyamika). Generally, all Tibetan meditators adhere to the common doctrine of the middle path, as enjoined by Buddha: "O monks, to view things as existent is one extreme, and to view them as nothing is another extreme." A meditator then seeks to attain a still higher vision of reality, namely the expanse of nonconceptual awareness, as urged by Buddha: "A wise devotee does not dwell on the middle path either." The "extreme" views were those dualistic tenets advanced by some ancient (non-Buddhist) dogmas. Buddhism treats dualism of any kind as the "thesis" and refutes it as being inherently contradictory while upholding nondualism as the "antithesis" that can stand up to any test. Since these two metaphysical standpoints are diametrically opposed to each other, the question of synthesizing them does not arise. In order to establish the validity of the nondualistic reality, Buddhism propounds the concept of "two truths," the conventional and the absolute. The two naturally encompass the two aspects of reality as interdependent and mutually compatible.

"Apparent truth" refers to the appearances of the mind and the material phenomena. This means that every visible or perceivable reality appears as "real" to deluded minds but as "unreal" to enlightened ones. "Absolute truth" refers to the primordial simplicity that the tradition calls "inherent voidness." It represents the ultimate reality of mind and materiality. The concept of voidness is very hard to explain and is even harder to comprehend. The tradition warns meditators against any premature conclusions, misconceptions, and improper approach. Voidness must be understood as representing far more than nothingness or the mere absence of (the crude and subtle entities of) the dualistic phenomena. Voidness constitutes the ultimate nature of all phenomena. More significantly, this voidness affirms all phenomena as being relative. While this reflects the view of the School of Valid Empiricism (svatantra madhyamika), a higher standpoint is presented by the School of Rational Reductionism (prasangika madhyamika) when it states that the voidness affirms the conceptually designated dimension of the relative phenomena. Thus the voidness, as the universal substratum, is the heart of the nondualistic phenomena. The two aspects of reality (visible and hidden) are inseparably unified. Such an insight into the nondualism of the apparent and the ultimate realities—existence and enlightenment—represents the beginning of "seeing things as they are." There is a distorted aspect to the apparent reality of mind. It consists of an imaginary vision of the existent self and of the substantive essence in respect to the material phenomena. Because they represent the deluded notion, which vitiates the pure perceptions of mind like a cloud overshadowing the sky, they are regarded as false and transient phenomena.

A crucial stage in the insight meditation consists of the rational determination and contemplative realization of the nonselfhood of personality and phenomena and, by extension, their innate voidness. The concept of "dualistic selves" and a "nondualistic nonself" represents the very root of our existence (saṃsāra) and enlightenment (nirvāṇa). The dualistic selves are naturally incompatible; the visions of "no self" and "no substance" are the antidote to the dualistic selves. All Buddhist schools hold that one cannot perceive the natural state of mind and materiality, namely the "nonself" and "nonsubstance," let alone the innate voidness of these phenomena, without first understanding the distorted ever-present notion of the dualistic selves. Once the "self" of mind has been determined, the understanding of its natural state of nonself will come about. One then focuses on the "nonsubstance" of the material phenomena, specifically as they are represented by the five psychophysical aggregates of one's existence.

There are three ideas of "self" (in respect to mind): a non-Buddhist dogma sees the self as being a solitary, independent, and immutable essence. The Buddhist schools treat this as a crude notion that has no relevance to the natural state of mind. Most ancient Buddhist schools pinpoint a less crude self and define it as being an independently existing self-entity. One school recognizes the subtle self and defines it as a separate self-entity. All these Buddhist schools look upon the diverse notions of self as being complete distortions that are in conflict with the natural state of mind. As long as this deluded notion of self persists, man's existential bondage remains and liberation cannot be realized. The philosophy of "no self" and "voidness" negates only the misconceived notions of mind and materiality, not the valid perception and the relative phenomena, nor the conceptually designated reality.

The meditator, in his analytical investigation, tries to negate both the less crude and the subtle self by the inferential logic of "mutually excluding one and many (entities)." He similarly negates the notion of the "substance of the phenomena" and affirms their merely relative nature through the rational principles such as "the four modes of negating self-emergent reality," otherwise called "the rationale of diamond particles." Among many other investigative principles is "the sovereign reasoning of interdependent arising" (pratītya-samutpāda).

As the meditator progresses toward an ever-higher insight into the nondualistic reality, he applies this principle of interdependent arising to the appearance of the phenomena. He will achieve the insight into the coemergence of the apparent and the ultimate realities. He will then attain the primordial awareness wherein all realities are perceived as being "the one perfect evenness." When applied to his mind, he perceives the coemergence of stream-consciousness and its intrinsic voidness; when applied to any perception as the self-realization process, he experiences an illuminating state that is the union of the immutable bliss and its innate voidness.

These are some aspects of the nondualistic vision and practice as revealed in the collected literature of the transcendental wisdom (prajñāpāramitā). The *Heart Sutra* (the essence of the prajñāpāramitā) sums up this principle of nondualism:

Form is inseparable from emptiness;
Emptiness is inseparable from form.
Sound is inseparable from emptiness;
Emptiness is inseparable from sound.
Smell is inseparable from emptiness;
Emptiness is inseparable from smell.
Taste is inseparable from emptiness;
Emptiness is inseparable from taste.
Touch is inseparable from emptiness;
Emptiness is inseparable from touch.
Consciousness is inseparable from emptiness;
Emptiness is inseparable from consciousness.

The glorious Nāgārjuna reaffirms this:

There is no phenomenon that is not emptiness;
There is no phenomenon that is not interdependent.

And the incomparable Tsongkhapa states:

Everything dependent on conditionality
Is empty of self-nature.
Such being the proclamation,
Is there anything more wonderful than this?

The joint development of the tranquility and insight meditations will lead to the practice of contemplative absorption (samādhi). For the Kagyüpas and some of their sister orders the perfect way to maintain and master this highest meditation is a simple observation, that is, a "no-thought" or nonconceptual meditation. This means avoiding all mental activities and the urge for and attachment to any sublime experiences, as well as avoiding any conceptual analyses. In the process of immersing one's mind in a nondual absorption, even the determinate notion of reality causes distraction and interferes with the tranquil absorption. The truly transcendental wisdom will emerge only when the tranquil absorption is completely unstained by any mental activities.

Here it seems relevant to refer to some of the current Tibetan approaches to the rational investigation and contemplative awakening. The Kagyüpas rely less on dialectical investigation as a means of determining the vision of reality. To support this position, they cite the couplet from the *Bodhicaryāvatāra*:

The ultimate reality is beyond intellectual investigation,
For the intellect is regarded as apparent reality.

The Gelukpa order, on the other hand, holds that one cannot gain a direct insight into the ultimate reality without first gaining a discerning insight into the deeply rooted notion of self and reality. It stresses exhaustive investigation through the proven rational methods, while at the same time relying on the contemplative process.

Despite the scholarly polemics among the different schools of Tibetan Buddhism regarding their respective interpretations and applications of the nondualistic views of reality, the Tibetan tradition upholds the respective sectarian positions as valid and effective. This is in keeping with the traditional saying: "All paths lead to enlightenment." A great Gelukpa teacher, Thukan Dharma Vajra, summed up this position: "The achievement of self-realization should be the practical criterion for judging the validity of the sectarian views of and approach to reality."

The distinctive aspect of the mahāmudrā meditation can be found in the way it has harmoniously blended the two aspects of the sutric meditation on tranquility and insight.

The history of mahāmudrā highlights the development of Tibetan Buddhism since its beginnings (Buddhism was introduced in Tibet during the seventh century C.E.). Tibetan Buddhism has synthesized many authentic Buddhist traditions while maintaining a dynamism and distinction all its own. Mahāmudrā—like the Nyingmapa's mahāsampanna—represents a special path that embodies a vision of the ultimate reality and an instantaneous self-realization process. The mahāmudrā teachings represent the essence of the vast doctrine of Buddha. The early Indian Buddhist teachers, starting from the second century C.E., preserved what was then designated as the "quintessence of reality" (*nyingpoi-don*). Gradually this was identified with the term "mahāmudrā." Among the enlightened teachers of the early period were Saraha, Nāgārjuna, Śavari, and Maitrīpa. Some great teachers of the later period included Tilopa and Nāropa and their Tibetan disciples Marpa, Milarepa, and Gampopa. Their songs of enlightenment contain much of the mahāmudrā's wisdom. The doctrine on the quintessence of reality has remained a closely guarded secret. These teachings are given only to those few who fulfill the requisite conditions mentioned earlier.

During the eleventh and twelfth centuries the mahāmudrā doctrine attained a distinct position within the Kagyüpa order in Tibet. According to the author of this treatise, it was the incomparable Gampopa who turned the mahāmudrā teaching into a special system of metaphysics and meditation, providing it with a strong foundation and institutional identity. The separate lineage described in the text highlights the role of the Indian and Tibetan Buddhist teachers.

Even though this mahāmudrā of the ultimate reality has drawn the essential concepts and methods from both the sūtras and the tantras, the system itself is considered an intermediary tradition. There are numerous other mahāmudrā texts in the Tibetan language. Some have incorporated the Buddha's teachings on the supreme yoga (anuttaratantra). Although all these mahāmudrā texts form the special literature for all Kagyüpas, only certain individual texts are studied by the various branches.

What the distinct mahāmudrā tradition is to the Kagyüpas, the prajñāpāramitā (transcendental wisdom) is to all other orders of Tibetan Buddhism. Both these systems provide the doctrine of the ultimate reality. Some orders also study and practice a specific mahāmudrā. For instance, the Gelukpas cherish "The Bright Lamp of Mahāmudrā," composed by the first Panchen Lama, Lozang Chögyn (1570–1662). And the Sakyapas have "The Eye-Opening Tools of Mahāmudrā," composed by the renowned Sakya Pandita (1181–1251), one of the original founders of the Sakyapa order. In Tibetan Buddhism the eclectic tradition has always encouraged the understanding and appreciation of intersectarian tenets and traditions.

The elucidation of the main mahāmudrā follows the wide-ranging information on its requisite preparations and various aspects, the four levels of self-realization (i.e., the four yogas of mahāmudrā), the postabsorptive views and practices, and so on. In the section on advanced insight meditation, the text provides the special Kagyüpa methods of determining the divisive states of nondualism as specified by terms such as *the spontaneous coemergence of mind* and *the spontaneous coemergence of appearance*. These terms mean an insight into the coemergent mind and its simplicity (i.e., voidness) and into the coemergent appearance and its simplicity. Besides, the term *mahāmudrā* itself connotates a coemergent awareness (sahajajñāna), a nondualistic union of transcendental insight and its innate simplicity as well as coemergence of awareness and bliss. In the exoteric sūtra this means the union of wisdom and compassion. The mahāmudrā that embodies the transcendental wisdom holds that all realities (external and internal) contain the nondualistic state. The mahāmudrā meditation is capable of instantaneously arousing the primordial awareness, a perfect union of voidness and bliss, regardless of a distorted consciousness. Once the quintessence of mind is brought about, it can be maintained under diverse and even adverse conditions.

What distinguishes the mahāmudrā (and the mahāsampanna) from other systems of Buddhist metaphysics and meditation are its special views of reality and methods of realization. The mahāmudrā metaphysics propound the extraordinary theory that an individual's "ordinary mind" (thamel shepa) represents his original stream-consciousness, defined as being an unaltered, natural state (machö nyukma). The mahāmudrā text provides an elaborate description of this which can be summarized as "lucidly clear and inherently simple." In terms of one's daily experience, the ordinary mind is identified with a pure and valid perception regarded as a natural enlightenment and usually called the "Buddha-nature." This inner purity will manifest itself fully and through all times upon the complete elimination of the mind's self-delusion and upon the simultaneous blossoming of all-encompassing evenness, sensitivity, compassion, and wisdom. Until then the meditator's authentic ordinary mind reveals itself through shadowy distortions like sunlight emerging through patches of clouds.

For the contemplative traditions of Kagyüpa and Nyingmapa the ordinary mind's vision of the clear and valid perception is not only the right approach but a reliable aperture to the dawn of insight. The ordinary mind and the worldly mind are the two aspects of human consciousness. The one is inherent and pure, the other acquired and impure. These conflicting inner realities can be differentiated in terms of the two truths. The ordinary mind, as a valid sensory perception, consists of a mirrorlike clarity and an awareness with an insight into its innate simplicity. The perceptive clarity, being conditioned, is on the level of apparent reality. The awareness of the innate simplicity, being unconditioned, is on the level of the ultimate reality. The two are compatible and, in fact, nondual. However, the worldly mind, being deluded, perceives reality in a distorted way. It cannot, therefore, be identified with any valid perception of an ordinary mind. The deluded mind and its distorted view of dualism represent the false nature of the apparent reality. Through each valid perception the ordinary mind reveals its primordial state and its intimate link with the ultimate reality. This is the reason why the ordinary mind is looked upon as natural enlightenment. However, such understanding and insight cannot automatically come to untrained minds. Only to an experienced meditator will the ordinary mind manifest itself as pure and simple but at the same time profound and transcendental.

The mahāmudrā's view of a deluded mind stands in contrast to the other three traditions of Tibetan Buddhism. The fundamental sutric tradition (Hīnayāna) looks at the deluded mind as being evil and therefore to be eliminated. The advanced sutric tradition (Mahāyāna) treats it as destructive and therefore sublimates it to a compassionate motivation for the good of others. The Buddhist tantra also perceives the negative reality as poison and therefore transforms it into transcendental states of consciousness. By contrast, someone well trained in mahāmudrā treats every deluded thought as a perfect state. Such a deluded thought, when directly observed, instantaneously reveals its innate simplicity, which in turn brings about the dawning of nondualistic wisdom. The mahāmudrā meditator looks into the negative experience with a direct insight or at least with a childlike innocence. He actually finds himself faced with the gentle smile of primordial beauty. The mahāmudrā tradition describes this experience as "holding a Buddha in one's palm." It is said that for a mahāmudrā meditator there will always be order in his life, even amid chaos; love amid hatred; light amid darkness; joy amid misery; enlightenment amid confusion.

The mahāmudrā contemplation on the ordinary mind represents the fundamental Kagyüpa meditation. A meditator with good training and experience instantaneously attunes himself to this "mind." A natural state of stream-consciousness, it is neither stained by self-delusion nor stirred by thoughts—good, bad, or neutral. The ordinary mind is known by such terms as "first thought," "pure perception," "valid reality," and "existential awareness." Mahāmudrā recognizes it as being a coemergent awareness (nondualism).

An even more extraordinary view advanced by the Kagyüpa mahāmudrā is that a deluded thought is the dawning of enlightenment. This was criticized by orthodox teachers as being tantamount to saying that "existence is enlightenment" and "delusion is pure consciousness." The exponents of the contemplative Kagyüpa tradition were not unduly concerned with the subtle conceptual distinction and hairsplitting. To them the most important thing was the fact that the fundamental and undeniable truth is that the ultimate simplicity (the inherent purity) permeates all realities, including deluded thoughts. And this vision is shared by all Tibetan Buddhist traditions. Besides, the Mahāyāna tradition holds that because noble and ignoble thoughts do not contain any innate essence, they have the innate simplicity or voidness.

In summary: the unaltered state of the ordinary mind is the true mahāmudrā. Only a good meditator can perceive this inner reality even through the clouds of delusion. As the traditional saying goes: "Once one knows the secrets of the mind, one will uncover the nature of all realities. By knowing the one, one will know all. This is the nature of mind."

The mahāmudrā wisdom shows that when one perceives all appearances without distortions, one will actualize them as authentic experiences of the earthly manifestation of enlightenment, because the perfect vision of the interrelatedness of appearance and its ultimate state represent the visible form of enlightenment (rūpakāya). The clarity of the ordinary mind represents the higher manifestation of enlightenment (sambhogakāya), whereas the innate simplicity of that mind represents the true enlightenment (dharmakāya).

Seen from a deeper psychological perspective, the mahāmudrā penetrates into the five forms of delusion and perceives them as being identical with the five perfect aspects of wisdom.

The mahāmudrā meditator contemplates his confused state (ignorance) as being the wisdom of the ultimate reality, his hatred as mirrorlike wisdom, his desire as discriminating wisdom, his jealousy as fulfilling wisdom, and his arrogance as equalized wisdom. The key to this penetrating insight into the deeper nature of such inner delusions lies in his awakened awareness.

THE FOUR YOGAS OF MAHĀMUDRĀ

The four yogas are so extraordinarily subtle and profound that only advanced meditators can understand them and grasp their significance. The mastery of them will lead to the realization of the diamondlike absorption that is said to represent the highest state (realized only by great bodhisattvas). The sublime nature of this supreme absorption was described by Buddha himself as follows:

> This transcendental wisdom is beyond expression, thought, and definition;
> It is unborn and unceasing, like that of space;
> It remains within the purview of a supreme awareness.
> This is the Mother of Buddhas, past, present, and future.

Meditation in the Tibetan Buddhist tradition is regarded as an all-encompassing self-realization process. It is a way of true insight into reality and of developing the enlightenment qualities such as serenity, collectedness, fearlessness, sensitivity, compassion, and wisdom.

A Reader's Key to the Riches of Mahāmudrā

This Reader's Key is intended to give the general reader an overview of *Mahāmudrā* and to give a quick orientation to the book's treasury of knowledge. Takpo Tashi Namgyal has written an encyclopedia of mahāmudrā tradition that is considered one of the classics on the stages of meditation for the Kagyü lineage. On the one hand, this book is a technical reference work for practitioners and teachers of meditation. However, it deserves a much wider readership. The general reader interested in self-actualization, psychologists interested in the mind and its conditioning or in typologies of meditation, students of religious experience, contemplatives of non-Buddhist traditions, and, of course, both scholars and practitioners of buddhadharma—all will find this a rich and provocative book.

THE SIGNIFICANCE OF THE WORK

The basic message of this book is the basic message of the buddhadharma: that suffering and negative conditions originate within ourselves, and that within us is a powerful potential to overcome this suffering and to actualize a life of compassion, transcendent vision, and beneficial activity. Moreover, the key to this actualization is the practice of meditation, guidance by an authentic spiritual lineage, and a proper understanding of discipline. In this sense the book has a universal message of the innate goodness of human life and its potential for profound fulfillment.

Mahāmudrā is the first extensive exposition of the mahāmudrā meditation tradition to appear in the English language. A variety of shorter translations have appeared, discussing the tradition in brief, giving the sudden-path instructions only, or presenting realization songs and life stories of the lineage founders. Although these works, discussed below, are highly recommended, the reader may come away puzzled as to how one actually gets into the mahāmudrā practice and unfolds it. This book answers that question.

In particular, *Mahāmudrā* is a synthesis of the direct or sudden-path oral instructions of the siddhas (realized ones) and the gradual-path approach stemming from the Indian Mahāyāna masters like Kamalaśīla. *Oral instructions* refers to pithy statements by the lineage masters, often received face to face in the presence of one's guru, which are full of meaning and intended to direct one to the main point. Such oral instructions are often kept private between master and disciple because in that context they are not only words but a direct demonstration of their meaning. Naturally, over the years, many of these pithy instructions were also codified and written down for the benefit of future students and made accessible to them once they had received appropriate previous training and transmission. In the case of the text of *Mahāmudrā*, His Holiness the Sixteenth Karmapa expressly requested that this book be made available to the Western public.

Psychologists, students of religious experience, and contemplatives of other traditions will find here a rich typology of meditative experience that may be somewhat different from the accounts of Buddhist meditation previously available to them. For instance, many people may be familiar with the meditative system of the classical abhidharma as set forth in Buddhaghosa's *Path of Purification*, in the Dalai Lama's *Opening of the Wisdom Eye*, and elsewhere. Some may be familiar with accounts of experience in the Zen tradition, although these are rarely presented in any sort of discursive exposition. (Naturally, in any exposition of advanced experience, one needs to read a lot between the lines!) The tradition of the Kagyü mahāmudrā expounded here derives from the great Indian masters Asaṅga, Kamalaśīla, Śāntipa, and Saraha. The educated reader will be able to discern that this system incorporates elements of the yogācāra, madhyamaka, and vajrayāna schools.

Of course, *meditation* can refer to many different types and levels of experience. Our author sorts these out in detail, with some indication of how the experience of each level can be developed, and the sidetracks to which meditators are prone at each stage. Speaking in very general terms, we can say that Takpo Tashi Namgyal discusses four aspects of meditative experience. These correspond more or less to the four yogas of mahāmudrā.

The first aspect is "settling the mind," stabilizing it and disengaging from the habitual preoccupation with external events, emotional dramas, and our own thoughts. In this way we gain initial perspective on ourselves and our life, and open up some chance to encounter the depth of our being, perhaps for the first time.

The second aspect, insight meditation, goes further by cutting through all kinds of conditioning forces that hinder our inner freedom. We are deeply and unconsciously shaped by hosts of hidden preconceptions, tenaciously rooted inner tendencies. These include specific emotional fixations imprinted by previous experience as well as our basic suppositions concerning who we are altogether as the center of our experience and what our world is.

The third aspect, "recognition of spontaneous coemergence," addresses the integration of liberated awareness with all circumstances of our ordinary world. This could be called "sacred outlook," or "pure appearance" (dag snang), the discovery of sacredness everywhere. All experience begins to show itself as the face of wider meaning and fulfillment. Even the so-called ordinary confused emotions cease to become obstacles; they are transformed into compassion and greater awareness. The boundary between sacred and mundane dissolves.

As for the fourth aspect, a liability of any form of discipline or training, even one aimed at freeing us from limitations, is that we become bound by the discipline itself. The very path to wider awareness subtly conditions us, because of our clinging to the means and the memory of the journey. In the instructions on "nonmeditation," we are concerned with letting go of any deliberate mental focus or "state of mind." In this way realization can become continuous, all-encompassing, and effortless.

In writing his book, Takpo Tashi Namgyal quotes extensively from both the philosophical and meditative traditions. Those of scholarly bent, as well as those primarily interested in practice, should find it illuminating how our author naturally integrates these two, demonstrating how doctrine and practice function together in the living tradition.

Cognitive psychologists and others interested in the process of mind and how we construct our experience will find this a challenging description of how our awareness can be deconditioned, entering thereby into progressively expanded realms of vision and meaning. Moreover, this book raises many epistemological questions about how we construct our realities. For instance, one of the central premises of the book is that "everything we experience is mind." This has at least three meanings: (1) a great deal of experience is conceptually projected over what is "actually there" (parikalpita, or false conceptions); (2) the structure of the world is integrally related with the collective conditioning of consciousness, of those who perceive it (paratantra, or dependent truth); (3) within every conscious creature there is intrinsic awareness inseparable from its deepest being; this intrinsic awareness does not belong to the subject or object of experience, is neither with form nor without form, and is the source of unending presence (kāya) and wisdom (jñāna).

Last and certainly not least, for meditators and meditation teachers, Tashi Namgyal sets out with great clarity how one should practice meditation, the view and oral instructions of the masters concerning that stage, the types of experience one is likely to have, and how to discriminate keenly between experience that is unerring and that which is misleading.

THE PLACE OF MAHĀMUDRĀ IN THE BUDDHIST TRADITION

Stemming from the activity of Śākyamuni (560–480 B.C.E.) the buddhadharma (teaching of awakening) flourished on the Indian subcontinent for

1,700 years, developing many different meditation practices, philosophical formulations, and forms of community. Buddhadharma spread to Sri Lanka and Southeast Asia (250 B.C.E.), Kashmir (140 B.C.E), China (300 C.E.), Korea and Japan (600 C.E.), and Tibet in two phases (750 and 1000 C.E. on).

The Earlier and Later Spreadings of the dharma in Tibet brought the complete Indian Buddhist heritage: the monastic discipline of the vinaya rules; the bodhisattva ethic of working to liberate all beings; the doctrines of the abhidharma (analytical psychology and stages of meditation), prajñāpāramitā and madhyamaka ("transcending knowledge" and "middle way" teaching on emptiness), and yogācāra (mind-only perspective); and the culture of the great monastic universities, which were centers of sacred and secular learning. Tibet also received the esoteric oral intructions of the siddhas and the meditation methods of tantra, as practiced both in the monastic institutions and by solitary yogins in the jungle.

The buddhadharma in Tibet developed many streams of transmission that interchanged teachings, practices, and controversies. Broadly speaking, they are all included in the four major schools, the Nyingma (Ancient Ones), the Kagyü (Oral Instruction Lineage), the Sakya (Grayish Land, referring to the locale where the founding monastery was situated), and the Geluk (Virtuous Tradition). While the essential teachings of these schools are very similar, each traces its transmission through a particular lineage of masters, and each developed a distinctive approach to training disciples, in particular to the final realization, or meditation on ultimate reality.

The Nyingma school originated from the Early Spreading, and the activity of the bodhisattva abbot Śāntarakṣita and his successor Kamalaśīla, as well as from the fruition tantra teaching of Padmasambhava, Vimalamitra, and Vairocana. Padmasambhava had twenty-five major disciples, including King Trisong Detsen and members of his court. They divide the Buddhist teaching into nine vehicles and emphasized as the final understanding atiyoga, or dzogchen, the "great perfection."

The other three schools derive primarily from the Later Spreading. The Sakya school comes from the Indian siddha Virūpa, through the Tibetan translator Drogmi Shakya Yeshe (c. 1050), to Khon Konchog Gyalpo, who also held direct Nyingma lineage. Their special teaching is called lamdre, or "path and fruition."

The Geluk school derives from the teachings of Tsongkhapa Losang Dragpa (b. 1350), who combined two main influences. One is the Kadam tradition of monastic discipline, the study of logic and debate, and "stages of the path" training of the prajñāpāramitā, all revived in Tibet by the Indian master Atīśa (c. 1050). The other stream is the tantric tradition of the New Translation School of the Later Spreading. Thus the Geluk school emphasizes the tantric practice combined with the view of the prasangika madhyamaka as the way to the highest understanding.

The Kagyü school descends from the Indian mahāsiddha Tilopa, who held four special lines of teaching from human gurus, in addition to receiving direct teaching from the dharmakāya. This legacy was passed on to Nāropa, whose "six doctrines," which are tantric yogas connected with mahāmudrā, form a main component of the teaching. In addition, a direct mahāmudrā lineage also comes from the great siddha Saraha through Maitrīpa. From Nāropa and Maitrīpa the teaching passed to their student, the Tibetan translator-yogin Marpa (1012–1096), and thence to the poet-hermit Milarepa (1053–1135) and Gampopa (1075–1153). Gampopa unified the mahāmudrā and tantric teaching he received with his background in the Kadam tradition, and founded many monasteries. Prior to his time, mahāmudrā seems to have been presented primarily in a fruition-teaching, oral-instruction style. From Gampopa's time onward, this perspective was integrated, at least in his writings, with a gradual, "stages of meditation" style; Takpo Tashi Namgyal writes in this tradition. In any case, for the Kagyü school, mahāmudrā, the great symbol, is considered the culmination and fulfillment of all practices. A longer explanation of the significance of mahāmudrā and its lineage of transmission is given in the chapter "Exposition Engendering Confidence." The question of the relation of mahāmudrā and the tantra as such is discussed below.

HOW MAHĀMUDRĀ IS INTRODUCED

It may be helpful to describe how, according to tradition, the mahāmudrā view can actually be understood and recognized experientially. Mahāmudrā is not a beginner's practice. To be sure, what is called the "foundation mahāmudrā" pervades all sentient beings as their inherent buddha nature. However, the actual mahāmudrā realization, the fruition mahāmudrā, is considered to be the enlightenment of all the buddhas. For this reason, recognizing the mahāmudrā view, even as an evanescent glimpse, is of great significance. In this sense, mahāmudrā meditation could be called practice of the fruition. Not surprisingly, this practice requires an aspirant's commitment and preparation.

A few unusual students may have evolved spiritual faculties enabling the guru to introduce them immediately to the basic nature. The great majority of people must be led gradually, stage by stage, from basic up to more advanced disciplines. The usual prerequisites in the tradition include training in meditation, study, and disciplined life-style in accordance with the "three vehicles" (yānas). These three vehicles, as applied in the Tibetan tradition, are not so much successive stages from which one graduates, one to another; they are more like concentric circles of understanding and discipline that proceed simultaneously.

Discipline in the "lesser vehicle" includes abandoning fruitless preoccupations and behavior, either internally in one's attitudes or externally through precepts and life-style, or both. Meditation entails the cultivation of mindfulness or "recollection," śamatha, or taming the mind's incessant discursiveness, and basic vipaśyanā (insight), such as with respect to impermanence, the shiftiness of internal and external experience.

In the "great vehicle" training, discipline includes the bodhisattva practice of working energetically for the benefit of others and making compassion and concern for others' welfare the basic motivation of life. Meditation entails cultivating bodhicitta, the "enlightened attitude," the union of nonfixed mind and compassion.

The Vajrayāna or "indestructible vehicle" training generally begins with meditation on the "extraordinary preliminaries" (discussed in Book Two, Chapter 2) followed by practice of the sādhanas (liturgical procedures) of various meditational deities. Generally the Vajrayāna places great emphasis on the master-student relationship. The master must be competent, that is, he must actually have attained realization, and he must be skillful in knowing how to develop students and help them overcome their obstacles. The student must have strong commitment and integrity.

These conditions are necessary because the Vajrayāna discipline is based on transmission and empowerment. Transmission is a meeting of minds between master and student in which the student, because of his training, is able to open himself, and the master, through the power of his spiritual blessing and understanding, is able to awaken the student to recognition of his own nature. Sometimes transmission happens in a formal ceremony, sometimes in a casual conversation with the teacher. Very often it happens circumstantially in situations around the teacher.

Transmission awakens something innate in the student; it is not the transplantation of something new. On the other hand, it is taught that one's ability to develop the mahāmudrā insight is principally dependent on receiving the blessing of one's master and lineage. In general, empowerment is said to ripen the students; that is, their inner potential is awakened and their obstacles are diminished.

Empowerment usually refers to a formal ceremony of transmission in which students are introduced to a specific meditational deity and its mandala. These deities and mandalas are not external entities but a kind of psychological geography of our mind, including our link with the lineage of realization, our relationship with our immediate world, our sense perceptions and emotions, all the way out to the flickering fringe of confusion, where awareness falters. A very extensive empowerment may include authorization to meditate with the symbolic forms of deities; a more advanced practice with the yogic energy body, carrying forward the essential kernel of the deity practice; and a still more advanced practice that is purely formless.

The practice regarding such deities and mandalas alternates between meditation on their forms and formless meditation (the "completion stage" or sampannakrama). As the practice progresses, the visualization stage and the formless stage, initially seeming so different, are increasingly discovered to be inseparable. Likewise, as one's awareness becomes more open, the boundary between visualization and perception begins to dissolve. In this way the practice of meditating on such deities is a natural bridge to mahāmudrā understanding. This should not be surprising, since these meditation methods are not "man-made" so much as themselves expressions of the mahāmudrā principle.

Having said this, we must clarify the relationship between mahāmudrā itself and the tantric methods. The tantric practice is one means among others to awaken the disciple to mahāmudrā. In the tantras themselves, mahāmudrā is referred to as the fourth or ultimate empowerment, which is the culmination of what has gone before and is not dependent on any particular symbolic means of being indicated. In line with this, Saraha, Maitrīpa, Gampopa, and Takpo Tashi Namgyal emphasize that mahāmudrā is not dependent on the tantric methods to be recognized or practiced. (Thus this book speaks almost entirely in the vocabulary of mental quiescence and insight practice, with only passing reference to the tantra.) However, such a "pure mahāmudrā" path is rather steep and difficult for ordinary people to grasp. Therefore, as our author says, these days, "the tantric methods and mahāmudrā are commonly blended to enhance the realization" in both directions.

SYNOPSIS OF THE CONTENTS

In what follows we present a brief synopsis of the topics covered in the book's thirteen chapters.

Introduction

All of confused existence, and all the wisdom of awakening, is the result of solidifying and conceptualizing the mind, or the absence thereof. Therefore, insight into the true nature of the mind is the crucial point.

Book One: The Outline of Tranquil Equipoise in General and the Removal of Doubts

As a prologue to his main subject, Takpo Tashi Namgyal discusses tranquility and insight according to the generally accepted Hīnayāna and Mahāyāna traditions inherited by all schools in Tibet. He characterizes tranquility meditation and insight (a distinction made by all Buddhist systems) and discusses the importance of joining them together.

Book One, Chapter Two: The Stages of Tranquility and Insight Part I: Tranquility

Tashi Namgyal mentions various meditations suitable for developing quiescence of mind. He begins with a number of subjects that actually combine tranquility and insight but are reckoned by most masters of the tradition as means of stabilizing the mind in preparation for more advanced insight practices. These include "analytical meditation," a means of counteracting the predominant conflicting emotions of the meditator, and "skillful investigation," bringing preliminary insight into the nonexistence of the "ego of personality." (The "I"-sense and accompanying assertion of "mine" and "other" is one of our fundamental misunderstandings, upon which all manner of thoughts and emotions base themselves. When this is seen through, many confusions are cut at the root and no longer arise, and for this reason, skillful investigation is included here as a stabilizing meditation.) The author discusses practices suitable at beginning stages of meditation, such as those based on mindfulness of body and visualization.

Finally he describes the classical teaching composed of the eight antidotes, the nine stages of resting the mind, the six powers, and the four attentions. The eight antidotes, discussed in more detail in the preceding chapter, are countermeasures to specific obstacles. The nine stages characterize the meditator's experience and application of mindfulness and effort. They span his journey all the way from the stage of reining in a wild and distracted mind to the stage of letting the mind settle naturally in effortless absorption. The six powers develop naturally in the course of the nine stages; they are both the result and motive power in the practice. (Readers who wish to investigate these topics further can refer to several contemporary expositions: His Holiness the Dalai Lama, *Opening of the Wisdom Eye* (Theosophical Publishing House), pp. 77–88; Chögyam Trungpa, Rinpoche, *1979 Hinayana-Mahayana Seminary Transcripts* (Vajradhatu Publications), pp. 20–45; Geshe Kelsang Gyatso, *Meaningful to Behold* (Wisdom Publications), pp. 222–234; Jamgön Kongtrul, *The Treasury of Knowledge: The Stages of Meditation of Shamatha and Vipashyana* (Dhagpo Kagyu Ling).

Book One, Chapter Three: Stages of Tranquility and Insight Part 2: Insight

The author enumerates a variety of ways in which insight meditation has been presented in the tradition, commenting in sum:

> Just as fire results from the rubbing of two sticks, so intellectual examination [of dualistic perception] will lead to a dawning of insight. Once the wood is consumed, the flames die. Thus, when insight dawns, both the image of the examiner and its examination fade.

After briefly characterizing the meditative procedure of the main Mahāyāna schools, Tashi Namgyal turns to the central issue, insight into twofold selflessness. He first discusses what "clinging to a self" means and then presents the classical way of meditating on the selflessness of personality based on examining the relationship between the "self" and the five psychophysical aggregates. Moving on to selflessness of phenomena, our author notes that in terms of the genesis of ego-clinging, first mind fixates subtly on substantiality, and then we identify ourselves with reference to these external projections. The refutation of substantiality or self-nature follows the standard madhyamaka observation that because all phenomena depend on causes, they cannot have a self-contained self-entity of their own. A second refutation follows Śāntarakṣita's way of investigating for a self-nature, which must be either unitary or multiple, if it exists. (Further elucidations of these contemplations may be found in Thrangu Rinpoche's excellent book *Open Door to Emptiness* in Geshe Kelsang Gyatso's *Meaningful to Behold*, and in other expositions of the middle way.) Then, under the headline "Emergence of Vision through This Meditation," Tashi Namgyal observes that "the negation of the two selves is meant to eliminate delusion, which perceives duality as true." On the other hand, it is quite erroneous to cling to a conceptualized negation of things and call this a realization of emptiness! Finally, in "The Specific Methods of Meditating on the Vision of Ultimate Reality," the author foreshadows the second half of the book, summarizing some of the key instructions of the mahāmudrā approach.

Book One, Chapter Four: The Stages of Tranquility and Insight Part III: Clearing Doubts Regarding the Methods for Maintaining the Vision of Reality and Meditative Absorption

In this chapter Takpo Tashi Namgyal· addresses issues of controversy between various schools of meditation. He especially clarifies how tranquility and insight should be unified, the correct role of analytical intellect in meditation, and the relation between various kinds of nonconceptual meditation and insight.

Our author compares the traditions of meditation based on the Mahāyanā schools of logic and the authoritative expositions of Nāgārjuna with the tradition of meditation on the nature of mind handed down by Saraha and Śavari. He criticizes a variety of meditative systems on the grounds that they violate the natural harmonization of tranquility and insight, that they misunderstand the proper use of analysis and so reintroduce deluded discrimination into meditation, and that by dwelling on inferential judgment, instead of on true nonconceptual vision, they reinforce a clinging to a conceptual notion of emptiness. Finally, in "The Meditational System of Our School," the author sets forth the Kagyü mahāmudrā approach to these issues.

Book Two, Chapter One: Exposition Engendering Confidence

Chapter One of Book Two intends to establish confidence in the mahāmudrā as a genuine and precious tradition. The author begins with the meaning and general significance of the term, then discusses how this tradition is reflected both in the sūtras and the tantras, and how it is the essence of the path of both, and its relationship to the tantric means. He refutes some false allegations made against the tradition. Finally, he gives an account of the lineage holders and progenitors of the tradition, both Indian and Tibetan, recounting their great spiritual qualities.

Book Two, Chapter Two: Preparatory Practices

Here the author presents the preparatory conditions and training necessary for someone to approach the mahāmudrā practice. He discusses the general conditions necessary for entering the Buddhist path and the need for the teacher to assess the spiritual maturity of the students in giving appropriate teaching, whether of the sudden-path or gradual-path variety. He discusses the uncommon or extraordinary preliminaries: meditation on impermanence, taking refuge and arousing the enlightened attitude, making offerings of a mandala of the universe, purification by meditation on Vajrasattva, and attunement to the lineage mind through the guru yoga. Here Tashi Namgyal just refers to each of these practices, stressing their importance and benefits, but without expounding them in detail. (Readers interested in more exposition can refer to several contemporary translations: Jamgon Kongtrul, *Torch of Certainty*, trans. Judith Hanson; Khetsun Sangpo, *Tantric Practice in Nying-ma*, trans. Jeffrey Hopkins; Geshe Rabten, *The Preliminary Practices of Tibetan Buddhism.*) The chapter ends with remarks on the format of a meditation retreat.

Book Two, Chapter Three: Guiding Meditators on the Path: Tranquility

The general topic of tranquility meditation is taken up from the mahāmudrā lineage perspective. Tashi Namgyal examines conditions of solitude and physical posture. In treating suitable means of concentration for the mind, he discusses, in turn, mental images derived from external perception; abstract mental images, that is, meditation based on awareness of breathing; and formless tranquility, that is, letting the mind settle in itself without any determinate object or image. This formless meditative absorption is the one to be cultivated as the immediate basis for mahāmudrā meditation. Tashi Namgyal discusses the important topic of balancing exertion and relaxation in the context of formless tranquility, and characterizes this settled state.

Book Two, Chapter Four: Guiding Meditators on the Path: Insight

The meditations described here establish one's mind and all emerging appearances to be empty and groundless, vivid and unceasing. They have the general tone of the second yoga of mahāmudrā, Simplicity or Nondiscrimination (see Chapter 9). They will be followed up in Chapter Five by the advanced insight meditations of spontaneous coemergence, which have the general tone of the third yoga, One Flavor.

Takpo Tashi Namgyal cites the main sources of insight as realized teachers, scriptures that show the ultimate rather than the provisional meaning of the dharma, and meditative examination.

The first stage of insight is to recognize the nature of the mind itself. Our author brings forward many citations from the sūtras, tantras, and oral instructions of the siddhas supporting this approach. The principal points are these: The mind is the root of all confused saṃsāra as well as of all realization. Moreover, the intrinsic nature of the mind is primordial enlightenment, as expounded in the *Uttara-tantra* of Maitreya, the *Kālacakra-tantra*, and elsewhere. As Asanga says,

> Understand that nothing exists apart from the mind.
> Know that mind itself is unreal.

This combines the yogācāra and madhyamaka insights. In practical terms, the meditator proceeds by recognizing every determinate experience as a projection of the mind according to conditions. At the same time this "mind" is utterly without determinable characteristics.

Tashi Namgyal instructs in the actual meditative investigation: having settled one's mind in tranquility, one has to examine whether it has any structure like a form or color; any basis or support, inside or outside the body; any distinctive identity, like a formlessness; any mode of manifestation, like blankness or brilliance. The fruit of successful investigation is firm conviction in the absence of any such graspable characteristic.

The second stage of insight is to investigate the dynamic manifestation of the mind—what arises from it. We conventionally divide this manifestation into "internal" experience (thoughts, conceptions, emotions) and "external" experience (sense perceptions and appearances of the external world). The meditator proceeds by examining thoughts, emotions, and perceptions, both gross and subtle, in the same manner as before with the mind itself. The insight of these meditations is not that appearances cease, but that appearances are recognized as indistinguishable from the nature of the mind, which is itself ungraspable. The essence of thoughts is unidentifiable and without form. Appearances arise in a union of brilliance and inherent emptiness.

A third stage of insight ("Clearing Assumptions and Skepticism about the Basic Root") deepens these realizations with three further investigations. The first examines the emergence, dwelling, and dissolution of thoughts, to elevate the practitioner's experience to a state where each discursive thought, as it arises, manifests its intrinsic clarity and emptiness. The second meditation erodes one's attachment to the "still mind" and the "appearing mind" as separate phenomena. In this way the meditator learns to maintain whatever state arises, whether still or emerging, as identical with his inmost awareness. The third meditation is called "certainty that appearances are nonarising." The meditator gives up notions of existence, because whatever emerges in experience never attains graspable substantiality. He gives up notions of nonexistence, because presence emerges ceaselessly and unobstructedly. He realizes that his previous notions of things emerging, dwelling, or ceasing were all conceptual fixations that are not supported by the intrinsic reality.

The author closes this chapter by discussing how insight emerges and the typical difficulties meditators have at this stage.

Book Two, Chapter Five: The Stages of Virtuous Practice

The virtuous practice of the title is the insight of spontaneous coemergence. This is also called coemergent wisdom (Skt. sahajajñāna, Tib. lhan.chig.kyes.pa'i.ye.shes), the natural state (gnas.lugs), natural awareness or ordinary mind (thamal.gyi.shes.pa), luminosity (od.sal), or simply "the mind." On the basis of the aspirant's preparation thus far, the guru can point out mahāmudrā more directly. This chapter seemingly reiterates the insight meditations previously given, but from this more advanced point of view.

Takpo Tashi Namgyal opens his exposition by clarifying the view and terminology used at this stage of teaching. First of all, one regards the essence of the mind as emptiness, its nature as luminous clarity, and its manifestation as all the qualities of saṃsāra and nirvana. Second, one introduces the view of spontaneous coemergence as that which pervades and encompasses all.

The heading "Actual Identification of Spontaneous Coemergence" refers to the guru's pointing out and the meditator's recognition. As before, the meditator goes through recognition of the mind itself. Here it is to be recognized as the inherent indivisibility of stabilization and insight, dharmakāya. Then follows investigation of the coemergence of thought and of external appearance. The central instruction here is to allow thoughts and appearances to arise unimpeded and to crystallize vividly, at the same time recognizing them as indivisible from the intrinsic nature.

Śamatha and vipaśyanā, or tranquility and insight, have a special meaning at this stage. Tranquility means no attachment or aversion as unceasing thoughts and appearances arise in the mind. Insight means a recognition of the inherent nature of the mind and its appearances to be emptiness, dharmakāya. Or again, tranquility and insight are the inseparability of emptiness and appearance.

The author quotes many "vajra sayings" of the realized masters of the Kagyü order, which point out the view at this stage, such as "cognizing discriminating thought as dharmakāya, and delusion as awareness." Maitrīpa says:

> A transient thought arises from that which is unborn.
> This very thought has the nature of all-embracing reality.
> The two are inseparable from the very beginning.
> Therefore I reveal these two as one even flavor.

And:

> Intrinsic in defilements is great awareness.
> It helps a meditator to consume them
> Like a conflagration that consumes a forest.

Again:

> Even form reveals enlightenment.

Having expounded the correct recognition, the author discusses at length typical misunderstandings whereby meditators go astray and styles of meditation that only partially hit the mark ("The Elimination of Flaws"). Some of these experiences are appropriate to a previous stage of practice, but are not the awareness of coemergence being expounded here.

The chapter concludes with an exposition of the correct manner of mahāmudrā meditation, which consists of identifying meditation with the "ordinary mind" ("The Recognition of Flawless Meditation").

Book Two, Chapter Six: Consolidation of Experience in Meditation: How to Maintain Absorption and Postabsorption

Tashi Namgyal emphasizes how important it is not to be content with a glimpse experience of mahāmudrā meditation but to carry it out fully. Thus the subject of this chapter is the main mahāmudrā practice, that is, having recognized it, how to continue and consolidate it both in absorption and postabsorption.

Our author expounds the importance of mindfulness in general and specifically addresses the significance of mindfulness in a tradition that repeatedly emphasizes as key instructions "no memory," "no effort," and "no mental constructions."

In ordinary terms, absorption (nyamshak, or meditative resting) refers to the formal meditation session, and postabsorption (jethop, or postmeditation) refers to the aspirant's awareness practice during meditation breaks. The author explains that in the context of advanced practice, absorption refers to spacelike equipoise undisturbed by any dualistic thought, even though the meditator may be walking or talking. Similarly, postabsorption refers to the emergence of thought projections, even though the meditator is still engaged in his formal session.

Explaining the subject in general, our author says:

> . . . the meaning of mahāmudrā consists of recognizing the intrinsic nature of every thought or appearance—with no concern for discrimination or nondiscrimination—and then maintaining that awareness unmodulated. . . . Nowadays, during actual meditation, beginners concentrate one-pointedly on absorptive equipoise, the awareness of the mind's essential nature. During the intervals between meditation they concentrate mainly on the postabsorptive perception by elevating all thoughts and appearances to awakened experience.

Takpo Tashi Namgyal then expounds some of the famous lineage instructions, equally appropriate for both absorption and postabsorptive perception. Among these are the similes handed down by Gampopa: vast as space, expansive like the great earth, stable as a mountain, bright like a lamp, like a clear crystal. Also among these are Tilopa's famous six topics:

> No recollection, no thinking, no thought,
> No meditation, no examination,
> But let the mind be in its natural state.

Having quoted the sayings of many masters of the tradition, Takpo Tashi Namgyal gives his condensed elucidation of their meaning in three points—(1) meditation without any conceptual fabrication, (2) undistracted awareness of the intrinsic reality, and (3) that these two together are the essence of meditation: nonmeditation and nondistraction.

The author then turns to practice in postabsorption—how to make one's mahāmudrā awareness continuous by merging it with all the experiences and activities of daily life. What is important here is mindfulness, which in this context means maintaining definite awareness of the mind's coemergence, as experienced through transmission and in the meditative absorption, while allowing thoughts and perceptions to crystallize vividly, without grasping or restraining one's mind as it unfolds. The previous recognitions of the coemergence of thought and of appearance come into play here. All thoughts and perceptions become meditation, self-recognized and self-released.

The author then discusses correct and incorrect attitudes to postmeditation perception as being "illusory." The yogin should perceive forms, sounds, and so forth as arising from immediate conditions by interdependent origination. This awareness of emerging appearances should be joined and strengthened by his awareness of the true nature of coemergent thought and appearance as being nonarising. In this way the meditator simultaneously acknowledges the truth of action and result, and the essencelessness of all things.

Takpo Tashi Namgyal concludes this aspect of his discussion by considering how absorption and postabsorption coalesce. The true coalescence of absorption and postabsorption takes place at the attainment of the great One Flavor and Nonmeditation stages, where the boundaries of meditation and postmeditation completely dissolve in the yogin's experience. The author gives his opinion that there is a good foretaste of this during the great stage of Nondiscrimination.

Book Two, Chapter Seven: Consolidation of Experience in Meditation: How to Get Rid of Meditative Deviation

Two general types of deviations are addressed here: (1) the four aberrations—various misunderstandings of the true experience of emptiness; and (2) three deviations—solidification or clinging to experience of bliss, clarity, and nonthought. These topics are also discussed in Wangchuk Dorje, *Mahamudra Illuminating the Darkness of Ignorance*, pages 121–125, and in Dilgo Khyentse Rinpoche, *The Rain of Wisdom*, page 336.

As to the four ways of straying regarding emptiness, Takpo Tashi Namgyal explains each of the four strayings in two aspects: (1) a primal aberration—how the mind strays from the primordial nature, missing the point; and (2) an immediate aberration—which is the erroneous attitude and approach in one's meditation. In brief, the four are: straying into nihilism by labeling the mind with conceptual negation; straying with regard to emptiness being the path; straying with regard to emptiness being an antidote; straying into labeling by identifying emptiness with some meditation experience such as that induced by the "oṃ svabhāva" mantra.

As for the three deviations: the meditator's attainment of the union of tranquility and insight may bring about various intense inner experiences, in particular those of bliss, luminosity, and nonconception. These experiences are the footprint of realization rather than the actual thing. Since they arise from the meditator's development, there is an inevitable tendency for the meditator to evaluate his experiences and to try to re-create them, and to be dismayed by their absence. Such a directed focus and bias of the mind will lead to deviation into the three realms of confused existence. The antidote to all this is to detach oneself from craving and then settle the mind in its natural state, unfabricated, and not distort it through accepting or rejecting. One prevents this by maintaining mindfulness of the certainty of nonarising with respect to these inner sensations.

Book Two, Chapter Eight: Consolidation of Experience in Meditation: How to Determine the Mind as Nonarising and Enhance Meditation

This chapter consists of advanced instruction on nonmeditation and bringing adverse conditions to the path. The first set of instructions on "nonarising" are sudden-path instructions aimed at helping aspirants to cut through quickly to the very essence in a short time. The second set, "enhancing the practice," are ways of making the realization completely applicable and thoroughgoing by bringing negativities and extreme conditions to the path.

The instructions on nonarising are aimed at bringing the meditator to swift realization of all appearances and existence as dharmakāya. Takpo Tashi Namgyal says that if applied at the correct stage, these special instructions can bring about immediate realization in those of high potential and can cause other meditators to advance rapidly from the lower levels of the four yogas to the higher ones. He discusses the proper timing of these instructions.

The basis of the instructions is that the abiding nature of all phenomena is nonarising, beyond subject or object, beyond reality or unreality, an unceasing stream that from the very beginning never was conditioned by past, present, or future. Thus it is not something acquired through mindfulness or lost through distraction.

Since the mahāmudrā in general belongs to the path of blessing, an additional requisite is for the meditator to rouse strong faith and devotion to his guru as the embodiment of the dharmakāya, and to invoke the guru's blessing.

The central insights here are as follows. First, one aims to dissolve the division of meditation and meditator, realizing them as an inseparable union without any essence. Second, one examines again the destination of past thought, the nature of present thought, and the source of future thought, until one comes to the conviction that these thoughts are not assignable to the three times and are uniquely pure and open, for all times. Third, one tries to dissolve any residual dualities between "internal" and "external," "subject" and "object," so that all experience is seen as a single stream, self-emerging and self-releasing.

Having recognized in this way, the meditator should dismantle his clinging to the subject of meditation, loosen his mindfulness, abandon his yearning for experience and his seeking for realization, and remain in a normal relaxed state. He should make this continuous throughout the day and merge it also with his sleep and dreams.

As for "Perfecting the Efficacy [of Awareness] through the Sublimation of the Path": The term "lam.khyer," "carrying on the path," "elevating or sublimating to the path," refers to directly engaging apparently negative and adverse conditions and turning them into powerful tools for advancing and extending one's realization.

Three kinds of situations especially call for these methods: (1) when the practitioner's mind is agitated or upset by powerful circumstances and he finds it hard to elevate his awareness spontaneously; (2) when he is at peace but finds that his awareness is becoming sluggish and he is unable to recognize the intrinsic nature of his thoughts; (3) when he has achieved an uninterrupted meditative state, a blending of absorption and postabsorption, and he wishes to further stabilize and test his realization. Many of these methods are also given in the tantric instructions on transformation.

At this stage it is actually of benefit for the meditator to be in an environment—such as awesome solitude, terrifying charnel grounds, or a haunted place—that arouses strong deluded thinking or conflicting emotions. This helps him develop fearlessness toward external and internal manifestations, as well as an unleashed and spontaneous mind that transcends hope and conventional discriminations. In very ordinary terms, this means that it is good if the meditator's path has some difficulties, crises, and challenges. Otherwise his approach to life becomes too indolent.

The instructions come in six categories: (1) elevating dualistic thought—allowing that thought, subtle or gross, positive or negative, itself to dawn as the meditative state; (2) recognizing the five wisdoms within the five basic kleśas; (3) dealing with apparitions of devas and demons, and the fascination and fear aroused thereby; (4) using grief and anxiety about suffering—one's own and others'—to heighten the bodhicitta, the union of compassion and essencelessness; (5) relating with disease through direct awareness of the pain and the symptoms, and their intrinsic nature; (6) making the death process a path of realization.

Book Two, Chapter Nine: The Resultant Dawning of Realization

In this final chapter Takpo Tashi Namgyal turns his attention to a discussion of how meditators actually develop realization and how the different levels of attainment can be assessed. The tradition distinguishes three types of aspirants—those with strong potential for immediate realization, those with potential for evanescent realization, and those who progress gradually from stage to stage. Our author explains their characteristic ways of understanding.

The path according to mahāmudrā has been divided into the four yogas, even in the early mahāmudrā tradition. Subsequently Lord Gampopa wrote on the four yogas in detail, and his disciples, especially Phagmo Drupa, propagated a threefold division of each yoga, of lesser, medium, and greater attainment, making the twelve yogas. Takpo Tashi Namgyal warns that "there is no certainty that experiences arising from the twelve levels of the four yogas will follow the regular order, like steps of stairs." For example, before completing the experience of inner sensation and realization of the great level of the One-Pointedness yoga, the experience of the two levels of the next yoga of Nondiscrimination may emerge, and so forth.

Nevertheless, since it is important, at least for the teacher, to be able to assess the level of evolution of the practice, Takpo Tashi Namgyal elucidates in vivid detail.

The author shows that the four yogas are foreshadowed and are in agreement with the expositions of sūtra and tantra by quoting the *Laṅkāvatāra-sūtra*, the *Hevajra-tantra*, and other texts.

He then characterizes the four stages of yoga in general, quoting the masters of the tradition ("General Meaning of the Four Stages of Yoga: The Distinct Nature of Each"). Then he differentiates each of the four stages according to (1) the distinct type of realization at each stage; (2) the type of dullness and obscuration to which each is prone; (3) the character of the postabsorptive perception; (4) the progressive elimination of subtle, residual stains; (5) how awareness fluctuates; (6) how absorption and postabsorption are blended or different at each stage; and so on.

The yogas are then described one by one in "The Detailed Elucidation of Each of the Four Yoga Stages." "The Differentiation" clarifies common misunderstandings concerning what is and is not this stage, and elucidates it according to the six criteria of Je Gyare, which assess the extent of the realization. Under "How Inner Sensation and Experience Will Dawn,"

Tashi Namgyal discusses in very experiential terms what a meditator is likely go through at each level. "How This Yoga Is Maintained" gives practical instructions for the meditator at this stage of practice.

The overall significance of these stages is to remove the mind's clinging to any conditioned experience and to the process of meditation itself. This brings transcendence of karma and the forces of rebirth.

As his final topic ("How the Various Grounds and Paths of Enlightenment Are Reached through the Four Yogas"), Takpo Tashi Namgyal entertains the question of whether any correlation can be made between the map of attainment according to the four yogas and the description of the stages in the sūtra tradition, namely the five paths and the ten bhūmis. He quotes the master Je Zhang:

> The mahāmudrā is attainable in one stride.
> It is deluded ignorance to divide it into bhūmis and paths.
> However, to delight the hearts of the confused,
> I shall divide it into bhūmis and paths,
> Adapting it to the system of logical definition.

Takpo Tashi Namgyal discusses various opinions of the great masters on this question, ending with his own assessment.

ASSOCIATED WORKS

The following works in English translation will be very helpful in understanding the present book and its context.

Any spiritual tradition is passed on in human situations, from master to student. Biographies of lineage teachers are often written to show the profound qualities of these people, their understanding of how to manifest spirituality, and their skill in guiding disciples. Thus these are not only biographies but also presentations of mahāmudrā teaching itself.

The Life and Teaching of Naropa, with a Philosophical Commentary Based on the Oral Transmission, trans. H. V. Guenther (Shambhala Publications, 1986)

The Life of Marpa the Translator, by Tsang Nyön Heruka, trans. Nālandā Translation Committee (Prajñā Press, 1982)

The Life of Milarepa, trans. Lobsang Lhalungpa (Shambhala Publications, 1984)

The Hundred Thousand Songs of Milarepa, trans. Garma C. C. Chang (Shambhala Publications, 1977)

The general context of training in which mahāmudrā is presented is given in Thrangu Rinpoche's little book, *Showing the Way of Liberation* (Manila:

Tara Publications, 1984), and *The Rain of Wisdom*, compiled by Karmapa VIII Mikyo Dorje, trans. Nālandā Translation Committee (Shambhala Publications, 1980). In particular, a concise summary of the entire teaching characteristic of *Mahāmudrā* is given in "The Song of Lodro Thaye," pages 81–90 in *The Rain of Wisdom*.

A short exposition of mahāmudrā meditation has been published as *Mahamudra Illuminating the Darkness of Ignorance* by Karmapa IX Wangchuk Dorje (commentary by Beru Khyentse Rinpoche), trans. Alexander Berzin (Dharamsala: Library of Tibetan Works and Archives, 1978). This short classic by the Ninth Karmapa is an excellent introduction that points out the view of mahāmudrā through a series of introductions and examination-meditations. The ground it covers is similar to that covered in Book Two, Chapters 4 and 7, in the present book. However, the implications of this view and how to consolidate one's meditative experience are discussed much more fully by Tashi Namgyal.

H. V. Guenther's groundbreaking work, *The Royal Song of Saraha*, presents mahāmudrā in a different style. This text, based on the realization songs of Saraha and oral transmission commentaries by Kyeme Dechen, Karma Thinley, and Nyime Avadhutipa, exemplifies the direct-path oral tradition. Here the guru awakens the view in the disciple through direct pointing out, "through symbols and other appropriate means." The student meditates with this, relying on the instructions embodied in the terms *memory* (all appearance is mind), *nonmemory* (mind is empty and groundless), *unorigination* (while it appears, it has never been produced or obscured by conditions, and manifests unceasingly), and *transcendence* (wisdom is all-encompassing). These are roughly analogous to the significance of the four yogas of mahāmudrā. This seems to be the type of teaching to which Takpo Tashi Namgyal refers when he explains (in Book Two, Chapter Two) that "those inclined to the instantaneous path should be engaged at the outset in the process of discovering the vision of inherent reality, and then in settling the mind in tranquil absorption" in it.

Dorje Loppön Lodrö Dorje Holm
Vajradhatu
Boulder, Colorado
March 1986

MAHĀMUDRĀ

Introduction

HOMAGE

1 B I prostrate myself before my guru and the indestructible mind.[1]
Though his inherent nature is detached from conceptual determination,
He manifests himself in diverse forms.
His voice—indestructible and indeterminable—surpasses ordinary speech and reverberates, like a melody.
His compassion with its intrinsic mark—unstained by the dualistic concept of "I and others"—remains the source of all benefits and peace.
The Buddha Vajradhara,[2] master of all realities—material and nonmaterial—
I prostrate myself before him.

2 F His body is incarnated in illusory forms throughout all realms;
His speech proclaims the way of the dharma through the three vehicles[3]
To aspirants in a language that each understands;
His mind embraces all sentient beings equally
With great nonconceptual compassion.
Buddha, the Incomparable Teacher, possessed of the three mystical qualities,[4]
The one friend of fortunate seekers,
I prostrate myself before him!

By receiving even a part of his compassion
2 B One is able to elucidate the many treatises
According to their apparent or ultimate meanings.[5]

Likewise, when one is propagating the dharma,
Debating, or composing,
He grants fearless wisdom without obstruction.

He awakens one to the deep intrinsic reality
That remains mysterious to ordinary minds.

O Perfect Deity, Terrifying Lord,[6] I pay homage to you!
May you grant me inexhaustible wisdom as your unsurpassable gift!

The Archer who had "the body of empty space" [Saraha],
Nāgārjuna, Śavari, Tilopa, Nāropa, Maitrīpa, Marpa, and Milarepa[7]
Saw the true nature of the mind as being deep and clear
And all conceptualized realities as false.
They realized that within the nondifferentiable unity
Of inherent emptiness and awareness are contained
The roots of freedom, the path, and its realization.
I prostrate myself before them . . . .

He [Gampopa] had attained enlightenment
Before [Śākyamuni] Buddha,
As the bodhisattva Candraprabha-kumāra.
3 F He is also known as Gelong Tsoje [monk-physician],[8]
As he appeared out of compassion for the people in the Land of Snow Mountains [Tibet],
Thus fulfilling the prophecy of the Buddha.[9]
Known as Gampopa, the second Buddha,
Throughout the three spheres of the universe,[10]
He proclaimed aloud the dharma of the ultimate reality[11]
In an age of decadence.
I prostrate myself before him.

Though learned and ordinary monks in this snowy land
Examined the nature of mind
Through dialectical analysis,
And self-proclaimed masters of mysticism[12]
Through experience,
They realized very little.

Those of you in the glorious Kagyü order of Takpo[13]
Who have seen the inherent face of the mind's nature
And who are also skillful in teaching others,
To you all I prostrate myself. May you bless me!

Your transmission of the teaching is known as mahāmudrā.
It clears the illusion of conceptual falsity
And refutes the many awarenesses created by the intellect.
This path embodies the ultimate meaning
3 B Of the sūtras and tantras.[14]

Those who conceptualize are like people pursuing a mirage for water;
Others watch the changing patterns of their thoughts,

And still others cling to sensory and meditative experiences,
Which are illusory, like rainbows.
These are not the ways to be followed by one wishing
To achieve early liberation.

Though one may listen to innumerable scriptures
Containing both the apparent and ultimate meanings
And properly examine and investigate them,
Any attempt at liberation will take longer
Without meditating on the meaning of intrinsic reality.[15]

Some say the present age is not the time for meditation.
This act of discouraging oneself and others is wrong discourse.
Those predestined seekers who refuse to believe this and keep their distance
Should meditate in all earnestness.

I will present an eloquent explanation of this moonlight [mahāmudrā].
In its full phase it will contain the meanings of the sūtras and tantras
And reveal the true nature of reality
As clearly as the outline of "the rabbit" [in the moon].[16]
Let there be peace in those who wander in the darkness of delusion!

Those of you who do not turn your backs on the great goal,
Who are not confused by perverted doctrines,
And who wish to meditate and realize the meaning
Of pure reality,
All you spiritually destined and intellectually discriminating ones,
4 F Listen in humility!

THE RESOLUTION TO COMPOSE THIS WORK

The way to practice the sacred dharma for those of us who have embraced the precious teachings of the fully and perfectly enlightened master, the Buddha, is known as the ten dharma practices.[17] Meditation on intrinsic reality alone is said to be supreme among these practices. The system of that meditation will be explained here.

Seeing that most of the listeners and investigators of the present time do not have any experience in the practice and that some practitioners have only a vague notion of the vital aspects of meditation [on the mahāmudrā of ultimate reality], I will elucidate it by arousing a completely benevolent attitude in myself for the sake of those relying on me. As most people might find the text, written mainly in conceptual terminology and poetic composition, hard to understand, I will expound it in an easily understandable manner.

In this work, I will provide:

4B 1. The reasons why meditation on the true nature of mind is essential
2. The stages of meditation

THE REASONS WHY MEDITATION ON THE TRUE NATURE OF MIND IS ESSENTIAL

The essence of Buddhist doctrine reveals that only by understanding the mind through meditation can one achieve insight into ultimate reality.

Stating the reason why meditation on the true nature of mind is essential, I shall deal with the two stages of meditation: (a) a concise elucidation of common meditative absorption [samādhi], and (b) an extensive elucidation of [mahāmudrā] the uncommon meditation. In this section, I shall show:

1. All realities are but mental phenomena
2. The deficiencies arising from not meditating on the true nature of mind
3. The benefits arising from meditation

All Realities Are But Mental Phenomena

All things encompassing the phenomena of existence and enlightenment [saṃsāra and nirvāṇa] are of the mind.

The *Daśabhūmika-sūtra* states:

> O sons of the victorious Buddha,
> The three planes of existence are of the mind only.

The *Vajrapañjara-tantra* says:

> Neither ordinary beings nor enlightened ones
> Exist outside of the precious mind.

In the *Samputa-tantra*, it is said:

> All things, external and internal,
> Are designated by the mind.
> Apart from the mind nothing else exists.

Guru Śavareśvara[18] says:

> All things are but inherent phenomena of the mind.
> Apart from the mind nothing exists, not even the minutest particle.

F If that is so, one might ask how the external world of form, sound, and so on appears to be real. The mind—being unaware of its true nature—has perceived the duality of "self" and "others" from beginningless time. Clinging to these, the mind builds up a sediment of impressions.[19] This causes external phenomena to appear as real to the deluded mind.

The *Laṅkāvatāra-sūtra* states:[20]

All things appear as perfect reality to the mind.
Apart from the mind no reality as such exists.
To perceive external reality is to see wrongly.

The *Sampuṭa* says:

All realities are of the mind's delusion.
Apart from the mind nothing exists.
All appearances are due to the mind's delusion.

Here again the illusion of an external reality that appears concrete is caused by the accumulating sediment of delusion, the way earth and rock are formed out of wind-stirred water.

Saraha says:

5 B Even though water is soft
It turns solid like a rock if stirred [constantly] by wind.
An ignorant mind, if stirred by thought,
Turns the formless into a solid entity.

How does such a mind fall into an existential cycle [saṃsāra] or attain a pure state [nirvāṇa]? A deluded mind does not know that the nature of duality is saṃsāra and the opposite is nirvāṇa.[20] This is supported by the following treatises.

The second section of the *Hevajra-tantra* teaches:

Ignorance gives rise to existential form.
Purged of ignorance saṃsāra becomes nirvāṇa.

The *Sampuṭa* comments:

"Enveloped by the darkness of many thoughts,
Overcome by madness as if struck by lightning,
Stained by impurity such as lust and the like,
All of which are difficult to prevent—
Such a mind is indeed saṃsāra," said Vajradhara.

One achieves liberation by realizing
The mind's nature is lucid clarity.
He who is unstained by lust and the like,
Who is without any duality of subject and object,

This superior enlightened mind
Is defined as supreme nirvāṇa.

Master Nāgārjuna says:

F By purifying that which is the cause of saṃsāra,
One achieves the purity which is nirvāṇa.
Thus the mind is the root of all deficiencies and attributes.
They originate only from the mind.

The *Laṅkāvatāra-sūtra* states:

The reflection of form in a mirror
Is an image without substance.
Duality—like that image—
Is a projection of the mind.
The perception of external phenomena as reality
Is caused by diverse thoughts
Rooted in the psychic residue of past lives.
This is the transitory mind.
It creates all forms.
What appears to be external reality
Is actually nonexistent.
The seeming self within the body
Experiencing the senses
Is only the mind; this I proclaim.

The *Avataṃsaka-sūtra* explains:

The mind is like an artist:
It creates.
All existential realms,
All these are created by the multifarious mind.

The *Ratnamegha-sūtra* comments:

The world is led by the mind.
The mind does not see itself;
Good or bad action is caused by the mind.
It revolves like a fire wheel
Moves like waves,
Burns like a forest fire,
Widens like a great river.

The *Vajrapañjara* says:

Ever since beginningless time phenomena have existed.
These have been called the external world.

All these are but creations of the mind
Which encompasses everything.

Further on, the *Vajrapañjara* says:

No external reality exists except for the mind.
Everything appearing as form and the like
Is a manifestation of that very mind.

The Deficiencies Arising from Not Meditating on the True Nature of Mind

A Buddhist who studies only the concept of the dharma by listening and investigating will achieve only a transitory benefit and will fail to realize the ultimate liberation. This has been illustrated by many examples.

7 F The *Gaṇḍavyūha-sūtra* states:

One cannot achieve realization merely by listening
To the perfect teachings of Buddha.
As a weak person may die of thirst
While being carried away by a great river,
So the dharma is ineffective unless meditated upon.

Like the man who has given food and drink to many people
And dies himself of hunger,
So the dharma is ineffective unless meditated upon.

Like the physician who possesses all the medicine
And dies of internal disease,
So the dharma is ineffective unless meditated upon.

Like the guardian of a treasury who counts the gems
Without owning any himself,
So the dharma is ineffective unless meditated upon.

Like the servant who is born into a palace
Yet does not own any food or drink,
So the dharma is ineffective unless meditated upon.

Like a blind artist who cannot be made
To paint a market scene,
So the dharma is useless unless meditated upon.

7 B Like a boatman on a great lake
Who transports many across but dies in the lake himself,
So the dharma is ineffective unless meditated upon.

Like someone who praises the prosperity of others
While standing at a crossroad,
Yet does not achieve anything himself,
So the dharma is ineffective unless meditated upon.

Furthermore, if one does not meditate, one's mind will succumb to defilement, causing it to fall into the lower realms.

The *Mañjuśrī-vikrīḍita-sūtra* states:

If the nature of mind is not realized,
It is drawn toward imaginary thoughts
And is forced to wander in the three planes
And six spheres of existence.

The *Bodhicaryāvatāra* says:

A man whose mind is totally distracted
Is caught between the fangs of defilement.

And the same work continues:

If one does not know the secret nature of the mind
Which is the essence of all dharma,
8 F One might wander aimlessly,
Though one wished to be happy and eliminate misery.
Wisdom does not arise without meditating upon tranquility;
Enlightenment does not arise without the emergence of wisdom.

The *Suhṛllekha* concludes:[21]

Wisdom does not arise without meditation on tranquility.

This requires all those engaged in observing ethical precepts and those studying through hearing and examining to practice meditation.

The Benefits Arising from Meditation

Boundless benefits will arise from meditation upon the true nature of reality. For the *Tattvaprakāśa-sūtra* states:

O Śāriputra, one will accumulate more benefits through meditation upon the tranquility of thatness,[22] even if only for a moment, than through listening to discourses for an aeon. Śāriputra, for this reason you should instruct others concerning the tranquility of thatness.

The *Mahoṣṇīṣa-sūtra* says:

Meditating for only a day on the meaning of the true nature of things brings greater spiritual benefits than hearing and examining the dharma for many aeons, as it removes one from the cycle of birth and death.

B The *Tokpa Gyepe Dho* explains:

> A moment's devotion to contemplative tranquility achieves greater benefit than saving all human life on the three planes of existence.

Furthermore, it is stated that meditating on tranquility produces revulsion for sensory pleasures, removes all doubts, and engenders perfect cognition, contemplative tranquility, and great compassion; it causes one to perceive the true nature of reality and enables one to set spiritual trainees on the path to enlightenment and to achieve other virtues.

The *Prajñāpāramitā-saṃcayagāthā* says:

> Meditative tranquility eliminates forbidden sensory pleasures and enables one to achieve the highest virtues, perfect cognition, and mental tranquility.

The *Daśacakra-kṣitigarbha-sūtra* adds:

> Doubts may be cleared by meditating upon tranquility. Nothing else can do that except the understanding of it [tranquility]. Therefore, to meditate upon tranquility is the best of all. O wise ones, strive toward it!

The *Dharmasaṃgīti-sūtra* says:

> By altering the mind to tranquil equipoise, one will reach its intrinsic
> 9 F purity. Through perfect perception of the inherent purity of reality, a bodhisattva practices in great compassion for the sake of all sentient beings.

The *Sūtrālaṃkāra* states:

> Merely through contemplation all sentient beings will reach the three kinds of enlightenment.[23]

BOOK ONE

A Concise Elucidation of the Common System of Tranquil Equipoise

THE OUTLINE OF TRANQUIL EQUIPOISE IN GENERAL AND THE REMOVAL OF DOUBTS

THE MEDITATION ON TRANQUILITY AND INSIGHT

Some texts explain methods of achieving tranquil equipoise according to both Mahāyāna and Hīnayāna traditions. The sūtras contain a clear explanation concerning contemplative absorption as it is known today. Specially known for their clarity are the *Saṃdhinirmocana* and other sūtras of the Buddha, the doctrines of Maitreya, the treatises of the bhūmis (*Sade*), and
B the *Abhidharmasamuccaya* by Asaṅga,[1] the *Prajñāpāramitopadeśa* of Śāntipa, which summarizes these texts, and also the three treatises of the *Bhāvanākrama* by Kamalaśīla, and others. Based on these texts I will elucidate the general meaning of tranquil equipoise.

The *Saṃdhinirmocana-sūtra* gives this concise description of contemplative absorption:

> Many aspects of the contemplative absorption of the śrāvakas, bodhisattvas and tathāgatas[2] shown by me should be understood to be comprised of meditation on tranquility and insight.

The second *Bhāvanākrama* says:

> All mystics [yogins] should constantly and surely dwell in tranquility and insight because all forms of meditational tranquility are unified in these two.

Tranquility and insight are the basis of all meditational absorptions of both Mahāyāna and Hīnayāna traditions. They are like the root that grounds the trunk, branches, and leaves of a tree.

10 F How do tranquility and insight contain the different kinds of meditations such as visualization and nonvisualization according to the meditational absorptions of the Mahāyāna and Hīnayāna, such varied meditations as the form and formlessness of Mantrayāna, and the numerous absorptions originating from bliss, lucidity, and nonconception according to mahāmudrā? Regardless of a meditation being conceptual or nonconceptual, visualized or nonvisualized, a meditation in which the mind has been fixed singly upon a sacred object is in harmony with tranquility. Wisdom being virtuous by nature discerns the true meaning [of the mind] so that it is in harmony with insight. Similarly, according to mahāmudrā, tranquility is the mind—either superior or inferior—undistracted from the object of concentration. The analysis and comprehension of the mind lead toward insight. Thus, all meditations culminate in tranquility and insight.

The *Mahāyānaprasādaprabhāvana-sūtra* states:

> Understand, O noble son, that the faith bodhisattvas have in the Mahāyāna teachings and whatever they have attained through them originates from the essence of the completely undistracted mind and from contemplation on the true reality.

10 B The undistracted mind is that which has focused itself one-pointedly upon a mental image[3] [of an object]. Contemplation upon the true reality is an act of a discerning intellect. Therefore, all qualities of Mahāyāna and Hīnāyana should be attained through the joint application of the one-pointed mind and discerning wisdom.

The third *Bhāvanākrama* sums it up:

> The Illuminated Conqueror showed different immeasurable and inconceivable absorptions of the bodhisattvas. Since tranquility and insight embrace all absorptions, the path of their joint application should be described.

CHAPTER ONE

The Ordinary Meditation of Tranquility and Insight

F This section is comprised of seven divisions:

1. The cause of tranquility and insight
2. Elimination of hindrances to tranquility and insight
3. Identification of the true nature of tranquility and insight
4. Distinctions of tranquility and insight
5. Examination of the stages of tranquility and insight
6. Meditation on joint tranquility and insight
7. The result of tranquility and insight

THE CAUSE OF TRANQUILITY AND INSIGHT

The *Saṃdhinirmocana-sūtra* states:

> Illuminated Conqueror, what is the cause of tranquility and insight?
>
> Buddha: Maitreya, tranquility arises from the purity of moral discipline, insight from hearing and examining.

The revered Gampopa spoke of this in a similar manner.

Tranquility is said to arise from a guru's spiritual blessing, the interaction of a good cause and condition, ever-growing virtues, and the purification of defilements. This is applicable to insight as well.

The second *Bhāvanākrama* enumerates the six causes of tranquility as arising from:

> A harmonious environment, curbing desires, contentment, limiting
> 11 B activities, maintaining moral discipline, and eliminating discursive
> thoughts.

> Insight arises from these three factors: association with holy persons, the acquiring of knowledge, and proper contemplation.

"To live in a harmonious environment" is to live in a place where sustenance can be obtained without much difficulty and where there is no harm from enemies and wild animals. "A good location" is one that is not affected by diseases, is not crowded during the day, is quiet at night, and is a place where one finds good friends following the same path of discipline and sharing similar views of reality.

The *Sūtrālaṃkāra* states:

> The environment where a wise man seeks realization
> Is one where proper nourishment is obtained,
> Where shelter is secure, the land congenial,
> Where friends are good,
> And where the yogin finds favorable conditions.

12 F "Curbing desires" means to harbor no sensual attachment to food and clothing for their quality or quantity. "To be content" is to be satisfied with frugal food and clothing. "To limit activities" is to abstain from harmful deeds such as trade, close association with lay people or monks, the practice of medicine, astrology, and so on.

"To maintain moral discipline" is to guard the foundation of the precepts as stated in the canon of individual liberation (*Pratimokṣa-sūtra*) and in the bodhisattva precepts, etc., and to apply spiritual remedies with repentance if one has, without self-control, transgressed these precepts. "To abandon desire and other discursive thoughts" is to be conscious of their evil consequences for this life and the next. It means eliminating desire through meditation on the impermanence of things, beautiful or ugly, from which one is soon to be separated.

12 B "To associate with holy persons" is to follow a spiritual guide who knows unerringly the importance of hearing, examining, and meditating, and who himself has realized tranquility and insight. "To seek extensive knowledge through hearing" is to listen to discourses on scriptures whose ultimate meaning is without flaws and to develop a discriminatory intellect. One does not achieve this by hearing teachings with conventional or intended meanings.

"To properly contemplate" is to ponder the ultimate meaning of the discourse and to apply inferences so as to realize intellectually the perfect view of reality.

THE ELIMINATION OF HINDRANCES TO TRANQUILITY AND INSIGHT

The elimination of hindrances to tranquility and insight requires:

1. The recognition of hindrances
2. Instructions in the remedies necessary to remove the hindrances

The Recognition of Hindrances

Concerning tranquility, the *Saṃdhinirmocana-sūtra* states:

> Maitreya: Illuminated Conqueror, of the five hindrances how many are hindrances to tranquility, how many to insight, and how many to both?
>
> Buddha: Maitreya, tranquility is hindered by sensual incitement and resentment, insight by sluggishness, drowsiness, and doubt; both are fogged by craving and malignity..

The *Abhidharmasamuccaya* says:

> 13 F What is sensual incitement?[4] It is the mind that lusts after beautiful forms. Its function is to disturb the state of tranquility. This wandering thought having focused itself upon an object of beauty causes interruptions in maintaining the stability of the mind.

The same text comments on resentment:

> Resentment[5] is formed by conscious or unconscious deeds of a positive or negative kind. It harbors indignance at some deeds, good, bad, or neutral, timely or untimely, worthy or unworthy, thereby unsettling the stability of the mind. Hence it belongs to the category of delusion (ignorance).

This lingering thought upon right or wrong, arising from positive or negative action, effectively disturbs the stability of the mind.

Concerning sluggishness it is said:

> What is sluggishness?[6] It is that which renders the mind inactive and maintains distortions and secondary distortions. Hence it belongs to
> 13 B the category of delusion.

The commentary on the *Abhidharmakośa* states:

> What is sluggishness? It is heaviness of body and mind.

It stupefies [the mind] making both the body and mind unmanageable.

Since sluggishness and dullness are considered alike, no separate comment has been made on dullness. The second *Bhāvanākrama* explains:

> Dullness occurs when the mind does not visualize clearly, like a blind man, a man in darkness, or one with his eyes closed. When the clarity of the mental image loses its sharpness on account of physical and mental lethargy, it is not quite the same as sluggishness.

The second *Bhāvanākrama* comments on sleep:

> 14 F What is sleep? Sleep causes withdrawal of thoughts, good, bad, or neutral, timely or untimely, worthy or unworthy. The effect of sleep is the cessation of activity; hence it belongs to the category of delusion. As stated here, sleep results in the loss of sensory functions causing the meditator to lose his mental focus.

Concerning doubt the same text says:

> What is doubt? It is having two minds about all aspects of truth, effectively preventing one from following the course of virtue.

It means entertaining doubts about the relative and absolute truths and the four noble truths. It creates confusion in the meditator's mind, causing him to doubt the aims of his meditation and its success or failure. Thus it saps his urge to practice.

Craving is a longing for any kind of sensory indulgence to which the mind clings. Malignity is evil intended to cause others harm out of hatred or jealousy.

14 B About the other obstacles to tranquility and insight the *Saṃdhinirmocana-sūtra* states:

> Maitreya: O Illuminated Conqueror, what are the distractions that cause mental divergences for a bodhisattva who dwells in tranquility and insight?
>
> Buddha: Of these there are five: divergence of the mind toward mental activities, external, internal, perceptive, and emotive divergence.

To identify them the same sūtra states:

> Buddha: Maitreya, divergence of the mind toward mental activities occurs when a bodhisattva has degenerated into the mental activities of "the Hearers" and "the Solitary Buddhas," having forsaken the mental application of Mahāyāna Buddhism. External divergence occurs when the mind turns toward the five senses, the gathering of people,
> 15 F duality, discursive thoughts and secondary defilements, and external images. Internal divergence of the mind occurs when one feels either

lethargic, drowsy, or when one indulges in the ecstacy of trance or in any subtle distortion of the meditative absorption. Perceptive divergence occurs when the mind visualizes an image of external form in the realm of pure contemplation. Emotive divergence occurs when the mind with its inbred tendencies assigns "I" consciousness to sensations arising from its inward activities.

The *Madhyāntavibhāga* states:

> Laziness, the forgetting of instructions, dullness and sensual incitement, nonexertion of the mind, and overexertion are the five defects that interrupt tranquility.

These five become six if dullness and sensual incitement are enumerated separately. These defects are also applicable to insight.

"Laziness" is the result of being either adverse or indifferent to any endeavors and lacking in vigilance, so that habitual idleness deprives the contemplation of any motive force. "Forgetfulness" consists of being unable to recollect the object of the meditational search and getting distracted. "Dullness" and "sensual incitement" have been described before. "Nonexertion" is the lack of any effort at eliminating dullness and sensual incitement and allowing the mind to idle. "Overexertion" is the excessive striving toward the mind's object, even after pacifying dullness and sensual incitement. It does not let the mind dwell in its natural state.

Instructions in the Remedies Necessary to Remove the Hindrances

There are two sections:

1. The general elucidation of remedies for hindrances
2. The specific means for removing dullness and sensual incitement

The General Elucidation of Remedies for Hindrances

16 F The texts mentioned before made no precise comment with regard to remedies for the hindrances. Most hindrances belong to the area of dullness and sensual incitement. By knowing how to remove these one will automatically know the remedy for others.

The remedy for sensual incitement lies in calming the mind by meditating upon impermanence. As for resentment, the remedy is to avoid thinking about its object. To counter sluggishness, one perceives joyful things. Dullness is removed by stimulating the spirit. Drowsiness is overcome by visualizing light. Resoluteness is a remedy for doubt. Contemplation on contentment and the evil consequences of sensory pleasures is a remedy for craving. Evil intent may be removed by engendering love and kindness for others. All these are very important. Similarly, one should adopt these remedies for the five distractions of the mind.

The *Madhyāntavibhāga* states:

> The eight remedies for the five interruptions.

16 B There are eight remedies for removing the five interruptions: for laziness it is (1) faith, (2) earnestness, (3) striving, and (4) perfect ease. Forgetfulness is relieved by (5) mindfulness. The cure for dullness and sensual incitement is (6) vigilance; for nonexertion it is (7) mental exertion. For overexertion it is (8) equanimity that lets the mind rest in its true state. Faith, earnestness, and striving are simple to understand.

Concerning perfect ease, the *Abhidharmasamuccaya* says:

> What is the state of perfect ease?[7] It is the suppleness of body and mind that pacifies harmful tendencies and hindrances.

The evil tendencies of the body and mind make them uncontrollable. The power of perfect ease removes heaviness and other defects, which hinder the practices of virtue, from the body. Perfect ease makes the body light and controllable through bliss. This is how the body can be controlled. It also eliminates misery through focusing it on a mental object that produces joy, bliss, etc. This is how the mind can be controlled.

17 F Master Sthiramati[8] says that mastery of the body eases physical activities and makes the body light. The docile mind is flexible and serene in contemplation. Possession of such a mind will enable one to contemplate without hindrance.

Perfect ease cannot be obtained at the initial stage of meditation; it is achieved through continuous effort. At first only a small measure of ease will be attained. However, through persistence this will increase until perfection is achieved. The *Śrāvakabhūmi* states that achieving a perfect ease of mind first will bring about the circulation and diffusion of the vital air in the body. Once this takes place meditators will achieve the perfect ease of the body.

On the nature of memory the *Abhidharmasamuccaya* states:

> What is memory?[9] Memory is not forgetting things one has familiarized oneself with; its function is to effect an undistracted concentration.

17 B Memory means not being distracted from a familiar mental image. The mind sustains the image vividly without lapse. For example, by thinking of a certain image often one does not forget it. This one has to practice at first.

With regard to vigilance the commentary on the *Madhyāntavibhāga* says:

> Vigilance[10] may be achieved [during meditation] by not forgetting the

object of concentration while remaining fully attentive to any emerging distraction such as dullness, sensual incitement, or thought.

With such a stream of awareness one remains on guard, forever watching and discerning any distraction upon its arising. This is described in the *Bodhicaryāvatāra*:

> When one dwells at the gate of awareness, forever watching, vigilance arises.

The same text continues:

> This examination of the physical and mental states means precisely watching with vigilance.

F With regard to mental exertion [thought formation][11] the *Abhidharmasamuccaya* says:

> What is mental exertion? It is a mental activity that is drawn into all channels—good, bad, or neutral.

This being a mental function, it activates itself or is drawn toward three kinds of thoughts—good, bad, or neutral. In this case it is a thought that strives to eliminate dullness or sensual incitement once vigilance detects them.

On the equanimity[12] that settles the mind in its natural state, the *Śrāvakabhūmi* says:

> Equanimity is that condition in which the mental focus of tranquil or insight meditation is harmonious and free from disturbance, the mind being settled in a perfect state, dwelling in its innate realm, and experiencing peace. Within this state the mind is tractable and can be redirected effortlessly.

18 B Once dullness and sensual incitement are eliminated and tranquility and insight harmonized, one stabilizes that harmony skillfully by releasing the pressure of effort and maintaining the mind in a tractable condition.

The same text further comments:

> What is the mark of equanimity? It is an even level of the perceived mind brought about through directing the mental focus or through maintaining it without excessive exertion. When should one work toward this evenness? When tranquility and insight are free from dullness or sensual incitement, one achieves equanimity.

THE SPECIFIC MEANS FOR REMOVING DULLNESS AND SENSUAL INCITEMENT

There are two ways of eliminating dullness and sensual incitement:

1. Refraining from the causes of dullness and sensual incitement
2. The elimination of dullness and sensual incitement.

REFRAINING FROM THE CAUSES OF DULLNESS AND SENSUAL INCITEMENT

Most veils clouding contemplative absorption may be summarized as dullness and sensual incitement. These arise from harmful acts of body, speech, or mind.

The *Sa'ingōshi* says:

> 19 F What are the marks of dullness? Dullness arises from the uncontrolled senses, gluttony, the avoidance of meditation at dawn and dusk, from living without vigilance or in mental torpor, from excessive sleep or an unskilled meditation. Sloth, which undermines eagerness, industriousness, contemplation, or investigation is another cause of dullness. Meditation on a fragment of tranquility without mastery of the whole, leaving the mind in darkness, and taking no delight in focusing it on a perceptive image—these actions foster dullness.
>
> What are the marks of sensual incitement? They include the four
> mentioned earlier: uncontrolled senses, gluttony, avoidance of medita-
> tion, and a lack of vigilance. Sensual indulgence, aggressiveness, and
> being unmoved by saṃsāra's conditions are other attributes of sensual
> incitement. Sensual incitement takes other forms such as attachment
> 19 B to the desire for meditation, failure to be industrious, and a lack of
> mastery over the power of concentration. Fragmented meditation and
> an attachment to one's family and friends also constitute sensual
> incitement. In this context, the term "mark" of dullness and sensual
> incitement can be read to mean causes.
>
> The term "sloth" applies to lack of perseverance, contemplation, and investigation. "Achieving the mastery of tranquility" means acquiring an intimacy with the sensations and perceptions of tranquility. "Attachment" refers to the desire for meditation, perseverance, contemplation, and investigation. These are causes of dullness and sensual incitement and should be avoided.

THE ELIMINATION OF DULLNESS AND SENSUAL INCITEMENT

It is said that overwhelming dullness can be eliminated by various means such as contemplation upon a mental image of light and the attributes of the Buddha, examination of the dullness with discrimination, visualization of an expanding mental image, and an elation of one's spirits through meditation on joy.

The first *Bhāvanākrama* states:

> 0 F When the focus upon a perceived image becomes dim and the mind turns sluggish due to lethargy or drowsiness, one clears this by meditating on a mental image of a light or the sublime attributes of the Buddha, which create joy. Once a perceived image has been attained, it must be maintained.

The *Prajñāpāramitā-saṃcayagāthā* says:

> If overcome by depression,
> One should elate the spirit through the power
> Of perseverance toward attaining insight.

The *Madhyamakahṛdaya* as well says:

> Depression is to be levelled by meditating
> Upon a perceived image of great size.

The *Śrāvakabhūmi* states:

> Grasp the image of light that originates from a butter lamp or a great blazing fire or from the disc of the sun.

Thus the mind should be fixed on everything that is being illuminated or
20 B brightened by these lights. Referring to the mind during periods of non-meditational activity, the text says that it should be continually elated by perceiving luminosity and the sixfold remembrance.

Dullness should be removed by contemplating its causes: sluggishness and sleep. It can be cleared by strolling, watching the moon and stars, or washing one's face.

To remove intense sensual incitement whenever it arises, one must engender a sense of revulsion [for the round of birth and death] by contemplating impermanence[13] or the consequences of distraction. Settling the mind in tranquility also counters sensual incitement.

The first *Bhāvanākrama* comments:

> When memories of past indulgences in sensual incitement or indulgence distract the mind, they should be pacified by contemplating impermanence and other facts that cause revulsion. One should then strive to redirect the mind toward the perceptive image without any thought formations.

The *Madhyamakahṛdaya* says:

> Concerning distractions and their causes:
> One looks upon them as being harmful and terminates them.

21 F The *Prajñāpāramitā-saṃcayagāthā* concludes:

> When the mind becomes distracted by sensual incitement
> One should eliminate it through tranquility.

A behavioral remedy for such distraction consists of controlling the senses, refraining from rigorous activities—as in the case of a sick person—avoiding perception of objects that arouse passion, and engaging in multiple prostrations. Concerning subtle dullness: when the mind sinks, it should be elevated through a contemplative effort. When the mind is restless, it should be calmed and relaxed, or some other well-known methods should be applied.

IDENTIFICATION OF THE TRUE NATURE OF TRANQUILITY AND INSIGHT

To identify the true nature of tranquility and insight,[14] the (*Saṃdhinirmocana-sūtra*) states:

> He who lives in solitude, settling the mind in inward purity, meditates on aspects of reality previously analyzed. Such a sentient being continuously draws his mind inward. By so achieving a state of tranquility and the ability to attain that state as many times as possible, one attains the perfect ease of body and mind. This is said to be "dwelling in tranquility."

21 B The same text says:

> Having achieved such ease one should settle in this state, abandoning all thought forms, and then proceed to analyze the focus of contemplative absorption. "Insight" is the process of investigating the totality of contemplative absorption with a view to discerning properly and perfectly the reality of knowledge. It is achieved through the exercise of discrimination, observation, examination, endurance, and yearning.

The *Ratnamegha* says:

> Tranquility is one-pointed concentration.
> Insight is analytical comprehension.

The *Sūtrālaṃkārā* states:

> Know this: the essence of dharma lies
> In the paths of tranquility and insight.
> Investigation of these paths
> Begets insight.

The same text adds:

> The mind settled in its purity
> Is in a tranquil state.
> Analysis of this state
> Is insight.

The master Vasubandhu says in his commentary to this text:

> The mind resting in harmony through meditational absorption is in tranquility. Analysis of this state causes insight. Without meditational absorption there cannot be tranquility and insight. Such is the description of the two states.

In general, tranquility is achieved by fixing the mind upon any object so as to maintain it without distraction. Insight is characterized as wisdom that analyzes the reality of knowledge. Tranquility is achieved by focusing the
B mind on an object and maintaining it in that state until finally it is channeled into one stream of attention and evenness. Insight is attained through a general and detailed examination of reality and the systematic application of intellectual discrimination.

The *Bodhisattvabhūmi* states:

> Focusing the mind on its ineffable essence and on images of reality, one maintains an awareness free from judgements and distractions. With a delight in all mental images one focuses the mind on the mark of inner absorption, maintains it, and channels it into a stream of attention and quietude. These methods produce a state of tranquility free from judgements and distractions. When one appreciates all images of meditation, which range from fixing the mind upon the marks of inward meditational trance and sustaining an absorption to intensely consolidating it into one stream and achieving meditational trance, this is called tranquility.

The same text continues:

> What is insight? Insight is attained when a meditator, having achieved tranquility, now contemplates the various aspects of the mind and
> 23 F analyzes properly and perfectly its conditioned and unconditioned realities. He thus achieves skill in investigation and the application of wisdom.
>
> Concerning the mental images of tranquility and insight, tranquility is nonconceptual.[15] It simply focuses on any given object without duality. Insight is sublime perception that examines the nature of the mind.

The *Saṃdhinirmocana-sūtra* states:

> Maitreya: O Illuminated Conqueror,[16] how many forms of tranquility exist?
>
> Buddha: There is only one, and it is nonconceptual.
>
> Maitreya: How many perceptions of insight exist?
>
> Buddha: Only one, and it is conceptualized perception.
>
> Maitreya: How many perceptions of the two exist?
>
> Buddha: There is the perception of the extent of the phenomenal world [tranquility], and there is attainment of meditational aim [insight].

The *Prajñāpāramitopadeśa* comments:

> Tranquility is a nonconceptual perception of phenomena that dis-
> 23 B cerns neither their extent nor their exact nature. Insight is a conceptual perception of phenomena that discerns their extent and exact nature.

The second *Bhāvanākrama* adds:

> Tranquility is so called because, having pacified distractions, one focuses always on an inward image joyfully, naturally, and without interruptions while maintaining perfect ease of mind. Insight is that which examines the nature of that tranquil state so long as it remains.

If this is so, what are tranquility and insight to be called when they are not attended by perfect ease? They are then defined as simulated tranquility and insight.

The *Saṃdhinirmocana-sūtra* says:

> Maitreya: O Illuminated Conqueror, what may we call the mental exercise of a bodhisattva who focuses inwardly upon the mind before he has attained perfect ease?
>
> Buddha: Maitreya, it is not the ideal tranquility but a simulated one created by a yearning for tranquility.
>
> 24 F Maitreya: Illuminated Conqueror, as long as a bodhisattva does not attain perfect ease, what may we call his contemplation on the perceptions of the mind, which he continuously examines, until the attainment of perfect ease?
>
> Buddha: Maitreya, it is not real but simulated insight created by yearning.

Likewise, the *Prajñāpāramitopadeśa* states:

> A bodhisattva living in solitude and contemplation abandons conceptualization and meditates continuously on the perceptions of the mind. This meditation is simulated tranquility. Real tranquility is
> 4 B only attained when he achieves a state of perfect ease of body and mind.

The *Prajñāpāramitopadeśa* continues:

> Having achieved perfect ease, he maintains this state, and with intense yearning analyzes his perceptions of the significance of the reality he has examined. As long as perfect ease is not experienced, this meditation remains only superficial; once he attains this ease, insight is gained.

How is the perfect path of tranquility and insight attained? It is said that tranquility is attained when sluggishness and sleepiness are eliminated, whereas insight is attained when sensual incitement and resentment are eliminated.

25 F The *Saṃdhinirmocana-sūtra* says:

> Maitreya: Illuminated Conqueror, when does one achieve the perfect path of tranquility?
>
> Buddha: Maitreya, when one completely eliminates sluggishness and sleepiness.
>
> Maitreya: O Illuminated Conqueror, when does one achieve perfect insight?
>
> Buddha: Maitreya, when one completely eliminates sensual incitement and resentment.

DISTINCTIONS OF TRANQUILITY AND INSIGHT

Tranquility is divided into three categories: the first describes its nature as being either transient or transcendental; the next describes the three categories of tranquility and mentions blissful tranquility as one of them; the last categorizes the nine methods of achieving tranquility.

The *Sūtrālaṃkāra* states:

> Fixing the mind's attention on a perceived image,
> One's stream of attention should not be distracted.

Master Vasubandhu says in his commentary:

> 25 B This stanza illustrates the nine steps of stabilizing the mind[17] in tranquility:

1. To stabilize the mind
2. To settle it completely
3. To settle it firmly
4. To settle it intensely
5. To clear it of obstacles
6. To pacify the mind
7. To completely pacify it
8. To channel the mind into one stream
9. To settle the mind in equipoise

The *Abhidharmasamuccaya* says:

> What is tranquility? It is to settle the mind in tranquility, regularly, attentively, intensely; to clear the mind; to pacify the mind completely; and to settle the mind in one-pointedness and equipoise.

These are the nine stages of tranquility. They will be further identified in the section on tranquility.

Concerning insight, the *Saṃdhinirmocana-sūtra* says:

> Maitreya: O Illuminated Conqueror, how many aspects of insight are there?
>
> Buddha: Maitreya, there are three, namely:
>
> 1. That which originates from conceptual judgment
> 2. That which is attained through perfect inquiry
> 3. That which is achieved through analytical examination

26 F The same sūtra explains further:

> What is that which arises from conceptual judgement? It is insight which originates from the analysis of a perceived image of contemplative absorption.
>
> What is that which arises from perfect inquiry? It is insight which arises from the intellectual investigation of the unknown aspects of the mind.
>
> What is that which originates from analytical examination? Insight arises from perfect analysis of the mental aspects of reality, which the intellect has understood in all its subtleties.

The *Abhidharmasamuccaya* states:

> What is insight? Insight is that which differentiates systematically and
> fully all things [with respect to their apparent and true nature]. It also
> 26 B examines fully and perfectly duality and nonduality. This investiga-
> tion remedies harmful and dualistic tendencies. Not only does insight

deliver one from the wrong course, but it also directs the mind to focus on the right path.

Insight is said to consist of four stages:

1. That which differentiates all aspects of reality
2. That which differentiates absolute reality
3. The examination of the concept of duality
4. The understanding of that duality

The *Śrāvakabhūmi* elucidates:

> Buddha: What are the four kinds of insight, virtuous mendicants? They are:
>
> 1. Differentiation of all realities
> 2. Perfect differentiation of all realities
> 3. Examination of conceptual duality
> 4. Perfect examination of this duality
>
> The mind must rest in tranquility during all this.
>
> Buddha: How does one differentiate the reality of all phenomena? One differentiates it through:
>
> 1. A crystal-clear analysis, keen intellectual perception, or a purifying mental image that eliminates distortions
> 27 F 2. Differentiation of the nature of reality as it is
> 3. A complete intellectual examination that must occur when the mind clings to duality
> 4. Perfect examination that results when one perceives reality perfectly

The *Śrāvakabhūmi* states further:

> There are three gateways and six methods of determining insight. In short, these contain all types of insight. Insight may be determined through six methods of investigating the nature of the mind:
>
> 1. Reality
> 2. Substance
> 3. Characteristics
> 4. Spatial dimensions
> 5. Time
> 6. Dialectical process

EXAMINATION OF THE STAGES OF TRANQUILITY AND INSIGHT

Most doctrinal treatises related to the sūtras state that tranquility should be attained first and insight afterward; as the *Sūtrālaṃkāra* states:

> 27 B Mastery of the preceding principle results
> In the realization of the succeeding principles.
> The former is inferior and coarse,
> The latter superior and subtle.

The above quote refers to the six principles of gone-beyond.[18] It is said that each principle may be realized through the preceding one, as every preceding principle is inferior and crude, while the succeeding one is superior and subtle.

The *Suhṛllekha* comments:

> Wisdom does not arise without concentration.

The *Bodhicaryāvatāra* states:

> Knowing that insight arises from tranquility
> And clears the defilements of the mind,
> One should first achieve tranquility.

Similar comments are made in the *Śrāvakabhūmi*, the *Bhāvanākrama*, and the *Prajñāpāramitopadeśa*. Those who rely upon this approach say that the stages of meditation necessitate the attainment of tranquility as *a priori* to
28 F the achievement of insight. They reason that one does not achieve tranquility without perfect ease. Without achieving tranquility and perfect ease one cannot realize insight and the attendant perfect ease. This approach is incorrect because one can experience both tranquility and insight without achieving perfect ease. Why is this so? As the *Bodhisattvabhūmi*, the *Abhidharmasamuccaya* and the *Prajñāpāramitopadeśa* state, the nine stages for achieving tranquility, beginning with the quieting of the mind, constitute the stage of tranquility, whereas the four insights achieved through the determination of aspects of reality comprise the stage of insight. It is hard for beginners at the early stage of tranquility and insight to achieve perfect ease. Furthermore, they believe there can only exist an ultimate kind of tranquility and insight, and perfect ease must accompany both. By extension, this position would only allow for the existence of one ultimate path.

28 B The *Saṃdhinirmocana-sūtra* and the *Prajñāpāramitopadeśa* state:

> If this is so, how is it that meditations unaccompanied by perfect ease are not meditations of tranquility and insight?

The preceding was intended to be a yardstick for measuring the realization of ultimate tranquility and insight. Were it not so, many internal contradictions and fallacies in terms of Buddha's words and logic would arise. The statement that one should meditate upon insight by relying on tranquility was intended for individuals on the gradual path. As there are those who realize insight without even achieving tranquility, the *Abhidharmasamuccaya* says:

> Some achieve insight without tranquility, and through insight they attain tranquility.

The *Sa'ingōshi* says:

> Some practitioners understand perfectly the doctrine dealing with existential miseries, which ultimately leads to the path. They have neither attained any stages of absorption nor have they determined the aspects of reality with a tranquil mind, yet they exercise a superior
> F mind through transcending wisdom. This statement is made without contention. Even the tantras and commentaries on transformation and perfection[19] urge one to visualize an object during the first part of the sitting and meditate on formlessness during the last. These meditations are not like those that seek insight by first achieving tranquility. Many great masters urge others to meditate from the beginning on insight, seeking tranquility separately.

MEDITATION ON JOINT TRANQUILITY AND INSIGHT

There are two sections:

1. The reason one needs both tranquility and insight
2. The method of combining these two

The Reason One Needs Both Tranquility and Insight

There is a reason for combining tranquility and insight. Without tranquility and mind stirs, like water, and cannot settle in tranquil absorption. Such a mind cannot attain a true understanding of its inherent purity. Insight
29 B devoid of tranquility is unstable like a butter lamp in the wind, and as such it cannot produce a clear perception of original awareness. Hence the need for combining insight with tranquility.

The first *Bhāvanākrama* states:

> Because the mind is restless like water, it cannot settle without the foundation of tranquility. The mind that has not settled in tranquil absorption cannot perceive its inherent purity. The Illuminated Con-

queror said that by settling [the mind] in tranquil absorption one will understand its inherent purity.

The second *Bhāvanākrama* says:

> Without tranquility insight distracts a meditator's mind toward objects, rendering it unstable like a butter lamp in the wind and hindering it from attaining a clear perception of original awareness. One should therefore work toward attaining a balance of the two.

30 F However much one meditates upon tranquility, without insight this merely temporarily neutralizes the mind's distortion but cannot eliminate it. Besides, this meditation cannot uproot hidden psychic defilements, nor can it liberate one from harm arising from the round of birth, decay, disease, and death.

The second *Bhāvanākrama* also states:

> Yogins[20] meditating upon mere tranquility do not eliminate the mind's defilement. It [tranquility] merely suppresses the mind's distortion but cannot engender the vision of wisdom. Hence such meditation is incapable of destroying the sediment of that distortion.

The *Saṃdhinirmocana-sūtra* confirms:

> Concentration merely suppresses the mind's distortion; wisdom destroys hidden root distortion.

The above text quotes the *Bodhisattvapiṭaka* as follows:

> 30 B People who consider meditational absorption to be adequate have heard neither the collected teachings of the bodhisattva nor the moral law of the arhats.[21] They are bound to fall victim to their pride. They will neither achieve freedom from birth, decay, disease, death, lamentation, suffering, anguish, and agitation of the mind, nor will they achieve freedom from the six spheres of sentient beings,[22] nor liberation from the psychophysical aggregates.[23] In view of this the Enlightened Conqueror proclaimed that he who has realized that which is in complete harmony with all other phenomena, will achieve liberation from decay and death.

Tranquility brings about concentration undistracted from the mental image, while insight brings about the realization of thatness [tathatā], rendering the mind like a mountain, unmoved by wrong views. Hence the need for both tranquility and insight.

The *Candrapradīpa-sūtra* states:

> Tranquility makes the mind unshakable;
> Insight makes it unmovable like a mountain.

The Method of Combining These Two

One may wonder about the means of unifying tranquility and insight. There exist methods of combining tranquility and insight at every meditational stage prior to the ninth. Concerning the union of the final tranquility and insight at the ninth stage: when one has achieved perfect quiescent absorption through the elimination of dullness and sensual incitement, one strives toward the insight that differentiates all aspects of reality. One is then drawn naturally into a state of insight where there is no need for exertion, for one has achieved effortlessness, which is the mark of the ninth stage. This pure and perfect insight merges with a tranquil mind, achieving unification, and thus tranquility and insight become nondual.

The *Śrāvakabhūmi* states:

> At which time do tranquility and insight merge and for what reason is this described as a unifying path? When one has achieved the ninth stage of contemplative absorption through the nine stages of tranquil-
> B ity. One then strives toward transcending wisdom that differentiates all aspects of reality so that one is naturally and effortlessly drawn onto the path of differentiating aspects of reality. As with tranquility, at this level insight requires no exertion. It is perfect and pure, resembling the quiescence and bliss of tranquility. At this stage tranquility and insight merge, resulting in contemplative absorption. Hence the designation "unifying tranquility and insight."

The third *Bhāvanākrama* states:

> When the mind settles naturally in quiescent absorption, free from dullness and sensual incitement, it vividly perceives its very essence. At this stage one should relax one's exertion, maintain an even state, and become aware that at this point one has achieved the union of tranquility and insight.

32 F After that, the *Prajñāpāramitopadeśa* says that one focuses upon the image of discriminative thought. When one experience both [tranquility and insight] through continuous contemplation, this is described as the unified path of tranquility and insight [Tib.: zung-drel]. The syllable "zung" refers to [both] tranquility and insight while "drel" refers to the interrelationship. "Image of discriminative thought" refers to insight.

It is generally held that nonconceptualization is a mental image in the meditation of tranquility, whereas conceptualization is a mental image in the meditation of insight. Based on this some meditators even think that in
32 B tranquility one does not contemplate anything, whereas in insight one engages in thoughts only. This assertion is not correct. Were it so, it would rule out the existence of tranquil meditation on any creative images such as

visualized forms. Why? Because one must then necessarily accept the fact that when engaged in tranquil meditation on the visualized form of the Buddha, one is neither visualizing that image nor analyzing it. And because they claim that during the meditation of tranquility one neither contemplates nor analyzes anything, this rules out the possibility of a union between tranquility and insight, since—as they maintain—tranquility is nonconceptual and insight is conceptual. According to this position compatibility between conceptual and nonconceptual [meditation] is not possible. Were it so, it would be held up to ridicule by logicians. If they say that an image merely appears to the perceiving mind but is not discriminative thought, the appearance will be meaningless unless it is designated by discriminative thought. Whatever appears does so because every mental image including visualization is said to be a result of such designation.

33 F Their assertion that all insights are conceptual is not correct, because the *Bhāvanākrama* makes mention of insight without mental activity.[24] Also, nonconceptual awareness is reality perceived through insight, which is perfect insight!

Furthermore, their postion would deny the possibility of tranquility endowed with differentiating wisdom, as they hold that tranquility accompanied by discriminative thought is not possible. For them tranquility must necessarily be completely nonconceptual. Also, this assertion contradicts the fact that tranquility is comprised of four kinds of mental activity. According to their view one would not exercise mindfulness and vigilance when meditating upon tranquility, as the mind in tranquility does not engage itself in mental activity.

One might ask, why are the mental images of tranquility and insight, as referred to above, prescribed? So far, reference has been made to them in general terms only. However, even in particular cases, such as the visual-
33 B ization of forms of a meditational deity, there are two aspects:

1. Tranquility, in which the mind lucidly visualizes such a sacred image
2. Insight, in which the mind analyzes the intrinsic reality of that mental image

Similarly, tranquility is a state of mental focus on a particular visualized mental image without thought of anything else. Insight is that which examines the nature of such tranquility while being definitely aware of the essenceless reality of that state and the discerning thought.

Consequently, the two [tranquility and insight] blend inseparably into one essential reality with two aspects. Such is the unification of tranquility and insight!

THE RESULT OF TRANQUILITY AND INSIGHT

The *Saṃdhinirmocana-sūtra* says:

> What are the results of these two?
> The results are complete purity of mind and perfect wisdom.

Purity of mind is said to be the result of tranquility, and perfection of wisdom that of insight. Purity of mind refers to the elimination of distorted thought, perfection of wisdom to purification of the sediment of delusion.

Referring to liberation from the two bondages by means of tranquility and insight, the same sūtra says:

> Maitreya: O Illuminated Conqueror, what are the roles of tranquility and insight?
>
> Buddha: Maitreya, they are to liberate [sentient beings] from the two bondages: the bondage of the conceptual perception[25] and the bondage of the harmful psychophysical tendencies[26] of human beings.

Furthermore, tranquility is said to prevent one from clinging to the sensory pleasures of this life; it brings forth the flowering of superknowledge and meditational absorption in their diverse forms. It will also cause rebirth in a celestial form, free from desire.

The *Prajñāpāramitā-saṃcayagāthā* explains:

> Concentration helps one to abandon sensory pleasures, which are shunned [by the holy ones], and brings forth sublime inner qualities, super knowledge, and quiescent absorption.

The *Suhṛllekha* states:

> Through the four levels of contemplation[27]
> One eliminates sensuality, joy, pleasures, and miseries;
> 4 B One achieves a well-being equal to that of the celestials
> In the heavens of Brahma, Ābhāsvara, Śubhakṛtsna, and
> Bṛhatphala.[28]

The *Bodhipathapradīpa* comments:

> When a yogin achieves tranquility,
> He will also realize superknowledge.

Insight, being an awareness of the intrinsic nature of phenomena, is said to produce peace and happiness for the present and to bring about liberation from the three planes of existence.

The *Prajñāpāramitā-saṃcayagāthā* states:

All experiences of happiness that abound in the buddhas,
In their sons, the awakened hearers, and the lonely buddhas,[29]
As well as in celestial and other sentient beings,
Originate from supreme transcendental wisdom.

The same text states:

Through wisdom one comprehends
The intrinsic nature of phenomena
And will pass beyond all three planes of existence.

The ultimate result of tranquility and insight is the attainment of full enlightenment.

The *Bodhisattvabhūmi* says:

Having achieved transcending contemplation, bodhisattvas have attained, are attaining, and will attain full enlightenment.

The *Saptaśatikā-prajñāpāramitā-sūtra* comments:

35 F Buddha: O Mañjuśrī, if a great bodhisattva practices transcending wisdom, he will soon achieve unsurpassed, full, and perfect enlightenment.

In dealing with tranquility and insight in general, the revered Gampopa said:

Tranquility and insight are the gate to all realms of phenomena.

There are five conditions in each meditation on tranquility and insight. These are: cause, function, obstacle, veil, and the perfect path. The cause of tranquility is purity of discipline; the cause of insight is wisdom born of hearing and examining [the dharma]. The function of tranquility is to liberate [seekers] from the bondage of a dualistic mark; the function of insight is to liberate them from psychophysical tendencies. The obstacle to tranquility is the concern for one's body and possessions; the obstacle to insight is a lack of appreciation for the words of the awakened ones [arhats].
35 B Dwelling in crowds and discontentment with meager provisions are obstacles to both [tranquility and insight].

The veil of tranquility comprises passions, resentment, and skepticism; the veil of drowsiness and lethargy obscures insight. Both tranquility and insight can be clouded by the urge for sensual indulgence and evil intent. The perfect path to tranquility is comprised of the complete eradication of lethargy and drowsiness; the perfect path to insight consists of the complete elimination of passion and resentment. Dharmakāya[30] as the fruit of meditation may be achieved by eliminating the two defilements through tranquility and insight. The general elucidation of tranquility and insight is thus completed.

CHAPTER TWO

The Stages of Tranquility and Insight
Part I: Tranquility

Tranquility is divided into three sections:

1. The preparation for achieving tranquility
2. The elucidation of its mental images
3. The methods of realizing tranquility

THE PREPARATION FOR ACHIEVING TRANQUILITY

One should not be detached from the aforesaid causes of tranquility. One should neither abandon control of the sensory faculties that engender dullness or sensual incitement nor should one fail to check gluttony. One should then sit on a comfortable cushion in a contemplative posture, with its seven aspects,[31] and harness the breath by regulating its inward and outward flow so gently as to render it effortless, without panting, breathing noisily or violently. One should seek realization through meditation and similar means such as enduring miseries joyfully, and the like.

The *Bodhipathapradīpa* states:

> If the conditions of tranquility are impaired,
> One may meditate intensively
> For as long as a thousand years
> Without achieving tranquil absorption.

The first *Bhāvanākrama* elucidates:

> Tranquility may be realized rapidly, provided one does not concern oneself with gain and similar desires, abides perfectly by the moral law, is capable of joyfully enduring suffering and the like, and makes serious efforts.

THE ELUCIDATION OF ITS MENTAL IMAGES

36 B This is comprised of the following points:

1. Elucidation of general concentration
2. Different meditations to meet differing needs
3. Visualization at the initial stages of practice [tranquility]
4. Maintaining a visualized image through mindfulness and vigilance

Elucidation of General Concentration

This has four sections:

1. Comprehensive visualization
2. Analytical meditation
3. Skillful investigation
4. Meditation on the elimination of mental defilements[32]

Comprehensive Visualization

Comprehensive visualization (1) deals with ways of focusing the three methods (2, 3, and 4) that follow it. This visualization is comprised of four aspects:

1. Focusing the mind on a perceived image with discrimination, by its nature, belongs to insight [comprehensive visualization refers to the conceptual image of meditational insight].
2. Focusing the mind on a perceived image without discrimination means sustaining the resultant state without analysis. The term "perceived image" refers to an apperceptive image, not the object of perception.
3. 37 F In visualizing the boundaries of phenomena, there must be certainty with regard to both their ultimate and apparent nature. The object of insight meditation is the ultimate nature of phenomena.
4. Focusing the mind on realizing its spiritual aim—this realization results from mastery through practice of that meditation which is aimed at eliminating uncontrolled tendencies of the body and mind.

Analytical Meditation

Analytical meditation on the elimination of specific mental defilements involves using mental images to purge desire and accumulated defilements and to prevent their reoccurrence. This practice comprises five parts:

1. Visualization of the disagreeable bodily wastes, hairs, and pores, and of the revolting features of a rotting corpse
2. Visualization of compassion that engenders an urge to help promote the welfare of all sentient beings and make them equally happy—be they loved ones, enemies, or strangers
3. Visualization of the interdependence of cause and condition through contemplation on the twelve links of this law[33]
4. Determination of the psychophysical elements, which involves critical
   B analysis of the nature of the six elements such as earth, water, fire, air, space, and consciousness
5. Practice of watching and counting and rhythm of one's breath in order to eliminate and guard against distraction of the mind

Skillful Investigation

Skillful investigation contains some special mental applications capable of eliminating the personal self[34] [from the stream consciousness], which are not incorporated in the analysis of psychophysical constituents or its elements. The skillful contemplation is comprised of five parts:

1. Understanding of the [five] psychophysical constituents, which brings about an insight into the nonexistence of "I" and "mine"
2. Understanding of the eighteen psychophysical elements,[35] which brings about an insight into the interrelationship of cause and condition of each of the elements
3. Skillful analysis of sense formations, which enables one to understand that the six sensory consciousnesses arise through the six sense faculties, that the six sense objects provide conditions for the sensory perceptions, and that every passing thought creates an instant condition for the next thought to arise. The cessation of one stream of mental consciousness is an immediate condition that gives rise to the next flow of consciousness.

38 F

4. Skillful contemplation on the law of interdependent arising, which helps one to understand its twelve links. They are by nature transient, sorrowful, and devoid of self.
5. Skillful contemplation on the principle of appropriate and inappropriate cause and effect, which gives an understanding of how virtue causes good results and vice negative ones. This principle works in a similar fashion as the foregoing one.

Meditation on the Elimination of Mental Defilements

The meditational antidote for the mind's distortions has two relative levels, coarse and subtle. Both focus on the realms of desire, form, and formlessness—the last includes unconsciousness. These are arranged in descending order of subtlety, with desire at the coarse end of the spectrum and unconsciousness at the subtle end.

Meditation on the four noble truths should be extended to include its sixteen subdivisions.[36] The four noble truths are: the truth of misery, its cause, its elimination, and the path. Understanding the first two noble truths weakens the roots of mental defilement, while the last two eliminate it. Although the foregoing meditative visualizations are common to meditations on tranquility and insight, most [teachers] incorporate them into the chapter on tranquility, which they consider essential to stability of the mind.
38 B However, in tranquil meditation one first focuses the mind on a [chosen] object and then the mental image thus formed is sustained without discriminating or examining.

Different Meditations to Meet Differing Needs

The *Śrāvakabhūmi*, quoting the *Namdrü Shüpe Do* states:

> If a monk-yogin, contemplating the innate purity, is overcome by lust, he should focus his mind upon the unsightliness [of a body]. If he is overcome by hatred, he should fix his mind upon compassion. If he is overcome by confusion, he should investigate the law of interdependent activation as it relates to his confusion. If he indulges in conceit, he should examine the differentiation of the elemental realms [of psychophysical aggregates].

[Again, the *Śrāvakabhūmi* states:]

> If he loses the discriminating faculty, he should instead focus on the
> 39 F exhalation and inhalation of his breath and then concentrate upon a pleasant contemplative subject.

Concerning different skillful visualizations for different individuals, the *Namdrü Shüpe Dho* says:

> If a monk-yogin is confused about the characteristics of all mental events, the self, sentient beings, life, the born, the living, and the substantiality of personality, he should focus his investigations on the [five] psychophysical aggregates. If confused about their causes, he should examine [the interaction of] the [eighteen] elements. If confused about their conditions, he should examine the [twelve] dynamic sense formations.[37] If confused about impermanence, misery, and nonselfhood, he should investigate interdependent arising, which produces appropriate and never inappropriate effects.

Concerning contemplation on eliminating the mental defilements for different people, the *Namdrü Shüpe Dho* states:

> If the monk-meditator wishes to be free from passion of the plane of desire, he should analyze both the coarse contemplation of the plane of desire and the subtle contemplation of the plane of form. If he wishes to be free from passion of the plane of form, he should examine the coarse contemplation of the plane of form and the subtle contemplation of the formless plane. If he desires to free himself from all ego perceptions of the transient psychophysical aggregates, he should investigate the realities of misery, their causes, elimination, and the means.

A person who succumbs equally to [different] emotions or who is not so passionate may choose any one of those meditations mentioned earlier; this is commented upon in the *Śrāvakabhūmi*:

> A person who is overcome equally by [different] emotions, should endeavor to stabilize his mind through that which delights him [tran-
> F quil contemplation], rather than analysis. Less passionate persons should do likewise.

Visualization at the Initial Stages of Practice [Tranquility]

Which—of all these images mentioned—should one visualize first? However familiar a person is with the visualization of an image of his choice, it is important for those given to discursive thought to meditate upon the breath. They should first rely on a single object for stabilizing the mind.

The *Bodhipathapradīpa* comments:

> Settle the mind in a virtuous way
> Upon any chosen object of visualization.

Noble Āryaśūra[38] states:

> Seek to achieve stability of mind by concentrating on a perceived mental image; refrain from focusing on different mental images lest they disturb the mind.

For the initial meditation on tranquility, no specific objects [of visualization] are recommended.

Master Bodhibhadra[39] said:

> 40 B There are two kinds of tranquility: the one achieved through inward and the other through outward concentration. The former refers to the visualization of the body and the things associated with it. This

visualization is comprised of perceiving one's body either in the shape of a meditational deity or a repulsive form like a skeleton, or visualizing it as sacred objects such as a khaṭvāṅga.[40] There are five kinds of visualizations of things associated with the body. They consist of focusing the mind:

1. on the breath
2. on a tiny imaginary symbol[41]
3. on a mentally projected sphere
4. on the spectrum of light
5. on joy and bliss

With regard to external visualization, there exist an ordinary and a special kind. The latter is a sacred image or syllable.

There are those who object to concentrating upon a stone, a piece of wood, or a sphere of light, and who have not applied this system of meditation. However, most texts on meditation recommend settling the mind upon the form of the Tathāgata. This is excellent because through it a great purpose
41 F may be achieved, such as increasing one's well-being, accumulating merit, and eliminating defilements.

The *Samādhirāja-sūtra* says:

> Of perfect beauty is the Universal Protector [the Buddha],
> His sacred form golden.
> A bodhisattva who focuses on this image
> Is said to achieve tranquil equipoise.

The third *Bhāvanākrama* explains:

> A yogin should first endeavor to realize tranquility by fixing his mind on the sacred form of the Tathāgata, exactly as he has seen or heard about it.

If one achieves an inward stability and firm concentration through fixing the mind upon a mental image of an object, one can then direct the mind upon any of the visualizations stated before.

The first *Bhāvanākrama* states:

> When one achieves stability of the mind, one focuses comprehensively on one's [psychophysical] constituents and their conglomerate elements, and so on.

Maintaining a Visualized Image through Mindfulness and Vigilance

Maintaining a visualized image is very important for achieving a state of mental absorption. Here one should know the nature of mindfulness, vigi-

lance, dullness, and sensual incitement. One consciously maintains the
B stream of mindfulness, which prevents distractions from the visualized image. At the same time vigilance detects whether the mind is projecting or not projecting itself away from that image.

The commentary on the *Sūtrālaṃkāra* explains:

> Concentrate well on mindfulness and vigilance, for the former prevents distraction, and the latter senses if the mind is projecting itself.

An analogy illustrates the meaning of this:

> The mind, like an untamed elephant, should be bound with the rope of mindfulness to the column of a visualized image. If the mind wanders, it has to be controlled with the hook of vigilance.

The *Madhyamakahṛdaya* says:

> As the elephant of the mind wanders,
> It should be bound with the rope of mindfulness,
> Tied to the rooted column of a mental image,
> 42 F And controlled with the hook of wisdom.

Restlessness of the mind arises from tensions due to intense exertion, while indolence causes the mind to submerge and sink, producing dullness. Flawless absorption should be sought through a harmonious balance between exertion and indolence, and this state should then be maintained.

Master Candragomin[42] teaches:

> Undue exertion causes restless thoughts to arise;
> Overrelaxation produces dullness;
> An even balance is hard to achieve.
> Why should one stir the mind?

A similar statement appears in the *Deśanāstava* by Candragomin:

> Overexertion in concentration will arouse sensual incitement,
> Overrelaxation will bring about depression,
> While the middle ground is hard to achieve.
> Why should one get agitated?

THE METHODS OF REALIZING TRANQUILITY

The four methods of realizing tranquility are:

1. The eight points of mental processes for stability
2. The nine stages of settling the mind
3. The six powerful methods for achieving these stages
4. The four mental applications for these principles

The Eight Points of Mental Processes for Stability

42 B Concerning the eight points of mental processes, the *Madhyāntavibhāga* says:

> All aims may be realized
> By settling in tranquility,
> Making the mind pliant
> Through abandonment of the five defects
> And deployment of the eight mental processes.
> Laziness, forgetfulness,
> Dullness, sensual incitement,
> Lack of mental vigilance,
> Or unnecessary vigilance
> Comprise the five defects.
> Settling the mind in tranquility is the cause,
> Tranquility is the effect.
> Remembering the object of visualization,
> Detecting dullness and sensual incitement,
> Abandoning defects,
> Applying remedies,
> Reaching intrinsic tranquility—
> These are the eight mental processes.

The identification of the five defects and the eight mental processes has been stated before.

How does one achieve contemplative absorption by abandoning the former [the five defects]? When initially overcome by the three forms of laziness,[43] one does not delight in the meditation on tranquility. One should then endeavor to be conscious of the benefits of tranquility and engender the three faiths that move the mind to meditation. Besides, one should be completely drawn toward mental tranquility and develop a strong and stable urge to strive toward it. Seeing the harm of laziness and the benefits of
43 F tranquility one should make an effort to abandon the first and to practice the second. In doing so one should joyfully endure the hardships of exhaustion and strain, so that one will gradually achieve perfect ease of body and mind.

When the mind, in meditation, forgets instructions and becomes distracted, one should continuously reinforce mindfulness by redirecting the mind to its original visualization. At that time, when dullness or restlessness emerge or one senses such a possibility, one should observe it with vigilance and identify it. Failure to exert the mind in concentration because of mental distraction caused by dullness or restlessness [sensual incitement] should be remedied by exertion [in the case of dullness] and relaxation [in the case of sensual incitement]. When the mind becomes exceedingly restless in counteracting the climax of dullness or sensual incitement, one should settle the mind in equanimity and maintain it wisely in an absorptive state.

This method of achieving tranquility is known to most treatises on meditation and their instructions.

The Nine Stages of Settling the Mind

To elucidate the "settling of mind" in the first stage, the *Sūtrālaṃkāra* comments:

> One should concentrate on the visualized image,
> And not be distracted from the stream of continuity.

This level requires one to focus the mind on the chosen image of an object by completely withdrawing the restless mind from any thought of external phenomena.

The same text comments on maintaining the concentration in the second stage:

> One should maintain that concentrated state.

Here the meditator, having fixed the mental focus earlier, should carry on with it while guarding against any distraction.

The above text comments on revitalizing the concentration in the third stage:

> Recognize instantly any wandering thoughts,
> Redirect the mind toward the settled state.

The meditator should revitalize the concentration by immediately detecting any inner distraction and absent-mindedness and then by redirecting the mind toward the contemplative object.

44 F About the fourth stage of "firmly settling the mind," the *Sūtrālaṃkāra* comments:

> A skillful meditator draws the mind
> Ever deeper inward and increases the concentration.

The meditator should repeatedly draw the mind away from distractions while settling it with ever increasing concentration and sensitivity.

The fifth stage is about "the mastery of the concentration." The mind is trained through appreciation of the virtues of tranquility and intensive meditation; this is commented upon by the same text:

> Realizing the virtues [of tranquility],
> One trains the mind in tranquility.

The sixth stage concerns "pacification." One pacifies the disinclination toward contemplative absorption by considering the unwholesome consequence of idleness; this is again commented upon in the *Sūtrālaṃkāra*:

> Realizing the harmful effects of idleness,
> One eliminates the disinclination for tranquility.

The seventh stage refers to "the complete pacification of mental blemishes." One pacifies lust, worry, sluggishness, drowsiness, and other disturbances to tranquility by applying the appropriate remedies for each.

The same text comments:

> When the mind is agitated by lust, worry, and the like
> Eliminate each as it arises.

44 B The eighth stage concerns "one-pointed concentration." One should strive to sustain tranquil absorption in order to render its subsequent attainment constant and effortless.

The *Sūtrālaṃkāra* states:

> Once a monk-meditator intensifies his contemplative efforts,
> He will achieve a perfect, natural absorption.

The ninth stage deals with "settling the mind in tranquil equipoise." Mastery of the eighth stage results in a spontaneous, effortless, and natural absorption.

The same text comments:

> The mastery of tranquil equipoise will enable one to meditate without effort.

The Six Powerful Methods for Achieving These Stages

As stated in the *Śrāvakabhūmi*, tranquility is sought through the six powerful methods:

1. The power of listening [to discourses]
2. The power of contemplation
3. The power of mindfulness
4. The power of vigilance
5. The power of effort
6. The power of practice

45 F (1) The settling of the mind is achieved through the power of listening. By merely listening to instructions on the way to settle the mind through visualization, one can learn to settle the mind upon any mental image.

(2) A sustained settling of the mind is achieved through contemplation. By repeated contemplation upon the image of an object previously examined, one is able to settle the mind a little longer.

(3) Through the power of mindfulness one achieves two stages: settling the mind firmly and focusing one's attention closely. If the mind wanders from the visualization, one draws it back to the image through mindfulness. In the first place, one should prevent distraction from the image by exerting the power of mindfulness.

(4) Mastery of concentration and pacification of the disinclination for tranquility is achieved through the power of vigilance. A vigilant mind detects the emergence of coarse and subtle defilements,[44] and the consciousness of their harmful effects prevents the mind from wandering.

(5) The stages of complete pacification of the mind and one-pointed concentration may be achieved through the power of effort. One abandons coarse and subtle defilements and seeks to attain a constant, harmonious absorption impervious to dullness or sensual incitement.

B (6) Tranquil equipoise may be achieved through the power of practice. By continuous practice and mastery of the previous stage one will attain the state of tranquil absorption effortlessly and spontaneously.

The Four Mental Applications for These Principles

To achieve the nine stages of tranquility mentioned above, one should also employ the four mental applications. They are:

1. The application of concentrated exertion
2. The application with intermittent pauses
3. The application without pauses
4. The natural and spontaneous application

Attainment of the first and second stages requires great endeavor; hence the emphasis on the application of concentrated exertion. The application with intermittent pauses should take place when the third to seventh stages of tranquility cannot be maintained because of interference by dullness or restlessness. The eighth stage of tranquility can be maintained through application without pauses, undisturbed by dullness or passion. On the ninth stage one attains tranquil absorption through natural and spontaneous application.

The *Śrāvakabhūmi* states:

46 F
> Know that in order to realize the nine stages of tranquility one should use the four mental applications. These mental applications are used to attain the different stages of tranquility. The application of concen-

trated effort has a bearing on the first and second stages of tranquility. The application with intermittent pauses refers to the stages from the third to the seventh, such as (3) fixed attentiveness through inward withdrawal, (4) more intense attentiveness, (5) the taming of the mind, (6) the pacification of the mind, and (7) the complete pacification of the mind. The application without pauses enables one to realize the uninterrupted tranquility of the eighth stage. The application of the effortless stage leads to the attainment of complete absorption.

The names of the nine stages of tranquility given here [based on the *Śrāvakabhūmi*] differ somewhat from those stated earlier, though they are essentially the same. Again, mental exertion with intermittent pauses applies to the first and the second stages of tranquility. Exertion also applies to the five subsequent stages. Why the difference? The term "mental exertion" is used for the first two stages because the mind, for the most part, does not rest in
46 B tranquil absorption; hence the need for exertion. The term "mental exertion with intermittent pauses" is used because, though the mind, for the most part, rests in tranquil absorption, exertion is necessary when this tranquility is absent. In seeking tranquility, if distraction is allowed to interfere with one's meditation, it [tranquility] will not be achieved even in a thousand years. On the other hand, if one strives to obtain all the favorable conditions, as stated, and works continuously without interruptions or distractions, it is said one will achieve tranquility before long.

The *Bodhipathapradīpa* states:

When conditions for tranquility deteriorate,
No matter how great one's meditation,
Tranquility will not be achieved
Even for a thousand years.

The *Prajñāpāramitā-saṃcayagāthā* states:

Strive to achieve tranquil absorption
Through uninterrupted contemplation
On inner purity.
Just as the striking of two flints
With long pauses in between
Will not cause sparks,
So occasional meditation
Will not lead to tranquility.
Do not give up until perfection is achieved!

This concludes the elucidation of the meditation on tranquility.

F # *CHAPTER THREE*

The Stages of Tranquility and Insight
Part II: Insight

The meditation on insight in divided into two major categories:

1. General meditation on insight
2. Methods for achieving the vision of insight: enumerating the methods employed by the Buddhist schools to attain this vision

GENERAL MEDITATION ON INSIGHT

There are three kinds of insight:

1. The insight of the mundane level
2. The insight of the supramundane level
3. The insight of the Mahāyāna tradition

The first insight perceives the superficial form of tranquility, the second perceives an insight that chiefly eliminates the self by focusing on the four noble truths, and the last is the insight of our meditations.

The *Saṃdhinirmocana-sūtra* mentions three insights:

1. The insight arising from perceptions refers to insight resulting from a penetrating analysis of these perceptions through various aspects of wisdom
47 B 2. The insight originating from exhaustive investigation refers to wisdom that enlightens an understanding of the doctrinal view regarding the unknown intrinsic reality
3. The insight originating from analysis of distinct realities refers to insight that arises through illuminating wisdom, which has perfectly examined the total reality. This refers to meditative practises, which follow after one has achieved a definite vision of reality.

The *Saṃdhinirmocana-sūtra* and the *Abhidharmasamuccaya* list four insights arising from:

1. General differentiation of the realities through wisdom, which examines all conditioned realities, including contemplative perceptions of mental defilements
2. Perfect differentiation through wisdom, which attunes itself perfectly to the true nature of the realities
3. Extensive examination, referring to the intellect that discriminates in general the relative nature of phenomena and the ultimate nature
4. Penetrating analysis, referring to the perfect wisdom that makes a fine determination of the diverse realities and their ultimate nature.

The *Śrāvakabhūmi* mentions:

> There are six ways of gaining insight, and these incorporate other
> 48 F methods. The six methods of attaining insight are through examining the conceptual significance of reality, its substantiality, its characteristics, space, and time and through logical investigation.

This passage refers to the means of discovering insight through investigation of the [apparent and ultimate] realities.

The *Sūtrālaṃkāra* states:

> Examine constantly
> The mind's manifestations.
> Differentiate their constituent aspects.
> Determine the single flavor of thoughts
> And their undefinable nature.[45]

Master Vasubandhu[46] elaborates in his commentary on the *Sūtrālaṃkāra*:

> These four lines illustrate the eleven performances of the intellect. They are: (1) to investigate all that is conceptual, (2) nonconceptual, (3) that which is neither conceptual nor investigative, (4) to focus on tranquility, (5) to contemplate insight, (6) to contemplate both tranquility and insight jointly, (7) to examine through logic mental perceptions, (8) to contemplate the rationale of tranquility, (9) to contemplate the rationale of equanimity, (10) to constantly contemplate the actions of the mind, and (11) to contemplate objects of reverence.

48 B These are the eleven ways to insight. Of these the first few are the means for determining the vision [of the ultimate reality]. The middle ones are meditations upon the attained vision of that reality, and the last few methods lead to strengthened vision. In short, the sūtras and treatises of meditation state that to discover insight one first relies upon wisdom to examine and determine the apparent and ultimate nature of the psychophysical aggregates and

thoughts. Just as fire results from the rubbing of two sticks, so intellectual examination [of dualistic perception] will lead to a dawning of insight. Once the wood is consumed, the flames die. Thus, when insight dawns, both the image of the examiner and its examination fade. Similar comments have been made by Dīpaṃkara Atīśa.[47] It is essential to achieve such vision of the ultimate reality in the meditation of insight.

METHODS FOR ACHIEVING THE VISION OF INSIGHT: ENUMERATING THE METHODS EMPLOYED BY BUDDHIST SCHOOLS TO ATTAIN THIS VISION

F While seeking the vision of the ultimate reality, the meditator should determine the reality of dualism through two premises. One premise, advanced by the Idealist School [Vijñānavāda], has it that the reality of phenomena is devoid of any independent substance, since one consciousness manifests itself in diverse external realities and such a consciousness coemerges with its perceptive images. This theory of the Consciousness Only School was expounded by Maitreya in his teachings to Asaṅga[48] who transmitted them to his brother Vasubandhu. The other premise, known as the principle of relative exclusion, holds that because objective phenomena are devoid of any substance, the perceiving intellect is bound to be without any essence. This represents the Middle Path School [Madhyamaka].[49] For both these schools of Mahāyāna Buddhism the fundamental doctrinal view [of reality] consists of nondual awareness.

Nāgārjuna and his spiritual son Āryadeva described the way the School of Valid Relative Phenomena [Svātantrika-Madhyamaka] determined the vision of reality. It holds that nothing essential or real can be found in all the dualistic realities when they are thoroughly investigated through logical analysis, known as the nonexistence of one or many [absolute entities]. It accepts an experiential phenomenon described as nonconceptual awareness, which is well-settled in its supraperceptive simplicity. Hence this transcending state is designated as inmost discerning wisdom.

Prāsaṅgika-Madhyamaka holds as the essential vision a transcending awareness of the unity of perceptive appearances and their inherent void, rejecting the two extreme modes—absolute reality and nihility. Meditators should seek to realize this perfect view of reality.

49 B Using the logical premises such as the mutual exclusiveness of the one and many, they should deeply analyze all subject-object phenomena, their essential nature, and their causes and effects with special reference to the coemerging delusion that clings to the concepts of "I" and "mine." This delusion is at the root of the cycle of existence. Meditators should determine the inherent void of phenomena so as to eliminate the concept of substantive

dualism. Using the logic of interdependent activation of cause and condition, they should analyze all perceptive appearances in order to refute the concept of nihility.

Diverse theories were proffered by Indian and Tibetan teachers. One theory advocates that the meditator be aware of the fact that subject and object realities are but mind-created. It calls on the meditator to establish the voidness of the mind by knowing it to be without essence and devoid of all conceptual identities such as being eternal reality or nonexistent, self-emergent being or the cessation of being. Finally, the meditator should develop the perfect view, which consists of being aware of the intrinsic nature of all phenomena as the undefinable, all-encompassing realm of [supreme] simplicity.

In this connection I shall now explain the methods for realizing meditative insight, as advocated in the Mahāyāna doctrinal treatises.

METHODS FOR ACHIEVING THE VISION OF INSIGHT: THE RELEVANT METHODS TO BE USED HERE TO ATTAIN THIS: THE GENERAL MEDITATION ON SELFLESSNESS

50 F There are three sections:

1. The reason for meditating on selflessness
2. Ways of meditating on the two kinds of selflessness
3. Emergence of vision through this meditation

The Reason for Meditating on Selflessness

To identify the self and the mind's clinging to it, it is said that although duality is devoid of essence, it is misconceived as possessing substantiality, due to inbred delusion. The mind develops attachments and clings to the two self-entities of subject and object. Conversely, the nonexistence of the two innate selves is nonduality.

Candrakīrti[50] in his commentary to the *Catuḥśataka* says:

> What is described as the self [ātman] is the essence or the inborn entity, the existence of which does not depend upon external conditions. Selflessness [anātman] is without such a self. Selflessness of material and mental phenomena are so designated because the two distinctions are made in the form of material elements and personality [dharma and pudgala].

Dharmakīrti says:

> The dual realities categorized according to their inherent characteristics are designated as "dharmas" [the elements of material phenomena] while personality is stated to consist of man's stream consciousness that coalesces with the physical constituents.

The *Do Silbu* summarizes:

> All [the realities of] the elements bearing inherent characteristics are designated as "dharmas." The stream consciousness is designated as personality.

B The self of personality [pudgala-ātman] consists of the innate consciousness that assigns to itself, as its own nature, an eternal, independent entity and thereby clings to the notion of "I" or "self." The self of material elements [dharma-ātman] is the product of the mind grasping to realities, such as the physical constituents of life, as being objective realities composed of innate substance and clinging to them as such. These two "selves" engender karma,[51] defilement, affliction, and harm.

Śrī Dharmakīrti comments:

> By conceiving the self,
> One perceives the existence of others.
> Differentiating between the self and others
> Causes attachment and hatred.
> Entanglement with these causes afflictions.

The *Ratnāvalī* elucidates:

> As long as clinging to the aggregates [of life] exists,
> So long does clinging to the self persist.
> Where there is clinging to the self,
> There is karma.
> Karma causes rebirth.

In order to eliminate the stream of existence caused by clinging to the self, it is essential to meditate upon the meaning of selflessness.

Dharmakīrti states:

> Without subduing the subjective base of this [self]
> One cannot eliminate it.

The *Catuḥśataka* comments:

> When one perceives nonselfhood in the perceptive base,
> The seed of cyclic existence will cease to exist.

51 F The *Madhyamakāvatāra* says:

> All defilements and afflictions originate
> From conceiving as real the transient aggregates of being.
> Only by perceiving this and investigating the realms of this self
> Can a yogin eliminate it [the self].
>
> Only by meditating upon the truth of nonselfhood
> Can one eliminate the deluded view
> And the clinging to "I" and "mine."
> Such an elimination terminates rebirth
> Caused by clinging, sensuality, and the rest.
> In this way liberation is finally achieved.

The *Mūlamadhyamaka-kārikā* says:

> Once "I" and "mine" are eliminated,
> Clinging comes to an end.

Again, the same text states:

> Upon the elimination of "I" and "mine,"
> Internal and external realities,
> The psychophysical aggregates, will cease.
> With this rebirth, karma, and defilements will cease,
> And thus liberation will be achieved.

Ways of Meditating on the Two Kinds of Selflessness

This meditation is accomplished through:

1. The negation of the self of personality
2. The negation of the self of phenomenal reality

The Negation of the Self of Personality

The *Ratnāvalī* enunciates the Madhyamaka view:

> Assertion of the reality of "I" and "mine" is a distortion of the sacred truth.

51 B The self of personality is thus stated to be nonexistent. The logic concerning the nonexistent self states that, if it exists, it must emerge either in oneself, in others, in both, or in the three periods of time. Since this self has not emerged in these, it is nonexistent. The same text states:

Since the self has not emerged
Out of oneself, others, or both,
Nor been born in the three periods of time,
Clinging to the self can therefore be eliminated.

Furthermore, if the self of personality exists, it must necessarily be either identical to the psychophysical aggregates or distinct from them. Both of these hypotheses are untenable.

The *Mūlamadhyamaka-kārikā* comments:

When one says that no self exists
Except for the rebirth-seeking aggregates,
It means that these aggregates are identical with the self.
Then the self is indeed nonexistent.

The same text states:

If the aggregates are the self,
Then it too will be subject to birth and death.

Thus the contention that the self is identical with the psychophysical aggregates has been refuted. If one assumes that the [independent] self is subject to the cycle of birth and death, this [self-contradiction] will be refuted through the following inferences. [The self that lost its enduring nature would make the possibility of] recollecting untenable. Memory of a past life would not be possible, committed karma would not produce results, and one would experience effects without karmic causes.

52 F The separate realities of the self and the aggregates are also refuted in the same text:

If the self is a separate entity from the psychophysical aggregates,
The characteristics of these aggregates become invalid.

The same text continues:

The self is an entity
Separate from the rebirth-seeking aggregates—
This is untenable,
For if objective reality
Without aggregates were possible,
Then cognition would be impossible.

In the *Madhyamakāvatāra*, it is said:

For all these reasons
The self does not exist
Apart from the aggregates;

Except for these aggregates
No perceiver exists.

Eliminating the self of personality by implication negates the existence [of the substantive nature] of its parts such as the eyes, nose, and the rest. The *Mulamadhyamaka-kārikā* states:

If the "I" does not exist,
How can there be the "mine?"

The *Madhyamakāvatāra* states:

Because there is no actor, there is no action,
For there can be no self of a person who is nonexistent.
Therefore, the seeker of truth who conceives
The emptiness of the "I" and the "mine"
Will achieve perfect liberation.

The following is a summary of the meditation upon the nonselfhood of personality, as stated in the first *Bhāvanākrama*:

52 B There is no personality to be perceived apart from the aggregates, elements, and sense faculties. The self is not the essence of the aggregates, etc., because they are essentially transient and composite, whereas personality has been defined by others [such as those of the Brahmanic tradition] as an eternal and independent essence. This self or another undefinable self cannot possibly exist as substantial entities, since there is no reality of substance. Establish all that is conceived as "I" and "mine" in the transient world as a total delusion!

The Negation of the Self of Elemental Reality

The basis of designating the personality consists of the "dharmas," such as the psychophysical aggregates, the elements, and the sense faculties. Therefore the way of negating innate being in them is shown in the *Mūlamadhyamaka-kārikā*:

It does not arise from itself
Nor from others,
Neither from both
Nor from causelessness;
Nowhere do composite realities so emerge.

The emergence of the self is thus negated through the four modes of
53 F inference. Through the first mode of inference, the existence of an external, independent self is negated. The same text states:

If it is an individual being, simply the fusion of cause and effect,
This would make the producer and production one entity.

The second mode of inference negates the self as arising from external causes. According to the *Madhyamakāvatāra*, it is said:

If the causation of the self were extrinsic,
Then this causation and causelessness would become identical.

Negating the last two modes of inference, the *Madhyamakāvatāra* then sums up:

The self does not emerge from oneself, nor from others,
Nor even from the fusion of the two factors.
There exists nothing that does not depend on causes.
Therefore, all realities are devoid of self-entity.

Because psychophysical aggregates and other realities are conditioned, they cannot contain intrinsic self-nature; the *Mūlamadhyamaka-kārikā* contends:

Conditioned innate nature
Implies creation.
How can an innate nature
Be conditioned?

All things—subject and object—are found to be without substance when examined and investigated. If they were substantive, their substantiality would have to consist of either unitary or multiple entities. However, neither of these exist. Dharmakīrti explains:

By examining things one will find
That there is no substance in them.
They are devoid of a unitary
Or multiple innate nature.

53 B The *Bodhicittavivaraṇa* comments on the nonexistence of a unitary self-nature:

Corporalities, particles, and sensory perceptions
Are not born [out of innate nature],
For it is outside of perceptive realities.
They are produced by the interaction
of causes and conditions;
[Innate nature] in them cannot be tenable.
Even subatoms are differentiated
In terms of [three] spatial dimensions;

How can there even be [ultimate] particles
Since they are determined by proportion?

Concerning the nonexistence of mulitple essences, the same text states:

An external phenomenon is perceived
Differently by differing levels of consciousness.
A body of enchanting beauty
Is looked upon differently:
A wandering yogin perceives it as a corpse;
A sensual man perceives it as an object of lust;
A dog looks upon it as food.
These are three different perceptions.

Why do these diverse realities of subject-object appear? They appear as external manifestations of distorted perception due to hidden defilements. The *Laṅkāvatāra* elucidates:

54 F The mind stirred by hidden defilement
Causes the appearance of external reality.
But for the mind, the reality does not exist.
To perceive external phenomena as reality
Is distortion.

The appearance of external reality is analogous to a conjurer's creation. The *Samādhirāja* illustrates this:

Magicians conjure up horses,
Elephants, chariots, and other forms.
These appearances are illusory.
Understand all things as such!

The first *Bhāvanākrama* comments on the condensed meditation:

Meditate upon the nonselfhood of all things, which are comprised of the five psychophysical aggregates, the twelve sense formations, and the eighteen realms of the elements. Ultimately, apart from being manifestations of the mind, these aggregates, sense formations, and elements do not have an independent reality. No object of attachment can exist, as the essence of reality itself is nonexistent. Their reduction to particles and finally to infinitesimal proportions will show this. Determining reality in this manner, one should contemplate that from
54 B beginningless time, due to their deep clinging to the apparent reality of phenomena, childish sentient beings have mistaken the mind's manifestations for external reality in much the same way as a dreamer holds his dreams to be true. Ultimately, all these are but manifestations of the mind.

Emergence of Vision through This Meditation

The negation of the two selves should be carried out to eliminate delusion, which perceives duality as the true reality. In a real sense it is wrong to even cling to the concept of nihilism and void with respect to duality.

The *Mūlamadhyamaka-kārikā* states:

All the victorious buddhas expound:
The void will liberate one
From all conceptual views,
But he who conceptualizes the void
5 F Will fail to realize liberation.

The *Mahāratnakūṭa* elucidates:

Buddha: Kāśyapa, viewing the self to be as great as Mount Sumeru is less confounding than clinging to the view of the void. Why? If the void liberates one from all views, he who holds on to the void cannot achieve liberation.

The *Bodhicittavivaraṇa* says:

Conceptualizing the void
As being nonarising, empty, or selfless
Is the meditation of an inferior mind.
This is anything but meditation on the void!

Atīśa clarifies this:

Only through the mastery of skillful means[52]
And the contemplation of transcending wisdom
Can one attain enlightenment rapidly,
Not by meditating on nonselfhood alone.

How is this so? Duality appears through the interdependent activation of causes and conditions. Upon investigation or examination of the phenomena they are found to be without self-nature or essence. Hence, there is no perfect reality or substance to be identified.

The *Mūlamadhyamaka-kārikā* comments:

Nothing exists
That is not interdependent activation.
Therefore, nothing exists
That is not void.

[The same text adds]:

55 B Do not conceptualize
Phenomena as empty

Or not empty!
Refrain from affirming or negating both;
Describe only to designate!

For to affirm is to hold it eternal;
To negate is to view it as nothingness.
Skillful meditators should neither
Affirm nor negate.

The commentary on the *Satyadvayavibhaṅga* explains:

For that reason, it is neither empty nor not empty,
Neither affirmed nor negated,
Neither nonarising nor arising—
Such is the teaching of the Illuminated Conqueror.

The human mind, accustomed to diverse perceptions of reality, is frightened upon finding the unreality [emptiness] of those perceptions of reality or objects of imagery, upon which the mind usually clings. The mind that delights in such perceptive bases clings to the concept of eternalism or nihility, emptiness or nonemptiness. This causes miseries in the transient world.

Hence, the *Ratnāvalī* states:

Human beings who are frightened
By the unreality of the perceptive realm
Delight in conceiving its reality.
Clinging either to the concept of eternalism or nihility,
Unwise people bring about their downfall.

56 F As all dualistic realities are neither substantive nor nothingness, should one then view these realities as being manifestations of inner awareness? This manifestation is experienced under some conditions. Even so, such inner awareness is without true reality.

The *Laṅkāvatāra* says in support of this:

External reality is neither substantive nor nothingness;
Even the mind is not an entity.
Elimination of all views is the criteria
For nonarising [emptiness].

The *Bodhicaryāvatāra* says:

The [autoconsciousness] can neither be perceived
By other senses,
Nor by itself;
To examine if the autoconsciousness is self-manifesting or not

> Is like describing the comportment of a sterile woman's son—
> It is an exercise in futility.

The same text continues:

> When, in the purview of the mind,
> There remains [no essence in] composite and noncomposite things,
> Then there is no other reality,
> And the clinging [to an imagery essence] pacifies
> Itself into a nonconceptual state.

The first *Bhāvanākrama* summarizes:

> Contemplate the three planes of existence as being of mental origin, since they are designated by the mind. By analyzing the mind, the meditator examines the essence of all things.

B In analyzing the essence of the mind he should contemplate that the mind itself cannot possibly be perfect reality. How can this mind be such when it conceives false external forms as perfect realities, even though these "realities" are but its manifestations? Just as corporality and other sensory objects are unreal, so is the mind. Sensory objects are of diverse appearances; they are neither of one essential entity nor of multiple entities. The mind is not different from such characteristics, as it is neither one essential entity nor multiple entities. The mine is ephemeral. One should establish the ephemeral nature of phenomena in the same way as is done with the mind.

Deep examination of the essence of mind through wisdom will reveal the
57 F mind in an ultimate sense to possess neither intrinsic nor extrinsic reality. Yet, without considering these two, the mind cannot be cognized. The mind is not of the past, present, or future. Emergent thought has no observable point of egress and is without destination upon its passage. The mind cannot be subject to tactile contact or demonstration; it is without structure. One may wonder about the essential nature of the mind, if it cannot be grasped or demonstrated and is without structure. The answer is stated in the *Ratnakūṭa*:

> Buddha: Kāśyapa, as one explores the mind, it cannot be discovered. This unknowable nature cannot be cognized. That which is uncognized does not have a past, a future, nor even a present.

57 B This method of meditation is far superior to those in which emptiness is conceived through analysis or conceptualization.

The *Sūtrālaṃkāra* concludes:

> Know that, apart from the mind, nothing exists,
> And that even the mind itself does not exist.

Understand, intelligent meditator, the nonreality of the two,
And settle—without duality—in all-embracing emptiness.

Master Vasubandhu, in his commentary, agrees:

> By understanding that apart from the mental image, there is nothing to be cognized, one realizes the nonexistence of the mind, because without external reality there is no internal reality. Comprehending this nonduality one settles in the nondual expanse of reality. Such is the direct relationship of the all-encompassing space of reality.

METHODS FOR ACHIEVING THE VISION OF INSIGHT: THE RELEVANT METHODS TO BE USED HERE TO ATTAIN THIS: THE SPECIFIC METHODS OF MEDITATING ON THE VISION OF ULTIMATE REALITY

This is divided into three sections:

1. Identification of the perfect vision of reality[53]
2. Meditation upon tranquil absorption
3. Achieving a postabsorptive perception

Identification of the Perfect Vision of Reality

58 F To meditate upon the true nature of the mind by assuming it to be substantive, nonexistent, both, or neither is to fall into the extremes of monistic eternalism or materialistic abnegation. Also, to meditate upon the concept of emptiness[54] as nonarising[55] or nonimagery is to intellectualize the void; hence it is not the true vision of inherent reality.

What then is the true vision? True vision may be determined either through prescribed doctrinal dialectics or the contemplative elimination of all distortions or skeptical views, according to the key instructions. True vision consists of the attainment of a determinate awareness that subject-object phenomena are but manifestations of the mind, and that true reality of the mind is not comprised of any essence whatsoever. Like space it is unstained by substance or conceptual mark and detached [from arising, enduring, or ceasing]. Transcending the purview of a penetrating intellect,
58 B it is an uninterrupted stream of being.

For an ordinary aspirant the vision of reality consists of perceiving [the mind] to be like an illusion. This is distinguishable from the subtle awareness of minds on advanced levels. A true vision of reality and mindfulness must be achieved through intellectual discrimination and experiential insight.

The *Chönyi Miyowai Dho* (*Dharmatāsvabhāva-śūnyatācala-pratisarvāloka-sūtra*) says:

> All things, by their innate nature, are nonarising, nondwelling in their true essence, divorced from all modes of absolute functions and activities, and beyond the realm of conception or nonconception.

The *Prajñāpāramitā-saṃcayagāthā* states:

> To perfectly understand all phenomena as being devoid of intrinsic reality is to exercise the transcending wisdom of the excellent path.

The same text adds:

> Not to conceptualize [phenomena] as being [absolute] arising or nonarising, or both, is to exercise the transcending wisdom of the excellent path.

The *Dharmadhātu-prakṛtyasambhedanirdeśa-sūtra* comments:

> The mind is not composed of forms; it can neither concretize nor radiate; it can neither be touched nor is it visible; it does not dwell within or without or in between. It is completely pure, being without any essence. There is no liberation[56] for the mind, since its innate nature is the all-embracing expanse of reality.[57]

The *Yumla Töpa* says:

> That which is inexpressible, inconceivable, and undefinable
> Is transcendental wisdom.

The *Mūlamadhyamaka-kārikā* defines:

> That which can neither be abandoned nor acquired,
> Neither disintegrates nor exists eternally,
> And is neither absolute ceasing nor arising,
> That is the state of nirvāṇa.

Atīśa elaborates:

> It is abstruse and nonconceptual,
> Lucid, and uncomposed;
> Primordially pure, it is neither arising nor ceasing;
> Its nature is nirvāṇa,
> Which is the all-encompassing reality (dharmadhātu),
> Devoid of a center and horizon.
> Watch it with sensitivity, with an insight detached from
> conceptualization
> And without sensual incitement and dullness.

Atīśa comments on wisdom:

All aggregates, elements, and sensory faculties
Are to be understood as being without absolute arising,
Their innate nature void.
This is described as wisdom.

Meditation upon Tranquil Absorption

59 B An undistracted vision of reality is generally considered to be meditation. Absorption in the aforesaid vision is to be sustained with mindfulness and vigilance, while abstaining from all discrimination and imagery. Thus the mind should be settled in its innate naturalness in "a fashion of no contemplation," and without efforts either in modulating, increasing or decreasing, or examining.

The *Namkha Tabü Tingnge-dzingyi Do* explains:

Through the ambrosia of a holy guru
One will understand the mind to be like the sky.
To remain singly aware of its significance
Is expounded as tranquil absorption.

The *Tingdzin Dampai Dho* says:

In the intrinsic nature of reality [dharmatā]
One settles the mind—which is identical to it.
There arises in one an undefinable experience.
This is tranquil absorption.

The *Saptaśatika-prajñāpāramitā* states:

Where there is no rejection, acceptance, or grasping
Of any aspect of reality,
There is meditation on the wisdom-gone-beyond.
60 F Noncontemplation and nonimagery are such a meditation.

The *Aṣṭasahasrika-prajñāpāramitā* adds:

Meditation of the wisdom-gone-beyond
Means not to meditate on anything.

The same text also says:

To meditate on wisdom-gone-beyond
Is to meditate on space.

And:

As space is nonconceptual, so is the wisdom-gone-beyond.

The *Namkha Rinpochai Dho* and Maitreya state:

> There is neither anything to be eliminated
> Nor something to be determined;
> Only the pure reality is to be perfectly perceived.
> Through this perception liberation may be achieved.

The *Avataṃsaka* states:

> He who aspires to enter the active realm
> Of the victorious Buddha,
> Should train the mind
> To be pure like space.
> By abandoning thought, discrimination,
> And the clinging to cognition,
> He should enter this realm
> With a mind like that of space.

The *Sūtrālaṃkāra* continues:

> Mainly by settling the mind in the expanse of intrinsic reality
> B And stabilizing the attention of pure awareness,
> One will soon cross the oceans of attainment.

The *Bodhicittavivaraṇa* says:

> The mind, separated from mental images,
> Possesses the innate characteristics of space,
> And this spacelike meditation
> Is regarded as meditation on emptiness.

Atīśa elucidates:

> In the expanse of intrinsic reality, detached from any conception,
> One settles the mind without discrimination.

Similar sayings of the great masters will be stated in the chapter on postabsorptive perception.

Achieving a Postabsorptive Perception

When the meditator perceives realities during a postabsorptive state—a phase different from tranquil absorption—he should maintain the glow or power of mindfulness previously acquired in the state of tranquil absorption. While maintaining an awareness that all appearances are, in reality, devoid of inborn essence, the percipient sees every aspect exactly as it appears. This is described as postabsorptive perception and is similar to ephemeral illusion.

The *Prajñāpāramitā-saṃcayagāthā* elucidates:

By understanding the five aggregates
To be like a magical illusion
61 F And not contradicting the aggregates and their illusory nature;
By detaching from diverse dualities
And settling in a tranquil state,
The meditator indeed practices the wisdom-gone-beyond.

The *Samādhirāja* remarks similarly:

Like a mirage, a phantom city,
A conjuration, and a dream
The meditation of perceptive reality
Is devoid of true essence.
Know all phenomena in the same way.

Concerning the analogy of "conjuration," the meditator—during his postabsorptive consciousness—conceives all perceptions as unreal and illusory. The focus is on the conceived identification of the appearance [of reality] with the analogy of "illusion." Hence the designation of conceptualized illusion. Although one sometimes perceives the illusion in this way, it is not exactly in accordance with the term "meditation on the analogy of a conjuration." How then does one deal with postabsorptive perception otherwise? One has to deal with this exactly in the way the magician handles his
61 B conjuration, perceiving it as unreal while remaining free from clinging. Even though spectators perceive the appearance of a conjured form in the same way, unlike the magician, they hold it to be something real.

Likewise, while ordinary humans are overcome by rigidly clinging to subject-object phenomena as though they are true reality, the yogin remains aware that all visions are appearances without real nature or essence. Just as the magician perceives the conjured-up images, the yogin perceives unhindered the mere appearance of relative phenomena. This he does with the awareness that ultimately all realities are devoid of real nature. Such a viewing of reality is said to be in accord with the meaning of the analogy of conjuration.

The *Samādhirāja* comments on the perception of illusion:

Magicians conjure up various forms
Of horses, elephants, and chariots.
Though they appear as such,
There is no reality.
Understand all phenomena to be the same.

The meditator who has realized the mind's primordial purity integrates the absorptive evenness, which is immutably settled in the recess of intrinsic reality, with the illusory postabsorptive perception. He thereby achieves twofold enlightenment, eliminating clinging to all dualities while perceiving all phenomena as being manifestations of intrinsic reality.

The *Prajñāpāramitā-saṃcayagāthā* states:

> He does not ponder being in or out of tranquil absorption,
> Because he has realized perfectly the true nature of phenomena.

Thus, as the meditator sustains the realized vision of superior seeing, he should know how to maintain it with undistracted mindfulness, guard it against dullness or sensual incitement through alertness, and strengthen the concentration of the unobstructed vision of reality. He should also achieve perfect equanimity, which protects the mind from sensory diversions, and should know how these contemplative states can be achieved through the four mental forces such as inward exertion, etc. These instructions are contained in the *Śrāvakabhūmi*. He should know their application to both tranquility and insight. Thus the commentary on the meditational stage of insight is completed.

CHAPTER FOUR

The Stages of Tranquility and Insight Part III: Clearing Doubts Regarding the Methods for Maintaining the Vision of Reality and Meditative Absorption

1. Distinction between analytical meditation and concentrative meditation (fixed attentiveness)
62 B 2. Application of analysis and concentration to tranquility and insight
3. Analysis and concentration on the vision of reality
4. Elimination of doubts about the essential vision of reality

DISTINCTION BETWEEN ANALYTICAL MEDITATION AND CONCENTRATIVE MEDITATION

Some consider the meditation of the learned teachers to be solely analytical and that of the mendicant seekers to be exclusively that of concentration. Others think Buddhist scholars only study and investigate through reliance on doctrinal texts, whereas seekers practice tranquil absorption through the sole reliance on practical instructions. This is not so.

Scholars need the fixed attentiveness of tranquil absorption, which concentrates on the subject of meditation, while seekers need analytical meditation in order to purify their view of distortion and scepticism. Otherwise the vision of inherent reality attained solely through analytical investigation reduces that vision to an intellectual exercise, whereas the vision achieved only through fixed attentiveness is a mere experience of the mind. Without both—fixed attentiveness and analytical investigation—the essence of meditation will be difficult to realize.

63 F What are the determining and differentiating factors of fixed attentiveness and analytical investigation? Fixed attentiveness and analytical inves-

tigation are designated according to their greater or lesser degree. Analytical investigation is a meditational stage that seeks to establish the vision of inherent reality through inferential examination and authoritative exposition. Fixed attentiveness is a meditational stage in which the vision of intrinsic reality is determined essentially through valid cognition leading to meditation on tranquil equipoise of the ultimate reality. The school of analytical investigation concerns itself with the meditational systems based principally upon inferential investigation and the authoritative expositions embodied in the works of Asaṅga and Nāgārjuna. The meditational system of fixed attentiveness seeks perfect vision through initial contemplation on the valid cognition and then through main absorptive meditation on the mind's ultimate nature. This system was handed down by the great sages Saraha and Śavari. The perfect vision arrived at by these two schools must necessarily be identical, insofar as the void being the ultimate nature is concerned.

3 B Je Götsangpa[58] comments on these systems:

> The ultimate object of the analytical school of Buddhist savants and the school of fixed attentiveness of the mendicant yogins is one and the same. The latter is regarded as being the more rapid path.

The realization of perfect vision solely through reliance on authoritative exposition and inferential logic is difficult. As master Candrakīrti reasons, "Investigation through authoritative exposition and inferential logic is analysis through concepts, which is incapable of determining valid cognition." According to the Buddhist tradition many of the great Buddhist savants such as "the two great chariots," Nāgārjuna and Asaṅga, attained liberation through their adherence to the pithy instructions of Buddhist esotericism. Other great savants such as Nāropa and Maitrīpa have achieved liberation by following the pithy instructions of the ultimate truth, though not without having first attempted to do so through the path of authoritative exposition and inferential logic. Most of the great saints of Tibet and ancient India have achieved liberation by following the pithy instructions of Buddhist esotericism.

There are those who hold that perfect vision cannot be realized without
64 F the general application of authoritative exposition and inferential logic and particularly the application of this logic according to the Madhyamaka of Nāgārjuna and Āryadeva, the spiritual father and son. This view seems to be a personal indulgence and is not quite correct. If this assertion were valid, it would follow that, prior to their composing texts on Madhyamaka logic, Nāgārjuna and Āryadeva had not realized perfect vision. Such a view further implies that the Buddha, the bodhisattvas, and most of the great awakened ones of Tibet had not realized the perfect view either.

From the etymological standpoint, the terms such as "investigation" and "attentiveness" denote analysis and quietening of the mind. Difficulty will arise if one were to differ from these definitions. Analytical meditation encompasses the entire doctrine, from the rarity of obtaining a blessed human state to impermanence and to the determination of the two types of selflessness, as the subject of investigation. Meditation on fixed attentiveness embraces all absorptive meditations on the determination made through preceding investigations. Such concentration is maintained through single-minded attention and vigilance.

64 B There are some who consider analytical investigation and fixed attentiveness to be mutually exclusive. They contend that the mind cannot be settled in tranquility while concurrently investigating with penetrating intellect. Similarly they hold that analysis is impossible while the mind remains settled in tranquility, which is a nonconceptual state.

The first *Gomrim* (*Bhāvanākrama*) states:

> While the mind is settled in tranquility, one investigates it through intellectual discernment. The intellect in absorptive equipose should examine itself [the nature of mind].

The master Vasubandhu, in his commentary on the *Sūtrālaṃkāra*, refers to the varieties of meditation on insight: meditations with or without both general examination and penetrating analysis, and those engaging only in penetrating analysis. Many of the analytical meditations are to be practiced without disturbing the state of fixed attentiveness. The application of vigilance in a settled tranquility is a form of examination [if only to detect the emergence of sensual incitement or dullness]. Many similar instances exist.

APPLICATION OF ANALYSIS AND CONCENTRATION TO TRANQUILITY AND INSIGHT

Some people assume that by alternating the meditation of fixed attentiveness with investigation, tranquility cannot possibly be realized. They insist that meditation on tranquility must always be a fixed state and hold that analysis through discerning wisdom—during the meditation on insight—might cause that insight to cease. These views are misconceived.

65 F If the aforementioned view of fixed attentiveness expressed by some people were correct, such meditation, as "exhaustive analysis,"[59] "the inward examination for the elimination of defilement,"[60] etc. cannot be used as objects of tranquil meditation. By extension, the application of discerning wisdom and strong vigilance in mastering tranquility would be wrong, too. The view of an exponent on insight would contradict the traditional viewpoint that upon completing the analysis the analyzing intellect finally quietens itself [into a tranquil state]. According to his position, the nonconcep-

tual and imperturbable insight mentioned in the *Bhāvanākrama* would not be possible. Moreover, he maintains that meditational analysis and tranquility, insight and fixed attentiveness are mutually exclusive. This view assumes analysis to be completely intellectual discrimination, and tranquility to be totally nonconceptual. It holds that the state of insight ceases when meditation on fixed attentiveness progresses. Therefore, insight must always remain attached to the discerning intellect. These assertions would render impossible the integration of tranquility and insight, and would
B negate the similarity between nonconceptual perception and insight. This is a great fallacy.

How then does one practice? At the stage of tranquility one meditates mainly on fixed attentiveness, according to the methods laid down in the nine stages of settling the mind. Even so, analysis must be applied once tranquil equipose is stabilized.

The first *Bhāvanākrama* states:

> When complete quietude of mind prevails, apply extensive analysis to all the psychophysical aggregates and elements [of one's stream of being].

There are many analytical methods recommended to be practiced during a stage of tranquility. These are contemplation upon ugliness as an antidote to lust, upon love against hatred, and upon the law of interdependent activation against ignorance. Similarly, investigation through three or four
6 F methods are predominant in the meditation of insight. Insight is not lost when the analyzing intellect finally quietens itself; so no trace of duality remains. This quietening of the analytical intellect is the stage of pure insight, at which meditation on a fixed attentiveness is required.

The *Kāśyapaparivarta-sūtra* says:

> Fire produced by rubbing together two sticks of wood
> Then consumes both sticks;
> Likewise, discernment of dualism engenders wisdom,
> Which then destroys the two [dualistic notions].

The *Madhyamakāvatāra* explains:

> Human individuals are bound by dualistic conceptions;
> Yogins who overcome dualism achieve liberation.
> The fruit of perfect analysis
> Is the reversal of discrimination.
> So proclaim the wise ones.

Once integrated tranquility and insight are attained, the principal meditative effort must be on fixed attentiveness, with occasional alternations to analytical investigation.[61] The authoritative expositions will be quoted

below. The following methods are recommended for ordinary aspirants.
66 B Meditate on tranquility, if overcome by inner diversion[62] arising from excessive analysis; meditate on insight, if overcome by depression due to excessive meditation on fixed attentiveness and tranquility; meditate on effortless equanimity when harmonizing tranquility and insight.

The first *Bhāvanākrama* states:

> Dullness, if not eliminated, will completely engulf the mind, turning it into a dark realm devoid of insight. The moment the mind sinks into dullness, it must be cleared. At times the intellect attains great sensitivity through insightful meditation; this causes the mind to become very restless. Its perception of true reality becomes shaky, like a butter lamp flickering in the wind. This mind is not capable of perceiving intrinsic reality. The remedy for this condition is the meditation of tranquility. As this tranquility stabilizes itself, meditation on discerning wisdom must resume.
>
> Once the meditator has harmoniously blended tranquility and insight,
> 67 F he must maintain it without undue exertion for as long as the body and mind can endure it. Once tranquility and insight are unified, the mind must settle in concentrative equipose, instead of alternating this with investigation.

The *Saṃdhinirmocana-sūtra* comments:

> Maitreya: At what stage do the blending of tranquility and insight and their harmonious union take place?
>
> Buddha: This takes place when the mind is settled in one-pointed concentration.
>
> Maitreya: What is the one-pointed mind?
>
> Buddha: It is a simple awareness of the perceived image of absorption, which is to be sustained.

Master Jñānagarbha,[63] in his commentary on the *Saṃdhinirmocana*, explains:

> The path of tranquility is not separate from the path of insight, since the former is concentration on the mind, which then becomes the object of investigation for the latter. The mind is the only object for both these visualized meditations. When tranquil meditation stabilizes the mind, insightful meditation analyzes it. Both the visualization and visualizer are just identical characteristics of the mind. Hence they are not separate entities.

ANALYSIS AND CONCENTRATION ON THE VISION OF REALITY

Some teachers have expounded the following methods, which I consider to be wrong: To maintain perfect vision a meditator should first investigate the ultimate reality, using the authoritative doctrinal expositions and logic. This should bring about a firm determinate awareness of the nonsubstantiality of dualism.[64] The meditator should focus his concentration on it for a short while. They contend that an extended concentration will reduce its determinate awareness to mere tranquility with the resultant loss of insight. Not only is the meditator to practice investigation in this manner, but he is urged to alternate the meditation of fixed attentiveness with that of investigation.

I shall explain why the determinate awareness of nonsubstantial reality, so engendered through the examination of the authoritative doctrinal expositions and logic, is, regardless of the explanations, nothing but the mind grasping at emptiness. Such a vision is not endowed with perfect insight, and it cannot be perfected through the meditation of fixed attentiveness either. This system may not result in the attainment of an absorptive equipoise endowed with perfect vision, since they hold tranquility to be unattainable through the alternating meditation of fixed attentiveness and investigation. The reason for settling the mind in tranquility and insightful vision is the same. To settle the mind in fixed attentiveness after investiga-
68 F tion is also wrong, as they maintain insight vanishes once the mind is settled in tranquility. With insight so vanished, a concentration on the perfect vision [of reality] cannot render the meditation perfect. It is also incorrect to say the union of tranquility and insight will degenerate into mere tranquility without the benefit of repeated examinations. When the vision of such a union emerges, a single-minded concentration on that vision will encompass both tranquility and insight. This is indeed the union of the two. It is incorrect to examine repeatedly after settling the mind in the attained vision, because such an examination through authoritative doctrine and logic still remains within the conceptual domain. This is deluded discrimination and is to be eliminated through the dawning of nonconceptual awareness.[65] The reference in the *Kāśyapaparivarta* and the *Bhāvanākrama* to nonconceptual awareness arising from analytical intellect merely indicates the initial need for wisdom to establish the perfect vision. They do not show the need for repeated examinations to maintain the attained vision.

68 B Since most forms of determinate awareness[66] are nothing more than inferential judgement[67] based on a rational intellect, they cannot be accepted as nonconceptual awareness. It is also incorrect [for these exponents] to assume a concentration on perfect vision and a contemplative tranquility as being the same. A vast difference exists between the two. Tranquility merely

maintains the stream of nondiscriminating mindfulness[68] of the visualized image,[69] whereas the mind focused on the perfect vision is the stream of nonconceptual awareness, which is in harmony with the determinate certainty of the void nature [of duality].

How then are analytical investigation and fixed attentiveness to be practiced in order to maintain the perfect vision? At first, when seeking the vision of reality, development of a determinate awareness can be helped by discarding all doubts and assumptions about the criteria of the individual marks of reality and their generalized marks through the intellect born of acquired knowledge. This is like the track training of a new horse. For the realization of perfect vision a discerning wisdom[70] arising from meditation is essential. While not dependent upon inferential judgement, this wisdom is capable of
69 F directly establishing all realities to be devoid of true essence or inborn nature. It will cause the meditator to experience the analytical intellect itself as being without identifiable appearance or essence. This is the fundamental tenet of perfect vision. Observations and examinations must be practiced through the contemplative wisdom with unceasing mindfulness of the tranquil meditation, and not through conceptual analysis.

The first *Bhāvanākrama* states:

> When the mental focus on the visualized image of tranquility becomes firm, if at that moment one examines it through wisdom, an illumination of pure awareness will emerge, like light clearing the darkness. Pure awareness arises when the harmony between the two [tranquility and insight] is achieved. This harmony arises in the same way as one's eyes and light harmonize to produce a visual perception, without the conflicting characteristics of light and darkness. This absorptive
> 69 B trance is, by its nature, devoid of darkness, its essential characteristic being single-mindedness. By such meditational equipoise[71] ultimate reality can be perceived as it is. Not only is this meditation compatible with wisdom, but it is in perfect harmony with it. Therefore, the inconceivable nature of all phenomena, established through analytical wisdom obtained in absorptive meditation, is the ultimate reality beyond conception. It is the criterion of the subliminal purity [of awareness], which is spontaneous perfection. There is nothing more to be observed beyond that.

As discerning intellect finally quietens itself [when primal awareness emerges], all realities are cognized as being empty of absolute self-nature. This is the meaning of perceiving the true reality.

The first *Bhāvanākrama* continues:

> What does the perception of ultimate reality signify? It signifies the noncognition [of any absolute self-nature] of all realities. The term

> "noncognition of all realities" should not be construed to be the same as the dark void experienced by a blind man, a person with his eyes shut, or someone lacking in mental application.

As the text states:

> ... the inconceivable nature of all phenomena, established through
> F analytical wisdom obtained in absorptive meditation, is the ultimate
> reality beyond conception.[72]

Therefore, a meditator seeking the perfect view must first settle the mind in absorptive equipoise and then conduct meditational investigation through discerning wisdom. This view attained, the meditator should repeat his investigation whenever the mind is overcome by nonvirtuous thoughts, caused by its attachment to duality. Once the unerring awareness of perfect view is established, meditation with fixed attentiveness alone, rather than alternating it with investigation, should be the practice followed, until that view is mastered. This will be illustrated through doctrinal expositions later.

ELIMINATION OF DOUBTS ABOUT THE ESSENTIAL VISION OF REALITY

There are two sections:

1. Review of other Buddhist schools
2. Establishing the meditational system of our school

Review of Other Buddhist Schools

It was not correct on the part of some earlier Tibetan teachers to have assumed the view of intrinsic reality as consisting of abandonment not only of attachment to duality, but also of virtuous thoughts. Some have regarded this line of thought to be identical to that of the Hwashang school,[73] as both
70 B are lacking in determinate awareness that comprehends the intrinsic reality.
This is considered to be either due to a confused mind or to indifference.

Other earlier Tibetan scholars assumed "perfect view" to be the stream of determinate awareness arising from their recognition of the nonexistence of duality, as a result of expositional and inferential investigation based on the three marks of syllogism.[74] This is incorrect. Master Gampopa described such a system as the abnegated concept of nonarising [void], because it is an intellectualized and superficial void based on inferential judgements.

The *Pramāṇasamuccaya* says:

If one is led to the truth
Along the path of dialectics,[75]
It debases the teaching of Buddha.

Master Atīśa says:

Through the two forms of awareness,
Primal cognition[76] and inferential judgement,
One will perceive the void.
So say those people
Confused by duality.[77]

Still other early Tibetans have assumed intrinsic reality to be the void of absolute nothingness, determined by examining the self and the psychophysical aggregates through the logic of the Madhyamaka. This is also incorrect. The *Kālacakra* places this assumption closer to nihilism. It therefore cannot be accepted as being identical with the void of supreme form.[78]

71 F Some [teachers] propound that one establish an undeviated view, free from any extreme theories, through authoritative exposition, logical inference, or practical instruction, and then settle the mind in a nondiscriminating awareness. Such is the nature of vision and meditation. And when the mind is in tranquil equipoise, there emerges a union of awareness and void that is vivid, transparent, and unblemished. This is the nonconceptual awareness of intrinsic reality.

Some others stated that the above-mentioned scholars criticized Hwashang's contemplative approach, yet practiced a similar contemplation themselves. However, I find that their position with respect to the vision of reality and the method of attaining tranquility is in accord with the treatises of the Buddhist scholars and saints. Nonetheless, these very exponents identify blissful experience, gained through control of the complex neuropsychical system[79] and the creative elements, with nonconceptual awareness. This should not be confused with real nonconceptual awareness. No matter how good the awareness, when it is not separated from the moisture of sensations and experiences, it is nothing more than an appearance arising from either a subjective or objective dimension.

Also, some savants—while refuting all other visions of intrinsic reality—
71 B content themselves with not having any formulation. Such a position is not only hypocritical, but is a nonacceptance of the classical treatises of the Madhyamaka of which they are professed followers. It is an expedient substitute for a definite awareness of the "thatness" [of ultimate reality].

Some assume that even though one does not discover the vision of intrinsic reality through examination of doctrine and logic, meditation on the meaning of true reality is fulfilled if the mind is settled in its primal state, detached from the notion of objective reality and from the process of discrimination. They assert that, since the void of true reality is devoid of all identity, there must be such a method for settling the mind. Others have refuted this approach by identifying it with the nihilistic system of Hwa-shang. Though such practice is without error, the manner of its description might well be incompetent. My own observation of this system is that a meditator can use this to discover the proper vision, provided he is aware of the inherent limitations of nonsubstantial objective reality and the essential significance of the void nature of true reality, which is beyond all identity.

Even without comprehending these essential points, if one begins to
settle the mind in a simple, nonconceptual state by first examining it through
F wisdom, and then maintaining that quietude through vigilance and mindfulness, one is adopting a method prescribed for new meditators to practice
tranquility and insight. It is somewhat close to the method for maintaining
a view of intrinsic reality, though not the same employed by those competent
meditators who have eliminated all doubts and exaggeration. Even a nonconceptual meditation accompanied by mindfulness and vigilance will serve
to maintain nonconceptual tranquility. Yet such a tranquil state can be
flawed by the lack of mindfulness and vigilance and clouded by a deep
dullness and sluggishness. This is recognized as depressed thoughtlessness.

Other exponents, while admitting the need for perfect vision through
2 B analysis of the doctrine and logic, assert that once perfect vision is attained,
the mind settled in a completely nonconceptual state constitutes the meditation of that perfect vision. Opponents of this hold that, if this position
were true, then all dimensions of thoughtlessness—such as deep sleep or
the meditation on simple tranquility—should represent meditation on
the perfect vision. The question as to whether a meditation deals with perfect view can be answered by determining the presence or absence of
vigilance and mindfulness, reinforced by a determinate awareness of that
view, in the nonconceptual state in question. My previous comments on the
value of simple nonconceptual meditation has application in this instance.

It has been asserted by some that once the true vision is achieved, all
subsequent meditation should begin with an examination of the vision
through discerning wisdom. After that, the mind should be settled in a
nonconceptual state. They hold this to be the meditation on the true vision.
This has been refuted by some on the same grounds as the preceding case;
it is argued that the mere settling of the mind in a nonconceptual state is
73 F similar to a deep sleep. On the criteria for determining whether a meditation
is that of perfect view, I refer to my observations above.

Some exponents do not accept the three above-mentioned meditational systems. To them meditation on the perfect view is forming a determinate awareness of its void nature and then firmly fixing attention on the significance of it. They, however, point out that the first system is not without any intellectual inclination toward the void, and the second does not lack mindfulness of the perfect view when settling the mind in a nonconceptual equipoise. The third system is not without fixed attention on the vision of perfect reality after the initial investigation.

However, this approach has drawn criticism on the grounds that the meditation prescribed in contradistinction to the three consists solely of fixing the mental focus on the perfect view through recollection of its previous understanding of that view. It is held by critics to be simply tranquil meditation on the void and therefore lacking in insight that arises from investigation. Holistic meditation must consist of tranquility and insight; this practice is incomplete, as it contains only tranquility. This criticism cannot be valid if the meditation in question is basically a concentration [as the critic pointed out] on insight attained earlier through analysis. Therefore, there is no need to repeat the analysis [in the same practice]. I find the approach to be well presented, though there may be some basis for doubt concerning the existence of attachment to the experience of the view.

A Tibetan savant asserts that in order to establish the vision of reality, the meditator should first eliminate the mind's grasping of dualism born of ignorance and, then, as a counterbalance, produce a powerful awareness of
73 B the void [nature of mind] through meditation. To merely master concentration of the mind on the awareness of that vision is to only maintain tranquility. Instead, there must be repeated examination and creation of a powerful awareness of certainty. Any comprehension of the meaning of intrinsic reality does not necessarily constitute a clinging to substantive dualism. All nonconceptual states, detached from discerning intellect, are similar to the meditational system of Hwashang.

Followers of this savant hold that in the emptiness of true dualism, established through the logical investigation of the Middle Way [Madhyamaka], lies the meaning of nonselfhood. The powerful certainty of selflessness or emptiness of true reality produced by an intellect inclined toward that position, is the definite awareness of the perfect vision. Seating that awareness of certainty on the horse of tranquility and thereby settling it in absorptive equipoise is regarded to be the true vision in meditation. The rest is as I have said before.[80]

I shall now examine the preceding assertion that creating a powerful
74 F awareness of the emptiness of innate nature involves conceptualizing the nonexistent self-nature or nonsubstance; this is not different from clinging to that emptiness. It is similar to the other position following it, according to which the intellectual grasping of the selflessness of phenomena or of the emptiness of true reality is but mental attachment. The greater the grasping, the stronger the clinging. Though the existence of the self is negated, the intellectual grasping of nonselfhood still persists; though clinging to sub-

stantive reality is negated, an attachment to that reality still persists. These are recognized as the great fallacies.

The *Bhāvanākrama* explains:

> Contemplate all things as devoid of self-nature; abandon even the idea of nonexistent self-nature through transcending wisdom.

The *Mūlamadhyamaka-kārikā* states:

> He who views his nature and that of others
> As being substantive or nihility
> Does not perceive the true nature
> According to the Buddha's doctrine.

And the same text adds:

> To affirm reality is to concede eternalism;
> To deny reality completely is to accept nihilism.

The *Bodhicittavivaraṇa* expounds:

> This is nonarising or emptiness,
> This is nonselfhood.
> Such is the meditation of an inferior mind.
> This is not the meditation on the void.

These expositions contradict the positon of the scholars mentioned earlier.

The *Mūlamadhyamaka-kārikā* states:

> By their erroneous perceptions of emptiness
> The less intelligent will come to grief.

The *Uma Tshiksal* (*Mūlamadhyamaka-vṛttiḥ Prasannapadā*) explains:

> The moment all phenomena are conceived as nihility
> A distortion of the view occurs.

There is a possibility of this risk. However, should such clinging persist, choose a positive view of reality, which is the better of the two evils.

The *Mūlamadhyamaka-kārikā* asserts:

> He who affirms will go to the realm of peace;
> He who denies everything will go to the realm of affliction.[81]

It is incorrect to regard as simple tranquility the state in which the mind is focused on a memory of perfect vision. The mind settled in a tranquil state contains insight; thus a union of the two exists. A vision without the two cannot be said to be a perfect vision. To designate every insight as conceptual and every tranquility as nonconceptual is to deny the harmony between the two. Such designation precludes the possibility of a synthesis of tranquility and insight. In the light of this approach, the following might also be incorrect. Concerning the unity of tranquility and insight master Uñānagarbha, in his commentary on the *Saṃdhinirmocana-sūtra*, writes:

> Since the path of tranquility concentrates primarily on the mind, which is at the same time the object of insight, the perception and perceiver are not separate entities but the complete state of the mind. With regard to the mind's grasping of emptiness or nihility, no other exponents of the ultimate doctrine, Tibetan or Indian, have accepted this as being valid.

This approach contradicts many authoritative positions. For example, the *Dharmadhātu-stava*[82] states:

75 B Abandon discrimination and conceptualization
Of all phenomena projected by mind;
Meditate on the inner expanse of reality
For in reality they are devoid of the innate essence.

The Great Saraha elucidates:

> The true essence of reality is unblemished
> By extreme concepts and impurities [prejudices];
> Pure from the beginning, it is beyond determination;
> To discriminate it is to arouse a poisonous snake.

Since conceptual discrimination or investigation is but the exercise of a conditioned and deluded mind, the conceptual discrimination of the ultimate reality is opposed.

Nāgārjuna says:

> The ultimate reality is beyond
> The realm of the mind's discrimination,
> For the mind is recognized as being conditioned.

It is incorrect to assume that grasping of the true nature of reality does not represent a clinging to conceptual reality.

The *Prajñāpāramitā-saṃcayagāthā* elaborates:

> If a bodhisattva considers
> The psychophysical aggregates as being "void,"
> He is grasping a conceptual reality,[83]
> Thus showing little reverence toward that which is "unborn."

The Prajñāpāramitā comments that to dualize all phenomena, from psychophysical aggregates to perfect knowledge, as being eternal or impermanent,
76 F empty or not empty, possessed of self or without a self, is to indulge in conceptual duality.

Saraha says:

> When the mind is enchanted [by the senses]
> And indulges in them with a passionate heart,
> Then even a pain as small as the husk of a sesame seed
> Is sure to cause constant affliction.

And he concludes:

> Abandon attachment to objects, whatever they may be.

There have been many statements to the same effect.

It is a little too audacious to say that all nonconceptual states, devoid of analytical investigation, are identical with the meditational system of Hwashang.

The *Bodhicittavivaraṇa* asserts:

> Nondiscrimination is emptiness.
> How can there be emptiness
> Where discrimination exists?

The *Madhyamakāvatāra* explains:

> Erroneous concepts are the results of discrimination—
> So proclaims the Wise One.

Atīśa, in elucidating the technique of settling the mind according to special Madhyamaka instruction, says:

> In the midst of meditation one does not discriminate nor cling to anything.

All such statements, which urge the settling of the mind in a nonconceptual state, might well be the meditational system of Hwashang [according to the critic of nonconceptual meditation].

6 B The teachings of Maitreya[84] refer to the wisdom that grasps at the emptiness of reality as the concept of eternalism. Since this concept is to be abandoned through nonconceptual awareness, it cannot be the perfect vision. Even if, as advocated, it is seated on the horse of tranquility, it would not be the perfect vision in meditation. According to his system, tranquility must necessarily be nonconceptual, whereas the tranquil mind, detached from discrimination, causes the loss of insight. The analogy of a horse and its burden is incompatible. It has been affirmed that analytical investigation itself must finally cease [in an absorption]. When this occurs, [if the critic is right] insight is lost and the meditation becomes similar to that propounded by the Hwashang school. Buddhist logic and doctrine can be used to counter this position; however, I will not elucidate here for fear of overelaboration.

Establishing the Meditational System of Our School

Much can be understood from the previous explanations on insight, the identification of the vision of reality and its maintenance, and also from the
77 F commentaries on the doctrine and logic. The realization of the vision of the void is said to occur upon achieving the stage of illumination. Here I shall only deal with the vision appropriate to the intellectual level of ordinary human beings. It is of the utmost importance to establish the vision of the void, whether through analytical or concentrative meditation. The sūtras state that nonrealized vision and meditation cannot destroy the roots of existence [saṃsāra].

The *Bodhicittavivaraṇa* remarks:

Those who are ignorant of the void
Cannot achieve liberation.
These confused minds wander
In the prison of the six realms.

It is futile to practice without discovering the unerring vision of reality. Nāropa, in his *Dṛṣṭisaṃkṣepta*, comments:

Through unerring vision,
Meditation and action well harmonized,
Enlightenment is achieved,
Like a trained horse skillfully negotiating a course.
77 B If the vision is not truly in accord [with intrinsic reality],
Meditation and action will take the wrong course,
And nothing of any worth will be achieved.
That is like the groping of a blind man without a guide.

The attainment of awareness through meditation is essential for a successful determination of the true vision. Mere intellectual understanding arising from hearing and examining will not suffice. All the sūtras, tantras, and illuminating instructions agree that the ultimate meditation is one that concentrates on the mind and culminates in realization.

The *Guhyasamāja-tantra* states:

When fully examined,
The mind is found to be the source of all realities.
This phenomenon is the space of indestructibility
In which the duality of phenomena and their intrinsic nature is absent.

The *Vajrapañjara* sets forth:

The precious mind is a dynamic force; the mind attuned to meditation attains enlightenment.

The *Laṅkāvatāra-sūtra* elucidates:

> Do not determine the external reality through mere reliance on the mind. Transcend the confines of the mind, by focusing on the suchness [of the void]. Settle the mind on the unreality of phenomenal appearance. A yogin who has realized the unreality of appearance will truly understand the Great Vehicle.

The *Sūtrālaṃkāra* summarizes:

> Know that nothing exists apart from the mind.
> Realize the mind itself is devoid of true reality.

Saraha says:

> The mind is in bondage, if tied by attachment;
> If this tie is broken, the source of confusion is eliminated.

Based on the *Laṅkāvatāra-sūtra*, the system of the Two Great Chariots,[85] "the stages of meditation" and "the instructions on the wisdom-gone-beyond" prescribe practices for attaining the nonconceptual state by focusing (1) on the mind, (2) on the awareness of the suchness [of the void], or (3) on the perception of the unreality of phenomena. When establishing the view of reality through meditation according to the sūtras or tantras with elucidating instructions, discerning wisdom is indispensable. This is stated in the third *Bhāvanākrama*:

> 8 B All realities in their essence are void, which cannot be understood without analytical intellect.

However, this intellect itself must finally be quietened, ushering in the emergence of a nonconceptual state.

The *Kāśyapaparivarta* states:

> Buddha: Kāśyapa, when two wind-blown trees strike each other, fire is produced. This fire then consumes the trees. Similarly, Kāśyapa, from the perfect analytical intellect is born the wisdom of the awakened ones, whose flames then consume the intellect.

The second *Bhāvanākrama* explains:

> The fire of the true understanding of ultimate reality emerges from the discerning intellect. This fire consumes the intellect, the way the flames consumed the trees. Such were the words of the Illuminated Conqueror.

79 F Analysis [of insight]—not of conceptual views—should be done while dwelling in a meditative absorption. A sūtra affirms this approach:

> Understanding of the pure truth can only be attained through absorptive meditation.

The *Bhāvanākrama* agrees:

> Perfect awareness will dawn only when the mind—firmly settled in tranquility—applies wisdom and investigates it.

At this level, the true vision of intrinsic reality is the dawning of nonconceptual awareness devoid of any entity. This occurs when the discriminating faculties become quiet. A sūtra says in support:

> Perfect insight is the nonperception of all phenomena.

The *Bhāvanākrama* adds:

> What is the insight into true reality? It is the nonperception of all phenomena.

At this stage the mind should be quietened in a nonconceptual, nonperceiving state, free from any dualistic though or consciousness, undisturbed by the cloud of dullness or sensual incitement.

A sūtra declares:

> Upon intrinsic reality as such is focused the mind with a similar
> 79 B nature. An undefinable experience will illuminate in one. This is described as absorptive equipoise.

Atīśa says:

> Settle the mind without discrimination in the nonconceptual expanse of reality.

And he adds:

> The infinity of reality is without center or horizon. Observe it with a deep nonconceptual mind, unobscured by any shadow of dullness or sensual incitement.

The *Madhyamakopadeśa* of Atīśa concludes:

> Thus, past thought has ceased, the future is yet to emerge, and the present is difficult to penetrate. Being nonsubstantive and spacelike, the mind is colorless and shapeless. It is neither one nor many entities. Its nature is the unborn [void] and luminous awareness. By examining the mind with the weapon of logic, one will comprehend its nonreality.

Neither the twin aspects of the mind [awareness and its void nature] nor the discerning intellect are composed of any essence. For example, the fire that
80 F results from the friction of two pieces of wood consumes the wood that begot it; when the wood is burnt, the fire dies. The moment wisdom establishes the

unreality of all perceptive and conceptual dualism, the meditator will realize the wisdom itself as being lucid and void, unobscured by perceptive duality and undistracted by dullness or sensual incitement. The mind should be rid of flaws such as dullness, sensual incitement, clinging, memory, and other mental activities. The meditator should maintain a nonconceptual state until interrupted by stealthy thieflike perception or discrimination.

This can be explained in a simpler way. When, at first, the meditator seeks perfect vision, he establishes the mind as being the source of all duality. The mind is then discovered to be without essence. These investigations are carried out through logical formulae known as: the three entrances of time, the mutual exclusion of the one and many, the nonexistence of absolute
0 B arising, cessation and duration, and the lucid, void nature of the mind. One establishes the mind to be devoid of any substantiality whatsoever through the [above-mentioned] logical investigation. Even the analytical intellect is [established to be] unreal. The analytical intellect dissolves itself finally into the nondual, luminous state in the way wood is consumed by fire.

This is the attainment of the perfect view. Once this occurs, the mind should concentrate totally on the realized view unless interrupted by perceptions or discrimination. During the absorptive period the mind should be cleared of any creeping dullness or sensual incitement. It should not allow discrimination, attachment, consciousness of duality, or other mental activities.

The *Bhāvanākrama* advises:

> Contemplate the nonsubstantiality of all phenomena. Eliminate even the very notion of nonsubstantiality through nonconceptual wisdom. Meditate on such a nonconceptual state that transcends dualism, both existence and nonexistence.

81 F There are those who seek to maintain the vision of reality through meditation and who thereby wish to harmonize the tranquil state with analytical insight into the void nature of phenomena, the nonexistence of an essence, or the nonexistence of the self. They will gain a definite understanding by contemplating the meaning of these quotations.

Many discourses refer to the need for nonconceptual meditation once the perfect way has been established. The *Samādhirāja* states:

> Wise understanding of the conditioned and unconditioned reality,
> Elimination of all perceptive duality,
> And the quietening of the mind in a nondual state
> Will bring about insight into the void nature of all phenomena.

The *Bhāvanākrama* quotes the *Ārya Ratnamegha*:

> A thorough examination of the understanding of the mind will bring about a realization of its emptiness. With this knowledge, the medi-

tator should withdraw into the pure state of nonduality. Understand-
81 B ing the mind's nonexistent essence through analytical insight is absorption in the state of nonduality.

The second *Bhāvanākrama* continues:

> When a seeker of the truth fully examines [the mind] through wisdom and refrains from clinging to its intrinsic nature as being the ultimate essence, he then reaches nonconceptual absorption.

Kamalasīla in his commentary on the *Avikalpapraveśa-dhāraṇī* explains:

> At the conclusion of the examination the mind should be quietened into a nonconceptual state.

The *Bodhipathapradīpa* supports this:

> First establish all phenomena
> As being devoid of self-nature and absolute condition
> Through doctrine and logic.
> Then meditate on the perfect nonconceptuality.

This completes the general elucidation on the removal of doubts concerning vision and meditation. This has been written as a general exegesis, to serve as a guide for the many methods of realizing the absorptive state in accordance with the sūtras, tantras, and illuminating instructions.

BOOK TWO

An Extensive Elucidation of Mahāmudrā, the Uncommon Meditation

PART I: PRELIMINARY EXPOSITION

F The elucidation of this part will comprise:

1. Exposition engendering confidence
2. Preparatory practices

CHAPTER ONE

Exposition Engendering Confidence

This is comprised of five sections:

1. The inherent significance of the teaching: Definition of *Chakgya Chenpo* [mahāmudrā]
2. Origin of mahāmudrā according to the sūtras
3. Origin of mahāmudrā according to the tantras, especially the Unsurpassed Link (anuttara tantra)
4. How mahāmudrā embodies the deep meaning of all the sūtras and tantras
5. The great qualities of the mahāmudrā practitioners.

THE INHERENT SIGNIFICANCE OF THE TEACHING: DEFINITION OF *CHAKGYA CHENPO* [MAHĀMUDRĀ]

This section will explain three points:

1. The various meanings of the [Tibetan] title
2. The substance and distinction of its inherent significance
3. The benefits derived from the knowledge of it and the harm ensuing due to ignorance of it

The Various Meanings of the [Tibetan] Title

Concerning the title *Chakgya Chenpo*: *Chakgya* denotes simultaneously seal [mudrā], symbol [nimitta], and sign [lakṣana]. Just as a seal leaves its impression on other objects, so *chakgya chenpo* (mahāmudrā), the ultimate
82 B reality, leaves its imprint upon all [dual] realities of saṃsāra and [nondual] nirvāṇa. Just as the coat of arms on a suit of armor establishes the wearer's identity, so *chakgya*, as a doctrine, indicates the inherent character or abiding reality of all things. *Chakgya* signifies binding authority, like the

uncontestable authority of a sovereign over his subjects. It also signifies the ultimate nature, which thus assigns to all realities their holistic qualities.

The *Gaganagañjaparipṛcchā-sūtra* renders further etymological meanings of *chakgya*:

> The realities are marked with the seal of the Tathāgata. It is the seal of suchness [of the void], which is inseparable from the realities, remaining impervious to discernment, penetration, or attachment. It is neither mover nor movement; hence it cannot be moved by the universe of beings, celestial, semicelestial, and human. This seal of the Tathāgata—the buddha nature—is unborn [nonconditioned]. It is the seal of complete emptiness, complete singleness, complete aspirationlessness, complete compositeness, and desirelessness. As suchness [of the void] it is the seal of purity and the seal of inner space.

The term *chenpo* [mahā] means the supreme deity. The *Guhyasiddhi* states:

> It originates from the highest tantra—the fourth division [of the vajrayāna system];
> It will bring about the perfect enlightenment.
> It is the meditation of mahāmudrā, which stands unsurpassed by anything.

The *Mahāmudrātilaka* comments:

> As regards the *chakgya chenpo*,
> *Chak* stands for awareness of vacuity [śūnyatā],
> *Gya* signifies its intrinsic quality that transcends existential duality,
> *Chenpo* symbolizes the union of the two.

The *Pañcakrama* on the term *chak*:

> *Chak* signifies the attainment of insight into innermost awareness;

and on the term *gya* adds:

> *Gya* symbolizes the void of awareness, which transcends the limits of saṃsāra and which has imprinted its mark upon all things.

The *Guhyasamāja* sets forth the nature of ultimate reality [mahāmudrā]:

> It is devoid of all substance,
> Devoid of subject-object duality
> That arises from psychophysical aggregates,
> Elements, and sense faculties.
> This is the selflessness of reality
> In which [saṃsāra and nirvāṇa] are equal.

Chenpo stands for the union of skillfulness and wisdom, etc. and is therefore the highest of all meditations. The *Dekhonanyi Chupa* (*Daśatattva*) describes:

> A true seeker unifies skillfulness and wisdom
> Through the highest meditation.
> He becomes one with the mahāmudrā.

The title of this doctrine is explained in the *Padminī*, a commentary on the *Kālacakra-tantra*:

84 F *Chakgya chenpo* stands for wisdom-gone-beyond which has produced Tathāgatas in the past, does so at present, and will do so in the future. *Chakgya* means nonabiding nirvāṇa or immutable bliss. Hence, it surpasses the seal of mystical performance [karmamudrā], and the seal of transcending awareness [jñānamudrā].

> *Chenpo* is so designated because it [wisdom-gone-beyond] is unstained by the psychic sediments of saṃsāra.

Je Gampopa says that *Chak* stands for the realization that all appearances and actualities, saṃsāra and nirvāṇa, are not separate from their unborn void nature. *Gya* stands for the primal purity that encompasses everything—perceptions and possibilities. *Chenpo* stands for the realization that freedom is inherent in the true nature of reality [dharmatā].

Lama Serdingpa's *Thektrön* declares:

> Regarding the definition of *chakgya chenpo*:
> *Chak* signifies the spontaneous dissolution of defiled thoughts and deeds, and the blending of the mind with the ultimate state of simplicity [dharmakāya].
> *Gya* signifies the power of this state which cannot be overcome by the perceptive mark of duality.
> *Chenpo* stands for the superior level of this system over all other vehicles [of transmitting the teachings], whether they be the vehicle of metaphysical dialectics,[1] the esoteric vehicles of external performance, and of physical and mental performance.[2]

84 B The synonyms for the designations of *chakgya chenpo* are the intrinsic nature, the supreme awareness, the universal excellence, the great seal, and the ultimate reality of all phenomena.

Indrabodhi's *Jñānasiddhi-sādhana* states:

> This ultimate reality
> Is also called the supreme indestructible awareness
> And the universal excellence.
> It is also known as the great seal.
> Understand this as being dharmakāya.

The *Yogasapta* also explains the title of this doctrine:

> The nonexistent self-nature, suchness [of the void], intrinsic reality, evenness of phenomena, and the ultimate realm are synonyms. They show nothing other than that which is devoid of self-nature.

The Substance and Distinction of Its Inherent Significance

The essential characteristic of mahāmudrā is described as being analogous to all-encompassing space; it rests nowhere and is detached from all conceptions. Indrabodhi defines it thus:

> As nondwelling space encompasses everything and defies definition, so it is with the ultimate reality.

Maitrīpa elaborates:

> Mahāmudrā is nondual awareness that transcends intellect; it is nonconceptual, lucid, like all-pervading space. Though manifesting boundless compassion, it is devoid of self-nature. It is like the reflection of the moon on the lake's surface. It is lucid and undefinable, without center or circumference, unstained, undefiled, and free from fear and desire. Like the dream of a mute, it is inexpressible.

The great seal is divided into three levels of interpretation: the foundation, the path, and the accomplishment. As the foundation it is, in general, the intrinsic reality of all phenomena which is, from the beginning, detached from concepts. With its inherent void and lucid nature, such reality embraces saṃsāra and nirvāṇa, yet defies description. This basis, applied particularly to the mind, is the true and primordial nature of the great seal. Clear, lucid, and without identifiable entity, it surpasses thought and definition.

5 B The great seal as the path consists of the understanding that underlies all phenomena, the understanding of saṃsāra and nirvāṇa, perceptions and potentialities. It is indivisible clarity and emptiness, devoid of [self-nature], i.e., absolute emergence, endurance, and extinction.[3] It can be realized through the doctrinal practices of listening, examination, and meditation,[4] but especially through attainment of the perfect vision and contemplation.

The great seal as the accomplishment is complete awareness, endowed with the twin purities.[5] This can be realized by perfecting one's insight into the foundation of mahāmudrā through consummate experience of the great seal as the path. The practice requires the purging of all dualistic perceptions in their infinitesimal subtlety to effect a clearness like that of a sky without clouds.

There are further distinctions in regard to the three principles [foundation, path, and accomplishment]. The *Uttaratantra* describes the foundation of mahāmudrā:

> Impure, impure,[6] pure, and supremely pure
> Correspond to the three mental states
> Of sentient beings, bodhisattvas
> And the Tathāgata respectively.

Thus the foundation of mahāmudrā is discerned through suchness [of the void] to be inherent in all three levels of the inner-stream [mind].

Concerning the aspects of mahāmudrā as the self-awakening process [path], the *Dechok Jungwa* (*Saṃvarodaya-tantra*) says:

> Emptiness differentiated
> Becomes contemplative absorption and wisdom.

The *Jñānagarbha-tantra* summarizes:

> The path of mahāmudrā is divided into four parts: the female consort as the sublimation of sensuality (karmamudrā); spiritual commitment (samayamudrā); the inner consort of manifest awareness (jñānamudrā); and all phenomena (dharmamudrā).[7]

Concerning mahāmudrā as accomplishment, Indrabodhi, in his
86 F *Jñānasiddhi-sādhana*, states:

> Just as a mirror reflects form, so ultimate reality [dharmakāya] reflects awareness. Such is the mirrorlike awareness.

The five awarenesses [pañca-jñāna] and the three perfect aspects [trikāya] should be understood as the differentiation of the mahāmudrā of accomplishment [enlightenment].

The Benefits Derived from the Knowledge of It and the Harm Ensuing from Ignorance of It

Lack of understanding the abiding reality of mahāmudrā will result in failure to attain liberation, even though the meditator may know a hundred thousand other absorptions into the pure state. Only by understanding that abiding reality will he comprehend all other realities and attain the enlightenment of the Indestructible Spirit [Vajrasattva].

The *Mahāmudrātilaka* says:

> He who does not understand mahāmudrā
> Is not a realized one, however illuminated.

He will not achieve supreme fulfillment
Without perfectly understanding
The essence of mahāmudrā,
Even though he may know
A hundred thousand tantras of yogatantras and yoginītantras,
He who has perfect knowledge of all dharmas [phenomena]
Is indeed a buddha.
He who has perfect understanding of mahāmudrā
Will realize the indestructible spirit [buddha mind].
The intrinsic awareness of this spirit
Is the characteristic of mahāmudrā.

The innate emptiness of phenomena is the same as mahāmudrā, according to the *Bodhicittavivaraṇa*:

Those who do not understand the void
Fail to realize liberation.
So, confused beings wander in the cycle of existence,
Prisoners within the six existential spheres.

Maitrīpa says:

By realizing the intrinsic nature of one's self,
One will realize the cosmic appearances and actualities as being
mahāmudrā,
The great, ultimate, and all-prevading reality.

And he also says:

He who has not attained this intrinsic reality
Will achieve nothing except temporary freedom.
Once he has realized this intrinsic reality,
What is there that can bind him?

ORIGIN OF MAHĀMUDRĀ ACCORDING TO THE SŪTRAS

The sūtras identify the meaning of mahāmudrā as being similar to various epithets of the same term [mudrā]. The *Sāgaramatiparipṛcchā-sūtra* declares:

> Buddha: O Sāgaramati, all realities are marked by the seal [mudrā] of innate freedom, which is completely pure and nondual. Like the
> 87 F expanse of space, all realities are without distinction because they are all marked by the seal of evenness.

The same sūtra mentions twenty kinds of seals, one of which is the unblemished seal, the mind that has been purged of clinging to the self. The sūtra describes:

> This dharma is pure, excellent, and lucid;
> Its state of evenness is like space;
> Being unborn [emptiness] from the beginning,
> It is devoid of absolute arising, origin, settlement, or cessation.
> This is the seal of the victorious Buddha.

In the *Maitreyaprasthāna-sūtra*, Buddha refers to fifteen seals:

> O son of noble spirit, all things bear the imprint of the seal of emptiness.

Ten seals are stated in the *Gaganagañjaparipṛcchā-sūtra*. The *Bumo Rinchengyi Zhüpai* refers to the following seals:

> The characteristics of phenomena
> Are similar to the characteristics of space.
> Whatever bears the mark of such a seal
> Does not regress or retrograde.

87 B The *Bhadrakalpika* makes mention of such designations as the seal of awareness, the seal of realities, etc. The *Varmavyūhanirdeśa-sūtra* also mentions the term the seal of realities. The *Mañjuśrī-mūlatantra* in the collected texts of the fundamental tantra refers to the postures of the hand as the great seal. The *Vairocanābhisaṃbodhi* identifies the implements of the meditational deities with the great seal. The Yogatantra categorizes the postures of the hand into four seals. Similar enumerations of the term mahāmudrā exist.

In summary, mahāmudrā of the foundation is shown in the tantras and sūtras as being the quintessence of the Tathāgata [buddha nature], which from the beginning permeates the stream of individual consciousness. This intrinsic nature of the mind is described as being lucidity [emptiness]. Mahāmudrā of the path is shown as being the creative methods for the blossoming of the innermost potentialities [the buddha nature lying dormant in every stream-being] and for unifying [such an awareness] with the ultimate simplicity of nonconception, intrinsic emptiness, unreality of phenomena, and evenness. Mahāmudrā of accomplishment is shown in the
88 F teachings on achieving all-knowing enlightenment, consisting of the four perfect aspects (caturkāya) and the five awarenesses (pañcajñāna).

ORIGIN OF MAHĀMUDRĀ ACCORDING TO THE TANTRAS, ESPECIALLY THE UNSURPASSED LINK [ANUTTARA TANTRA]

This section covers three topics:

1. Exposition of the system of three and four mudrās
2. Exposition of the extraordianary mahamudrā
3. Clearing away the confusion of other schools

Exposition of the System of Three and Four Mudrās

The *Kālacakra-tantra* states:

> Out of critical determination, one dissociates from the female
> consort (karmamudrā)
> And abstains from the inner consort of manifest awareness
> (jñānamudra).
> By concentrating on that which is supreme and immutable,
> One meditates on mahāmudrā.

And it continues:

> As the intimate union with the female consort
> And the delightful application of an inner consort of manifest
> awareness
> Are unified with the seal of the great mother[8]
> Into a single state,
> An immutable bliss will increasingly arise.

Padmavajra in the *Guhyasiddhi* advises:

> The female consort of transformation is tumultuous and devious.
> So is the inner consort of manifest awareness.
> Abandon these, which are replete with discrimination
> And meditate on mahāmudrā.

88 B Mañjuśrī, in his *Tawe Döpa Dortenpa*, says:

> Crazy and malignant is the female consort;
> The inner consort of manifest awareness is the same.
> Abandon these in the dualistic realm
> And practice mahāmudrā.

The three forms of the great seal are: the female consort, the inner consort of manifest awareness, and mahāmudrā. This has met with the concurrence of some great sages. These three seals are also mentioned in the fourth chapter of the *Pradīpoddyotana*:

> The three seals are phenomena, the perceptive mark, and the great seal (mahāmudrā).

The four seals are mentioned in the exegetical tantra, the *Vajramālā*:

> Thus spoke the indestructible Illuminated Conqueror:
> Many are the mudrās—the mudrā of phenomena,
> The mudrā of the inner consort of manifest awareness,[9]
> The mudrā of spiritual commitment, and the great seal,
> To mention them in their order.

The *Candraguhyatilaka* affirms:

> The first is the seal of phenomena,
> The second, the seal of spiritual commitment,
> The third, the great seal,
> And the fourth, the seal of the inner consort of manifest awareness.

The *Jñānagarbha-tantra* refers to four divisions of the great seal: the female consort, the seal of spiritual commitment, the inner consort of manifest awareness, and phenomena. The commentary on the *Sangye Nyamjor*
89 F (*Buddhasamāyoga*) by Garap Dorje also gives the four as the great seal, the seal of spiritual commitment, the seal of phenomena, and the seal of the female consort. Master Abhayākara, in his commentary on the *Buddhakapāla*, enumerates the following mudrās: the mudrā of visualized transformation, inner perfection, and final attainment.[10] Each of these is further divided into four: the seal of the female consort, the seal of phenomena, the great seal, and the seal of spiritual commitment. The four seals are all mentioned by Nāropa in his commentary on the *Hevajra-tantra*: They are the female consort, the inner consort of manifest awareness, the great seal, and the spiritual commitment. Each of them is necessary: first as a condition for preceiving the lucid awareness [of one's stream-being], second as contemplation, third as inner realization, and fourth as consolidating it without impairment. Maitrtpa in his *Caturmudrāniścaya* also mentioned the four mudrās. The treatises of great sages contain these four with different orders and identifications.

Regarding this a certain [teacher][11] contends:

> Whatever are the great seals of Nāropa and Maitrīpa,
> 89 B They are the seal of the female consort,
> The seal of phenomena, the seal of spiritual commitment, and the great seal.
> These are stated as such in the tantras that these [sages] have accepted.

This contention is based on mere assumption, because the four seals referred to in the esoteric texts of the two great saints contain different orders and identifications. These he has not ascertained. Apparently he has not seen the other texts by the two saints on the ultimate meaning of the great seal [nitārtha mahāmudrā]. Their elucidation on the four seals contains a different order and identification. The critic's quotation does not correspond with them. It is implicit in his statement, when examined, that the two saints did not compose separate texts on nitārtha mahāmudrā apart from their elucidation of the four seals in accordance with the tantric treatises. Such a contention is completely unacceptable.

Despite his intellectual achievement which encompassed the ocean of sūtras and tantras, Nāropa was dissatisfied with it. He associated himself with great Tilopa. During the period of undertaking the twelve near-fatal ordeals as commanded by his teacher, Nāropa realized the secret oral teachings on the quintessential great seal. It was stated that this resulted in his liberation, which was not dependent upon the esoteric path of tantra.

If Nāropa and Maitrīpa elucidated only the four kinds of mudrā embodied in the tantric treatises as indicated by this critic, Nāropa would not be the author of the mahāmudrā treatises such as the *Chakchen Tsikdü*, *Yeshe Selje*, and *Dṛṣṭisaṃkṣepta*. Besides, there are Tilopa's mystical songs [dohā] and his mahāmudrā texts, such as the *Mahāmudropadeśa* given by the Ganges river. Similarly, Maitrīpa would not be the author of his mystical songs and such mahāmudrā texts as the *Chakchen Tsikdü* as well as others. Besides, the texts on the quintessential great seal he advanced included the mystical songs of the great and lesser Sarahas.[12] Maitrīpa, also, having been dissatisfied with his proficient knowledge of the sūtras and tantras followed [the mystic teacher] Śavarīśvara and received the illuminating instructions on the quintessential great seal, which were not based on the tantric teachings. Maitrīpa then achieved spiritual liberation. If this critic accepts Nāropa and Maitrīpa as being the authors of those mahāmudrā texts, he
0 B contradicts himself since he stated that the mahāmudrā accepted by Nāropa and Maitrīpa [consisted of the four seals]. [This implicitly rules out their authorship of other texts on mahāmudra.]

Exposition of the Extraordinary Mahāmudrā

Some of the aforesaid texts, which refer to three or four mudrās, also show the extraordinary mahāmudrā. The reference in the *Kālacakra* to mahāmudrā is apparently to this extraordinary mahāmudrā. With the passage, "This immutable bliss is mahāmudrā," it affirms the complete transformation of the emptiness of supreme form and the immutable bliss into oneness, characterized as "one flavor." The *Kālacakra* makes it clear that this immutable bliss is a spotaneously coemerging bliss and not a mentally conceived awareness brought about by the use of a real or higher psychic consort for inner transformation.

91 F The *Vajramālā* in the forty-sixth chapter refers to the mahāmudrā of foundation:

To expound among others
The meaning of the mahāmudrā, the characteristics,
And the resultant quiescence of the great yoga,
The significance of great awareness is summarized,
Thus providing a tremendous opportunity for great bliss
That possesses one great flavor..
It is a grand illusion with subtlety,
A vast space—greater than the greatest.
This mudrā is the awareness of tathāgata.
Enter this state without discrimination;
It is the realm of indivisible mind,[13]
Full of bliss, free from dualistic movements.
It is like space that is unclouded.

The same text comments on mahāmudrā as path:

All processes for attunement with the primal purity
[Of one's stream-being] involve awakening awareness
To its undefinable characteristics of nonduality and nonselfhood,
To its innate nature and inherent basis.
[To actualize this awareness]
One abandons discrimination
Arising from the aggregates of stream-being,
Their elements, and the sensory formations;
One abandons the duality of meditator and meditative absorption,
And the two stages of esoteric meditation as well.[14]
One avoids creating the duality of consciousness and awareness
While abstaining from incantation of sacred syllables and
transmutation with a meditational deity.

The *Vajramāla* finally describes mahāmudrā of accomplishment:

Understand that only through tremendous appreciation
Can one achieve the great realization of expansive awareness,
Which transcends all realms of knowledge,
91 B For it is the unsurpassed mahāmudrā.

These verses are explained in the commentary by the master Alaṃkakalaśa.

The *Mahāmudrātilaka* gives a similar description of the mahāmudrā of foundation:

"O Illuminated Conqueror,
All supremely awakened ḍākinīs revealed
The mystic path like the sun,
Which dispels the darkness of ignorance,
Yet none has expounded mahāmudrā.
Supremely Victorious One, may you reveal it."

The Illuminated Conqueror replied,
"Listen devī,[15] the supreme state of bliss is mahāmudrā.
This sublime mystery
Is undefinable, inexhaustible, and unborn.
Although formless it is the body of all realities;
Although formless it dominates forms supremely.
Its intrinsic nature is indeterminable,
Unaffected by concepts of formal qualities such as proportions or size;
The state of unstained lucidity is without a specific confinement.
Neither momentarily emerging nor dissolving,
2 F It remains a steady illumination of sublime expanse;
Free from the time-space dimension,
It is thus not subject to birth and death."

Besides expounding the true nature of the existential foundation, these [verses] show the methods of realizing it, and the benefit and harm arising from understanding or not understanding it. Master Zabpai Dorje (Gambhīravajra) explains these verses in his commentary.

The *Jñānatilaka* states:

Being ten million times superior to the highest heaven [brahmaloka],
You [the great seal] have left your indelible imprint
Upon the countless things.
You are therefore renowned as the great seal.

Its commentary, the *Guhyatattva*, elaborates:

[Great bliss] arises from or with the support of luminous awareness,
Which in turn may be actualized through the innerfire [caṇḍālī][16]
According to conceptual mahāmudrā.
Thus one attains nonconceptual bliss, which is the true nature of
  mahāmudrā,
By experiencing the various levels of natural bliss.

Again the same text comments:

All sentient beings possess buddha nature
Which is identical with the illuminated mother, mahāmudrā.
92 B Thus there is a cause-effect identity between them.

The great seal is so described because it leaves its imprint on all things. The same text identifies mahāmudrā with nonconceptual awareness, natural bliss, and the nature of the existential foundation. The commentary by Saraha on the *Buddhakapāla* explains the phrase "she who has the intellect of mahāmudrā" as follows:

> Because the intrinsic nature of the great void has made its imprint on all tathāgatas it is the great seal.

Thus the great void of sublime form is identified with the great seal.

The *Padminī*, a commentary on the *Kālacakra*[17] explains:

> What is designated as the great seal is wisdom-gone-beyond, which produced tathāgatas in the past, does so in the present, and will do so in the future.

The doctrinal view of wisdom-gone-beyond is thus identified with mahāmudrā.

Rāmapāla's commentary on the *Sekanirdeśa* elaborates:

> 93 F Since it has left its imprint on the three levels [of foundation, path, and result] of mudrā, it is indeed the seal, and a great one at that. Its essence being nonabiding [emptiness], it [i.e., the mahāmudrā of foundation] cannot be established through analyses. By actualizing awareness of the path [mahāmudrā of the path] through ceaseless discipline and veneration one may realize the mahāmudrā [of accomplishment—the great union of great bliss and its void nature]. This [true] awareness—devoid of reality and intellectual confusion—ever remains the source of all manners of excellence. In their intrinsic nature saṃsāra and nirvāṇa remain identical. It rebounds in great inconceivable compassion, for this is great bliss.

Such are the definitions and identifications of mahāmudrā as the existential foundation, the path, and the accomplishment. Similar descriptions are found in such tantras as the *Buddhasamāyoga*, the *Saṃvarodaya*, the *Vajrapañjara*, the second section of the *Hevajra-tantra*, the *Sampuṭa*, and others, and also in the doctrinal texts of great sages, like those entitled the *Seven Sections of Accomplishment* (*Truppa Dedün*). However, no further elaboration is needed.

In summary, one should understand that mahāmudrā is referred to in all
93 B the tantras and doctrinal texts through such terms as the intrinsic nature of the existential foundation [with regard to all things], the inherent emptiness, spontaneous coemergence, evenness, as well as immutable bliss, great bliss, nonarising, nonexisting, and nonceasing, depth, tranquility, and nonconceptuality. Even so, a certain teacher[18] criticized this system by saying, "We do not accept mahāmudrā, which is not expounded in the tantras."

This utterance shows that he failed to investigate or study the intention and meaning of the sutras and tantras.

Clearing Away the Confusion of Other Schools

The [same] critic states:

> Present-day [Kagyü] mahāmudrā is not different from the Chinese Mahāsandhi [Tib.: Dzokchen], i.e., the Ch'an contemplative system. The only change made[19] was from its original designation "the swooping down path" to "the path of sudden realization" and from its designation for Indian Buddhism as "the climbing up path" to "the path of gradual realization."

Such a statement was probably made out of the sheer wish to criticize.
94 F The mahāsandhi belongs to Atiyoga and as such is regarded to be the highest secret teaching, whereas the meditational system of the Chinese teacher Hwashang has been affirmed as having been based on the eighty sūtras. Therefore, the two differ not only in their system of meditation, but also in their source. No authority has ever described the Chinese system as being mahāsandhi. To designate it as being the meditation of Hwashang is tantamount to degrading the religion to the level of nonreligion.

This critic seems to lack understanding of the meaning of mahāmudrā, which is in accord with the spirit of such texts as the *Triad of Mystic Songs* [*Dohā Korsum*], the *Dochung Dzögye*, the *Trupnying*, the *Amanasi*, and others. Likewise, this critic commented on the historical account that begins with "concerning the emergence of religious systems such as these. . . ." This is pure imagination, which contradicts an authentic account given by Kamalaśīla's disciples contained in the preface to his *Bhāvanākrama*.

Again [this critic says]: "Even though it was based on the writing of the
94B Chinese abbot, the designation was changed to mahāmudrā. Present-day mahāmudrā is virtually the Chinese Buddhist system." This statement is completely false for it reflects the critic's personal feeling rather than the truth. There is neither evidence nor logic in the contention that, even though the system was based on the texts of the Chinese abbot [Hwashang], the name was changed to that of mahāmudrā. This name was already known in the tantras and the exegetical treatises, and to the Buddhist scholars and sages. He arbitrarily equated this system with a wrong one while concealing his own shortcomings in the tantric treatises that refer to mahāmudrā. To make such a comment without a definite understanding is not the dispassionate way of scholars.

Some contend that the Chinese abbot did not accept the theory of interdependent arising[20] with respect to man's psychophysical behaviour.

He advocated the negation of all thoughts—positive and negative—with respect to doctrinal vision and meditation, even though these are based on the eighty sūtras. On the level of attainment he accepted no enlightenment other than the realization of the mind. Thus, critics contend that contem-
95 F porary meditators of mahāmudrā seem to be following the Chinese system. During recent times some arrogant scholars have repeated such comments without examining the facts. All these irresponsible utterances are nothing but slander, showing the utter lack of insight of these critics into the vital aspects of the vision and meditation, as well as the doctrinal principles advocated by the exponents of mahāmudrā.

Some, in their refutation of the Chinese system, quote the third *Bhāvanākrama* which refers to this subject:

> There are those who think and say that all sentient beings wandering in the various spheres experience diverse levels of existence owing to the force of their actions—either virtuous or nonvirtuous—which arise from dualistic mind. Those who shun all thoughts and actions will achieve liberation. For this reason one should neither entertain any thought nor practice such virtues as generosity. Such practices are prescribed for the benefit of ignorant people.
>
> Those who think and speak in this way have abandoned the Great
> 95 B Vehicle [Mahāyāna] completely. By abandoning this vehicle one abandons all other vehicles, for the Great Vehicle is the root of them all. Thus, to urge meditators not to discriminate in meditation is to abandon discerning wisdom, for perfect discernment is the root of sublime awareness. If one abandons it, one would be abandoning transcending wisdom. Besides, to implore [seekers] not to practice generosity and the other virtues is to reject all the practical means [to enlightenment].

This is the quotation from [Kamalaśīla's *Bhāvanākrama*] that rejects Hwashang's position. Although the Chinese system appears to have discarded not only discriminating wisdom on the path of vision and meditation, but even the virtues such as generosity and others, for the critic to say that that system [mahāmudrā] has not accepted the karmic law of cause and effect is to show his utter lack of understanding. The *Bhāvanākrama*, restating the Chinese system, mentions at the outset its position regarding the relationship of cause and effect to virtue and vice. The Chinese master would certainly have known about karma through the eighty sūtras since these are the source of his teachings. So unreliable is the critic's treatise on the detailed account of the debate between Hwashang and Kamalaśīla that it is irrelevant, slanderous, and self-contradictory. The refutation of Hwashang's
96 F position [by Kamalaśīla] was inappropriately quoted. Similarly, this critic contends that the meditation on mahāmudrā of intrinsic reality is akin to

that of the Chinese system. This is sheer fabrication, but I do not wish to extend any refutation for fear of enlarging the volume.

However, the distinction between mahāmudrā and the system of
Hwashang may be briefly dealt with here in order to clear this misrepresentation. With regard to practical means, Hwashang holds that the pursuit of
virtue and the purging [of inner defilements] are devised for ignorant people
who lack understanding of suchness, thus ignoring spiritual performance.
Mahāmudrā expounds a way of perceiving the inner action of cause and
effect to be of the void in nature, that is to say, it is essential for a seeker to
devote himself intensely to the principle of causal law even after having
realized the void of reality. Similarly, many subtle distinctions exist [be-
B tween the two systems] concerning whether one perceives or does not
perceive one flavor [i.e., intrinsic unity] through the divergent relativity,
whether one has mastered the conditioned [mental phenomenon], and
whether one knows how to create the cause for achieving the highest
manifestation.[21]

With regard to meditation, Hwashang's system advocates complete
negation of thought or mental activity whereas mahāmudrā requires a
meditator, even during the early quietening of the mind, to maintain a
concentration that is undisturbed from the image of an object and to keep a
vigilance that is capable of detecting any interference of dullness or sensual
incitement. Hwashang, in meditational absorption, maintains nonconceptual quietude, discerning neither benefit nor harm, whereas mahāmudrā
considers nonconceptual quietude defective as such, being a nonconscious
inertia. Hwashang does not employ any means of investigation or analysis in
meditation. This system [mahāmudrā] requires investigation or analysis in
every way regarding the meaning of meditation. Through discerning wisdom Hwashang maintains a state of nonconceptual quietude,[22] whereas this
97 F system [mahāmudrā] requires avoidance of distraction from mindfulness
and awareness. Hwashang is content with the complete negation of thought,
while this system considers such an approach to be a deviation and digres-
sion and requires one to adhere to its precepts.

Concerning doctrinal vision, Hwashang does not accept wisdom emerging from examination and meditation respectively, whereas this system requires one to seek the vision of intrinsic reality through wisdom gained through intellectual analysis and meditation respectively, and then to achieve the realization of it. Hwashang's system is divorced from the vision that comprehends the thatness [of emptiness], while this school cuts off the roots of all dualities and maintains the awareness of intrinsic reality. Concerning accomplishment, Hwashang asserts that liberation consists of the simple mastery of the stream of the nonconscious state. This system considers it essential [for a meditator, having once gained the insight into thatness (of the void), to work toward the consummation without any

distraction so as] to purge dualities in all their infinitesimal subtlety through continued expansion of awareness, once having awakened to thatness [ultimate reality]. For this reason it is improper to criticize, out of jealousy, the
97 B meaning of ultimate purity. This would mislead those who are trusting into abandoning the dharma.

The [same] critic asserts his own system to be as follows:

> As for our system of mahāmudrā, it is an awareness [first] brought about through mystical empowerment and nurtured through meditative absorption, known as the two contemplative levels. Thus it is an inborn awareness.

Having examined this position, I have no doubt about the possibility of perceiving the four mudrās in general and the intrinsic reality of mahāmudrā in particular. It is highly incorrect to claim as the state of mahāmudrā an experience of bliss that pervades the body and mind and which is transmuted with [awareness of] void as if through the process of imprint. This is because the sensation of bliss has emerged from the cyclic flow of the sexual fluid brought about by means of the third empowerment.[23] Indrabodhi upheld my view:

> A wicked human being claims,
> "Bliss [of the transient kind] arising from sexual union
> Enables one to perceive thatness [tattva], the intrinsic reality.
> The Supremely Victorious One has not proclaimed
> That to be great bliss.
> Since the former [transient bliss] has arisen from sexual interaction
> It could not possibly contain the awareness of thatness.
> For such bliss does not last for all times as an essential state.
> [Conversely] the awareness of all the Tathāgatas[24] cognizes its intrinsic nature
> And stands out as supreme among all blissful states.
> Hence it is described as the great bliss.
> This great bliss is not a transient phenomenon, but permanent great bliss.

98 F Many other writings have opposed [his standpoint]. Since it [sensual fulfillment] arises from the cyclic flow of sexual fluid and is transient by nature, it contradicts immutable bliss, which the *Kālacakra* identifies with mahāmudrā. It is even more incorrect to say that this [fulfillment] has to be unified with the sealed-off void, the awareness of which arises from an intellectual examination. The *Kālacakra* refutes this as follows:

> The void perceived by analyzing the aggregates of stream-being
> Is without essence, like a bamboo tree.

> But the void supreme in all forms
> Is nothing like that.

The section in the *Kālacakra* on awareness (jñāna) dealing with the realization of supreme, immutable awareness advises:

> ... to be completely detached from the void of total negation, as determined through the analysis of the phenomenon composed of atomic particles.

Thus it is said that the void determined through an analysis of the psychophysical aggregates represents the void of total negation.

Besides, the system of the critic is highly incorrect as it identifies modal awareness [peyi yeshe] with transient bliss, which arises from the cyclic flow of seminal fluid as effected during the third empowerment. It is also incor-
8 B rect to identify the ultimate awareness in the fourth empowerment with the void of total negation, which is designated as a nonconceptual state. By doing so, he would be accepting the opposite position stated in the *Kālacakra* and the *Jñānasiddhi*. Although these two levels of awareness—the modal and the ultimate—must of necessity be similar and interrelated, like cause and effect, the critic, however, seems to describe the two as being unrelated and contradictory. Again, he is wrong to infer, as he did in the *Thupgong*, that mahāmudrā [as the spontaneous union of bliss and void] must necessarily originate from the initiatory process. If this were so, he would have to state that mahāmudrā of the existential foundation—the primordial nature of all things—also originated from the initiatory process. If such a mahāmudrā of the existential foundation is not accepted, mahāmudrā of the path and of the accomplishment would have to be denied, because one has to achieve the accomplishment by gaining perfect experience on the path with regard to that which lies hidden in the existential foundation. It would also mean that one would have to commit sacrilege by abandoning many treatises on
99 F mahāmudrā given by the senior and junior Sarahas, Tilopa, Nāropa, Maitrīpa, etc., as well as the other texts such as the *Truppa Dedün*. Furthermore, it would also mean that the great sages who were the authors of these treatises would have to be refuted on account of his distorted vision.

HOW MAHĀMUDRĀ EMBODIES THE DEEP MEANING OF ALL THE SŪTRAS AND TANTRAS

There are two sections:

1. Identifying the essence of the path
2. Condensing the deep meaning of the sūtras and tantras

Identifying the Essence of the Path

Concerning the manner of identifying the essence of the path, some of the mystical songs and the transmission of symbolic mahāmudrā recognize this system as belonging to the tantric tradition as opposed to the sūtra tradition, and specifically to the third subdivision of tantra—the path of directly perceiving reality. The other two are the path of spiritual blessing and the path of giving inner solace. It is said that [in order to facilitate the practice of this system] one is required to receive either a short or an elaborate initiation as a means of germinating [the hidden seed of illumination].

It is further said that—since the paths preceding the esoteric mantra are regarded as being stepping stones—one should meditate on any of the aspects of these paths and not ignore them. According to the tradition of the
99 B secret mystic practice, since there are three levels of spiritual trainees—inferior, average, and superior—the path has been divided into three, viz.: the definitive vehicle of wisdom-gone-beyond, the vehicle of innermost mystical formula, and the vehicle of the unsurpassed essence. Mahāmudrā is regarded as belonging to the third. It has been said that mahāmudrā does not conform directly to the first, it is not in conflict with the second, and while in accord with the third, it even surpasses all three. It is said that one [who wishes to practice mahāmudrā] should receive a short or elaborate blessing and initiation and should also meditate on a meditative deity [yidam] at an appropriate stage. In such a case, mahāmudrā should be included in the vehicle of the innermost mystical formula. Nonetheless, if one examines the treatises by Saraha [one would find that] he designated mahāmudrā as "the essential path" and considered it an intermediate path [seng lam]. He states as follows in his mystic song:

> This supreme, essential path of the Great Vehicle
> Enables one to bring into actuality the accomplishment.
> [This is possible] because the accomplishment
> Has been inherent [as the seed] from primordial times on.

He continues:

> It is empty of any mystic circle [of transcending awareness]
> And empty of devotees who make burning offerings.
> Detached from any mystical formula, gesture, and consecration,
> It cannot be realized through tantras and śāstras.[25]
> This indestructible awareness is of perfect beauty
> In its natural realm.

100 F He further states:

> It does not need either tantra or mantra, examination or
> contemplation,
> For they all cause delusion of the mind.

Again he says:

> What do you need any butter lamps or cakes of grain for?
> What does one do with it and why does one apply the innermost
> mystical formula?

Sayings such as these describe the path of mahāmudrā in its essence and show that it is not based on tantric mysticism. Mahāmudrā is regarded as being detached from the three subtle cognitions,[26] while transcending the four kinds of joy[27] and even surpassing the mind's innate transparency. Nevertheless, it can be treated as being related to tantra because the *Queen Dohā* mentions [three factors]: associating oneself with a female consort, training her in order to germinate the seed of illumination in her, as well as carrying out the secret enactment of the self-realization process.[28]

The incomparable Takpopa says:

> There are, in general, three spiritual paths.
>
> 1. Concerning the application of inference on the path, one ascertains the absence of innate nature in all things by examining through the deductive formula that negates one or many self-entities of individuals.[29] And then, one meditates with the certainty that [intrinsic
> 0 B reality] is not anything but the void of self-nature.
>
> 2. Regarding the application of spiritual blessing on the path, one seeks to gain control over the nervous system and the internal energies through the meditational visualizations of the form of a yidam.
>
> 3. The path of direct awakening through open reality is the mahāmudrā of inmost purity.

Gampopa mentions another three kinds of paths as follows:

> 1. "The path of eliminating the existential foundation" is the vehicle of wisdom-gone-beyond. Through this path one differentiates between the countermeasures and the unacceptable behaviors, and thereby one eliminates them.
>
> 2. "The path of the inner transformation of the existential foundation" belongs to tantric mysticism. According to this path, the transformation of external phenomena refers to the meditative transmutation of one's body into the form of a yidam and also the male and female sexual organ into the sacred scepter [vajra] and lotus [padma] respectively.

Transformation of reality refers to transformation of mental defilement into a spiritual experience. One turns every dualistic thought into [nondual] awareness. Thus, as has been stated, impurity purges impurity, duality eliminates duality.

3. "The path of knowing the existential foundation" is mahāmudrā. In this path there are neither unacceptable principles that must be abandoned nor are there antidotes against them; neither is there a transformation nor one who transforms, for all realities are only manifestations of the mind. Only by understanding that the meaning of the mind's nonarising [void nature] from the beginning is intrinsic dharmakāya and by perfecting such an awareness will one attain enlightenment.

There is yet another category of three paths. A person of inferior intelligence embraces the path of spiritual merits as being the vehicle of wisdom-gone-beyond. A person of average intelligence who possesses discriminating faculty and passion follows the path of skillful-
101 F ness, which is the vehicle of mysticism. A person of superior intelligence enters the path of intrinsic reality, which is mahāmudrā.

Thus he [Gampopa] considers mahāmudrā to be a separate path and independent of the sūtras and tantras.

At certain times mahāmudrā was also designated as the path of spiritual blessing. That is to say that an awakened guru is required to guide his predestined disciple—who has renounced this worldly life—toward liberation through mahāmudrā—the only path of instantaneous illumination, which doesn't depend on the paths of the sūtras and tantras. In recent times meditators of mahāmudrā sought to make adjustments according to both the sūtras and the tantras. They have incorporated [in the mahāmudrā tradition] many practices that require preparations such as the mystical empowerment that sows the seed of a spiritual blossom, devotion to preliminary exercises, and methods of enhancing experiences. It is for that reason that it is not contradictory to regard mahāmudrā as identical with the common and profound path of the sūtras and tantras, due to the fact that many superior and inferior minds are going to benefit from it.

Condensing the Deep Meaning of the Sūtras and Tantras

101 B It has been said that all the teachings of the sūtras and the tantras expounded by the victorious Buddha are a means to realize the thatness[30] [intrinsic reality] of all things. The intended meaning of all these [teachings] are condensed in this thatness upon which the ultimacy of the practice rests. It is also the direction into which the vast and profound teachings inevitably must

lead. A sūtra makes this point:

> All teachings of the Tathāgata are condensed in thatness; they rest on it and lead toward it.

The second *Bhāvanākrama* states:

> The teachings of the Illuminated Conqueror were perfectly expounded to directly or indirectly elucidate thatness, and they all focused on this.

Dīpaṃkara Atīśa says:

> The entire eighty-four thousand forms of the dharma[31]
> Expounded by Buddha come down to thatness.
> No sūtras and tantras were expounded
> Other than those dealing with
> The methods of realizing the void nature of reality.

F The *Pañcakrama* asserts:

> The concept of thatness expounded in the various sūtras and tantras revealed nothing other than the intrinsic void.

The praise to the Illuminated Conqueror by *Nivaraṇaviṣkambhi*[32] affirms:

> You expounded the dharma concerning that which is
> Tranquil and nonarising from the beginning.
> You set in motion the wheel of doctrine
> That deals with that which transcends all miseries [saṃsāra].

Thus two paths as means to realizing the void were expounded. The depth of the sūtra path generally embraces the three courses, namely, listening, examining, and meditating, and particularly the practice of the six principles of wisdom-gone-beyond. All these are concentrated in the meditation on abiding reality.

The *Vajrasamādhi-sūtra* states:

> If one does not move away from the awareness of void,
> One has combined the six principles of perfection.

The *Khyepar Semkyi Zhüpai Dho* defines:

> Nonduality means generosity;
> Nonexclusion, morality;
> 02 B Nondiscrimination, patience;
> Nonacceptance and abandonment, striving;
> Nonattachment, tranquil absorption;
> Nonconception, wisdom.

Saraha sums up:

> That nonconceptual awareness is reading, comprehending, and meditating as well as cherishing the dharma.

The *Raptu Minepe Gyü*

> By eating food that is natural and unmodified,[33]
> One may satisfy all schools of the doctrine,
> For everything appears in the light of mental characteristics.
> Only an ignorant, childish mind relies on conventional words.

Furthermore, all creative applications on the two meditational stages constituting the inmost depth of the esoteric path were explained in order to realize nonconceptual awareness, because the ultimate intent [of the Buddha] is the attainment of that ultimate simplicity. The *Dorje Khado* (*Vajraḍākinī-tantra*) explains:

> In order to realize the mode of intrinsic purity, a meditator applies the creative processes such as meditation and the repetition of sacred syllables. Having once realized the mode of intrinsic purity, the practitioner of outwardly creative processes should no longer apply them.
> 103 F Just as someone crossing a river on a board leaves the board behind once on the other shore, so should the meditator cease the creative processes.

The *Hevajra-piṇḍārtha* commentary on the *Vajraḥridaya* states:

> He who is bound by dualistic thoughts and latent impressions
> Should at the outset employ rituals of dualistic dimension.
> Upon realizing the inmost nature of dualism,
> He should elevate himself to a nonconceptual state.

For that reason it is stated that inherent in the thatness [the void nature] of nonconceptual awareness is the meaning of the mystical practices for actualizing the inmost purity. The *Taknyi* (*Hevajra-tantra*) reiterates:

> Upon the intrinsic nature of the nonconceptual state
> Rests the significance of the sacred syllables
> And the supreme illusory forms.

The same text adds:

> It [nonconceptual awareness] embodies [the essence] of repeating
> sacred syllables, asceticism, fire sacrifices,
> And the assembly of supreme forms and mansions.
> In summary, the mind brings about the unity of all forms.

The *Amṛtaguhya-tantrarāja* says:

For one who has discovered the intrinsic nature of the mind,
This [state] embodies all the diverse actions and performances
Such as worship, offering of sacrifical cakes [torma], etc.

It has been stated that in order to realize pure awareness, the key instructions of mahāmudrā are essential. Without them the realization of mahāmudrā as being the lucid awareness of true reality is difficult to achieve through the path of the sūtras and tantras. Saraha states:

Having thus renounced the world, these devout celibates
Are designated to be full-fledged monks, elders, and novices.
Some teach the sūtras,
Some grasp the single flavor of the mind's nature,
While others apply the Mahāyāna teachings as the cause [of liberation].
These teachings originate from the classical treatises on the conceptual marks [of realities].
Still others meditate on the sublime cosmic dimension and the divine assembly [maṇḍala].
Some elucidate the significance of the fourth empowerment;
Others contemplate the element of space;
Still others view the void.
Most have embarked upon the path of disharmony [leading in an unfavorable direction].
Whoever contemplates the nature of nirvāṇa
Without spontaneous awareness
Will not realize the ultimate.

Tilopa supports this position:

Whether by expounding the tantric mysticism,
The transcending wisdom, the sacred canon, and the concise sayings,
Or by following the various classic treatises
And the doctrines of conceptual determination,
One may not realize mahāmudrā as lucid awareness.

It is said that true reality may easily be realized if one follow the key instructions on mahāmudrā, the ultimate reality. The *Abhidhāna-tantra* urges:

He who devotes himself to meditation on mahāmudrā
Will achieve direct meditative awakening
And also will attain perfect liberation and enlightenment.[34]

The *Sūryacandra-sādhana* comments:

Seekers with superior intellect should follow
The mahāmudrā of true reality;
Through mastery of unperturbed concentration
They should meditate with consistency
On the nondual state of bliss and its void
For a period of three years and three months.[35]
They will attain the supreme realization; thus it is stated.

THE GREAT QUALITIES OF THE MAHĀMUDRĀ PRACTITIONERS

These teachers are described in two sections:

1. The lineage of the realized ones in India
2. The lineage of the meditative system in Tibet

The Lineage of the Realized Ones in India

104 B Buddha Vajradhara expounded the unlimited, unsurpassed tantras, especially the *Mahāmudrātilaka*, the *Śrī-anāvila-tantra*, the *Raptu Minepe Gyü*, and others belonging to the quintessential tantra. They were entrusted to Guhyapati as the custodian who then transmitted them to the awakened women [ḍākinīs] in Uḍḍiyāṇa [Swat]. The incarnate king Viśukalpa had traveled to Uḍḍiyāṇa where he received the key instructions and elucidations from the ḍākinīs. He brought to India the extensive teachings of tantric mysticism. Having examined the potentiality of all would-be disciples, he found Saraha to be of vastly superior mind—a perfect human devotee—who was predestined to attain instantaneous liberation. As a result of his giving the key instructions to him, Saraha achieved liberation. He [Saraha] then sang the essential instructions and brought about the liberation of many fortunate people. Thus, the lineage of inmost realization came into being, a fact well known to this tradition.

According to the accounts contained in the *Dohās*, the *Datsa*, the *Gyagar Sangchö*, etc., the perfectly enlightened Buddha saw that the time was opportune for transmitting the wonderful quintessence of the dharma. This occurred around the time he was contemplating nirvāṇa and showing signs of his passing away, after having set in motion the wheel of dharma in three
105 F phases in response to the needs of the three levels of sentient beings. At the behest of Mañjughoṣa and Avalokiteśvara he traveled to the South and transmitted this quintessential dharma to an assembly of innumerable bodhisattvas gathered together at the city of Vidarbha.[36] At that time the

Buddha prophesied that some time in the future there would emerge exponents of this quintessential dharma. These were the two bodhisattvas [Mañjughoṣa and Avalokiteśvara], Saraha, Nāgārjuna, Śavari, and others. Some time later the bodhisattvas Mañjughoṣa and Avalokiteśvara—having reincarnated as Devaputra Ratnamati and Devaputra Sukhanātha—transmitted this teaching to Saraha. It was said that he achieved liberation instantly. Another tradition, while mainly agreeing with this account, states that Ratnamati was the reincarnation of Buddha himself and Sukhanātha that of Guhyapati [bodhisattva Vajrapāṇi]. This and other variations are not
B contradictory because, in the ultimate sense, the five perfectly accomplished ones[37] and others like them were stated to be reincarnations of the Buddha.

So the Buddha Vajradhara transmitted his teaching to the reincarnated bodhisattvas who in turn gave it to Saraha, who was the father of all the great saints of India and who helped them to achieve liberation. Saraha transmitted it to Nāgārjuna, who was renowned as the second Buddha. Both of them were the gurus of most of the great Indian saints. Nāgārjuna especially guided Śrī Śavarīśvara toward his liberation. He belonged to the caste of dancers and was a perfect devotee, predestined to attain instantaneous liberation. According to certain traditions, Śavari later received the quintessential dharma from the two bodhisattvas and also from Saraha. They had achieved enlightenment through illusory form or the spacelike mystical form.[38] It is said that these masters appeared before fortunate devotees at the mountain retreat of Śrīparvata[39] until recent times.

106 F Having come down through a succession [of teachers], the quintessential instructions such as the *Druppa Dedün* of mahāmudrā, the *Nyingpo Kordruk*, the twenty-four sections of *Amanasi*, and the extensive and concise texts of the *Dohā* were known in India. Because of all these, most of the wise scholars and saints of subsequent periods were so overcome with a sense of marvel at this quintessential instruction that they sought out the gurus and the instructions of this lineage.

Similarly, the learned saint Maitrīpa who had also heard of the greatness of this quintessential dharma and that of the lineage traveled to Śrīparvata in the South, experiencing immeasurable hardship. When his initial search for Śavari was in vain, he made an attempt to take his life, whereupon Śavari appeared before him. By and by Maitrīpa received the instructions on the quintessential dharma. All this resulted [during his sojourn at Bodhgayā in Magadha] in the recognition of this outstanding teacher as the great lord Maitrīpa, and in his making available the numerous commentaries on the
106 B instructions that he had composed himself. The quintessential instructions contained in the *Dohās*, *Datsa*, *Sangchö*, etc. became extensively known, especially as they were passed on to the Indian Vajrapāṇi [Gyagar Chakna] and from him to others.

Furthermore, according to [some sources] known to this meditative tradition, the renowned great saint, the superhuman Tilopa, was a reincarnation of Cakrasaṃvara, the illuminated conqueror, while others claimed that of the bodhisattva Cittavajra.[40] He was said to have visited the Akaniṣṭha buddha realm in his subtle illusory manifestation and to have listed to Buddha Vajradhara expounding the doctrine in all its profundity and vastness. Consequently he became the preeminent master of tantric mysticism, like its custodian Vajrapāṇi. Tilopa compiled all forms of creative visualizations into four or six segments, all higher meditations of perfect fulfillment belonging to the father tantra into five levels, while those of the mother tantra into four mudrās or six segments.

Tilopa was then said to have visited the great country of Zahor in East
107 F India [Bengal]. By expounding the teachings to a gathering of people, hundreds of thousands of people found their way into the realm of ḍākinīs,[41] thus rendering the city deserted. This account refers to Tilopa's miraculous subjugation of the eight saints who in turn liberated innumerable sentient beings, and to the tradition that Tilopa continues to live, performing acts of inner purity in his illusory form as long as the teaching of Buddha survives. Tilopa's assertion that he had no human teachers caused others to be skeptical. So, in order to satisfy critics, he created the impression of having associated with earthly gurus and achieved liberation. Among the gurus from whom he received the four mystic transmissions[42] were Nāgārjuna, Kṛṣṇācārya, mahāsiddha Lavapa, and ḍākinī Subhaginī. Having attended other great male and female gurus such as Ṭeṅgipa and Dārika, who were disciples of Lūyipa, and his dharma brothers Indrabodhi and Vajraghaṇṭa, he manifested the way of liberation.

Then there was the great master Nāropa who had achieved the mastery of the sūtras, tantras, the sciences, and arts as well as the realization of mysti-
107 B cism. Following the prophetic guidance given by Cakrasaṃvara and a ḍākinī, Nāropa went to Zahor looking for the great master Tilopa. Having found and pleased him with his service and hospitality, such as performing the twelve personal ordeals, Nāropa received all the key instructions just as the entire contents of a vase are completely poured into another vase. On his return to Magadha, Nāropa brought about fulfillment for innumerable disciples. Among the eminent ones were the seven who were comparable to him, such as Maitrīpa, the hundred and eight saints like Paiṇḍapa, the fifty-four male yogins, who attained the purest state through transformation of adverse conditions, and the one thousand female mystics. Besides, there were Phamthingpa of Nepal and the great translator Marpa of Tibet. Nāropa also attained enlightenment with the rainbowlike manifestation.

The Lineage of the Meditative System in Tibet

F The preeminent Marpa the translator visited India three times. He studied for a good period of time with venerable masters like Nāropa, Maitrīpa, and others who had attained realization. Having practiced the most profound instructions, he cleared away doubts and assumptions. The venerable Marpa was the most outstanding among all the bilingual scholars and was widely known to be a realized master. Of all the Tibetan translators educated in India, Marpa was known to have excelled in the vital instructions that were vast and profound. He had many realized disciples such as the three—Mey, Ngok, and Ram, as well as Tsurtön, Golek, and others, and especially Mila Shepe Dorje of Kungthang.

Milarepa pleased the preeminent Marpa by willingly undergoing innumerable physical ordeals. As a result he was given the general teachings and the quintessential instructions on mahāmudrā, as well as the special secret oral instructions. He raised the victorious banner of meditation through so much hardship and asceticism that upon hearing about them one becomes awe-struck and deeply moved. As a result, Milarepa became the
8 B most renowned mystic of Tibet. Among the numerous awakened disciples were the four great cotton-clad *repas*,[43] the eight minor ones, and the six masters.

The teachers of this meditational lineage up to Milarepa meditated mainly on the key instructions of the Mantrayāna mysticism while at various times incorporating vital instructions on mahāmudrā from the discourses on the yogas of inner heat and lucid awareness.[44] Yet, the great master Gampopa, having been moved by immeasurable compassion, expounded mainly on the quintessential instructions on mahāmudrā. As a result it became widely known as the single path for all predestined seekers. In connection with this there appeared to be a special causal link established in the past, which may be briefly mentioned.

09 F The venerable Gampopa was formerly known as the bodhisattva Da-ö Zhonnu (Candraprabha) amongst the disciples of Buddha, the Supreme Sage and Illuminated Conqueror. Once, when expounding the *Samādhirāja-sūtra*, the Supreme Master asked the assembled audience of bodhisattvas, "Who among you wish to be the one to propagate this sūtra and make it widely known in the future when the dharma will be declining?" Thereupon Candraprabha stood up and pledged to do so. The Supreme Master, having placed his right hand on his head, called upon the great disciples such as Ajita [Maitreya] and the celestial beings of the universe and prophesied, "When in the future the dharma will be declining, Candraprabha will always maintain the principle of chastity, make this sacred meditative absorption widely known, and open up the dharma treasure of the Sugata [supremely attained Buddha]. He will instruct no less than five hundred

disciples. He will attain enlightenment and become known as the victorious buddha Drimay Ö (Vimalaprabha). The Buddha then blessed bodhisattva
109 B Candraprabha so that he would not be overcome by obstacles. At that point the eight hundred teachers of the dharma also stood up and pledged to preserve the meaning of the same sūtra. Then devas, nāgas, and kuberas,[45] eight hundred million in number pledged to protect these holy sages. This was stated in the *Samādhirāja-sūtra*.

Again, the Supreme Master, in giving solace to Ānanda prophesied in the *Mahākaruṇāpuṇḍarīka-sūtra* that after his passing into nirvāṇa a monk by the name of Tshoje (Jīvaka) would appear in the region of the North and that he would spread Buddha's teachings widely. Buddha, having praised him well, prophesied that this monk, immediately upon his death, would attain enlightenment and become the tathāgata Vimalaprabha in the buddha realm known as Guṇālaṃkāra, within the Blissful Pure Land [Sukhāvatī] of Buddha Amitābha. It was further prophesied that in the snowy land, north of Bodhgayā, close to the river Lohita [the river Brahmaputra in part of its
110 F course through East Assam] running along the rocky and forested mountains, a monk-physician and dharma master by the name of Jīvaka [Tshoje], along with an assembly of disciples numbering no fewer than five hundred, would partake of the enlightened awareness of the Tathāgata. Although there exist more of such prophecies, they are not mentioned here for fear of overstatement. Those who desire extensive references may read the relevant sūtras.

Thus, in accordance with the prophecies, the revered master Gampopa and assembled disciples numbering no fewer than five hundred, having appeared amidst the rocky, forested mountains of glorious Takla Gampo, north of Bodhgayā, practiced the quintessential instructions of mahāmudrā and then made them known far and wide among disciples. Similarly, in keeping with their pledges the eight hundred dharma master bodhisattvas were reborn in Tibet and became either the personal disciples of Gampopa
110 B or the disciples of his disciples. Many of them were great awakened masters who not only absorbed the teachings but also preserved and spread them widely. The snowy land of Tibet resounded with such a great echo of their fame that it could have easily shaken the whole world. The glorious Kagyüpa order of Takpo became widely known in other countries such as India, Nepal, China, and Mongolia. As everybody can clearly see, even in this day and age of rapid degeneration, there are still human beings who completely renounce attachment to a materialistic life and surpass others in raising the victorious banner of meditation while wandering through terrifying cemeteries, passing amidst mountain hideaways, and living in lonely caves and deserted regions.

With this I complete the elucidation on enhancing one's faith.

CHAPTER TWO

Preparatory Practices

PREPARATION

These practices are discussed in two sections:

1 F 1. The systematic path of general teachings
2. The description of the preparatory exercises for this meditative path

The Systematic Path of General Teachings

A practical system of the sacred dharma is enumerated for persons who, having been agonized by the miseries of existence [saṃsāra] and having sought liberation, embraced the precious teachings of Buddha. At the outset devotees should look for a fully qualified spiritual guide, since he or she is the basic support of the path. After critically assessing the teacher, they should associate themselves with him and practice the requisite precepts of morality that brings forth blossoms of good qualities. They should thoroughly study the collected words of the victorious Buddha and, in particular, devote themselves to dharma as the integrated path for the three seekers,[46] which is the path that evokes an inward response toward the sacred teaching and protects one from any degradation. It is not sufficient to grasp only once the meaning of what one has heard. They should contemplate it again and again in order to arouse a strong dislike for attachment to
111 B this life and thereby engender an extraordinary yearning for attaining permanent peace in a future life. Examining the conduct of those who profess to be devotees of the dharma with that kind of attitude, one will understand that for some of them the dharma is a casual practice, for others a means of livelihood, a subject for lectures, or a form of hypocrisy. The understanding that such practices not only will not be beneficial for future lives, but will also be harmful, will produce a sense of joy in directing oneself toward meditation and realization in the right manner.

Nāgārjuna comments:

Wisdom will expand
If one listens to and contemplates [the dharma]
And devotes oneself to meditation;
One will attain the supreme realization!

The *Abhidharmakośa* emphasizes:

He who maintains moral discipline
And has listened to and examined [the dharma]
Should embark upon the meditational process.

The *Bhāvanākrama* explains:

112 F At the outset one should seek to develop wisdom by listening [to the dharma], for it enables one to grasp the meaning of the authoritative scriptures. Then, with analytical intellect one differentiates between the apparent and the ultimate meaning. With an understanding of the meaning so differentiated, one should meditate on the reality of the pure state and not on its apparent aspect. If one meditates wrongly and fails to clear away all doubts, one will not achieve perfect awareness. As a result, the meditation becomes fruitless, like the meditation of the radical dogmatists [tīrthika].

This being the case, those who are less capable of embracing the deep meaning at the outset may best be guided gradually through the "integrated path of the three persons" just as if they were climbing steps. The *Caryāsaṃgraha* explains:

To enable all new devotees to search for the sacred truth,
The fully enlightened Buddha expounded the methods
In stages, like the rungs of a ladder.

The *Hevajra-tantra* summarizes:

Those sentient beings—beset by less favorable conditions—
Are difficult to train spiritually.
By what means may they be trained?
112 B The Illuminated Conqueror answered:
"First give them the method for self-purification,
Then the ten moral precepts.
Impart the doctrines of the Vaibhāṣika,
Sautrāntika, and Yogācāra;
Following that you should teach them the Madhyamaka doctrine.
After they have learned the tantric system,
You should reveal the teaching of Hevajra.

When the disciples apply this with a deep veneration,
Realization will dawn upon them without any doubt."

Thus it is indicated that the teachings are to be imparted stage by stage—first the graded path of the exoteric vehicle and then the classes of tantra.

The Description of the Preparatory Exercises for This Meditative Path

There are two kinds of persons seeking out the deepest meaning of the path. It is imperative to clearly know the necessity for imparting the profound path instantly to those predestined learned seekers and gradually to beginners. The *Kapey Sarnying* (earlier and later *Āhapramāṇasamyak*) enunciates:

According to the distinct levels of intellect,
There are persons inclined toward either the gradual or the instantaneous path.
A great medicine for gradual seekers
Becomes a poison for instantaneous seekers.
A great medicine for instantaneous illumination
Becomes a poison for gradual illumination.
3 F Persons with inborn creative abilities should be shown
The instantaneous path,
While young minds should be guided through
The gradual path.

Regarding the manner of imparting the profound path [of mahāmudrā], the venerable Gampopa considered it to be an independent path of tantra. So he did not make the esoteric empowerment a prerequisite for receiving the mahāmudrā teachings. He spoke about the method of directly guiding the disciple toward the intrinsic reality of the mind. This [simple] method consists of seeking refuge in the guru and the three jewels, offering to them the symbolic cosmos [maṇḍala], accounting for all one's harmful deeds, and invoking them with intense faith and veneration. This practice includes meditation on love, compassion, and an enlightened attitude [bodhicitta]. In this respect, the prodigious intellects inclined toward the instantaneous path should be engaged at the outset in the process of discovering the vision of inherent reality, and then in settling the mind in tranquil absorption, similar to the contemporary training of the mahāmudrā of four syllables. The
113 B inferior intellect, inclined toward the gradual path, should be put through the practice of tranquility leading to the meditation of insight. This is similar to the contemporary training through what is known as "harmonizing with the coemergent awareness."[47] One understands that the reason for these

[two ways] is to be found in his [the venerable Gampopa's] written commentaries, the oral testament, the answers, and his oral testament recorded by Pal Phagmo Drupa[48] and Je Düsum Khyenpa[49] in their respective collected works.

Lately the followers of this meditative order adapted mahāmudrā to the practice of tantric mysticism. Known as "mahāmudrā in five sections,"[50] it comprises among others development of an enlightened attitude, elevating the mind to the purest state through meditation on a meditative deity [yidam], on the guru, and as well as on mahāmudrā, while concluding with the dedication of merits for the liberation of others. Before explaining other mahāmudrā treatises like the *Lhenchik Kyejor* and the *Yige Shipa*, the four preparatory exercises are prescribed at the start, as a means of actualizing the meditation. These exercises are concerned with the meditation on impermanence, the visualization of Vajrasattva followed by repetition of the mantra, making an offering of the cosmos [maṇḍala], and harmonizing the mind with the perfect awareness of the guru. Since these mahāmudrā meditations incorporated tantric elements, practitioners are required at the
114 F outset to receive an elaborate or abridged initiation as a means of activating their inner potentiality. The *Mahāmudrātilaka* comments:

> Without an initiatory empowerment one cannot achieve self-realization,
> For it would be like crushing sand to extract butter.

The *Buddhakapāla* states:

> Just as one cannot play a harp without the strings,
> Even though all the other components are assembled,
> So one cannot realize the mystic mantra and meditative absorption
> Without the empowerment.

On the other hand, if one follows venerable Gampopa's system in elucidating mahāmudrā alone, it is not necessary to bestow the empowerment upon devotees. In keeping with his system one should adhere to the preparatory exercises he prescribed without incorporating the tantric meditation of Vajrasattva, the utterance of mantra, the transformation of oneself into yidam, and the visualization of one's guru in the form of Buddha Vajradhara, the source of the mystic empowerment.

In this respect one might ask if the exercise of counting the breath rhythm and retaining it, which is incorporated in tranquil meditation, originated from tantric mysticism. The answer is no. Because the counting of and focusing on the breath rhythm and many such exercises are prescribed even for attaining meditative tranquility, according to the exoteric sūtra.

114 B In the present age, mahāmudrā and mantrayāna [tantric mysticism] are being blended and meditated upon in order to enhance realization. Many

tantric elements are also incorporated into the preparatory practices. For those who wish to do so, the empowerment for actualizing the inner potentiality is certainly essential. One should receive either an elaborate or short empowerment, based on a genuine tantra, associated with a realization deity such as Cakrasaṃvara with his consort. Such a tradition must be sustained by the living masters of a spiritual lineage, for they are the source of blessing.

THE RELEVANT PREPARATORY PRACTICES: THE ELUCIDATION OF THE UNCOMMON PREPARATIONS

There are five different practices:

1. Contemplation on impermanence and the like for overcoming laziness
2. Taking refuge in the three jewels and engendering an enlightened attitude for clearing impediments in the practice
3. Making an offering of the cosmos [maṇḍala] for enhancing personal virtue
4. Meditation and mantra recitation for purging inner defilements
5. Contemplative harmonization with the perfect state of the guru for drawing in spiritual blessing

Contemplation on Impermanence and the Like for Overcoming Laziness

It is always important for a practitioner to produce an intense yearning for liberation, since it is the root of dharma practice. This is possible through serious contemplation on the rarity of attaining a human body endowed with good qualities and conditions, on how through this existence great aims may
115 F be realized, on how the body succumbs to aging rapidly, on how the force of karma controls one's destiny even after death, on how white [good] and black [bad] karma works, on what the distinction between light and heavy karma is, on how inexhaustible karma produces an effect, and on how one experiences the results from the three kinds of karma. The contemplation is further focused on the sufferings of sentient beings in the six existential spheres and the maladies of all apparent pleasures of life. Aversion for cyclic existence is known as the basis[51] for meditation or the master of meditation. If one is content with merely comprehending these principles once, or even if one initially experiences a meditation, one will not only fail to overcome delusion, lust, and hatred, but will succumb to the force of materialistic ambition for wealth, pleasure, and fame. Herein lies the reason why so few seekers achieve realization.

As Tilopa urges yogins:

O look at the reality of the material world.
It is transient, like a dream or illusion.
Dream and illusion are devoid of existence!
Produce a sense of aversion,
Abandon the pursuit of the transient world,
Cut the tie with companions and habitation,
Which cause attachment and hatred to arise.
115 B Meditate amidst forests or mountain solitudes.

Taking Refuge in the Three Jewels and Engendering an Enlightened Attitude for Clearing Impediments in the Practice

It is very important for those who strive toward liberation—out of horror for the miseries of saṃsāra—to place themselves under the protection of the three jewels and to go to them for refuge, for this constitutes the foundation of Buddhist practice. A sūtra states:

When one goes for refuge to the Buddha,
The dharma, and the saṅgha[52]
And the four noble truths—
The truth of suffering in saṃsāra,
The truth of the cause of suffering,
The truth of attaining freedom from suffering,
And the truth of the noble eightfold path of the awakened—
One will realize peace in nirvāṇa.
In perceiving through wisdom
The four noble truths of the awakened
Lies the refuge that is principal and supreme;
By trusting it one will achieve
Liberation from all suffering.

Regarding the benefit for going to the three jewels for refuge, the *Prajñāpāramitā-saṃcayagāthā* states:

If the spiritual merits from taking refuge [in the three jewels]
Were material substances,
Then the three planes [of the universe]
Would be too small a container.
The great ocean is the treasure of water;
116 F It cannot be measured in ounces.

The benefits are inconceivably great, particularly in terms of the eight benefits, namely: (1) the taking of refuge brings one into the community of the dharma, (2) it constitutes the basis for receiving all levels of precepts, (3) it enables one to wear out past karma and the mind's defilements, (4) it helps one to accumulate spiritual merits, (5) it prevents one from falling into the lower realms, (6) it shields one against harm from human and nonhuman beings, (7) it helps one to fulfill spiritual aspirations, and (8) it enables one to achieve enlightenment rapidly.

Besides, it is said that further benefits may be realized by taking refuge according to the Mahāyāna tradition. Devotees will be saved from deviating into practices that are devoid of skillful means[53] and those contained in the Primary Vehicle [Hīnayāna].[54] One should therefore take refuge with a definite and thorough understanding of the objective, the periods of time to be employed, the motivation, the form, etc. Nowadays some consider the stage of taking refuge to be meant only for beginners. Ignoring it as being unimportant for a later stage, they fail to apply the precepts of refuge. Such an unwise action does not bring them into the rank of Buddha's disciples.

Engendering an enlightened attitude [bodhicitta] provides an entrance for all those who wish to follow the Great Vehicle. As such it is the foundation of the path to enlightenment. Nāgārjuna describes:

If oneself and other worldly beings
Wish to attain supreme enlightenment,
They should establish its foundation—bodhicitta—
As solid as that of Mount Sumeru,
King of all mountains.

The *Gaṇḍavyūha-sūtra* states:

> O noble son, bodhicitta is like
> The seed of all the teachings of the Buddha.

Such bodhicitta is to be brought forth through the development of love and compassion. Love and compassion will arise from the consideration that all sentient beings have once been our "mothers" and "fathers" from time immemorial and that one fervently wishes to repay them. One meditates on this [cosmic interrelatedness] with a deep understanding. The spiritual benefit from meditating on love, compassion, and an enlightened attitude is described in the *Rinchen Trengwa* (*Ratnāvalī*).

> The spiritual merit earned by a merchant
> 7 F From feeding three hundred people three times a day
> Cannot equal even partially the merit earned
> By one who engenders love even for a moment.
> He who does so will receive love and protection
> From human and celestial beings.
> He will enjoy inner peace and well-being

And will remain free from being poisoned and injured by weapons.
His aspirations will be fulfilled without his having to strive.
He will attain the highest level of the cosmos [Brahmaloka].[55]
Even if he has not achieved liberation,
He will realize the eight attributes of love.

The life story of bodhisattva Avalokiteśvara contains this passage:

The application of one virtue will attract
All other virtues of enlightenment,
Just like having them all in your palm.
What is this one [virtue]?
It is great compassion.

Candrakīrti describes:

For producing a perfect crop of victorious enlightenment
Compassion is like the seed
And is like the water that germinates, grows, and ripens it into crops.
May this be enjoyed for a long time.
With such a consideration I begin with a praise to compassion.

The *Vīradatta-gṛhapatiparipṛcchā-sūtra* declares:

If the spiritual merit from an enlightened attitude
117 B Were material substances
And were to fill the cosmic space,
The magnitude [of the merit] would be vastly greater.

The same text continues:

If one submits oneself to bodhicitta
With hands in reverential posture,
One is making an offering beyond limitations,
For it is far superior
To making offerings of precious gems to all
Those passed into tranquility [buddhas],
That fill in as many buddhafields as sands
In the Gangetic plain [northern India].

Numerous other sayings exist [concerning the benefits to be obtained from an enlightened attitude]. In addition, the following are benefits obtained from a yearning for bodhicitta. It brings one to the level of the Great Vehicle, which constitutes the basis for all bodhicitta precepts. It eliminates all harmful deeds and brings the accumulation of spiritual merits through which one pleases all buddhas. It enables one to bring spiritual benefits to sentient beings. One achieves enlightenment rapidly.

Further, the application of bodhicitta enables one to continuously fulfill one's aspirations and the diverse needs of others. Many other benefits are mentioned. One therefore meditates persistently with the definite knowledge of the object such as love, compassion, an enlightened attitude, and their intrinsic nature. It has been stated that without an enlightened attitude, any application of the fundamental virtues, in general, and meditation on the void, in particular, are neither in accord with the Mahāyanā path nor do they form a basis for supreme enlightenment.

Making an Offering of the Cosmos [Maṇḍala] for Enhancing Personal Virtue

Generally, one cannot achieve temporary or permanent happiness without accumulating moral virtues [spiritual merits]. Particularly, [in attempting to realize the ultimate goal] one has to enhance the real virtue arising from transcending awareness. Yet, one cannot realize the vision of the void without the spiritual merits. Therefore it is important to work first on them. A sūtra states:

> One achieves peace through spiritual merits.
> So human beings should accumulate spiritual merits;
> They should do so very frequently
> And do it resolutely this very day.

18 B The *Prajñāpāramitā-saṃcayagāthā* emphasizes:

> As long as the root of virtues is not completely perfected,
> One cannot realize the ultimate void.

Regarding the accumulation of spiritual merits or the purposes, the *Acintyaguhya-sūtra* says:

> Through real virtues arising from awareness one completely purges all mental defilements. Through spiritual merits arising from moral virtues, all sentient beings will maintain their well-being. O Illuminated Conqueror, this being so, a bodhisattva, a great bodhisattva should strive toward accumulating the moral and real virtues of awareness.

The *Ratnāvalī* states:

> In summary, the rūpakāya[56] arises from the accumulated sovereign moral virtue.
> The dharmakāya arises from the accumulated sovereign virtue of awareness.

In short, the two levels of spiritual merits represent all spiritual benefits to be derived from the practice of the six principles of the wisdom-gone-beyond.

Concerning the method of accumulating moral virtues one generally practices the ten virtues of the dharma[57] and the four ways of winning
119 F [devotees].[58] In this respect it has been stated that the accumulation of merits may be achieved through the sevenfold devotion, making the maṇḍala the principal offering. In offering a maṇḍala, followers of this meditative order should visualize before them any forms of refuge to be the source of spiritual merits. Regarding the offering of the maṇḍala, it is said that the whole universe [maṇḍala] is offered to the precious refuge through the visualization or mental creation [of the myriad cosmos]. This one should do with an imagination of owning and giving it away without any expectation.

One further enhances the moral virtues through the practice of the sevenfold devotion. Out of these seven performances, prostration, worship, petition, and invocation are the means to gain moral virtues. The admission of moral offenses enables one to purge mental defilements, delighting [in the good deeds of others] increases virtues, and the sharing of one's spiritual merits with others not only prevents these merits that originate from accumulation, purification, and perfection from diminishing but even expands them. It is stated that through these practices one gains immeasurable spiritual merits. One should endeavor to make a special effort.

Meditation and Mantra Recitation for Purging Inner Defilements

119 B While seeking understanding of the path of liberation and of all-knowing buddhahood and their realization, devotees are confronted with powerful inherent defilements that originate from the effects of harmful karma one committed throughout previous lives from time immemorial. Unless they purify these mental defilements, they will continue to wander aimlessly, experiencing miseries throughout limitless cyclic existences like an ever rotating water wheel. Illustrating this, the *Tsom* (*Udānavarga*) comments:

> Even by committing a minor negative karma,
> The consequence in the next life will be great fear—
> Like that of just having swallowed poison—
> Misfortune and misery.

Again, the same text states:

> Whoever has committed harmful deeds through wild passion
> In order to achieve personal happiness,
> He will—crying helplessly—suffer the consequences.

As for the methods for purging evil karma, the four principles are mentioned in the *Caturdharmanirdeśa-sūtra*:

> Buddha: O Maitreya, a bodhisattva, a great bodhisattva, who possesses the four dharmas will overpower all accumulated evil karma. What are the four [dharmas]? They are (1) the power of regular practice for complete elimination [of evil karma], (2) the power of regular application of antidotes [against it], (3) the power of abstention from harmful deeds, and (4) the power of refuge.

It has been explained that the first power lies in remorsefully admitting
past harmful actions [committed]; the second in memorizing or reading the
sūtras, joyously contemplating the void, reciting [the sacred mantra], painting or sculpturing images and stūpas, worshiping and invoking the buddhas
and bodhisattvas; the third power in [the virtue of] abstaining from the ten
evil deeds; and the fourth power in taking refuge in the three jewels and the
engendering of an enlightened attitude. In this practice, the remorseful
)B admission of evil karma is through meditation and mantra recitation. However, a sincere repentance and firm resolution for self-control represent the
application of all four powers. Regarding the purification of harmful deeds
through mantra recitation, the *Subāhuparipṛcchā-sūtra* explains:

> Just as a wild forest fire in the summer
> Effortlessly consumes all trees and plants,
> So is evil karma consumed by the fire of mantra recitation,
> Fanned by the wind of morality
> And burnt by the power of exertion.
> Just as snow is melted by sunlight,
> So is the snow of evil karma dissolved
> By the heat of morality and mantra recitation.
> Just as a small butter lamp brightens the darkness,
> So does the lamp of mantra recitation illuminate the karmic darkness
> Accumulated during thousands of past lives.

One should often reproach oneself for evil deeds, because it is harmful to
accumulate them from moment to moment through transgression of the
precepts originating from any one of the four causes, viz. ignorance, com-
121 F plex emotionality, voluptuousness, and lack of devotion. The *Udānavarga*
urges:

> Do not ignore harmful deeds however negligible,
> Thinking that they will bring no harm.
> Even by collecting mere drops of water
> One can gradually fill up a big pot.

The *Lekdrup* (Susiddhi) says:

In nightly meditation one should reproach oneself
For each uncontrolled deed of the day;
Each day one should reproach oneself for any evil deed committed at night.
Having done so properly one should rejoice.

Concerning the meditation of Vajrasattva and the recitation of the "one hundred syllables," the *Dorje Nyingpo Gyan* (*Vajrahṛdayālaṃkāra*) advocates:

Visualize properly Vajrasattva seated on [the disc of] the moon and a white lotus;
Recite the hundred syllables
Twenty-one times according to the ritual.
He [Vajrasattva] will terminate the moral transgression,
As enunciated by the realized masters.
Practice the mantra in between meditations
By reciting it a hundred thousand times.
You will attain the perfect state.

Contemplative Harmonization with the Perfect State of the Guru for Drawing in Spiritual Blessing

121 B The sūtras and the tantras generally state that the guidance of a guru constitutes the root of the path through which one seeks liberation. Besides, they describe what his characteristics should be, how he should be approached, and also the purpose or spiritual benefits to be derived from this. The treatises of Mantrayāna particularly comment that an esoteric master is the source of realization, while speaking extensively about how one should take utmost care in associating with him.

More particularly, this meditational order, which is regarded as possessing the power of transmission of spiritual blessing, advocates two ways of (1) gaining a new experience in meditation and (2) of perfecting it. Both are depending upon the blessing of the guru. Hence, a meditator should try his utmost to actualize the purest state of a guru through intensive meditation. If one asks the reason for this, it is given in the *Mañjuśrīnāma-saṃgīti*:

He is the object of worship, praise, and prostration.
He is worthy of constant service.
He is the excellent one, worthy of reverence.
He is the supreme guru worthy of homage.

Another comment about a guru says:

His body unifies all the buddhas;
He is the true essence of Vajradhara.
He is the root of the three jewels.
He is the guru; I prostrate before him.

F The purpose of [guru yoga] is to gain temporary as well as ultimate realization, as explained in the words of Bhavilha:[59]

The reason, says Vajradhara, is that
Realization is dependent upon an esoteric master.

Again it is said:

One should bow before the lotus feet of the guru
For he is the source of attaining to the level of glorious Vajrasattva.

Concerning the way of meditating on the guru, the *Vajrahṛdayālaṃkāra* teaches:

A disciple who reveres the guru
Should look upon him in this manner:
The guru is the equal of all buddhas,
He is Vajradhara for all times.

The *Vajrapañjara* states:

He who is known as Vajrasattva
Has assumed the body of an esoteric master.
Considering the well-being of all sentient beings,
He [Vajrasattva] manifested himself in an ordinary body.

Bhavilha also says:

Do not look upon your guru and Vajradhara
As two separate entities.

The *Vajraḍākinī* describes the way of meditating upon the guru as the master who has unified in himself all the buddhas:

His body, by nature, represents all the buddhas;
22 B His limbs represent the bodhisattvas;
The hair in his pores represents the arhats;
His crown represents the five classes of buddhas;
His seat represents the beings of the transient world;
The rays represent gods of wealth such as Nöjin Sang and others.
Yogins should always look upon his body
As representing all these attributes.

A similar statement is made in the root text of the *Dorje Danzhi* (*Catuḥpīṭha*) and its commentary. Deducing from this, one should learn more. The purpose of guru meditation according to master Śāntipa is "to inculcate in oneself an equal faith in Vajradhara and one's guru, to stabilize one's inmost awareness of Vajradhara, and to fully and rapidly realize him through the accumulation of spiritual merits with the least striving. The *Pañcakrama* spells out the benefits to be derived from making special offerings to one's guru in this way:

> Abandoning all other forms of offerings,
> One should make a perfect offering to one's guru.
> By so pleasing him one will realize supreme awareness.

The *Guhyasamāja* states:

> To worship only one hair of the body of one's guru
> Brings one more merit
> Than worshipping all the buddhas in the three periods of time.

123 F The *Sampuṭa* proposes:

> One offers to one's guru
> Every beautiful object without any expectation.

The *Vajrahṛdayālaṃkāra* states:

> With every effort,
> Worship your guru who represents the Buddha Vajradhara.
> By pleasing him after his heart
> One indeed pleases all the buddhas.

Bhavilha says:

> He who wishes to realize the inexhaustible thatness
> Should offer to the guru the gift of a special kind—
> One that delights his heart.
> By doing so he will be worshiping
> All the buddhas for all times.
> Such worship produces spiritual merits
> Which, in turn, lead to supreme realization.

Concerning the reason why such worship of the guru should be done with strong faith and veneration, the *Daśadharmaka-sūtra* elucidates:

> To have faith in the spiritual guide
> Who extricates one from inner bondage
> Is in accord with the supreme vehicle.
> For this reason a wise person
> Approaches him through faith.
> No positive quality will ever grow

In a person without faith,
For no green sprout will spring from burnt seeds.

The *Ratnolkā-dhāraṇī* gives this precise comment:

Faith precedes [every practice] or brings forth like a mother,
It protects all good qualities and develops them,
It removes doubts and transports one across the river [of saṃsāra];
Faith symbolizes the city of peace and perfection,
It crystallizes the mind without causing confusion.
Being the root of veneration it removes conceit.
Faith is like wealth, like a treasure, like excellent feet;
It is like the hand that gathers and is the root of everything.

By remembering the spiritual benefits the guru brought, one engenders such faith and yearning that one is moved to tears. The *Gaṇḍavyūha-sūtra* describes the role of spiritual guides:

> Buddha: "Zhonnu Norzang (Kumāra Sudhana), spiritual friends protect one from the lower realms, help to realize the evenness of all things, show the way of differentiating the path of happiness and misery, counsel in practices for consummate perfection, show the path to the city of omniscience, transport one to the realm of omniscience, take one to the ocean of all-embracing reality, expound the oceanic knowledge of the three periods of time, and initiate one into the maṇḍala of the awakened assembly. Spiritual friends help one to enhance the practice of virtue. Such a yearning for them will move one close to tears.

If one has faith and veneration one is bound to receive the spiritual blessings [of one's gurus]. With the guru's blessings realization will come about as has been indicated in the second section of the *Hevajra-tantra*:

That which is spontaneously arising [i.e., inmost awareness]
Can neither be described by any outward expressions
Nor can it be found anywhere.
Understand that it arises inwardly
By the guru's timely guidance and skillful methods
And also as a result of one's spiritual merits.

Nāgārjuna elucidates as follows:

Once one has fallen from the summit of Mount Sumeru,
One keeps falling despite one's desire to the contrary.
If one has discovered the illuminating path through the kindness of one's guru,

One is bound to achieve liberation
Even though one may desire otherwise.

124 B The supremely venerated Gampopa sums up in this manner:

> Our's is the lineage of spiritual blessings. A deep understanding of mahāmudrā is not possible without the infusion of a guru's blessing. Such an infusion of blessing can take place without any difficulty. It comes through invocation originating from one's faith and veneration. A devotee with deep faith receives a powerful blessing. One with medium faith receives a medium blessing. One with lesser faith receives the lesser blessing. It is the nature of things that one cannot receive spiritual blessing without faith. For those practitioners who have failed to gain deep understanding, there is no other way except that of worshiping the guru with faith and through meditation invoking his blessings. Even those who have gained understanding should continue to have faith in their guru as a means of strengthening and perfecting their inner development.

The manner of invoking a guru should be in accordance with the practices of this order of meditation:

A meditator invokes even as he travels,
125 F While sitting or awakening from his sleep.

The methods of guru yoga meditation were established by the masters of vital instructions. In order to conduct a meditational self-reproach in case one [a devotee] has, along the way, weakened one's sacred commitment, one should begin the meditation by visualizing the guru as a helmsman standing either up in front of oneself or sitting [in the lotus position] on the crown of one's head. In this [exoteric meditation] it will not be right for the devotee, functioning on a normal, human level, to visualize receiving empowerment [from the guru]. [First] he should meditationally transform himself into a realizational deity[60] and then visualize upon his crown the guru in the form of Buddha Vajradhara who unifies in himself all the buddhas. He then performs the devotion in worshiping the guru with outer, inner, and inmost offerings[61] and invoking him with intense faith. In the meditation he visualizes himself receiving the mystical empowerment. Finally [the radiant guru] is dissolved into himself. [He remains in a state of awareness.] This method is excellent because it seems to represent many vital aspects of the path for activating inherent potentiality and achieving liberation.

Concerning the centers of the meditator's body wherein the guru is to be visualized, the *Abhidhāna* states:

125 B By visualizing the gracious guru
At the center of one's heart or on the crown

Or in the palm of one's hands,
The meditator will realize
The attributes of the thousand buddhas.

The supremely venerated Gampopa said that one should visualize the guru in the space up and in front of oneself. The venerable Yangönpa[62] said:

When worshiping [the guru] with offerings and a ritual feast,
One visualizes [him] in the space up and in front of oneself.
When invoking [him], one visualizes him upon the crown of one's head;
One always visualizes the guru at the center of the heart.

Now I will refer to the signs of one's having persistently meditated on the doctrine and practice at the preparatory stage. The result of meditation on impermanence should be such that one has turned away, both in thought and deed, from the materialistic pursuit of this life and from attachment to sensory pleasure. As one becomes convinced of the futility of such ambitions one is bound to perceive the transient reality of life, pacifying the eight worldly emotions[63] while achieving a tranquil mind. As a result of the refuge meditation, the meditator achieves inner peace, joy, amiability, and equanimity. The offering of the maṇḍala results in gaining a radiant look and
F a sense of well-being, so that one will not feel hunger even when one abstains from eating. Besides, one will experience lucidity of mind and an increase in intelligence. As for other inner experiences, the meditator will dream of a rising sun or moon, flowers, or climbing heights. Meditation on Vajrasattva and the mantra recitation will result in the meditator's achieving a lightness of body, lessening of dependence on sleep, a feeling of well-being, and joy of heart. The meditator may dream [as a sign of purification] of pus and blood flowing out from the body, vomiting, or emptying of the bowels, etc. Meditation of guru yoga will produce in one such admiration and yearning for the guru that one may feel like touching his body or invoking him day and night. One will also experience dissolving of concrete perceptions and an all-pervasive inner illumination. One will dream [as a good sign] of meeting the guru, of him giving a discourse, or an empowerment. The meaning of dreams is given in the works of the masters of this meditative order.

Those who consider these preparatory practices to be simply a means of establishing beginners in meditation but to be insignificant at a later stage only show their great ignorance with respect to the vital factors of dharma, because these practices constitute the central pillar of the Mahāyāna path.
26 B These practices are very important as the root of the dharma and the pillar of the path. I could not provide a detailed elucidation, but only a partial description, for fear of increasing the volume of my writing. However, it is very essential for devotees to study hard by listening to and examining the

vast teachings integrated into the stages to enlightenment and then to determine the meanings in all their subtlety.

THE PRACTICE PRECEDING THE MEDITATIONAL STAGES

There are two sections:

1. To begin with, one must understand the definitive precepts
2. How to maintain sessions for meditation

To Begin with, One Must Understand the Definitive Precepts

One endeavors to cultivate what the *Abhidharmasamuccaya* refers to as the five principles conducive to liberation. [The first principle], morality for individual devotees, consists of feeling aversion to and turning physically and mentally away from violence against others, and of strengthening a nonviolent attitude. The *Bodhicaryāvatāra* implores:

> Wherever there are fish and the like in need of protection,
> Transport them safely without causing death.
> By developing a nonviolent attitude
> One will reach the yonder shore of morality.

127 F Devotees should mindfully and vigilantly abide by the precepts received through the ordinations for [lay devotee] and others,[64] while abandoning all inexcusable offences through self-control. As the *Suhṛllekha* describes:

> Just as the earth supports all things dynamic and static,
> So is morality the foundation of all virtues.

The *Śīlasaṃyukta-sūtra* concludes:

> Just as a blind person does not see any forms,
> So an immoral person does not see the dharma.

[The second principle] concerns the control of sensory impulses. The six sense faculties are stimulated through the interaction between the six objects and the six sense organs, and are then altered by the faculty of intellect causing either attachment or aversion to any sense object. By not clinging to the cognitive image or the mark of perception one should not only guard against greed and hatred but also settle the mind either in a virtuous or a
127 B neutral state. A quotation from a sūtra reiterates the above passage:

> Even though the eyes see forms, they do not grasp them, either as cognitive images or perceptive reality.

[The third principle], to apply vigilance, means that whenever one engages oneself in any action—physical or otherwise—one should act scrupulously and with vigilance, consciously discriminating what is positive or negative, what is to be accepted or rejected. This is indicated in this passage from the *Bodhicaryāvatāra*:

> One observes again and again
> The state of one's body or mind;
> Every such observation means
> Watching with utmost vigilance.

The *Prajñāpāramitā-saṃcayagāthā* comments in a similar fashion:

> One should maintain vigilance through all such movements,
> Walking, resting, and sitting.

A sūtra says:

> Be conscious of every action you engage in:
> Now being aware of the act of standing,
> Now attentive to being seated.

The *Ratnakūṭa-sūtra* describes the purpose of vigilance:

> If one continuously applies awareness and vigilance,
> One cannot be affected by any distorted thoughts.

128 F [The fourth principle] concerns the regulation of daily food. Meager food makes one hungry and weak. An excessive quantity causes heaviness in the body and increases lethargy and drowsiness. Eating food that is hard to digest or unsuitable worsens an already existing sickness, causes new diseases, and makes the body intractable for the practice of virtues. Food obtained through greed or violence—being food contaminated by an evil mind—will cause one to resort to unspeakable offences and will make the mind uncontrollable. Meditators should instead eat food in moderate quantity, but not the kind just mentioned.

Glorious Nāgārjuna in the *Suhṛllekha* states:

> By looking upon food as medicine
> One eats, unstirred by greed or hatred,
> Neither for satisfying hunger,
> Nor for gratifying sensuality,
> Nor even for a radiant appearance,
> But simply in order to sustain the body.

Whether or not one regulates food depends on the attitude toward the consequences of one's craving for food. One therefore contemplates thus, "Overeating will immediately produce a loathsome feeling, like seeing dis-

128 B tasteful vomit, and may even cause sickness while increasing impure waste that must be eliminated. Besides, on account of searching for food and provisions one [often a poor meditator] suffers such hardship. Food causes lust, hatred, and confusion leading to harmful deeds so that one eventually degenerates to the lower realms." On the subject of moderation in eating food, the awakened master Vasubandhu said that when one eats moderately, one will do well to engender a benevolent attitude toward one's benefactor. One should also maintain a compassionate thought of serving sentient beings and of nurturing microscopic organisms in the body.

[The fifth principle] concerns how one should strive to devote oneself to meditation at dawn and dusk. A devotee should strive to meditate with mindfulness and vigilance not only during the greater part of the day, but also during two-thirds of the night, i.e., at dawn and at dusk. The *Dho Dhupa* (*Prajñāpāramitā-saṃcayagāthā* refers to the striving for meditation:

> Striving does not cause virtues to decline;
> It enables one to discover the treasure of the victorious Buddha,
> The limitless awareness.

The *Suhṛllekha* comments in the same way:

> O master of wisdom, meditate on mantras
> During most of the day, at dawn and dusk.
> Not wasting the nightly rest
> You should contemplate until sleep.

129 F If one wonders whether the [preceding] sayings imply a certain manner of nightly retirement, they are meant to show the four aspects of it. (1) Concerning the body posture, one lies in the relaxed manner of a lion, on the right side with the left leg resting on the right one, during the middle of those three quarters of the night. It was stated that this posture, by nature, will neither produce physical inertness nor deep sleep, yet it helps one to maintain awareness even while sleeping and prevents one from getting disturbing dreams and from committing any harmful deeds. (2) The "awareness" retains the conscious image of daytime contemplation until one falls asleep. This will elevate the meditator to a virtuous state even during sleep. (3) Vigilance enables the mind to instantaneously detect any impure thoughts so as to eliminate them. This will shield one against [discomfort in] sleep and delusion in dreams. (4) In desiring to wake up the meditator should resolve to arise in time next morning and to practice meditation. He goes to sleep for
129 B a moderate time in order to enhance his physical well-being since a proper rest nurtures the generative elements in the body. While sleeping he should visualize a disc of light on which to focus. This will prevent darkness from descending on the mind, render the sleep light, allow him to wake up in time, and make him energetic for the morning meditation.

How to Maintain Sessions for Meditation

Generally two or three sessions of meditation per day are necessary; most prefer four sessions. The latter is the tradition of this meditational order. Meditators are urged to have four sessions a day: at dawn, in the morning, in the afternoon, and at dusk. Each session consists of three parts: viz., the preliminary, the main part, and the final part. Concerning the preliminary practice, the meditator may set up an altar with sacred images, if he has any, and arrange offerings not defiled by any impure motivation. Sitting on a
F comfortable cushion he brings body and mind into a harmonious state. He should then abandon all sensual craving and discursive thoughts. Unless these outflowing thoughts are pacified, their persistence will produce an adverse effect on the main contemplation. The meditator should begin with an enlightened attitude, for it turns every aspect of the actual practice into a creative process that will bring about enlightenment.

Concerning the actual practice [of meditation], one should regularly meditate on impermanence and the other principles stated earlier. Familiarizing oneself with the system and order of the meditations, at this stage, be it a formal or abstract kind, one then meditates with mindfulness and vigilance in an orderly manner. In doing so one should resolve never to get entangled in a diverse visualization such as starting with part of one meditational system and ending with part of another system. Also, substituting
0 B the visualization one has virtually mastered with an unfamiliar one, or any other diversification, will surely harm the practice for the rest of one's life. It is therefore important, from the start, to train the mind in firmly focusing upon a [chosen] object.

If a beginner during the early period of meditation concentrates too long [in each session], he will be overcome by dullness or sensual incitement. He will form a habit [of indulging in these mental flaws], which will be difficult to change. So one should meditate for many short periods a day. A short period makes a meditation flawless. Repeating it often increases the quality, so it is said. Besides, by stopping when one experiences the clear vision of the image, one will feel less tired and will have a yearning for meditation. Long sessions can generate mental irritation and cause enthusiasm to wane. Only when one has achieved lasting concentration should one gradually increase the duration of meditation. Once one masters concentration one should be able to strengthen one's endurance so as to reach a deep absorption. On the other hand, if one makes short meditations a permanent practice, not only does the mind become habituated to it, but it will not reach the innate excellence.

131 F When one stops each meditative session, one performs a devotional ceremony for sharing with all sentient beings the spiritual merits arising from the practice. The meditator solemnly dedicates these merits to other

sentient beings for their supreme enlightenment and sincerely expresses his wish for its fulfillment. This, it was stated, will not only counteract against the impact of future negligence but will also strengthen the spiritual merits.

During the interval between sessions the meditator engages in such relevant practices as controlling sensual impulses and applying the moral precepts, like the ten actions of dharma. These include prostration and circumambulation [of holy temples] considered as means of gaining spiritual merits. There can be no real progress in this practice if the meditator allows the mind to run astray and thereby neglect an appropriate visualization through mindfulness and vigilance. Intervals are also to be devoted to the study and contemplation of the relevant teaching and to the regular application in each case of mindfulness and vigilance. It is also necessary to learn how to apply this procedure—appertaining to intervals—to every meditation, from meditation on impermanence to mahāmudrā meditation and
131 B vision. This, however, does not include certain special methods of mastering contemplation

With this I complete the discourse on the preparatory practices.

PART II: THE MAIN MEDITATION OF MAHĀMUDRĀ

This contains two sections:

1. The differentiation of mahāmudrā meditation
2. Stages of the actual meditation

THE DIFFERENTIATION OF MAHĀMUDRĀ MEDITATION

This first section shows, in general, two paths. There is the rapid path, which is designed for a person with superb intellect, well disposed to an instantaneous illumination. He has to master, at the outset, the doctrinal views of reality [through analytical insight and] through the clearing away of doubts and distortions. He then concentrates wholly on the vision of reality [established through wisdom]. Then there is the gradual path, which is for a person of an average or inferior intellect disposed toward a gradual illumination. He has to master first the meditation on inner tranquility, and then seek to gain analytical insight.

Teachers such as the glorious Saraha, Śavari, Indrabodhi, Tilopa, Maitrīpa, and others expounded the teaching designed to suit persons with
32 F superb intellect. The teachings for the average intellect are given in the treatises such as the teachings of Maitreya, the treatises on the bhūmis (*Sade*), the *Bhāvanākrama* of Kamalaśīla, and the *Prajñāpāramitopadeśa* of Śāntipa. In Tibet some of the ancient masters of the Kadampa order maintained the tradition of meditation on the quintessence of reality.[65] This meditation they received from the supremely revered Atīśa who in turn had obtained it from Ḍombipa,[66] whose lineage is traceable back to Indrabodhi. This system seems to have been transmitted down through Atīśa's disciples such as Neljorpa and Gönpawa. Much of the [Atīśa's] other teachings transmitted down through the three brothers[67] represent [the gradual path] mainly the meditational stages of the sūtra,[68] which was embodied in the *Changchup Lamrim* [The Integrated Path to Enlightenment].

Gampopa's system of elucidation embraces the aforesaid paths of gradualism and instantaneity as well as the key instructions on the perfect stage of tantra [sampannakrama]. But the principal system, being the meditational stage of mahāmudrā, consists of the methods for [achieving a pefect view of

132 B reality] by clearing doubts and distortions and then seeking a concentrated absorption. The fact that the mahāmudrā instructions, made known in Tibet by Maitrīpa's disciples such as the Indian Vajrapāṇi by way of the treatises like the *Dohā*, the *Datsa*, and the *Sangjor*, were identical with those of Gampopa's affirmed the authenticity of the mahāmudrā system. This being so, some [teachers] asserted that any meditation on the perfect meaning of reality must be based only on the classical commentaries of the sūtras. They criticized the key instructions of the great saints [of the mahāmudrā lineage], which emphasized the attainment of insight from the beginning. Such criticism would imply their disregard for the exponents of the tantric instructions, especially their sources like *Nyingpo Kordruk* and the *Truppa Dedün*. Moreover, they certainly did not understand the meaning of the following passage from the earlier and later *Āhapramāṇasamyak*:

> The great medicine for seekers of gradual illumination
> Becomes a poison for seekers for instantaneous illumination;
> The great medicine for seekers of instantaneous illumination
> Becomes a poison for seekers of gradual illumination.

The classical treatises of the sūtras hold that no tranquility can be achieved without first obtaining perfect ease of body and mind, no insight without achieving tranquility, and no realization of Thatness [tattva] [of true reality]
133 F without these two [tranquility and insight]. Those who were influenced deeply by this statement not only concluded that no one at present or in the future would achieve the meditation, but went so far as to pronounce that the present age is not meant for meditation. It was utterly wrong for them to turn their backs on meditation and to mislead others. Moreover, such an assertion would imply that the many different dharmas expounded by Buddha according to the different levels of seekers were wrong. If this were their attitude, they would be committing the karma of abandoning the key instructions of the great esoteric path, which produces great results through little striving, and many distinct paths that originated from the illuminating experience of the great saints.

The meditational system of the Takpo Kagyüpa order consists of two systems. The first system, which meets the needs of seekers inclined toward an instantaneous illumination, directs them, at the outset, to master the vision of reality by clearing doubts and distortions concerning the natural foundation of existence[69] and then settle the mind [in a nondual] state. The
133 B second system, which meets the demands of seekers of gradual illumination, directs them first to achieve tranquility of mind and then gradually strive toward insight. The former method would be more suitable for highly intelligent and passionate persons. Nevertheless, I shall elucidate the latter at this stage because it is widely known in the country.

STAGES OF THE ACTUAL MEDITATION

This is elucidated in four sections:

1. Guiding meditators on the path (Chapters 3 and 4)
2. The stages of virtuous practice (Chapter 5)
3. Consolidation of experience in meditation (Chapters 6, 7, and 8)
4. The resultant dawning of realization (Chapter 9)

Guiding Meditators on the Path

There are two ways of guiding meditators:

1. Guiding through tranquility
2. Guiding through insight

CHAPTER THREE

Guiding Meditators on the Path: Tranquility

INTRODUCTION

The meditation on tranquility is comprised of seven aspects:

1. The means of mastering tranquility
2. Physical conduct and posture
3. The method of concentrating on an object
4. The actual mental images for attaining settled quiescence
5. How to maintain the tranquil state
6. The stages of realizing the settled mind
7. The purpose of realizing tranquility

THE MEANS OF MASTERING TRANQUILITY

One should know at the outset about the requisite conditions for meditation on tranquility, particularly the method of detecting dullness or sensual
134 F incitement which interfere, and of eliminating them. The instructions were provided earlier in the general elucidation on tranquility and insight. The place of meditation should be quiet—not frequented by others—during the daytime and even less noisy at night, and one where water, wood, and other requisite conditions are favorable. As one resolutely works toward realization, one remains in solitude, with slow movements and a gentle manner as if one were convalescing. Abandoning all those things that cause physical and mental distractions, one should control the senses and emotions, watch every behavior with vigilance, and consume food moderately. To behave otherwise would make the realization of inner tranquility very difficult. Atīśa comments:

> However hard one may strive to meditate on tranquility,
> If the requisite conditions are defective

One will not realize tranquil absorption,
Not even for a thousand years!

PHYSICAL CONDUCT AND POSTURE

Nāropa said that in a skillful posture of the body lies a vital quality of meditation. It is recommended by this meditational order that one should
B [first] master the physical management if one wishes to attain inner tranquility. Skillful control of the body will help, in a relative sense, to bring forth inner realization. In applying what is known as the sevenfold meditational posture, a meditator (1) sits on a soft seat with his legs in the vajra posture,[70] or if he cannot do that, in the bodhisattva posture;[71] (2) the hands are in the contemplative posture, held close to the abdomen and about two inches below the navel, placing the [back of the] right hand in the open palm of the left hand, with the two thumbs raised upright, touching each other; (3) the backbone is straightened, with the vertebrae being upright so as to stiffen the whole body; (4) arms and elbows are held straight down from the shoulders without bending them; (5) the chin is pressed down so as to bend the neck slightly; (6) the tip of the tongue touches the front palate while the upper and lower teeth are set in a barely touching position, with lips closed lightly; and (7) the eyes are serenely gazing at the space a little beyond the tip of the nose,
35 F without moving the eyeballs. These are called the "seven aspects of Buddha Vairocana" because of their identical nature. Some say the lips and teeth should be in a more natural position but the aforesaid position is preferable. Besides this, the modulation of the breath may be made the eighth aspect as urged by Kamalaśīla in two of his *Bhāvanākrama*. One inhales and exhales gently and without effort, even without feeling it. One should not pant, neither should one breathe heavily or violently.

The *Vajramālā* advises:

Keep arms stretched down evenly,
The tongue touching the palate,
Teeth and lips in a relaxed position,
The eyes gazing at the space close to the nose.

Master Pagme Dorje also mentions:

Sit in the vajra posture on a comfortable cushion,
The two hands held in the contemplative posture,
The body held upright while the neck is [slightly] bent.

135 B Nāropa explains:

The vital aspects of the body are to be described here.
The [spinal column] should be straight,

Like precious beads strung together on a reed;
[The neck] should be bent slightly;
[The body] should be erect, like a wild lily;
The arms extended and parallel
[As if to form] a square knot;
The hands in a meditative posture
Should press [the spot below the naval].
[The legs] should be crossed, like lines on a checkerboard.

Thus he refers to postures such as a straightened spinal column, a bent neck, a stiff body, stretched arms, and contemplative hand postures,[72] while [the crossing of legs], like the lines on a checkerboard, is to be done in some special exercise.

Regarding the purpose or benefit derived from these vital body postures, the effusive energy can be controlled by the cross-legged posture, thermal energy by pressing on the navel, diffusive energy by straightening the spinal column and holding the body erect, the vital life energy by straightening the shoulders, arms, and elbows, and the ascending energy by bending the neck slightly and touching the palate with the tongue.[73] Once one is able to control these fundamental energies in the body, one can automatically gain control over all secondary energies. The latter can be especially controlled
136 F by the immobile gaze of the eyes. With these postures all of one's nervous system, energies, and "enlightening spirit"[74] [i.e., the creative element, the seminal fluid] may be revitalized and stabilized within their respective planes. It was stated that as a result of all this the elements of the body will achieve harmony, the complexion will be radiant, and good, tranquil absorption will arise naturally, since discursive thoughts have been pacified [by the meditative postures]. The mind will be less overcome by dullness or passion. Awareness will manifest itself with clarity.

Adverse effects would arise from defective postures. If the body slants to the right, [the mind] would be drawn to sensory objects despite an initial calmness. If the body slants to the left, [the mind] will be overcome with much discursive thought, even though it has initially been tranquil. If the body bends forward, the mind will be agitated, even though it has initially been clear. If the body bends backward, [the mind] will be overcome with much distraction, even though it has at first been lucid and relaxed. If the focus of the eyes shift, form consciousness will be aroused, thereby causing discursive thoughts. These instructions came from the masters of this meditational order. The *Śrāvakabhūmi* comments on the benefits:

136 B These body postures will soon produce perfect ease,
Prevent physical exhaustion, and enable one to persevere for a very long time.
They are distinct from those adopted by dogmatists or hostile critics.[75]

If one were seen in these postures,
The beholder would delight.
They were the postures adopted by Buddha and his disciples.
Meditators are urged to adopt them.

THE METHOD OF CONCENTRATING ON AN OBJECT

Meditation should commence with a joyful mind. This depends upon one's appreciation of the benefits arising from tranquil absorption. The benefits are described in a sūtra as follows:

Unless this teaching is meditated upon,
The intrinsic reality [of all things] cannot be perceived.
However much one may hear about or look at water,
One's thirst cannot be quenched until one drinks it.

Such is the general reason why meditation on the teaching is essential. Describing the benefits of tranquil absorption, the *Prajñāpāramitā-saṃcayagāthā* states:

Firm concentration pacifies craving for
Objectionable sensory pleasures;
It brings forth a realization of awareness,
Supranormal cognition, and tranquil absorption.

7 F Besides the general benefits, specific benefits may be gained through concentration done consistently with proper appreciation and awareness. The specific benefits are that the body will be permeated with bliss and the mind with joy, making it disposed toward concentration. Any unworthy disposition of the mind will be overcome; maleficent behavior abandoned, spiritual power such as supranormal cognition,[76] transfiguration, etc. achieved. Above all, through tranquility insight will dawn. Then, by sustaining and strengthening insight, liberation from saṃsāra is achieved, and transient and ultimate qualities are realized. The *Madhyāntavibhāga* explains this aspect by saying:

There exist a dwelling and a process of settling in it,
And [also] a cause and effect.

The term "dwelling" refers to the dimension of striving, which means an intense yearning for tranquil absorption. "Process of settling" refers to "an intense striving," which means consistency and regularity in striving. "Cause" refers to the "cause of yearning," which implies faith, born of admiration for and appreciation of the qualities of tranquil absorption. "Effect" refers to the outcome of striving in meditation, which means that body and mind have achieved perfect ease. By understanding these concepts, one directs the mental focus on a visualized image.

THE ACTUAL MENTAL IMAGES FOR ATTAINING SETTLED QUIESCENCE: VISUALIZATION OF A MENTAL IMAGE, USING THE IMAGE OF AN OBJECT

137 B This visualization consists of:

1. The actual meditation
2. Identification with a tranquil state of mind

The Actual Meditation

A person of average intelligence who seeks to achieve mental tranquility may endeavor to sustain fixed attentiveness by employing any of the methods as expounded by Tilopa:

> By gazing and other techniques
> For sustaining concentration,
> One trains the mind until it attains tranquility.

Although the sūtras and the three *Bhāvanākrama* of Kamalaśīla state that, as a first visualization, one should seek to achieve a tranquil mind by focusing on an image of the Tathāgata's figure, the meditational lineage considers it very difficult for an inferior intellect to visualize an image of the Tathāgata at the beginning. They suggested that the settling of mind may be achieved
138 F easily, if one focuses on some ordinary object such as a pebble or a piece of wood. One may later be able to focus on a sacred object such as an image of the Tathāgata. The focusing of the mind on a pebble or a piece of wood may be done during the daytime. If one finds it somewhat difficult, one may focus on some small object in a shaded place. And at night one visualizes a disc of light—large or small, either white or black, at the center of one's forehead, between the eyebrows, or sometimes underneath oneself, and then concentrates on it. This is done by directing the mind in a relaxed manner to the visualized object without letting the thoughts flow or the mind be distracted. While so focusing the mind firmly on an object, one avoids analyzing its color and shape.

In summary, one has simply to achieve a settled mind imbued with sharpness and lucidity, without any thought whatsoever. Every time the mind has achieved a momentary settled state, one stops [the meditation]. After a brief rest, one resumes the practice of settling the mind. Each [sitting] should be brief and repeated many times, because if one adjourns the meditation joyfully, one will be happy to resume it. If one drives oneself too hard, one might become so tired that one's sense of delight in resuming the meditation will diminish.

Some people criticize the use of a pebble, a piece of wood, or an imaginary disc of light for concentration. Their contention is that this method is not mentioned in any other treatises as means for realizing a settled mind. This only shows the ignorance on the part of their advocacy. It is unfair criticism. The purpose [of this method] is to enable an inferior mind to easily discover a settled mind and to achieve much through little striving. Such is the significance. It is not true that other texts do not mention this [method]. For instance, master Bodhibhadra states:

> There are two kinds of mental tranquility.
> One is achieved through focusing the mind inwardly
> And the other through focusing outwardly.

Again he states:

> What has been referred to as "focusing outwardly" is comprised of a special and ordinary kind. The ordinary kind involves the method of
> F focusing on a pebble, a stick, or any such object.
>
> The five components of human life used for concentration are (1) breath, (2) a tiny symbol, (3) a disc of light, (4) a ray of light, (5) joy and bliss.

This refers to the fixation of the mental focus on a disc of light.

If the critic says that the use of external objects such as a pebble or a stick for realizing a settled mind is wrong since the attainment of a settled mind must necessarily depend on mental perception, [we say] there is no truth in this reproach because the eye consciousness is the primary faculty that influences the outer sense perceptions as well. The vital fact about this is that mental consciousness for the most part is aroused through sensory perceptions. By keeping a steady gaze one not only renders the eye consciousness immobile and reduces the movements of the other senses, but one also
39 B achieves a mental tranquility. A pebble or a stick is used simply to focus the mind through eye consciousness and thereby to keep the mind undistracted. This is like someone being able to recollect a certain thing through a token of memory. However, no clearly refined rule exists in the use of material objects for fixing the mental focus. Even in regard to the use of repulsive, ugly objects such as a putrid corpse, etc., a number of similar objects are prescribed. The mental focus can also be fixed on other things such as a syllable, a sound, a light, or a name, etc.

The *Bhāvanākrama* reveals that there is no well-defined set of mental images for tranquility. Nonetheless, a sacred image of Buddha is highly recommended as an object of concentration. One of the many sayings in the *Bhadrapālapàripṛcchā-sūtra* illustrates this as follows:

> [Buddha:] O Bhadrapāla, just as I am seated in front of you teaching the dharma, so should a bodhisattva visualize the Tathāgata. He should be perceived as being seated while delivering a sermon, his body, endowed with perfect form, symmetry, radiance, charm, and
> 140 F beauty. Meditate on each of the Tathāgata's attributes. [This will] produce a multitude of spiritual merits.

The *Samādhirāja* says

> His body is like radiant gold. . . .

The third *Bhāvanākrama* comments:

> Numerous statements were made on various stages of the visualization. *Āryasūra*[77] and Atīśa said that it is better to concentrate on one suitable visualization in order to realize the tranquility of mind.

The first *Bhāvanākrama* says:

> Once one has realized tranquility,
> One may practice any other visualization.

[For further practice] the system of the sūtras speaks of many methods such as a contemplation on (1) the elimination [of wrong views] through critical examination and (2) the purification of defilements. These were
140 B explained before. The followers of this meditational order use either a real pebble, a stick, or a disc of light and a similar imaginary thing as an object of concentration.

Identification with a Tranquil State of Mind

Even though many distinct methods for attaining tranquility exist, at this point one should achieve a settled nondiscriminating state in a manner as stated by Tilopa:

> Abandon all body movements and let the body relax in a natural way.
> Do not indulge too much in talking, which is like an echo.
> Do not indulge in thought but watch the natural awareness.

Master Diṅnāga implores:

> Subject and object, duality and nonduality,
> Self and others, as well as saṃsāra and nirvāṇa—

All these are discriminations.
Abandon them and let the mind settle in a tranquil equipoise.

Thus, one is concerned with the search for a settled state of mind. Yet at this point it is hard for most [beginners] to achieve a flawless absorption. So, by constantly visualizing one of the objects mentioned one retracts from the incorrigible indulgence in sensory distraction. If one is able to maintain a
1 F relaxed, tranquil mind with simple mindfulness, without any thoughts, for any length of time, one has found, to a certain extent, the settled quietude. Being once in such a state, one should gently break it up. After a brief rest one should resume the practice. On the other hand, such a nondiscriminating quiescent state may well turn into an unconscious inertness. It is a defect one should guard against. In such an event the meditator should wake up and reinforce the mindfulness. [As a remedy] he should practice tranquility for a number of short periods. If during his [regular] practice he finds himself in a somewhat sullen state where mindulness has not completely faded, this [subtle] defect will automatically clear up. The same practice should be carried on for a shorter session.

If this settled state seems to lose its stability and the flow of thought seems to increase, despite the presence of mindfulness, this happens because one is now able to detect every flow of thought, the streamlike movement of which had not been recognized before. This [momentary, inward] attentiveness signals a certain level of calmness. Hence it should not be construed to be faulty. Through repeated practice one should try to free oneself from deeply instilled sensory attachment, to neither usher in a new thought nor to pursue its track. One thus maintains an undistracted state in which there is neither negation nor affirmation.

141 B It is a sign of dullness when the mind fails to still itself or detect its movements. At this point the meditator should learn directly the actual meaning of "unconscious inertness." He should listen to a sudden crack of sound that is so loud that it shocks him, interrupting one thought [or perception] while preventing for a moment the emergence of the next. What has taken place between these two is the state of nakedness and stillness. He should then resume the meditation for each short session as to retain the same stillness. This method should be applied to any visualization of breath, to be dealt with later.

ATTAINING QUIESCENCE WITH A MENTAL IMAGE, WITHOUT THE IMAGE OF AN OBJECT

This is done in two ways:

1. Using the breathing
2. Not using the breathing

Using the Breathing

Both sūtras and tantras spoke in general terms about the realization of tranquility through breathing. Tilopa comments:

> If a person of inferior mind cannot settle in tranquility,
> He should control the vital air energy
> By means of retention and release.

Focusing the Mind on Counting Each Breath Rhythm

Breathing as a form of meditation was prescribed in the sūtra meditational discourses for persons with a strong sense of discrimination. The autocommentary of the *Abhidharmakośa* also comments:

> There are six aspects [in the breathing exercise]:
> 142 F Counting, retrospection, fixation [of mental focus],
> Comprehension, transmutation, and complete purity.

The term "counting" refers to the rhythm of the breath. One counts twenty-one times [with exhaling and inhaling being one unit], then up to sixty seconds and then to sixty minutes. The meditator focuses his attention on the counting. "Retrospection" refers to the retracing of the breathing exercise one has just performed. The meditator examines inwardly whether the movement of air has permeated some parts or the whole body. "Fixation" refers to the settling of the mind in a complete nondiscriminative state. "Comprehension" refers to understanding the inconceivable nature of the air energy. "Transmutation" refers to the process of transforming the concentration of the air energy into another object of tranquility. "Complete purity" refers to meditation on a nondiscriminative state, which has purified all dualistic thoughts.

Although the tantric treatises contain the descriptions of innumerable meditations on breathing, I do not propose to elaborate here. Instead I would, however, speak about methods of realizing a tranquil state through
142 B counting the rhythm of breath and saturating [the whole internal system]. The *Sai Nyingpo Khorlo Chupai Dho* elucidates:

> How does one perceive through the force of mindfulness the inward and outward movements of the breath in keeping with one's inmost purity? One counts them exactly while keeping in such a state. Similarly, he who has withdrawn himself into concentrated absorption focuses his attention on the inward and outward movements [of the breath]. Such a sentient being may be described as the one who dwells in the ultimate, purest state and who concentrates in perfect harmony with the purest state.

Thus this statement is made with a pleasing comment.

The *Saṃvarodaya* adds:

> A yogin who dwells in a state of tranquil equipoise
> Should count constantly and without sound
> The rhythm of his breath
> Until the count reaches one hundred thousand.
> A seeker who completes this "utterance" a hundred thousand times
> Will doubtlessly live for five more years,
> Even though the final day of his life has arrived.

At this point the meditator settles the mind in a state of purity by means of the vital body postures and the gazing. Thus, by gently breathing in and out through the nostrils, without panting, making hissing or swishing sounds, he focuses the concentration on the inward and outward movements of the breath. Unmoved by any distraction he should concentrate from the beginning on the breath movement, counting up to three, five, and then seven times. After a rest period he should resume the concentration on the counting of the breath rhythm, with mindfulness, until the count reaches a hundred. Each count includes both an inhalation and exhalation. In case someone has already achieved a settled tranquility through sustained concentration, the breathing meditation will help to consolidate it further. On the other hand, if he has not achieved it, it is important that he tries his utmost. This is a splendid instruction on the concentration of mind.

Focusing the Mind on Its Inward Retention

For the control and diffusion of the air in the whole system of the body one inhales the breath in a normal way or deeply [a few times] so as to retain it in
3 B the way a vase holds something. The *Dorje Khadro* (*Vajraḍākinī-tantra*) describes:

> By diffusing [the air] in the whole system
> The body may be purified;
> Poison and fever of a flu may be purged.
> By retaining the air as if in a vase,
> The aperture of the senses may be controlled.

The *Saṃvarodaya* explains the benefits:

> Alternately, by retaining [the air] as in a vase
> One will fully triumph over death.
> With the insight into one's self-nature
> One saturates the body down to the heels
> And firmly retains [the air] in the fashion of a vase.

To explain the retention in the fashion of a vase, it is said that the upward and downward flow of air is brought to converge [at the spot of the navel]. The *Saṃvarodaya* follows up with this description:

> Air that ascends and descends
> Should be brought to converge by [the power of] the concentration,
> And by perfecting this yoga
> One will reach a level of stability.

The *Kālacakra* elucidates further:

> Drawing in fully the air through the nostrils with the mouth closed,
> One stirs the life breath[78] forcefully and blends it with the descending energy,
> Which is like pure lightning.
> By continuously mastering this unification
> Through the "sun" and "moon" [the two arteries],
> One harmonizes these energies with the "fire" [of caṇḍālī]
> In the mystical center [solar plexus]
> And achieves the harmonious flavor [of all things].
> This will eliminate hunger and thirst
> 144 F And will even bring the gift of immortality.

It is necessary to know the significance of the fourfold exercises. Nāropa comments:

> There are four [breathing exercises]:
> Drawing in, saturating, diffusing, and darting, like an arrow.
> Without knowing these four,
> Meditators run the risk of the practice deteriorating.

The treatises contain no detailed instructions on the relevant breathing exercises. As part of sustaining the concentration, one breathes to diffuse the system in the body and retain the air so as to seek a nondiscriminating tranquility. How should one do this? Following the harnessing of the breath and the purging of the body of foul air one forms the body postures and then remains fixedly in the gazing position as before. One gently inhales the air fully through the nostrils, without swishing, hissing, or panting, and then retains it by relaxing the chest and pressing [the air] down briefly into the
144 B abdomen as long as no discomfort is felt. The moment one feels discomfort and the pressure to exhale, one releases the air gently without hissing or any noise. During all these exercises of drawing in, retaining, and releasing air one maintains undistracted mindfulness. Especially during the retention of the breath one maintains the stream of nondiscriminating state silently and vividly.

Breathing exercises are done by first repeating breath rhythms three, five, and seven times and so on, while alternating them with rest periods. As one gains proficiency in it, the retention should be extended. When the mind tends to be restive, one relaxes deep inside to the point where it is not distracted. However, if the restiveness persists, one might get exhausted. Any suitable method of resting and refreshing should be employed. If one feels dizzy or depressed, it is due to a deprivation of internal energy. One should take nourishing food and apply body relaxation techniques [kum-nye]. Owing to the impact of control of the internal energy a cloud of dullness might appear. In such a case the meditator should elevate his spirit by means of firm gazing, crystallizing the awareness. When faint thoughts arise, they should neither be treated as a meditational deficiency nor should
5 F the meditator fall into an unconscious inertness. Instead, the force of mindfulness should be revitalized while the mind should be alert but relaxed. All these practices concern themselves with stabilizing the mind. They are based on the key instructions on training beginners in inner tranquility. However, meditators must try their utmost to achieve a state of nondiscriminating tranquility before the end of this stage.

Not Using the Breathing

45 B The meditation not using the breathing is an [advanced] method for training those who have achieved some level of tranquility. It shows how they can now meditate on the mind without a supporting basis or a focal point. In this practice the postures of the body should be the same as before. Without having to focus the mind on an external object, rhythm of breath, and so on, the meditator should concentrate on the mind and try to attain an absorption in its natural state. He should not let the mind seek a supporting basis nor should he stir it through discriminating thoughts. He should neither recall past events he has done, recounting any of the bygon happenings, nor should he anticipate the future with a plan to do this or that, nor should he let the mind indulge in present thoughts, for instance, about his immediate plan or how it looks. In this way the mind should be settled in its natural, relaxed state. The *Guhyasamāja* comments on this:

> In elevating the mind to a nondiscriminating state
> One should not indulge in thought.

The *Dohā* states:

> By completely abandoning thought and the object of thought
> One should let the mind settle in the natural state of an infant.

When the mind is as quiet as space, free from any thought whatsoever, psychic energy will be harnessed so that the mind will become stable. The *Dohā* makes an identical comment:

By attaining a spacelike quietude
One's psychic energy will be harnessed.
By comprehending the equality of all things
One's mind will be pacified, unmoved by distraction.
By realizing the mind power
One will hasten liberation from all that is transient and fluid.
So proclaims the Archer [Saraha].

After achieving a stable, nonconceptual state one will experience a certain manifest effect arising. From the harmonious absorption [into the vital system] of external and internal energies one will attain liberation from the
146 F substance of the existential realm.

The *Kālacakra* declares on quietening of the mind:

In seeking pacification of thoughts
One observes oneself inwardly for one day.
If no effect arises at all
My word would be a lie!

The *Dohā* states:

Whenever someone has quieted the mind in an undistracted state
Then he will gain liberation from the conditions of saṃsāra.

In so seeking to settle the mind a meditator should practice as stated before for many periods, refreshing the mind if dullness clouds it or relaxing [tension] if passion overcomes it. If he is in a mood of torpor in which he loses the clarity of consciousness and his mind becomes intractable, he should act according to the key instructions. Engaging himself in pure devotion, he should repeatedly prostrate before the sacred symbols, purify all harmful thoughts and deeds, and invoke [the threefold refuge] to bless him so that he may soon experience the dawn of tranquil absorption. The meditator has already achieved some measure of tranquility during the earlier training. If he now does not make serious efforts in enhancing the tranquil state through concentration in which he should seek to settle the mind in its innate quiescence without any aid of an object or image, no progress in this pure concentration is possible. Hence the importance of
146 B mastering it. Since this method of attaining concentration either with or without a breathing exercise excludes the method of focusing on the shape or colour of a material object such as a pebble or a stick, the masters of this meditational order characterized it as "concentration without concrete object," or the key instructions on consolidating a partially stabilized mind.

FORMLESS TRANQUILITY, WITHOUT A MENTAL IMAGE

This is comprised of two aspects:

1. The methods for achieving flawless tranquility
2. Recognizing its absorptive state

The Methods for Achieving Flawless Tranquility

There are three approaches:

1. The importance of knowing the vital point of balance between exertion and relaxation
2. The meditation with mental exertion
3. The relaxed meditation

The Importance of Knowing the Vital Point of Balance between Exertion and Relaxation

There is an agreement between the passage on this method contained in the meditational treatises of mahāmudrā and the passages in the sūtras on the methods for removing flaws of tranquil absorption such as dullness and sensual incitement. The meditator who has realized a level of tranquility through the previous concentration engages in visualization with a mental exertion. If a cloud of dullness looms, a little more mental exertion will help clear it, just as sensual incitement will be arrested with more relaxation.

7 F Referring to the clouds of a contemplative trance, the *Dho Gongdrel* (*Saṃdhinirmocana-sūtra*) enumerates sensual incitement, resentment, torpor, drowsiness, doubt, desire, longing, evil intent, etc. Most flaws are condensed into two kinds: dullness and sensual incitement. And although there is a distinction between torpor, drowsiness, and dullness the reason why this sūtra has not specified dullness is that dullness and torpor are considered as belonging to the same category. Even though there exist countermeasures for each of these flaws, most treatises of meditation mention the methods for clearing away only flaws of dullness and sensual incitement because these texts point out that other flaws are purged automatically when these two are eliminated. Therefore the meditator should know the flaws described previously in connection with tranquility and insight. He should be able to identify the factors that cause dullness and sensual incitement and recognize their characteristics, with a view to abandon them by employing the necessary means to clear them up. In short, a flawless absorption of tranquility must be the one in which perfect clarity of

mind is harmonized with its one-pointed concentration in a nondiscriminating state.

Dullness is a flaw that clouds the clarity whereas sensual incitement disturbs the concentration. For such reasons these two defects are the chief
147 B obstacles in maintaining an absorptive tranquility. Hence the importance of employing means to clear them. The meditational system of the sūtras states that the meditator should heighten his spirit when overcome with dullness by thinking of delightful scenes, visualizing the form of light, and so on. To overcome sensual incitement he should contemplate impermanence and the undesirable consequences of mental distractions, and especially meditate on tranquility. All flaws in this meditation on tranquility must be detected, especially dullness and sensual incitement. They may be cleared mainly by means of mental exertion and relaxation respectively. A vital point here is to know the exact level of the balance between exertion and relaxation, which is either afflicted by dullness or sensual incitement.

The Meditation with Mental Exertion

The visualization with mental exertion is directed mainly against dullness and can be also good against sensual incitement. As for dullness, a pronounced dullness looms when the mind is already in a nondiscriminating tranquility. Clarity of mindfulness fades out so gradually that finally the
148 F concentrative image is completely lost. The mind becomes dim or stilled inertia, a subtle [lesser] dullness[79] in which the mental image remains untarnished but loses clarity of focus. Thus the mind becomes still and semiconscious. An unskilled meditator considers the latter to be flawless tranquility. As long as the subtle dullness is sustained instead of being eliminated, one cannot achieve a vivid mental focus, and the mind gets duller and more forgetful. These are flaws in the meditation on tranquility. To remove such flaws the meditator forms the body postures and gazes, with the eyes turned up—as described before—while lifting the mind out of the depression or torpor, which arose owing to prolonged withdrawal, by expanding the mental perspective and by relaxation. These methods are capable of clearing such dullness. The *Prajñāpāramitā-saṃcayagāthā* points out:

> One should elate the mind if overcome by depression.

The *Uma Nyingpo* (*Madhyamakahṛdaya*) states:

> When a depressed mood looms,
> Meditate on an expansive mental image.

148 B If subtle dullness persists after its more pronounced condition has been

purged, the mind should first be invigorated by exertion and by being relentlessly attentive. The mind should be settled in one-pointed concentration serenely, vividly, and sharply, without any inclination toward sensory enjoyment. After a while this [tranquility] should be broken. With due exertion, the mind should again be settled in tranquility without distraction. Through such practice the meditator should attain not only evenness or stillness of the mind but should also develop such a sharp sensitivity that it recognizes the mind's natural serenity, vividness, transparency, and freshness. In short, the focus of the mind in a nondiscriminating state should be so sharp and vivid that it can detect an emerging dullness or sensual incitement. The *Madhyāntavibhāga* agrees:

> Recognize dullness and sensual incitement.

The second and third *Bhāvanākrama* repeat:

> Detect dullness or its emergence.

And again it says:

> Detect sensual incitement or its emergence.

By following this method, even an agitated mind may experience an acute vividness, but its nondiscriminating quiescence may be short-lived. Rather than regard this as faulty, the meditator should repeat a brief practice many times so that flawless tranquility may be realized. However, when such concentration fails to be stable, the meditator should know how to loosen the rigidity of concentration without losing the vividness and should then maintain it.

The Relaxed Meditation

Even though many forms of relaxation generally exist, the purpose here is to clear away the flaw of sensual incitement. The term "sensual incitement" is described as a form of lust that focuses on an object that delights the lower emotions. In this case it encompasses all thought flows and emotions such as resentment, doubt, evil intent, etc. The meditator should therefore work toward the pacification of all mental distractions. The way of pacifying them is said to consist in remembering the evil consequences of mental distraction in general and of lust, etc., in particular. The *Dhodigyan* (*Sūtrālaṃkāra*) says:

> If one realizes that distraction brings harm,
> One will not only treat it with disinclination
> But will seek to eliminate it.
> Similarly one will pacify agitations like lust and anxiety.

The *Uma Nyingpo* (*Madhyamakahṛdaya*) states:

> If one is overcome with distraction,
> One should retract and regard it
> As being a harmful sign of perceptive diversion.

149 B Distraction can be overcome by refusing to focus the mind on any object of distraction and by releasing the thought of abandonment and application. The *Pharchin Düpa* (*Prajñāpāramitā-saṃcayagāthā*) urges:

> When the mind tends to be restless
> It should be pacified by tranquility.

In such a case the meditator performs the same body posture as before, lowers a little the gaze of the eyes, and then relaxes the mind in an expansive mood. In so practicing tranquility he should not concern himself with what form of meditation he should or should not choose; neither should he feel excited when the mind is tranquil nor should he feel disturbed when thoughts flow. The meditator should quiet the mind in a relaxed and natural state, without modulating or altering it through a thought of acceptance or rejection. With a firm resolution never to be distracted he should continue to maintain that tranquility. If any vivid thoughts arise abruptly, the meditator should not let them flow freely, neither should he pursue them, which will only distract the mind, nor should he even supress them. He should maintain the continuity of an undistracted state by revitalizing mindfulness.
150 F Even if dim, subtle thoughts occur, he should neither rejoice nor get upset, neither abandon nor accept them but should extend the tranquility through a relaxed state without losing the natural mindfulness. When the mind remains in a state of lucidity and serenity one should interrupt it and take a rest.

Now, when the practice is resumed, the meditator will perceive the progress. Up to this time whenever he applied exertion so as to achieve tranquility, he perceived that all forceful and feeble thoughts seemed to fade as if through suppression. The mind became momentarily so serene and still that the meditator was obliged to control it with one-pointed attention. It was not a very easy condition. At the present stage he finds that when the mind is relaxed it can be settled naturally and easily while not losing the vigor of mindfulness. When a forgetful or feeble thought arises and when the focus of mindfulness is well set, it will not distract but will quiet the mind in the first or following moment so that it rests in tranquility. If one knows the secret of releasing whatever inner craving has emerged, one will know how to relax the mind and still it. One will then achieve further proficiency in the practice of releasing. Saraha refers to this practice:

> By releasing the tension that binds the mind,
> 150 B One undoubtedly brings about inner freedom.

And again he says:

> A mind in bondage tries to run in ten different directions;
> If released it settles firmly and immutably.
> Reversing that [mind], [one] will be like a [restless] camel—so I understand.

Maitrīpa comments:

> When any discriminating thoughts arise in a yogin's mind,
> He should remain relaxed and unmodulated, like cotton wool.

Some critics misconstrue the saying of this meditational order that "the best meditation lies in the best relaxation" is applicable to meditation at this stage. They contend that dullness, looming large owing to laxity in mindfulness and vigilance, is being mistaken for meditative tranquility [by the meditators of this order]. Such remarks indicate that they are only too eager to comment despite the height of their ignorance. The foregoing saying was a quotation from Saraha's teachings. It is supported by Tilopa when he states:

> Relax the mind in the unmodulated primal state.
> For if the mind is released from inner bondage,
> Freedom will doubtlessly prevail.

Saraha again advises:

> Any form of attachment should be released.

Such conceptual terminology was composed as a means of breaking the mind's attachment to inner sensations and experiences during the main
1 F meditation. The great saint Zhang also elucidates this point:

> When consciousness unwinds in a relaxed manner,
> There arises a sublime quality of vividness and nondiscrimination.
> This state emerges like the deep, pure sky.
> This is the luminous clarity of dharmakāya.

This Meditational Order considers a steady inertness the state of complete dullness and confusion, arising from inactive mindfulness and vigilance which, in turn, are caused by an unskilled relaxation of the mind. Who [among us] identifies this [steady inertness] with the best relaxation and best meditation? The critics should not slander this system in such a manner.

When the vigor of mindfulness and vigilance becomes weak, any unskilled relaxation will cause the mind to submerge into a semiconscious dullness. Such a mind cannot perceive any distraction, nor any movement or stillness. If, in the face of mindfulness, thoughts scatter or swirl, it indicates either an insufficient relaxation or pressure from craving [for inner expe-

rience]. The meditator should know the appropriate stage and time to strike the balance between exertion and relaxation. In summary, beginners should learn to maintain the mind in a relaxed state. The meditator should not reinforce the mindfulness again and again unless necessitated by a weaken-
151 B ing of its attentiveness and alertness. Only when the mindfulness and vigilance appear to lose their vigor should some mental exertion be applied so as to revitalize it. One should know how to maintain the concentrated state and clear away all its flaws. By doing so the mental awareness will stabilize and crystallize without a flow of thoughts. If, during this quiescent state, the mind unceasingly perceives forms, sounds, and the other senses gently, serenely, fearlessly, vividly, and quietly, tranquility has been realized.

Recognizing Its Absorptive State

At last a flawless absorptive tranquility is realized through the previously imparted methods of settling the mind. Such a mind must of necessity be a coalescence of a serenely stable state in which the mind rests with one-pointedness and a discriminating awareness, coupled with an unimpaired sharpness of clarity arising from mindfulness and vigilance. In this respect the flaws of tranquil absorption are the projection of thoughts toward diverse objects through failure in focusing the mind one-pointedly on the image of an object, a restlessness brought about by the steady decline of mindfulness, and a fading mindfulness without sharpness of clarity, which renders the state unsuitable for any kind of evenness.

152 F Furthermore, if mindfulness and vigilance are lacking in sharpness of clarity, this indicates a fog of dullness, whereas if the mind has not settled in one-pointedness, this indicates a discursive thought, which is a distraction. Hence the importance of the methods for clearing away dullness and thought flow. These have been and will be further elucidated. In short, sharpness of clarity should be improved and crystallized whenever dullness looms large. Mental exertion born of a yearning [for advancement] should be appropriately relaxed whenever thoughts flow vigorously. When the desired harmony between exertion and relaxation is achieved, no mental examination should be conducted but its natural tranquility should be maintained without any interruption. Nāgārjuna states in the *Tüshi Nyamjor*:[80]

> Heighten the spirit when dullness or heaviness loom large,
> Settle the mind in its innate naturalness
> When thoughts swirl and scatter.

With regard to mindfulness and vigilance, the former averts mental distraction from a visualized image while the latter detects dullness or the flow of thoughts. Besides having intensified one's resolve not to be distracted, even for a moment, from the visualization, and having continuously maintained the settled state, one vivifies mindfulness. Being in such tranquility, one should simply observe while remaining alert, without specifically examining if the mind is affected by dullness or thoughts, by mindfulness or forgetfulness. The tradition of the sūtras separately comments on mindfulness and vigilance. According to the instructions of this order, the two aspects are usually incorporated into awareness or mindfulness alone. If one wonders about this, there is no flaw. The *Bodhicaryāvatāra* clarifies:

> When mindfulness dwells in the mind's entrance
> In order to keep a watchful eye,
> Then, at that moment, vigilance will emerge.

Accordingly, mindfulness and vigilance have been distinguished in terms of their being pronounced or subtle, crude or refined, because a vigorous and vivid mindfulness encompasses vigilance. This is stated in the commentary on the *Madhyāntavibhāga*:

> Whoever dwells deeply in mindfulness will also possess vigilance.

At this stage prudent meditators who concentrate on a visualized image with one-pointed mindfulness and vigilance might wonder how to proceed in a situation such as this. They feel that to engender vigilance in order to detect whether or not the concentration is focused on the [chosen] mental image or
3 F whether it is distracted either by dullness or thought flow means to produce some subtle thought. With subtle thought tranquility cannot be nondiscriminating. To be otherwise means there is no vigilance to detect distracting elements of dullness and thought flow.[81]

Those unskilled in meditation, having considered any subtle thought to be a flaw, seem to sustain a settled mind with a certain degree of vividness, but nevertheless they lack a sharp vigilance. [Vigilance] as subtle thought should be employed since it is not an active thought but is an alertness or awareness in the category of insight. The second *Bhāvanākrama* states:

> Thus, by concentrating on a visualized image of one's choice, the meditator should continuously focus on it. Having done so perfectly, he should examine if the concentrating mind has a firm grip of the visualized image, if it is being clouded with dullness, or if it is wandering toward external objects, thus being distracted.

Regarding the way of activating such thought, rather than abandon the
153 B uninterrupted mindfulness, the mind should simply be watchful while, at the same time, not letting the tranquil state fade out. Yet, repeated invigoration of that watchful mind will arouse adverse thoughts that will blunt

the mindfulness. Through every succeeding moment one simply watches the vigor of definite awareness that passes undiminished through every moment.

In short, the meditator should acquire the skill of evenly balancing his inner exertion and relaxation. This is the most significant of all the methods for achieving tranquil absorption. What has been described as tranquil absorption is comprised of the stream of mindfulness of the visualized image. The clarity of such an image remains free from the uncommendable flaw of dullness or thought flow, and the mind is settled in its intrinsic purity, filled with joy. The visualized image, in this case, is nondiscriminating and vivid. As such it is a sustained stream of mindfulness and vigilance. Similarly the *Śrāvakabhūmi* elucidates:

> Very well, what then is a one-pointed mind? The answer is: it is the recollection that repeatedly focuses on an image that is the reproduction or resemblance of what one's memory has retained; it is the stream of thought, unstained by any uncommendable moral offenses, but full of joy. It is therefore described as tranquil absorption and also as virtuous, one-pointed thought.

154 F The phrase "recollection that repeatedly focuses on an image" refers to the resumption of meditation on the tranquil absorption when the mind is periodically being diverted to listening or examining [the dharma]. The same text explains:

> What then should one recollect again and again? The answer is: you, who have listened to or assimilated the dharma, who have received instructions from gurus, and have stabilized the mind, you should directly realize the perceptive mark of tranquil absorption and should closely follow and focus on the visualized image with a stream of mindfulness.

HOW TO MAINTAIN THE TRANQUIL STATE

A devotee should know the methods for settling the mind in tranquility for each session. At the outset, before meditating, he should contemplate the attributes of tranquil absorption, then regenerate faith [resolution], striv-
154 B ing, and preparation to achieve perfect ease. Failure to produce these four factors of mental thrust will soon wear out the delight in meditation on absorption and thereby lead one to indulgence in idleness. The aforesaid flawless absorption is maintained in regular meditation by means of vigorous mindfulness, unaffected by distraction and forgetfulness. If such mindfulness lacks vigor, then forgetfulness sets in, making the mind incapable of

retaining the visualized image. In order to detect instantly an emergence of dullness or thought flow in the sustained tranquility, an ever-alert vigilance should be brought into being out of mindfulness.

If one's vigilance is inactive or inattentive, flaws of tranquility cannot be detected, because one cannot recognize flaws of tranquil absorption if one's mental vigilance lacks sharpness of clarity and keenness of sensitivity. One should try one's utmost to inwardly employ methods for clearing away the flaws of dullness or sensual incitement described before. Thought flow must be cleared by the factors of mental thrust stated before. Laxity in this effort will bring the mind under the domination of dullness or thought flow, which will prevent flawless absorption from emerging. Once dullness or thought flow have been cleared, the mental thrust should cease and the mind should
F rest in a natural equilibrium. Without quieting the mind in such an equilibrium [as a stepping stone] tranquil absorption will dissipate, making it difficult [for the mind] to settle in tranquility. These methods are summed up in the *Madhyāntavibhāga* as follows:

> The mind settles and settles perfectly;
> The first is the cause and the other the result.
> By not forgetting the visualized image,
> By detecting and dislodging dullness and thought flow,
> By applying mindfulness,
> The mind attains tranquility, resting in its innate purity.

There are some meditators who, at the outset, do not develop faith in and yearning for tranquil absorption. Nevertheless, they attempt in their own way to settle the mind in tranquility. Since this mindfulness lacks vigor, the mind is overcome by too much distraction. Because vigilance lacks sharpness, dullness and thought flow are left undetected. Even if it [vigilance] detects these distractions, these meditators misconstrue them to be thoughts and as such objects to be abandoned. They thus weaken the vigor of clear awareness. Having failed to understand true absorption, they mistake any kind of sensory or perceptive experience for tranquil absorption. And even if a kind of flawless absorption does come about, instead of settling it in its
55 B intrinsic purity, they apply too much mental thrust, causing thoughts to swirl wildly. They thus lack skill in mastering tranquil absorption.

It is for this reason that beginners should produce a vigorous mindfulness at the outset. In the case of a highly passionate mind, a familiar sensual incitement is bound to emerge. They may be able to pacify only the crude passion by detecting it with vigilance. But when thoughts and sensualism in their subtle form flicker, these beginners should not get agitated but should simply release their yearning a little so that the thoughts may automatically quiet down. After that the meditator should apply a slight exertion as a caution against possible fading away of the mind's sharp clarity due to either dullness or thought flow in their pronounced or subtle forms. After a while the force of dullness or thought flow will diminish and a flawless tranquil absorption will emerge. By applying the same logic the meditator, whose mind is clouded by deep dullness, should clear the dullness in both pronounced and subtle forms. Once this is done he should then be cautious of sensual incitement and should seek to realize tranquil absorption. When flawless tranquil absorption emerges, it should be maintained in an even state so as not to let the absorption fade away. Too much thought and mental exertion are the great obstacles that interfere with and destabilize the process of settling the mind in absorption.

156 F As for mindfulness—as long as it is strengthened and sustained by determined resolve, the mind will not be distracted in any way from a visualized image. Any tendency toward even a slight diversion indicates a certain decline in the vigor of mindfulness. A distracted mind has lost complete mindfulness. In such an event a meditator should not let the vigor of mindfulness diminish through every passing moment but should strengthen it. In short, he should not allow any interruption in mindfulness between the passing and emerging moment so as to link one phase of mindfulness with another.

Vigilance arises from the great force of mindfulness. A vigilant mind with sharp focus should simply observe the emergence of dullness or thought. In this tranquil meditation it is wrong to expand the scope of vigilance so as to examine, dissolve, or interconnect [thoughts, perceptions, or experiences], because to do that is to invite great obstruction to the practice of one-pointed concentration.

Mental effort or exertion refers to the application of methods for clearing away dullness or thought flow whenever one or the other clouds the mind. It is wrong to apply these methods even after dullness or thought flow have been cleared because it is contradictory to stir the mind and [at the same
156 B time] to settle it imperturbably. The second and third *Bhāvanākrama* also state:

> To stir the mind in tranquil absorption is to completely distract it.

Evenness of mind refers to settling the mind in its innate purity upon achieving a proper balance between exertion and relaxation as a result of purging dullness and thought flow. It also refers to skillfully maintaining such a tranquil absorption by abandoning any mental exertion or thrust. The second *Bhāvanākrama* explains:

> When dullness and thought flow have been eliminated and the mind is naturally focused on a visualized image, one should release exertion, harmonize the state of mind, and maintain it as long as one wishes.

What about the duration of each session for practicing the aforesaid

methods? If a beginner meditates too long in each period, he is bound to lose the force of mindfulness and vigilance. This will result in making him absent-minded and prone to distraction. The inability of the mind to recognize dullness and thought flow stems from the fact that the mind [tired from a long session] is easily overpowered by dullness or thought flow. So a beginner would do well to meditate for a short period and repeat it again and again. Longer periods of meditation will not be disadvantageous once he has achieved a certain level of proficiency, has acquired the skill to maintain
F mindfulness and vigilance, and has achieved a flawless tranquil absorption. To sum up, he should settle the mind in tranquil absorption until it is interrupted by physical and mental flaws. These flaws should be eliminated and the meditation should be resumed. No definite duration has been indicated [in the sūtras and śāstras].

In this chapter, I have explained mainly the vital points on how to maintain a settled mind. The obstacles or defilements in tranquility, the identification of mental thrusts designed to eliminate the obstacles, and the description of them are commented upon in the section dealing with the general elucidation on tranquility and insight. Hence no further explanation is given here.

THE STAGES OF REALIZING THE SETTLED MIND

Concerning the system for realizing a settled mind, the great saint Tilopa states:

> In the early practice the mind is
> Like a stream rushing through a gorge.
> In the middle the mind is
> Like the river Ganges flowing along gently.
> At the end the mind is like the rivers [joining the ocean],
> Like the reunion of daughters with their mother.

The application of this passage is not definitely confined to tranquility alone, but also applies to a beginner who experiences diverse conditions rang-
157 B ing from the swirl of thoughts, powerful or feeble, at the start up to the attainment of a level of nondiscriminating tranquility. This stage is like a stream rushing through a narrow gorge because the mind here is habitually restless and unstable. Once the meditation becomes more proficient, he may be able to pacify mainly powerful thoughts, or at least they will flow in a sober and serene manner, causing no interruption. He may find this state somewhat easier to maintain for it is like the river Ganges gently flowing along. Even though his mind remains mainly tranquil, it occasionally will fail to quiet powerful thoughts that arise from various conditions, sensory and other-

wise. Following that the meditator will attain a level where no powerful or subtle thoughts arise, but even if they do, they are naturally pacified. This state is like rivers joining the ocean the way daughters join their mother. Emerging thoughts and sensations are harmonized with the expanse of mindfulness and vigilance as one flavor. Such a tranquil state cannot be stirred by waves of thoughts.

In this particular case the different stages of a settled mind are shown to be three. According to the sūtras, there are nine levels [or parts] in tranquil meditation. At the first level the meditator seeks to realize (1) fixed attentiveness by withdrawing inward and focusing upon the image of an object.
158 F Similarly, (2) prolonged attentiveness is achieved by extending the duration of a settled, undistracted mind. (3) Stable attentiveness is achieved by bringing the distracted mind into that state. (4) Refined attentiveness is achieved by repeated withdrawal and actualized sensitivity. (5) A trained mind is achieved by reinforcing the meditation through appreciation of the benefits arising from tranquil absorption. (6) A pacified state is achieved by clearing away flaws of distractions. (7) A perfectly pacified state is achieved by clearing away such flaws as lust and other passions. (8) One-pointed concentration is achieved by mastering tranquil absorption with conscious endeavor. (9) Tranquil evenness is achieved by mastering one-pointed concentration and thereby entering into tranquil evenness effortlessly and naturally. The *Sūtrālaṃkāra* comments on the significance of this:

> Focus the mind upon the image of an object;
> Undistractedly maintain the stream of mindfulness.

158 B The six forms of power required in tranquility are: (1) listening to dharma teachings and instructions on tranquil absorption produces the intellectual power; (2) practicing the dharma produces the power of examination; (3) mastering undistracted mindfulness produces the power of mindfulness; (4) cognizing dullness or thought flow produces the power of vigilance; (5) striving for tranquil absorption produces the power of striving, and (6) adapting perfectly to the contemplative process produces the power of mastery.

The four mental performances required in the mastery of tranquility are: (1) an assiduous exertion in meditation, which provides a much needed one-pointed thrust at the outset in order to achieve tranquil absorption; (2) an intermittent exertion, which may be applied every time one's concentration is interrupted by either dullness or thought flow; (3) an unceasing application [not exertion], necessary for carrying on with the concentration when it is not interrupted by dullness or thought flow; and (4) a spontaneous application, which is achieved when one finally attains tranquility effortlessly. These have been elucidated before.

With the powerful thrust emanating from confidence in and yearning for

tranquil absorption, mindfulness, and vigilance, an assiduous striving through the levels from the first to the sixth will lead to the realization of the
F seventh and eighth levels respectively. This, in turn, will lead to the ninth level where tranquil absorption will emerge effortlessly and naturally. With perfect mastery in tranquil absorption the meditator begins a session simply by reviving his resolve and mindfulness. Thus he will, in all subsequent sessions, attain complete absorption without the need for uninterrupted mindfulness and vigilance. Such an attainment may be compared to the analogy of a mastery in literacy. A beginner must always strive to perfect reading or chanting through unrelenting mindfulness and vigilance. Once mastered, it comes through effortlessly and naturally by simply getting into the act, for it does not need continued striving through mindfulness and vigilance.

The experience of absorption, endowed with bliss, lucidity, and nondiscrimination, will sometimes harmonize with the postabsorptive perception. Unskilled meditators assert this to be an excellent practice. But this meditational order considers it as an experience arising from a settled mind, but certainly not as an excellent practice. In fact, one may wonder if this is true tranquility. According to the sūtra meditation, tranquility is attained after
59 B perfect ease has been realized. Without achieving [perfect ease], no matter how good the tranquil absorption may be, it is merely a one-pointed concentration on the plane of desire. Not only that, but it is also far from being the main tranquility. It is not even regarded as "approximate tranquility"[82] because preparatory tranquility is stated to be one in which perfect ease must be realized. Therefore, a simple, one-pointed tranquility on the plane of desire is designated as being the "approximate tranquility," which is a nonabsorptive state, whereas the tranquility on the plane of sublime form is regarded as being on the level of absorption. However, the method by which the [beginner] meditator may achieve gradually the perfect ease is elucidated in the *Śrāvakabhūmi*:

> The meditator in one-pointed concentration, typical to those on the plane of desire, first attains a tractable mind at ease. To achieve this, he strives unhesitatingly and with increasing joy to maintain the meditation that vigorously unfolds a nondiscriminating awareness with inherent lucidity and bliss. Then, by virtue of this mind power, the internal air permeates the whole system of body and a perfect physical ease arises.

With this perfect ease, the next state of meditation incorporates the congenial factors, viz., differentiation, enthusiasm, quietude, increased joy, investigation, and assiduity. The meditation will advance through the levels,
160 F beginning with the preparatory contemplation known as the first tranquil state on the plane of sublime form. This will be followed by the realization

of advanced levels called absorptive evenness, associated with the plane of sublime form and the formless plane. The *Bhāvanākrama* provides a brief description of the four preparations for absorptive states:

> The first absorptive state is known as the unstirred process. The meditator experiences equanimity in which are carried on general and thorough examinations [of the psychophysical realities]. The first
> 160 B absorptive state is realized when the meditator who has purified himself of any sensual craving and harmful indulgences carries on the examination and analysis while in a state of joy and bliss. The special quality of this state is even attained when the examination itself ceases. When the processes of examination and analysis cease completely, yearning for the first absorptive state is pacified, and when joy, bliss, and inner lucidity permeate his whole being, the meditator has reached the second absorptive state. When yearning for the second absorptive state is pacified, joy, equanimity, mindfulness, and vigilance are accomplished, and he has reached the third absorptive state. When yearning for the third absorptive state is pacified, the meditator achieves a states of equanimity and mindfulness, free from the sensations of both misery and bliss. He has reached the fourth absorptive state.

No further explanation is offered here.

Once perfect ease is realized, even without repeating the tranquil absorption for many [days and] nights, the meditator will experience that nonvirtuous tendencies of his body and mind cease as joy and bliss permeate his whole stream-being. He will again be able to dwell in tranquil absorption. For instance, the supremely venerated Takpopa was able to remain in tranquil absorption for thirteen days and nights with a butter lamp placed on
161 F his head.The gurus of this meditational order regard the attained tranquil mind to be merely the basis or support for meditation. They also accept as tranquility the ability of a meditator, who has yet to achieve perfect ease, to actualize tranquility either effortlessly or with a minimum of effort. And this is regarded as an indication that he now be guided toward insight.

Three forms of one-pointed meditation on unified tranquility and insight are usually expounded. In this case, the method used is designed to help establish and master the virtuous practice of unified tranquility and insight rather than to exclusively strengthen tranquility. Regardless of the distinct nature of meditations on absorption, which every meditator seeks to master, every meditation is maintained by means of the three [supports]: mindfulness, vigilance, and effort. The way in which every tranquil absorption or equipoise is actualized and dawns remains the same in all cases. I see that the mastery of pure tranquility would be better for persons who are inclined toward the gradual path. The *Bodhicaryāvatāra* says:

3 ... with insight supported by tranquility...

Similarly, this meditational order has such sayings as "Where there is no contemplative tranquility, there is no insight" or "If one seeks insight too early, one will not achieve tranquility."

THE PURPOSE OF REALIZING TRANQUILITY

It is essential to accomplish tranquility of mind since this is the common ground of all [Buddhist] paths—mundane and supramundane.[83] The mundane path is comprised of the three planes of existence. Meditation on the plane of desire is designed to bring about a specific insight by eliminating the mind's defilement and strengthening psychological antidotes against negative thoughts. Based on the tranquil state, insight will perceive the spiritual level on the plane of desire as being unrefined while those on the plane of sublime form as being refined. An insight, arising from each level of the eight approximate and eight actual absorptions on the [higher] plane of the form and formless planes, perceives every preceding insight as being less refined, or every succeeding one as more refined. Tranquility, all along, forms the basis of insight.

52 F Similarly, tranquility on the supramundane path forms the basis for insight that perceives the four noble truths and exposes as false the sense of a personal self, according to the Primary Vehicle [Hīnayāna]. Tranquility is also essential for realizing the insight of nondual awareness, which focuses on the unreality of true self-entities [viz., personality and phenomena], according to the Mahāyāna path. Besides, tranquility is the foundation of such transcendental attributes as the four feet of miraculous transformation,[84] the [eight levels of] absorption on [the plane of sublime form and] the formless plane,[85] the eight processes of liberation,[86] the supranormal cognitions, and such absorptive powers as [the eight] overpowering contemplative manifestations,[87] and [the ten] all-encompassing contemplative transformations.[88] The first *Bhāvanākrama* summarizes:

> By carrying out the eight kinds of resolve to eliminate negative factors, one will realize tranquil absorption. Through such absorption the great power of miraculous transformation may be accomplished.

For similar reasons the sūtras urge us to meditate on the feet of miraculous transformation with the eight kinds of resolve. The same source says:

> Through a one-pointed concentration the meditator in due course will accomplish tractability [of body and mind] and will attain various levels of absorptive evenness, endowed with the special quality of

162 B visualization on the planes of form and formlessness as well as perfect liberation.

Moreover, tranquility is used for many purposes, such as subduing active emotionalities and releasing oneself from the bondage of dualistic marks. The principal purpose is to achieve insight. Of the two levels of insight—namely, (1) superficial and subtle insight of the transient world, which leads one to the pinnacle of the existential planes, and (2) transcending insight, which not only perceives reality as being devoid of an inborn self, but also eliminates the seed of existential bondage—transcending insight is the object of realization. Here, too, tranquility is the basis.

The reason why tranquility is sought is as follows. Since insight by nature is fluid, like a waterfall, or flickers, like a butter lamp in the mind, a settled equipoise cannot be achieved without [first realizing] tranquility. One can neither understand nor clearly perceive perfect reality as it is without realizing a settled equipoise. The first *Bhāvanākrama* comments:

> Because the mind is shaky, like water, it does not settle without the
> 163 F foundation of tranquility. The mind that has failed to achieve settled equipoise can in no way understand perfect reality as it is.

The middle *Bhāvanākrama* further explains this point:

> Insight without tranquility renders a yogin's mind susceptible to the distraction of sensory objects. Because it is unstable, like a butter lamp exposed to the wind, it fails to attain the illumination of awareness.

How then should one seek to realize tranquility? It is highly praiseworthy for someone to achieve simple tranquility on the preparatory level of the first concentrative absorption [on the plane of sublime form] as stated before. Failing that, one would do well to realize a one-pointed concentration on the plane of desire. Master Pawo in his *Ngakwö Ngaktö* describes:

> People who are blinded by ignorance,
> Who do not follow your teachings,
> Wander through the cycles of existence afflicted by miseries,
> Even if they reach the pinnacle of existence.
> Those who follow your teachings, even though they might not have realized
> The main absorptive state [on the plane of form],
> Turn away from the round of existence,
> Despite the forces of obstruction staring at them.

CHAPTER FOUR

Guiding Meditators on the Path: Insight

INTRODUCTION

3 B There are six sections on insight meditation:

1. The reason why meditation on insight is necessary
2. The preparatory practice for insight
3. The systems of meditation on insight
4. The relevant meditation on insight
5. The characteristics of emerging insight
6. The blending of insight with that of other systems

THE REASON WHY MEDITATION ON INSIGHT IS NECESSARY

Seekers of liberation and of all-knowing awareness would do well to meditate on insight—which perceives the nonselfhood of dualism—rather than remain content only with tranquil absorption. Without meditation on insight, tranquility alone cannot bring about liberation from the round of existence, because it can only bring about temporary pacification of inbred defilements and is incapable of eliminating them. The middle *Bhāvanākrama* maintains:

> Yogins cannot completely eliminate inner defilements by accomplishing
> 164 F ing tranquility alone. It temporarily pacifies, but cannot destroy defilements until and unless wisdom [insight] illuminates.

The *Ārya-saṃdhinirmocana-sūtra* reaffirms:

> Concentrative absorption subdues inner defilements whereas wisdom destroys their inbred sediments.

For these reasons those who wish to eliminate all defilements and attain the pure awareness should meditate on wisdom after having perfected settled tranquility. The *Samādhirāja* says:

> Even though men of the world meditate on tranquil absorption,
> Since this does not destroy consciousness of the self,
> Mental defilements will again stir up violently,
> As in Udraka's meditation on tranquil absorption.[89]
> One determines from every mode the selflessness of all things
> And meditates on discerning wisdom.
> One will achieve nirvāṇa through this source of fulfillment;
> No others will lead to such peace.

164 B People on the mundane level meditate on tranquil absorption, such as the four kinds of concentration, but tranquility by itself cannot destroy clinging to a self, which is the root of cyclic existence. The power of self-delusion causes the root and attendant defilements[90] to arise, which, in turn, lead one to commit harmful deeds and consequently to wander in the lower realms. The analogy for this is to be found in the meditation of such ascetics as Udraka who believed in an external creator. On the other hand, the determination of nonselfhood [in one's psychophysical aggregates] through discerning intellect followed by meditation will result in attaining permanent peace. No other means can completely eliminate misery and defilement.

THE PREPARATORY PRACTICE FOR INSIGHT

The *Saṃdhinirmocana* says that "perfect vision arising from listening and examining is the condition for realizing insight." The middle *Bhāvanākrama* mentions three sources of insight. They are associating with holy persons, listening to [the dharma] extensively, and then examining it perfectly. Holy persons in this case mean those who have realized tranquility and insight. Without such realization they cannot assimilate the true aim of life however proficient their scholarship may be in the conceptual doctrine
165 F with its assigned meanings.[91] Listening to the dharma extensively refers to those unblemished scriptures that reveal the ultimate doctrine. One may listen to the apparent teachings with conceptual terminology but they do not reveal the meaning of certainty. Even with respect to thorough examination, one should apply the instructions transmitted by the realized ones because sacred truth transcends dialectical investigation and examination.

One might wonder about the difference between the scriptures containing the contrived or intended meaning and those containing the true meaning. The former principally enunciates apparent reality through conceptual terms and definitions, while the latter reveals the view of ultimate reality that is deep and inconceivable. The *Lodrö Mizepae Tanpa* (*Akṣayamatinirdeśa-sūtra*) states:

> What are the ultimate-guidance sūtras and the provisional-guidance sūtras? The sūtras that expound the means of realizing apparent or conventional truth are designated as bearing an intentionally fabricated meaning. The sūtras that reveal the means of realizing the absolute truth are designated as bearing the true meaning. Concerning the sūtras that reveal diverse conceptual views, they are designated as bearing fictitious meaning conceived for guiding adherents gradually toward the profound truth. The sūtras revealing that which is deep, B difficult to perceive, and hard to realize are designated as those containing the true meaning.

What then are the apparent and true realities themselves? Apparent reality refers to the transient aspects of phenomena such as the self, life, sentient beings, living beings, etc. Ultimate reality is referred to as the [all-pervasive void of] phenomena characterized as nonarising, nonselfhood, etc. The same sūtra further states:

> The elucidations on the apparent truth are revealed in those sūtras—designated as containing the fabricated meanings—through diverse concepts and terms such as: self, life, sentient beings, living beings, human beings, personality, bearer of karma, and product of karma,[92] and performer of karma. Besides, the provisional-guidance sūtras speak of self when in reality no such self exists, simply in order to skillfully lead seekers to the illuminating truth. The elucidations of absolute truth are enshrined in those sūtras that bear the meaning of the entrances to liberation, such as the void, signlessness, aimlessness, the nonarising and unborn unreality of discrimination, consciousness, life, personality, self, and inborn controller.

The *Samādhirāja* reiterates the same points:

> The void revealed by He Who Attained The Sublime Peace
> [Sugata] is to be understood
> Through the specific sūtras containing the true meaning.
> The sūtras that refer to sentient beings, personality,
> Human beings, and all similar things are to be understood
> As containing the fabricated meanings.

This indeed is so. The factor that causes insight to emerge is stated to be the understanding of the vision of reality. Such an understanding may be gained by knowledge arising from listening to and examining the classical treatises—whether they are the teachings of Buddha or their exegetical texts by great saints and scholars—that elucidate unerringly and clearly the real meaning. This is followed by meditation with the requisite processes, namely, the elimination of dullness or thought flow, the control of sense faculties, vigilance of behavior, and moderation in food. This meditational order particularly considers that in order to realize the vision of true reality, the contemplation of guru yoga and fervent supplication for blessing are vitally important. The second section of the *Hevajra-tantra* elucidates:

> This spontaneous coemergence[93] can neither be described by any external means
> Nor can it be discovered anywhere
> Except by receiving a timely empowerment from a guru
> And by virtue of one's own spiritual merits.

Again the same text says:

166 B
> This inmost perceiving awareness transcends all verbal expressions.
> Being an object of contemplation it arises
> Through the guru's blessings.
> Such is the awareness of the all-knowing ones.

THE SYSTEMS OF MEDITATION ON INSIGHT

Among the many levels of insight are superficial and subtle insights according to the transient world, and insight into the four aspects of truth according to the exponents of the Primary Vehicle [Hīnayāna]. They are excellent in their own way, but are not indispensable [in this tradition]. Insight into the truth of selflessness is the one to be sought here because it is through this that the abiding nature of the realities that manifest in duality must be determined. Regarding the process of awakening such insight, the *Saṃdhinirmocana-sūtra* and *Abhidharmasamuccaya* elucidate the four kinds of insight in their extensive forms. The former text refers to three kinds of insight in their average forms, and also to insight that perceives the two
167 F categories of selflessness—in a condensed form. With regard to the two selflessnesses, most expounders of Buddha's teachings and logic, having relied on the exegetical treatises of Nāgārjuna and Asaṅga, spoke extensively about the methods of meditating on the vision of emptiness. This vision emerges from the fact of having determined all dualities as being unreal by examining them through the great rational formulae such as "the mutual exclusion of one and many." There were those in Tibet who had realized the perfect vision of intrinsic reality through these doctrinal systems. Nowadays most meditators seem to contemplate the overall meaning of emptiness by relying upon inferential judgement. With the support of the original exposition and logic I stated earlier, this kind of approach reduces emptiness to a

conceptualized pseudo-emptiness such as the emptiness conceived through a complete negation, the emptiness of inertia, and so on.

This stage concerns itself with the way of realizing the vision of [all-encompassing] emptiness through contemplation on the mind alone and then through determination of all dualities [as being devoid of an inherent essence], which is elucidated thus in the instructions on directly actualizing
B valid reality. This method is based on the major and minor treatises including the miscellaneous instructions that were transmitted down from great Saraha, Śavari, and the sovereign yogin Tilopa. They contain a wealth of powerful methods, capable of bringing about the realization of great aspiration through little hardship. It is also amazing that this approach is virtually identical with those contained in the sūtra meditational treatises such as the *Prajñāpāramitopadeśa*, the three *Bhāvanākrama* of Kamalaśīla, and the *Madhyamakopadeśa* of Atīśa. Such being the case, I shall elucidate this system to the best of my ability.

The relevant meditation on insight consists of

1. Determining the intrinsic nature of diverse mental perceptions
2. Clearing assumptions and skepticism about the basic root [of saṃsāra and nirvāṇa]

Determining the intrinsic nature of diverse mental perceptions is divided into three parts:

1. The reason why one achieves insight into the mind
2. The determination of the mind's true nature as being the basis for everything
3. The determination of mind's dynamic manifestations

THE RELEVANT MEDITATION ON INSIGHT: DETERMINING THE INTRINSIC NATURE OF DIVERSE MENTAL PERCEPTIONS

The Reason Why One Achieves Insight on the Mind

All realities are generally shown to be mind-made. The consequences or benefits of not meditating or meditating on the true meaning of the mind have been stated before. The deficiencies of saṃsāra and the virtues of
168 F nirvāṇa are precisely dependent on the mind or originated from it; hence the importance of meditating on the mind. The *Dharmasaṃgīti-sūtra* states:

> Thus the bodhisattva Vikrāntamati spoke: Illuminated Conqueror, what has been designated as dharma is the dharma that neither dwells

> in any sensory objects nor in any spatial dimension. On the other hand, the dharma based on mind is an exception. Therefore, one should gain a complete hold on the mind, reach its ultimate level, tame it thoroughly, settle it in absolute evenness, and subdue it completely.

Similarly it is said that understanding the mind means understanding all things, and liberating the mind means liberating it from all forms of bondage. According to the *Ārya-Ratnamegha-sūtra*:

> The mind precedes all things. Only by understanding [the nature of] the mind will one gain the understanding of all things.

The *Atyayajñāna-sūtra* remarks:

> Because understanding the mind means transcending awareness,
> One should meditate perfectly on it with a resolve
> Never to seek buddhahood through any other means.

B Saraha comments on meditation:

> If one binds the mind, it will be overpowered by bondage.
> If released, it will remain free from doubt.

And he says further:

> Oh, if only ignorant beings would direct the mind toward an inward examination,
> They would achieve liberation from all erroneous views.
> If they would settle perfectly in that state,
> Through the power of great bliss,
> They would gain the sacred realization.

Tilopa also says:

> Just as cutting the roots of a tree
> Full of branches and leaves causes the death of all its myriad branches,
> So it is with cutting off the roots of saṃsāra.

Thus, by cutting the root of the mind's delusion, the stream of cyclic existence is said to cease. According to Śāntideva, ignorance of the mind is the cause of all miseries. On the other hand, understanding and gaining control of the mind is described as the best of all self-mortifications. He says in the *Bodhicaryāvatāra*:

> If he does not understand the secret of the mind
> Which represents the supreme, sublime dharma,
> He will wander in vain,
> However much he desires happiness and loathes misery.

And again he says:

> Thus, one should have a firm grip on the mind, should guard it vigilantly;
> Other than watching the mind—the only form of self-mortification—
> What benefit can one gain by practicing self-mortification?

Some exponents of philosophical concepts argue that "it has been said that liberation may be achieved by meditating on the void. If liberation is achieved by meditating on the mind or by assuming the mind to be of primordial enlightenment, then it would mean that all sentient beings will achieve liberation without any effort." Such an argument indicates that they discriminate the void as being good and the mind evil. This exposes their negative understanding of intrinsic reality and their personal deficiencies due to utter lack of learning. I will explain gradually how the characteristics of the void are identical with the abiding nature of the mind and, similarly, how meditation on the two is identical. Since meditators can understand it from the latter explanation, no further elucidation is given here.

Concerning the exposition that the mind's intrinsic nature is primordial enlightenment, the *Laṅkāvatāra-sūtra* elucidates:

> The intrinsic nature of mind is detached from discrimination;
> It is this state with which consciousness seeks transmutation.
> Because it is awareness of all things,
> I proclaim this mind to be enlightenment.

The *Kālacakra-mūlatantra* states:

> 9 B The innate mind of sentient beings is luminous clarity;
> From the beginning it is detached
> From the absolute attributes of arising, ceasing, and settling.
> Since beginningless time it has been the primordial supreme Buddha,
> Because it has been unmodulated by cause and condition.

The *Dügyü* (*Tantrasaṃgraha*)[94] comments:

> All sentient beings are buddhas because no other great buddhas exist in the transient plane of the universe.

The *Vajraḍākinī-tantra* says:

> A sentient being is a primordial buddha
> By virtue of understanding his own mind.

The *Hevajra-tantra* adds:

Nowhere in this transient plane of the universe
Can one find a buddha,
For the mind is a complete buddha,
And no other buddha has been revealed.

The *Jampal Zheylung* (*Dvikramatattvabhāvanā-nāma mukhāgama*) summarizes:

If one realizes the intrinsic nature of the mind,
Which is supreme among all things,
One is on the level of buddhahood!

This profound method for realizing primordial buddhahood is characterized as being the meditation on mind. How through that a perfect liberation may be achieved, the *Yulkhor Khyongyi Zhupai Dho* (*Rāṣṭrapālaparipṛcchā-sūtra*) explains:

170 F By relying upon and meditating on the mind
One should understand everything to be empty!

The *Vajrapañjara* states:

Motivated by the precious mind [bodhicitta]
One meditates on the intrinsic nature of mind
And thereby attains enlightenment.
This dawning of the sacred truth is buddhahood!

And again, the same text says:

The meditation on the indivisibility on the void, awareness, and compassion
Represents the expounded path
Of Buddha, dharma and saṅgha.

One should know the meditation indicated by such conceptual terms as "the relative mind of enlightenment,"[95] and "the ultimate mind of enlightenment."[96]

The Determination of the Mind's True Nature As Being the Basis for Everything

There are four sections:

1. Which of the scriptures deal with this subject?
2. The actual stages of this meditation
3. How this meditation compares with the original exposition
4. How to determine the nature of the mind

Which of the Scriptures Deal with This Subject?

One may wonder which of the scriptures deal with meditation on the vision of reality, which arises from insight and which is capable of resolving doubts and assumptions. Such a vision is attained after having determined that all things are only mind created, and that even the mind's intrinsic nature is devoid of true essence. The *Sūtrālaṃkara* illustrates this:

> Understand that nothing exists apart from the mind.
> Know that the mind itself is unreal
> An intelligent person, comprehending the unreality of the two,
> Settles in the expanse of the nondual reality."

The *Bodhicittavivaraṇa* expounds:

> Having once established pure idealism,
> Blessed seekers reject the reality of mind itself.
> For the exponents of the Consciousness Only school
> All the diverse appearances are the manifestation of mind.
> What then is the self-nature of consciousness?
> This is to be elucidated here.
> "All things are but a product of the mind,"
> The Supreme Sage expounded
> To protect seekers with childish minds who might otherwise be terrified,
> Even though this statement was not truly so.
> All the conceptually designated, dependent conditionality
> And established reality are but empty.[97]
> This is the singular essence of the abiding reality,
> And should be determined in terms of one's own mind.
> For those who delight in the Great Vehicle,
> Reality is perfectly even, without a self-essence,
> Because the mind is nonarising right from the beginning.
> Thus it was summarized by Buddha.

The first *Bhāvanākrama* elaborates:

F ... Thus, one contemplates that the three planes of phenomenal existence are the product of the mind only, and then one realizes that everything conceptually designated is simply of mental origin. If one examines every aspect of the mind, one is analyzing the intrinsic nature of all phenomena. In so examining one may further examine in the following manner. The mind as such cannot be real from the standpoint of ultimate truth. How can the mind be real when it clings to images of what are essentially false sensory forms, etc., manifesting themselves externally in diverse appearances? Just as sensory forms, etc. are false, so the mind is also false since it is not any different from the former. The senses—emerging in diverse forms—are devoid of either one or many essences. The reality of the mind is not different from the senses; it is also devoid of either one or many essences. For these reasons the mind by nature is indeed like a magical scene. Like the mind, all phenomena in their intrinsic nature are also like a magical scene.

Similar elucidations are found in other treatises on the stages of meditation.

The Actual Stages of This Meditation

171 B During the earlier meditation on tranquil absorption the settling of mind in a nondiscriminating absorption[98] was predominant. Here, in this meditation on insight, the analyses of mind through discerning wisdom should be the predominant factor. By settling the mind in undistracted tranquility, one enhances the quality of mind's lucidity and then examines this state. Here the method of determining the mind's innate essence is similar to those of the sūtra tradition for determining selflessness of personality. To meditate on insight at this stage, the body posture should be the same as stated before. As for the manner of gazing, one should keep the eyes wide open, watching, looking straight ahead, just the way Saraha states:

> In seeking the pure awareness beyond meditation,
> It is also said, "Meditating with open eyes
> Surpasses all other meditational methods."

He also says:

> Meditators of the brahmanic order look upward,
> Calm śrāvakas look downward,
> While [mystics] gaze straight ahead with "vajra eyes."[99]

172 F A meditator should first settle his mind in tranquil equipoise, which is both clear and nondiscriminating. He should then let the mind focus sharply on itself in a relaxed manner as if "gazing" inwardly or outwardly. To determine the nature of mind, meditational analysis is applied. The examination concerns itself with structure, luminosity, basis, support, identity, and mode. The analysis begins with the structure of mind to find out if it has a certain form, like round or square, or the shape of the ground, a stone, a rock, of a human being, or of any particular animal. The examination is then shifted to other processes to find out whether the mind has any color: white, black, red, etc. and also whether the mind has an inbred basis or support, an

external kind like another sentient being, a material object, or even a specific basis within one's own body. Should the mind appear to rest on one's body, the meditator should examine if it rests on any particular part or portion of the body between the head and heels or if it permeates the whole body. If the mind appears to rest on the whole body, the meditator should find out exactly where it rests, whether inside, outside, or on the integrated realm of the two. If the mind appears to rest on the integrated realm, the meditator should examine how the mind projects toward form or any objects.

In determining the mind's innate identity or manifesting mode the meditator should examine if the mind can be identified with the void or with the formlessness of the void. To determine if the mind has a definite manifesting mode, the meditator examines if it can be identified with the lucidity or with the form of lucidity. Should the mind appear to be of the void state, the meditator should examine if it is a nonexistent void or the void like that of space. Should the mind appear to be of luminosity, the meditator should examine if this luminosity is like the radiance of the sun, moonshine, or the flame of a butter lamp, or if it is inborn lucidity without light or color. Thus, the meditator should examine the mind in numerous ways. No definite understanding or determinable certainty can be achieved regarding the mind's abiding reality through mere knowledge or intellectual comprehension and without thorough examination. A meditator should therefore examine thoroughly with a persistence in the manner of an inquisitive person crushing a bone with a stone!

73 F Having arrived through such an investigation at the conclusion that no aspect of things—external or internal—is composed of any core substance, one then meditates on the tranquil mind in a unified state of clarity and emptiness. The one who has not realized the true nature of the mind, apart from experiencing a settled tranquility, should perform a contemplative supplication to the gurus with intense faith and veneration. When in a resumed meditation he experiences the clarity of mind [nondiscriminating awareness] or the void, he should examine each in terms of its mode of existence. By doing so, he will find himself at an utter loss, being unable to describe [the awareness of inner reality] in terms of form or color, basis or support, identity or manifesting mode; he will experience a kind of complete inward cognition, which is an inmost lucid awareness.[100] This lucidity is neither luminous nor colorful, and like an inner emptiness, it is devoid of any identity. It remains a perceivable experience when mindfulness is present. When mindfulness is diverted, the awareness leaves the mind at once, reverting back to an ordinary level. Such a stage indicates that a
173 B relevant experience has dawned. At that time the meditator concentrates—with mindfulness remaining undistracted not even for a moment—on the awareness that is self-cognizing but unidentifiable. Then, without losing the mindfulness, he examines that state with a discerning intellect. No exami-

nation should be conducted with the mind inclined to be distracted as in case of ordinary thinking.

Saraha comments:

> O, you should look inwardly for the sign of intrinsic reality.
> By failing to watch your mind attentively
> And thereby getting distracted,
> You will not see the very intrinsic nature of the mind!

The *Bhāvanākrama* concludes:

> Thus, when the mind is firmly settled in tranquility, one should examine it with a discerning intellect so that perception of pure awareness will emerge.

How This Meditation Compares with the Original Exposition

The followers of the meditative order describe the aforesaid meditation as
174 F discovering the mind. Some [critics] argue that there is nothing to discover since the mind is not composed of any substance. It is an exercise in futility to search for something that does not exist. By such a statement they reveal their ignorance concerning the vital significance of ultimate reality. On the term "discovering the mind" the *Ratnakūṭa* states:

> Thus one should search the mind fully.

The *Tsugna Rinpochey Dho* (*Ratnacūḍaparipṛcchā-sūtra*) concurs:

> One should make a complete search for the mind.

The *Sumchu Tsasumpai Liu* (*Trayastriṃśat-parivarta*) adds:

> A learned person should search for the intrinsic nature of the mind.
> In his search he perceives the mind and its intrinsic nature,
> For there is no innate essence, neither in the mind thus sought
> Nor in the seeker himself.

Many similar passages are found in the scriptures. Searching for the mind through a contemplative analysis—even though [the mind] is not composed of any substance—serves the purpose of realizing that the mind is empty of an innate essence. The *Bhāvanākrama* quotes the *Phakpa Könchoktrin* (Ārya-ratnamegha):

174 B If those who meditate on the void analyze every discursive thought and every joyous contemplative state, they will realize that everything is void [free from an essence]. If they examine what the mind is, they will realize that it is void. If they search for the essence of the investigating

mind, they will realize that it is also void. By realizing this, they will elevate themselves to inmost purity, detached from the mark [of duality].

Concerning the search for or examination of the mind, the *Dharmadhātu-prakṛtyasambheda-nirdeśa* of the *Ratnakūṭa* states:

> [The incarnate monk said:] O venerable ones, examine your mind in order to determine if it is identical with what has been designated as blue, yellow, red, white, maroon, or a crystal shade, or if it is pure, impure, eternal, impermanent, material, or immaterial.
>
> They [the multitude of monks] replied: O venerable one, the mind is formless, undemonstrable, without appearance, intangible, groundless, and invisible.
>
> Thereupon the incarnate monk spoke: O venerable ones, concerning the mind which is formless, undemonstrable, without appearance, intangible, groundless, and invisible, can it be conceived as dwelling inside, outside, or in between?
>
> The monks replied: No sir, this is not so.
>
> The incarnate monk asked: Venerable ones, if the mind is formless, undemonstrable, without appearance, intangible, groundless, and invisible, then there is nothing to observe inside, outside, or in between. Do you suppose that it has not evolved as a perfect reality?
>
> They replied: No sir, this is not so.

5 B The *Ratnakūṭa* says:

> Search for the mind should be conducted thus: What is a lustful mind, a hateful mind, or an ignorant mind? Has the mind emerged in the past, does it do so in the present, or will it do so in the future? Very well, you should contemplate the fact that the past mind has ceased to exist, that the future mind has yet to arise, and that the present mind does not endure. O, Osung (Kāśyapa), the mind cannot be perceived as dwelling inside, outside, or even inbetween. O, Osung, concerning the nature of mind, there is nothing to investigate, nothing to demonstrate, nothing to support, nothing to make it appear, and nothing of visible form.

Again, the Buddha explains in the *Ratnakūṭa*:

> O, Osung, one does not find the mind through a complete search. Whatever is undiscoverable cannot be conceived. Whatever is inconceivable did not arise in the past, nor will it in the future, nor does it

176 F arise at the present time. That which is neither past, nor future, nor present indeed transcends the three periods of time. That which so transcends the three periods of time cannot be construed as either existing or nonexisting.

The *Ratnacūṭa-sūtra* states:

> He who searches for the mind cannot find it inside or outside of himself, or both outside and inside. He can neither find it in his psychophysical aggregates, in the elemental realms, nor in the sense faculties. Then, because he cannot find the mind, he explores inwardly the stream of his mind with the assumption that a thought arises from a perceptive image. He contemplates whether a perceptive image and mind exist distinctly from one and another or whether they are iden-
> 176 B tical. If the image is separate from the mind, then there are two kinds of mind. If the image is the mind itself, then how can the mind "see" the mind, because the mind cannot "see" the mind itself.

The *Namnang Ngönjang* (*Vairocanābhisambodhi*) further elucidates:

> [Buddha Vajradhara:] O Master of the Secret Path [Guhyapati], if a seeker wishes to understand his own mind he explores it in this manner. One examines the mind in order to find out if it has any form, color, or shape, or if it exists as a sense object, or as form, feeling, cognition, mental categories, or consciousness, or if it is identical with the sense of "I," "mine," or with subjective or objective phenomena. One continues to determine if inner reality exists as a pure or impure entity, or exists in the elemental realms, or the sense formations. Despite this exhausitve investigation one will not find the mind!

The same text provides the guidance:

> [Buddha Vajradhara:] O Master of the Secret Path, a seeker should strive hard for enlightenment and all-knowingness in terms of his own mind. Why? Because the mind in its intrinsic nature is completely
> 177 F pure. The mind cannot be conceived as existing inside, outside, or in between the body. O Master of the Secret Path, the mind has never been seen by all fully enlightened, supremely attained ones—who conquered inner adversaries—nor will they ever see it. Being formless, the mind has no color such as blue, yellow, red, white, maroon, or crystal shade. The mind has no shape either short or long, either round or square; it is neither light nor dark. It has no sexual identity such as female, male, or sexless.
>
> O Master of the Secret Path, the mind is not of the nature of either the plane of desire, the plane of sublime form, or of the plane of formless-

ness. It is not of the nature of any classes of sentient beings such as celestial beings, nāgas, kuberas, gandharvas, demigods [asuras] garu-
3 ḍas, kinnaras,[101] great serpents, humans, and nonhumans. O Master of the Secret Path, the mind does not reside in the eyes, nor in the body, nor in the consciousness. Why? The mind has the characteristics of space, because it is by nature detached from all thoughts and discriminations.

The sūtras and the tantras are replete with many such words of wisdom. In summary, it has been stated that examination of the mind has to be so exhaustive as to embrace all the external and internal phenomena with special reference to color, shape, dwelling place, support, identity, and mode of mind. Only after a thorough examination will one understand that the nature of mind is formless, undemonstrable, without basis externally or internally, and is detached from discriminating thoughts. Thus, the intrinsic nature of mind is identical with space! The *Bodhicittavivaraṇa* expounds:

> The mind is but a conceptual designation.
> Nothing exists apart from this designation.
> Perceive it as being a designation—pure and simple.
> Even the very designation is devoid of any innate reality.
> 78 F The victorious buddhas have not discovered it,
> Neither within, without, nor in between.
> The mind with its illusory nature
> Is devoid of color, shape, an objective or subjective essence, a male, female, or sexless identity.
> The mind by nature does not have a basis.
> In short, enlightened ones have neither seen the mind
> Nor will they see it.
> Since the mind is devoid of a self-essence
> How can they see it?

The *Chödü* (*Śikṣasamuccaya*) quotes the *Teshin Shekpa Tamchekyi Menngak Yangdakpar Drowa*:

> The mind is something that is hard [for an ordinary mind] to comprehend perfectly; it has always been the object of attention of or associated intimately with the buddhas. It is not so with those who seek inner solace through external means. The mind is devoid of a foundation, dwelling, basis, shape, or color. Because of its intrinsic nature the mind is not only detached from any mark of dualism, but it transcends the senses and is beyond the reach of dialecticians.

And again the same text says:

178 B Being formless or colorless, mind in reality is a simple lucid state, identical with space. Like ultimate reality, the mind's true nature is hard to grasp.

How to Determine the Nature of the Mind

One now endeavors to systematically determine the mind through meditational methods such as those already described. The meditator will ultimately perceive the mind [in its natural simplicity]. Apart from being incorporeal, formless, colorless, or without a dwelling or support, the mind is—like space—empty of any identity and unaffected by any concepts. The mind is even beyond its manifest expressions! The *Mahākaruṇānirdeśa-sūtra* states:

> Mind is like space; it has the nature of space;
> Equal to space, it encompasses everything.

The *Jamzhukyi Dho* (*Maitreyaparipṛcchā-sūtra*) remarks:

> [Maitreya:] O Illuminated Conqueror, how should one observe the mind inwardly?
>
> [Buddha:] Like space, the mind is without shape.

The *Vairocanābhisambodhi* adds:

> 179 F Mind bears the characteristics of space, because it is detached from thoughts and discriminations.

Numerous expositions compare the mind to space. Saraha advises:

> Comprehend the mind to be similar to space,
> Comprehend the mind to be of the nature of space!

Śavari concurs:

> The mind that is cut at the root[102] is like space.

Even though the mind is repeatedly compared to space, this analogy points to a meditative state of nondiscrimination that arises as a result of the dissolution of the discerning process through which the analysis of the mind has been conducted. The way this nondiscriminating state has emerged is shown here to be identical with the way mental images fade away while one gazes at space. Tilopa repeats the analogy:

> Just as perceived images fade away
> While one gazes at the expanse of space,
> So do discriminating thoughts

When one watches the [inmost expanse of] mind,
And illumination is attained.
For example, mist and clouds loom over a wide space,
And neither proceed toward any destination nor do they dwell
anywhere.
9 B Likewise, although discriminating thoughts arise from [the inner
expanse] of mind,
These thought waves dissolve themselves when the meditator
perceives the mind.

And he says again:

Just as empty space is designated with a term,
But there is nothing to predicate space as being such and such,
So is the mind described as being of luminous clarity,
Yet there is no ground for designating how and what the mind is
composed of,
Because the nature of the mind is identical with that of space.

Śavari declares:

However completely one explores the entire space,
Seeing will completely cease, for space is infinite.
Similarly, one explores inner and outer reality,
But one will not find any essence—not even a subatomic particle!
The mind thus explored is inconceivable;
Hence seeing nothing is seeing it indeed.

The *Kāśyapaparipṛcchā-sūtra* elucidates:

Fire emerges by rubbing two sticks together,
Yet the rising flame consumes the sticks.
180 F Similarly, a discerning process is activated by analytical wisdom,
Yet the wisdom consumes the dualistic thoughts.

Starting the meditation on insight one examines the mind by means of discerning intellect. When the process of discrimination is finally pacified, a nonconceptual awareness arises. If one wonders whether some difference exists between mind and space, the answer is: "Yes, there is!" Space is not self-cognizing awareness! The realization of mind is said to be self-cognizing awareness. The *Saṃdhinirmocana* comments:

Self-cognizing awareness lies in the realm of marklessness [beyond
sensory perception];
It is undefinable, avoids any conceptual formulations,
And is beyond the scope of intellectual disputation.
By its characteristics it transcends all dialectical limitations.

The *Gongpa Lungtangyi Dho* (*Saṃdhivyākaraṇa-sūtra*) describes:

> Concerning the definitive meaning of an enlightened mind,
> One has to ascertain it repeatedly.
> Such a mind is neither within nor without, nor both.
> 180 B It is neither mutable, nor eternal, nor momentary,
> For it is self-cognizing awareness.

The second section of the *Hevajra-tantra* says:

> For this self-cognizing awareness is in the realm of transcendence,
> Beyond the avenue of speech.

And it again says:

> By inwardly cognizing this self-awareness,
> One will achieve enlightenment.

These sublime words identify the meaning of inmost awareness with that of ultimate reality. Being an immutable bliss, it is beyond sensory perceptions, conception, and definition. In this respect, the term "self-cognizing awareness" simply signifies an understanding of its primordial nature—which is completely detached from all perceptive marks—as a result of having examined the mind. Self-awareness does not mean that it encounters an identifiable object and cognizes it the way a visual image is perceived through the contact between the eyes and an object. Tilopa makes this clear:

> Lo! This is self-awareness!
> It surpasses all avenues of speech and thought.
> 181 F I, Tilopa, have nothing to reveal.
> You should know it yourself through inward examination.

In this respect, some untutored [meditators]—having experienced the sensation of the even state of tranquility, the meditation known as "mind watching the mind"—asserted that they had achieved insight into the mind. Others asserted that they had gained insight into the mind when they perceived some perceptive visions, due to the activation of hidden psychic imprints, even though they held on to them as solid forms. There were still others who asserted that they had gained insight into the mind when actually they were forcefully clinging to the sensation. They perceived either mind's clarity or intrinsic emptiness, and they not only clung to the experience but also sought to repeat it. All of these [meditators] seem to lack a definite understanding with respect to the mind's abiding reality, which is detached from all perceptive marks. Besides, they were overcome by clinging to the appearance of experience arising from an interaction of immediate causes and conditions.

The term "seeing the mind" is a simple designation for understanding the mind's unreality that is detached from the beginning from all modes of existence or nonexistence. The nature of mind is such that there is nothing—not even the infinitesimal end of a hair—that is a conceivable or perceptible object or observer. The intrinsic nature of mind is undefinable and unimaginable, yet it is timeless and immutable. The *Prajñāpāramitā-saṃcayagāthā* explains it thus:

> Sentient beings speak of having seen the sky,
> But one should examine how one has seen the sky!
> In the same manner the Tathāgata has shown
> The way of seeing reality.

Saraha says:

> The nature of mind is pure like space from the beginning.
> In the process of looking, seeing comes to an end.

Śavari elaborates:

> In the process of searching for all that manifests as mind and matter
> There is neither anything to be found nor is there any seeker,
> For to be unreal is to be unborn and unceasing
> In the three periods of time.
> That which is immutable
> Is the state of great bliss.

He further states:

> In the act of self watching the self,
> A solitary self remains;
> In observing this self, one does not see it.
> This is undefinable where there is neither observer nor observation.
> Who can comprehend
> That which is undefinable?

Nāropa comments:

> The mind has the nature of luminous clarity,
> Wherein there is no substance,
> Not even the infinitesimal end of a hair.

Beginners may gain an experience of such an undefinable state, coupled with mindfulness and awareness of certainty. This is stated in the *Tingdzin Tampe Dho*:

> By focusing the mind
> On the suchness of intrinsic reality,
> Which is so similar to the mind,
> One will gain an undefinable experience.

Tilopa describes:

Amidst the intrinsic reality of nondiscriminating simplicity,
There emerges a sudden illumination of awareness[103]
With regard to intrinsic reality, which is completely detached from all concepts.

Maitrīpa concludes:

The mind is simply the flux of consciousness:
A force of air-energy, it is without self-nature.

The Determination of Mind's Dynamic Manifestations and Dualistic Appearances

This is divided into three sections:

1. Showing all appearances to be the products of mind
2. The realization of mind, which will bring about an insight into all appearances
3. The actual stage of this meditation

Showing All Appearances to Be the Products of Mind

182 B To those who have not gained insight into the suchness of the mind, all discriminating thoughts arising from the dynamic power of the mind and all appearances such as form, sound, etc. appear to be real and distinct from the mind owing to their inner delusion. In reality they are only manifestations of the mind. The *Laṅkāvatāra* explains:

External reality appears as such to human beings
From whose minds originate diverse dualities
Due to an interaction between their discriminating thoughts and psychic imprints.
External reality is the product of the mind;
All appearances are, therefore, completely unreal,
For they are all the manifestations of the mind!

The *Vajrapañjara* states:

Form, sound, smell, flavor, and touch
Arise from interacting causes and conditions,
Characterized as being the product of this precious mind.

These sensory cognitions are pacified in the all-encompassing
supreme reality.
Concerning form, feeling, cognition, mental categories, and
consciousness,
Those are all products of the mind,
For the Enlightened Sage did not indicate otherwise.

How then do manifestations such as form appear to be external reality? The mind—having been unaware of its intrinsic reality and unable to rely on itself—conceived the duality of itself and others. Attachment to and dis-
F crimination of dualism continuously stored the seeds of defilement, which so deluded the mind that all appearances seem to be external reality. The *Laṅkāvatāra* comments:

External reality appears as such to the mind,
Which has been distorted by psychic sediment.[104]
Apart from the mind, no external reality exists.
To perceive it so would be an utter distortion.

The *Vajrapañjara* concurs:

Since the beginningless state of existence,
External reality has been perceived as such.
But all things are the manifestations of the mind,
Because everything is the projection of the mind.

If that is so, how is it that not only external phenomena appear as such but even exist as real, marked with the quality of solidity? Because the mind formed a complex sediment of delusion,[105] things appear not only as external, but even as solid reality. For this reason Saraha states:

When stirred constantly by [cold] air
183 B Even gently flowing water solidifies like a rock;
When a confused mind is stirred by a craving for dualism,
Even the formless becomes solid.

Such is the analogy for the meaning of "hardened psychic imprint." In any case, a mere appearance before a deluded mind cannot be true reality. For it is like a distorted vision in which strands of hair or dark patches appear to people with infected eyes. Though to the infected eyes this distorted vision appears real, yet it does not to normal eyes. One may wonder if there is an external appearance at all by which to understand the abiding nature of the mind. There is not. As long as one's collective karma and seeds of delusion—which are like the eye infection—remain unaltered, a mere knowledge of the way the mind was overcome with delusion or of what abiding reality means cannot alter external appearance, since such knowledge, like that of the eye infection, is mere information. Virūpa wrote:

If unsettled in an awakened state,
One is distracted by grasping of perceptions,
One cannot alter the psychic imprint of dualism.[106]
Even though one knows that the lingering of dark patches
184 F Means an eye infection,
One cannot eliminate it
Until and unless the disease has been cured.

However, when one realizes unerringly the abiding nature of the mind, appearances will not cease but will emerge as indistinguishable from the intrinsic nature of the mind. The *Vajrapañjara* clarifies:

All appearances such as form
Do not have any external reality apart from the mind.
They are all but manifestations of the mind.

The *Bodhicittavivaraṇa* states:

All the conceptually designated, dependent conditionality,
And established reality have the one intrinsic quality of emptiness.
This the meditator should determine with respect to his mind.

The Realization of Mind, Which Will Bring About an Insight into All Appearances

Saraha comments:

Since the mind alone is the seed of all [possibilities],
It is this that unfolds saṃsāra and nirvāṇa.

The mind alone is thus stated to be the root of all realities, saṃsāra and nirvana. He further says:

184 B Intrinsic in everything projected by the mind
Is the nature of the Enlightened Master.
Existence and its evenness [inner emptiness]
Are of the nature of space.
Are the sea and its waves distinctly separate?

All that which is projected by the mind is thus stated to be nothing but the nature of the mind. A sūtra describes the nature of the mind:

Mind does not possess a mental entity
Because the mind's intrinsic nature is luminous clarity.

The nature of the mind is thus described to be of emptiness in luminosity. Therefore, if one realizes the mind's intrinsic nature as being of emptiness, one automatically can realize emptiness as being the nature of external appearances. A sūtra comments on the universality of intrinsic emptiness:

> If one understands suchness [of mind's emptiness],
> One will understand suchness of all things.

Āryadeva provides a similar comment:

> He who sees suchness of one thing,
> Will see suchness of all things.

Again he says in the *Catuḥśataka*:

> Whoever has a [perfect] vision of one thing,
> Has the [perfect] vision of all things,
> For the emptiness of one thing
> Is the emptiness of all things.

He who is an analyst or visionary of the nature of one thing such as form is an analyst or visionary of the nature of all other sense objects. Similarly, the emptiness of the self-essence of one thing such as form is the emptiness of the self-essence of all other sense objects. Atīśa in his *Satyadvaya* says:

> Where emptiness is concerned
> There is not even one division.

A meditator would do well to understand the method of determining all external appearances by extending the logical investigation previously applied in order to determine the essence of the mind. As stated in the *Samādhirāja*:

> Just as you understand cognition of the self,
> So should you apply your intellect to all other things.
> Since all phenomena remain ever pure, unstained by any inborn essence,
> 5 B They are as pure as space.
> Through one thing one will know all things,
> Through one thing one will see all things.

As it has thus been stated that by knowing or seeing the nature of one thing one will know or see the nature of all other things, this meditational order also holds the same view as indicated in this phrase: "Through knowing one, everything will unfold itself."

While determining—at this juncture—the essence of external appearances, one must perceive the unity of the two: the intrinsic emptiness of all appearances, which are unstained by any essence, and the appearances emerging ceaselessly.

The *Bodhicittavivaraṇa* describes the nondual state of reality:

> As rock sugar has the nature of sweetness,
> And fire has the nature of heat,
> Likewise, all things have the nature of emptiness.
> This has been so affirmed!

Again the same text states:

> Apparent reality is stated to be empty [of essence].
> Emptiness itself means apparent reality.
> Ascertain this through the logic of mutual exclusion,
> Because it is identical with the interdependence
> Of what is conditioned and impermanent.

186 F *The Actual Stage of This Meditation*

At this stage, the determination of thoughts and appearances is similar to the determination of the selflessness of things according to the sūtra system. Although the different mental events are the manifestations of the mind, they are individually analyzed in order to gain immediate and better understanding. To determine thoughts first, one should adopt the aforesaid procedure for the body posture and manner of gazing. The meditator settles the mind briefly—without a moment's distraction—in a tranquil equipoise, a state in which there is an unidentifiable union of the mind's lucidity and emptiness. Soon, in the same state, he visualizes or revives deliberately a vivid and vehement emotionality such as violent anger. Immediately upon its emergence he looks at it penetratingly and begins to analyze every aspect of it. He seeks to find out if this emotion has any perceptible shape or color, a base or a support, or an identifiable essence or a form. He repeats this examination many times in the proper order as shown before. Should he fail to cause such emotionality to arise, he is left with no object of inward investigation. The mind should thus be briefly diverted and then an emotion
186 B of hatred should be aroused by recollecting how a certain personal enemy had afflicted him with injury and harassment. He then examines it. Similarly, during other sessions, he arouses an emotion of lust for an object of sensuality so that he may examine it. This method of examining may be extended to other crude emotionalities. Similarly, he should arouse or recollect a less powerful thought and then subject it to thorough examination. By so examining he will understand that thoughts—crude or subtle [positive or negative]—are unreal, devoid of shape, color, base, support, and identity.

After a while, in the course of such analytical meditation, he will find that his mind attunes itself to a nondiscriminating awareness, which unmasks its intrinsic lucidity and emptiness. This indicates that the recollected emotions have been pacified in the tranquil absorption. However, he should repeat the examination of thoughts instead of quietening them. By maintaining the lucidity of thoughts—which he neither suppresses nor quietens—he should so strengthen his experience. Unlike before, he now does not cling to the cognitive reality but discovers the essence of the vivid thoughts as being unidentifiable and undefinable. Should this occur, he should expand his experience and determine the nature of thoughts commensurate with this stage. From then onwards he should—without distraction—maintain the same undefinable state while perceiving the vividness of thoughts—crude or subtle.

In imparting meditational instructions, Je Takpopa [Gampopa] included all dualistic thoughts into external appearances. To understand this better, the meditator should regard all six consciousnesses[107] as external appearances and examine each thoroughly. Immediate appearances of form
B in every shape and color arise unobstructedly as valid cognition[108] from the interaction between the sense organs and objects, a kind of common occurrence. These appearances [of dualism] are the result of individual karma and seeds of delusion. Yet, here the appearances per se should not be analyzed into the infinitesmal particles or proportions to determine their unreality and lack of essence. It has been affirmed that by determining the mind that clings to sense objects one will gain self-release from bondage of external objects. For this reason the meditator should examine mainly consciousness itself since it is the perceiver of all appearances.

As for determining the appearances, one first actualizes the mind's intrinsic lucidity and emptiness. And, then, upon perceiving an appearance one conducts a thorough examination in the same order as stated earlier in order
F to determine if the perceiver has any shape, color, base, support, identity, or mode of manifestation. The analysis must now shift in succession to the mind as perceiver of sound, smell, etc., to a specific internal and external phenomenon, to lust, hate, and other deluded emotions, as well as to the mind as experiencer of happiness or misery. In doing this in proper order, the meditator either simply perceives a sense object or recollects an emotion or an experience. Thus, when one examines the perceiver of an emerging appearance, the perception fades away instantly, or becomes unclear while the mind attains a harmony with its intrinsic lucidity and emptiness. By so pacifying the emerging perception along with the mind's clinging, one has realized the tranquil equipoise.

Yet even this cannot bring about definite insight into the duality of the perceived and the perceiver. One should specifically examine the perceiver of each specific perception. In short, the meditator has gained some little

188 B experience if he—while focusing on an "unobstructed" appearance with clarity—cognizes the perceiving mind as empty of intrinsic nature or identity. At the same time the appearance—without luster—is detached from attachment and clinging. Such a state is hard to describe! From then on he should maintain a contemplative awareness of the union between the lucidity of every perception—gross or subtle—and its intrinsic unreality [emptiness].

Some systems of meditational guidance advocate the analytical methods only for attaining insight into nondiscriminating lucid awareness. The analytical system that excludes active thoughts and perceptible appearances seems to be somewhat crude. By following this system one may achieve more easily a settled tranquility, but may find it hard to achieve a meditative state when the objects are active thoughts and perceived appearances.

Similarly, there are those who say that by looking at inward activities or outward appearances, duality will dissolve and awareness with its intrinsic lucidity and emptiness will dawn. This may be all right for some beginners. However, this system does not seek to determine active thoughts and perceived appearances in order to elevate the meditator to the path, but only to
189 F pacify through mindfulness the active thoughts and perceived appearances into an absorptive equipoise.

THE RELEVANT MEDITATION ON INSIGHT: CLEARING ASSUMPTIONS AND SKEPTICISM ABOUT THE BASIC ROOT [OF SAṂSĀRA AND NIRVĀṆA]

This is achieved through:

1. The definite sense that thoughts and appearances are of mental origin
2. The attainment of certainty about the intrinsic nature of both tranquil and active states of mind
3. The sense of certainty that all appearances are only nonarising

The Definite Sense That Thoughts and Appearances Are of Mental Origin

What is the difference between the aforesaid determination of thoughts and appearances and the one being elucidated here? The previous analysis sought to establish the nonexistence of the self-essence as a perceivable form with a shape, color, etc., whereas this contemplation examines thoughts and appearances through their emergence, dwelling, and destination in order to determine that their intrinsic nature is nondifferentiable from that of the mind. These examinations should be detailed and complete.

First, thoughts are to be determined as being identical with the mind itself. The mind is brought to an equipoise—a state of indivisible lucidity
B and emptiness. This done, one then causes an emotion of hatred to arise and examines its nature in terms of any perceivable source, basis, and destination. By determining the source of such hate, one will not discover any other source except the mind itself. If one assumes that the hate has originated from mind itself, one should then examine if it arises in a tangible form—the way a mother gives birth to a son—or if it arises from [the mind's] innate potential—the way sun and moon emit light—or if the mind itself has been transformed into that emotion.

In the middle, as one looks at the way that emotion has sustained itself, one will not discover any perceivable basis on which it settles. However, if one assumes that this hatred is self-sustained, one should examine if it is coupled with a clinging to reality of a violent state or if the hatred is devoid of any identifiable essence.

In concluding the meditation, one examines the destination of the emotional outflow but will find only the nonexistence of such a terminal point. Thus, having found nothing, one should examine if the hatred disappeared owing to a deliberate suppression, or if it pacified itself. If there has been a suppression, one has to find out who suppressed it, and what were the circumstances that brought about the suppression. If the hatred pacified itself, one finds out how it happened or whether it simply ceased by itself.
190 F This method of examination may be extended to every other discriminating thought, either in a vigorous or mild form.

During the next sessions one arouses in oneself two conflicting thoughts, one after the other, such as the emotions of happiness and of misery. One examines one by one their perceivable patterns and essential nature. Finally, one tries to find out whether any distinction exists between the two regarding their essence and their good and bad qualities. Although such an examination cannot establish the identity of the thoughts through their emergence, dwelling, and destination, it should help one to destroy the mind's clinging to dualities. The deluded one senses that thought and mind are separate entities, that the mind's inward and outward movements are separate and are distinct segments, like the body and its limbs.

This should also help to bring about an elevated state wherein each discriminating thought manifests its intrinsic lucidity and emptiness. Henceforth the meditator should be aware of the indivisibility of the mind and thoughts, which are like water and its waves. The waves are not different
190 B from the water, for the water itself appears as waves, which retain the intrinsic nature of water. Similarly, diverse thoughts—from the moment of their emergence—are inseparable from the mind's intrinsic lucidity and emptiness, because the mind—as unceasing movement—manifests itself in dualistic thoughts. The meditator should, therefore, resolve that diverse

thoughts are the manifestations of the mind, but they are also inseparable from the intrinsic lucidity and emptiness of the mind that is devoid of any essence or identity.

To determine appearances as being mental products, the meditator settles the mind in tranquility as in the earlier case and then perceives or visualizes vividly an appearance of form. He begins to analyze if that appearance has a perceivable origin, a dwelling, or a destination as was done with respect to thoughts. He then examines that appearance to determine whether such an appearance and the mind are separate or identical phenomena. If he perceives them to be separate, he should find out whether they exist as opposites or dualities, existing concurrently inside and outside, or above and below. If they are dualities, he should further find out whether they exist as two independent entities or whether the mind simply manifests itself as an appearance. If he perceives that the mind simply manifests itself as an external appearance, he should find out the nature of nondual percep-
191 F tion in view of the fact that there is only one mind. The meditator should continue to determine whether this nonduality has emerged simply because the mind manifested itself as appearance or because the appearance has merged itself with the mind.

Using the same logic the meditator examines other vivid and subtle appearances arising from the senses such as sound, smell, etc. He specifically visualizes opposite appearances one after the other such as a beautiful and an ugly form, or a pleasant and an unpleasant sound, and then examines each in regard to its pattern and essence. Finally he seeks to find out if each of these appearances has a discernible innate quality that is either good or bad. By examining it in this way the meditator should be able to free himself from inborn clinging to dualities such as mind and appearance, external and internal realities, or those existing side by side.

By thus examining diverse appearances the meditator will experience the indivisible union of appearance and its intrinsic emptiness as being devoid of any identifiable essence. This union of mind and appearance should be understood to be like the union between the consciousness in a dream and its
191 B appearance. For instance, in a dream the emergence of diverse appearances is not different from the mind's unceasing manifestation. The emergence of the diverse appearances and the mind should, therefore, be understood as being an indivisible union. In this manner a meditator should establish that appearance and mind are a nondual phenomenon, without bifurcating the diverse external appearances and internal movements of the mind. However, as long as one's collective karma and its psychic residue remain impure, there is no way of averting the emergence of common appearances—gathered together by the force of karma—arising immediately from the interdependence of and interaction between sense objects, faculties, and consciousness.

I have provided only the relevant explanations for this portion. The harmonious blending of appearance and mind will be achieved later at the great level of single flavor, after one has completely eliminated all one's assumptions about appearances and the mind and one has detached oneself from expectation and fear.

The Attainment of Certainty about the Intrinsic Nature of Both Tranquil and Active States of Mind

The meditator first settles his mind in the evenness of lucidity and its intrinsic emptiness. Observing its serene and nondual aspects he then examines the even state through a discerning intellect to determine if it has an absolute mode of emerging, dwelling, or destination.[109] He now causes a thought to flow and examines it as was done before. In either examination he will find neither the source, dwelling, nor destination of an emerging thought, nor an essential identity. However, by means of the contemplations he will be able to perceive [simultaneously] two distinct aspects of the mind: the settled tranquility and the transient movement.

The meditator then examines whether these two aspects are endowed with any identifiable essences, whether they are empty or not empty, and whether they possess a quality, i.e., are either good or bad [or both or neither]. He is not likely to find such a differentiable nature. Even if he comprehends the nature of the two aspects as nondifferentiable, he should
B further examine if this is so because of the fact that the two aspects—the tranquility and movement—are the same or identical or are indistinguishable in form despite their separate existences. If he contemplates that the two aspects are one and the same, he should find out if they are one in the beginning of their emergence, in the middle, or in the end. If he contemplates them to be identical, he should examine how they are identical.

Having examined the settled and dynamic aspects of the mind thoroughly, he will turn away from attachment and clinging to them as two separate phenomena. He will then cognize all the diverse appearances arising from the interaction of the senses and objects, including the mind's stable state and dynamic movements, as being the manifestation of the mind alone. He will be able to actualize an inmost awareness wherein the diverse manifestations and their intrinsic emptiness of any identity are unified as "one flavor" in the way waves arise from water or light emerges from the sun. Consequently he resolves that affirmation or rejection, acceptance or abandonment of a settled or active mind [perceiving it either in concord or conflict with what is usually perceived as a contemplative equipoise] are unwarranted. He has simply to maintain whichever state arises, simply by being aware of the fact that a settled or active state is identical with his inmost awareness, which is the union of a [perceivable] lucidity and its intrinsic emptiness and which has natural self-clarity, self-manifestation, and self-release.

193 F Well, then, if the two mental states are identical with the mind's intrinsic nature, why do they emerge separately? They emerge separately due to the immediate interaction between sense objects, sense faculties, and consciousness as well as to the ripening of karmic conditions and activation of subpsychic delusion. The activation of karma and delusion are affected through the movement of the psycho-neurotic energy[110] within the body as the collector of karma. Saraha writes:

> Mental currents are gathered together
> And are stirred violently by the waves of energy and emerging senses
> So that [the mind] turns into a vicious state.

Maitrīpa also comments:

> The mind also is merely a flux of memory and awareness;
> Empty of self-nature it consists of the force of air-energy.

For example, just as an inanimate object like a log is tossed around by the waves of the ocean, so is the source consciousness stirred through the support of the body as if by a wave of air. If detached from the body, consciousness is stated to be the differentiating inner awareness. The *Bodhicittavivaraṇa* describes:

> Just as an inanimate object like a log
> Is tossed around in the ocean,
> So source consciousness
> 193 B Becomes energetic through the support of the body.
> Where there is no body, there is no energetic consciousness.
> Understanding this means a differentiating self-knowledge.

Referring to the meaning of the identical nature of the mind's settled and dynamic aspects at this point, (1) some [masters] contend that the mind's movement does not happen independently of settled tranquility. Settled tranquility does not exist independently of its dynamic aspect. (2) Others assume that by watching the mind's movement the movement itself turns into a settled state. (3) Most masters contend that one cognizes the inner identity of the mind's movements through its settled state while recognizing the identity of its settled state through movements.

The first assumption is not correct, because it means that a meditator—apart from knowing that the mind itself becomes identical now with a settled, now with an energetic state—lacks a definite understanding about the essential unity of the two mental states. The second assumption is not correct, because their position appears to be that the mind's dynamic state should cease without even any understanding of its intrinsic nature. The third position is also somewhat wrong. It is not explicit enough on the essential nature of the two aspects except for its identification of an insight into the settled state with its energetic aspects for its letting the energetic state quiet itself without any differentiations.

F How are they actually to be cognized? At this stage the settled and energetic aspects in their nature are to be perceived as being empty of any identifiable essence and therefore of one flavor in terms of emptiness, while the two aspects manifest separately in the realm of experience as has been indicated by the analogy of water and its waves. Saraha comments:

> Just as placid water stirred by wind
> Turns itself into billowing waves,
> So does this Archer,[111] the sovereign yogin,
> Cognize the diverse forms arising from a single source.

Further discussion will be given later on the designation that the settled and the energetic aspects are essentially one with respect to one's inmost awareness, but are separate in their manifesting forms.

The Sense of Certainty That All Appearances Are Only Nonarising

The meditator—while remaining in a harmonious state of clarity and emptiness as before—lets the mind examine the mind itself. He considers that the emerging thoughts and diverse appearances manifest themselves as such, simply due to the vigor of the mind. He then contemplates—with a fixed
194 B gaze—as to what really is the inherent disposition or the abiding nature of the mind so designated.

At the beginning he examines the origin of the mind's abiding nature. Finding neither the origin of the cause nor the determinable condition, neither a producer nor a creator, he concludes that it is primordial nonarising [emptiness], not born from the interaction of cause and condition, and that it is devoid of support or root. In the middle, he examines how the mind settles itself. He does not find—not even to the infinitesimal point of a hair—any identifiable form with shape or color, dwelling or support, nor any identity or a mode of being. He, therefore, concludes that the mind does not have any ground for settling itself. At the end, while he examines the destiny of every thought flow, he finds neither a destination nor a trace of its movement; he finds that it can neither be obstructed nor can its emergence cease by itself. So he concludes that [the abiding nature of the mind] can neither be destroyed nor can it cease to reemerge.

Furthermore, he contemplates that, if the mind is identical with past

events, it must necessarily come to an end or dissolve itself; if it is an event of the future, it has yet to emerge or appear; if it is a present event, it must have
195 F something identifiable. Since it cannot be identified with the three periods of time, it is detached from the extreme assumption of an eternal entity. Though empty of any substance, it is the root of all possibilities, of saṃsāra and nirvāṇa. As such it emerges in diverse forms and is detached from extreme nihility. Since it is not composed of any substance or mark of duality, it cannot be fully described by an analogy. It has not been produced by any cause in the beginning. It is free from birth. Being empty of all identity in the present, it is without a dwelling. Finally, neither can its passage be traced nor can its emergence cease; it remains ever unceasing. Since it has not been born from a cause, it cannot be destroyed through conditions. Because its origin is not rooted in time, it encompasses all times. Being detached from a substantive reality of arising, settlement, or cessation, it remains an uninterrupted stream [of consciousness]. The intrinsic nature dwells indiscriminately in all beings alike—awakened and unawakened, good and bad—transcending finite progression and degression. It
195 B exists in all sentient beings whether or not they are aware of it, leaving no possibility for anyone to either gain or lose it. It is immutable as it is not subject to transient increase or decrease.

By thus examining the significance of the nonarising [emptiness] of the mind through discerning wisdom, the meditator should examine thoroughly its fundamental root or intrinsic nature—the way someone analyzes a bone by crushing it with a stone—until he discovers the depth of the mind. By so examining the meditator will experience the mind's abiding nature, which transcends thought or expression, and will finally achieve the extinction of the discerning intellect itself and the dawning of nondual awareness. Saraha comments:

> The nature of mind, like space, is pure from the beginning.
> As one gazes at it, the act of seeing as such ceases.

And he again says:

> The mind may be described through the analogy of the mind itself.
> When dualistic thoughts are cleared
> The mind becomes stable and immobile.
> Like salt dissolves in water,
> So the mind dissolves itself in its intrinsic nature.

On determining the mind to be nonarising [emptiness], the second *Bhāvanākrama* states:

196 F
> Thus, when one examines the essential nature of the mind through discerning wisdom, one may find that the mind in its ultimate sense

can be conceived as neither an internal or external entity, nor even as the nonexistence of both. Similarly, the essential nature of the past mind cannot be conceived, neither can the future mind nor the present mind. When a thought arises, it does not come from any perceivable source. A dissolving thought does not proceed anywhere, for the mind is formless; it can neither be seized nor can it be demonstrated.

The second *Bhāvanākrama* quotes the *Ratnakūṭa*:

> [Buddha:] O Kāśyapa, the mind cannot be found through a complete search. What is impossible to find is inconceivable. What is inconceivable is neither past, future, nor the emerging present. What is neither past, present, nor future is empty of any essence. What is empty of any essence does not have any origin. What has no source of emergence has no cessation.

B The *Chokyi Gyalpoi Dho* (*Dharmarāja-sūtra*) elaborates:

> [Buddha:] O virtuous son, if you aspire to achieve release and liberation, you should detach yourself from any sensual indulgence and should contemplate the mind as being one but not as dualistic phenomena. The mind that contemplates its own reality is empty of any reality. The emptiness of essence constitutes the essential nature of the mind. It is devoid of any movement, projection, or achievement; hence it has been characterized as enlightenment.
>
> [The disciple:] Since mental cognitions are of an inconceivable extent, how could they be designated as being empty of movement, projection, or achievement?
>
> [Buddha:] If one enters a fully concentrated state observing and examining inwardly, one will achieve the state of purity that is nonarising [emptiness].

The *Dampaicho Yongsuzinpai Dho* (*Saddharmaparigraha-sūtra*) teaches:

> . . . for that reason you should understand the mind to be empty of any essence and as undependable and unreal. You should not grasp the mind as being immanent with an essence because it is empty of essence. Phenomena, which are empty of essence, do not have a true existence of their own. All phenomena are conceptually designated. Such is their intrinsic nature and has been so revealed. The wise
> 197 F abandon the two extreme views [absolute reality and total nihility] and explore the middle path. Things that are empty of essence constitute the path of enlightenment. I, too, have revealed this path.

Many similar passages are to be found in both the collection of the sūtras and the tantras.

THE CHARACTERISTICS OF EMERGING INSIGHT

Concerning the analytical meditation on insight through discerning wisdom, some meditators could not gain definite insight into intrinsic reality—despite their persistence in their investigation—due to their excessive strengthening of tranquil mind. However many analyses they conducted, they nevertheless found themselves in an absorptive tranquility. While doing so a sense of certainty dawned on them that the significance of the analyses was revealed through the tranquil state. They mistakenly identified this experience with the gaining of insight into the intrinsic nature of mind. Some meditators experienced in their meditation on tranquility a strong sense of unreality about the essencelessness of all phenomena, which they
197 B mistook to be the insight into the intrinsic nature of the mind. In such cases the meditator should immediately use the methods prescribed [by the teacher] to clear the sensation and experience of tranquility and the mind's clinging to it. By removing the moisture of such a sensation from his inmost awareness and by meditating on insight, he will achieve the result.

However, some people with a deep mental defilement and low intelligence may not gain the insight into the mind no matter how much they may examine it. They should devote themselves, for a while, to the practice of expanding virtues and eliminating defilements, and then to the meditation on tranquility with an increased clarity. Only thereafter should they resume the meditation on insight. Some intelligent [meditators] mistook an intellectual comprehension of the mind's ultimate nature as the dawning of insight. Others who are learned and eloquent in imparting a discourse on the doctrine lack illuminating experience. Still some others who lack an aptitude for eloquent speeches, gain experience commensurate with the appropriate level of meditation. For meditators such differentiation is very essential.

However good a meditation may be, without insight it will be nothing more than the ordinary meditations known to the adherents of the dogma[112] or to lay Buddhists. If this kind of meditation does not match the meditation of the Primary Vehicle [Hīnayāna], it is needless to say that it cannot be
198 F comparable with the middle path meditation of the Mahāyāna, particularly with that of mahāmudrā [the great seal]. For all these reasons an emphasis on meditation on insight is of utmost importance.

How then does one determine the level of insight that has dawned in oneself? An infallible insight,[113] which directly perceives the truth of the all-encompassing expanse of reality, cannot be realized except on the great level of the nondiscriminating state. The insight being referred to here is simply an approximate insight, which dawns in the mind of an ordinary individual. This insight is compared to the waxing moon which, in effect, fulfills the same function as the moon; hence the designation of moon is applicable to both. Insight, at this stage, must consist of (1) the understanding that all dualities including the mind, its manifest thoughts, and appearances are in an ultimate sense empty of any absolute mode of arising, settling, or cessation and (2) of the awareness with a deep certainty that all these dualities are empty of true essence or self-nature.

The authoritative sayings about this either have been or will be quoted. Should a meditator fail to achieve [even this simple insight], he would do well to seek an understanding of what the masters of this meditational order consider to be the beginner's insight. Such an insight should consist of a harmonious blend of the mind's intrinsic characteristics: self-comprehending, self-crystallized awareness and its innate emptiness of any essence. Thus, by attaining such an insight first, the meditator will gradually achieve the infallible insight as well.

Regarding the standard level of realized insight, the meditative tradition of the sūtras holds that the ideal insight is achieved when the meditation on insight brings about a greater perfection of ease, already achieved earlier during the meditation on tranquility. Insight on the lower level means approximate insight. However, our meditational order does not maintain such a differentiation. Most systems of the vital instructions hold that just as one-pointed concentration—before attaining perfect ease—constitutes meditation on tranquility, so the general detailed analysis of the meditation
F on insight—before it has achieved perfect ease—falls within the fold of insight. Besides, it is relevant to incorporate into the subject matter of insight its varied categories such as the differentiated types of insight, like the insight arising from a perfect differentiation of things, and the three other types such as the insight arising from the analyses of perceptive marks, and so on.

The *Śrāvakabhūmi* states that the fourfold mental applications elucidated in the section on tranquility are applied to the meditation on insight. It is, therefore, not contradictory to regard [the four mental applications] from the uninterrupted exertion downward as belonging to the realm of insight, because at this stage the meditator achieves an uninterrupted state of insight. This elucidation on the methods for attaining tranquility and insight, identifying their characteristics and harmonizing the two meditative states, is based on the system of the vital instructions as opposed to the various other methods detailed in the sūtras and tantras.

9 B

THE BLENDING OF INSIGHT WITH THAT OF OTHER SYSTEMS

The insight [of this meditational order] may be described in light of the four kinds of insight, such as the insight arising from the perfect differentiation of things stated in the *Saṃdhinirmocana-sūtra* and other sūtras. According to

this order, the intellectual determination of all dualities—embodied in one's thoughts and appearances that originate from the innate power of mind—represents (1) the insight arising from the differentiation of things, because with analytical penetration the intellect differentiates all objects of knowledge. Perceiving dualistic reality as being empty of any innate essence represents (2) the insight arising from the perfect differentiation of things, because with analytical penetration the intellect differentiates the significance of the exactness of all knowledge. Determining in general these two kinds of
200 F significance with a grasping of the perceptive mark represents (3) the insight arising from a general investigation, because with the support of the perceptive mark the discerning intellect investigates the broad significance of the exactness and the extent of all phenomena. Investigating with a penetrating precision the two kinds of significance represents (4) the consummate, analytical insight, because this investigation is directed toward the subtlest significance of the exactness and the extent of all things. Such being the case, the *Śrāvakabhūmi* explains:

> How does one differentiate between [the two aspects of things]? One may differentiate by such means as perfect analysis, skillful discernment, and thorough examination, which is designed to eliminate mental defilements. Besides, one differentiates exactly the specific characteristics of phenomena. One examines through a discerning intellect the mind that grasps any perceptive marks. One also examines with penetrating discernment all dualistic thoughts.

Furthermore, our system of insight may be explained in light of the three kinds of insight, such as the insight arising from the analysis of perceptive
200 B marks, etc., as stated in the *Saṃdhinirmocana-sūtra*. According to this meditational order the methods of examining all perceptions as the object of analytical insight represent (1) the insight arising from any perceptive marks, because the investigating intellect focuses completely on the dualistic thoughts since they form the object of insight. The methods for determining [these dualistic thoughts] as empty of any essence represent (2) the insight that emerges from a thorough investigation, because this exercise of intellect enables the meditator to realize the object of realization, which has thus far remained unknown to him. The methods through which one achieves self-deliverance with the realization of the essencelessness of all phenomena and which help one to stabilize this experience represent (3) the insight arising from the discerning intellect, for through such an intellect one realizes the abiding nature of all phenomena, and through consolidating that realization
201 F one will achieve inner peace and self-release as well. The *Saṃdhinirmocana-sūtra* explains:

> What is that [insight] which emerges from the perceptive mark? It is an insight that focuses mainly on discriminating thoughts as the object of

tranquil absorption. What is that [insight] which emerges from complete inquiry? It is an insight arising from intellectual appreciation and realizing perfectly the aspects of phenomena that the mind has not fully realized. What is that [insight] which arises from an analytical intellect? It is an insight arising from a discerning intellect that seeks to achieve inner peace and deliverance through perfecting a good comprehension of phenomena.

The sūtras and the commentaries expound on the types of insight but the
B treatises on meditation do not explain the methods of differentiating every insight.

Our intellectual system of determining the two kinds of selfhood may now be summarized here in comparison with the sūtric system that was widely known in Tibet and [ancient] India. Our way of determining the intrinsic nature of the mind is similar to the sūtric way of determining selflessness of personality. The sūtras consider that a sustained consciousness of the stream of life's aggregates constitutes the personality; that a consciousness clinging to the notion of an eternal and independent entity of "I" or "self" constitutes the self of personality; and that understanding the unreality of such a self represents the selflessness of personality. Similarly, our meditational order establishes that it is the mind that not only holds the self to be an eternal and independent entity, but also clings to it as "I" or "self" and that such a mind should be determined to be empty of any self-nature. The method of this order for determining thoughts and appearances
2 F is similar to the sūtric method of establishing the selflessness of phenomena (dharmanairātmya). According to the sūtra tradition, the self of an individual holds to the psychophysical aggregates, elements, and so on, as realities [dharmas], clings to these valid cognitions as substantially real. This is grasping the self of phenomena (dharmātman). The understanding of these phenomenal realities as empty of self-nature means the selflessness of phenomena. Similarly, our meditational order establishes all categories of thought, which the mind has so designated, and the reality of appearances, such as external form, sound, etc., as being devoid of any innate self-nature.

However, [the two systems] differ on the sequential order of determining the nature of subject and object. The sūtras hold that the mind that perceives sensory objects cannot be determined without first determining these objects. Dharmakīrti affirms this:

Without first challenging sensory objects
One cannot eliminate [the self].

Āryadeva agrees:

202 B Only upon perceiving sense objects as being empty of self
Can one terminate the seed of the existential circle.

If our Meditational Order follows the sūtric approach, it could make any subsequent determination of the perceiving mind very difficult. It has therefore established that the determination of the mind first can easily make the determination of sense objects a spontaneous self-release. This process of nullifying [the mind's clinging to the self of personality] was compared by Tilopa to the analogy of a tree. By cutting the roots of a tree first, its leaves and branches will dry up automatically. The same approach is found in the vital instructions on the significance of the quintessential doctrine [mahāmudrā].

This completes the discussion of the methods of guiding [meditators] toward insight.

CHAPTER FIVE

The Stages of Virtuous Practice

There are three sections:

1. Understanding the system of absorption at the start
2. The actual identification of spontaneous coemergence
3. The elimination of flaws and the appreciation of the meaning of meditation

UNDERSTANDING THE SYSTEM OF ABSORPTION AT THE START

This is divided into two sections:

1. Determining the abiding nature of mind
2. Explaining the definitive meaning of spontaneous coemergence

Determining the Abiding Nature of Mind

There are three things to be determined:

1. The essence of mind
2. The nature of mind
3. The characteristics of mind

The Essence of Mind

203 F Although the abiding nature of the mind has generally been designated by three terms, namely, essence, nature, and characteristics, they are in reality not different from the essence of mind. The *Āmnāyamañjarī* states:

> Emptiness constitutes the intrinsic nature of all things [mental and material]. The essence of such emptiness is not different from what has been designated as the mind's self-nature and its manifesting mode. However, from the standpoint of the [mental aspect] it can be divided into three: essence, nature, and characteristics, which are identified accordingly.

Regarding this the venerated Gampopa wrote:

> The essence of the mind consists of three aspects: essence, nature, and characteristics. Its essence consists of the state of clarity and nonconception, its nature is devoid of any substantive mode of arising, dwelling, and ceasing, and its characteristics refer to the dualistic appearances of cyclic existence and permanent peace [saṃsāra and nirvāṇa].

Again he comments:

> The mind consists of nature, essence, and characteristics. The designated term "nature of mind" means that in its intrinsic nature it is pure and uncreated, and thus encompasses all realms of saṃsāra and nirvāṇa. The term "essence" means that innermost awareness is detached
> 203 B from arising and ceasing. The term "characteristics" means the diverse appearances of images arising from conditioned psychic imprints.

Je Phagmo Trupa concurs:

> Mahāmudrā means nondual [awareness].
> Its three aspects are
> Essence, nature, and characteristics.
> "Essence" means the emptiness
> Of arising, ceasing, or conceiving.
> "Nature" means unobstructed lucidity.[114]
> "Characteristics" mean the diverse appearances
> On the levels of saṃsāra and nirvāṇa.

The essence and nature of mind are stated to be identical in reality. The aspect of mind is identical with the characteristics. This is affirmed by Je Rangjungpa [the third Karmapa]:

> The essence [of mind] is empty, its self-nature is lucid,
> And its aspect consists of diverse, unceasing appearances.

The essence of mind is, from the beginning, devoid of any substantive arising, dwelling, or ceasing. It is unstained by dualistic concepts of life's psychophysical aggregates, the elements, and the sense faculties. It bears the same nature as those of phenomena that are empty of any self-essence but are all-encompassing evenness.

This is emphasized in the *Guhyasamāja*:

> It is empty of all substances
> And detached from dualistic discriminations
> Such as aggregates, elements, and sense faculties.
> It is selfless and even.
> This mind is unborn from the beginning,
> Because it is empty by its innate nature.

Referring to the essence of mind as bodhi, the *Bodhicittavivaraṇa* explains:

> The enlightened minds [bodhi] of the buddhas
> Are unclouded by any view of dualities—
> The self and the aggregates of life—
> Because the characteristics of these minds
> Are void at all times.

As stated earlier, when one looks into and examines thoroughly the mind's intrinsic nature, one finds no substantive basis at all. Instead one experiences that the analytical process is quieting itself down or effacing itself. This state is described as being the ultimate reality, the all-encompassing emptiness that is intrinsic in all things and at all times. The *Dennyi* (*Satyadvaya*) states:

> Apparent reality appears in the way it does
> Yet is [seen to be] empty of any substance
> When subjected to a thorough logical investigation.
> This discovery [of emptiness] represents the ultimate truth,
> Which is inherent in all things and at all times.

Such intrinsic emptiness of mind is indeed emptiness of all things, which encompasses all the appearances and existences of saṃsāra and nirvāṇa.
4 B Āryadeva comments:

> One substance represents the essence of all other substances;
> All other substances represent the essence of one substance.

Āryadeva also says in his *Catuḥśataka*:

> The emptiness of one thing
> Represents the emptiness of all things.

The *Satyadvaya* declares:

> There is no division whatsoever in emptiness,
> Not even in the slightest degree.

The Nature of Mind

The *Gyetongpa* (*Aṣṭasāhasrikā-prajñāpāramitā-sūtra*) teaches:

> The nature of mind consists of luminous clarity.

The *Laṅkāvatāra* states:

> Mind's nature consists of luminous clarity,
> Which is the intrinsic nature of the Tathāgata.

There are many such passages that describe the nature of mind as being luminous clarity. The term "luminous clarity" means that it is pure, unstained by any discriminating thoughts such as arising, dwelling, or ceasing. Undefiled [by any mental blemishes] and detached from the particles of the aggregates it remains immutable at all time, like space, or even inseparable from the nature of space. The *Upālipariprcchā* explains:

> This mind in its nature is pure and luminous.
> 205 F It is nonsubstantive, undefiled, and detached from any subatomic particles.

The *Gyü Lama* (*Uttaratantra*) says:

> This luminous clarity, being the nature of the mind,
> Is immutable, like space.

The *Yeshey Nangwa Gyan* (*Jñānālokālaṃkāra-sūtra*) elaborates:

> [Buddha:] O Mañjuśrī, enlightenment by its innate nature consists of luminous clarity, because the mind's intrinsic nature is luminously clear. Why is it so designated? The mind's intrinsic nature is detached from any inner defilement and is equal to or possesses the nature of space, while encompassing space through its identical characteristics. For all these reasons it is designated as being luminous clarity.

The *Namnang Ngönjang* (*Vairocanābhisambodhi*) remarks:

> The nature of the mind is pure, yet it cannot be conceived dualistically as being external, internal, or in between.

And again it says:

> 205 B Whatever is the nature of space is the nature of mind. Whatever is the nature of mind is the mind of enlightenment. For this reason the mind, the expanse of space, and the mind of enlightenment are nondual and inseparable.

The *Guhyasamāja* explains:

Since all things in their nature are luminously clear,
They are pure from the beginning, like space.

This being so, some unwise meditators, when they experience any kind of inner clarity, consider it to be the mind's luminous clarity and even assume it to be radiant like sunlight. This is a very serious error, because, as proven by earlier quotations, the term "luminous clarity" has been used to simply mean that the mind is of intrinsic purity, which is unstained by discriminating thoughts or emotional afflictions. If the nature of the mind consists of anything radiant and colorful, the mind would have to be a light and have a
F color. Then the [Buddhist] doctrine that holds the nature of the mind to be pure, i.e., detached from any self-essence, would be wrong.

Well, then, how about certain experiences in which yogins perceive self-awareness with self-clarity as if it were a psychic manifestation, an inner light that even surpasses appearances, or a normal color or light? Nāropa clarifies this in the *Tawa Dhordü* (*Dṛṣṭisaṃkṣepta*):

All things of appearance and existence
Do not exist apart from self-awareness,
For things appear and crystallize themselves
Just as, for example, the mind experiences
Its own self-awareness.

And again he says:

This self-awareness is detached from discrimination;
It manifests while being intrinsically empty;
Being empty it manifests itself.
Appearance and emptiness are, therefore, inseparable.
They are like the reflection of the moon on water.

Such [an experience of the mystics] is simply the inward dawning of the mind's lucidity and awareness. Although this inner experience is currently designated as awareness for the practical purpose of contemplation, it is still on the level of duality and as such cannot be an actual awareness, because it
206 B is not the supreme emptiness of all forms nor the all-pervading power. The great commentary on the *Dükhor* (*Kālacakra*) [the *Vimalaprabhā*] explains:

> What, then, is awareness? The answer is that this awareness, so designated, is the innermost awareness of a nondiscriminating kind. It is the supreme emptiness of all forms. Besides being an immutable and blissful awareness, it transcends all concepts. This awareness is the master of cause and effect. Cause and effect coalesce in it like the light and heat of fire.

The *Jampal Tshanjhö* (*Mañjuśrīnāma-saṃgīti*) describes the awareness:

It is all-knowing, complete, and ultimate awareness.
As such it transcends the realm of consciousness.

And again it says:

It comprehends everything, oneself and others.

For this reason Je Drikhungpa[115] says:

What is known as the great seal is this innermost awareness.

All forms of awareness shown here as objects of meditation should be understood in the light of these passages. Even so, the inner perception that
207 F mystics experience cannot be construed to be the discerning awareness and the mind's intrinsic lucidity. The *Saṃdhinirmocana* explains:

Discerning awareness is in the nondual state.

The *Sangwa Samgyi Mikhyabpai Gyü* (*Guhyācintya-tantra*) states:

By abandoning eternalism and nihilism,
Arising and cessation, and such other extreme views,
The mind achieves transcending awareness,
Which from the beginning has been detached from any dualistic distortions.
The meaning of this is indeed beyond a conceptual dimension.

Thus the meaning of being aware of [or having insight into] every aspect of reality is stated to be nondual and beyond a conceptual dimension. The meaning of the mind's intrinsic lucidity has been explained earlier.

The Characteristics of Mind

The intrinsic purity of the mind was clouded by a transitory defilement. Ensuing confusion distorted the consciousness of its natural state. Through its interaction with fundamental discrimination emerged sentient beings of the six existential spheres, with their [capacity for experiencing] transient
207 B pleasure and misery. When the defilements are eliminated, the intrinsic nature of mind is actualized, and the interacting process of self-realization is completed, one attains the enlightenment of ultimate reality so that its supremely illusory manifestations will appear for the benefit of sentient beings. The *Dṛṣṭisaṃkṣepta* comments:

Alas, the six levels of sentient beings are
Emanations of deluded minds.
Through the infinite realm of space
They ramble in unimaginable misery and delusion.

And again this text points out:

Lo! From minds undefiled emerge
Emanations in sublime forms.
Appearing as the pure realms
And the enlightened assemblies in their diverse forms,
These wonderful emanations
Pervade the infinite cosmic space!

Saraha says:

Mind alone is the seed of all realities,
From which unfolds saṃsāra and nirvāṇa.

The *Sampuṭa* explains:

Mind defiled by passion and other uncontrolled impulses
Is indeed the mind of cyclic existence.
F Discovering the mind's intrinsic lucidity is liberation indeed.
Undefiled by lust and emotional impurities,
Unclouded by any dualistic perceptions,
This superior mind is indeed the supreme nirvāṇa!

If the mind in its natural state is pure from the beginning it cannot possibly be stained by any transitory impurity. Were this possible, the mind, after purifying the impurity, might again be stained. The mind's impurity has been designated as transitory since it can be eliminated. It is not something that suddenly emerged from nowhere. In fact, the mind's impurity has been coexisting with the mind since time without beginning. The *Uttara-tantra* explains it through an analogy:

Intrinsic purity [bodhi] is like pollen in the common lotus,
Like grains in chaff, and gold in dirt,
Like a treasure under the soil, and seeds in pods,
Like an image of Buddha wrapped in rags,
Like a prince in the womb of a common woman,
208 B Like a heap of gold beneath the earth.
Thus, the nature of enlightenment remains hidden in all sentient beings
Who are overcome by transitory defilement.

As long as the mind remains clouded by transitory defilement, even though its intrinsic state is pure, the qualities of enlightenment will not crystallize themselves. They will, however, emerge spontaneously upon the elimination of the mind's defilement. The *Hevajra-tantra* affirms this:

All sentient beings are buddhas,
Only they are overcome by transitory defilement.

> They become Buddhas at the moment of eliminating their defilement.

Nāgārjuna expounds:

> Though precious vaiḍūrya
> Is always translucent,
> If left uncut,
> It does not shine.
> So is the all-encompassing reality [dharmadhātu];
> Though intrinsically undefiled,
> It is clouded by defilement.
> So it remains latent in saṃsāra
> But crystallizes itself upon attaining nirvāṇa.

209 F The characteristics [of the mind] are thus described as that which manifests itself in the diverse forms of saṃsāra and nirvāṇa.

The mystics of the present time experience even the mind's manifestations as being indeterminable and unobstructed diversity. Due to the force of their diverse inbred tendencies they perceive inner manifestations as outer realities. They appear exactly as designated or modulated by the interaction of karma and inbred tendencies of the meditators. Even though the intrinsic nature [of the mind] does not change, its manifestation takes many diverse forms, like a woolen fabric that is transformed by the use of dyes. The *Laṅkāvatāra-sūtra* elucidates:

> The mind in its nature remains pure and lucid. It nevertheless manifests exactly as the intellect wills it to be, just in the way a white woolen fabric is transformed by the use of dyes.

In order to determine the mind's actual state and how it manifests itself in diverse forms, one would normally study the exegetical texts on the eight forms of consciousness including the source-consciousness and the mental categories. However, I have given here only the relevant information.

Explaining the Definitive Meaning of Spontaneous Coemergence

This will be examined in three ways:

1. The essence and the terminology of spontaneous coemergence
2. The differentiations and their identification
3. The significance of spontaneous coemergence

The Essence and Terminology of Spontaneous Coemergence

The essence of the mind's spontaneous coemergence consists of luminous clarity. Like space, it is an all-pervading sovereign that encompasses all
B things, static and dynamic, saṃsāra and nirvāṇa. Of the many elucidations the *Hevajra-tantra* comments:

> The great awareness exists
> In the bodies of all sentient beings,
> Neither as duality nor nonduality,
> Neither as substance nor nonsubstance,
> But as the supreme state
> Pervading all things, dynamic and static.

The experience of this [coemergent awareness][116] is the object of analytical insight since it is beyond intellectual expression, discrimination, and definition. The *Yumla Töpa*[117] identifies awareness with wisdom-gone-beyond:

> Wisdom-gone-beyond[118] is inexpressible,
> Inconceivable, and undefinable.
> With the intrinsic nature of space it is nonarising and unceasing;
> It is the object of analytical insight.
> You, mother of the buddhas in the three periods of time,
> I pay thee homage.

10 F Tilopa proclaims:

> O wonder, this is innermost awareness.
> It is inexpressible and beyond discrimination.

The *Hevajra-tantra* comments:

> Spontaneous coemergence cannot be described by external means.

Concerning the literal meaning of the term spontaneous coemergence, it is so designated because all substances drawn together in dynamic and static phenomena and intrinsic suchness [emptiness] of each and every aspect of these realities have been coexisting from the beginning, without either preceding or succeeding. The above text also says:

> Whatever has simultaneously arisen,
> It is described as being spontaneous coemergence.

Ḍombipa states in the *Lhanchik Kyedrup* (*Sahajasiddhi*):

> Because it is in the nature of spontaneous coemergence,
> It is described as inexpressible coemergence.

Indrabodhi states in his commentary to the above text:

> That which has arisen simultaneously with something else
> Is therefore described as coemergent.
> What has been thus described as intrinsic coemergence
> Has been coexisting with all things, mobile and immobile.

The Differentiations and Their Identification

210 B Generally, there are three kinds of coemergence, namely: coemergence as being the existential foundation, the path, and the accomplishment. Spontaneous coemergence as the existential foundation signifies the mind's intrinsic lucidity, which constitutes the basis or the heart of all things—saṃsāra and nirvāṇa. Coemergence as the path consists of insight into the inherent emptiness of all phenomena, attained as a combined result of knowledge through studying [the dharma], examining, and meditating. Coemergence as the accomplishment consists of perfecting experience on the path and thereby transforming the mind's coemergence on the existential level into the twin states of purity. This indeed is the coemergence of accomplishment.

Furthermore, the *Hevajra-tantra* and other texts mention two kinds of coemergence, namely: inbred coemergence and coemergence in a blissful state. The latter is a method by which the creative fluid [in the central nervous system] is harnessed by virtue of the inner fire with the coemergence of bliss and emptiness. This is mentioned in the texts of the Drubnying. There are three kinds of processes. Inbred coemergence means the mind's luminous clarity, which here signifies mahāmudrā as perfect reality. Coemergence in a blissful state means luminous clarity, which arises due to the
211 F refinement of "bodhicitta" [i.e., the creative fluid in the central nervous system]. The ultimate luminous clarity in the nondual state means the coemergence of bliss and its intrinsic emptiness.

Relevant at this stage are what the venerated Takpopa enumerated as the two kinds, viz., coemergence of the intrinsic mind and coemergence of external appearances. He incorporated the categories of thoughts into the dimension of appearances. Conversely, Je Gomchung separated the coemergence of emotional discrimination from the dimension of appearances. In doing this he seemed to have taken into consideration a certain distinction that exists between the appearances of external objects—which are perceived by most individuals as the result of their common karma—and the appearances of discriminating senses. As stated before, coemergence of the intrinsic mind means that the mind's essence or its self-nature consists of lucidity, nondiscrimination, and nonduality. Coemergence of appearance means that the mind's innate power or characteristic manifests itself unceasingly in the various aspects of saṃsāra and nirvāṇa. Spontaneous arising of emotional discrimination is considered to be the unfurling of various mental afflictions such as the three poisons.[119] The last two are to be regarded as belonging to the coemergence of appearance. The reason for using the term "coemergence" for these two has been stated earlier.

The term "coemergence" means the spontaneous coexistence—from the very beginning—of the characteristics of things or phenomena and their intrinsic reality or inherent emptiness, much the way as rock sugar and its sweetness or fire and its heat coexist. Coemergence of the intrinsic mind and coemergence of appearance are stated to be indivisible like the sun and its light or sandalwood and its fragrance. Nāgārjuna explains:

By their self-nature rock-sugar is sweet
And fire is hot;
So the intrinsic nature of all things
Is said to be empty [of substance].

And he says further:

Apparent reality is stated to be empty;
Emptiness means apparent reality,
For their mutual nonexclusion is a certainty,
Like the interrelatedness between the conditioned and their
transitory nature.

2 F The venerated Gampopa instructs:

Coemergence of the intrinsic mind represents dharmakāya;
Coemergence of appearance
Represents the illumination of dharmakāya.

Coemergence of the intrinsic mind means the mind's true or actual state, whereas coemergence of appearance means all the recollective and discriminating thoughts. These two kinds of coemergence are indivisible, like the sun and its light or sandalwood and its fragrance. Je Gomchung restates:

Coemergence of mind is the real dharmakāya;
Coemergence of appearances
Is the illumination of dharmakāya;
Coemergence of emotional discrimination
Is the stream of dharmakāya.
[These three as] indivisible coemergence
Are the meaning of dharmakāya.

Well one might wonder whether the mind and appearances perceived by ordinary individuals might not also be the same coemergence. Whether or

not seekers on the path realize spontaneous coemergence, it is coarising [immanent in every individual]; hence it is neither subject to change nor
212 B does it cease to exist. For example, a butter lamp and the sun shine without discrimination. The only people who fail to perceive the light are the blind. Saraha comments in the same manner:

> Even when a home is well lit,
> Blind people still remain in darkness.
> Likewise, coemergence encompasses everything
> And remains close to every individual.
> Only the ignorant mind moves far away from it.

Virūpa sums up:

> Thus all apparent things that appear or exist
> Are empty of any essence,
> And have only a conceptual or nominal identity.
> Not the slightest distinction exists between the designation
> And the nature of things that it symbolizes,
> For there is a constant coemergence,
> Which cannot be realized by external means.

The Significance of Spontaneous Coemergence

Why is the vital instruction on mahāmudrā described as the identification of spontaneous coemergence? The venerated Takpopa [Gampopa] mentions
213 F in general the way of identifying discriminating thoughts with the four aspects [kāya] of enlightenment. As explained before, the mind as the superficial perceiver, the discriminating thoughts issuing from it, and their intrinsic emptiness have all been coarising from time without beginning and as such are indivisible. Yet, ignorant minds erroneously discriminate and divide these realities. They are to be recognized as being a spontaneous arising from beginningless time through the vital instructions of ultimate mahāmudrā and through experiential guidance. The sense of their identity thus attained is to be harmonized with the mind itself, for it encompasses their intrinsic nature as well. This process is described as the harmonization with coemergence. According to Je Phagmo Trupa:

> The mind, the emotional discriminations, and their intrinsic
> emptiness [dharmakāya]
> Are spontaneous coemergence from the beginning.
> They are to be harmonized with the mind
> By applying the instructions,
> As indicated by the term "harmonizing with coemergence."

Besides, there exist the methods of harmonizing normal thoughts and appearances with coemergent awareness, or of harmonizing the appearance of dualistic mind with emptiness that has coemerged spontaneously. In summary, the term "coemergence" may be applied to other realities with dual aspects, such as the mind's intrinsic lucidity and its emptiness, perceptive appearance and its emptiness, awareness and its emptiness, bliss and its emptiness, etc. I do not propose to elaborate these terms.

THE ACTUAL IDENTIFICATION OF SPONTANEOUS COEMERGENCE

The actual identification of spontaneous coemergence may be carried out in the following manner:

1. Identifying coemergence of the mind
2. Identifying coemergence of thought
3. Identifying coemergence of appearance

Identifying Coemergence of the Mind

The mind is settled in a natural state, attuned to its pristine purity, without getting distracted either by dullness or sensual incitement, by expectation or aversion. Then, as the mind observes its own intrinsic nature or mode of existence, all discriminatory thoughts in their forceful or feeble forms dissolve or pacify themselves without suppression. The mind remains in an indeterminable state with inbred lucidity and quietude. This contemplative attainment is described as tranquility.

14 F Now, to attain insight, the meditator is required to maintain the same tranquil state, not letting its lucidity and mindfulness become sullenness, unmindfulness, or even a neutral inertness. In determining the nature of the mind, he observes it in a state of awareness with unceasing lucidity and self-crystallization. He finds the exact way this self-crystallization and self-cognition has dawned within him. It is undefinable, yet the experience remains one of vivid awareness and a sense of certainty. The *Sūtrālaṃkāra* defines tranquility and insight:

> Having settled in its intrinsic state,
> The mind first concentrates on itself
> And then properly differentiates all perceptive realities.
> These are tranquility and insight respectively.

This description is according to the root text of the *Sūtrālaṃkāra* and its commentary. Although tranquility and insight are treated as separate as-

pects, they are in fact inseparable [coemergence]. Tranquility is inherent in the insight of self-awareness and self-crystallization, while insight is inherent in the quiet nature of the mind. Tranquility and insight are therefore a
214 B coemergent state, concentrating one-pointedly and indivisibly, because insight by itself comprehends and crystallizes a state of tranquility unstained by any perceptive marks. The *Saṃdhinirmocana-sūtra* expounds on this nondual state:

> [Question:] At what state may tranquility and insight become blended and brought to an even state?
>
> [Buddha:] When the mind contemplates with one-pointedness only.

The identification of tranquility and insight and elucidating quotations were provided in the previous section on the general description of tranquility and insight. The fusion of tranquility and insight with the mind is considered to be the coemergence of ultimate mind [dharmakāya]. Many of the designated terms will be given later.

He who has realized the mind's intrinsic purity or discovered its identity is called a yogin. Maintaining that state is called meditation or tranquil
215 F absorption. The *Jñānamudrā-sūtra* states:

> All things are marked with the seal of the mind;
> The mind is marked with nonsubstantiality.
> He who discovers the identity of the mind
> Lives in its intrinsic purity.

The *Saṃdhinirmocana* comments:

> [Question:] How long should a bodhisattva meditate?
>
> [Buddha:] He should continuously contemplate the intrinsic characteristics of the mind.

The *Samādhirāja* teaches:

> [Buddha:] O young one, what has been designated as tranquil absorption is a definite awareness of the mind's intrinsic nature that is unborn [void].

Again the same text says:

> Because it is [a state] devoid of any thought or discrimination,
> And it is beyond sensory cognition and intellectual definition,
> A state wherein the mind itself is unimaginable,
> It is described as tranquil absorption.

The *Namkha Tabui Tingnge Dzingyi Dho* explains:

Through the ambrosia of a holy master
One will understand the mind to be like space.
Remaining undistractedly aware of the significance of this state
Is described as tranquil absorption.

B The meditation on nondiscriminating awareness has been highly praised. The *Buddha-avataṃsaka-sūtra* declares:

He who wishes to enter the realm of the victorious buddhas
Should quieten the mind, like space.
By eliminating thought, discrimination,
And clinging to dualistic notions,
He should enter this realm with a spacelike mind.

The *Lalitavistara* asserts:

I have discovered this ambrosialike dharma
That is deep, tranquil, nondual,
Luminously clear, and uncomposed.

The *Samputa* says:

If one abandons the network of thoughts,
One's experience in deep virtue will expand.
The sacred path expounded by the Tathāgata
Should neither be idealized nor discriminated against.
Discrimination means great ignorance.
It throws one into the ocean of saṃsāra.
If the mind is settled in nondiscriminating absorption
It will realize an unstained purity, like space.

The *Saṃvarodaya* states:

Similarly by meditating on the mind
As being of one flavor just like space,
One will go beyond the planes of sublime form and formlessness.
216 F One who abandons dialectical skepticism
And who pacifies all mental events in absorptive awareness
Will harmonize with the intrinsic [buddha] nature
That is immanent in every sentient being.
Like a formless state that is immersed in space.

The sūtras, the tantras, and the vital instructions all agree on this meaning [of coemergent awareness]. I have not given any further elucidation. Students will understand it from what has been and will be stated. Various designations [of coemergence], as found in other texts, have the same meaning. The *Dṛṣṭisaṃkṣepta* enumerates various designations:

Inmost awareness, unstained by dualistic thoughts
And detached from all discriminations,
Is nondwelling nirvāṇa.[120]
It is the Indestructible Being [Vajrasattva],
It is the sixth mystical form Buddha [Vajradhara],
It is the sixth family [of all the buddhas],
It is the Glorious Gentle Youth [Mañjuśrī-kumāra],
It is the Supreme Illuminator [Vairocana],
It is the ultimate nature of things [dharmakāya] and the great bliss,
It is also the nondual state of bliss and its intrinsic emptiness,
216 B It is the state actualized in the fourth empowerment,
It is the joy of spontaneous coemergence,
It is the innate purity.

This text further says:

It is also the enlightened mind [bodhicitta],
It is the family of the enlightened ones,
It is the intrinsic buddha nature [tathāgatagarbha].
From the flavor of its experience
Arises great bliss.

The same text continues:

It is the innermost awareness.
As awareness it is lucid;
As self-cognizing awareness it is nondiscriminating.

And again it states:

Nondiscriminating awareness
Is the actual basis of cyclic existence,
It is the ultimate peace [nirvāṇa],
It is the great middle path.
It is to be observed,
To be meditated upon,
And to be realized.

217 F In summary, it [coemergence] is the basis or the root of various designations, such as the ultimate nature of all things, the great bliss, the coemergent awareness, the self-emerging awareness, the self-cognizing awareness, the ultimate enlightened mind, the essence of the tathāgata, and the suchness of intrinsic reality. The *Chakgya Chenpo Rabtu Mineypai Gyü* sums it up:

This [coemergent] mahāmudrā
Is not stained by any defilement;
It is neither to be negated nor affirmed;

It cannot be cultivated
Through the spiritual path and antidotes;
This perfect structure of all the enlightened ones
Is the source of all excellent qualities
And spontaneous accomplishments.

Identifying Coemergence of Thought

This meditation begins with a tranquil equipoise of the mind's coemergence, as stated earlier. The meditator should produce an emotion of joyousness, lust, or malignance with clarity and vitality. Gazing sharply at its appearance, the meditator observes the clarity of unobstructed thought patterns, as he had done before while determining it. This [reconstructed] emotion is somewhat different from those of real life. Here the contemplative mind does not have the deluded clinging to inbred reality. Besides, the mind perceives the emotion as being empty of any identifiable essence or self-entity. Furthermore, the mind perceives the union [coemergence] be-
7 B tween the intrinsic lucidity of thought and its undefinable emptiness, the inseparability of emptiness from the thought stream, as well as the inseparability of the thought stream from its intrinsic emptiness. This experience means a supercognition of the coemergent nature of the emotion, which is analogous to the inseparability of waves and water. The movement of water forms waves; hence they are not different from the water. Likewise, the emotions do not exist apart from their intrinsic emptiness, yet they arise due to the interaction of causes and conditions, which in turn is brought about by the nonobstructing inner avenue of their emptiness.

At this stage the natural pacification of the mind's clinging to every unceasing thought represents contemplative tranquility, while a definite awareness of its intrinsic emptiness or unborn ultimate reality [dharmakāya] represents insight into the intrinsic nature of every thought stream. If the intrinsic nature of such a thought stream is emptiness, emptiness is the
218 F thought stream itself. In short, the inseparability of emptiness and thought stream represents the coemergence of tranquility and insight. This means that discriminating thoughts arise in the dharmakāya or become pacified in it. On the basis of this view the Takpo Kagyüpa order formulated such concepts and terminology as "cognizing discriminative thoughts as dharmakāya" and "delusion as awareness." If one were to ask how the sūtras and tantras show the meaning of this particular concept, the *Lodrö Mezepe Tanpa* (*Akṣayamatinirdeśa*) *states:*

> The understanding of the mind's defilement is enlightenment [bodhi], because the intrinsic nature of defilement is also the intrinsic nature of enlightenment.

The *Lodrö Zhüpa* (*Sāgaramatiparipṛcchā*) comments:

> Sāgaramati: O Supreme Illuminated Conqueror, this tranquil absorption is indeed difficult to attain!
>
> Supreme Illuminated Conqueror: This is because consciousness and awareness are to be realized as being an even state.

This text continues:

218 B [Buddha:] By realizing the evenness of all things one attains enlightenment. Therefore, bodhisattva, do not consider enlightenment to be far away.

The *Chöthamche Jungwa Meypar Tanpa* (*Sarvadharmapravṛttinirdeśa-sūtra*) comments:

> Desire is proclaimed to be nirvāṇa;
> So are hatred and ignorance,
> Because enlightenment is inherent in them.

Again this sūtra says:

> Enlightenment and desire do not have two separate natures.

The *Ratnakūṭa* states:

> Everything arises from that which is unborn [emptiness];
> At the moment of its arising it is devoid of [absolute] arising.

The *Hevajra-tantra* teaches:

> Between the state of pure awareness
> And the discriminating mind of cyclic existence
> There exists not the slightest distinction.

It continues:

> What is designated as saṃsāra is also nirvāṇa.

Again it explains:

> Hatred and the afflictions of cyclic existence are in reality nirvāṇa.

The *Sampuṭa* affirms:

> Saṃsāra and nirvāṇa
> Do not exist as two realities;
> Understanding the intrinsic nature of saṃsāra
> Is designated as nirvāṇa.

219 F Saraha comments:

A sunlike awareness through its pure light illuminates ignorance;
This supreme awareness transforms every experience into sublime bliss,
The way alchemy changes [base metal] into gold.

Nāgārjuna teaches:

There is not the slightest distinction
Between saṃsāra and nirvāṇa.
Nirvāṇa is not different from saṃsāra,
Not even to the slightest degree.

Āryadeva states in his *Nirvikalpaprakaraṇa*:

Nirvāṇa is a state that transcends dualism.
It does not emerge
Except when the mind has pacified all discriminating thoughts.

Virūpa explains:

If one realizes the intrinsic purity of mind
As revealed by a guru,
Diverse forms of consciousness pacify themselves
Into all-embracing reality.

Tilopa observes:

All aggregates, elements, and sense faculties
Arise from [the mind's] innate nature that is mahāmudrā
And pacify themselves into it.

219 B The *Tsigdü* of Nāropa and Maitrīpa states:

Intrinsic in defilements is great awareness.
It helps a meditator to consume them,
Like a conflagration that consumes a forest.

This text adds:

Deliverance from discriminating thoughts means great awareness.

Maitrīpa elaborates:

A transient thought arises from that which is unborn [emptiness].
This very thought has the nature of all-embracing reality;
The two are inseparable from the very beginning.
Therefore, I reveal these two as one even flavor.

The venerated Marpa says:

The mind's habitual dualistic discrimination
Is to be dissolved into the nondiscriminating dharmakāya.

The Great Master [Milarepa] sang:

This mental consciousness—the inner movement—
Is the source of karma and mental defilements;
It remains ignorant as long as it lacks any understanding,
Yet, when understanding dawns, it becomes self-comprehending awareness
And the source of all virtues.

Je Gampopa concludes:

Dualistic thoughts that arise from the senses
Should be firmly seized as dharmakāya.

The numerous other sayings of indestructible truth by the precious Kagyüpa lineage are all in agreement with these views. At this point some [Kagyüpa meditators] have assumed that the meaning of the identity of
220 F discriminating thoughts with dharmakāya consists of the pacification of thoughts—during inward observation—into a nondiscriminating state. Others have assumed that the understanding of discriminating thoughts represents dharmakāya, and that the absence of such an understanding means the nonexistence of dharmakāya. Both are wrong. The former position seems to hold that the purity achieved through pacification would become dharmakāya. This simply lacks the understanding that the intrinsic nature of discriminating thoughts represents dharmakāya. Hence it cannot be the valid reason for identifying thoughts with dharmakāya. The latter position seems to make the identification of thoughts with dharmakāya dependent upon the presence or absence of understanding. It thus lacks the understanding that dharmakāya is in reality the incessant, indwelling nature of all discriminating thoughts. This view reduces such a state of dharmakāya to a transient level.

What should be their authentic positions? Referring to the former position, the term "thoughts as being dharmakāya" is designated to mean an extraordinary experience and an awareness of certainty with respect to the coemergence of thought patterns and their intrinsic emptiness. Regarding
220 B the position of the latter, there can be either understanding or lack of understanding, but this is not the basis for affirming or denying the existence of the dharmakāya. For instance, the act of affirming or denying the sun as being a luminous body does not depend upon whether the observer does or does not have eyes, because the luminous sun exists and will continue as long as it exists. The scriptural quotations to illustrate this point were given earlier.

221 F Again, a certain [teacher][121]—despite his metaphysical concept known as "the nondifferentiability of saṃsāra and nirvāṇa"—refuted such conceptual terms as "perceiving discriminating thoughts as dharmakāya" and "cogniz-

ing delusion as awareness." This was simply due to his desire to find fault. Whatever his logic for validating the nondifferentiability of saṃsāra and nirvāṇa, it is similar to validating these conceptual terms. His refutation of our position may well be redirected at him. Besides his statement [propounding the doctrine of his order] was erroneous. At such a [meditational] state reality—in the main—is nirvāṇa, whereas cyclic existence is mere appearance and is therefore not reality. If the appearance of cyclic existence [saṃsāra] is not accepted as cyclic existence, no other basis to designate it can be found. Besides, if his view of it is valid, it leaves no ground for designating saṃsāra as the other constituent aspect of that which is a nondifferentiable union. Without saṃsāra this union would be reduced to nirvāṇa alone. By implication the correlative terms like "the union of method and wisdom" would be reduced to wisdom, etc., and then many harmful consequences could result.

Identifying Coemergence of Appearance

All appearances, being the mere manifestations of individual minds,[122] do not depend on the interacting sense objects and conditions otherwise necessary for what is apparently external reality. The appearances that emerge before the mind due to psychic imprints of the past[123] are not different from the coemergent appearances[124] of dualistic mind. What is being identified here is the appearances—such as form, sound, and so on—known to ordinary minds as valid cognitions. These appearances in reality depend upon and arise from the effects of individual karma that are common to all [ordinary] minds.

Now the meditator—as in the preceding case—should fix the mind in a tranquil equipoise of coemergent mind.[125] By gazing sharply at the perceptive image of a mountain, a house, or a vase he will experience the undefinable emptiness of that form while at the same time he will perceive the vividness of its formal characteristics. Here the perceiver should not limit himself to merely the mind's lucidity and emptiness. He should not let the lucidity of the imagery or appearance dim or die.

In short, when the meditator perceives the clarity of perceptive form and its unidentifiable emptiness as being the inseparable, denuded union of appearance and emptiness or emptiness and appearance, he has gained insight into the intrinsic coemergence of appearance. The analogy of a dream illustrates well this experience. Whatever diverse forms a dreamer dreams such as the material world, the outer container, sentient beings, and the inner flavor, they are nothing more than the functions of the dreamer's subconsciousness. So are the immediate appearances [of dualistic distortions], which arise out of the unobstructed vitality of the mind's innate

emptiness and continue to arise until [the meditator's] common collective
222 F karma is purified. From the moment of its emergence an appearance is not different from the mind's intrinsic emptiness. Je Lingrepa[126] provides an appropriate comment:

The rootless mind dreamed
A dream during the third part of the night;
This was the teacher who showed the identity of dream-appearance
with the mind.
Do you understand?

The same method of exploring the appearance of form may be applied to the remaining appearances of the six senses. Nāgārjuna explains extending the inference of one thing to every other:

He who sees the suchness of one thing
Sees the suchness of all other things.

Here I have simply shown the appropriate synchronization of appearance and mind. However, it is said that the perfect synchronization can be achieved only at the meditational stage of great one flavor.[127] At this stage "the mind's settled tranquility" consists of a sustained stillness free from evaluating and clinging, while perceiving vividly the appearance of an object one has focused on. "Insight" here consists of an awareness of certainty or understanding, based on the determination of a perceived appearance and
222 B its emptiness. "The union of tranquility and insight" consists of the appearance as inseparable from its intrinsic emptiness or of the emptiness itself appearing as a form. Based on such experience and understanding, the Takpo Kagyüpa order has formulated such conceptual terms as "the principle of realizing appearances as dharmakāya" or "realizing every appearance and existence as dharmakāya." To show that these terms have originated from the sūtras, tantras, and vital instructions, the *Prajñāpāramitāhṛdaya-sūtra* states:

Form is empty; emptiness is form. Emptiness is not other than form; form is not other than emptiness.

The *Prajñāpāramitā* elaborates:

Form is not one; suchness [emptiness] of the form is not another.
This is why form and the suchness of form
Are neither duality nor can they be bifurcated,
Because they are neither individuals nor separate entities.

The *Nyampanyi Nampartröpa* (*Sarvadharmasvabhāvasamatāvipañcita-samādhirāja*) says:

Even form reveals enlightenment.

It continues:

> Since form and enlightenment are equal
> One cannot find them to be separate entities.

And it further teaches:

> All things intrinsically are equal;
> They are identical with nirvāṇa.

The commentary by Mañjuśrīkīrti on this sūtra says:

> The intrinsic nature of form is enlightenment. Enlightenment itself is form.

Again this commentary explains:

> Sound and nirvāṇa are neither dual nor separate entities.

The *Samādhirāja* states:

> Do not view form as one and the intrinsic nature of form as another.
> Do not view the intrinsic nature of form as one and the tathāgata as another.

The *Hevajra-tantra* explicates:

> The grass, plants, vines, etc.
> Constitute the dynamic and static reality.
> Based on one's perception of the nature
> Of these phenomena
> One meditates on that which is ultimate!
> Such an ultimate is devoid
> Of any absolute entity,
> Yet it is inmost awareness, which is of great bliss.

223 B The *Vajrapañjara* remarks:

> Diverse appearances of form and the other senses
> Are the manifestation of the mind alone.

The *Samputa* advises:

> When looking at forms,
> When listening to sounds,
> When speaking or laughing,
> When relishing different flavors,
> When performing different actions,
> A true meditator who controls his mind
> Will experience a constant dawning of the natural state,

For this is the supreme enlightened mind [bodhicitta].
It is the indestructible one, the glorious indestructible mind [Vajradhara],
The completely purified enlightenment [samyaksambuddha].

The *Lhankye Samgyi Mikhyabpai Gyü* proclaims:

Spontaneous coemergence of the mind is dharmakāya;
Spontaneous coemergence of appearance is the illumination of dharmakāya;
Thus the indivisible union of appearance and thought
Represents spontaneous coemergence.

Saraha says:

Earth, water, fire, air, and space
224 F Are not distinct from the flavor of their innate coemergence.
He who does not bifurcate nirvāṇa and saṃsāra is stated to [adhere to]
The abiding nature of all-encompassing reality.

Śavari instructs:

All appearances and sound vibrations are like an illusion, a mirage, or a reflection;
They are substances without the marks of reality.
The mind that cognizes illusion is also like space;
Without a center and frontier, it is beyond intellectual conception.

Virūpa explains:

All marks of duality, like pleasure and pain,
Are the manifestation of the [mind's] unmodulated,
All-encompassing nature—that is mahāmudrā.

According to Tilopa:

The aggregates, the elements, and the sense of realities
All arise without any exception
From the [mind's] intrinsic nature of mahāmudrā
And dissolve themselves into it.

Nāropa affirms:

All these things—appearances and realms of existence—
Do not exist apart from the innermost awareness of the mind.

The *Tsigdü* states:

The self-delivering nature of appearances is dharmakāya.

And it continues:

> He who realizes the intrinsic nature of reality
> Has realized all appearances and existences
> As being mahāmudrā.

Maitrīpa declares:

> Diverse manifestations arise from the mind's intrinsic nature;
> It is mahāmudrā uncomposed by causes and conditions.

Je Marpa proclaims:

> Concerning this illusory wheel of external appearance,
> I realize it as being the nonarising great seal [mahāmudrā].

Jetsün [Milarepa] explains:

> Whichever way external appearances emerge,
> It deludes unrealized minds.
> Their attachment to external reality confines them in bondage,
> Yet this very reality appears as illusion to realized minds,
> And diverse appearances emerge in support of them.

Je Gampopa concludes:

> These appearances and sound vibrations arise
> From the conceptual imprint of the psyche;
> Seize them promptly for they embody the ultimate reality.

These are but few of many indestructible sayings of the precious lineage of the Kagyüpa order. I have not included any more for fear of overillustration.

THE ELIMINATION OF FLAWS AND THE APPRECIATION OF THE MEANING OF MEDITATION

There are three sections:

1. The areas of erroneous meditation
2. The flaws of partial meditation
3. The recognition of flawless meditation.

The Areas of Erroneous Meditation

25 F To achieve tranquility one has to attain one-pointed concentration, free from the flaws of dullness or thought flow and endowed with a sublime state

of bliss, clarity, and nonconception—just like the one described before, at this stage of tranquility. Although this is a contemplative absorption especially capable of producing the psychic power of transformation and supercognition, this can hardly be the appropriate cause for complete enlightenment, as it doesn't have the development of an enlightened spirit [bodhicitta]. When this is achieved, such meditation can still not be a distinct path to enlightenment, i.e., actual liberation, if the mind has failed to direct itself toward its intrinsic emptiness. Nāgārjuna explains:

> Those who do not understand emptiness
> Will fail to achieve liberation.
> Thus, ignorant beings wander helplessly
> In the prison of the six cyclic existences.

Insight is capable of determining [emptiness] as the fundamental nature of the mind or as the nature of the two kinds of nonselfhood. Hence it is indispensable for understanding emptiness. A simple tranquility unconnected to insight can neither be meditation on emptiness nor mahāmudrā. The *Samādhirāja* states the reason:

> Even though some people in the world meditate on tranquil absorption,
> Such meditation cannot eliminate the deep consciousness of a self-entity.

225 B Meditators who have listened to a few discourses and have had little association with teachers may experience a superficial meditation. They are prone to many errors. Being ignorant of the method for maintaining a definite awareness of insight, they automatically lose that state but also erroneously identify any nonmeditative sensation with meditative experience, for the former arises from a lax mindfulness and vigilance.

I shall now explain these kinds of experiences. As one tries to maintain tranquil meditation, dullness or depression will increase. First the image of the object, large or small, with dim, blurring the clarity until finally the appearance of that form completely ceases as the result of the eye consciousness having dissolved in the process. Similarly, the perception of sound through the auditory organ will gradually decrease until it ceases altogether. It is also possible that when encountering such a condition, all sense consciousness might finally cease, and the meditator will fall into an unconscious state, similar to fainting. This is similar to the freezing of a lake.
226 F As the water turns into a sheet of ice, its lucidity and transparency disappear, concealing the things lying below.

Or the meditator might experience a contemplative state with a little more clarity, combined with a momentary mindfulness. Even though the appearance of form or sound does not cease altogether, it becomes a faint image or perception. His mental vigilance—far from crystallizing itself—either becomes dull, befuddled, or indifferent. These conditions are said to be in the category of ignorance of a secondary defilement.

Yet another condition might arise—a state devoid of any consciousness or cognition of either clarity or dullness with respect to the appearances of the six senses. The mind becomes passive, almost unconscious. It is an inertial stillness that overcomes the mind, a condition similar to the former one. Therefore, the mind is not tractable for meditation.

All these states are clouded with ignorance and are stated to be the cause of an animal existence. For that reason the *Ratnāvalī* states:

B Stupidity results mainly in an animal existence.

There might be yet another experience that is somewhat different from these earlier ones. This happens when meditative tranquility consists of a kind of lucidity, but since coalescing attentiveness and vigilance are lacking in the desired crystal clarity, such a concentration cannot represent the one-pointedness of virtuous thought. However, it is not a thought of counter-virtue but is a neutral state. Similarly, a mind settled in tranquility without lucid mindfulness and vigilance, without affirmation or rejection, means that it must necessarily belong to an even cognition and thus represents a neutralized mind. The activities of a neutralized mind may possibly be transformed through circumstances, yet will not necessarily produce any definite results. Some people have identified this with the immutable karma [of the formless plane]. This is not quite right. The difference between the two is enormous! At best these two minds may become the cause of non-
27 F cognizing absorptive states. They could possibly turn themselves into sources of defilement. If either state cannot even be a flawless absorption of the four concentrative levels of the plane of form and formless plane, it cannot represent the meditation to be pursued here. The *Bodhicaryāvatāra* explains:

> Thought detached from [the awareness of] emptiness
> Dissolves itself and arises again,
> As in a noncognizing trance.

So this is the cause of certain celestial beings being so immersed in a noncognizing trance that the conscious senses along with their attendant factors cease to arise.

Furthermore, many meditators who experience a blank consciousness for a certain period, which emerges between the preceding and succeeding thought, mistake this for meditation. Lacking in the definite awareness of insight, this is a mere noncognizing state, similar to deep sleep, unconsciousness, the stupor of a drunkard, or a mind in sudden shock. Even if such

227 B a mind crystallizes itself or becomes stable, it can still not be meditation focused on the mind's intrinsic emptiness. A meditator may experience a kind of definite awareness of insight, but lacking in a secured tranquility, this state can become like that in which the mind is forcefully suppressed, making it easily susceptible to interruption or irritation by even a faint thought or appearance. So he will find it hard to continue the meditational absorption. This can be considered a beginner's meditation. It cannot be accepted as meditation on determining the mind's intrinsic nature. Je Gampopa provides this instruction:

> When the mind remains settled, a state of nondiscrimination has to be maintained. But to apply and sustain nondiscrimination with respect to the mind's essential nature is to show no understanding of the crucial point of the dharma.

He also says:

> Some other [meditators] suppress every emerging thought as they focus their mind on a nondiscriminating state. They look upon this as a positive quality, but it cannot help them to advance on the meditational path, since such a state is "a crippled awareness."

Without seeking the definite awareness of insight, none of the following meditative states is to be sought: meditation in which (1) the mind is settled
228 F blissfully, (2) in which the mind remains quiet in an empty state without any sense of past, present, or future, or (3) in which the tranquil mind perceives a lucid state with such clarity that it is as if it were reflecting all external and internal phenomena. Such meditation may bring about an inner sensation of bliss, lucidity, and emptiness separately or collectively. Je Gampopa described these meditations known as "undetermined appearances."[128] They are likely to become the cause of a noncognizing absorption. The consequence of these fallacious meditations might make the kind of rebirth for a meditator uncertain.

A certain meditation system[129] advocates the application of an uninterrupted mental grasp of unreality and emptiness with respect to every emerging thought, appearance, or to every noncognizing awareness. This is not the meditation to be sought here, because this meditation on the sustained mindfulness of intrinsic emptiness does not seem to contain a definite
228 B awareness of insight. Even if it does, it appears to sustain a mental clinging to unreality and emptiness. Thus, it becomes a great view of nihilism. Nāgārjuna gives the reason as follows:

> He who holds on to emptiness
> Cannot perfect the inner development.
> Thus it has been proclaimed.

Again he advises:

> By erroneously viewing emptiness
> Unintelligent minds bring about their own destruction.

A certain [critic][130] has stated [the following criticism] by simply relying on all kinds of sayings without carefully examining them:

> Ignorant ones who meditate on mahāmudrā
> Create the cause for animal existence,
> Or for rebirth on the formless plane,
> Or for degenerating into Hearers in an absorptive trance.

This statement is extremely erroneous and was made simply out of a desire to criticize [the system of mahāmudrā]. Why is this so erroneous? Because it implies that meditation on mahāmudrā would be the cause for rebirth as an animal. It also implies that ignorant people cannot be worthy of meditation. By the same logic ignorant people should not engage them-
F selves in the threefold study through hearing, examining, and meditating. It would further mean the existence of a common cause for animals, sentient beings on the formless plane, and hearers in absorptive trance. Inevitably this would mean they are all on the same level.

Furthermore this critic claims:

> Mahāmudrā in our order consists of an awareness
> That arises out of empowerment.

If this were so, the ignorant could not even meditate on such an awareness and would not be "worthy recipients" of such an empowerment. Then the reference in the *Hevajra-tantra* to "ignorant and wicked people" as worthy recipients would be wrong. Besides, ignoramuses who meditate on awareness attained through empowerment might well be creating the cause for animal existence, because this critic has affirmed that meditation on mahāmudrā by ignorant people would be the cause for their [rebirth as] animals and that the initiatory awareness itself is mahāmudrā.

This critic might have wished to say that a lack of knowledge about mahāmudrā meditation might produce such [undesirable] results. It would
9 B still remain a faulty statement. To illustrate this point, one could say that ignorance about Mahāyāna meditation could lead one toward becoming an adherent of Hīnayāna. However, one cannot say that meditation on the Mahāyāna will create such a cause. Similarly, one might possibly be reborn in any lower realm as a consequence of being ignorant of the dharma, but one can never say that practicing the dharma creates a cause for one's rebirth in a lower realm.

Moreover, in order to realize the formless plane, the meditator would have to attain not only an even absorption with a clear perception on each

main contemplative tranquility of the four subtle cognitive modes, but also insight with its superficial and subtle levels—all of this constituting [the contemplative zenith] in the mundane state. It is stated that this is not easy even for [aspiring] arhats to achieve. It is exceedingly improper for this critic to equate this state with the cause for an animal existence. If by his statement "degenerating into hearers in an absorptive trance," he means the deep absorption realized by arhats in general and by nonreturning arhats in particular, he by all means cannot equate it with the cause for an animal existence, because it must necessarily contain an insight into the nonselfhood of personality. It is even more difficult to conclude that "a stupid per-
230 F son who meditates on [mahāmudrā], the cause for that absorptive trance" is necessarily stupid, as the critic would have us believe. By his contention the critic has contradicted what is stated in the third *Bhāvanākrama*, that a meditator who has not realized the fourth contemplative tranquility can in no way attain the absorptive trance of an arhat. If by using this term he means "the arhat" who figures in some popular anecdotes, then it is nothing more than an ordinary verbal story. Thus, this term does not and cannot mean the arhat in a true sense. The critic should have only expressed himself after a careful consideration regarding this matter.

Some have criticized the Kagyüpa method of instruction on mahāmudrā meditation with the following passage:

> Nowadays some [meditators] identify mahāmudrā experience
> As a momentary nondiscriminating state,
> Which emerges through the power of faith in their guru.
> The [experience] could well be either an act of obstructing forces
> 230 B Or the result of coalescing psychophysical energies and elements.

To advance such a contention is utter nonsense. It would mean that they assume that the blessings of their gurus and the act of obstructing forces are identical. Such skepticism is highly improper. As explained before, any nondiscriminating state devoid of insight has not been accepted as mahāmudrā meditation. It is also an overexaggeration to say that a meditational state that has arisen from the coalescing energies and elements in the human body would mean that all methods for arousing awareness by channeling and absorbing the mental energy into the vagus of the central nervous system are wrong. And, by implication they are refuting mahāmudrā meditation, which they have already accepted.

The Flaws of Partial Meditation

There are some who recognize mahāmudrā meditation as the mind that has settled serenely in a nondiscriminating state while crystallizing its inherent clarity. This is nothing more than an absorption in tranquility unclouded by dullness or thought flow and is not quite mahāmudrā meditation. Except for the inmost sensation of clarity and emptiness it lacks insight with an awareness of certainty. If discriminating thoughts are naturally pacified, awareness crystallizes its innate clarity and cognizes with certainty its indeterminable experience. Such a meditation may be regarded as a beginner's meditation. Since this nondiscriminating state seems to depend on the suppression of thoughts or appearances, it is not quite meditation on unmodulated natural awareness. Consequently, with this very method it is difficult to achieve postabsorptive cognition.

Some [meditators] suppress or control every emerging thought or appearance to settle the mind in a coalescent state of clarity and nondiscrimination. Others assume that it is necessary to maintain vivid mindfulness in order to settle the mind in its state of lucidity and emptiness. Such meditations may be regarded as [correct] beginner's meditations if they are supported
B by an undistracted mindfulness or awareness of the mind's intrinsic nature, which has been explored in the way someone examines a bone by crushing it with a stone. Many beginners fail to clear their doubts and assumptions regarding the essential nature or thoughts or appearances. Consequently, thoughts and appearances could cause harm to arise. All these represent fragmented experiences due to the meditator's failure to discover the naturally loosened mind and due to overexertion.

However, if skillfully maintained, this kind of meditation will continuously progress toward mastery. Gradually, emerging thoughts and appearances will pacify themselves naturally so that at last the meditator will eliminate doubts and assumptions about them. Yet at the outset, some may experience clear and diverse manifestations of the mind. Should they fail to gain a deeper sense about the abiding nature of these thoughts, it is most probable that the meditator might find it hard to maintain the contemplation and thereby might become irritated by the practice. In any case, the meditator must recognize and determine the nature of the three kinds of coemergence: namely, coemergence of a nondiscriminating state, of discrimination,
232 F and of appearances. If [in guiding his disciples a teacher] identifies [the essential nature of mind] with the nondiscriminating state, most meditators might construe this to be an archtype for their meditation at all times. This will greatly constrict meditators, and therefore it is not a good method. What is most important is to have an inner sense of understanding the identity of the emerging thoughts and appearances.

The Recognition of Flawless Meditation

This section consists of three points:

1. The mind's abiding nature is said to be identical with ordinary mind

2. The recognition of the distinctive characteristics of ordinary mind
3. Its undistracted state is shown to be meditation on mahāmudrā

The Mind's Abiding Nature Is Said to Be Identical with Ordinary Mind

Some uninformed people assume that what is known as ordinary mind is deluded ordinary awareness. This is not so. The Sanskrit equivalent "prākṛta" of the Tibetan term [thamal] has two meanings, viz., an ordinary and a natural state. Here it denotes the natural state. Hence this ordinary mind consists of luminous clarity, intrinsic purity, and a self-existing state
232 B that is unmodulated and unpolluted. The Takpo Kagyüpa order is not the only one that enunciates the term "ordinary mind." The *Dekhonanyi Raptu Mineypai Gyü* refers to the same term:

> The intrinsic nature of ordinary mind is supreme fruition.
> If maintained without modulating,
> It is the threefold enlightenment [trikāya];
> If let go of, it is ultimate awareness.
> If settled unaltered in its intrinsic purity and indestructible nature,
> It is undefinable.
> It is the mother of the buddhas throughout the three periods of time.

Śrī Śavari advises:

> Ordinary mind consists of natural simplicity.
> Do not distort it through intellectual construction,
> For the pure nature of mind needs no modulation.
> Let the mind be in its natural state
> With no attempt at grasping or releasing it.

Mahāsiddha Koṭali[131] explains:

> When ordinary mind awakens its inmost recess
> And the six sensory perceptions are purified,
> A stream of bliss will flow incessantly.
> 233 F All designations are meaningless and become the source of misery.
> Settle the mind in its primal simplicity and nonmeditative state.

The Great Master [Milarepa] proclaims:

> Having continuously maintained ordinary mind
> I have already forgotten the delusion of ignorance.

Je Gampopa affirms:

This meditation relies solely on ordinary mind. I have discovered it through the grace of [my guru], the Buddha in a human body.

The Recognition of the Distinctive Characteristics of Ordinary Mind

Many such references to ordinary mind[132] give a few descriptions of its identity. This I will provide. The *Tsokchö Chenmo* of Je Gampopa describes it as follows:

> If at this moment one wishes to achieve liberation from the cycle of existence, one must recognize ordinary mind, for it is the root of all things. That which is designated as "ordinary mind" is one's own awareness. Left in its natural state, this awareness remains unstained by any [nonordinary] perceptive forms, unmuddled by any levels of existential consciousness, and unclouded by dullness, depression, or
> B thought. If one has discovered the identity of that mind one has discovered the self-cognizing awareness. If one fails to gain such an understanding, this ordinary mind remains with the coemergence of ignorance. However, the understanding of that mind is called awareness, the essence, the coemergent self-knowing, ordinary mind, unmodulated simplicity, nondiscrimination, and luminous clarity.

Thus Je Gampopa gives the description for identity of ordinary mind and the synonyms for this term. He also makes the comment that the discovery of ordinary mind is superior to most sublime qualities.

The aforesaid term "unstained by any [nonordinary] perceptive forms" means that [ordinary mind in its intrinsic nature] is uncorrupted by the intellect's grasp of conceptual formulation or by a supernormal sensation of bliss, lucidity, nonconception, and the like. The term "unmuddled by any levels of existential consciousness" means [this ordinary mind] remains unblemished by lust, hatred, and any passions or by any anxiety about one's
4 F immediate or future plans. The term "unclouded by dullness, depression, or thought" means that the mind's abiding nature or its existential mode has not been veiled by the confusing force of dullness or depression, remaining undistracted by discursive thought or sensual incitement. The term "in its natural state" means the essential nature of mind, the inmost disposition, or the existential mode that is undistorted by any concern for acceptance or rejection. Je Yanggönpa comments:

> "Nondual awareness" is the [Tibetan] classical term. "Naked ordinary mind" is the naive term used by mendicant mystics. Both mean the same thing.

Nowadays some people, having derived the idea from some odd sayings of previous gurus of this meditational order, construe the term "ordinary mind" to be a pure nondiscriminating state and use it as such. They may not
234 B have grasped the proper meanings as explained by Je Takpopa and his nephew Gomchung. According to them ordinary mind means the mind in its natural mode, unveiled by any substantiality of dualistic concepts. In a general sense, accepting a state of nondiscrimination and rejecting the discriminating mind [in meditation] cannot be the meaning of ordinary mind and its unmodulated naturalness. Gampopa in his instruction to master Gomchung explains:

> In summary, ordinary mind is an unmodulated simplicity, which must be left to manifest freely and unaltered by any exertion of accepting or rejecting it as being positive or negative, empty or not empty, conceptual or nonconceptual, good or bad, superior or inferior.

Je Gampopa further provides the meaning of the relevant terminology:

> Leaving aside "unmodulated," the term "ordinary mind" refers to primordial awareness, not distorted by any dogma or dialectics. The term "unmodulated" refers to letting [that awareness] be as it is, without altering it.

235 F If one wonders about the meaning of the adjective "naked" that Je Yanggönpa uses to denote ordinary mind, it means the essential or intrinsic nature because it is detached from any conceptual discrimination, and being undeluded, it is identical with nondual awareness. What is generally known as "nondual awareness of intrinsic reality" is immanent in every substance of reality. If one realizes the intrinsic nature of every thought or appearance, it is not different from awareness itself. Based on this standpoint Yanggönpa states:

> In summary, this natural, unmodulated ordinary mind, which cognizes its own identity, is described as the dawning of mahāmudrā meditation.

It is of the utmost importance for the meditator to understand perfectly
235 B the intrinsic nature of mind, thoughts, and appearances. Otherwise, he can neither understand exactly the meaning of unmodulated ordinary mind, nor can he achieve the awareness of certainty about it. He would be like a blind person trying to examine a body. Once he gains such an understanding he will in due course attain a deep awareness of certainty that the unmodulated, uncorrupted existential or abiding mode of the mind is no other than ordinary mind itself and that it is indeed the dharmakāya. Such a realization is achieved through a proper and persistent meditational practice because an exact understanding of the abiding mode of ordinary mind will be difficult

to achieve. Je Yanggönpa further comments on ordinary mind:

> There are many gurus who arouse [in their disciples] an inner sensation and a certain absorptive state, which they identify with meditation. Yet gurus who are skilled in making disciples recognize ordinary mind as meditation are rarer than visible stars in daylight.

Knowing the intrinsic nature of ordinary mind is described as "having seen the essence of the mind." The way one sees it does not depend on the emergence or nonemergence of a nondiscriminating state through the mastery of meditation. It happens the moment the meditator discovers it through the discriminating mind itself—which is exactly like the mind of an unreligious person—without losing sight of its segment or aspect. Je Gampopa describes:

> To observe perfectly the perceiving mind exactly as it is,
> Without impairing its form or missing any aspects,
> Really means to encounter the real buddha.

Je Gomchung elaborates:

> First there is primordial awareness,
> Second, ordinary awareness,
> Third, perceiving awareness.
> He who has perceived the intrinsic nature of these three
> Has discovered his own mind,
> Has attained all-seeing awareness,
> Has perceived the essence of its unmodulated simplicity,
> And has seen it through dualistic thoughts;
> In short, this is the awareness of an untutored lay person.[133]

Je Gyare concludes:

> This awareness of an ordinary person is dharmakāya;
> One can realize this
> Without having a guru to reveal it.

6 B More of the illuminating sayings of this meditational lineage will be made known later.

Its Undistracted State Is Shown to Be Meditation on Mahāmudrā

Having discovered the intrinsic nature of ordinary mind, the meditator remains aware of it without getting distracted, and at the same time maintains unmodulated whatever immediate mode of mind or thought arises.

This is described as the meditation. Je Gampopa describes:

This undistracted state of ordinary mind
Is the meditation.
One will understand it in due course.

If in order to meditate, the meditator retracts from maintaining the
mind's natural state through being mindful of its identity, and alters it or
adds a new element, he will be contradicting the meaning of unmodulated
mind. It cannot be meditation on this level. In any case, he must not allow
himself to be distracted—not even for a moment—by his deluded awareness
237 F with its ingrained clinging to duality. Affirming the practice by which to
attune oneself to the mind's natural naked state, the *Sangwa Dütsi Gyalpoi
Gyü* (*Amṛtaguhyatantrarāja*) states:

Neither by meditation nor by nonmeditation
Can one discover the [mind's] intrinsic emptiness and luminous clarity;
Meditation itself involves discrimination
And nonmeditation consists of discursive thought.
There is really nothing to meditate on, not even a particle,
And nothing to distract one, not even for a moment.

Śavari says:

Do not view anything as being faulty;
Perceive everything to be nonbeing;
Avoid craving after inner warmth for the sign of progress;
A nonmeditational state has been revealed,
Even so, do not fall through laziness and indifference.
Meditate regularly with mindfulness.

The *Gomdön Drubpa* clarifies how one meditates on the naturalness and simplicity of ordinary mind:

Do not contemplate anything while meditating;
This process is designated as meditation.

Even as the reflective consciousness perceives the mind's quiescent emptiness, ecstasy, streaming thoughts, or diverse appearances, the meditator
should neither cling to nor have concern for any of these experiences. He
should instead know the intrinsic identity of each and maintain that awareness in a relaxed manner without modulation and distraction. The medita-
237 B tion that requires the mind to quiet itself into a nondiscriminating state by
first retracting outflowing thoughts or stopping emerging appearances is
described by Je Tsangpa Gyare as being "meditation like a hook," because
the vibration of this meditation is rather limited.

The essence of mind, the discriminating thoughts, and the emerging appearances are all devoid of any separate, independent substance. They are the diverse manifestations of the innate power of awareness, the way rays emanate from the sun or the waves rise from the ocean. Whatever thoughts or appearances emerge in the self-abiding nature of the mind are devoid of intrinsic goodness or evil. Apart from recognizing the identity of an outflowing thought when it arises, or the identity of the settled mind when it is settled, as well as recognizing the identity of an emerging appearance once it arises and then maintaining it through mindfulness born of innermost awareness, one need not alter, divide, or modulate each experience. Je Gampopa comments:

> Whether one is absorbed in a nondiscriminating state, neither affirming nor rejecting anything,
> Or cognizing diverse thoughts,
> If one is able to maintain a tranquil mind,
> Unmodulated by dualistic discrimination,
> 8 F And if one realizes the inner sense that this state is nondiscriminating awareness,
> One has discovered the essence of mind,
> Its inmost disposition, and mode of abiding nature.
> When such an understanding is dawning,
> One need not make efforts in meditation.
> It will come automatically to him
> So that he can neither stop nor abandon it.
> Similarly, as diverse thoughts arise
> Without his being able to obstruct them,
> So does nondual awareness arise in the same manner.

Je Gomchung gives a similar comment:

> This intrinsic nature of lucid awareness
> Remains inseparable, undistractable, and uninterruptible.
> Every emerging memory and thought
> Contains the same intrinsic identity as awareness
> If ordinary awareness remains undistracted;
> Every memory and thought is identical with awareness.
> Do not view this as deficient.

238 B One may wonder whether it is proper for beginners to focus the mind on every emerging thought with mindfulness instead of going through the stages of meditation according to the exegetical method. This can be done in the case of meditators who are predestined to be awakened by the instantaneous path. This, however, will not work in most cases because without leading them through the stages of meditation, they will not be able to

eliminate doubts and assumptions regarding the mind, thoughts, and appearances. Besides, they will neither gain insight into the nature of these inner realities, nor will they attain the awareness of certainty with respect to them. A meditation with general mindfulness will not serve the purpose unless it has the inner sense of the mind's [selfless] identity with the mindfulness. Je Gampopa elucidates:

> One may wonder if there is any distinction between the common thought of ordinary people and a common consciousness of yogins. If the distinction does not exist, then does that mean that ordinary people also automatically achieve inward release? Ordinary people do not cognize the identity of nonduality due to their ignorance of the vital instructions—something that the yogins know. What they experience mostly is the mind's habitual clinging to duality, like affirmation and rejection. Even if they have received the vital instructions, they lack the trust in the diverse indefinite ways nondual awareness manifests itself and thus remain at the level where there is no possibility of
> 239 F liberation from their ingrained clinging to dualism. Devotees of dharma are also afflicted by the miseries arising from their clinging to duality of learning through hearing, examining, and meditating. Experienced meditators [yogins] who have detached themselves from the causes of dualistic affirmation and rejection experience nondual awareness through diverse ways, like indeterminate discrimination and great bliss. In this significant state lies the distinction [referred to earlier].

With this I complete the discussion of the stages of identification.

The consolidation of experience in meditation will be explained in three sections:

1. How to maintain absorption and postabsorption (Chapter 6)
2. How to get rid of meditative deviation (Chapter 7)
3. How to determine the mind as nonarising emptiness and enhance meditation (Chapter 8)

CHAPTER SIX

Consolidation of Experience in Meditation: How to Maintain Absorption and Postabsorption

THE REASON FOR MAINTAINING MEDITATION EVEN AFTER GAINING INSIGHT INTO THE IDENTITY OF VIRTUOUS CONTEMPLATION

B This section will be explained in three ways:

1. The reason for maintaining the meditation even after having discovered its intrinsic state
2. In general, how to maintain the meditation with the support of mindfulness, vigilance, and self-restraint
3. In particular, how the role of mindfulness is vital in meditation

The Reason for Maintaining the Meditation Even After Having Discovered Its Intrinsic State

It is said that, if the meditator, after having realized the meditational state, retrogresses into an ordinary level and indulges in ignoble deeds the way unscrupulous people do, his inner qualities will decline so that he will fall victim to existential bondage. Saraha comments:

> Ah, once having realized the abiding nature of the mind,
> If he indulges in ignoble deeds,
> He is acting like a king who prefers to sweep dirt.
> If he abandons inexhaustible bliss
> And indulges in debauchery,
> He will be bound by the touch of sensuality.

Je Gyare remarks:

He who abandons the meditational state once it is realized
Is like the victim of a cyclone who leaves behind all his wealth.
He is like a lion who roams with stray dogs;
He is like a precious gem fallen in a swamp.

Moreover, a meditator—having realized the vision of nondiscriminating simplicity[134] and still being preoccupied with the meditation on creative images and with the virtuous exercise of body, speech, etc.—is described as one who deviates from the true course. He is like a person who prefers an ordinary stone to a precious gem he has already discovered. Saraha again comments:

Alas, a yogin who has realized the innate simplicity of mind
And who still carries on with formal religious practices
Is like someone who has discovered a precious gem
But who still searches for an ordinary stone.
However much he may strive,
His practice is devoid of essence.

240 F Tilopa advises:

What is transcendent cannot be perceived by the intellectual faculty;
What is unconditioned cannot be realized by conceptual formulation.

Atīśa says:

When one has firmly settled the mind in one-pointed equipoise,
One should not devote oneself mainly to the virtues of body and speech.

Jetsun [Milarepa] teaches:

When the mind's innate simplicity dawns,
Do not crave after any conceptual forms,
Lest you might fall in the trap of the eight worldly principles.[135]

And he says further:

When meditating on mahāmudrā,
Do not strive for the virtue of body and mind,
Lest you might lose your nondiscriminating awareness;
Settle [the mind] in unmodulated simplicity.

Just as a fire is produced by continuously rubbing together two sticks, so will inborn freedom dawn by continuously meditating on nonvisualization.

This should not be interrupted by excessive visualized meditation. The master Vīra (Aśvaghoṣa) illustrates:

A fire will not emerge
By rubbing sticks with too frequent interruptions;
It is the same with meditation on primordial purity;
B Do not give up until this sublime state is realized.

A continuous examination and meditation is highly recommended. For instance, the *Abhisamayālaṃkāra* states:

The aspects of differentiation constitute the path of seeing.
The path of meditational attainment
Is composed of frequent contemplation,
Direct perception,
And definite understanding.

In General, How to Maintain the Meditation with the Support of Mindfulness, Vigilance, and Self-Restraint

Generally, all such meditation just described must be supported by mindfulness, vigilance, and self-restraint under all circumstances. The following quote from a sūtra supports this approach:

By constantly applying mindfulness and vigilance,
No perceptive mark of any defiled thought can overpower one.

The Bodhicaryāvatāra agrees:

All those who wish to protect their mind
I would implore
To safeguard mindfulness and vigilance
Even at the cost of their own lives.

Mindfulness means being conscious of the meaning of meditation with-
241 F out ever forgetting it. Concerning this the *Tsukna Rinchengyi Zhupa* (*Ratnakūṭaparipṛcchā-sūtra*) states:

Where mindfulness persists, no mental defilements can arise,
No obstructive forces can harm, and one will not degrade oneself to an evil level.
What is described as perfect mindfulness
Is that which does not open itself—a door—
To a nonvirtuous consciousness or the categories of emotive impulses.

Thus, mindfulness as a constructive state of mind protects one from non-virtue and elevates one to the level of virtue. Concerning the different categories of this constructive source of mind, the *Dharmasaṃgīti-sūtra* explicates:

> Well, what is the meaning of perfect mindfulness on the path to enlightenment? It is the mindfulness through which one will understand all things [dharma], will examine them, will deeply penetrate them, will contemplate them, and will recollect them all. Through
> 241 B such mindfulness one will understand the intrinsic characteristics of things.

These functional categories of mindfulness are proclaimed to be the aspects of enlightenment! The *Lodrö Mizepey Zhüpai Dho* (*Akṣayamati-paripṛcchā-sūtra*) maintains:

> Well, what is the meaning of perfect mindfulness? Perfect mindfulness means that which remains ever-present, imperturbable, straight-foward, unequivocal, and scrupulous about life's inherent deficiency. Mindfulness leads [one] toward nirvāṇa and makes one ever-conscious of the exalted path.

Such are the attributes of the perfect mindfulness. The *Chö Yangdakpar Düpa* (*Dharmasaṃgīti*) continues:

> O noble son, I will answer your questions, "What is the steadfast mindfulness of a bodhisattva? What is mindfulness? What is the level of mindfulness?" O noble son, mindfulness is the knowledge of the unborn characteristics of all the things that bodhisattvas possess. They
> 242 F have fulfilled their aspiration for realizing that which is unborn. The mindfulness of these bodhisattvas is completely purified by awareness of the unborn. Such mindfulness is always in an unmovable and unperturbable state, the depth and extent of which cannot be comprehended by ordinary people, hearers, and the silent, solitary buddhas.

Although the all-round mindfulness of a bodhisattva is designated with many different terms, the *Catuḥśataka* says:

> When an object [once] perceived is not present
> And the mind has failed to retain the event,
> Upon the return of what is called "memory,"
> There emerges that very thought.

Candrakīrti describes the way mindfulness arises from the coalescence of preceding and succeeding sensory events:

> Mindfulness is brought about
> Through the coalescence of undistorted senses and objects.

Perceiving them to be dual realities
Is deluded discrimination.

The *Abhidharmasamuccaya* explains:

B What is mindfulness? It is a retentive power that does not forget something already familiarized. Precisely its function is to prevent the mind from being overcome with distraction.

It is, therefore, a special kind of mindfulness, and an indispensable means for realizing tranquility. The two other types of mindfulness stated before represent discriminating mindfulness, which has a role in differentiating or analyzing things but which must be abandoned in meditational equipoise. One may bring about a vigilance capable of discriminating between acceptance and abandonment by relying upon such mindfulness and being watchful of the deeds of the three entrances [body, speech, and mind]. The *Bodhicaryāvatāra* elucidates this as follows:

When mindfulness stands on guard
At the entrance to the mental realm,
Vigilance will emerge.

Again it says:

That which examines again and again
The body and mind
Is the precise definition of vigilance, the watchful guard.

This being so, the essential requisite at this stage is the joint application of mindfulness and vigilance in order to maintain awareness of the mind's intrinsic nature and advance it through the exercise of discrimination with respect to what is to be accepted and rejected. Regarding the harmful consequences of not applying mindfulness and vigilance, the *Bodhi-*
243 F *caryāvatāra* states:

However much one might hear, examine or meditate on [the dharma],
If one is lacking in vigilance
One cannot retain anything,
Like a pot with a hole that cannot retain water.
Many who lack vigilance
May easily retrogress from their moral precepts,
Even though they possess knowledge,
Faith, and dedication.
When they fail to be vigilant, mindfulness vanishes,
Passions, like robbers, stealthily pursue them and rob them of their spiritual merits.

They will then fall into the lower realms,
The way victims of robbery fall into poverty.

Self-control will come naturally to those who command mindfulness and vigilance. The essence of self-control lies in the fact that it shields the mind against all harm of defilements and causes the virtues of the transient
243 B and transcending levels to bloom. The *Dezhin Shekpai Sangwai Dho* (*Tathāgatācintyaguhyanirdeśa-sūtra*) teaches:

> The term "self-control" is defined so as to denote not only the taming of the mind and the delighting of others, but also the eliminating of attachment to inner defilements and the joyful striving toward the dharma.[136]

It continues:

> Self-control is defined as being devoid of any unwholesome and harmful thoughts.

Furthermore, the *Dawa Dönmai Dho* (*Candrapradīpa-sūtra*) observes:

> Self-control remains the root of all virtues,
> Such as morality, learning, generosity, patience, and the like.
> Cherish it as an inexhaustible treasure,
> As implored by he who attained inner tranquility.[137]

The *Suhṛllekha* comments:

> Concerning miserliness, stealth, craft, lust, idleness, conceit, desire, hatred,
> And also pride in caste, physique, learning, youth, and in vast property—
> You should look upon them as your adversaries.
> The great sage proclaimed
> Self-control as the omnipotent ambrosia,
> Sensual indulgence as the realm of bondage.
> 244 F Therefore, in order to perfect the practice of virtue,
> Strive always to maintain self-control with reverence.

These [words of wisdom] are reflected in the following sayings of this meditational lineage that urge one to devote oneself to meditational realization by drawing away from distraction and settling in the natural stillness of the mind:

> Revulsion for saṃsāra constitutes "the feet" of meditation or the master of meditation; faith and reverence constitute "the crown" of meditation or the harbinger of spiritual progress; mindfulness constitutes "the guard" of meditation or its foundation; love, compassion,

> and the spirit of enlightenment constitute the ever-unfolding "action" of meditation; conscientiousness and honesty constitute "the armor" of meditation.

The meditator should be conscious of these maxims and should devote himself persistently to meditation and self-realization by drawing himself away from distraction and settling the mind in inner tranquility.

In Particular, How the Role of Mindfulness Is Vital in Meditation

Mindfulness is generally considered indispensable not only in the threefold religious training through hearing dharma discourses, examining, and meditating, but particularly in maintaining meditational absorption. The meditator should, therefore, maintain one-pointed mindfulness. If he loses his mindfulness, he is bound to miss the focal point of realization through it. In this respect the *Suhṛllekha* advises:

> O sovereign, those who attained sublime tranquility
> Showed the mindfulness of all elements within your body
> To be the one common path to liberation.
> You should therefore guard that mindfulness closely
> And with the utmost endeavor.
> If you lose your mindfulness,
> All your dharma practices are bound to decline.

Je Gampopa teaches:

> Meditate on the vision of reality with the support
> Of sovereign mindfulness;
> Strive to maintain it unperturbed
> Under different circumstances;
> Seek nothing else but the stream of mindfulness.

Je Phagmo Trupa warns:

> Unless one is on guard with mindfulness,
> The four evil robbers[138] are bound to encircle one.
> There is the danger of one's losing the gem of awareness.

Je Drikhungpa concludes:

> The uninterrupted stream of mindfulness
> Is indeed the central path of the buddhas in the three periods of time.
> If one does not know how to achieve an unperturbed mindfulness,
> One will fall prey to restive tendencies of body and mind.

Mindfulness is divided into two functional aspects according to the tradition: (1) an anticipatory mindfulness and (2) a retentive mindfulness. The former merely resolves to be mindful of a chosen object while the latter
245 F focuses the mind on the object and maintains it without distraction. Beginners will perceive the sequential order of the two but later will experience them as one single movement when proficiency in meditation is achieved. The [gurus of this] Meditational Lineage have described them as an active mindfulness and a spontaneous mindfulness respectively. They then expanded the active mindfulness into a vigorous mindfulness or strenuous mindfulness and reflecting mindfulness of emptiness or the identifying mindfulness. Then the spontaneous mindfulness is further expanded into mindfulness of the union of duality and a transcending mental state.

Regarding the vigorous mindfulness, (1) the focus of the mindfulness is fixed vigorously on the experience dawning with an awareness of certainty. (2) The reflective mindfulness maintains the definite awareness of the inherent emptiness of every thought and every appearance that emerges. (3) The mindfulness of nonduality brings about the transformation of mental effort and its habitual grasping of certainty into nondual awareness regardless of the retentive mindfulness. (4) The nondiscriminatory mindfulness helps to achieve the pacification of all dualistic notions into the state of unmodulated equipoise, thereby heralding the ceaseless mindful wheel of awareness.The
245 B saint-scholar Ogyenpa believed in synchronizing these four kinds of mindfulness with the four pure states of meditation, not withstanding the subdivision of the latter into twelve. He considered it to be profoundly effective to meditate with great effort on each preceding mindfulness in order to herald the emergence of each succeeding mindfulness.

Amongst these various kinds, beginners should, at this stage, concentrate mainly on the vigorous mindfulness.[139] Once they have achieved the awareness of the unborn [emptiness of all appearances], they may apply the retentive mindfulness.[140] There are two courses for this practice. One is an intensified application of each of the two forms of mindfulness just stated. In the second, mindfulness stabilizes itself automatically. Je Götsangpa considers the former [vigorous mindfulness] to be intensely concentrated, in the manner of a kingfisher catching a fish. It is a coalescence of two events of mindfulness where the fading vigor of the preceding mindfulness is revitalized through a renewed effort.

246 F One may wonder why this system stresses mindfulness so much, whereas the scriptures and exegetical texts repeatedly refer to "no memory"[141] and "no mental activity."[142] These are applicable only to meditational equipoise. Concerning the meaning of the term "no memory," the *Lodrö Gyatshö Zhüpa* (*Sāgaramatiparipṛcchā*) states that a meditator:

> Maintains first the all-round mindfulness
> Without memory or mental activity.

The *Phakpa Sangye Drowa* (*Ārya-buddhasaṃgīti*) says:

> Question: O Mañjuśrī, what is meant by the term "settled in the all-round mindfulness?"
>
> Mañjuśrī: All things are memory or of mental activity.

The *Drenpa Nyerzhak* (*Smṛtyupasthāna*) and the *Anusmṛti* contain many passages that refer to all-round mindfulness without memory or mental activity. One such instance is illustrated by this couplet:

> Meditate on the all-round mindfulness of the enlightened,
> Which is devoid of memory or mental activity.

Again, regarding the distinctive forms of mindfulness, the following descriptive terms are given:

46 B The all-round mindfulness is mindfulness that is unperturbable, straightforward, unequivocal, recollective, retentive, and unforgetful of the sublime path.

The term "no memory" is used to mean the pacification of discursive thoughts. Hence it is not considered to signify the confusion arising from forgetfulness, loss of mindfulness, or such unconscious states as fainting or sleep. Similarly, the term "no mental activity" is elucidated in the *Nampar Mitogpala Jukpai Zung* (*Avikalpapraveśa-dhāraṇī*):

> [Buddha:] O noble son, what is the reason for designating the expanse of the nondiscriminatory state as disengagement from mental construction?
>
> [The disciple:] Because one has transcended the cognitive marks of all dualism. This term "no mental activity" signifies that through this process [of disengagement] one transcends all dualistic thoughts.

The *Bhāvanākrama* quotes the *Avikalpapraveśa-dhāraṇī*:

> By disengaging from any mental constructions one may abandon the cognitive marks of form and the like.

247 F The term "disengagement from mental activity" is intended to mean a cessation of investigation once the inconceivable nature of the mind has been determined through discerning wisdom. The same text states, "This term does not encompass mental activities as a whole." Thus, it is used to signify a specific contemplative stage at which one disengages from any discriminatory thoughts and other habitual inner movements. Obviously, it does not mean a total absence of mental activity, as indicated by Saraha:

> O yogin, settle in this one primal mind.

Śavari reiterates:

> One masters the process of realizing
> The state of simplicity.

The *Nyensa* (*Śrāvakabhūmi*) also says:

> He who contemplates should do so from the outset
> Without any memory or mental activity
> In order to neither drift toward any cognitive marks
> Nor become distracted.

Thus, the terms "no memory" and "no mental activity" are stated to mean "no cognitive marks of dualism" and "nondiscrimination." The third *Bhāvanākrama* explains:

> If, however, a mere absence of memory and mental activity is taken to mean no mindfulness and no mental activity, then one should at this
> 247 B moment examine by what process these two are to be nullified. Nonexistence cannot possibly be the cause [for the pertinent result]. How can the nondiscriminatory state emerge from these two—no cognitive mark of dualism and no mental activity? If they simply attain the nondiscriminatory state, then this would mean that fainting, which lacks both memory and mental activity, could well become a nondiscriminatory state.

I now summarize the numerous elucidations already referred to. It has been stated that the terms "no memory" and "no mental activity" mean maintaining the stream of nondiscriminatory awareness[143] discovered earlier through investigation by wisdom. The third *Bhāvanākrama* explains further:

> Thus, one should understand that perfect analysis precedes the contemplative state of "no memory" and "no mental activity," revealed in the holy teaching, for perfect analysis alone can effectively bring about
> 248 F this nondiscriminatory state of "no memory" and "no mental construction." Thus, when a yogin investigates through his discerning intellect, he does not consciously cognize the absolute emergence of reality at that moment, in the past, or in the future. At that moment he enters the meditative state described as "no memory" or "no mental activity." Only by reaching this state will he realize the emptiness [of reality] and will then eliminate all intertwined misconceptions.

Accordingly, meditators would do well to know how to eliminate dualistic mind, memory, and mental construction, and how and when to maintain the stream of nondiscriminatory mindfulness and relevent mental activity. To consider that in meditation mindfulness and other mental activities are to be rejected altogether is to go to the extreme.

The instructions as to how to specifically maintain absorption and post-absorption are divided into five sections:[144]

1. Identifying the nature of absorption and postabsorption
2. The methods of maintaining a general meditative state
3. The method of maintaining absorption
4. The method of maintaining postabsorption
5. The method of blending absorption and postabsorption

IDENTIFYING THE NATURE OF ABSORPTION AND POSTABSORPTION

Absorption and postabsorption can be differentiated on the exact state of nonconditionality and at other higher states. Since exact absorption and postabsorption at the one-pointed state cannot be actualized due to an overbearing perceptive appearance and inner sensation, it is considered that an approximate absorption and postabsorption relevant to this level can be differentiated. An absorptive equipoise consists of a state of mind, undistracted by thoughts or dullness, which has settled itself in its coemergent intrinsic nature already grasped through the teacher's guidance. Such an absorptive equipoise should be maintained until distracted by a perceptive mark or a discriminatory thought. Atīśa in his *Madhyamakopadeśa* says:

> Clearing all flaws such as thought and dullness
> Settles the mind in a state of nondiscrimination,
> Nongrasping, no memory, no mental application,
> As long as possible or until interrupted
> By an enemylike or robberlike cognitive mark or dualistic thought.

As discussed earlier, the meaning of "no memory" or "no mental application" does not mean the abandonment of mindfulness or mental application altogether. It means that one should abandon only an instantaneously arising memory or mental activity. A thought does not arise as long as mindfulness remains undistracted. The moment it is distracted, a vivid thought will emerge. But when the mind is completely distracted, there emerges either a deluded thought or the appearance [of a sensory object] with an inbred clinging to its perceptive mark. These two—thought and appearance—have the nature of deluded consciousness. They are described as post-contemplative thought and post-contemplative appearance[145] respectively. Once mindfulness has been revived and unobstructed thought and appearance have been sustained by the glow of mindfulness, the meditator perceives their intrinsic state as the unceasing indeterminate union of appearance and emptiness. Because mindfulness was interrupted and revived, this contemplation is described as a "restored state." The absorptive equipoise itself is compared to space and the postabsorptive experience to an illusory form.

If during or after meditation the meditator experiences one-pointed equipoise, it is regarded as the actual absorptive equipoise. If, on the other hand, during the actual meditating it is interrupted by a momentary distraction but the meditator is able to quickly apply what is usually termed as "the
249 B coating of mindfulness," such a state is regarded as a postabsorptive state. Je Shang elaborates on this as follows:

> Like the center of pure space
> It is clear, empty, open, and infinite;
> It is vivid and crystal.
> Such is the equipoise of the first yoga.
> If this state is interrupted by a thought projection,
> It turns into a postabsorptive perception,
> Even though the meditator is actually engaged in it;
> As long as his mind remains in a state of crystal clarity and intrinsic emptiness,
> He is in an absorptive equipoise,
> Even though he may be talking, sitting, or moving.

At this stage of meditation there emerges an apparent coalescence of absorptive equipoise and postabsorptive perception[146] as a result of one's having mastered the spontaneous stream of mindfulness. Although not the real coalescence of absorptive equipoise and postabsorptive perception, this is regarded as "the cycle of inner experience."

In this regard, the meaning of mahāmudrā consists of recognizing the intrinsic nature of every thought or appearance—with no concern for discrimination or nondiscrimination—and then maintaining the awareness unmodulated. Such a state cannot be altered at all through any exertion of acceptance or rejection. Nowadays, during actual meditation, beginners
250 F concentrate one-pointedly on absorptive equipoise, the awareness of the mind's essential nature, until they achieve the coalescence between absorptive equipoise of attained insight and its postabsorptive perception. During the intervals between meditation they concentrate mainly on the postabsorptive perception by elevating all thoughts and appearances to awakened experience. They rightly construe this approach to be the intention of this Meditational Lineage. In this way, most beginners may be able to build a firm foundation of absorptive equipoise and to turn postabsorptive experience into effective practice. The progress of meditation is greatly enhanced by using these two practices for mutual perfection.

THE METHODS OF MAINTAINING A GENERAL MEDITATIVE STATE

Je Gampopa has spoken of three kinds of proficiency in meditation. The first proficiency refers to the skill in starting the meditation. The meditator forms a proper posture of the body, adjusting the vital centers well. Then, as prescribed before at the state of tranquility, he tries to clear the mind of its concerns and conflicts and arouse in himself an intense faith in and yearning for the meditation by appreciating its beneficial effects. The second proficiency consists in skillfully maintaining awareness of the mind's intrinsic nature while clearing the flow of dullness or thought flow as well as detaching the mind from a feeling of heaviness. The third proficiency is the skill in terminating each meditation conveniently and in repeating short, lucid meditations many times [each day] to prevent the meditator from losing interest in meditation and to have a pleasant recess. This procedure is formulated for the benefit of beginners. Je Gampopa again comments:

> At the beginning a meditator should avoid any strenuous exertion and should thereby completely relax body and mind.

By this he means keeping the body with its vital parts in a natural posture without strong pressure. The mind is to be relaxed in its own state without any vivified anxiety or strong exertion. Gampopa continues:

> In the middle, the meditator should settle the mind in its natural state without the slightest restlessness.

By this passage he means not altering or modulating the mind's primordial nature, and abandoning any scepticism about the mode of its reality and unreality.[147] He concludes:

> At the end, the meditator should understand all flow of thoughts and sensations as being nonarising [emptiness].

This passage of Gampopa's means that once the meditator establishes the intrinsic reality of every thought or every sensory perception, he will realize that it is detached from an absolute mode of arising, dwelling, or ceasing, and that every thought and perception attains self-release into the mind's unmodulated simplicity.

Moreover, when he says, "Raise [the spirit] as high as the blue infinity," Je Gampopa means expanding the vista of one's mental perception to the extent of infinity. With the phrase "Spread out widely like the earth," he means enlarging the scope of mindfulness and vigilance. "Stabilizing the mind as firmly as a majestic moutain" means fixing the mind in concentration [without any movement]. "Light up like a butter lamp" means increasing the intrinsic clarity of awareness. "Be unstained like a crystal" means maintaining lucid awareness, free from the veil of inner sensation. Since most of these methods are equally appropriate for absorptive equipoise and postabsorptive perception, they are elucidated as a common means of maintaining them.

THE METHOD OF MAINTAINING ABSORPTION

This will be described in two ways:

1. Enumerating the methods for maintaining the mind's intrinsic nature
251 B 2. The condensed elucidation of these methods

Enumerating the Methods for Maintaining the Mind's Intrinsic Nature

This will be elucidated in three ways:

1. The six methods for maintaining the absorptive state
2. The well-known methods of settling the mind
3. The other methods of settling the mind

The Six Methods for Maintaining the Absorptive State

According to Tilopa these are as follows:

> No recollection, no thinking, no thought,
> No meditation, no examination,
> But letting the mind be in its natural state.

The term (1) "no recollection" refers to having no thought of past events, for as long as a meditator recollects so long will he be distracted. (2) "No thinking" refers to not modulating or evaluating the focus of mental cognition for it will interfere with the present mind, which is to be settled in an absorptive equipoise. The term (3) "no thought" refers to not anticipating any ideas of future activities, because this will divert the mind to those ideas, which will make it unstable. These three points are very widely known. Saraha also comments:

> Abandon thought and the object of thought;
> 252 F Remain innocent like an infant.

Again he says:

The mind cannot be viewed
As being an external or internal reality.
He who abandons thought and the object of thought
Dwells in the mind's natural state,
Singing the song of indestructibility.

And finally he sums up:

That from which [the intrinsic mind] is detached
Is contemplation.
What is there to be contemplated?

Śavari points out:

Thus, the mind that detaches itself from activities
Throughout the three periods of time
Remains unclouded by any modes of discrimination.
Maintaining this innate simplicity is designated as meditation.

The above-mentioned term (4) "no meditation" means not contemplating any objects such as a visualization, a nonvisualization, etc. To do so would be to engage the mind in a dualistic discrimination. Saraha explains why:

Ah, do not prescribe a contemplation
On the mind's intrinsic reality, which is devoid of any self-nature.
By contemplating the duality of meditation and meditator
One will abandon the enlightened spirit.
Such a person will bring afflictions on himself.

Furthermore, he adds:

For a mind detached from self-nature
252 B There is neither meditation nor a meditator.
The ultimate freedom from hope and fear
Is the indivisible mind.

Śavari says:

If an ignorant mind has nothing to meditate on,
A realized mind has no duality of meditation and meditator.
The latter, by nature, is like space,
For space does not conceive another space.

Virūpa explains:

The expanse of the mind's intrinsic reality
Is empty of an essence;
Therefore, it is detached from the duality of meditation and
meditator.

The term (5) "no examination" means that once the mind has actualized its nondiscriminatory simplicity, an examination should not be repeated. To indulge in discursive thoughts at such a stage will herald dualistic appearances and a clinging to perceptive marks. Saraha comments:

The intrinsic nature [of the mind]
Is unblemished by any modes of discrimination and deficiency.
Being pure from beginningless time,
It cannot be intellectually determined.
To do so would be like provoking a poisonous snake.

Also he says:

By examining the mind through logic,
Negating one or many substantive realities,
One will lose the mind's innate clarity
And will thereby wander through the realms of saṃsāra.
253 F What can be more pitiful than someone
Walking straight into an abyss in open view?

Finally, he sums up:

A mind unstirred by examination remains still, like space.
This nondwelling space transcends all conceptual definitions;
Such a nondiscriminating mind need not be examined or analyzed.

Śavari explains:

A critical analysis will confine the mind in bondage.

Virūpa declares:

The self-nature of the mind is inexpressible.
Its essential identity remains detached from all interdependent relativity.
It can neither be examined and analyzed
Nor can it be illustrated through an analogy.

The aforementioned term (6) "letting the mind be in its natural state" means leaving the mind in its natural or existential mode without ever altering it. To do otherwise would distort the abiding nature [of the mind]. Referring to this, Saraha states:

In keeping the mind in its exact nature
Lies the unobstructed fruit
That is inherent from beginningless time.

He continues:

Do not corrupt the mind's natural purity by an act of
concentration.
Do not agonize yourself so, but settle in tranquility.

Śavari advises:

The innate purity of the mind does not need any alteration;
Let it be in its natural state without clinging or projecting.

Virūpa elaborates:

Be aware of the mind's ultimate purity and nonattachment;
Let the mind remain in its natural pleasant mode,
Without accepting or rejecting, craving, controlling, or staining,
For this is the perfect ultimate.

Maitrīpa concludes:

Keep [the mind] in its pure state without modulating it.

These methods for maintaining the mind's absorptive equipoise incorporate most of the vital principles that deal with one-pointed meditation on the mind's intrinsic nature. They are wonderful methods for determining intrinsic reality [dharmatā]. Tilopa reaffirms:

By not recollecting, thinking, examining,
Meditating, practicing, expecting, or fearing,
One will gain self-release
From the mind's clinging to these dualities,
And one will thereby arrive at intrinsic reality.

The Well-Known Methods of Settling the Mind

Je Gampopa in his *Tsokchö* mentions four kinds:

In watching the intrinsic nature of the mind one should (1) loosen it, (2) let it rest in its primal nature, (3) keep it in a delightful state, and (4) let it rest in a relaxed mode.

To (1) "loosen the mind" refers to a very effective method of relaxation, the knowledge of which enables one to clear assumptions and doubts regarding the mind's mode of existence and immutable nature. Je Gampopa elucidates this as follows:

The best loosening means the best meditation;
Average loosening means an average meditation;
While inferior loosening means an inferior meditation.

Why is this so? When the mind is utterly relaxed in whatever perceptive form or existential mode it is in, without letting attachment [or anxiety] interfere, every sensory consciousness will [automatically] pacify itself and nondiscriminatory awareness with its intrinsic lucidity will dawn. This awareness of the unborn [emptiness] with the vigor [of intrinsic lucidity] represents the inseparable union of tranquility and insight as well as the mind's coemergence with its intrinsic nature. Shang, the great realized one, states:

> Upon loosening the mental consciousness through relaxation,
> Inner sensations of clarity and nondiscrimination emerge,
> Like the expanse of the clear sky.
> 254 B This represents the luminous clarity of dharmakāya.

Saraha teaches:

> A mind bound by tension will undoubtedly gain
> Its self-release through relaxation.

He also says:

> If the mind is under pressure, it succumbs to bondage;
> If it is released, distortions will clear by themselves,
> For what fetters ignorant people
> Liberates thoughtful people.

Tilopa agrees:

> Loosen the mind in unmodulated simplicity;
> By loosening the fetter, self-release will doubtlessly come about.

And he continues:

> Like the expanse of space, the mind [in its intrinsic nature]
> transcends intellect.
> Let it remain in its relaxed nature,
> Withoug directing or settling it,
> For mind without a manipulated focus
> Represents mahāmudrā;
> By deepening intimacy with it,
> One will attain supreme enlightenment.

The aforementioned term, (2) "let it rest in its primal nature [soma]," refers to settling the mind evenly in its primordial state, which is to say, the meditator should simply let the mind rest in the intrinsic coemergence of mind. This is its indeterminable nature of primordial simplicity, as has been identified [through the initiation process] by one's gurus. This is like the

5 F intrinsic nature of gold, which has remained unchanged from its existential beginning up through the refining processes such as smelting, etc.

Some [texts] refer to the same term [the primal nature] as a settling of the mind without any hesitation, the same way a dove enters its nest. Others refer to it as maintaining the mind in an unmodulated state. Saraha comments:

> In order to contemplate intrinsic reality, detached from any root,
> One will attain it through the pith instructions of one's gurus.

He comments further:

> To meditate on inconceivable awareness
> Means to meditate on total realization.

Śavari maintains:

> When one has perfect understanding of the mind's innate simplicity,
> One has achieved what a mountain dweller has realized.

Virūpa:

> That which has coemerged with the mind from the beginning,
> Which cannot be discovered by any other means,
> Is mahāmudrā, intrinsic emptiness and simplicity, as it is conceptually designated.

The phrase (3) "keep it in a delightful state" means letting the abiding nature or existential mode of the mind remain delightful and exact as it is. If it is fettered by a directed focus or by a strong desire, the mind will become
255 B intractable, like a prisoner who remains agitated with thoughts of escape, but regains his equilibrium once in freedom. So it is with the mind. Saraha explicates:

> Those who are shackled will attempt to escape toward the ten directions.
> If released, they remain firm and still.
> I understand that turning them back would be like turning back a camel.

This example is identical with the [sixth method of Tilopa] already referred to as "letting the mind be in its natural state."

The phrase (4) "let it rest in a relaxed mode" means letting it remain quiet without being fettered by the bondage of affirmation or rejection, reality or unreality, good or evil, and attachment or clinging. As hay lies loosely on the ground when unbound, so the unbound mind remains relaxed. Saraha implores:

Abandon the attachment that fetters you.

And he advises further:

Substance and nonsubstance shackle the mind,
Preventing it from achieving the supremely attained state [sugata];
Rather than bifurcate, actualize the evenness of saṃsāra.
256 F O yogin, dwell one-pointedly in the pristine simplicity of the mind!

Je Gampopa describes the intrinsic reality of the mind in three terms: primordial, unmodulated, and loosened. In the unmodulated state it is identical with the mind in its natural mode. By maintaining the mind unaltered even when disturbed by an adverse circumstance, its agitated form will then quietly release itself into intrinsic simplicity and spontaneous fulfillment. Such a clear mind, free from dualistic clinging, is like that of an infant's. Śavari describes:

Ordinary awareness is simple in its own mode.
Let it remain unblemished by any contrived ideas and images,
For the mind's innate purity does not need any modification.

And he emphasizes:

Neither holding the breath nor fettering the mind
Let unmodulated awareness remain like that of an infant's.

Maitrīpa says:

The unmodulated and simple mind is dharmakāya.
The innate purity cannot be actualized through a modulating intellect,
So release the mind into the sublime peace.

256 B He continues:

A modified procedure of body and mind does not produce meditation.
Meditation is settling the mind in an undistracted state.
Indeed it is not alterable through antidotes
For equipoise or against nonequipoise.

The Other Methods of Settling the Mind

Nāgārjuna gives the instruction:

Do not discriminate, do not reflect,
Do not alter, but let the mind be relaxed,

For the unmodulated mind is the natural treasure of the unborn
[emptiness],
The nondual path of wisdom-gone-beyond.

Thus he enumerates four methods, namely, not to discriminate, not to reflect, not to modulate, but letting the mind be relaxed. The *Semnyi Ngalso* (*Cittaviśrāmaṇa*)[148] advises:

O listen, my son, in order not to be fettered or bound
By whatever way you may discriminate,
Remain undistracted, unmodulated, and natural,
Thus relieving yourself of afflictions.

This refers to the three methods of maintaining the natural state of mind, i.e., to rest the mind (1) in a natural way, (2) without modulation, or (3) without distraction.

Je Gampopa proposes:

Let your mind remain like the sky without clouds!
Let your mind remain like an ocean without waves!
Let your mind remain like a butter lamp without a breeze!

257 F He mentions three methods, namely, nondiscrimination, imperturbability, and clarity of mind.

The *Chakgya Chenpo Yigeshipa*[149] mentions six ways:

> Keep your mind in its immutable simplicity, free from pressure or exertion, like a great eagle soaring through space. Settle the mind in stillness, like a tideless ocean! Maintain complete clarity, like the unclouded sun! Know that perceptions and feelings arise from the mind, like waves appear upon a river, and therefore settle the mind in its natural state. Let your mind be clear, unobscured, and without clinging, like that of a child gazing with wonderment at a temple. Maintain trackless consciousness, like a bird flying across the sky!

Khedrup Chegompa[150] refers to four sets of methods. The first set is (1) to maintain the mind's lustrous clarity, (2) nondiscrimination, (3) nonconfusion, and (4) supportlessness. The second set consists of three methods: (1) no modulation, (2) no distortion, and (3) simplicity. The third set has three methods of letting the mind settle (1) in its primordial state, (2) in a loose state, and (3) in its inborn luster. The fourth set consists of two methods of recognizing (1) the state of no meditation and (2) of no distrac-
257 B tion. I have not elucidated these methods. One will know them from what has been and will be said.

Besides, the works of the ancient masters refer to the methods for stabilizing the mind as being soft, quiet, serene, and loose. They also refer to the methods of maintaining the clarity of the mind as clear, lucid, vivid, fresh, lustrous, and distinct. However, for beginners to maintain pure awareness during their meditation, Je Gampopa instructs:

> In the beginning, learn to actualize lucid awareness,
> To protect it from distraction,
> And to maintain it in its essential mode.
> Once a deep intimacy is achieved,
> An awareness of certainty will emerge.

And he continues:

> Clarity is an inner sensation. Remaining undistracted means stability, and insight into the unreality of awareness is the realization.

However, without penetrating insight into the essential nature of the mind, the experiences of blissfulness, clarity, and nondiscrimination, however good, are merely undetermined, cognitive appearances. Without achieving a one-pointed equipoise, focusing on the mind in its intrinsic nature will be a
258 F mere intellectual exercise. Jetsün [Milarepa] comments as follows:

> That is only an intellectual perception,
> But not awareness;
> It is only the trunk, not the fruit;
> It is only an attribute, not nondiscrimination.

Thus, whatever the deviation, every contemplative equipoise must achieve the union between the clarity of awareness and an undistracted stability. This precisely constitutes the one-pointed, inseparable state of tranquility and insight.

The Condensed Elucidation of These Methods

This will be dealt with in three ways:

1. Meditating without intellectual effort
2. Maintaining an undistracted awareness of intrinsic reality
3. How these two methods contain the vital instructions on meditation

Meditating without Intellectual Effort

To meditate on mahāmudrā is to maintain undistractedly the mind's innate mode of existence. To meditate anew on something conceived is to depart
258 B from a natural meditation on the mind's abiding nature. I have already given the reasons and will repeat them briefly. The mind, by its nature, is impar-

tial. One should neither discriminate between affinity for or aversion against the unfolding perception of appearance, awareness, and emptiness. Similarly, as the essence of the mind is devoid of any identity, one should not meditate by identifying the essence of the mind with reality or unreality; neither should one affirm or deny it. The intrinsic nature of mind being indeterminable, the meditator should not objectify it so as to let it be loose, fixed, or focused. Since the intrinsic nature of mind is immutable, one should meditate without agitating it through hope, fear, or motivation. As the mind is by nature devoid of a good or evil entity, the meditation should not be altered through affirmation or negation. The intrinsic mind being inconceivable, one should not modify the meditation through visualization or intellectual alteration.

In summary, the essence of mind is beyond meditation. Therefore, one does not meditate about it. To indulge in such meditation is to engage in intellectual exercise, objectify mental images, discriminate perceptions, or cling to dualism. Therefore, such meditation cannot represent either the perfect vision of or the perfect meditation on the abiding nature of mind. A prajñāpāramitā text confirms this approach:

> To meditate on wisdom-gone-beyond means not to meditate on anything.

The *Guhyasamāja* explains:

> There can be no meditation
> On that which is devoid of substance.
> Meditating on something [conceived] is not meditation.
> Since reality is neither substance nor nonsubstance,
> Meditation must be without a conceptual image.

The *Gur* (*Vajrapañjara*) says:

> One should meditate neither on the concept of emptiness
> Nor on nonemptiness.

Saraha advises:

> One should abandon attachment.

And he explains:

> Focusing on any conceived image
> Will cloud the path of liberation.

He sums up:

> A person, enchanted by something delightful,
> Clings to it out of attachment.
> He is bound to be afflicted, even by a pain as small as a sesame seed.

Śavari comments:

Mahāmudrā is a state of no-discrimination
In which there is nothing [conceivable] to meditate on,
259 B Not even an atom;
So do not meditate [intellectually].

Virūpa explains:

It is a deviation to conceptualize the abiding nature of the mind,
To either develop attachment to inner sensations,
Or to conceive their intrinsic nature.

Tilopa urges:

Do not contemplate any mental activities.
Watch the nature of your determinate reality [awareness].

Maitrīpa summarizes:

Apart from letting the mind remain in its own nature,
There is no meditation through the manipulation of body and speech.
There is no meditation through an antidote
For an equipoise and against a nonequipoise.

Maintaining an Undistracted Awareness of Intrinsic Reality

[In the mahāmudrā system] there is nothing to meditate on intellectually but only a way of maintaining undistracted mindfulness, which is impervious to normal consciousness. By merely remaining undistracted, the mind cannot differentiate its distinctive role [in the four stages] until one has perfected [mahāmudrā] meditation. So, mindfulness on each stage of the four stages must be firm, undistracted from the relevant meaning of the mind it embodies. Mindfulness in this respect must be completely undistracted from the significance of the mind, coemerging with its intrinsic nature, which the
260 F meditator discovered previously through an initiatory process. New meditators, who have not yet resolved their assumptions [about the intrinsic nature of mind], should practice concentration, similar to one-pointedness, which enables them to remain undistracted in any meditation relevant to their respective level. Saraha comments:

O, watch your own self,
For it represents intrinsic reality.
If unable to watch with an undistracted mind,
You will fail to penetrate the forest of substance

And will lose the gem of true reality,
For a distracted mind is incapable of realization.

Śavari repeats:

Lo! Look at yourself with an undistracted mind.

Virūpa declares:

Keep your undistracted awareness
Without conceptualizing it as real or unreal.

Tilopa explains:

To remain undistracted is to be a king among meditators.

Maitrīpa sums up: .

There is nothing else to do but remain in an undistracted state. . . .

Some inferior intellects do perceive the inner sensation of an undistracted
state, yet they may not know if they are distracted from being conscious of
the mind's abiding nature. How does this happen? The abiding nature of the
260 B mind transcends intellectual perception. When the meditator conceives its
conceptual meaning, he is somewhat distracted from the meditation on
equipoise. Similarly, the true meaning of mind is beyond knowledge. The
moment the meditator conceptualizes it, he is distracted to a certain extent.
The intrinsic nature of mind is not the object of intellectual examination; the
moment the meditator applies critical analysis with respect to the mind's
intrinsic emptiness or nonarising, he is distracted from meditative equipoise. The nature of mind is not an object or a direct object of mental focus;
the moment the meditator focuses on the inner sensation of bliss, clarity,
and nondiscrimination, he is distracted. In short, the intrinsic nature of
mind transcends all dimensions of intellect. The meditator will be distracted
from that state either by creative visualization, conceptual abstraction, or
261 F even by simply resolving to end all activities. Saraha explicates:

A mind cleansed of defilement
Coemerges with its intrinsic nature;
Such a mind remains free from disharmony.

He further explains:

By turning the mind into "a nonmind state" [nondiscriminatory],
One will achieve supreme enlightenment.

Virūpa affirms:

To conceptualize or dualize ultimate reality
Is to create the foundation of saṃsāra

And become a helpless wanderer.
Watch the intrinsic nature of the mind,
Which is the basis of all things.
As one ceases all mental activities
And perceives nothingness,
One will certainly achieve liberation.

He continues:

To exercise the intellect on emptiness, nonarising,
On the mode of reality or unreality
Is to move away from the abiding nature of mind.

Śavari urges:

Watch, keep watching, but do not watch anything.
Meditate! Keep meditating! But do not meditate on anything!

261 B One may wonder how new meditators, who have not realized the exact meaning of the mind's transcending nature, should practice. Those who have yet to realize the meaning of the mind's intrinsic nature, as has been explained, should continuously meditate on the mind coemerging with its intrinsic nature and maintain awareness of certainty and inmost experience. They should remedy every deviation or remove every obstacle [as explained by their teacher]. They will in due course realize unerringly the meaning of the mind's transcending nature through the four stages of inmost clarity. This gradual process is like the waxing of the moon, the growth of a lion's cub or of a child. They will know more through further elucidation.

How These Two Methods Contain the Vital Instructions on Meditation

All the aforesaid methods of maintaining meditative equipoise are condensed into two: nonmeditation and nondistraction. The term "nonmeditation" embraces no recollection of the past, no contemplation [of the present], no anticipation [of the future], no modulation, no distortion, no examination, etc. The term "nondistraction," in fact, encompasses such terms as a primordial quietude or a loosened state, the intrinsic nature, the
262 F mode of existing, and the intrinsic nature of reality. Similarly, the passage "to settle the mind in its nonmeditative naturalness" indicates the settling of the mind in tranquility; "not to be distracted from awareness" signifies insight; and "the even blend of nonmeditation and nondistraction" encompasses the merging of tranquility and insight. This is described in the sūtras as nondual awareness, nonconceptual, undiluted consciousness, and natural emptiness. The treatises of the Mantrayāna describe it as coemergent aware-

ness, natural clarity, and total emptiness. This tradition [mahāmudrā] describes it [the coalescence of tranquility and insight] as coemergent mind, the intrinsic essence of mind, the abiding nature of mind, etc. These are wonderful means to achieve absorptive evenness. The *Prajñāpāramitāsaṃcayagāthā* emphasizes this:

> Sentient beings claim to have seen space.
> They should examine how they have perceived it.
> The Tathāgata applies such an analogy to perceiving reality.
> This cannot be explained in any other way.
> He who perceives space in this way will perceive all realities.

According to the *Sampuṭa*:

> To settle the [mind] in nondiscriminatory absorption
> Is to remain pure, like space.

The *Bodhisattvabhumivṛtti* states:

> Letting the nonvisualizing mind
> Maintain the characteristic of space
> And meditating on space
> Constitute meditation on emptiness.

The *Chöying Töpa* (*Dharmadhātustotra*) urges:

> Abandon discrimination and analysis of realities—
> Mainly those of a mental nature.
> Meditate on the expanse of intrinsic reality,
> Which encompasses the nonsubstantiality of all things.

The *Bodhicaryāvatāra* describes:

> When neither substance nor nonsubstance remains real
> Before a perceiving intellect
> And since no alternate reality exists,
> A mind detached from conceptual images is peaceful indeed!

Atīśa says:

> Settle the mind without any discrimination
> In the nonconceptual expanse of reality.

Illuminating sayings of great saints were quoted before, hence no further elaboration is needed.

F Beginners [in the mahāmudrā meditation] should know that "no meditation" here connotes a state of tranquility and relaxation. However, an excess of relaxation will produce dullness. "No distraction" belongs to the dimension of insight and exertion. An excess of exertion will produce sensory incitement.[151] The meditator should know that the methods of clearing away dullness and sensory incitement and of maintaining even absorption and insight were discussed earlier. At this level it is necessary to maintain absorptive equipoise with a harmonious balance between relaxation and exertion in the manner indicated by the analogy of a brahmin spinning yarn evenly, neither too loosely nor too tightly. Je Gampopa advises:

Let your mind remain loosened and unmodulated
In its primordial naturalness;
Do not direct it, let it remain as it is;
Do not cogitate but fix the mind in a nonconceiving state.

Among the many similar sayings is one from Je Phagmo Trupa:

To meditate on the unaltered dharmakāya
Means to let the mind relax and remain unaltered in its primordial state,
The way a brahmin spins yarn.
When obscured either by the dullness of tranquility
Or by swaying from a directed focus,
263 B Meditate on unification with the mind's coemergent nature.

Some teachers have criticized the content of this saying in the following manner:

It was stated, "Let the mind relax and remain unaltered in its primordial state,
The way a brahmin spins yarn.
This is mahāmudrā meditation."
I find that resting the mind in its primordial state
Is like letting the wool remain natural,
But spinning it into yarn implies a modulation of the natural mind;
Therefore, this analogy is faulty.

These critics did not know that the simile describes only the state of balance between slackness and exertion necessary to maintain evenness of the mind. They are not only ignorant of the meaning of the primordial state [soma], but are also wrong in assuming that the mere resting of the mind in the primordial state is mahāmudrā. Regarding the method of maintaining absorptive equipoise Je Götsangpa states:

Observe your mind with penetrating sharpness;
You will perceive nothing, for it is devoid of substance.
Let the mind rest in that emptiness loosely and lucidly,
Without imagining and clinging.

The nature of mind cannot be observed by letting "the mind watch the mind" penetratingly. When experiencing the nonsubstance of mind, one should let this awareness rest loosely in its natural mode. In order not to let it fade into a neutral state, lucid mindfulness and unimaginary simplicity, devoid of directed focus, should be maintained, without clinging either to affirmation or abandonment. This summarizes well the vital points of mahāmudrā meditation.

THE METHOD OF MAINTAINING POSTABSORPTION

This may be elucidated in four ways:

1. Recognition of mindfulness in postabsorption
2. The method of maintaining meditation through postabsorptive mindfulness
3. Sublimating discriminating thoughts
4. Perceiving postabsorptive perceptions as being like a magical scene

Recognition of Mindfulness in Postabsorption

The meditator has properly maintained a one-pointed equipoise of the mind in its coemerging essence during the meditation. What then is the procedure for his practice during the postabsorption? The meditator should first learn to maintain the stream of mindfulness and vigilance through continued effort. Je Drikhungpa counsels:

> He who has realized mindfulness becomes the master of meditation.
> O my sons, cherish mindfulness!

Mindfulness in this case refers mainly to definite awareness and the experience of mind's coemergence, which he was made aware of through initiation. However, the meditator should, in a slightly different way, sustain the mindfulness of whatever virtuous deed in such a way that it will not lose its power or lucidity, while crystallizing every immediate thought or perception of form or sound, without any concern for affirmation or rejection of any perceived reality. He should do this through an extended effort, in order to actualize the lucid, expansive mindfulness that is detached from any clinging, like an infant looking at a shrine.

In summary, the meditator should maintain the perfect state of the two virtuous absorptions, namely, the mind's coemerging thoughts and the coemerging appearances, as has been explained before. The *Bodhicaryāvatāra* summarizes:

Concerning the perception of form, sound, or knowledge,
These are not the object of negation;
What must be rejected is conceptualized dualism,
Which is the cause of all miseries

The Method of Maintaining Meditation through Postabsorptive Mindfulness

265 F How does one maintain virtuous practice through mindfulness? It is done in the same way an experienced cowherd watches his cattle. Without rounding them up or following every animal, he keeps them all under his observation, letting them graze freely, even though some may wander. In a similar fashion the meditator should not obstruct the unfolding of a thought or appearance in his attempt to suppress or vitiate it as if to constrain the meditative mind. Besides, the meditator should not let the mindfulness of every thought or appearance lose its sharpness due to distraction, while in pursuit of an object, and due to his inborn clinging to the idea of acceptance or rejection. He should forthwith crystallize each of the six cognitive manifestations and, at the same time, maintain a definite awareness of its indeterminable nature. He should specifically maintain in an unwavering and nongrasping manner the awareness of every unfolding thought as being a vibrant movement in intrinsic emptiness, and of every appearance as a
265 B manifestation of immanent emptiness Je Götsangpa advises:

Every time a thought arises,
Seize it firmly,
Release it into its natural state;
Without doubt one will achieve inward liberation!
Watch external appearance with sharpness,
It is an illusion like the mind itself;
Focus the mind on that which appears, without any clinging.
Let the intermediate consciousness uncoil itself,
It flows like the wind devoid of substance.
Let this flow remain free from clinging.
This is described as thoughts arising as meditation,
It is an insight into one's inner identity
Where there is neither affirmation nor negation.
There exists no other meditation
Apart from remaining so undistracted.
Do not deviate from the nonmeditational state.

This condensed explanation is easy to understand. As beginners try to maintain coherent mindfulness of the fourfold daily conduct,[152] they will initially find themselves frequently distracted. However, through the combined power of intensified mindfulness in meditational absorption and F sustained mindfulness during postabsorption, they will not only be mindful, but will in due course become undistracted from the clarity and emptiness of every thought and that of appearance and emptiness. If they continuously fail to gain such an experience, it means that contrary to their claim they have not yet eliminated their exaggeration and slander with respect to the mind's coemerging thought or that of appearance. They should then produce a thought or perceive a sensory appearance in an absorptive state and examine it from the standpoint of its origin, dwelling, and movement, as well as its intrinsic nature in various ways. Having so determined every thought and every appearance, they should maintain absorptive evenness, as was done previously.

Saraha teaches:

> All things empirically established are empty of any essence;
> Even conceptual designation cannot exist
> Without interacting causes and conditions.
> If one understands the self-released nature of intrinsic reality,
> One realizes that it transcends the visual, auditory, and other
>   sensory faculties,
> For it is devoid of any self-nature.
>
> Understand the dual appearances of self and others
> As being monistic reality;
> Remain fully aware of this without distraction,
> 266 B But abandon clinging lest it afflicts the mind.
> Realize peace without attachement to anything.

Śavari says:

> All the different rivers, the Ganges and the rest,
> Become of one flavor in the salty ocean.
> Understand that all discriminating mind, the mental events,
> Become of one flavor in the expanse of intrinsic reality.

Virūpa concludes:

Thus all appearance and existence of conditioned phenomena
Are empty of essence.
They are mere epitomes, symbols, or designations.

Sublimating Discriminating Thoughts

Je Gampopa mentions three ways of actualizing the path:

1. Recognizing the contemplative identity
2. Reviving the awareness of intrinsic reality
3. Sublimating recreated afflictions

Recognizing the Contemplative Identity

The method of recognizing the contemplative identity has been evolved for the benefit of those who have some experience in postabsorption. Such a meditator, with an inbred familiarity, recognizes the spontaneous self-release of a thought or an appearance into the mind's nonarising simplicity. This process is analogous to the instant recognition between friends upon a sudden encounter.

Saraha points out:

> Intrinsic reality is everywhere,
> Before you, behind you,
> 267 F And each of the ten directions.

He asks:

> All that manifests from the mind
> Contains the identical nature of the Master [Buddha];
> Therefore, can waves be distinct from the water?

Maitrīpa declares:

> Diverse appearances are but the manifestation
> Of the mind's intrinsic nature.
> They have not evolved a real identity
> Through the interaction of senses and sense objects.
> They are mahāmudrā.

Reviving the Awareness of Intrinsic Reality

Concerning (2) reviving the awareness of intrinsic reality, this practice has evolved for those who have had little experience, like snow melting through contact with warm rocks or a river. Such meditators experience the spontaneous self-release of every emerging thought or appearance into the emptiness of nonarising. Saraha comments:

> This is like a crow that flies from a boat,
> Soaring around and afar,
> And that returns to it.

Śavari uses the same image:

Just as a crow that flies from a sail
Returns to it after circling and soaring,
So a passionate mind that pursues the trail of thought
Returns to the primordial purity of mind.

Sublimating Recreated Afflictions

"Sublimating recreated affliction" refers to the way experienced meditators should perceive intuitively the spontaneous self-release of virtually all thoughts and appearances into the emptiness of nonarising. Furthermore, these advanced meditators should produce heavy and disturbing thoughts or appearances and thereby perceive them to be the manifestation of the mind's innate emptiness of nonarising. This is analogous to a great fire that is fueled by the forest and fanned by the wind, yet these elements do not aid a small fire [which is like an inexperienced meditator].

Saraha says:

> You should let all these appearances
> Unify themselves into their fundamental emptiness,
> The way a spreading fire embraces a forest.

Maitrīpa observes:

> A deluded mind [by its intrinsic nature] is great awareness;
> It aids meditators greatly.
> The way a forest fuels a great fire.

He further states:

> The emerging senses dissolve
> Into the expanse of intrinsic reality.
> Emerging thoughts spontaneously release themselves
> Into great awareness.
> The harmonious unity of senses and thoughts
> Is dharmakāya.

Je Phagmo Drupa elaborates:

> If one meditates for four periods (a day)
> And pacifies dualistic thoughts in the nondual path,
> One will gain four experiences, described as
> The meeting of an old friend,
> The melting of snow on a hot rock,
> The spreading of a forest fire,
> And an inner sensation of bliss, clarity, and emptiness.

The first experience is like the reunion of old friends,
Who recognize each other instantly upon their meeting.
So the yogin, perceiving emerging thoughts instantly,
Comprehends them to be identical with the mind's intrinsic emptiness.
Hence its description as the reunion of old friends.

The second experience is referred to as "snow melting on a hot rock."
Snow that falls from water-bearing clouds
Melts upon touching warm rocks.
Likewise thoughts arise from a discriminating mind;
If one perceives them as originating from the mind itself,
Without striving one will realize
That the mind is the nondiscriminatory dharmakāya.
Hence the term "the revival of the awareness."

The third experience refers to the simile "spreading like a forest fire."
A raging forest fire burns everything indiscrimately—
268 B Trees, grass, and animals, clean and unclean land.
Winds and hailstorms cannot stop it,
Instead they intensify the flames.
Similarly, when the fire of thought flares,
Let it consign to the emptiness of nonarising
All discrimination, good and bad, self and others,
All emotions, lust, and hatred,
Without acceptance and abandonment, affirmation and rejection.
The more numerous thoughts are,
The more powerful an aid they become for inner transmutation.
Hence the description "sublimating recreated affliction."

The fourth experience refers to a secured realization
In which the mind becomes clear, open, transcending,
Blissful, lucid, nondual, and detached.
Even a pinprick turns into ecstasy;
The same experience will prevail throughout intermissions day and night,
When one walks, sits, rests, and so on.
Such is the fourth illuminating experience
Of bliss, clarity, and so on.

Perceiving Postabsorptive Perceptions As Being Like a Magical Scene

This will be examined in two ways:

1. The meaning of a magical scene and the rise of illusion
2. Perceiving postabsorption as being like an illusion

The Meaning of a Magical Scene and the Rise of Illusion

269 F Some assume the analogy of illusion to mean a mere appearance without reality that emerges before the purview of mental delusion. Others view illusion as being the emergence of thoughts or appearances, more like dull, misty scenes, as an aftermath of having experienced an inner sensation of tranquility and emptiness. Still others hold illusion to be a sustained consciousness that every emerging thought or appearance is an illusion.

The first view is incorrect. Although it has not rejected the appearance of the senses, it nevertheless embraces the negation of interdependent activation. The second view is false, because it merely perceives the outer appearance of inner sensation without ascertaining the nature of such appearance. The third standpoint is also incorrect, because it merely conceptualizes every appearance as being an illusion.

What then is the exact approach? It is said that the term "illusion" is generally applicable to two categories: (1) intrinsic reality [dharmatā] and complete knowledge [sarvajñāna] and (2) phenomena such as the form aggregate [rūpa-skandha] and the rest. Intrinsic reality or complete knowl-
269 B edge is established only through inference [and experience] as it does not manifest itself in a visible or tangible way. The latter [phenomena] are described as illusion since they manifest as apparent reality, even though being devoid of any essence. This is relevant to the nature of illusion under review. The *Prajñāpāramitā-saṃcayagāthā* explains:

> Understand that the five aggregates are illusory phenomena.
> Do not treat illusion as being different from the five aggregates themselves.

The *Samādhirāja* states:

> Meditation on perceptive marks
> Is empty of the unborn essence,
> Like mirages and the phantom city of the gandharvas,[153]
> Like illusions and dreams.
> Understand all things as such.

Thus many examples of illusion are given. I will provide a simple explanation. A magician conjures up an illusory vision of a horse or an elephant
through the manifestation of tools and use of incantations. Both the
270 F magician and the visually deceived spectators see the magical figure. The
difference is in the way the latter perceive this figure, i.e., as if it were a
self-existing reality. Therefore, the spectators create an inbred clinging to it.
The magician, who knows the unreality of the figure, is not deceived by it.

Likewise everyone perceives all sense objects such as form, sound, etc. and cognizes discriminating thoughts. Just as the magician understands the intrinsic unreality of the magical form, so the meditator, after having established subject-object reality as being empty of an innate essence or self-nature, perceives reality to be a mere appearance, without an innate entity, i.e., as a magical figure.

The *Samādhirāja* affirms:

> Magicians produce phantom forms—
> Horses, elephants, and others.
> Whatever their appearance
> They are devoid of reality.
> Know all things as such.

Perceiving Postabsorption as Being Like an Illusion

To perceive reality to be an illusion, two factors must be present simultaneously: one, the external appearance perceived by the sense consciousness
and two, the definite awareness of emptiness. For example, a master magician perceives the appearance of the phantom horse or elephant through his
270 B eye consciousness. At the same time he is certainly aware of the fact that
the form is unreal. He, therefore, remains certain of the sensory falsity.
Similarly, during postabsorption a yogin unmistakenly perceives diverse
mental experiences, due to immediate circumstances, or appearances of
form, sound, etc. that emerge through the interaction of diverse factors. At
this point the yogin's perception should coincide with his awareness of the
intrinsic emptiness of all postabsorptive experiences and appearances. Such
an awareness must be strengthened by coherent mindfulness of inner sensation and certainty of the mind's coemerging thoughts and appearances. As
a result of this, the meditator will perceive the illusion for what it is during
the postabsorptive state. Śavari elucidates:

> If reality is examined, it is devoid of the three conceptual images.
> Being unreal it is like a dream or illusion.
> A dispassionate mind remains joyous
> And free from sorrow.
> He is like a master magician performing the art of magic.

He continues:

1 F Every appearance or sound is like an illusion, mirage, or reflection;
It is substance without the mark of reality.
The mind that perceives such illusion is like space.

In order that the emergence of such illusionlike postabsorption be established in the awareness of emptiness, it is essential for the meditator to attain the awareness of mind's coemerging thought as being nonarising [emptiness]. He should revitalize his inmost awareness through meditative absorption. It is equally essential for him to strengthen the awareness of the true nature of both coemerging thought and appearance. No special efforts are necessary when determining the dimension of external manifestation, since normal thoughts and appearances emerge through the power of interacting causes and conditions.

Some people who are overcome by their attachment to emptiness seem to negate the interdependence of action and effect. This represents great nihilism, which is totally wrong. They should remedy this by seeking a
271 B definite understanding and a clear vision of the subtle aspect of interdependent karma and its effects. In short, it is essential to realize the following two concepts simultaneously: a perfect understanding of the unfailing consequences of one's action and a definite awareness of the emptiness and essencelessness of all thing. This is described as the object of wonderment by the *Bodhisattvabhumivṛtti*:

Being fully aware that all things are intrinsically empty,
One abides by the principle of karma and its consequences.
This is wonderful, supremely wonderful!
This is marvelous, supremely marvelous!

The examination for the self-nature or the essence of all things will bring about an awareness of total nondiscrimination. Even though devoid of a self-nature or essence, [intrinsic emptiness] manifests itself as form, sound, etc. These two aspects [of reality] are characterized by the ancient masters as the spacelike emptiness and the illusionlike emptiness [appearance] respectively. Following this, the present-day exponents of ultimate reality
272 F describe the two aspects as the spacelike equipoise and the illusionlike post-equipoise, sometimes the former is called transcending awareness, while the latter is called awareness of the transient world.

272 B The sublime sayings of this Meditational Lineage contain references to the methods of maintaining the mind's inherent mode steadfastly and unmodulated while not altering the agitated consciousness, which is due to circumstances. Having misconstrued this, some hold that agitated consciousness must be sustained as an spontaneous experience. Others misunderstand

the sayings to mean that even a deluded awareness must be maintained without alteration. They are all completely wrong because they fail to differentiate the exact level and condition [of the mind and meditation], and also to differentiate between what is to be accepted or rejected. The sayings refer to the method of maintaining agitated consciousness without alteration and the emerging thoughts without modulation, acceptance or abandonment, at a particular level only. It is a definite level where the meditator is required to maintain unmodulated every emerging perception and also to maintain any agitated consciousness, without attempting to alter it. This is done only after the meditator has gained insight into the mind, its essence, nature, and characteristics. This is the level where the aforesaid sayings may be applied literally.

It is stated that, if one has failed to realize the crystal clarity of inmost awareness through penetrating analysis, in the same manner as someone examines a bone by forcefully crushing it, one must immeditately purify the intense experience of bliss and clarity, must detach the consciousness from the emotion of these sensations, and must then maintain the awareness perfectly. Otherwise, to maintain a deluded awareness of conditioned reality, without altering or reorienting it through devoted meditation, means to create for oneself a cause for cyclic existence. In this connection, Je Drikhungpa differentiates the meaning of "unmodulation" and the different levels:

> To remain unaltered in defiled consciousness
> Is to live on the three planes of saṃsāra.
> To maintain an inner sensation and experience
> Is to create a cause for rebirth in a higher celestial realm;
> To realize the mind's unalterable intrinsic nature
> Is to elevate oneself to the level of nirvāṇa;
> To realize the unalterable nonduality of saṃsāra and nirvāṇa
> Is to attain the union of the two on the self-transforming path of Buddhism.
> He who has realized that which transcends intellect,
> Which is unmodulated, ultimate,
> Self-arising, and spontaneously accomplished,
> Will fulfill the aims of others without striving.
> The ultimate accomplishment is the state transcending inner development.

273 F What then is the meaning of the aforesaid term "unmodulation?" Maintaining the mind in its natural mode without altering it when one has realized its abiding nature is phrased "maintaining the mind in its unmodulated natural mode." "Not altering consciousness" refers to abstaining from activating the awareness of the abiding nature of reality. Craving for an affir-

mation or a rejection is designated as "unmodulating the conditioned consciousness." Similarly, the term "blending [the mind] with every sensory appearance" means to be truly mindful of the intrinsic nature of mind. The term "releasing oneself into every emerging sensory consciousness" is so stated with the consideration that the meditator will reach a natural level of mind by releasing his concern for affirmation or rejection.

In summary, if the meditator maintains an unceasing mindfulness of the mind's intrinsic essence throughout the postabsorptive consciousness or the emergence of appearances, all one's undistracted consciousness or appearances will become the postabsorptive perceptions. By maintaining an unceasing awareness of the mind's intrinsic reality, one will be able to maintain every emerging perception in its natural mode during the postabsorptive state, and one will also attain the determinate awareness with respect to the abiding nature of every sensory appearance without attempting to alter it. It is of the utmost importance to continuously maintain undistracted mindfulness of the intrinsic nature [of thought or appearance]. This is the reason why mindfulness constitutes the main meditation. Je Gampopa affirms:

> Meditate on the vision of reality with undistracted mindfulness,
>   which is like a king.
> Strive toward that state while guarding it against fleeting diversions;
> Seek nothing but the stream of undistracted mindfulness!

Again he says:

> As long as the peg of clinging is not removed,
> So long will the outflowing thoughts create karma.
> One had better be on guard with undistracted mindfulness!

THE METHOD OF BLENDING ABSORPTION AND POSTABSORPTION

It is not at all easy to describe how exactly the coalescence of absorption and postabsorption comes about, mainly due to the different ways people experience it. I have not seen many treatises on this. In some of the written dialogues with Je Gampopa, he addresses the question, "What does the term 'coalescence of the essence of an absorptive evenness[154] and that of a postabsorption' mean?" He replied:

> Such a coalescence comes about if the mind always remains
>   essentially conscious of its intrinsic nature,
> Undetached from its luminous clarity
> Throughout the four modes of daily conduct.

Asked if "no coalescence" means when mindfulness fades and the mind cogitates in discrimination, and upon regaining mindfulness, it becomes aware of its intrinsic nature, Gampopa replied, "That is no coalescence."

Je Drikhungpa comments:

> He who has mastered absorption and postabsorption on separate levels
> Is called a bodhisattva.
> He who has mastered the union of absorption and postabsorption
> Is called a buddha or mahāsiddha.

According to this quotation it would appear that the true coalescence of absorptive evenness and postabsorption does not come about until the meditator has reached the great level of one flavor and no meditation [the final stages of yoga]. Nonetheless, it was stated that the complete, luminous clarity of the mind that has pacified dualistic discrimination does not even emerge after the postabsorption on the great level of nondiscrimination. Solid sensory appearances would be perceived momentarily on the intermediate level of one flavor.

Je Gomtsül asked Gampopa the following question:

> 274 B What is the standard for coalescing absorption and postabsorption? Can one engage in activities [during postabsorption] without being separated from one-pointed absorption? Are postabsorption and dualistic discrimination compatible? Is postabsorption identical with a dream or illusion? Did those who perceived a dualistic discrimination during postabsorption establish its intrinsic nature?

In response to this question on whether one can engage in activities [during postabsorption] while being separated from one-pointed absorption, Je Gampopa replied:

> If one experiences it in the way indicated in the earlier inquiry, it is excellent, though it rarely happens. Concerning the second inquiry [whether postabsorption is identical with a dream or illusion], yes, it should be so. Concerning the last inquiry, if dualistic discrimination remains ordinary without the determinate awareness of its intrinsic nature, coalescence of absorption and postabsorption has not taken place.

Deducing from the sayings of some ancient gurus belonging to this Meditational Order, it appears to me that no contradiction will arise in using the term "coalescence of absorption and postabsorption, when one is absorbed in the great level of nondiscrimination." Where such coalescence has taken place, the entire experience in postabsorption need not be of luminous clarity only, but it can well be associated with illusionlike thoughts. It is stated that when the mind is occasionally distracted for a moment, one may do well to immediately perceive the abiding nature of such apperception and thereby reestablish that which has been determined. Such experience takes place just before or on the level of the great nondiscrimination. The *Prajñāpāramitā-saṃcayagāthā* states:

> This absorption is free
> From discriminating senses of being in it or departing from it,
> For it [the absorption] embodies a complete awareness
> Of the intrinsic nature of all phenomena

The stated reason is that where there is understanding of the true nature of phenomena, there is bound to be a coalescence of absorptive evenness and postabsorption. Śavari confirms:

> Having realized the intrinsic nature of one's self,
> Even a distracted mind dawns as mahāmudrā.

It is thus stated that when one realizes intrinsic reality, one experiences the dawning of the meditative state, no matter whether one is mindful or distracted. An opportune moment comes even on the great level of non-discrimination in which the meditator may experience the coalescence of absorptive evenness and postabsorption. I shall describe the way of blending absorptive evenness and postabsorption. This blending is expected to take place on every level of the four stages of yoga; however, one must still keep in view how it is experienced at each level.

The ideal coalescence of absorption and postabsorption is absent at the stage of one-pointedness, because the mind has yet to purge its clinging to
275 B inner sensation and experience. However, there can be a superficial coale-scence of absorption and postabsorption on this level. During a certain period of the postabsorption on the average level of one-pointedness, what used to be a strong apperception or appearance now pacifies itself. So much so, that it emerges far less frequently as solid reality. When an apperception or appearance arises, it is either pacified or fades away. This shows some tendency to amalgamate to a certain extent, the contemplative absorption and postabsorption on their own level. The reference to an incessant perception of inner sensation and experience on the great level of the one-pointedness must be regarded as the coalescence of absorption and postabsorption on their own level. The ideal coalescence of absorption and postabsorption arises on the level of nondiscrimination. However, during the time of postabsorption, on the average level of nondiscrimination, the meditator may not always achieve the awareness of mind's intrinsic nature, but retentive mindfulness is present in this postabsorptive consciousness. At this time, when the meditator experiences awareness and its emptiness

and appearance and its emptiness, and meditation comes very easily, it indicates a slight amalgamation of absorption and postabsorption.

On the great level of nondiscrimination when the meditator is able to maintain the absorption for a day and night without interruption, in a state detached from any inner sensations, this should be recognized as the amalgamation of absorption and postabsorption. Similarly, on the average level of one flavor, the meditator may experience much less postabsorptive delusion at the occurrence of appearances by reason of his meditation. Thus, at this level a slight amalgamation of absorption and postabsorption is achieved.

276 F During the time of postabsorption, on the great level of one flavor, the meditator perceives without any clinging all appearances as clear and empty as someone's vision of an ephemeral illusion. This is to be regarded as an amalgamation of absorption and postabsorption. For these reasons the great trio Gampopa and his two nephews, as well as Je Phagmo Trupa and Je Gyare, together with their disciples, affirmed that a natural amalgamation of absorption and postabsorption would take place on the level of one flavor. Besides, many distinctions exist between the virtuous practice, the absorption, and the postabsorption of the yoga of nondiscrimination and one flavor. They will be dealt with later.

CHAPTER SEVEN

Consolidation of Experience in Meditation: How to Get Rid of Meditative Deviation

This will be dealt with in two ways:

1. The elimination of aberration and deviation with regard to absorptive equipoise
2. The methods of removing obstacles to meditation

THE ELIMINATION OF ABERRATION AND DEVIATION WITH REGARD TO ABSORPTIVE EQUIPOISE

This elimination has two sections:

1. The elimination of the four aberrations
2. The elimination of the three deviations

The Elimination of the Four Aberrations

276 B There are two further sections:

1. The identification of the four aberrations
2. The methods of guarding against these aberrations

The Identification of the Four Aberrations

The four aberrations [each having two parts] appertains to the way the meditator reduces the overall significance of emptiness to a certain intellectual comprehension. Hence, each is designated (a) as a primal aberration; and (b) in terms of the error in each meditation on emptiness is designated as an immediate aberration. Two of the four aberrations appertain to the way the intellect reduces emptiness to the area of conceptual knowledge.

The first aberration contains the two parts. (a) The primal aberration is committed when the meditator remains ignorant about the supreme emptiness of all forms,[155] a meditational state described as nondifferentiable appearance and its emptiness, which is the nondualistic mode of emptiness and relativity. In this situation the meditator concludes that the nature of emptiness consists of absolute nihility, unrelated to the discrimination of good and evil, and consequently disregards the efficacy of karmic effects with respect to vice and virtue. In other words, the meditator shows a totally nihilistic tendency by conceiving the intrinsic emptiness of things to be "absolute emptiness." Carried away by this intellectual appreciation of emptiness he has failed to understand apparent relativity that arises from interacting causes and conditions.

277 F (b) The aberration, designated as "immediate aberration," is committed when the meditator, regardless of his understanding of the overall meaning of emptiness and his ability to explain it to others, perceives it to be existing elsewhere. Thus he fails to understand it with respect to his own mind and to achieve true experience.

The second aberration splits into two parts. (a) The first, the primal aberration, is committed when the meditator assumes that by meditating on emptiness to sublimate his experience on the path, he will attain, in a different form, enlightenment consisting of three supreme aspects [trikāya], endowed with five transcendental awarenesses [pañcajñāna]. This happens when the meditator has failed to realize that immanent in the abiding nature of mind is the spontaneously fulfilling dharmakāya, the object of realization, and also that indivisibly integrated in the mind's intrinsic nature is the basis of existential life, the process of inner transformation and realization. The integrated mental aspects mean that the meditation, the path, and the goal are nothing else but the intrinsic aspects of mind.

(b) The second, the immediate aberration from meditation, is committed when the meditator, ignoring through lack of confidence and consistency the adequate methods of meditation he already possesses, seeks to find something different or better elsewhere, or when he focuses in his meditation on immense sensational delight and lucidity, as if they were superior to the intrinsic nature of mind.

277 B The third aberration consists of two kinds. (a) The first aberration from emptiness occurs due to the meditator's erroneous understanding of emptiness as being an integral aspect of the deluded mind and of perceiving it as a natural antidote inherent in all inner malaises. The "primal aberration" is committed when the meditator, after having created the duality of defilement and emptiness, considers it necessary to eliminate his defilement first and then meditate on emptiness as the spiritual antidote. This is due mainly

to his failure to understand that the very nature of mental defilements consists in emptiness, which remains as the inherent antidote against them, thus rendering unnecessary a contemplative differentiation between the application and rejection of any alternate antidotes, and that by the intrinsic voidness of the defilements he can experience the defilement dawning as awareness, which is the inmost antidote. It is also a part of the same aberration to focus the mind firmly on the conceptual conclusion, arrived at after an intellectual appreciation, that the nature of defilement is devoid of any self-nature. (b) The second, the "immediate aberration," occurs when the meditator fixes his mind in meditation by pacifying emerging thoughts or appearances instead of remaining mindful of their intrinsic emptiness after having reascertained them.

The fourth aberration has two forms. (a) The primal aberration from the understanding of emptiness takes place when the meditator fails to perceive emptiness as being the very nature of all realities, which includes among others the contemplative nondifferentiation of skillful means and transcending wisdom [i.e., the union of bliss and void-awareness], visualized and nonvisualized meditations, and so on. He consequently meditates on the perceptual image or the conceptual view of generosity and other such skillful means. And then, by deductive reasoning or by being aware of the "no essence mantra"[156] he determines the perception [of generosity] to be devoid of an innate self-nature. (b) The immediate aberration from the stabilization of absorption occurs when the meditator—in his attempt to sustain it—fails to bring about coherence and order. At the same time, he fails to elevate emerging thoughts to an absorptive level and vivifies them, believing that this is the proper contemplation. Owing to his oscillation, he even fails to elevate a postcontemplative awareness to the level of the practice and, as a consequence, stops the flow of thoughts, as he considers this to be the meditation.

The Methods of Guarding against These Aberrations

Of all these aberrations the aberration in which emptiness is reduced to conceptual knowledge is the most fallacious. Saraha indicates this in the following quotation:

> To hold on to nothingness
> Is even more foolish.

Nāgārjuna concurs:

> An inferior intellect brings about its own downfall
> By misconceiving emptiness.

Such is the great view of absolute nihility. The consequence of this will bring one down to the lower realms, as it is said that he who holds on
278 B to absolute negation will descend into the lower realms. Je Gampopa comments:

> By reducing emptiness to the realm of knowledge
> One shows a lack of understanding, even though one is
> detached from any clinging.

Meditators must not fall victim to any of the other aberrations. Even though these other meditational aberrations are slight by comparison to such misconceived views of reality, they do not necessarily lead to insight that fully penetrates abiding reality. What has been designated as mahāmudrā is by its intrinsic character nonarising [void], completely empty of identity, be it existent or nonexistent, transitory or eternal, real or unreal. Yet, from its unceasing abstract "tone" arise the diverse phenomena [interdependent arising]. Thus, by understanding that the void is the heart of interdependent arising and that interdependent arising is the intrinsic void, [the meditator's awareness of] the void will not deviate into an intellectual aberration. The *Mūlamadhyamaka-kārikā* explains:

> There is nothing that is not interdependent arising;
> Therefore, there is nothing that is not of emptiness.

The *Bodhisattvabhumivṛtti* illustrates:

> Apparent reality is designated as emptiness; emptiness is inherent in apparent reality.

279 F By perceiving mahāmudrā, the intrinsic nature of ordinary awareness, which like a sovereign embodies or commands all things, including the existential foundation, the path, and the accomplishment, the meditator may avoid deviating from the nature of emptiness on the path of self-realization. In this regard Saraha exhorts:

> Mind should investigate mind regarding pure awareness,
> For it unites all the existential ground, the path,
> And enlightenment into one flavor.

He continues:

> To meditate on the inconceivable self-emerging awareness
> Is to meditate on the complete accomplishment.

He concludes:

> The unobstructed accomplishment is always within oneself.
> So, do not imprison your consciousness by any fear or doubt.

Āryadeva clarifies:

> One substance represents all other substances;
> All substances embody the nature of one substance.[157]

Je Gampopa sums it up:

> Now I understand that this inmost awareness,
> Clear and empty, is dharmakāya.
> Now I understand this beginningless, pure awareness
> As the inherent accomplishment.
> Oh! In this vast expanse of the precious mind,
> B The source of cyclic existence,
> Is enshrined the spontaneous inner accomplishment.

Deviation from emptiness through one's disregard for spiritual antidotes will not happen to the meditator, once he has understood the unity of all things and knows that mental defilement and awareness, the object of abandonment and the means of remedy, are the spontaneous coemergence of even flavor. The *Hevajra-tantra* affirms:

> There is not the slightest distinction
> Between a perfect awareness
> And discriminating thoughts on the existential plane.

Again it says:

> Cyclic existence, hate, and such other emotions
> Indeed embody nirvāṇa.

Nāgārjuna teaches:

> No distinction whatsoever exists
> Between saṃsāra and nirvāṇa.

Maitrīpa says:

> Underlying mental defilement is the great awareness.

The meditator will not commit an aberration by intellectualizing emptiness, if he bears the seal of dharma, i.e., through understanding unmodulated mahāmudrā as the sovereign who commands all appearances and existences, and if he thereby comprehends that the intrinsic nature of
280 F visualization and all such practices is nothing other than natural, pure emptiness. Virūpa comments:

> Happiness, misery, and all other things that bear dualistic marks
> Are but manifestations of the intrinsic nature, mahāmudrā;
> Even as manifestations they are unreal, impermanent, and mutable,

Yet they bear nothing but the seal of abiding emptiness,
Which is the true nature of all things.

Śavari says:

All thoughts always arise
From all-encompassing reality.

Maitrīpa summarizes:

If one realizes the intrinsic nature of oneself,
One has realized all appearances and existences
As mahāmudrā, the all-pervading dharmakāya!

Furthermore, Je Gampopa refers to two other deviations: (1) deviation from an exact appreciation of realization to sublimated sensations, and (2) deviation from an understanding [of their intrinsic void] to sublimated sensations. The former, upon experiencing the sensations of bliss, clarity, and nondiscrimination, holds them to be an unsurpassed state. But these sensations are simply the effect of the meditation on the mind's intrinsic
280 B nature, which employed a special technique of harmonizing the vital energies within the psychic centers of the central nervous system. The latter deviation refers to the meditation that focuses on the meditator's yearning for these sensations or his displeasure at their absence. The sensations of bliss, clarity, and nondiscrimination are the by-product of his mind, which has through the blessings of his guru glimpsed the essence of mind as devoid of any identity or essence. Je Drikhungpa comments:

This blissful bliss and this clear clarity
Sometimes emerge, other times disappear!
A meditator who longs for them
And who meditates on absorption
Is like a child gazing at an elusive rainbow.
It becomes dimmer and dimmer
Until it disappears in the sky!

In this respect some made a critical comment as follows:

The intention to abandon the four aberrations
Is a dualistic discrimination; it is incompatible with mahāmudrā.
If it is not dualistic thought, it cannot be abandoned;
If it can be abandoned even though there is no dualistic thought,
Why then can intrinsic mahāmudrā not arise in all sentient beings without effort?
If this were actual mahāmudrā meditation,
There could be no areas of aberration or deviation.
Where these exist, it cannot be mahāmudrā.

This comment has been made merely to criticize the system. What is the explanation for it? By the aforementioned sayings of Maitrīpa and others such as "self-releasing thought represents great awareness," it has been confirmed that on the level of insight into the abiding nature of thoughts they spontaneously become mahāmudrā. This system has not accepted as mahāmudrā the emerging mental cognition that purports to abandon general meditational aberrations. Therefore, this criticism is unjustified. If one could not eliminate [inbred] defilements in the absence of any dualistic thoughts, the sayings quoted below would be incorrect. The *Sūtrālaṃkāra* maintains:

> By continuously harmonizing
> With the power of nondiscriminatory awareness,
> Intelligent meditators destroy the dense forest of defilement,
> In the same way that a powerful medicine eliminates poison.

The *Bodhicaryāvatāra* declares:

> Emptiness is the countermeasure against the dark cloud
> Of the knowledge and emotionality.
> He who wishes to achieve enlightenment soon
> Should meditate on emptiness.

The implications of the criticism would mean that those who meditate on nondiscrimination would not be able to eliminate inner deficiencies, and
31 B that sentient beings would remain free from any dualistic discrimination, which would be ridiculous. By stating that no aberration or deviation would take place in the meditation on mahāmudrā, the critic repudiates his own statement:

> For most ignorant people to meditate on mahāmudrā might cause their rebirth in the animal realm.

Again the critic has stated that no aberration or deviation takes place in the meditation on mahāmudrā. By the same token no deviation could possibly take place at any stages of the path to enlightenment. Such a position would invite a serious refutation based on [Buddhist] logic and doctrines.

The Elimination of the Three Deviations

This has three sections:

1. Particular experiences as a possible ground for aberrations
2. How the aberrations turn into deviations
3. Methods to prevent deviations from taking place

Particular Experiences as a Possible Ground for Aberrations

It is said that a potential for deviation exists in experiencing many astounding sensations. This can happen only to a few energetic meditators. When,
282 F as a result of continuously meditating without ever slackening the control over any habitual indulgences, the meditator overcomes sullenness, attains a lucid awareness, and when, specifically, he experiences numerous sublime sensations, a lasting harmony of and an easy mastery over the central nervous system and the vital energies will come about. Then, among the potentials for deviation are visions of forms, an inner sensation of sound, smell, and other distinct sensory perceptions, and diverse thoughts that flow the way the tidal waves rise. Much of the latter is considered to be the manifestation of defiled psychic imprints and karmic power. However, those who alternate meditation with ordinary activity do not experience this, except for a few inner sensations.

282 B According to this meditational system there are three kinds of subliminal sensations [arising from meditational absorption]: bliss, clarity, and nondiscrimination. The first may consist of the sublime bliss that permeates the body, the bliss that arises through the tactile sense, or the bliss that makes one forget the body as well as the difference between day and night. It includes tranquility, happiness, and a sense of mirth. The second inner sensation consists of the clarity of mind, which like a crystal reflects a variety of inner sensations and is like a bright light. The clarity of mind emerges so much like a bright light that even in the dark night things far and near seem visible. Besides this, the power of clarity consists of supercognition, which reads the thoughts of people. The third inner sensation arises from absorption in a nondiscriminatory state. Some teachers consider the vision of an "empty image" that arises from the meditator's psychic potential as the sublime sensation of emptiness. I prefer to treat it as belonging to the sensation of clarity. The third sensation will consist of the cognition of all
283 F static and dynamic phenomena as intrinsically empty, of faintly perceiving the senses, and of form fading, like a mist. Besides, the meditator will perceive the dualistic appearances of himself and others as manifestations of emptiness and perceive the complete paling of thoughts into all-pervasive emptiness, which is like pure space.

As in the passage quoted below, some teachers refer to inner sensations that emerge through the meditator's body, speech, and mind as prophetic signs that the realization of the abiding nature of mind is imminent due to the blessing of the three indivisible sources [trivajra].

> When one cognizes the first glimpse of the mind's abiding nature, one will receive significant dreams and sublime sensations. The masters of the three supreme indivisible sources embody this deep, abiding reality, which is the sovereign of all phenomena. The blessings of the

> indivisible bodies [vajrakāya] will arouse in the meditator the body movements of shivering, shaking, levitating, moving, jumping, and running. The blessing of the indivisible speech will cause an outflow of diverse vocal expressions of talking, laughing, crying, and lamenting.
> B The blessing of the indivisible mind will cause the realization of perfect absorption and supercognition.

Despite many similar references these sensational experiences happen to only a few—and not all—meditators as a result of the control of the vital life force and the harmonious interaction of the central nervous system and the creative energies with the mental state. This Meditational Order has regarded them as experiences representing these three: the sublime sensation of mental tranquility, of an integrated tranquility and insight, and of inward realization. According to Je Gampopa "the experience of mental tranquility" means "the bliss of the outflowing senses," which in its wake creates a perfect well-being of body and mind as a direct result of controlling and channeling the vital energies into the vagus of the central nervous system. The "sensation of clarity" means experiencing this blissful state. "Nondiscrimination" means submerging into a deep absorption of a nondiscriminating state, aided by "memory" [i.e., primal awareness]. Gampopa comments further:

> The five inner signs[158] of channeling the vital energies into the vagus and the eight beneficial results[159] will come about by virtue of a combined meditation on tranquility and insight and certainly not through a short stabilized focus on a subtle image.

284 F It is impossible for sublime sensations not to arise once realization has dawned clearly. Realization consists of perceiving the intrinsic state of awareness, which the guru signals at the initiatory ritual by exclaiming, "This is it!" so that the initiate gets the sense of identity as if he knew it himself from the beginning. As for the "sublime sensation of bliss," it is an elevated state of great bliss, transcending the outflowing senses. "Clarity" refers to a clear awareness, which might seem like a clear light permeating the body or like a spontaneous transformation of what hitherto has been a concept or a tinted clarity into the natural one. "Nondiscrimination" refers to such a [clear and blissful] state not remaining clouded by even the slightest thought, and this state emerges without the duality of sublime sensation and mental experience.

How the Aberrations Turn into Deviations

When a meditator seeks to revive the inner sensations of bliss, clarity, and nondiscrimination—either collectively or separately—owing to his craving

for them and his dismay at their absence, this is committing a deviation from the intrinsic nature of things. The reason why these sensations often become obstacles to true realization is that generally any directed mental focus
284 B becomes an impediment to liberation. Particularly the clinging to sensations of bliss, clarity, and nondiscrimination as superior levels will cause one to be reborn in a higher realm, [which is still saṃsāra], whereas discriminating against negative mental states as inferior will cause one to be reborn in a lower realm. In short, all craving, attachment, and directed mental focus are considered as deviations from the noble path. Saraha illustrates this:

> Directing one's mental focus on any images impedes liberation;
> Clinging to these images as superior experiences
> Will drive one into the whirling sphere of existence;
> Discriminating against inferior experiences as such
> Will afflict one with incessant misery.[160]

And again he says:

> O, do not crave any sensory gratification,
> For this great malaise will distort the state of supreme bliss.
> By craving the object of attachment
> You might strike the unblemished mind
> With the weapon of desire.

Finally, he advises:

> If you should cherish that which delights your heart
> While musing about its enchanting quality,
> 285 F You will be afflicted by pain,
> Even as small as the husk of the sesame seed.

According to Virūpa:

> A deviation from the path occurs
> When one intellectualizes the abiding nature of mind,
> When one craves sublime sensations,
> And when one meditates on the conceptual image of reality.

As to how a particular inner sensation can cause a meditator to deviate from the meditative course, [craving] bliss will lead him toward the plane of desire, [craving] clarity will impel him to deviate from the path and will lead him toward the plane of higher form, and [craving] nondiscrimination will lead him toward the plane of formlessness. Thus it will not be the relevant cause for enlightenment. After consummating sensory pleasures on any of the higher planes, which are only a temporary freedom from the sufferings of the lower realms, he will go to the three lower realms and wander about endlessly. Je Gampopa elucidates the three areas of deviation as follows:

> To crave the sensation of bliss that permeates body and mind and to look upon such sensations as sublime experience causes one to drift toward rebirth on the plane of desire. Such a meditator will, after his
> B death, be reborn on that plane [where he will indulge in sensory pleasures] and will wander endlessly through the three lower realms. To crave the sensation of clarity, which the meditator has achieved through the clearing of dullness or sullenness, and to look upon this sensation as sublime experience causes one to drift toward the plane of higher form. After he has indulged in the pleasures there for a while, he will easily descend into the lower realms. To crave the tranquility of mind, unstirred by a storm of thought, and to look upon such sensation as sublime experience causes one to drift toward the plane of formlessness. If the meditator dies while in this meditation, he will be reborn on this plane. After he has exhausted the enjoyment of peace there, he will wander endlessly through the three lower realms.

Je Phagmo Trupa states:

> By practicing the vital instructions received from one's guru
> One will experience bliss permeating body and mind.
> But by craving for this experience
> One will drift toward the plane of desire.
> 86 F Clarity [of mind] is like the clear sky;
> Its luminosity is like the rising moon.
> One will perceive it as illuminating both inside and outside,
> Whether one opens or closes the eyes.
> If one seeks this experience out of craving,
> One will drift toward the plane of higher form.
> By watching oneself outwardly and inwardly,
> One will perceive the mind
> As being devoid of the subtlest thought.
> By viewing this state as dharmakāya
> And maintaining it with hope and fear,
> One will drift [from the path]
> Toward the plane of formlessness.

Je Lingrepa remarks:

> Some great hermits,
> Behaving like a simple-minded child,
> Crave a rainbowlike vision and sensation.
> They do not realize that this is a deviation.

Je Barawa explains:

Deviations from mahāmudrā meditation are:
When a meditator settles his mind in an absorptive equipoise
And conceives it as infinite, like cosmic space,
He drifts toward the "spacelike, infinite consciousness."
286 B When he conceives consciousness as being infinite,
He drifts toward the "infinite consciousness."
When he conceives phenomena as nothingness,
He drifts toward "nothingness."
When he conceives phenomena
As neither reality nor unreality,
He drifts toward the "perception of neither reality nor unreality."

[The four concentrated states]

When the meditator analyzes the absorptive state
Consisting of joy and bliss
Arising from one-pointed concentration,
He drifts toward the first level of contemplation.
When he meditates with a one-pointed mind
On joy and bliss,
He drifts toward the second level.
When he meditates with one-pointed mindfulness and vigilance
On nondiscerning equanimity and bliss,
He drifts toward the third level.
When he meditates with a one-pointed mind
On perfect evenness and perfect mindfulness,
While transcending bliss and pain,
He achieves the fourth level.

[The deep absorption of arhats]

When the meditator is absorbed in an approximate
nondiscrimination
By suppressing mindfulness and the six sense faculties,
287 F He drifts toward the "deep noncognitive absorption."
When the meditator absorbs himself in an unconscious inertia,
Devoid of mindfulness,
He drifts toward a neutral state.
When the meditator maintains simple nondiscrimination,
A state of stupor, sluggishness, and confusion,
He drifts toward the level of animals.

Je Phagmo Trupa adds:

By meditating without attachment on the three inner sensations,
Bliss, clarity, and nondiscrimination,

One can attain the levels of arhats [awakened hearers]
And pratyekabuddhas [solitary buddhas].

Je Yanggönpa sums it up thus:

By attachment to bliss, clinging to clarity,
And cogitation in nondiscrimination,
By craving for them one will drift
Toward the three planes of existence.
Even if unaffected by craving and clinging,
A meditation that lacks insight
Into the inner face of abiding reality,
Can cause the meditator to drift
Toward the levels of the arhats and pratyekabuddhas.

B On the other hand, Je Gampopa considers that one might drift toward the level of the Hīnayāna either by intellectualizing emptiness, or through lack of compassion and love.[161] Yet it is stated that in order to attain the level of the awakened hearers and solitary buddhas, one must completely eliminate mental defilements and attain both perfect tranquility and transcending insight, which perceive the nonselfhood of personality. I consider it untenable to hold that one will attain the levels of the awakened hearers and solitary buddhas by dispassionately maintaining absorption coalescing with bliss, clarity, and nondiscrimination, since this represents only an ordinary contemplation on the mundane level.

Then how about Je Gampopa's statement that [absorption on] an indeterminate appearance carries the risk of turning it into the "incognitive" absorption? In his public discourse entitled *Tsokchö Tashi Phüntsok*, Gampopa states:

A guru who has attained the dharma eye [perfect knowledge] and who has realized emptiness should help a meditator gain a definite understanding of the abiding nature, the nonarising of the three experiences—bliss, clarity, and nondiscrimination. If the latter fails to perceive this with an awareness of certainty, his meditation will turn into what is characterized as meditation focused on indeterminate appearance. This is identical with a deep nondiscerning absorption. Such a way of meditating on the common path renders the destiny of the meditator uncertain.

88 F Concerning this, the *Abhidharmakośa* comments:

That which permanently precludes [any consciousness] from arising
Is the nondiscerning absorption, as opposed to the other incognitive absorption.

The autocommentary on this text elucidates it this way:

> The nondiscerning absorption permanently precludes any forms of consciousness from arising and is different from the other pacified absorption. It pacifies consciousness through dissociation with discernment, for this state cannot be realized through an analytical process.

As has been elucidated, this is an incognitive state, which through the absence of relevant conditions precludes the emergence of any sensory outflows [on the mundane level] and also of any supercognitions [on the supramundane level]. Hence it is different from the absorption with discernment. Regarding the consequences [of such meditation] on the meditator's next life, the *Bodhicaryāvatāra* states:

> Because absorption lacks the awareness of emptiness,
> Consciousness will arise again.
> This is like an incognizant absorption.

No matter how a mundane mind may meditate on absorption, it cannot destroy the inbred cognition of the self. Consequently the mind is stirred deeply by defilement. It is like the absorption practiced by Udraka. A
288 B meditator "without consciousness" will be reborn as a noncognizing celestial being with a complete cessation of cognitive functions. As for the "unconscious evenness," it is actualized in the fourth contemplative state, where consciousness remains inoperative in terms of both general and specific mental functions. Such a meditator will misconceive this state to be liberation. "Incognitive absorption" is actualized when cognizance and noncognizance change roles. This takes place when the meditator, who yearns for tranquility in order to pacify cognitions and sensations, embarks upon the practice of incognitive absorption with a thrust of determination.

The reason why these absorptive levels constitute deviations is that they lack the awareness of nonselfhood. Therefore they cannot help pacify any clinging to the self, which is the root of the whirling cycle of existence. Consequently these individuals will continue to create more karma and defilement, which in turn will toss them in the round of existence. Dharmakīrti elucidates:

> Where the self is perceived,
> 289 F The concept of others emerges.
> From the duality of self and others
> Flow clinging and malignance.
> All afflictions result from this involvement.

This is the reason why a meditator who meditates the way the mystic Udraka did will likewise fail to gain liberation from saṃsāra, even though he might have attained the highest mundane consciousness.

The absorption with discernment is described as an incognitive absorption, free from any outflowing senses. This is the climax brought about through concentration on the meaning of the four noble truths established by a discerning wisdom on the unimpeded path.[162] Certain uninformed people did not know much about the concept appertaining to the incognitive absorption of awakened hearers. Having misunderstood the warning that meditating on such an indeterminate appearance carries the risk of drifting toward that state, they made many remarks, most of which are simple utterances originating from their own ignorance. Even some reputed scholars remarked "lest one might drift toward the incognitive absorption of the hearers." This comment has since been repeated in the same manner as the widespread rumor about a monster.[163]

B Those who had the ability to attain the incognitive absorption of the awakened hearers were the nonreturning ones and the conquerors of inner adversaries. This critic[164] did not seem to know that in order to attain such a deep absorption, one must first achieve the transcending insight into the nonselfhood of personality. Had he understood this, he would have been ashamed of his criticism, which said that for an ignorant mind to meditate on mahāmudrā is to create a cause of rebirth in the animal realm.

Dorje Sherap, who follows the one thought system[165] of the Drikhung Kagyüpa order, states:

> Those who do not turn bliss into lust will attain the plane of desire. Those who do not turn clarity into clinging will attain the plane of higher form, and those who do not turn nondiscrimination into flowing discrimination will attain the plane of formlessness.

Much harm has been done by implying that meditators should turn inner sensations of bliss into lust, clarity into clinging, and nondiscrimination into discrimination. A state of nondiscrimination, without the definite understanding of nonarising, will make the meditator cling to emptiness and thus drift toward absolute nihility. Consequently he might descend to a lower
90 F realm. I have stated in the earlier segment on how to get rid of meditative deviation the reason why a dispassionate mind, a constituence of bliss, clarity, and nondiscrimination, and other intermediate mental states might become a meditational deviation. Je Gampopa speaks further on some essential points:

> The knowledge of the emptiness of duality may be free from
> attachment,
> But it lacks the awareness of the mind's abiding nature.
> Meditation not detached from duality
> May bring the inner sensations,
> Yet it lacks the awareness of the mind's abiding nature.

A view without realization may surpass all conceptual modes,
Yet it still remains an act of the intellect.
A great mystic who has not eliminated his attachment
Will create the cause of his cyclic existence.
No matter how good his meditative absorption,
A dharma devotee who lacks compassion
Will drift toward the path of the hearers.

Methods to Prevent Deviations from Taking Place

The factors that are likely to turn much of the sublime sensations of bliss,
clarity, and nondiscrimination into deviations arise from (1) the meditator's
lack of awareness that the sensations are, in reality, nonarising [i.e., empti-
ness], devoid of any absolute arising and ceasing, and from (2) his miscon-
290 B ceiving them as real and grasping their substance. They only appear to be
real, being the mere manifestation of his psychic imprints activated by the
direct integration of the central nervous system with the creative fluid and
vital energy. However, no deviation is possible if the meditator maintains
coherent mindfulness of the certainty of nonarising with respect to such
inner sensations, without grasping them to be of substance. Je Gampopa
urges:

> Be aware of the nonarising [emptiness] of bliss, clarity, and nondiscrimination. Not to be aware of their nonarising [emptiness] is described as "an undetermined appearance."

Furthermore, a little clinging to these sublime sensations impels the
meditator to deviate from meditation [on the mundane level] of the three
planes, the four concentrated states, and the four higher sense faculties.[166]
Deviation from meditation on the incognitive absorption [on the supramundane plane] of the dispassionate hearers is caused by [inappropriately]
examining emptiness. No such deviation is possible when the mind settles in
its intrinsic nature without clinging. Deviations are usually caused either by
craving or clinging. Therefore meditators should first detach themselves
from craving and clinging and should then settle the mind firmly in its
291 F natural state. They should let the mind rest calmly, while not distorting it
through acceptance or abandonment, because keeping the mind unmodulated is designated as meditation. The *Pradīpoddyotana* illustrates it thus:

> Settling the mind unmodulated in an even state
> Is designated as meditation.

If one wonders whether inner sensations of bliss, clarity, and nondiscrimination are essential, since the inmost certainty of nonarising [the abiding nature of mind] seems adequate in meeting the needs of meditators, this is not quite so. Je Gampopa makes the following observation:

> A meditative state that is aware of the mind's intrinsic nonarising nature but that is without bliss, clarity, and nondiscrimination is like the one described by guru Milarepa: "It is simply [partial awareness] but is not the actual one [complete awareness]. The former is like the trunk of a tree but not the fruit; it is an attribute [of the mind] but not the nondiscrimination."

Atīśa refers to the necessity of both sublime sensations and realizations:

> He who lacks an urge to escape miserable saṃsāra
> And to experience sublime sensations
> Cannot perceive the pure state of his mind.
> His practice will be like bees seeking [nectar]
> From [nonexistent] flowers in space.

How should one go about it? In keeping with what is defined as "the view based on understanding" the meditator must gain a direct realization of the mind's essence and nature not only as being empty of any substance but as something inexpressible and indefinable. At the same time he should not rest content with a mere intellectual comprehension of the mind's intrinsic nature as free from all modes of existence or as conceptual simplicity. The meditation on the perceived view, enriched by experience, means that he must have a clear awareness of the significance of such comprehension instead of holding on to it as an intellectual exerçise. Je Gampopa urges:

> At the beginning, practice to achieve a vivid awareness and an undistracted state. Never get distracted from the mind's intrinsic nature. Upon mastering this, you will gain the awareness of certainty.

He further explains:

> Clarity of awareness means the sublime sensation.
> Remaining undistracted from that clarity means stability.
> Watching it through wisdom as being devoid
> Of innate essence is the realization.

These are described as the self-unfolding realizations or manifestations of the intrinsic state and as an unblemished meditation on the inseparable union of sublime sensation and realization. Je Gampopa describes:

> What is the meditation endowed with inner sensation? It is the expression of the intrinsic state, an inborn experience of the mind's coemergent nature of inmost purity, an inborn experience of mahāmudrā. What does each designation indicate? It refers to the intrinsic

nature of mind. What then is the intrinsic nature of mind? The intrinsic nature of mind is nonexistent, for it contains no identifiable entity, not even to the minute degree of a one-hundredth of a hair. Yet, the mind is not an absolute nonexistence, because it can be experienced or realized. Indeed, it must and will dawn upon one as the unidentifiable union of clarity and emptiness, which manifests as such unceasingly. Such an experience may be described as meditation endowed with experience, a simultaneous dawning of experience and realization.

292 B In connection with this some teachers have made the following observation:

Bliss, clarity, and nondiscrimination
Are the three sensations in which deviations occur.
Bliss, clarity, and nondiscrimination constitute
The pinnacle of all meditations.

The former implies the craving for and clinging to inner sensations in the meditation, while the latter implies the experience of actual realization.

Some have made the following remark:

If the mere elimination of the three deviations
Represents mahāmudrā meditation,
Then it it indeed an incognitive absorption
On the part of the arhats.

This remark stems from the desire to criticize mahāmudrā meditation. To merely abandon the three areas of deviation has never been considered as actual mahāmudrā meditation. Such abandonment, however, is a necessary condition for this practice. "The three areas of deviation" means the three planes of existence. Since there are other meditations wherein one does not drift toward these three, it is irrelevant to single out the incognitive absorp-
293 F tion achieved by the arhats. As for those arhats who had the ability to enter the incognitive absorption, there were two types: those who realized the nonreturning state,[167] similar to nirvāṇa, through the body [i.e., physical tranquility] and those who achieved release from the two inbred obstacles.[168] By maintaining the body [i.e., the living physical residue] on the planes of desire and higher form respectively, they did not eliminate the three meditational deviations.

Other teachers made the following comment:

One should familiarize oneself with the void
But should not actualize it.
So states the wisdom-gone-beyond.
By meditating on the void alone

> One cannot realize the void itself.
> Even if one were to realize it,
> One might deviate toward the incognitive absorption of the arhats.

This is not good. One cannot familiarize oneself with emptiness without realizing it. The claim that this idea is contained in the wisdom-gone-beyond turns out to be false. To meditate on the "supreme emptiness of all forms" does not represent a fallacious meditation on simple emptiness. These two fallacies rebound back on [the critic's] view of total emptiness established through a logic of reductio ad absurdum. Such emptiness established through critical analysis is described in the *Jñānasiddhi* of the *Kālacakra* as emptiness conceived as absolute nothingness. As such it should be abandoned.

THE METHODS OF REMOVING OBSTACLES TO MEDITATION

This subject will be dealt with in two ways:

1. Removing obstacles to general absorption
2. Removing other external or internal obstacles

Removing Obstacles to General Absorption

In general, whatever meditative absorption one seeks must be the one that combines two qualities. The mental image to be maintained must be very clear, without obscurity, and it must remain firm and undistracted. The obstacle to clarity comes from dullness, while the obstacle to nondistraction arises from thought flow. Dullness and thought flow, therefore, constitute the root of obstacles to meditational absorption. Dullness includes other aspects such as torpor, stupor, and drowsiness. The different aspects of thought flow are resentment, skepticism, desire, longing, and spite. Since these mental conditions hinder the progress of a beginner's meditation, they must be cleared. I have explained the methods of identifying them and applying countermeasures in the chapter on general tranquility and insight.

A meditator who perceives the intrinsic nature of all things will not only understand the true nature of dullness and thought flow but will turn them into the meditation.

Venerated Milarepa elucidates:

> Do not clear away dullness and thought flow,
> Let them be the meditational state.

To clear away defects like stupor, dullness, and thought flow
Is like lighting a butter lamp in broad daylight.

Je Gampopa declares:

Watch any emerging dullness or thought flow!

Removing Other External or Internal Obstacles

The *Vairocanābhisambodhi* enumerates:

The two kinds of obstacles [to meditation]
Are the external and the internal.

It further advises:

294 B Know the internal obstacles:
Cold, asthma, influenza, cholera, gastritis,
Complicated by high fever, neurosis, gonorrhea, etc.
The external obstacles can come from humans or nonhumans.
These obstacles to awareness prick like a thorn;
By emerging in diverse forms
They undermine the world of meditators,
Yet meditators can confound them by maintaining
Inner tranquility through relentless striving.

The external obstacles can come from one's relatives or associates, inducing the meditator to a materialistic outlook of life, or in a violent form from enemies or robbers. He is likely to be overcome by them and easily give in to such obstacles. Among the obstacles emanating from a nonhuman source are the invisible obstructive forces, harmful or hungry spirits, who seek to undermine meditation through their miraculous acts, and also forces in the form of harassment by apes or other wild animals.

295 F The internal obstacles can come from the disharmony of the four primal elements or of one's whole psychophysical constitution in the form of diseases such as neurosis, jaundice, or consumption. The [other] internal obstacles can come in the form of uncontrolled thoughts that represent each of the five mental defilements or in the form of unrestrained indulgence in any of the eight worldly principles through failure to sublimate the view and meditation on the realization process. These obstacles should be perceived and then eliminated.

According to the saint-scholar Chegompa, "the force that obstructs through depression" brings the mind into a lethargic condition vitiating its clarity; "the force that obstructs through speech" makes the meditator very talkative to the point where he disregards the inner discipline to remain silent on his own experiences; "the force that obstructs through a restless mind" makes the mind too energetic, unable to quieten down into a tranquil state; "the force that obstructs through physical restlessness" makes the meditator too active and longing to get away from solitude.

The meditator should be able to overcome each obstacle by visualizing his guru sitting above his crown, inside the throat, or inside the heart respectively, and by invoking him fervently in order to clear it. Thus he will achieve pacification. In short, if the actualized spiritual merits and common psychic power impede the perfection of the meditator's vision and meditation, they will obstruct the realization of the supreme goal. These problems should be remedied through spiritual countermeasures and the methods of elevating the practice to the level of the spiritual path.

This ends the segment on the elimination of meditational deviations.

CHAPTER EIGHT

Consolidation of Experience in Meditation: How to Determine the Mind as Nonarising [Emptiness] and Enhance Meditation

This will be dealt with in two ways:

1. Determining the mind to be expansive, open, and nonarising
2. Perfecting the efficacy [of awareness] through the sublimation of the path

DETERMINING THE MIND TO BE EXPANSIVE, OPEN, AND NONARISING

This section is to be elucidated in five ways:

1. The epithet, significance, and time of determining the mind
2. Determining the abiding nature of the mind
3. Watching the mind's inner face as the basis of determination
4. Being aware of the mind's nonarising openness
5. Remaining in the state of determinate awareness throughout the day and night

The Epithet, Significance, and Time of Determining the Mind

The term "lada" denotes the awareness of certainty beyond any doubt,
296 F [which is achieved through the process of determination]. In this case it means the resolve [through analytical determination] that the mind's intrinsic nature consists of nonarising [emptiness], great openness, which is detached from any conceptual modes of absolute arising, ceasing, or dissolving and which is unaffected by the three periods of time. Tilopa comments precisely:

Watch that which has been determined
Without any mental activities.

Saraha describes it:

Receiving the vital instructions from one's guru
Is an adequate means to contemplating
The mind's ungrounded intrinsic reality.

He adds:

This is nonarising [emptiness] from the beginning.
Today realization has dawned [in me]
Through the elucidation of my glorious guru.

Śavari advises:

Remain in a state of nondiscrimination, nonconception, and primordial purity
Throughout all the three periods of time.

Tilopa states:

A mind without directed focus is mahāmudrā.

Maitrīpa summarizes:

All things are intrinsically even, like space;
Hence the designation of mahāmudrā.

These sayings show [the epithet of mahāmudrā and its significance]. This is consistent with the tradition of this Meditational Order that upholds the
296 B [original] intent of the incomparable Takpopa, as revealed in his "unfolding of the secret instructions." Numerous methods of focusing on the awareness of certainty were enunciated in recent times by devotees of this meditation.

As for the appropriate time to maintain the awareness of certainty, it is when the meditator, having cleared the strong sensations of bliss, clarity, and nondiscrimination, achieves clear awareness coupled with emptiness, which is just like space and lasts throughout the day and night or at least for a whole day. Or it is when he cognizes with cogent mindfulness every outflowing thought in its [indivisible] emptiness and clarity or emptiness and movement and cognizes every appearance of the six senses as a union of appearance and emptiness. In short, the meditator has perfectly determined [the abiding nature of internal and external realities] when he experiences the dawning of the determinate awareness of it coupled with an illusionlike sensation, perceiving every thought as being the union of clarity and emptiness and every appearance as the union of appearance and emptiness.

If the meditator starts the process of determination prematurely, he will

297 F not only fail to build a secure foundation of spiritual experience and fail to gain the awareness of certainty but might also drift toward a mere comprehension of the doctrine in such a way that he will become a degenerate dharma student who is given to ambition and vainglory. Consequently he will be overcome with passion and delusion. Even if others perceive him to be a realized person, he will remain the same person, bearing a deceptive appearance without substance, like an attractive but deserted house. Thus he will fail to realize the true aim of dharma and will deceive others.

If the meditator is too late in starting the process of determining the intrinsic nature of thought and appearance, he might not achieve proficiency in it. Predestined meditators will realize their inner liberation by looking upon their mind as the spiritual guide and by pacifying their craving for and clinging to any sublime sensations and experiences. But many meditators might drift toward the deviation described as "great meditators fettered to the luster of experiences," due to their ever-increasing clinging to the thought of a good experience. Je Gyare comments:

> Many meditators know how to meditate,
> But only few know how to dismantle [mental clinging].

The process of determination contains special instructions. If applied at the right time they will be a most effective means whereby predestined
297 B meditators will achieve liberation instantaneously. They will help other meditators to advance rapidly from the lower to the higher levels of the four yogas of mahāmudrā. It is stated that these methods will help those meditators with an indifferent attitude or even deluded mind to realize the meaning of the meditation in a few days, which would otherwise require many years of practice.

Determining the Abiding Nature of the Mind

The object of determination is nonarising [emptiness] as the abiding nature of existential phenomena. In fact, this has been explained before at the stage of determining the essence or intrinsic nature of the mind. I might however speak here briefly. All phenomena incorporated into saṃsāra and nirvāṇa are mainly manifestations of mind. The mind's essence or nature is empty of an evolved essence; it cannot be conceived as having either substance or nonsubstance, appearance or emptiness, reality or unreality. It is detached from all perceptive marks of subject and object and is unaffected by any movements, transference or transformation, going or coming. Because it is
298 F an unceasing stream, it is unaffected by the three transient periods of time. Like space, it is unstained and immutable. Saraha comments:

This coemergent nature of mind
Is neither of any substance nor nonsubstance.
Thus this Archer always proclaims.

Śavari elaborates:

It is neither going nor standing still,
Neither static nor dynamic,
Neither substance nor nonsubstance,
Neither appearance nor emptiness.
The nature of all things, like space,
Is without any movement.
One may call it "space"
But it is empty of any essence
And as such transcends definitions
Such as real or unreal,
Existent or nonexistent,
Or anything else.
Thus not the slightest distinction exists
Between space, the mind, and intrinsic reality.
Only their designations are different,
But they are unreal and false.

Virūpa affirms:

But for its designation the mind is empty
And nonconceptual, which means mahāmudrā.
It is empty from the beginning, like space.
298 B The essence of mind is unborn [emptiness]
And is detached from any substantive reality.
Like space, it is all-pervasive.
Neither transferring nor transforming,
It has always been empty and selfless
From the very beginning.

Such being the nature of the mind from the very beginning, it has never been conditioned nor mutated. Like the nature of space it is beyond definition, even though such qualifying terms as "empty" or "not empty" have been uttered. That is why Tilopa elucidates:

Space is designated as empty,
Yet its exact nature cannot be verbalized.
Similarly the mind is designated as luminously clear,
Yet its exact nature is empty, with no ground for definition.
Thus the self-nature of mind is and has been
From the very beginning like that of space.

Because from the beginning the nature of mind and everything that manifests from it are devoid of any self-nature, any unconditioned arising,
299 F dwelling, or ceasing and are neither mobile nor mutable, the mind is not something that can be acquired through mindfulness nor lost through distraction. It is indeed the great expanse and nonarising [emptiness]. Śavari elucidates:

> If the mind were real, all other phenomena would be real.
> Since the mind is unreal, who can understand
> That the real thing exists?
> Neither the mind and the appearances
> Nor the investigator can be found.
> Being unreal they are unborn and unceasing
> Throughout the three periods of time.
> The intrinsic nature [of mind] is immutable, abiding great bliss.

He also says:

> The primordial purity of mind
> Is of the nature of space;
> There is nothing one can receive or reject.

Watching the Mind's Inner Face as the Basis of Determination

This will be explained in two ways:

1. Watching the nature of mind and of appearances
2. The nature of meditation and meditator

Watching the Nature of Mind and of Appearances

This being the path of blessing in general, the meditator should strengthen his faith in and veneration for his guru, because his progress in meditation
299 B depends especially on his faith. All followers of this order agree on this. Je Drikhungpa elucidates this:

> Faith in the holy guru is a means
> For advancing meditation of mahāmudrā.

He further says:

> If the sun of faith does not touch
> The snowy mountains of the guru
> Who embodies the four enlightened aspects,[169]

The stream of his blessing will not flow.
Strengthen the faith in your guru!

Saraha implores in the *Queen Dohā*:

Only a holy guru can bring about the understanding
That in emptiness all diverse phenomena
Are one and the same.
This supremely noble one is like the water unto swans.
Pay your homage to him with deep veneration!

At this stage, before embarking on the main meditation, the meditator should devote himself to an appropriate preparatory practice. He should especially practice the guru yoga by arousing faith in his guru as the embodiment of dharmakāya. He should invoke him for his blessings so that he may realize all appearances and existences as dharmakāya.

As stated earlier, when the meditator begins the [main] meditation, he should eliminate any somber mood and crystallize the lucidity of awareness
300 F by settling the mind one-pointedly in an absorptive equipoise. He should maintain this undistracted awareness in a relaxed state without directing the focus of his mind. He should then produce a subtle thought, unconnected with anything pleasurable or painful, and should watch the intrinsic clarity of that thought. This [neutral] thought should then be substituted by a vigorously enjoyable or agonizing emotion. He should observe this attentively and then discern the distinction between the intrinsic nature of this vigorous thought and that of the subtle one. Once this has been determined, he should differentiate between the nature of these diverse thoughts and the mind's tranquil state. Similarly he should observe each of his eight worldly thoughts—desire and the other defilements. Sometimes he should cease thinking altogether or produce many thoughts or pursue a single stream of thought. He should observe them with a view to gaining a determinate
300 B awareness of the mind and its manifestations. He should similarly observe every sensory appearance including forms of varying sizes, shapes, and looks as well as sounds of varying qualities, pitches, octaves, and inflections.

In the course of these observations the meditator should create and observe different appearances of each form by altering his body posture and manner of watching, with his eyes sometimes open, sometimes closed, sometimes watching sideways to the right or left. The meditator should observe every sensory appearance for a few days at a time in order to determine its intrinsic nature, then check if any distinction is perceivable between the nature of each thought and each sensory appearance. Such observation and determination should result in the meditator's gaining absolute certainty that the intrinsic nature of all thoughts consists of the union of clarity and emptiness and that of all appearances consists of the union of appearance and emptiness. Since the meditator is thus aware of the spontaneous clarity of every thought or every sensory appearance, whose intrinsic essence remains devoid of identity, he has no need for controlling or suppressing it. This has been explained before in the section dealing with mind's coemergent thought and appearance. Here I quote the illuminating saying of Saraha:

301 F Harmonize all that which emerges before you
With its fundamental nature of emptiness.

Śavari teaches:

The Ganges and all other rivers
Flow into the salty oceans to become one flavor.
The mind and mental events
Rest in the expanse of intrinsic reality
Designated as one flavor. Understand this!

According to Virūpa:

Just as a mirage is without water,
So memory and thought are without reality.
Neither bound nor released,
They are inseparable from their primordial purity.

Tilopa states:

Like mist and clouds that arise in the sky
And neither proceed toward a destination nor settle anywhere,
The diverse thoughts that arise in the mind
Flow like waves through the realized state.

Maitrīpa observes:

Transient thoughts arise from the unborn [emptiness],
Thus dwelling in the expanse of reality.

And he adds:

Mahāmudrā is the intrinsic nature of mind,
Which manifests itself in diverse perceptions,
Yet it is detached from interacting causes and conditions.

The Nature of Meditation and Meditator

301 B The object of meditation here is the intrinsic nature of mind. The meditator should not be content merely with his intellectual cogitation and compre-

hension that the nature of mind is detached from unconditioned arising, dwelling, or ceasing and that, being empty of a identifiable essence, it transcends the dimension of the intellect. Instead, he should attain the awareness of certainty with respect to the sensations and experiences through which a mind attuned to its intrinsic purity directly perceives [ultimate reality]. In order to do this, the meditator should first maintain undistracted awareness in a relaxed manner, as he did in the earlier meditation. After focusing sharply again and again on the intrinsic nature of the meditational subject, without distraction or clinging, he should shift the focus to the nature of his consciousness. In doing this, should he perceive any duality, like two opposites or an internal/external one, it would mean that he has not as yet eliminated doubts and assumptions. Hence the need for him to repeat the process of determination until he realizes the determinant awareness.

In short, the meditator must achieve a retentive consciousness of the inseparable and indifferentiable union of meditation and meditator, which must be like an ephemeral illusion. At the same time he must be certain that this retentive consciousness is nothing more than a designation and that in reality it is completely empty of any identifiable entity or essence. This is to say that no reality exists, not even the infinitesimal particle of a hair.

2 F Once this is achieved, the meditator changes [the subject of meditation]. He now focuses on the thoughts of the three periods of time and examines them in order to find out if any discernable difference exists between them. Besides that he examines each temporal phase separately to trace the destination of a past thought, the nature of a present thought, and the source of a future thought. Should he perceive these thoughts of the three periods of time as being the objective realities of arising, dwelling, or ceasing, he has not as yet achieved the determinate certainty. He must therefore carry on the meditation until he fully attains a sense of certainty that these thoughts are but an uninterrupted stream and are not only nondifferentiable in terms of the three temporal phases but are like space—uniquely pure and open—at all times.

The duality of consciousness should be examined in a similar fashion: first that which clings to the "I" or "self" and then that which clings to others. When, in the course of examining them, the meditator perceives dualistic appearances, external and internal or two opposite realities, this indicates that he has not cleared his doubts and assumptions. He should
302 B therefore continue to observe and examine as before until he is able to achieve the inmost certainty that all these dualistic perceptions are but the manifestation of mind and that mind itself has from the very beginning been empty of substance, ground, or support and that it is a single stream, self-emerging and self-releasing. Furthermore, he should achieve the awareness of certainty that the dualistic consciousnesses of self and others, of meditation and meditator, and of thoughts in the three periods of time are only

distinct appellations or designations. These diverse manifestations are not separate from the stream consciousness, whose intrinsic nature is devoid of a real essence and whose natural state [of purity and emptiness] is unaffected by either transient delusion or attained liberation. The intrinsic nature transcends the duality of good and bad, attainment and abatement, integration and separation. In order to realize the awareness of certainty, the meditator should focus for many days on whatever thought or appearance arises, letting it be in its natural relaxed mode, unaltered and unmodulated, without ever affirming it, abandoning it, or clinging to it.

Saraha comments:

> Do not claim to meditate on intrinsic reality,
> Which is devoid of self-nature.
> If one conceives meditation and meditator as duality,
> One is abandoning the spirit of enlightenment
> And thus will bring much affliction upon oneself.

He elucidates further:

> The mind without self-nature
> Should detach itself from the duality
> Of meditation and meditator,
> 303 F For the ultimate freedom from hope and fear
> Is the indestructible mind [vajracitta]

Finally, he says:

> The mind in its great sublime bliss
> Is nondual, neither self nor others,
> For it perceives intrinsic reality,
> Which is before one, behind one, and around one in all the ten directions.

Śavari states:

> For a realized mind the duality
> Of meditation and meditator does not exist.
> Just as space cannot perceive itself as an object,
> So emptiness cannot meditate on itself.
> In a state of nondual awareness
> The diverse perceptions blend uninterruptedly,
> Like milk and water, into the one flavor of great bliss.

Virūpa agrees:

> No duality of meditation and meditator exists
> In the expanse of the mind's intrinsic reality,
> Which is empty of any identity.

And he continues:

> By detaching itself from the duality of observation and observer,
> The mind achieves self-liberation from division;
> By thus smashing the [contrived] practitioner
> The mind frees itself from striving and seeking;
> By discarding the [concern for the] fruit of inner development,
> The meditator unshackles himself from hope and fear;
> By eliminating the [sense of the] "self" or the "I,"
> The mind emerges victorious in its battle against inner adversaries;
> By dismantling the clinging to substance,
> The meditator will gain liberation from both saṃsāra and nirvāṇa.

B **Being Aware of the Mind's Nonarising Openness**

Once the meditator gains the awareness of certainty regarding the objects of investigation mentioned earlier, he should dismantle the inbred clinging to the subject of meditation, ease his mindfulness, abandon his yearning for experience, give up his striving, ignore the object of realization, and pacify the mind's orientation toward self-realization. In short, such an [advanced] meditator should abandon every cognition of and cogitation about what this or that is; he should abandon all his desire to meditate, to remember, to experience, to be aware of, etc. He should not even think of engaging himself in any thoughts but should let his mind remain in a normal, relaxed state without altering or modulating it. In doing so, the meditator should allow any thought or appearance to flow freely without rejecting, altering, or splitting it. He should not pursue any thoughts, nor should he worry,
4 F disapprove, or even examine, when momentarily distracted. Once he has regained mindfulness, he should keep up the ordinary awareness in its unaltered state, not even thinking of meditation, experience, or practice.

During the intervals between meditative absorption and even while eating, strolling, or resting, the meditator should as far as possible maintain a nondiscriminatory state, neither cognizing vigorous thoughts nor contemplating any plans. Except for a little invocation and making of a "torma" offering he should not only avoid any physical activities but should even avoid reciting the texts or doing other forms of religious exercises. When retiring, the meditator should sleep with the mind in its ordinary, unmodulated expanse, free from any craving. By so abandoning any mental activities, he should remain in a pleasant mode for many days. He will attain an inner release from his attachment to good experiences or from his clinging to a sensation of joy. His aversion to harmful or deluded thoughts will clear itself. Whatever ordinary thought emerges, he will cognize it as

304 B being the expression of emptiness, which is the meditational state, devoid of unconditioned arising or ceasing, unaffected by attainment or abatement, acceptance or abandonment. Regardless of whether he is mindful or distracted, attentive or inattentive, experiencing or not experiencing, realizing or not realizing, when he cognizes any appearance or existence, he must be able to bring about an awareness of certainty that every thought emerges or dissolves by itself and is an open, unsupported single stream, that everything is the meditational state, and that meditation pervades and continues throughout [the day and night].

At this stage some meditators might find themselves remaining in a mind of tranquil inertia[170] as a consequence of exerting too strong a control over the mental functions and thought flows. Or some might experience a feeling of uneasiness, discomfort, or depression due to confounding the introspection of the mind and the psychosomatic energies. In such a case these meditators should rest, relax through appropriate recreation, and should let thoughts flow freely for a while.

However, when a flawless experience arises, it should be well assimilated for a few days. During that period meditators should find out occasionally if there is a mind and a mental event that is not in the meditational state.
305 F Should they detect that a distracted or drowsy mind is not meditational, they should examine the essential or intrinsic nature of each mental event so as to realize its abiding nature Saraha elucidates this:

> Whoever meditates upon self-emergent, noncogitating awareness
> Meditates on spontaneous accomplishment.

He continues:

> One neither looks elsewhere for nonconceptual mind
> Nor searches for its natural qualities
> Except by clearing adverse conditions.
> This one cannot discover through the tantras and śāstras.
> A mind without craving and clinging
> Remains free from existential defilement.

And again:

> The essential nature of the mind is detached
> From either good or bad qualities.
> To actualize this no process of inner development is necessary,
> For the mind that has abandoned such processes
> Is the great sublime bliss.

He sums it up with:

> He who turns his mind into a nondiscriminatory state
> Will attain supreme enlightenment.

And:

When the mind remains firm and immovable
In its natural state, inner liberation
From saṃsāra's conditions will come about.

And:

B One will not depart from the mode of oneness,
If one understands all these actions
To be an extension of the mind—
Seeing, hearing, touching, and remembering,
Eating and smelling,
Wandering, walking, and sitting,
Talking and gossiping.

Following are a few of the other innumerous illuminating sayings. The first is by Śavari:

He who perceives the realities of saṃsāra and nirvāṇa
Realizes that they contain no self-nature whatsoever.
Through this he eliminates hope and fear.
How can there be striving to accept or reject?

He also proclaims:

Ah, does a mystic who has realized the pure nondual state
Need to accept or reject anything?
I have neither objectified nor abandoned any realities;
You, my son, should not command anyone to do otherwise.

Virūpa elaborates with:

For one who transcends the duality of knowledge and knower
There is neither discrimination nor partiality;
For one who attains pure evenness
There is no duality of separation and integration;
For one who has realized this
There is nothing to ask of others;
For one who perceives all diverse forms as dharmakāya
There is no thought of accepting or abandoning;
For one who has gone beyond the duality of meditation and no meditation
306 F There is no stain of deluded perception.
This [state] does not depend on sensory appearances or no appearances;
Being detached from all conceptual images,

It is free from any concerns for action and actor;
It has turned away from yearnings, hope, or fear.

And:

Where mind detaches itself from discrimination
There is neither defilement nor doubt;
Where mind perceives intrinsic reality directly
There is no duality of knowledge and knower.

And again:

Actualize the significance of that which is pure, ultimate reality!
This is the best means to let awareness
Remain blissfully in its natural state
Without any concern for abandoning or accepting,
Acting or obstructing.

Tilopa says:

The [nature of] mind is neither modulated nor unmodulated.
Understand it to be of primal purity, beyond concepts.

And he explains with:

By abstaining from cogitation or contemplation,
Examination or analysis,
Meditation or performance,
As well as from hope or fear,
The mental clinging to them will be pacified spontaneously
And the mind will attune itself
To the primordial intrinsic reality.

And:

A strong desire clouds the mind's luminous clarity;
It leads one to transgress
The discriminatory precepts and sacred commitments.
When a mind does not cogitate
And is not bound by desire,
Any emerging thought will quieten itself,
The way the waves of an ocean calm themselves.
306 B When the mind neither succumbs to its conditioned mode
Nor forgets the meaning of inconceivable reality,
This will prevent the mind from breaking the sacred commitments,
The way light prevents darkness from reemerging.
He who shuns all inner yearnings
And extreme views [of reality]

Will realize the doctrines
Embodied in the three collections of scriptures [tripiṭaka].[171]

Je Gampopa comments:

By neither accepting nor abandoning,
Neither seeking the path of self-realization
Nor conceiving the result,
I have pacified hopes and fears.
By realizing the false designation of reality
I have cleared the inner deception.

He continues with:

From beginningless time the mind
Has never had any real existence.
For one who has realized awareness
Through the mind's dynamic and settled conditions,
All striving and seeking will seem
Like a futile effort to grow crops in space.

And:

The mind has to be let loose without directing.
Sustained mindfulness has to be cast away
Without objectifying it.
The mind has to be left in its ordinary state without meditating.
Thus, with nothing controlling it,
The mind is joyous and at ease.

And further:

Where there is no nurturing of mindfulness,
There is no fear of distraction;
Where there is no separation between absorption and
postabsorption,
There is no intermediate state;
307 F Where there are diverse perceptions in the expanse of reality,
There is no acceptance or abandonment;
Where there is a false designation of everything,
There is an awareness of the falsity.

Gampopa concludes:

For the one who has realized the unreality of mind,
All cosmic appearances and existences are an expanse of emptiness;
For the one who does not ascribe values to discrimination,
All [emerging thoughts] are spontaneously released;

For the one who shuns inner yearnings and attachments,
All things remain harmonious evenness;
For the one who has realized all these,
Meditation is an uninterrupted stream.

Many similar expositions exist. Meditators may read the *Khappa Ngön-chung* for further elucidation.

Remaining in the State of Determinate Awareness throughout the Day and Night

The meditator should continue the all-round meditation, blending the two aspects—absorption and postabsorption—during each day and later also at night. The methods for maintaining the harmonized meditation have already been explained. At the stage of determination, if the meditator overexerts his sustained mindfulness, there is a possibility that not only inner sensations but even a craving and clinging might arise. When revitalizing the mindfulness, the meditator should abandon not only his attachment to it, but even the mere thought of abandoning it and should thus maintain a perfect meditation. This meditation integrates absorption and postabsorption without
307 B any exertion or modulation. It is like saying that perfect meditation lies in perfect relaxation. Je Shang counsels:

When one meditates on mahāmudrā,
One does not contemplate to do it this way or that way,
For it transcends the temporal phases of first and final.
Relax while refreshing the mindfulness!

One might wonder whether by doing so one might not sink into an inert stillness and lose the meditation. There is no such problem. Letting mindfulness go while refreshing it is by itself nonclinging mindfulness. Remaining in a nondiscriminatory state constitutes perfect mindfulness of the exact nature of mind. This is far superior to the controlled mindfulness and the retentive mindfulness. Śavari elucidates:

In the discipline of quiescent mahāmudrā
There is nothing to meditate on, not even an atom.
Do not meditate, for the perfect meditation
Is to remain inseparable
From the state of nonmeditation.

If, however, the meditator should momentarily lose the postabsorptive consciousness, he will do well to revitalize it and to cognize its abiding reality. If the postabsorptive consciousness is well determined, it may be incorporated into the integrated meditation of absorption. Such a meditation may be described as the all-encompassing meditation.

Similarly, the meditator extends the complete daily meditation into the night. While getting ready for his nightly rest, he should revive, at first with requisite effort, the quiescent state that he attained during the day's virtuous practice. Were he able to elevate his conciousness to the contemplative state during his sleep and dream, this would be the perfect practice for him. This happens only to a few meditators at this stage. Ordinarily, as they lose the active consciousness during sleep, they may still cognize dream as a delusion so that, when they wake up, they may well be aware of the abiding nature of the dream. Even this kind of practice is considered to fall under the designation of all-encompassing meditation.[172] Je Gampopa comments in his *Shülen* [*Answers to Questions*]:

> [Question:] When mindfulness is absent, the mind's essential nature is not cognized. When, however, mindfulness has its focus on a certain ordinary thought, does this mean that the previous thoughts become pacified? Is it necessary for mindfulness to perceive all emerging and fading thoughts or appearances?

> [Answer:] Once mindfulness focuses on hitherto uncognized ordinary
> B thoughts, these thoughts will pacify themselves. It is not necessary for mindfulness to maintain all emerging and fading thoughts. However, if the meditator can maintain an undistracted mindfulness, it will help him achieve the blending of absorption and postabsorption. Even if the mindfulness is not focused on all thoughts, they will neither harm nor cloud his mind nor even impede his practice. Luminous awareness is inherent in his sleep and dream. Once awake, the meditator retrospects that which passed unattended by his mindfulness, but realizes that it was not different from the luminous awareness itself. This is the uninterrupted stream [of meditation].

If the meditator feels distressed by the intermittent distraction of mindfulness, this means that the meditator has drawn a premature conclusion-from his determination of the mind's intrinsic nature and also has not as yet realized the uninterrupted stream of its abiding reality. Je Gampopa explains:

> When the mind is distracted, delusion emerges;
> When mindfulness is present,
> The mind's essential state emerges.
> This is indeed deluded duality.
> Such alternation of abatement and attainment
> Escapes my comprehension.
> 309 F If such duality were inherent in meditation,

> Both acceptance and abandonment would be worthwhile
> And to eliminate them would be fallacious.

He explains further:

> Attainment through mindfulness and delusion through distraction
> Are the creation of mind.
> In reality neither attainment nor distraction exist.

If the dawning of the awareness of certainty with regard to the object of conclusion takes place, the meditator should maintain determinate awareness without involving visualization or discursive thoughts for five consecutive nights. This should be followed by a day's pleasant rest. He then resumes and carries out intensive practice for up to a week or ten days, each time alternating with a period of rest. With the understanding of the mind's abiding nature the meditator seeks to consolidate his determinate awareness for a whole day at a time. Once this is achieved, he extends it to a night, until he is able to perfectly link his daytime and nighttime meditations.

The purpose of determining the mind is to settle it harmoniously in its abiding nature or its "existential ground" by dissolving any craving for and clinging to dualities such as meditation and meditator, experience and
309 B experiencer, realization and realizer. Similarly, any clinging to emptiness should also be eliminated. After a certain number of days a meditator with superior or average intellect will realize the abiding nature of mind, unclouded by any dualistic clinging. There is no certainty regarding the way that such realization may dawn in any individual, since it depends on his mastery of the meditation.

If some meditators fail to achieve such realization, they should carry on the meditation for a considerable period of time according to the previously elucidated methods of maintaining the absorption and postabsorption. Gradually, by detaching the mind again and again from inbred clinging to duality and emptiness, realization will dawn by stages. In the dawning of perfect realization lies the quintessence of Buddha's expoistions—the sūtras, tantras, and vital instructions. This system is therefore far more profound and effective than other paths and orders of transmission.

PERFECTING THE EFFICACY [OF AWARENESS] THROUGH THE SUBLIMATION OF THE PATH

This will be explained in three ways:

1. The ideal time conducive to the practices
2. The vital significance of this practice in general
3. The six ways of sublimating the practices

The Ideal Time Conducive to the Practices

The ideal time for a meditator to sublimate the practices is when, in general, he has gained insight into the intrinsic nature of the mind's spontaneous coemergence, and in particular, he has gained insight into the spontaneous coemergence of thought and appearance, and as well when, through mindfulness, he cognizes consciousness and appearance as the postabsorptive state. Without such insight into the essential identity of these three kinds of spontaneous coemergence one cannot sublimate the consciousness arising from immediate circumstances to the path of self-transformation.

Concerning the time when the meditator may elevate himself to the noble path, it is the time when, regardless of his awareness, the meditator, who confines himself to an ordinary life and who is still overpowered by concern for and clinging to the material pursuit of this life and by earthly desires and hatred, finds it hard to elevate his mind naturally to the path, since it is agitated by powerful circumstances. Or it is the time when, while enjoying peace and rest, he cannot perceive the intrinsic identity of any thoughts. In summary, the time to sublimate the mind to the path of self-transformation is when the meditator finds it hard to elevate himself to the path simply by being mindful of the virtuous absorption, or when his mind is uncontrollable owing to anxiety and agitation caused by hope, fear, etc.

0 B On the other hand, if a meditator in solitude experiences an uninterrupted meditative state, this calls for stabilization of the practice by testing [the mind] through adverse circumstances. The meditator performs the process of self-transformation specifically when the mind is agitated and anguished. Conversely, if after achieving an undistracted mindfulness of absorption and postabsorption, he stops maintaining the spontaneous flow of the mind's abiding nature and if he then tries to sublimate the practice and to meditate in order to apply antidotes [against the agitated mind], he has committed the kind of deviation mentioned before.

The time to engage oneself in such practice of self-transformation is referred to in the *Hevajra-tantra*:

> If a meditator achieves some degree of "inner heat"
> And wishes to practice self-transformation,
> He should do so only after such realization.

Accordingly the meditator engages himself in the practice only after achieving "inner heat" as the sign of realization.

311 F This Meditational Order also considers that the practice of self-transformation must be undertaken at an appropriate time. It seems that some people undertake the practice of self-transformation when they experience any sublime sensation arising from their meditation on tranquility, without even having realized insight into the intrinsic nature of mind.

Others embark upon the practice even without as much meditational experience as the former, by wandering about at crossroads and in wilderness areas, where dead bodies are disposed of. The motivation of such "mystics" is purely worldly, aimed at recognition and material benefits. And some people who start with such zeal and bear all the rigors of the practice, nevertheless degenerate into complacent renegades. Such an approach to the process of self-transformation will not result in any progress at all. It only shows their ignorance with regard to the abiding nature of mind and the essential nature of thoughts—the former as the basis and the latter as the object of self-transformation. The purpose of such practice is not entirely to elevate one's sensory enjoyments to higher experiences, but to achieve the blend of the dynamic and stable aspects of mind into one "even flavor." The *Hevajra-tantra* illustrates this:

> Whatever the elucidation [of self-transformation],
> It has not been expounded for practice
> In remote and terrifying places
> And for indulging in sensory enjoyments.
> It was expounded for testing the mind's dynamic and stable aspects
> As well as every other aspect.

Regarding the actual practice of self-transformation, the father tantra mentions three kinds of practice:

1. Discrimination
2. Nondiscrimination
3. Complete nondiscrimination[173]

311 B The mother tantra enumerates another three kinds:[174]

1. The secret practice
2. The uninhibited practice
3. The practice of triumph [over all adverse circumstances]

The *Trubnying* of Saraha mentions four:

1. The transformative practice of all-encompassing excellence
2. The secret practice
3. The practice of reversed consciousness
4. The practice of being triumphant over all adverse circumstances

And in addition yet another four practices for self-transformation exist:

1. The transformative practice for beginners
2. The practice of dominating awareness
3. The practice of completely dominating awareness
4. The practice for spontaneous liberation

It seems to me that if the practitioners of mahāmudrā happen to be tantric mystics [already] well versed in the vital tantric instructions for creative visualization and complete attainment, they can adapt the tantric practices of self-transformation to this specific mahāmudrā meditation. This is because [the texts dealing with mahāmudrā such as] the *Trubnying*, the dohā of Saraha, and the treatises on mahāmudrā by Śavarīśvara, Virūpa, and Tilopa state that any of these transformative practices should be carried out during this phase of mahāmudrā meditation.

However, the *Kālacakra* virtually forbids ordained monks to practice self-transformation through sexual application. In order to enhance the progress of their meditation they are allowed to carry out certain appropriate practices such as the practice for all-encompassing excellence, that of noncreativity, that of complete noncreativity, and the practice of being triumphant over all adverse circumstances. Monks can well carry out some of these practices for rapid progress as long as their vow of celibacy remains unaffected.

With regard to specific places for these practices, monasteries and cities are too relaxing and too pleasant, and thus lack the external and internal conditions crucial to sublimating the afflicted consciousness. These places cannot easily arouse deluded thoughts and coarse passions in the meditator. And without this kind of deluded thinking and passions rapid progress in elevating the mind to the path of mahāmudrā is not possible. A mind overcome by indifference and indolence cannot possibly rise above any afflicting circumstances in enhancing the progress of the path, even though the meditator may spend years or his entire lifetime deluding himself that he is engaged in meditation. For as long as he enjoys a peaceful and leisurely life, he will have a meditation purely oriented to such a condition and will instantly degenerate to an ordinary worldly level the moment an emotional crisis erupts.

2 B This order considers that progress can be achieved more rapidly during a single month of self-transformation through terrifying conditions in rough terrain and in "the abode of harmful forces" than through meditating for a period of three years in towns and monasteries. For this reason meditators are urged to begin the practice first by making an offering of kusului tsok[175] and then by performing the practice of self-transformation in utter silence on terrifying or forbidding peaks, in mountain solitude, in the abode of "nonhuman forces" who [are said to] produce frightening apparitions, in horrifying cemeteries where corpses and skeletons are disposed of, beneath a solitary tree possessed by serpent-gods or a powerful *tsen*, in deserted towns, and at intersections of roads haunted by hungry spirits and ghosts.

Concerning the meditator's confidence in himself to execute the secret practice for self-transformation, the ancient teachers of the Kadampa order have established five essential conditions for [a meditator to possess]:

1. To be honest in observing the precepts while in mountain solitude
2. To be capable of overcoming all adverse circumstances through spiritual countermeasures
3. To have mastered the vital instructions
313 F 4. To have revitalized one's whole stream of being through faith
5. To be capable of clearing subtle harmful influences

Je Gampopa has enunciated the following four essential requirements:

One must achieve confidence:
1. In one's knowledge of the vital instructions
2. In the mind's power
3. In one's experiences
4. In the view [of intrinsic reality]

Mahasitha Shang enunciated these four essential requirements:

1. To have mastered the treasure of the vital instructions
2. To be able to overpower the internal and external armies of harmful forces [māras]
3. To be honest in observing the precepts
4. To be capable of living alone in mountainous solitude

The actual practice of self-transformation is comprised of five kinds:

1. "To behave like a wounded deer." A wounded deer shuns companions and shows no interest in anything else. Thus a meditator should live by himself, not depending on friends, and should abandon any materialistic aims for this life, which would help vanquish his enemies, protect his friends, and flatter his benefactors.

313 B 2. "To behave like a lion." A lion is not afraid of any other animals such as deer or wild beasts. Thus a meditator should fear neither external obstacles [to his performance] created by human or nonhuman beings, nor internal obstacles arising from one's own deluded discrimination.

3. "To behave like the wind blowing through space." The wind blows freely through the expanse of space. Thus the meditator should let his thoughts flow freely and openly, without any attachment to his body, possessions, happiness, or fame.

4. "To behave like space." Space is without any support. Thus the meditator should neither direct his mental focus toward any specific object nor create a mental support for any image such as a visualized form or a formless object. Neither should he direct his mental focus toward any specific action.

5. "To behave like a crazy person." A mad person lacks any objective

direction. Thus a meditator should not have any attachment to anything, such as affirmation or rejection, acceptance or abandonment.

These five principles are considered to be a means of sublimating any emerging perceptions and emotions arising from adverse external or internal conditions and thereby to greatly enhance one's vision of abiding reality.[176]

F The Vital Significance of this Practice in General

At this point every deluded thought should be elevated to the path of self-transformation, because they bind sentient beings to cyclic existence [saṃsāra]. The *Vairocanābhisambodhi* states:

> Dualistic thoughts constitute great ignorance;
> They throw sentient beings into the ocean of saṃsāra.

However, when dualistic thought is brought to the illuminating path instead of being let run astray, it will through its intrinsic nature emerge as transcending awareness. The *Hevajra-tantra* says:

> A dualistic thought purifies a dualistic thought;
> And existential phenomenon purifies an existential phenomenon.

And Saraha says:

> A dualistic thought in its essence is great awareness.
> As such it will dry up the ocean of saṃsāra.

Both Nāropa and Maitrīpa make identical comments:

> A dualistic thought is self-releasing great awareness.

Someone may ask, "If that were so, would not the previous elucidation on identifying dualistic thought with dharmakāya be adequate for self-realization? Why is it essential for a meditator to sublimate every dualistic thought to the illuminating path?" Meditators predestined to an instanta-
314 B neous self-realization will achieve liberation by perceiving every thought to be dharmakāya. Most meditators must apply the crucial methods of elevating all discursive thoughts to the illuminating path. [Without such methods] only subtle, not strong thoughts can be transformed into transcending awareness by maintaining a state of mindfulness; neither can much of the mental cognition in the postabsorptive stage be transformed. Also, meditators can achieve sublimation of only a few intermittent thoughts to the meditational state. Many meditators may even commit a deviation by losing track of normal thoughts and subsequently conceiving these to be of the

nature of dharmakāya. Furthermore, at the [second] yoga stage of nondiscrimination, all subtle thoughts will arise as dharmakāya simply by the meditator's maintaining an undistracted mindfulness, but powerful motions such as desire, hatred, etc. still cannot attain the same sublimation. Even at
315 F the [third] yoga of one flavor, the mind, deeply agitated by violent circumstances, cannot easily be sublimated without the meditator's applying the crucial methods for their transformation. Hence these methods are essential even on the higher levels of meditation.

Nowadays some meditators who early on achieved the meditative state and who meditated for many years fail to make much progress and seem to succumb to idleness out of sheer frustration. All these [problems] arise from the meditator's failure to comprehend the vital significance of sublimating the mind to the illuminating path. For this reason all meditators, including beginners and great ones, should value this special method and master it. The essence of it lies in being skillful in maintaining the stream of mindfulness appropriate at every stage. Je Drikhungpa emphasizes:

> O my sons, summing up everything
> I cannot but state
> "He who is skillful in mindfulness
> Is skillful in meditation."

He says further:

> Undistracted mindfulness is essential
> Even for meditating on the stream of the pure state.

All other practices of elevating diverse practices to the illuminating path are the constituent parts of sublimating thoughts. Indeed, the latter consti-
315 B tute the root of the former. One aspect of mind must be understood to be identical to every other, for by knowing the hollowness of one reed, one knows the hollowness of all other reeds. Considering this, Je Gampopa enunciates mainly the elevation of dualistic thoughts to the path of dharmakāya. He considers that this principle of practice should be extended to all other practices of elevation.

Although there are six kinds of meditational elevation enumerated by the present-day practitioners of this order, this does not mean that Gampopa has not made similar comments. In his *Zer Nampa Ngai Menngak* [*The Five Naillike Instructions*], recorded in writing by [his disciple] Dülwa Dzinpa, he mentions the methods of awakening consciousness through transforming:

1. obstacles to the path
2. diseases
3. death
4. emotionality

5. dualistic thoughts
6. gods and demons

The last one refers to an investigation of the four demonic forces.[177] In addition Gampopa dealt with this matter in his precious collected works, though in a fragmentary way. Later, Je Gyare rediscovered certain written instructions of Je Rechungpa [on the same subject], which had been buried
F underground and were entitled "The Hidden Treasure." These instructions have since become widely known as "the even flavor" [ronyom][178] to all followers of the glorious Drukpa school of the Kagyüpa order.

There are three vital methods for all forms of elevating consciousness to the path:

1. "To identify every dualistic thought" means that a meditator should first identify every emerging thought or sensory appearance arising from either good or bad circumstances. While not letting it stray he should seek to establish its identity.

2. "To abandon clinging to self" means that whatever thought or appearance emerges, he should let it be in its natural state, unpolluted by lust or hatred, acceptance or abandonment, neither ascribing good nor bad qualities to it nor clinging to the inbred notion of self.

3. "To abandon the chasm of hope and fear" means that the meditator should abandon hope for success and fear of failure as well as the expectation to achieve the spiritual elevation or the doubt about the outcome. It also means that even if a certain subtle hope or fear were to arise, he should let it flow freely without modulating, altering, or clinging to it.

These three methods should be applied to all forms of the spiritual elevation.

16 B

The Six Ways of Sublimating the Practices

This is comprised of six sections:

1. Elevating dualistic thoughts to the path by transforming any agonizing crisis into blessed conditions
2. Elevating crude emotions to the path through the spiritual process called "transforming poison into ambrosia"
3. Elevating obstacles emanating from the superior and subordinate spiritual forces to the path
4. Elevating miseries to the path by transforming them into the spirit of enlightenment [bodhicitta]
5. Elevating the afflictions of disease to the path, the even flavor of the elements
6. Elevating one's dying to the path by unifying one's primal consciousness

and recollected contemplative awareness, the way a mother and her daughter are reunited

Elevating Dualistic Thoughts to the Path by Transforming Any Agonizing Crisis into Blessed Conditions

The *Hevajra-tantra* comments on the elevation of thoughts to the illuminating path:

> Just as water in one's ear
> Is flushed out with certain other liquids,
> So any thoughts of dualistic substance
> Should be purified with the certainty of nonduality.

Thus dualistic thoughts are to be purified through discerning thoughts. As for the method of purification, all deluded thoughts should be pacified by transforming them into their transcending nature. Je Gampopa instructs:

317 F Instead of abandoning discursive thoughts one should look upon them as being the source of benefits and as being useful and delightful. These deluded thoughts contain the nature of ultimate reality. They are friends and are the path to and the fuel for [the fire of] wisdom.

Je Gampopa mentions many such ways of elevating thoughts to the path.

As for identifying dualistic thoughts, to begin with the meditator should recollect either a subtle or a strong thought of a good or evil kind, which arouses a sense of delight or dislike. He should then establish the identity of that thought through mindfulness, without letting it run astray. In the middle of this process he should endeavor to eliminate the mind's clinging to the self. But in order to achieve this he should neither abandon that recollected thought nor should he control it in order to turn it into a nondiscriminatory awareness, which is regarded as a spiritual countermeasure. He should neither analyze the same thought in terms of its origin, dwelling, or movement in order to establish the emptiness of any essence nor should he let it run astray and then pursue it in order to focus on it through mindfulness. Instead, the meditator, upon establishing its identity, should use that thought in an undiminished form as the actual meditation and should maintain its clarity, looseness, and openness without altering or modulating
317 B it. In doing so he should not cling to that state, neither ascribe good or bad qualities to it nor suppress or pursue it. Without any attempt to accept or abandon, affirm or reject, alter or modulate, change or divide it, he will experience the dawning of that very recollection into a meditative state. This is regarded as the actual elevation of deluded thoughts to the illuminating path. Maitrīpa states:

A transient thought arises from the unborn [emptiness].
It embodies the nature of all-embracing reality.
These two have been inseparable from the very beginning.
I therefore proclaim the two to be of one flavor.

Je Gampopa comments:

Unaltered thoughts bear the nature
Of intrinsic reality.
Know that left unmodulated they are self-releasing.

F Je Götsangpa explains:

Each time a thought arises
Seize it firmly by its image,
Let it relax in its natural state;
It will doubtlessly release itself.

And he advises:

It flows like the invisible breeze;
Let it flow without grasping it.
This is described as "thought turning into meditation."
As insight into the intrinsic nature of one's self
It is free from affirmation or rejection.

Meditators who have practiced the vital methods of self-transformation may nonetheless experience some strong swirl of emotion which seems to create an inner disquiet and render the meditation somewhat difficult. This is due mainly to a disharmony between his thoughts and internal energies, since the two have an identical dynamic nature. However, this state of mind is in reality not completely detached from meditation. He will gradually and blissfully achieve the elevation of mind to the illuminating path. Once he masters the practice, he will experience the dawning of the meditational state through every thought the moment he recognizes it.

18 B Finally, in order to abandon the chasm of agitation and anxiety, division and integration, and particularly hope and fear [of fulfillment or failure] and thus elevate the practice to the path, the mind should be left in a trackless state without any evaluation or clinging. This same method should be extended to the other practices of elevating the mind to the path.

Elevating Crude Emotions to the Path through the Spiritual Process Called "Transforming Poison into Ambrosia"

The *Hevajra-tantra* states:

Just as the suffering of burns
Can be alleviated by applying heat,
So can someone burnt by the fire of desire
Be pacified by the fire of desire.

The *Samputa* says:

Desire can be purified by desire,
Hatred by hatred,
Jealousy by jealousy
All emotions by grasping
That which is the supreme indestructibility.

And so, by elevating the different emotions to the sublime path and harmonizing them with the mind's intrinsic nature into an even flavor, one will perceive the dawning of the five transcending states of awareness through these manifest emotions. Discerning awareness will dawn through desire, the expanse of emptiness through hatred, the mirrorlike awareness through ignorance, the harmonious awareness through conceit, and the sponta-
319 F neously fulfilling awareness through jealousy. The level of the five victorious buddhas will thus be realized. The *Samputa* describes:

Transcending awareness and emotion
May be merged evenly.
The former consists of the five buddhas
And the five transcending awarenesses.

If a meditator, who has applied the vital instructions of self-transformation, partakes of the six sensory enjoyments, he cannot be harmed by their transient deficiencies. For he is capable of transforming them the way a poison is transmuted into ambrosia. The *Hevajra-tantra* elucidates the point:

Human individuals are fettered
By their inexhaustible karma.
Yet by applying skillful methods
They can break the bondage of cyclic existence.

Saraha says:

One will not be defiled
Simply by partaking of sensory pleasures,

As the petals of the waterlily
Are unstained by mud.
He who seeks refuge in
The root of inmost purity
Is like a master with a secret formula
To purify poison.
How can he be harmed by poison?

He also explains

The salty water of the oceans
Turns to delightful freshness
Through interaction with the clouds,
And poison can be turned into ambrosia.
B Likewise a secure mind transforms [self-concern]
Into a genuine concern for others.

During the practice of elevating the mind to the illuminating path the meditator should first recognize and recollect his intense and vivid desire either for some material object or for a human individual. When using hatred as the basis of the practice, he should produce a heart-shattering ill-will and detestation for his enemies or for "obstructive forces." When dealing with ignorance, he should recognize it in such conditions as sullenness, drowsiness, dullness, inertia, confusion, or idleness. To use conceit as the basis of the practice, he should perceive it as being an attachment to oneself and to a superiority complex. When dealing with jealousy, he should recognize it as being such a rigid intolerance that it agonizes over the wealth and knowledge of others.

320 F The meditator should know that having thus recognized the identity of each defiled emotion, he should abandon his clinging to the self, his hope and fear, in the way indicated. Sometimes the meditator should deliberately produce an even more intense feeling of lust or hatred for some object of passion—one that makes him pant, change his facial expression, and even shiver. He should recognize this violent emotion [in order to transmute it into discerning awareness or nondiscriminatory compassion]. It has been proclaimed that the more powerful an afflicting thought, the more effective it becomes as a means to elevate the mind to the illuminating path and thus to achieve mental purification. Maitrīpa explains:

Emotions arouse great awareness
And support meditators
The way a forest feeds a great fire.

Based on the earlier practice, the meditator should know whether or not he has achieved the power of mind through the sublimation of his emotions.

Elevating Obstacles Emanating from the Superior and Subordinate Spiritual Forces to the Path

Discriminatory thoughts by themselves constitute obstacles. All "obstructive forces" originate from such thoughts. Nāropa says:

320 B In these dualistic thoughts lie diseases and "obstructive forces."
When illness afflicts one,
The illness lies in the very thought of it;
When harm befalls one,
The harm lies in the very thought of it;
When one dies,
The death lies in the very thought of it;
When one is reborn,
The rebirth lies in the very thought of it;
Pleasure, pain, or others lie in dualistic thoughts,
Yet the mind is empty of any reality.
When one has eliminated the root of dualistic thoughts,
Neither disease nor harm
From "obstructive forces" will befall one.

The great master Milarepa comments:

Concerning these three—the apparition of the obstructive spirit,
The mental grasping of that spirit,
And the discrimination of it—
They all originate from the yogin's mind
And will dissolve into his mind.
For obstructive spirits are
Only manifestations of his mind.
The yogin is overcome by his own delusion
When he conceives the reality of these forces
And fails to realize the emptiness of such appearances.

The demoness of the cave spoke thus to Milarepa:

Unless your dualistic thought manifests itself as your enemy
Due to your own inner delusion,
How can this cave demoness become your enemy?
Besides, this demoness of your hidden delusion
Originates from your own mind.
Unless you realize the mind's intrinsic nature
I shall not leave just because you asked me to.

321 F All one's mental clinging to the concept of malicious spirits is but the manifestation of one's own mind. Apparent figures of gods or spirits that might appear before one are purely an inner sensation that has arisen from

the mind's clinging to the very thought of them. It is indeed like someone mistaking a rope for a snake at that instant when his mind first conceives the image of a snake. The immediate cause and condition of such delusion consists of the interaction between the absorption of air-energy into the psychoneurotic system, which is the basis of the three inner poisons in the body [the vehicle of individual karma], and the mental grasping of dualistic thoughts.

Thus ignorance is considered to be the specific source of the deluded appearances of serpent-gods and earth protectors. Hatred is the source of the appearances of the vicious *tsen*[179] and other male spirits. Desire is the source of the appearances of demonesses and female spirits. Once the meditator has successfully elevated these thoughts and appearances to the illuminating path, he will achieve one after the other, like the rising and falling of a scale, a meditational state, the elimination of fear and other mental delusions, the disappearance of apparitions, the submission of spirits, and a feeling of well-being.

1 B Concerning the elevation of thoughts of spirits to the transcending path, Je Gampopa refers to a method for determining the unreality of spirits known as "investigation of the four kinds of spirits." This method is somewhat different from those applied at the stage of harmonizing diverse experiences into the one flavor. This method consists of letting that deluded thought remain unaltered in the mind's nondual awareness. The other methods he referred to elsewhere also deal with the same subject. Both are appropriate practices at this stage.

Regarding the elevation [of the delusion of] gods and spirits to the path, the meditator should seize such deluded thoughts either instantly when he perceives such terrifying apparitions [of gods and spirits] or seize them once he is overcome by the fear of encountering them. After having become aware of his mind under such circumstances, the meditator should keep [this insight] as the main meditation, as in the case of every previous meditation. To pacify greater or lesser threatening apparitions, the meditator should imagine that he is encountering far more frightening and unbelievably menacing apparitions, that he is being attacked by an army of malicious spirits whose movements sound like a clashing of heaven and earth, and that
322 F his body is being cut up with their swords, burned, and dragged in the water. After thus increasing his fear, he should then turn this mental condition into the meditational state.

Elevating Miseries to the Path by Transforming Them into the Spirit of Enlightenment [Bodhicitta]

Je Gampopa, in his *Tsokchö*, refers to similar methods for enhancing the practice: (1) regarding the miseries of life as a source of benefits, (2) perceiving the nature of these miseries as nonarising [emptiness], and (3) using these miseries as an impetus to produce love, compassion, and the spirit of enlightenment.

I will now give instruction in conformity with the general methods for elevating the mind to the path. The meditator should first establish the identity of the mind that is typical of individuals who follow the teachings of the Hīnayāna tradition. People with such a mind do not feel true compassion for other sentient beings in misery. Instead they become so visibly afraid of suffering similar afflictions due to their own deluded mind and evil karma that they even feel acute agony. This happens when, in general, such practitioners perceive or hear about how other sentient beings are afflicted by the three kinds of miseries[180] and when, in particular, they see how they
322 B torment, cut, and kill another, or when they see how still others are afflicted by various other miseries due to their own evil karma. Such meditators therefore long to practice the dharma simply to pacify their own evil karma and delusion and achieve liberation for themselves. Then the meditator should perceive the identity of the mind of Mahāyāna practitioners and should develop love and compassion for all sentient beings suffering from diverse afflictions. This has to be done by adopting an extraordinary attitude with which to look upon these sentient beings as "gracious fathers and mothers."

Thus, when the meditator first arouses a serious concern and acute anxiety for his own liberation and then that of other sentient beings, he should cognize the identity of each and elevate it to the sublime path, as was done before. When concluding the practice, the meditator should engender the spirit of enlightenment born of love and compassion for all sentient beings, while maintaining the sublime sensation of this meditation. He should then express the solemn wish that his high aspiration for the well-being of others be realized. This kind of practice has been highly praised. For instance Nāgārjuna proclaims:

323 F For oneself and others of this world
Who yearn for supreme enlightenment,
The foundation consists of bodhicitta,
Which is as solid as the sovereign Mount Sumeru,
Of boundless compassion, and of nondual awareness.

The spirit of enlightenment [bodhicitta] is defined as the union of compassion and emptiness, which is the quintessence of the path, the luster of unceasing compassion that cannot bear the suffering of sentient beings, and the nondual awareness that cognizes the compassion as being empty of any essence or self-nature. This is the essence of Mahāyāna Buddhism. The *Hevajra-tantra* comments:

The union of emptiness and compassion
Is described as the spirit of enlightenment.

The *Vajrapañjara* explains:

The meditation on the union
Of emptiness and compassion
Is indeed the teaching
Of the buddha, dharma, and saṅgha.

The *Sampuṭa* says:

The nondiscriminatory simplicity [of mind]
Is described as wisdom;
B That which fulfills the wishes of sentient beings,
The way a wish-granting gem does, as compassion.

Saraha states:

He who seeks emptiness without compassion
Will not realize the supreme path;
Yet he who meditates mainly on compassion
Will not realize liberation.
He who unifies the two
Will neither remain in saṃsāra nor in nirvāṇa.[181]

Śavari declares:

He who has attained nonevaluating awareness,
Who is unable to bear the misery of confused sentient beings,
And who sheds tears of compassion
While working for their benefit
Turns concern for himself
Into concern for others.

Elevating the Afflictions of Disease to the Path, the Even Flavor of the Elements

Diseases are generally the result of [individual or collective] karma and emotions, both of which originate from primal ignorance.[182] The immediate cause is the disharmony of the four basic elements of the psychophysical system and the constitution of every individual. This imbalance is brought about by the flow of his karmic energy [karmaprāṇa]. Thus he suffers from
324 F affliction of body and mind. Diseases were originally estimated to number 424. They are divided into four categories:

1. Diseases caused by the psychophysical energy [prāṇa]
2. Diseases caused by the humor of bile
3. Diseases caused by body fluids
4. Diseases caused by a combination of the other three humors

Pathological texts speak of many methods for healing diseases. A meditator removes the cause of his disease by applying the effective method of maintaining discerning awareness through an absorptive meditation. This is an antidote for the deeper cause, which is ignorance. In order to remove the immediate cause of the disharmonious flow of karmic energy, the meditator maintains his primal awareness without altering it. This is an effective antidote against the immediate cause. The vital significance of this method lies in the fact that both mind and internal energy have the same dynamic nature. To effectively neutralize and nullify the affliction, he should medi-
324 B tate on abiding emptiness. These methods of elevating the affliction to the iluminating path are considered to be far more effective than others for curing chronic or new diseases.

Regarding the practice of elevating any affliction of disease to the path, the threefold method mentioned by Je Gampopa agrees in principle with this approach. His reference to "over-powering the affliction at the beginning" means that a meditator should through his own imagination intensify his agony so much that it becomes an unbearable experience [thus creating a strong basis for the practice of self-transformation]. "Subjugation of the disease in the middle phase" means that the meditator should analyze this affliction in terms of its origin and movement and should examine whether it has any perceivable form or color. "Elevating the affliction to the path as the final phase" means that the meditator should consider that it is the mind that conceives the affliction of the disease and that the mind itself is nonarising [emptiness], like space.

However, at this point the meditator should neither examine the cause, condition, and way it afflicts, nor should he determine its emergence, endurance, and movement. He should simply observe the intrinsic nature of the feeling in his body and mind, which arises from the agonizing pain. In maintaining this observation as the main meditation he should keep the clarity of the awareness [of the affliction] without either altering or modulating it through intellectual acceptance or rejection or entertaining any attach-
325 F ment to or detestation for it. Occasionally he should analyze the mind's clinging to and concern for the afflicted self as the experiencer of the pain. Once the meditator has subdued the disease he should apply those [three] methods of Gampopa referred to earlier.

At the end the meditator remains free not only from hope or fear for his affliction but also resolves that the mind [in its intrinsic nature] is of great evenness. If the meditator wishes, he may repeat the method of overpowering the affliction. Nowadays one can elevate to the illuminating path the discomfort or pain caused by prolonged sitting in a cross-legged posture [vajrāsana] or any pain one has purposely created. Thus, by prolonged meditation on elevating the affliction of disease and the clinging to the self to the sublime path, the meditator will finally realize these very adverse experiences as the meditational state, thus making it unnecessary for him to treat them as his adversaries or to abandon them. Simultaneously he will experience the healing of the disease through the restored harmony amongst the psychosomatic elements, together with an evenness of body temperature and tremendous progress in meditation.

B The statement urging practitioners of even flavor to abstain at this stage from taking medicine and treatment conforms with the purpose of practicing even flavor, which is designed to eventually eliminate one's concern for hope or fear. This was also the traditional approach of the great saints [mahāsiddhas]. Many anecdotes speak of how Je Drikhungpa and Je Götsangpa brought about their complete recovery from many serious ailments only by practicing even flavor.

Nowadays the turning of one's ailments into a meditative absorption continues to be a characteristic practice of meditators. Since this human body as the invaluable support for seeking enlightenment cannot possibly be left to the fate of the live-or-die attitude of ignorant ones, meditators must rely upon the conventional healing methods and relevant practices for curing their ailments. They must also meditate on the ultimate awareness to eliminate any materialistic hope and fear. This has been accepted as being consistent with the purpose of this practice.

Elevating One's Dying to the Path by Unifying One's Primal Consciousness and Recollected Contemplative Awareness, the Way a Mother and her Daughter Are Reunited

Through meditation the meditator masters the sublimation of his deluded thoughts or appearances, which arise from diverse conditions of his life. He seeks particularly to achieve the elevation of the quietening process of sleep and of the clarity of awareness obtained in meditation to the illuminating
26 F path. As a result he will achieve the power to sublimate the dying phases through visualization in order to enable him to apply that power to the actual phases of death when it occurs and to bring about the union of the lucid awareness perceived in meditation with the actual awareness that emerges during a normal death, the way an infant returns to its mother's lap.

When, at a certain time, the meditator perceives that death is approaching, he should free himself from attachment to his country, his relatives, his companions, and his material possessions. He should then make over part of his possessions to his gurus as a gift, arrange the offering of sacrificial cakes and other delicacies to the meditational deities, guardian ḍākinīs, and dharma protectors, and provide a ritual feast for the brethren of the Vajrayāna order as well as a ceremony for purification. He should try to avoid any adverse conditions while performing virtuous deeds that will produce

spiritual benefits for his future life. When the moment of his death arrives, he should either lie down [on his right side] in the reclining "lion's posture" or sit upright and adjust every vital part of his body. He should begin the practice of elevating [the process of dying] to the illuminating path by first visualizing his guru on his head and by producing an intense faith in him. The dying process begins with the agonizing realization that one is finally being separated from everything one has clung to with intense craving. Thus one is overcome with heart-chilling anguish. Meanwhile one loses consciousness proportionate with the appearance of inner sensations arising from
326 B the disintegration of the four natural elements and from the dissolution of the subpsychic states, viz. the [white] illumination, the [red] diffusive glow, and the descending darkness.[183]

Regarding the way of turning these experiences into spontaneous attainment on the path, one will only impede one's practice if one allows oneself to be overcome by a detestation for these events or by a clinging to deluded discrimination of this or that experience, or if one is concerned with a hope of realizing the luminous awareness or with a fear of failure. The meditator would do well to simply recognize these thoughts and inner sensations at the outset and then to turn each as it arises into an essential meditation. While maintaining such an absorptive state, he should neither distort it by clinging to it nor by affirming or rejecting it. The rest of the procedure is as stated before.

The Mahāyāna teachings on the "training of the mind"[184] contain many highly praised instructions on the transference of stream-consciousness [to a buddha realm] at the final moment of death. None is more effective than the method to maintain every emerging thought or appearance without ever distorting it through mental clinging. When the disintegration of the psychophysical elements in the dying process is complete, the inherent luminous clarity [of one's primal awareness] will emerge by itself. The [dying] meditator perceives the spontaneous blending of this state with the luminous awareness he had experienced in his meditation. The union of these two states, the former as the "mother" and the latter as the "daughter," is like
327 F water being mixed with water or space being merged with space. And then enlightenment in dharmakāya is realized.

The tantras illustrate death as follows:

> What has been designated as death means dualistic thought
> And should be guided to the realm of the ḍākinīs.

The *Sampal Tsenjö* (*Mañjuśrīnāma-saṃgīti*) states:

> Through perfect discernment in that one moment
> Complete enlightenment is achieved in that moment.

Je Gampopa says:

How can there be death
When one thought current follows another?
How can there be death
For that which is perfect dharmakāya?
How can there be death
For that which disappears, like a rainbow?
How can there be death
For the mind, which is devoid of birth and death?

However, it has been declared that should a meditator fail to achieve enlightenment during his life through the union of his primal awareness with all-encompassing emptiness, due to his inadequate practice in turning the mind into attainment on the path, he may realize the mind's intrinsic power through the various methods of self-transformation, so that he may be able to control his destiny during the bardo [intermediate state] and rebirth. Such a meditator will be able, at least in his next life, to reestablish his religious practice, owing to the power of his karma.

Thus ends the chapter on determining the mind's intrinsic state of nonarising [emptiness] and on rapidly enhancing the experiences through the elevation of the mind to the illuminating path.

CHAPTER NINE

The Resultant Dawning of Realization

This is elucidated in three sections:

1. Differentiating the ways of realization
2. How realization of the four stages of yoga takes place
3. How the various grounds and paths [of enlightenment] are reached through the four yogas

DIFFERENTIATING THE WAYS OF REALIZATION

It is said that realization of the four states of yoga will dawn in the meditator in accordance with his or her spiritual potential in one of three ways. Meditators are divided into three groups—great, average, and ordinary—according to their present spiritual potentials, which are considered to be the result of achievements in their past lives. A "great person" means a meditator who has a strong potential for instantaneous realization [cik-charwa]. An "average person" means a meditator who has the potential for an evanescent realization [thögalwa], and an "ordinary person" means a meditator who has the potential for a gradual realization [rimgyipa].

A meditator with a strong potential will instantly comprehend, understand, and realize first the meditation on tranquility and then transcending
328 F insight. He will then, during a higher tantric initiation [bestowed upon him by his guru], instantly discover the inner identity of his whole being. Such a meditator will instantly realize the one-pointed stage alone or each of the three remaining yoga stages of mahāmudrā—the nondiscriminatory stage, the stage of one flavor, and the stage of nonmeditation.[185] Since these realizations will be of a stable kind, they are considered to be like the rising sun, which warms the rocks and ground.

An [average] meditator will attain in an evanescent manner[186] first an intellectual comprehension, experience, and understanding and then each of the four stages of yoga. So fluctuating is his experience that before stabilizing the first one he has a glimpse of the next one, like the sun appearing and disappearing alternately through patches of clouds. However, such a meditator can stabilize these experiences by strenuously meditating in solitude and by invoking his guru for his blessing with intense faith and veneration. Should the fluctuation persist due to his insufficient devotion, he will nonetheless achieve realization in the bardo stage.

An [ordinary] meditator with steady potential will first gradually gain an intellectual comprehension, experience, and understanding and then the realization of each of the four stages of yoga. Only after stabilizing the preceding experience can he gain the next one. Because he gradually realizes each stage, he cannot eliminate the inner deficiencies immediately or apply countermeasures. This kind of experience is similar to the rising sun on the far horizon, which can neither heat the ground and rocks nor melt the ice right away. However, the last two types of meditators can achieve an instantaneous realization without difficulty provided they have deep faith in and devotion to meditation. The experiences of meditators differ from individual to individual. Those who have at some point achieved instantaneous realization will gain the determinate insight [into intrinsic reality]. Others may fail to recognize the intrinsic nature of the realization that they have attained. They thus remain indifferent and nondiscerning. It is essential that such meditators seek the guidance of their gurus and spiritual friends.

The differentiation of the three processes of realization is (1) intellectual comprehension [gō], (2) experience [nyong], and (3) understanding [tok].[187] The term "intellectual comprehension" refers to the meditator's inferential determination based on his cognizance of the nature of his meditation at whatever level, high or low. The term "experience" refers to the absorption of perceived reality and to his experiencing it in terms of his awareness. The term "understanding" refers to his direct understanding of a nondeceiving reality and to his awareness of its determinate certainty. Je Gyare comments:

> Intellectual comprehension arises from examination;
> Dawning or decreasing sensations of bliss and clarity are
> experiences;
> Recognizing the mind's abiding nature is understanding.

The distinction [between the three processes of realization] may be deduced from this analogy. Intellectual comprehension is like someone visualizing the general scene of Bodhgayā as he listens to a description of it. Perceptive experience is like the same person having a quick glimpse of the place. Understanding is like the same person actually gaining a detailed knowledge of the place [through prolonged contact with it].

This tradition holds that a perceptive experience is that in which a meditator clearly maintains a specific meditational state in his awareness,
329 B that tranquil equipoise is that in which he maintains that absorption one-pointedly and without any distraction, and that realization is that in which the determinate certainty achieved through wisdom is devoid of the duality of observer and observation. Je Gampopa elucidates:

> Perceptive experience is a serene clarity [of one's awareness];
> Settled tranquility means maintaining such clarity undistractedly;
> Understanding means cognizing [the mind]
> To be empty of any essence, as determined through analytical wisdom.

In answering the question about the difference between inner sensation [nyam][188] and understanding [tok], Gampopa says:

> An inner sensation does not transcend the mind but arises within its realm. Like the sun's rays emerging through patches of clouds, the inner sensation of bliss, clarity, or nondiscrimination fluctuates, rising high one moment, falling low the next, or remaining steady. If the meditation on inner sensation is maintained without the mind becoming attached to it, mental defilement will clear by itself and understanding will emerge. Understanding consists of an unceasing stream of the mind's luminous clarity, without the duality of appearance and
> 330 F thought, meditator and meditation. This is described as simultaneous realization and perfection.

Some teachers described the three aspects of experience as follows:

> Concerning the three phases of experience—
> Inner sensation, intellectual comprehension, and understanding—
> Inner sensation [nyam] is inferior,
> Intellectual comprehension [gō] is moderate,
> And understanding [tok] is superior.
> This has to be examined.
> If inner sensation is
> Identical with experience [nyam nyong],
> Then all sentient beings would gain meditational experiences.
> If [by inner sensation] they mean an experience in meditation,
> Then this is attainable in all meditations
> From the path of consummate virtue
> To the stage of perfection.
> If inner sensation were identical
> With self-comprehending awareness,
> This would degrade the sublime experience of the awakened ones

> To a [mundane] inner sensation.
> These two terms "inner sensation" and "understanding"
> Are synonymous, meaning one and the same thing.
> They are two Tibetan renditions
> Of an original Sanskrit term.

This statement is not valid. Its description of the three aspects of meditational experience as being superior, moderate, and inferior is an exaggeration. No one has concluded that inner sensation must necessarily be of an inferior kind. The "inner sensation" has not been conclusively defined as an inferior experience. Therefore, his reference to the sensations experienced by awakened arhats is unwarranted. Even if such a definition were valid, the possibility of differentiating the inner sensation and experience of the arhats exists. Besides, this Meditational Order accepts certain levels of meditation where an inner sensation of experience [tokpai rangnyam] and an inner sensation of understanding [nyam tok] are not differentiable.

If, as they claim, intellectual comprehension and understanding were always one and the same, one would have to accept that the distinctive term lung-tok—the original exposition [lung] and understanding [tok]—is identical with that of lung and gōwa [the original exposition and intellectual comprehension]. Moreover, one would have to accept that understanding attained on the grounds of and the path to enlightenment as being intellectual comprehension. This is going too far. For certain reasons the Tibetan translators [lotsawa] and the Indian scholars [paṇḍitas] translated these terms separately.

Again, the same teachers wrote:

> If one wishes, one could describe clear and unclear thoughts
> As intellectual comprehension and understanding respectively.

This is wrong. According to them the very distinctive term "clear and unclear thoughts" ought to be identical with those of intellectual comprehension and understanding. Thus this position contradicts what has been stated earlier. By identifying vague thought with understanding they have
1 F gone too far in contradicting the system of lexicology. This also implies that the understanding of nondual awareness ought to be accepted as dualistic thought.

HOW REALIZATION OF THE FOUR STAGES OF YOGA TAKES PLACE

This is shown in three sections:

1. How the sūtras and tantras show the four stages of yoga

2. The general meaning of the four stages of yoga
3. The detailed elucidation of each of the four yoga stages

How the Sūtras and Tantras Show the Four Stages of Yoga

The *Laṅkāvatāra-sūtra* states:

> Mahāmati: O Illuminated Conqueror, all bodhisattvas and mahāsattvas who possess the four dharmas will attain to the yoga of the great perfection. What are the four dharmas [yoga stages]?
>
> [Buddha:] They are: (1) meditation on the lucidity of one's mind, (2)
> 331 B abandonment of the view of [absolute] arising, dwelling, or dissolving, (3) understanding that external reality is without substance, and (4) a deep yearning for discerning awareness. O Mahāmati, all bodhisattvas and mahāsattvas who command these four dharmas will attain the great stage of yoga.

This passage shows the four stages of yoga.

I shall now elucidate these one by one. The phrase "meditation on the lucidity of one's mind" indicates the one-pointed yoga [the first stage]. The same sūtra states:

> Mahāmati: How did the bodhisattvas and mahāsattvas achieve their skill in meditation on the lucidity of their mind?
>
> [Buddha:] They contemplated thus, "The three planes of cosmic existence are only of mind. The mind [in its intrinsic nature] is immutable, detached from the duality of "I" and "mine" as well as from the concern for affirmation and rejection. Yet it has from beginningless time been deeply stained by its attachment to the ignoble psychic outflow and has been intimately linked to one's actions per-
> 332 F formed in previous lives throughout the three planes. Thus one craves after this deluded mind, body, possessions, habitation, and movement."

This sūtra passage agrees in principle with the meaning of the one-pointed stage of yoga.

By referring to "abandonment of the view of absolute arising, dwelling, or dissolving," this sūtra shows the nondiscriminatory yoga [the second stage]:

> Mahāmati: How did the bodhisattvas and mahāsattvas abandon the view of an absolute arising, dwelling, or dissolving?

> [Buddha:] They abandoned it in this manner. They cognized that all phenomena are like an ephemeral illusion and dream, that they are detached from the duality of self and others, and that they are therefore unborn [emptiness]. They focused on the mind's manifestations and cognized external reality as unreal. By perceiving the unreality of phenomena, they brought about the cessation of the outflowing sensory consciousness. Because they cognized the unreality of their psy-
> B chosomatic aggregates and the interacting conditions of the three planes of cosmic existence as originating from their deluded mind, they saw external and internal phenomena as devoid of any inherent nature and as transcending all concepts. Having abandoned the view of an absolute arising [of phenomena], they realized the illusory nature and thereby attained insight into the unborn dharma [expanse of emptiness].

This sūtra exposition agrees with the meaning of the non-discriminatory stage of yoga.

The sūtra's phrase on being skillful in "understanding that external reality is without substance" shows the yoga of one flavor [the third stage]. The same *Laṅkāvatāra-sūtra* states:

> Mahāmati: How did the bodhisattvas and mahāsattvas achieve the skill to understand that external reality is without substance?
>
> [Buddha:] They attained this realization by penetrating into the intrinsic emptiness of phenomena and by perceiving their self-nature as being like a mirage, a dream, or a comb entangled with hair. They did so by understanding that from beginningless time all substantive reality has originated from the deluded mind with its attachment to the diverse ignoble psychic outflows.

333 F This sūtra's exposition agrees with the meaning of the one-flavor stage of yoga.

The sūtra's phrase "a deep yearning for discerning awareness" indicates the nonmeditation yoga [the fourth stage]. The same sūtra states:

> Mahāmati: How did the bodhisattvas and mahāsattvas achieve such penetrating analytical awareness?
>
> [Buddha:] They achieved it in this manner. After gaining insight into the nonarising [emptiness] of all things through the power of tolerance, the bodhisattvas dwelled on the eighth ground of enlightenment. They attained the state of awareness because of their penetrating awareness of thought, mental events, and mental consciousness, of the five senses, the nature of these five senses, and the two kinds of selflessness.

This exposition agrees with the nonmeditation stage of yoga.

The *Laṅkāvatāra-sūtra* further states:

Do not conceive external reality
Through the inference of the mind.
Focus your mind on the suchness [of emptiness]
And then transcend the mind itself!
Settle the mind in the emptiness of appearance
By transcending the phenomena of appearance.
333 B A yogin who has settled his mind in the emptiness of appearance
Will indeed see the Mahāyana.

The meaning of this quotation, as given in *Bhāvanākrama* and the *Prajñāpāramitopadeśa*, agrees with the meaning of the four stages of yoga. The *Sangwa Samgyi Mikhyappai Gyü* shows that the four levels of tranquil absorption and the four stages of yoga are identical:

First, the tranquil absorption like that of a lion in repose
Vivifies one's consciousness
And establishes a one-pointed, immobile state.
Then self-cognizing awareness will dawn,
And inner heat and power over rebirth will come about.

Secondly, the illusionlike tranquil absorption
Leads to great nondiscriminatory equipoise.
This will usher in the power of inconceivable absorption
And will steadily bring forth the pinnacle of awakening.

Thirdly, the tranquil absorption of a great hero
Brings about a supernormal cognition of diverse realities
As one flavor.
He will attain the tenth ground of enlightenment,
Will become a son of the buddhas in the three periods of time,
And will seek relentlessly to fulfill the wishes
Of other sentient beings.
With his power of tolerance
He will remove the miseries of those in the lower realms.

Fourthly, the diamondlike tranquil absorption
334 F Ushers in the sublime state of nonmeditation
So that the [awakened] meditator will cognize
The inconceivable pure realm of the all-knowing ones.
He will thus attain the spontaneously fulfilling level
Of the great supreme dharma!

The *Hevajra-tantra* also shows [the four stages of yoga]. The one-pointed stage is shown in this passage:

Settle the mind in equipoise throughout the day and night,
Like the constant flow of a river,
Like the steady tip of a flame.

The nondiscriminatory stage is indicated as follows:

The essence, form, and seer are all unreal.
The sound and the listener are also unreal.

And also as follows:

The beginning, middle, and end are unreal;
So are saṃsāra and nirvāṇa!

The one flavor stage is shown by this:

The state of evenness is achieved
By meditating on one flavor.

The nonmeditation stage is shown by this:

There is neither meditation nor meditator.

Saraha comments on the one-pointed stage:

Remain tranquil, like an infant,
By abandoning subject-object duality.

For the nondiscriminatory stage he says:

34 B Meditate on that which is empty of any real basis.

And for the one flavor stage:

All things have the nature of one even flavor.
That is inconceivable and supreme awareness!

Thus all references to one-pointed absorption found in the sūtras, tantras, and vital instructions should be treated as the one-pointed yoga; references to the state of nonarising [emptiness], detached from all conceptual modes, should be treated as the nondiscriminatory yoga; references to unreality and evenness should be treated as the yoga of one flavor; references to the [transcending] stage, devoid of any dualistic concern for or cogitation of what is to be accepted or abandoned, eliminated or established, should be treated as the nonmeditation yoga.

Je Yanggönpa and others consider the system of the four stages of yoga as originating from the personal realization of Je Takpopa [Gampopa], although the term "four yogas" is found in the tantric treatises and is known to have the same meaning. We remain indebted to Je Gampopa for having

composed a clear elucidation on each of the four yogas of mahāmudrā with a fine differentiation between the high and low levels of experience and understanding, which is designed to help present-day meditators. The
335 F crude terminology "four stages of yoga" apparently already existed in very early times. As stated earlier, it is found in the tantric treatise entitled *Sangwa Samgyi Mikhyappai Gyü* and also in the *Lhenchik Kyejor*, which was transmitted to Gönpawa by Atīśa. A system of the four stages of yoga is found in the songs of the great master Milarepa. The methods of realizing any tranquility and insight through meditation were available in the past and are even more so in the present. I have never seen other orders having such a system as ours for determining the level of inner sensation and understanding arising from the meditation [on tranquility and insight], nor methods of enhancing the progress or of differentiating the high and low stages of realization. This system shows the unexcelled characteristics of the Takpo Kagyüpa order.

335 B The General Meaning of the Four Stages of Yoga: The Essence of These Four Stages of Yoga

First I shall comment on the oral testaments concerning the four stages of yoga by Je Gompa che-chung [the senior and junior Je Gompas] and the ideas of teachers contained in their numerous works, such as the vital instructions on the subject by Je Gampopa to Je Gomtsül, Je Gomchung and Je Phagmo Trupa. I will also deal with the instructions of Je Shang, the disciple of Je Gomtsül, Je Gyare, and other disciples of the great saint Ling.

Je Gomchung refers to the method of identifying the essential nature [of the four yoga stages] as follows:

> To rest in quietude is the one-pointed stage;
> To terminate assumptions is the nondiscriminatory stage;
> To transcend the duality of accepting and abandoning is the one flavor stage;
> To perfect experiences is the nonmeditational stage.

Je Gampopa defines them thus:

> A lucid, unceasing, momentary awareness
> Is the one-pointed stage of yoga.

336 F
> Understanding the essential state of that awareness
> As nonarising [emptiness],
> Which transcends conceptual modes or reality and unreality,
> Is the nondiscriminatory yoga.

Understanding diverse appearances as being one
From the standpoint of their intrinsic nature
Is the one-flavor yoga.

An unceasing realization of the union
Of appearance and its intrinsic emptiness
Is the great equipoise of the nonmeditation yoga.

I shall summarize several other descriptions. The one-pointed stage means resting firmly, serenely, and lucidly in clear and empty awareness, without center and circumference, like space. This is the fusion of the dynamic and stable aspects of the mind.[189] Je Phagdru explains:

When one-pointed absorption first dawns in one's stream-
  consciousness,
Its serenity and lucidity is beyond any description.
It is clear and without any substance, like space.

Je Shang elaborates:

When the one-pointed stage dawns,
One realizes the intrinsic nature of one's mind
To be an unceasing stream of clarity and emptiness,
Devoid of any center and circumference,
Like the expanse of space,
Settled in serenity and lucidity.
This is absorptive equipoise
B On the first stage of yoga.

The nondiscriminatory stage consists of a determinate awareness that all subject-object dualities are but nonarising [emptiness]. The meditator will have achieved this state after having delivered himself from the mind's inbred attachment to the perceptive marks and to the distorting concept of absolute arising, dwelling, or dissolving. Je Phagdru comments:

Then the nondiscriminatory stage will dawn!
This the holy ones describe as the seeing of the mind's essence.
Such an intrinsic state is but nondiscriminatory simplicity,
The expanse of all realities.
No matter how one distinguishes buddhas and sentient beings
From the standpoint of knowledge and ignorance,
In reality they all have one ultimate nature,
Which is nondiscriminatory simplicity.
It is detached from the modes of eternalism and nihilism
As well as from the view of absolute arising, dissolving, etc.
It transcends not only the worldly concern for acceptance and
  abandonment,

But also all conceptual determinations.
Such is the middle path!

Je Shang concurs:

When the nondiscriminatory stage of yoga dawns,
The meditator will realize the essential nature of mind.
This is an unceasing awareness of pure simplicity.
When such a mind is absorbed in dharmakāya,
Which is free from any view of absolute arising or dissolving,
Acceptance or abandonment,
There arises the meditative equipoise
On the second stage of the nondiscriminatory yoga.

337 F The stage of one flavor consists of the mind settled evenly in its primal purity without affirming or rejecting the concepts of whether all things of saṃsāra and nirvāṇa are empty or not empty and of whether the mind has detached itself from the view of phenomena as absolute arising or dissolving. Je Phagdru explains:

By meditating on the one flavor of all things.
The meditator will cognize the one flavor of all these things.
The diversity of appearances and nonappearances
Mind and emptiness, emptiness and nonemptiness,
Are all of one flavor, nondifferentiable in their intrinsic emptiness.
Understanding and lack of understanding are of one flavor;
Equipoise and postequipoise are nondifferentiable;
Meditation and absence of meditation are unified into one flavor;
Discrimination and lack of discrimination are one flavor
In the expanse of reality.

Je Shang says:

When the one flavor stage dawns,
One will cognize the characteristics of mind;
One will realize that the diverse things of saṃsāra and nirvāṇa
Arise from the mind's nondiscriminatory dharmakāya.
Appearance and absence of appearance,
Stability and absence of stability,
Emptiness and absence of emptiness,
Clarity and absence of clarity
Are all of one flavor in the luminous dharmakāya.

337 B The nonmeditation stage is [an enlightened mind] that has cleared all stains of inner sensation and experience and has achieved a harmonious blend of the understanding of the illuminating process with the abiding nature of the

mind. Such a mind is completely detached from the duality of absorption and postabsorption, mindfulness and distraction. Je Phagdru writes:

> By perfecting this [nonmeditation stage]
> The meditator attains naked, unsupported awareness.
> This nondiscriminatory awareness is the meditation!
> By transcending the duality of meditation and meditator,
> External and internal realities,
> The meditating awareness dissolves itself
> Into its luminous clarity.
> Transcending the intellect,
> It is without the duality of equipoise and postequipoise.
> Such is the quintessence of mind.

Je Shang concludes:

> When the nonmeditation stage of yoga dawns,
> The essence of awareness detaches itself
> From any inbred supports.
> The yogin will find nothing to meditate on,
> Because the unreality of the meditator has been exposed.
> It is proclaimed that the potential of enlightenment
> Is contained in every mind.
> Adorned with the three transcending forms[190]
> And the five aspects of awareness,[191]
> One will discover this by oneself.

Since there is agreement among most of the oral transmissions concerning the identification of the four stages of yoga, I have not elaborated on them here.

The General Meaning of the Distinct Nature of Each [of the Four Yoga Stages]

This topic will be elucidated in eight sections:

338 F
1. The difference of realization between the yoga stages
2. The somber realm of inner sensations
3. How a postabsorption is maintained
4. How stains of the mind are purified
5. How postabsorption is pacified
6. The difference between absorption and postabsorption
7. The time of realization for each of the four yoga stages
8. Some other characteristics of these four

The Difference of Realization between the Yoga Stages

Je Gomchung comments:

> The essence [of mind] is cognized at the one-pointed stage;
> The nature [of mind] is cognized at the nondiscriminatory stage;
> The charcteristics [of mind] are realized at the one flavor stage;
> All-encompassing understanding is achieved at the nonmeditation stage.

The meditator should know the explanation of these three principles—the essence, nature, and characteristics of his mind. According to this order the realization of the mind's essential state at the one-pointed stage is the determinate awareness of the mind's intrinsic clarity and nonidentity. The realization of the nature of mind at the nondiscriminatory stage means that the meditator has attained insight into the nature of mind. As such he cognizes its nature to be an uncomposed state without any self-nature and to be detached from any absolute arising, dwelling, or dissolving. The realization of the mind's characteristics at the one flavor stage means that the
338 B meditator has attained the transcending awareness that all the diverse thoughts and appearances that arise from the mind's latent psychic imprints are of the one even flavor in the mind's nonarising expanse, and that at the same time he cognizes that all these diverse thoughts arise from the interactions between them and the power of the mind's intrinsic emptiness. At the nonmeditation stage the meditator will realize an all-encompassing, great, primordial awareness in which dualities of meditation and meditator, realization and realizer are of one even flavor and inseparable. Je Gampopa gives the following definition:

> The essence, nature, and characteristics of mind are the three aspects to be defined. The essence of mind consists of clarity and nondiscrimination. The nature of mind is [emptiness] detached from any absolute arising, dwelling, or dissolving, while its characteristics manifest themselves on the levels of both saṃsāra and nirvāṇa. The meditator will therefore realize the essence of mind at the one-pointed stage, the nature of mind at the nondiscriminatory stage, and the characteristics of mind at the one flavor stage.

[Contrary to this] Je Phagmo Drupa and Je Shang, along with others, state that the nature of mind will be realized at the one-pointed stage and the
339 F essence of the mind at the nondiscriminatory stage. This [disagreement] makes no difference, since the essence and nature are two aspects of mind. If one wonders whether the realizations of the one-pointed stage and the nondiscriminatory stage are also one and the same, the similarity between these two is limited to the essence of awareness at both stages.

But a great difference exists between the first and second yoga stage with respect to inner sensations—whether they are stained with the mind's clinging to them—and also with respect to the level of realization—whether these are endowed with the awareness of the nonarising [emptiness] of all external and internal realities. The meditator will know about them through an elucidation given later on.

The Somber Realm of Inner Sensations

Je Gomchung comments:

> The one-pointed stage may be overcome with darkness;
> The nondiscriminatory stage may succumb to nihilistic
> assumptions;
> The one flavor stage may drift away on the waves of duality;
> The nonmeditation stage may become obscured,
> Like the sun overshadowed by clouds.

Line one means that while the meditator's mind [at the one-pointed stage] remains merely settled lucidly and serenely in the union of clarity and emptiness up to the moment when he realizes the essential nature of mind, it might nevertheless be overshadowed by inner sensation, like someone who is confined to a dark place. Consequently the meditator might fail to appreciate or feel certain about the awareness of unceasing clarity.

B Line two refers to the meditator's error on the various levels of the nondiscriminatory stage. He might be overcome by his own clinging to the nihility of external and internal phenomena and also by a sense of certainty about it. Consequently he might either fail to master it or might ignore the law of interrelated cause and condition that encompasses all realms of appearance.

Line three refers to the meditator's error at the one-flavor stage. While experiencing the fusion of thought and appearance, he might lose sight of the objects of faith or compassion, thereby becoming confused about the methods for perceiving the goodness of others and feeling compassion for them. As a consequence he might retract to the level of the Hīnayāna. This is considered to be a great pitfall, like someone being tossed around by the waves.

Line four refers to the meditator's problems on some levels of the nondiscriminatory stage. Even though awareness without the duality of meditation and meditator will dawn upon him, he might fail to clear his illusionlike dualistic perception, so that obscurity still remains. This condition is compared to the sun being overshadowed by clouds.

How Postabsorption Is Maintained

Je Gomchung comments:

> Postabsorption at the one-pointed stage is solid;
> Postabsorption at the nondiscriminatory stage is a perceived illusion;
> Postabsorption at the one flavor stage is the awareness of emptiness;
> Postabsorption at the nonmeditation stage is dynamic compassion.

340 F Line one shows that because the meditator has failed to purge his inbred clinging to inner sensations during his meditation on the one-pointed stage, he will fail to eliminate a clinging to the reality of dualism during his postabsorptive perception. As a consequence he will perceive the appearances of reality as being solid.

Line two shows that because the meditator at the nondiscriminatory stage has realized all phenomena as being nonarising [emptiness], he will, during postabsorption, perceive the subject-object duality as a mere form, like an illusion.

Line three shows that because the meditator at some levels of the one flavor stage did not perceive all appearances during postabsorption as the nondual unity of appearance and emptiness, and because he perceived these appearances in an one-sided manner as pure emptiness, his postabsorptive perception also becomes completely partial to emptiness.

Line four shows that because absorption and postabsorption are blended together, no distinct postabsorption as such exists. Yet, nondiscriminatory compassion emerges representing a dynamic attainment. Hence the term "dynamic compassion" for the postabsorptive perception.

The *Prajñāpāramitā-saṃcayagāthā* advises:

> Understand that all these psychophysical aggregates
> Are void and nonarising from the beginning.
> Act with compassion for the plane of sentient beings
> 340 B Who have no experience in any absorptive equipoise!
> Do not deviate from the teachings of Buddha
> During this transitional stage!

And Saraha says:

> This sacred tree of nondual awareness spreads
> Throughout the three planes of the universe.
> It blossoms with the flower of compassion
> And with the fruit of benevolence.
> Such a mind is supremely magnanimous.

Je Gyare explains:

A residual perception of substantive reality
Is of the nature of an ephemeral illusion.
This happens on the middle level of the nonmeditation stage.
However, no such perception will arise
On the highest level of the nonmeditation stage.

Thus Je Gyare has accepted the illusionlike postabsorptive appearance even at the nonmeditation stage. In such a case an illusionlike compassion must arise in any postabsorption.

How Stains of the Mind Are Purified

Je Gomchung comments:

The stain on the one-pointed stage is the mind's clinging to substantive reality.
The stain on the nondiscriminatory stage is the nondetermination of the inner essence.
The stain on the one flavor stage are the inner sensations.
The stain on the nonmeditation stage is knowledge.

The stain of mind on the one-pointed stage is the clinging to substantive duality. It is the mind's attachment to inner sensations and to the awareness of certainty. The stain on any levels of the nondiscriminatory stage is the nondetermination of the inherent unity of appearance and emptiness. This
1 F is because of his [one-sided] conscious certainty of and attachment to pure emptiness, which inevitably puts him at ease with it, while at the same time causing an impediment to perceiving or practicing on the level of relativity. The stain on the one-flavor stage consists of the mind's subtle clinging to emptiness, owing to the imperfect determination of the intrinsic union of appearance and emptiness. Even if such a union were perceived, there would still remain some stain owing to the [residual] inner sensations that appear like illusions. As for the stain on some levels of the nonmeditation stage, there is what is described as the nonrecognition of nonconceptual simplicity during the postabsorptive perception. This is identified with the source consciousness, which is a nondiscerning neutral state. Since, in such a state, intrinsic reality does not emerge spontaneously, it has been designated as the stain of knowledge.

How Postabsorption Is Pacified

Je Gomchung comments:

In the one-pointed stage one will possibly lose the meditation
And will not realize it exactly.

In the nondiscriminatory stage one will possibly lose the meditation,
But one will realize it.

In the stage of one flavor one will not lose the meditation
And one will realize it.

In the nonmeditation stage one will transcend
The loss and realization of meditation.

Thus, at the one-pointed stage, there exists a possibility of losing the meditation every time through a lapse of mindfulness. When the mindfulness is revitalized, the stream of meditation is re-established, but true meditation will not emerge here.

341 B At the nondiscriminatory stage there exists a possibility of losing the meditation through a lapse of mindfulness. But once the mindfulness is revitalized, meditation capable of perceiving the nonarising [emptiness] of all things will emerge.

At the stage of one flavor there is no possibility of interruption in the meditation, since the stream consciousness of realization continues during postabsorption, even in the absence of sustained mindfulness. A possibility exists that the meditator will gain insight into the unity of appearance and emptiness through perfect mindfulness.

At the nonmeditation stage there is no separation between the meditator and meditation from the moment mindfulness dawns as a complete cycle of awareness. Because it encompasses every sensory appearance and every mental cognition, there is no need to realize the meditation anew.

The Difference between Absorption and Postabsorption

Je Gomchung comments:

At the one-pointed stage there arise
Both appropriate equipoise and postequipoise.

At the nondiscriminatory stage there arise.
Differentiable equipoise and postequipoise.

At the stage of one flavor there emerges
The union of equipoise and postequipoise.

At the stage of nonmeditation
There is an all-round absorption.

Since no exact nondiscriminatory awareness emerges in the one-pointed stage, there is no distinctive meditative absorption. Similarly, there is no

F distinctive postabsorption, since illusionlike postabsorption does not arise without the realization of the nonarising [emptiness] of all appearances. However, it is possible for the meditator, on this level of practice, to absorb his mind into the meditation and also to regain it immediately after getting distracted by simply revitalizing the mindfulness.

The distinctive meditative absorption is achieved in the nondiscriminatory stage, because the awareness that dawns consists of a dimension of nonduality. As a nondifferentiating awareness it is detached from the mind's clinging to the dualities of subject-object, external and internal. The distinctive postabsorption is achieved when the meditator cognizes the [inevitable] simple appearance of duality as only ephemeral illusion. And thus meditative absorption and postabsorption are differentiated.

In the absorptive equipoise at the stage of one flavor all dualities such as appearance and emptiness are perceived as being nondual. Even during postabsorption, whenever the meditator through mindfulness of nonduality cognizes appearance and emptiness as nondual and illusionlike, his practice is merely described as a blend of absorption with postabsorption.

In the stage of nonmeditation, even though sensory appearances con-
42 B tinue to emerge, they arise and dissolve in nothing other than the absorptive equipoise. Hence there is considered to be nothing but total absorption.

Je Shang sums it up thus:

> Whenever one is absorbed in primordial awareness,
> Whatever one may be doing—jumping, running, murmuring, or talking—
> One is still in equipoise.
> Whenever one is detached from primordial awareness,
> One slips into postabsorption,
> Even though one may be sitting in meditation.

He continues:

> However high the spiritual attainment,
> As long as one has not mastered meditation,
> There will emerge the dualities
> Of absorption and postabsorption,
> Sustained and unsustained mindfulness,
> A distracted and undistracted mind.
> Once the meditational state dawns
> Without any need to strive for it,
> Then this is described as the stage of nonmeditation.

Whenever an innermost awareness encompasses each of the first three yoga stages, the meditator is in an appropriate equipoise, even though he

may be engaged in jumping, running, or talking. But whenever such an awareness is absent, the meditator's mental stage is reduced to a postabsorptive perception, even though he may be sitting in meditation. As long as the meditator has the need to strive for meditational perfection, there will be such dualities as equipoise and postequipoise, sustained and unsustained
343 F mindfulness, a distracted and undistracted mind. It must be noted that the actual nonmeditation stage consists of the union [of luminous awareness and the supreme illusory form] on the path of noncultivation.[192]

The Time of Realization for Each of the Four Yoga Stages

Je Gomchung comments on the time thus:

> It comes when one is deeply absorbed in the one-pointed stage,
> When one masters both equipoise and postequipoise in the nondiscriminatory stage,
> When one succeeds in blending equipoise and postequipoise in the stage of one flavor,
> And when one realizes the stage of nonmeditation [enlightenment].

The meditator achieves a definite experience in meditative equipoise at the one-pointed stages, when he maintains the inner sensation and the conscious certainty through revitalized mindfulness. He reorients his meditation to the perception during the period of postabsorption through a vigorous mindfulness. The meditator masters both equipoise and postequipoise at the nondiscriminatory stage when he meditates first on the spacelike absorption with sustained mindfulness and then on the illusionlike postabsorption during the period of postabsorption. The meditator achieves the one even state of all things at the stage of one flavor when he meditates on the union of absorption and postabsorption by being perfectly aware of the nonduality of appearance and emptiness. The meditator achieves the indivisible union of equipoise and postequipoise at the stage nonmeditation when he perfects this meditation to its ultimate limit.

343 B Je Gampopa comments on the realization:

> A spontaneous fulfillment is achieved
> When one masters the one-pointed stage;
> A nondual awareness is achieved
> When one masters the nondiscriminatory stage;
> The inconceivable nature of mind is realized
> When one masters the stage of one flavor;
> The ultimate perfection is realized
> When one masters the stage of nonmeditation.

Some Other Characteristics of These Four

Je Gyare comments:

> At the one-pointed stage
> Inner sensations dawn and diminish;
> Karma is accumulated,
> For this is the path of the transient world.
>
> At the nondiscriminatory stage one perceives
> Things directly, the way one always sees one's fatherland,
> By alternately meditating
> On absorption and postabsorption.
>
> At the stage of one flavor
> Appearance emerges as meditation,
> Which lasts
> For an uninterrupted period of time.
>
> The stage of nonmeditation
> Is the seat of dharmakāya.
> This means a pure concept
> For most meditators on this level.

Thus the one-pointed stage is described to be the path of the transient world. The nondiscriminatory stage is [the transcendental path] where the meditator perceives the abiding nature of [mind's] existential foundation. The stage of one flavor is where appearances are cognized as the meditational state. The stage of nonmeditation is the actual dharmakāya. It is considered that for most of the present-day meditators this stage of nonmeditation remains a conceptual designation.

Je Gyare explains further:

> By meditating on the one-pointed yoga for a long time
> The meditator will inevitably eliminate
> His attachment to sensory pleasures
> And will gain certain powers achieved by the ancient ascetics,
> Such as the power of supercognition, transformation, and the like.
>
> By maintaining the awareness of the nondiscriminatory yoga
> The meditator will perceive the great spectacle
> Of uncertain reality and its false appearance.
> He will attain certain vital qualities of a bodhisattva,
> Such as compassion without any self-concern,
> According to the intensity of his training
> And the level of his intelligence.

By maintaining the state of one flavor for a long time
He will perceive the great spectacle of the pure lands of the buddhas.
No matter what he does, whether sitting in a reclining position,
Standing on his head, or walking,
[His absorption] is immobile, like a king who is firmly seated;
[He perceives] the interrelated unity
Of the apparent and ultimate realities,
Like the sight of a magnificent silk cloth in the sunlight.
He attains certain qualities of enlightenment
And will then fulfill the hopes of innumerable sentient beings.

When the meditator reaches the highest level of nonmeditation,
He will achieve the transcendental qualities
And will then carry out his spiritual functions
To their ultimate limit.

These verses describe how the inner signs emerge within and the great qualities dawn in the meditator at each of the four yoga stages of mahāmudrā.

Je Yanggönpa gives a further description:

At the one-pointed stage one will detach oneself
From the impact of one's psychophysical aggregates
And will purify the five sense consciousnesses.

At the nondiscriminatory stage one will detach oneself
344 B From the aggregates of feelings and cognitions
And will also purify one's mental consciousness.

At the stage of one flavor one will detach oneself
From the diverse mental events
And will purify the deluded source mind.

At the stage of nonmeditation one will detach oneself
From the mental consciousness
And will purify the source consciousness.

The preceding passage shows how the eightfold consciousness[193] may be purged through meditation on the four yoga stages.

Je Yanggönpa comments on the distinctive inner sensation and understanding that will arise from the four pure states:

On the stage of one-pointed yoga
Inner sensation and understanding are stained.

On the stage of nondiscriminatory yoga
Inner sensation and understanding are differentiated.

On the stage of one flavor
They are perceived as a union.

On the stage of nonmeditation the awakened mind
Will remain an all-round realization
Throughout the cycle of time.

Yanggönpa shows the cause and effect factors of the four yoga stages:

Realism as the effect of inner delusion
Manifests itself in the one-pointed yoga.

Perceiving everything to be like an illusion
Is the effect of meditation on the nondiscriminatory yoga.

Perceiving everything to be like space
Is the effect of meditation on the yoga of one flavor.

Supreme knowledge, attained through the yoga of nonmeditation,
Is the insight that perceives reality to be pure relativity
Without any innate foundation.

Concerning this description, some people asserted that once a meditator had
45 F discovered the inner identity of his own mind, he could sow no more karmic seeds, just as one cannot sow any seeds in space. This statement is absolutely inaccurate. The term "discovering the mind's identity" is used in connection with meditation on the one-pointed yoga. The meditator [on that stage] continues to create karma through his perceiving solid reality, due mainly to uncleared mental clinging. Even though it is said that such self-discovery may be achieved on the stage of nondiscriminatory yoga, the meditator can still create distinct karma during an unstable meditation, which intermittently fades and reemerges. Even a meditator who has realized the yoga of one flavor is said to momentarily perceive a solid reality and thus to create new karma. For as long as the mind clings to anything, man still creates karma. The *Ratnāvalī* elucidates this:

As long as clinging to a psychophysical aggregate remains,
Clinging to the self will persist.
From this clinging will arise karma;
From karma will emerge rebirth.

Je Gampopa urges:

Until the peg of clinging to an object is removed
Dualistic thought will continue creating new karma.
345 B Watch yourself with undistracted mindfulness!

Such is the way karma is created in relation to either a vigorous or sub clinging of the mind. Until one has realized all appearances as illusions, one will create karma through clinging or attachment to the solid appearance of reality. From the moment one has realized the illusory nature of appearances up to the time one achieves its perfection there will be possibilities [for the meditator] to create karma, either through imperfectly cognizing reality or through imperfectly perceiving appearances. Je Gampopa comments on the relevance of karma to the stages of realization:

> Regarding the dividing line between the operative and inoperative law of causality, the karma originating from attachment will remain operative until the time that one achieves direct insight into true reality and the perfect, illusionlike perception of all appearances. Karma originating from the way [such an advanced meditator] perceives mere appearances will continue to operate until he perfects his attained insight into intrinsic reality and the illusory nature of all appearances. In summary, karma will remain operative up to the moment when the meditator realizes dharmakāya. Once this has been achieved, the law of causality ceases to exist, even as a concept.

Some people say that the exalted arhats cannot create any new karma, since they have realized the emptiness [of reality], as indicated by the saying, "The exalted arhats have completely eliminated disease, decay, misery and death." This shows their confusion in differentiating between the levels of miseries—those that have been eliminated and those that are still being eliminated. A meditator who has established a stable insight into emptiness and has destroyed the vigorous clinging to substantive reality will no longer
346 F create any strong karma. He will, nevertheless, continue to create an illusion-like, subtle karma until he has eliminated all his latent psychic imprints. The *Bodhicaryāvatāra* clarifies this point:

> By assimilating the emptiness of reality,
> One eliminates one's psychic imprints of substantiality.
> This view of emptiness that one has assimilated
> Will also be nullified.

The same text says further:

> A magician creates the illusion of a woman
> And then feels desire for her.
> Because the magician himself has not abandoned
> His inbred clinging to sensory objects,
> His inclination toward emptiness is feeble,
> Even though he sees her as unreal.

With this I complete the general elucidation of the four yoga stages and on the way to realize them.

THE DETAILED ELUCIDATION OF EACH OF THE FOUR YOGA STAGES

3 This will be done in two sections:

1. Differentiating each of the four yoga stages
2. Differentiating the levels of each stage separately

Differentiating Each of the Four Yoga Stages

The collected works of Je Takpopa [Gampopa] contain no reference to the twelve levels of the four yoga stages, but the oral transmission of his discourses seems to have included them. The oral instructions given to Je Gomtsül refer to three subdivisions of each of the four yoga stages, viz., the excellent, intermeditate, and inferior level.

Je Phagmo Trupa subdivided each of the four yoga stages into three levels—the great, average, and lower level. These came down through an unbroken lineage of teachers to Je Gyare and his disciples. Je Rangjung Dorje [the third Karmapa, 1284–1339] and his disciples, particularly Je Khachöpa, subdivided the four yoga stages into twelve and then into twenty-four levels. These are now very well known to this precious meditational order and are found to be a wonderful and pertinent means for differentiating the various levels of inner sensations and realizations. Out of all these only Je Phagmo Trupa's methods for subdividing the four yoga stages into twelve levels became widely known. These will be elucidated here:

<u>The one-pointed yoga</u>

7 F 1. On the lower level of the one-pointed yoga the meditator will perceive the true nature of bliss and clarity.
2. On its average level he will achieve inner control over absorptive equipoise.
3. On its great level he will be able to experience the inner sensations uninterruptedly for a period of time.

<u>The nondiscriminatory yoga</u>

1. On the lower level of the nondiscriminatory yoga the meditator will realize his own mind as nonarising [emptiness].
2. On its average level he will realize [his mind] as empty of any ground.
3. On its great level he will eliminate doubts and assumptions about the duality of external and internal phenomena.

The yoga of one flavor

1. On the lower level of the yoga of one flavor the meditator will achieve the blend of saṃsāra and nirvāṇa.
2. On its average level he will destroy the root of duality.
3. On its great level he will blend [the perceptions] of all phenomena into the state of evenness.

The yoga of nonmeditation

1. On the lower level of the yoga of nonmeditation the meditator will attain a nondual awareness, detached from any dual images of meditation and meditator.
2. On its average level he will realize the inherent ground of spontaneous perfection.
3. On its great level he will unify his meditative luminous clarity with the ultimate luminous awareness.

The meaning of these can be understood from the elucidation to be given later. There is no certainty that experiences arising from the twelve levels of the four yogas will follow the regular order, like the steps of stairs. For example, before completing the experience of inner sensation and realiza-
347 B tion on the great level of the one-pointed yoga, experiences of the first two levels of the next yoga of nondiscrimination may emerge. Similarly, before completing the inner sensation and realization on the level of the nondiscriminatory yoga, experiences of the first two levels of the one flavor yoga may emerge. And also, before completing the experience of the great level on the yoga of one flavor, the inner sensation of the lower and average levels on the yoga of nonmeditation may emerge. Thus it is obvious that experiences may not follow the order of the levels of yoga, as described before.

Most of the descriptions of the inner sensations and realizations are based on the experiences of the ancient meditators of the Meditational Order, who raised the banner of meditation by completely devoting themselves to meditation in mountain solitude. Besides, the teachings that they imparted mainly for seekers of the gradual path might not be suitable for seekers of instantaneous realization and of evanescent realization. Moreover, since many present-day meditators succumb easily to idleness and distraction, there is no certainty that they may gain these experiences in the same order as stated. However, even at the present time meditators endowed with inborn wisdom and those who are awakened by the power of their guru's blessings will gain insight into the nature of their realization.

348 F Since the determination of the level of the virtuous practice seems very important, I shall elucidate it here by referring to the sayings of the ancient teachers of the Meditational Order.

Differentiating the Levels of Each Stage Separately: The One-Pointed Yoga

This will be explained in three sections:

1. The differentiation of the one-pointed yoga
2. How inner sensation and experience will dawn
3. How this yoga is maintained

The Differentiation of the One-Pointed Yoga

The one-pointed yoga is so designated because the meaning of the term consists of either one-pointed mindfulness, which is focused undistractedly on the meaning of the mind's abiding reality, or the spontaneous blend of fleeting thoughts with the settled nature of mind. One may wonder if this [definition] contradicts the statement that the exact meaning of the mind's abiding reality will be realized at the stage of nondiscrimination, but there is no contradiction. [If discerned well,] a marked difference on this point exists between the two stages. One realizes the simple abiding nature of mind on the one-pointed yoga stages, whereas the realization on the nondiscrimina-
8 B tory yoga encompasses the exact abiding nature of all realities, external and internal, while at the same time eliminating the mind's inbred clinging to inner sensations, experiences, and awareness of certainty.

Some people epitomize the meditation on tranquility as one-pointed mind. They mistakenly identify the tranquil mind with that one-pointed mind on the grounds that the former is a nonconceptual single-minded state, sustained by the clarity of vigilance. Others mistakenly identify the tranquil mind, unified with an understanding of emptiness, with the one-pointed yoga. The first assumption is quite wrong. Even though [the tranquil mind] appears to be flawless, it is completely devoid of the conscious certainty of insight. The second assumption is not correct either. It is only a simple consciousness, which is inclined toward emptiness, but it is devoid of the conscious certainty of emptiness with respect to the mind.

The one-pointed yoga must therefore be one in which the focus of awareness is entirely on the significance of the mind's essential nature. It must also be fully aware of one's inner identity while achieving a harmonious blend of the dynamic thought currents with the mind. This is in keeping
349 F with the saying that one will realize the essential nature of mind at the one-pointed yoga stage. Je Yanggönpa spoke about the way of maintaining the one-pointed stage:

> The importance of the practice lies
> In understanding one's inner identity

Through fleeting thoughts.
This serves as the entrance
To the mind's abiding reality.
By looking at one's inner face
One may harmonize it with oneself.
See if mindfulness and thought
Exist apart from oneself;
This will unify the fleeting thoughts
With the settled mind.

Of the three levels of the one-pointed yoga the lower level consists of a progressive experience ranging from the moment when the meditator attains absorption, accompanied by the inner sensations of clarity, emptiness, and bliss, to the moment when he is able to revive and sustain the absorption at will. He may find it somewhat hard to do so in the beginning. The average level is attained when the absorption sometimes emerges automatically, even without the meditator making any efforts, or comes about steadily, as the meditator gains control over the meditation. The great level of the one-pointed yoga is attained when the meditator experiences an uninterrupted inner sensation of absorption and is able to maintain the union of clarity and emptiness [of awareness] throughout the cycle of day and night, throughout all his absorption and postabsorption, and throughout the four regular conducts of his life.

349 B Differentiating the four yoga stages with respect to whether the realization of each stage is perfect or imperfect, Je Gyare mentions six pairs of criteria:

1. Realization with or without insight into the mind's intrinsic nature
2. Whether the attained mind power is complete or incomplete
3. Whether dualistic thoughts have dawned as meditation
4. Whether spiritual qualities have blossomed
5. Whether insight into apparent reality has been attained
6. Whether the seeds of the supreme manifestation [of the buddhas] have been sown [in the stream consciousness]

This system of determination is excellent and appropriate for this course. I shall therefore elucidate it here.

(1) The meditator has realized the one-pointed yoga when he has with conscious certainty gained insight into his own inmost awareness, which is an inseparable blend of its intrinsic clarity and emptiness. Like the expanse of space, this simplicity of mind is detached from any substantive entity while manifesting itself clearly and uninterruptedly. On the other hand, the meditator has not gained insight into the mind's essential nature through the one-pointed yoga if he has not achieved such an awareness of certainty, even

though his mind is settled quietly and serenely in the state of bliss, clarity, and nondiscrimination. Such an experience of indeterminate appearance is like an infant's perception of the moon's reflection in the water.

F (2) The mind's power over the one-pointed yoga has been achieved when the absorptive state of bliss, clarity, and nondiscrimination with awareness of certainty lasts throughout the entire cycle of day and night. Such power has not been achieved if the one-pointed yoga is interrupted by a shifting focus of the mind.

(3) The moment one's mindfulness focuses itself on an emerging thought or appearance, it turns itself into a meditative state, rendering its abandonment unnecessary. Besides, if the meditator can bring his sleep into luminous awareness, he has achieved the mind power to perceive every thought as a meditative state. Such turning of every appearance into the meditational state has not been realized if the meditator has to strive to do so through the force of mindfulness.

(4) The meditator has realized sublime qualities through the meditation on the one-pointed yoga when he feels revulsion toward his eight worldly reactions, when no external and internal "microorganisms" emerge inside or on his body, when he can produce diverse miraculous transformations such as the contemplative power of transformation and the overpowering manifestations (zepar and zilnön, see notes 86 and 87), when he has gained a supernormal cognition, etc. The meditator has not realized the essential qualities if his mind has not become tractable and tranquil and if he has not experienced any common signs such as the spontaneous inner heat.

(5) The meditator has achieved insight into apparent reality when, following his lucid absorption, he has perfectly understood the natural law based on interacting causes and effects, external and internal, which does not fail to produce results commensurate with major and minor karmas, and when he regulates his life, attitude, and behavior according to moral principles. On the other hand, the meditator has not achieved conscious certainty with respect to the natural law if he has neglected a scrupulous adherence to the principle of karma.

(6) The meditator has sown the seeds of the supreme manifestation in himself when he has engendered compassion, during postabsorption, for all sentient beings and has solemnly expressed his wish for the good of others.
350 B On the other hand, the meditator has not sown the seeds of the supreme manifestation in himself if he has not engendered compassion, due to the veiling of his mind by the inner sensations that have arisen from absorptive equipoise, and if instead he has sought the tranquility and bliss [of nirvāṇa] for himself.

How Inner Sensation and Experience Will Dawn

At the lower level of the one-pointed yoga the meditator will through his mental attachment maintain a determinate absorptive state of bliss, clarity, and emptiness. When experiencing such an inner sensation, almost every thought or appearance dissolves by itself, being unable to stabilize itself. The meditator might construe this to be a meditational state and thereby produce a definite clinging. He might sometimes fail to let an emerging thought flow freely. Most sensory appearances during postabsorption emerge as solid reality, while at the same time bringing forth a sensation of joy. During the period of postabsorption, every time the mind focuses itself on an inner sensation of clarity and emptiness, the meditator cannot but be
351 F conscious of it as either empty or a manifestation of mind. The meditator's dreams might not be very different from earlier ones, except for their greater clarity. Some meditators may dream of many things with little consciousness of certainty.

Sometimes the meditator may experience a lot of fluctuation in his meditation. Sometimes he may find it hard to achieve absorptive equipoise, causing him concern that he might never realize the meditation. At other times he may achieve a good meditation, thus making him feel good. In such an event the meditator should increase his faith in his guru, should adopt a positive or noble attitude toward his spiritual companions, and also should engender compassion for all other sentient beings.

At the average level of the one-pointed yoga the meditator will achieve a firm absorption of clarity, emptiness, and bliss. Sometimes he will achieve an absorption without making an effort and will experience fewer thoughts or appearances. Besides, whatever he perceives, it will flow smoothly, as if releasing by itself.

During the postabsorptive perception the meditator will in an open and expansive mood experience the sublime sensation of clarity and emptiness, which may get distorted by an appearance of solid reality. During a period of postabsorption his consciousness will turn into a meditative state the moment he applies mindfulness. He will or will not dream of experiencing any inner sensations. Some meditators will have fewer dreams but will expe-
351 B rience joy at the very thought of meditation. At the great level of the one-pointed stage there will emerge an uninterrupted absorption of clarity, bliss and emptiness. Any thought flows during absorption and postabsorption and even dreams will dissolve in an orderly fashion into the absorptive state. He will, with a stain of attachment, remain aware of the sublime sensations, which in their wake imbue in him a vigorous sense of emptiness. Thus, while experiencing the bliss, awareness, and clarity of thought and appearance, he perceives the emptiness in each as its intrinsic nature. Throughout all these experiences he will vividly perceive every appearance, like a dream or an

illusion, and will achieve certain psychic powers, such as a subtle supernormal cognition, etc. He will come to regard such a meditation as unsurpassed and his meditative faith and noble attitude will be enhanced.

How This Yoga Is Maintained

At the third level [great level] of the one-pointed yoga, the meditator should remain silent in a mountain solitude, with the entrance [of his cell or cave] blocked and cemented. He should take the maximum precaution against any [physical and spiritual] befoulments. A great befoulment is likely to render his mind intractable and to diminish his wisdom. Even a little befoulment is likely to vitiate his absorption and to create many impediments in his
F meditation. When he notices a sign of any befoulment, he should avoid the contamination resolutely and should, at the same time, apply the established remedies for clearing them.

In most cases where the meditation is interrupted by either dullness or though flow, the meditator should employ the specific methods for clearing them and should watch the essential nature of mind as often as possible. If his mind is vitiated by a torpid condition, his meditation will be greatly impaired. He should apply various spiritual remedies such as performing self-purifications, receiving empowerments from his gurus, practicing meditational empowerments many times, officiating at a ritual feast, making devotional offerings [to the supreme refuge], and even distributing gifts [to the needy]. Besides that, he should seek the understanding and blessing of his guru and spiritual friends in order to clear the befoulment.

If the meditator has maintained a negative attitude toward his guru or a spiritual friend, this transgression of religious affinity has caused him to experience an inner befoulment. He should clear this by seeking the blessing of his guru or friend. On the other hand, if the meditator has been harboring a more serious ill feeling toward either of them, or if he has even reneged on his faith in them and does not want to seek their understanding and blessings, this could well be an impediment caused by obstructive forces. The meditator must then apply the remedy himself by seeking refuge with an enhanced faith [in the guru as the living embodiment of the three jewels]. He must further meditate on the miseries of sentient beings, feel revulsion at and sorrow for their plight, and vigorously engender a noble attitude toward and compassion for them. Having done this well, he should relax for a few days and should do suitable physical exercises.

The meditator should now practice absorption through coherent and
352 B sustained mindfulness, the way a kingfisher gazes at a fish in the water. In maintaining the absorption he should not pursue analytical comprehension, the domain of nonconception, the dawning of experience, and the perceptive

appearance of postabsorption. He should neither allow the mind to crave a good experience nor should he detest a bad one. Even when a thought arises, he should simply perceive it without agitating either to accept or reject it. Since a dense inner sensation is likely to cloud [the awareness of] the mind's essential nature, the meditator should repeatedly try to detach himself from the "moisture" of such inner sensation. He should strengthen the vitality of his awareness and should keep up this primordial state. Since the biographies and the illuminating songs of the ancient masters of this Meditational Order describe the manner in which they mastered meditational practice, reading them occasionally may strengthen his determination to follow their examples in pursuing the path of liberation.

353 F Should the meditator, even after years of meditation on the one-pointed yoga, fail to attain an awareness developed to the level of nondiscrimination, it is essential for him to practice the "three abandonments." The first is abandoning his attachment to the self. The meditator should cut the cord of lust for and attachment to this life, to its materialistic aims, to his body and mind, and should disassociate himself from the company of fellow beings. He should stop discriminating between friend and foe based on his love and hatred. The meditator should [through his contemplative practice] make an inner offering of his body to the guru and should repeat "the mendicant's sacrificial performance." During such meditation he offers his [transmuted] body as a [higher] offering [to the three jewels and also to sentient beings].

The second abandonment consists of abandoning attachment to one's possessions. The meditator should distribute all his possessions by making gifts to his gurus and spiritual companions and by making sacrificial torma offerings[194] to and ritual feasts for [the meditational deities and the initiated brethren of the Vajrayāna order]. He should abandon not only his craving for pleasure, food, ostentatious dress, and recognition, but should abandon his father's home or other habitats that are likely to distract him. He should live in solitude in the manner of a deer, as stated before. In case he does not abandon all these, he should at least meditate in silent solitude for a number of years.

The third abandonment consists of abandoning attachment to absorption. The meditator first dissolves all sublime sensations such as joy and delight as well as the feeling of faith. He then reinvigorates his inmost certainty that there is no such thing as absolute good and absolute evil in the intrinsic nature of any emerging thought and appearance. Without any attempt at meditation he simply maintains undistractedly his pure and naked awareness, which is detached from any sublime sensations. Je Gam-
353 B popa offers these instructions:

> When at first learning how to meditate, learn to achieve a lucidity of mind. Next learn how to remain undistracted. Then how to maintain

ever-present awareness. When one establishes a true affinity with one's awareness, one will attain a conscious certainty of the ultimate reality.

Je Gyare advises:

Upon achieving the state of the one-pointed yoga
One should dissolve all inner sensations
And remain in that pure state
Without any attempt at meditation.

At the stage of the one-pointed yoga there is the possibility and great risk that a meditator may confuse any inner sensations with realization and drifting toward a deviation. Less intelligent meditators, who have not devoted enough time to training under their gurus despite the fact that they have meditated for many years, are liable to cling to the luster of inner sensations. This clinging is bound to prevent them from gaining insight into the true nature of mind. Even though they have glimpsed it, they are bound to lose it. In this respect Je Gampopa points out certain vital fallacies:

Any intellectual vision without realization
Is only an idea, though it is designated
To be free from any extreme views.
Great meditators who have not severed
The anchor of their attachment
Create causes for their cycle of existence,
No matter how good their absorption.

And Je Drikhungpa warns:

The unaltered inner sensations
Will cause one to be reborn in the higher celestial realms.

354 F It is essential for meditators to not even cling to or crave for the intrinsic nakedness of mind. Saraha urges:

Abandon your attachment to any object!

And Je Gampopa says:

A great meditator, who clings to duality,
Might achieve some experience,
But it is not real attainment.

By keeping up the meditation [on the one-pointed yoga] the meditator will achieve steady progress. He will, in due course, experience the purification of inner sensations and of attachment to them, which is typical of this first yoga. He will free himself from his clinging to subject/object duality and will realize a meditation detached from any modes of conceptual determination.

Differentiating the Levels of Each Stage Separately: The Nondiscriminatory Yoga

This will be explained in three sections:

1. The differentiation of the nondiscriminatory yoga
2. How inner sensation and experience will dawn
3. How this yoga is maintained

The Differentiation of the Nondiscriminatory Yoga

The term "nondiscrimination" refers to the abiding nature of mind, which, like space, is detached from any absolute arising, dwelling, or dissolving, from any conceptual determination such as eternalism and nihilism, or from inward and outward movements. The *Mūlamadhyamaka-kārikā* states:

> It is neither dissolving nor arising,
> Neither nihilism nor eternity,
> Neither going nor coming,
> Neither separate nor the same,
> Completely detached from all conceptual determination,
> It is the perfect quiescence.

354 B Some people assert that the yoga of nondiscrimination means the absence of subject/object duality. Others hold that its meaning consists of a definite awareness that directly cognizes the emptiness of all things. Both are incorrect. If the former were correct, even simple nonconceptual tranquility would become nondiscriminatory yoga. According to the latter even the attachment with which the mind clings to the conscious certainty of emptiness and unreality would be nondiscriminatory yoga. It has been stated that the abiding nature of mind is realized at the stage of nondiscriminatory yoga and that such a nature is unconditioned simplicity, like space. It is neither transferable nor changeable.

A popular sūtra saying describes it thus:

> It is deep and tranquil, nondiscriminatory,
> Lucid and uncomposed.

The *Uttara-tantra* declares:

> The intrinsic nature of mind is luminously clear;
> It is unchangeable, like space.

The stage of nondiscriminatory yoga is differentiated into three levels. The lower level consists of the understanding of mind's intrinsic emptiness, which is devoid of any unconditioned arising or dissolving. Yet this understanding is not detached from the stains of inner sensations and the conscious certainty of that emptiness. Consequently, the mind is agitated either by fear of its possible wandering about aimlessly in saṃsāra or by a desire to achieve liberation in nirvāṇa.

The average level of nondiscriminatory yoga consists of the realization that the nature of mind is devoid of any basis or root and that its attachment that clings to the cognitions of appearance and emptiness has been eliminated. Even so, the meditator has not completely rid himself of doubts and delusions about the appearances of external phenomena.

The great level of nondiscriminatory yoga consists of the meditator's inner release from his inbred clinging to the conscious certainty of the emptiness of both external and internal phenomena, which are encompassed by the terms appearance and existence, saṃsāra and nirvāṇa. This realization also includes the elimination of his doubts and delusions, hopes and fears.

The methods of differentiating between achievement and failure in mastering the great level of nondiscriminatory yoga are as follows. The meditator has realized nondiscriminatory simplicity as the essential nature of mind if he is able to maintain that state free from any discrimination. This is the result of his having delivered himself from the mind's clinging to the awareness of certainty and also of having dissolved the root of the experiencer in himself. On the other hand, the meditator has not yet gained insight into the nondiscriminatory yoga if he still has a slight clinging to the consciousness of emptiness or a slight determinate certainty, because all such mental clinging constitutes the inner sensations on the stage of nondiscriminatory yoga.

55 B The meditator has attained the mind power of this yoga stage once he has realized perfect insight into the nondiscriminatory simplicity of all things. Such insight must be unstained by the slightest attachment to emptiness or by hope and fear. The meditator has failed to gain the mind power of this stage if he has not cleared the sensation of his clinging to emptiness and if hope and fear, in partaking of sensory appearances, still linger on, even though he understands the innate intrinsic nature of cognitions and senses to be devoid of unconditioned arising.

The meditator has realized discriminatory thoughts as meditation when he establishes that all flowing thoughts are but empty [of any reality] and that all sensory appearances are also in the nature of emptiness, and as a result, perceives all his thoughts and appearances during the postabsorption to be like an absorptive state. He has failed to realize all emerging thoughts as the meditational state if he is unable to elevate his consciousness and sensory appearances to the state of absorption.

The blossoming of spiritual qualities on the nondiscriminatory stage has taken place only if the meditator, having encountered favorable circumstances such as obtaining the skillful methods for bringing forth the blossoms of great qualities, is able to unify the spontaneous signs of his supernormal powers [the by-product of self-realization] and his awakened state. On the other hand, the blossoming of great quailites has not come about in the meditator if he has not perceived the illuminating signs of the supernormal powers, due to his having failed to obtain the favorable circumstances and the skillful methods, regardless of the fact that he has gained insight into ultimate reality.

The meditator has attained perfect insight into apparent reality if, having cognized emptiness to be identical with the law of cause and effect, he has gained the understanding that even though the essential nature of mind is completely devoid of any substantive entity, the interaction between cause and condition is so powerful that it enables the meditator to sublimate his mind in diverse ways. On the other hand, the meditator has not gained insight into apparent reality if he lacks the understanding of interdependent
356 F relativity due to his ignorance.

The meditator has sown the seed of the manifestation of enlightenment in himself when he knows how to establish an illusionlike cause during his postabsorption by engendering enlightened thought and solemnly expressing the resolve to fulfill the wishes of other sentient beings. On the other hand, he has failed to sow this seed of the manifestation of enlightenment if he has not brought about the interaction of magnanimous causes and conditions and if he has found it difficult to produce compassion, even though he has realized emptiness.

How Inner Sensation and Experience Will Dawn

The meditator on the lower level of this yoga stage achieves an awareness of the nondiscriminatory simplicity of phenomena, which is detached from unconditioned dwelling or dissolving. Even so, he still retains a mental clinging to emptiness. During the period of postabsorption he will experience a vivid clinging to love for friends and hatred for enemies. Delusion will continue to prevail through most of his sleep and dreams. His virtuous practice will fluctuate. He will develop faith in his gurus, in his spiritual companions, and in his consciousness of certainty with regard to his practice, but sometimes this might be upset by emerging doubts about any one of them.

356 B On the average level of the nondiscriminatory yoga, the meditator clears his grasp of emptiness. This in turn makes him far less attached to anything. At the same time he cuts the root of deluded thoughts and puts doubts about flowing thoughts to an end. In spite of all this he will still be overcome by

fragments of hope and fear with respect to sensory appearances. His postabsorptive consciousness and dreams will alternately remain clear of delusion and be affected by it. The rise and decline of his faith in and doubts about his gurus and spiritual companions as well as his virtuous absorption will take place alternately. Occasionally there will arise in him the feeling that there is no possibility of enlightenment or of rebirth in the realm of great affliction.

On the great level of the nondiscriminatory yoga, the meditator eliminates all his doubt and delusion about external and internal phenomena as a result of having realized the very root of all dualities encompassed by saṃsāra and nirvāṇa. At the same time his mind becomes open, expansive, and unclouded by the feeling of certainty or skepticism about all things being either empty or not empty. He attains the true vision of the emptiness and selflessness of all appearances. However, during the postabsorption he may not as yet achieve the perfection of all discriminations. But his meditational state will persist a whole day without any interrupton. It will contain a sublime sensation of the intrinsic union of awareness and empti-
F ness as well as of appearance and its emptiness. Even so, he may not yet command uninterrupted mindfulness. Hence the need to master sustained mindfulness. His dreams will be partially affected by delusion and mental clinging to appearances. Sometimes there might arise such negative thoughts that there is neither a possibility of enlightenment nor of understanding abiding reality nor of rebirth in the sphere of great affliction. The meditator will now understand the deep meaning of the dharma. He will realize that his innate mind is the guru. Appearances will become an aid to his virtuous practice. He will be free from attachment to anything and will feel revulsion for his eight worldly reactions. However, there is always the danger of his getting so conceited, arrogant, and disdainful that he might consider himself to be no longer in need of his guru.

How This Yoga Is Maintained

During the practice of the three levels of the nondiscriminatory yoga the meditator should abandon the three attachments and should live silently in complete solitude [in a cell or a cave][195] whose entrance is blocked and cemented with a wall. Many formal practices of virtuous absorption are said to be disagreeable. He should abandon them except for a short invocation of his guru and the making of offerings of consecrated cakes [to the supreme refuge]. It is essential for him to concentrate on sustained mindfulness and
57 B to thereby maintain the mind's nondiscriminatory state without ever getting distracted or clinging to it. The meditator should occasionally devote himself to conditioned virtue such as giving alms [to the needy], making offerings to and engendering faith in the supreme refuge, perceiving the purity of

others, contemplating the law of interdependent relativity, and meditating on compassion. Besides, he should discuss the deep meaning of the dharma with his gurus and experienced dharma friends. He may read the songs of spiritual experience by the awakened saints and may even sing them himself.

In the event that his inner sensation of bliss diminishes or he has an urge to wander or to eat, he should practice the esoteric methods for harnessing the creative fluid and for reactivating the air-energy through the psychic channels of the central nervous system. He should also practice the inner fire [tummo] and some physical yoga exercises.

If the meditator had a glimpse of realization on the great level of the nondiscriminatoy yoga but has not made much progress even after a year-long practice, he would do well to apply the following methods. He should abandon the three attachments, should receive empowerments, should recognize and repent his transgressions of the precepts, and should invoke the refuge for increasing his understanding. He should meditate on the visualization of his own body as the form of his yidam [meditation deity]. Contemplating the miseries of the realm of affliction, he should resolve that all these miseries originate from the mind and should then settle his determinate awareness in the nondiscriminatory yoga.

358 F Similarly, he should repeat this meditation of quietening the mind in the nondiscriminatory yoga immediately after each of the following practices: contemplating respectively the happiness of the celestial beings, the conditions of the existential cycle, and the state of nirvāṇa. He should settle the mind in the nondiscriminatory state after climbing the summit of a mountain and sometimes amidst a crowd of people. He should repeat the same meditation by inhaling and retaining the breath and then gazing with his eyes widely open. These are the methods to enhance the meditation. Je Gampopa comments:

> It is vitally important for the meditator at the great level of the nondiscriminatory stage to revitalize his awareness and not to let it slip into indifference.

Je Gyare states:

> When one has reached the level of the nondiscriminatory yoga,
> One meditates by blending all forms of dualities.

Thus the meditator should meditate on the nondiscriminatory yoga by reinforcing his awareness and by blending the diverse forms of dualities. Je Yanggönpa instructs:

> Do not let your undistracted mindfulness lose its focus;
> Do not modify or meditate on the abiding nature of phenomena;
> Do not desire to define that which transcends the mind;

Do not distort it by investigation.
Maintain this state openly!
You will unify the meditation on and attainment of
The nondiscriminatory yoga,
Like the reunion of a mother and her only duaghter.

This instruction urges meditators not to be distracted from the nondiscriminatory yoga but to maintain it by revitalizing mindfulness. It implores the meditators not to distort this absorption by meditating anew, since the abiding nature of that state cannot be modified. It also urges meditators to maintain awareness naturally, without examining it, since it is undefinable, inconceivable, and inexpressible.

By thus mastering this nondiscriminatory yoga, meditators will realize all sensory appearances in their entirety as being one flavor of mahāmudrā. This very process of realization is completely detached from any concern for affirmation or rejection and also from any contemplation of whether all things of saṃsāra and nirvāṇa are nondiscriminatory or discriminatory, empty or not empty, acceptable or unacceptable.

Differentiating the Levels of Each Stage Separately: The Yoga of One Flavor

This consists of three sections:

1. The differentiation of the one flavor yoga
2. How inner sensation and experience will dawn
3. How this yoga is maintained

The Differentiation of the One Flavor Yoga

9 F The term "one flavor" generally means that all things epitomized by the appearance and existence of saṃsāra and nirvāṇa bear one flavor, emptiness, which is their ultimate nature. Saraha points out:

The holy guru bring forth the realization
That all the diverse things
Are one and the same in emptiness.

Śavari elucidates:

Various rivers, such as the Ganges and the others,
Merge into one ocean of salty water.
Similarly the mind and mental events
Are of one flavor in the expanse of reality.

Thus the term "one flavor" encompasses the blending of many opposite realities, such as appearance and nonappearance, into one single flavor. Je Phagdru explains:

> All these diverse things—
> Appearances and nonappearances,
> Thoughts and emptiness,
> Emptiness and nonemptiness—
> Are of one flavor in emptiness.
> Understanding and the absence of understanding are of one flavor;
> The distinction between absorption and postabsorption
> Is dissolved into one flavor;
> Meditation and nonmeditation are pacified into one flavor;
> Discrimination and nondiscrimination are of one flavor
> In the expanse of reality.

359 B Je Shang also says this in a similar manner.

Some people stated that, like the general concept of one flavor, the essence of all things consisting of the one flavor of emptiness is identical with the pure state of one flavor at this stage. This is incorrect. If this were so, one would have to state that this kind of yoga is identical with the yoga of one flavor [as practiced in this order]. One would then have to accept the lower and average levels of the nondiscriminatory yoga as identical with the yoga of one flavor. Although the possibility of realizing emptiness on the stage of nondiscriminatory yoga exists, the meditator who is at ease with the dimension of emptiness will find himself ill at ease with the dimension of appearances. He may therefore not realize the exact unity of appearance and emptiness. Only after having realized the perfect yoga of one flavor will the meditator experience the dawning of appearance in all its completeness as being inseparably blended with its intrinsic emptiness. Therefore it is proper to state that the one flavor, nondual nature of all opposite realities represents the meaning of the one flavor yoga.

360 F Of the three levels of one flavor the lower level is realized when one understands the one flavor of nondual mahāmudrā as the intrinsic nature of all conflicting dualities, such as saṃsāra and nirvāṇa. The average level of one flavor is reached when the meditator eliminates his mental clinging to the conscious certainty of one flavor through diverse appearances and realizes directly the inseparable union of appearances and the mind, thus erasing the perceptive division of reality into external and internal phenomena. The great level of one flavor is reached when the meditator realizes how the awareness of one flavor manifests itself in diverse forms and how these appearances and existences are of one flavor in primordial evenness. Prior to this the meditator realized the one flavor of all the diverse things.

The meditator has achieved insight into the essential nature of one flavor

when he discovers the intrinsic identity of every appearance as a self-manifesting objectlessness and evenness in its primordial nature. This he has achieved perfectly without any concern for affirmation or rejection, acceptance or abandonment. On the other hand, the meditator has failed to
B gain insight into the essential nature of one flavor if he still has a subtle clinging to his consciousness of certainty, which is an inner sensation on this stage, and to other inner sensations that arise from the spontaneous blending of any emerging thought and appearance. The other object of his subtle clinging is every thought and appearance that are to be unified into one flavor.

He has realized the consummate power of one flavor when he perceives every emerging appearance as a manifestation of the inherent power of mind's primordial evenness. On the other hand, he has not realized the consummate power of one flavor if he has failed to perceive one flavor through diverse appearances. This is because of his failure to detach himself from the [unwarranted discriminatory] concern for affirming [those that he considered good] and rejecting [those that he considered bad].

The meditator has realized all dualistic thoughts as the meditational state when he is completely at ease with whatever emerges [in his mind] through the entrances of the six senses and when he does not long for inner release or loathe his bondage. This happens after he has cleared the mind's clinging to any dualistic appearances, such as perception and perceiver, subject and object. However, he has not realized all dualistic thoughts as the meditational state if he has still to attain that state or inward release by means of retrospective mindfulness, which recognizes the identity of the six sensory appearances.

The great qualities of one flavor have arisen in the meditator when he has achieved the supernormal power to reintegrate his own body and mind as well as external appearances and thereby to transform them into any desired forms or emanations. The great qualities have not arisen in him if he has failed to acquire the supernormal power of transformation, [which would otherwise be the clear indication of his attainment]. His failure might well be due to his having less favorable conditions and less effective practices. Nonetheless, he has achieved a simple realization of the one flavor of appearances.

61 F The meditator has gained perfect insight into apparent reality if he knows how to differentiate saṃsāra and nirvāṇa in a single momentary vision of awareness and is certain of the efficacy of karma. He has gained this insight by cognizing emptiness, [the intrinsic nature of all things], as the basis of dynamic cause and effect and by understanding clearly their interrelationship and interaction. He has not gained such perfect insight into apparent reality if he has not realized emptiness through the interactions of diverse causes and effects.

361 F The meditator has sown the seed of the manifested body [of enlightenment] when all-pervading compassion has dawned in him, thus opening up the treasure of magnaminity for the benefit of other sentient beings. This is the result of his having experienced the dawning of emptiness as compassion. On the other hand, the meditator has not sown the seed of the manifested body [of enlightenment] when he has failed to manifest the power of his own self-realization in compassion and when, consequently, he becomes very limited in the application of skillful means, such as compassion, and thus fails to fulfill the wishes of others.

How Inner Sensation and Experience Will Dawn

On the lower level of the one flavor yoga the meditator realizes the essential nature of phenomena as primal purity. Yet there still remains the clinging to his own consciousness of certainty and to the inner sensations [arising from meditative absorption]. During a period of postabsorption the meditator
361 B might find himself ill at ease when he attempts to transform each of the six sensory experiences, which are violently disturbed by external and internal conditions, into sublime experience. He will occasionally perceive a solid appearance of duality. Because of its impact on his deeper psyche, his dreams will be briefly influenced by his mental delusion and attachment. He will experience a sublime sensation of the inseparable blend of his body, mind, and appearance. However, there is a possibility of his losing the vigor of appreciation with respect to the law of cause and effect and also of his faith and compassion diminishing.

On the average level of one flavor the meditator will achieve inner release from his inbred clinging to dualities such as realization and realizer, experience and experiencer. He will cut the root of that dualistic clinging to perception and perceiver. Besides, the meditator, during the period of postabsorption, will not experience much solid clinging to duality, while the delusion in his dreams will also diminish. It is said that such a meditator will gain sufficient inner power capable of helping or harming his fellow beings.[196]

On the great level of one flavor the meditator will realize nondual awareness, detached from any mental clinging, which lasts throughout the cycle of a day and night. This realized state cognizes all diverse appearances as the manifestation of the unceasing power of mind's primordial purity and evenness. He will also achieve a perfect union of absorption and postabsorp-
362 F tion, which will continue, like the flow of a river. Thus, while absorbed in nondual awareness, he will cognize the inner sensations of a few indeterminable appearances with some degree of clarity. During his postabsorptive

consciousness he will perceive appearances in the manner of seeing an ephemeral illusion, which is just a vision of emptiness. Even though such postabsorptive perception is detached from any clinging, it will occasionally contain some subtle dualistic appearance originating from the stream consciousness of the meditator. He will either have some uninterrupted and lucid dreams without any attachment or else will not dream. At this stage the meditator will acquire some power of supernormal cognition and will receive prophetic directions from his yidam and ḍākinī. In addition, his jealousy will clear completely.

How This Yoga Is Maintained

During the period of mastering the three levels of the one flavor the monk-meditator should mainly confine himself to a place of solitude, though he may occasionally join the assembly [of monks]. The methods for enhancing the progress of this meditation are, for the most part, the same as in the case of the great level of nondiscrimination. Even though he sometimes feels no perceivable difference between meditation and no meditation, between being mindful and not being mindful, it is vitally important for him to remain in solitude and maintain the undistracted mindfulness of the essential nature of his realization.

During the practice of the lower and average levels of the one flavor there
62 B might be some danger of the meditator neglecting skillful means, whose main features consist of the scrupulous application of karmic law, the development of faith in and veneration [for the supreme refuge], and compassion for all sentient beings. [In order to prevent such negligence] the meditator should strengthen his meditation on these dynamic practices. Besides, it is important for him to create a congenial circumstance by way of some asupicious events [in order to bring about favorable interactions and bring forth desired results], while avoiding the negative ones. He should conscientiously observe the moral precepts. Je Gomtsül exhorts:

> You may have realized the state of nonduality,
> But do not abandon the noble dharma.
> You may have realized the state of nonmeditation,
> But do not neglect skillful means.
> You may have transcended the level of acceptance and
> abandonment,
> But do not cause others to commit spiritual offenses.
> You may embody the spontaneous fulfillment
> Without indulging in hope or fear,
> But do not let your deluded mind run astray.

If the meditator has failed to acquire the spiritual power capable of producing both beneficial and baneful effects, has failed to gain supernormal cognition, and has also failed to receive any prophetic directions from the ḍākinīs[197] despite the fact that he has realized the great level of one flavor, then this condition might well be the consequence of his having violated the sacred bond or having been affected by a close associate who has abandoned his faith. In the case of the former all he has to do is to recognize the
363 F transgression of his spiritual commitments with deep remorse and resolve to fulfill these commitments. In general he is advised to produce a thousand sacred figurines [and to have them consecrated]. [Conducting the devotional ceremony himself], he makes the offering of one flower to each [sacred figurine] and invokes [the supreme refuge] in order to clear his spiritual befoulment. He also recites some specific mantras for clearing his inner befoulment. But whatever the circumstances, he must continue his practice of the noble path.

If, after having attained supernormal power, the meditator becomes either arrogant or succumbs to his volatile feelings—being pleased [one moment by a good experience] and dismayed [the next by a bad one]—this could mean that he has been overpowered by "the forces of obstruction." He would do well to contemplate in this way, "The 'forces of obstruction,' those that help or harm others, are all only the product of mind, and mind [in its intrinsic nature] is like space, without any center and circumference."

Nonetheless, once the state of one flavor dawns in him, the meditator can be overcome neither by a fear of discursive thoughts nor by a volatile feeling of either being pleased or dismayed by good or bad experiences. If, however, he finds himself [unusually] overpowered by intense and strong defilements like jealousy, crude thoughts, oversensitivity, or feelings of pleasure or dismay, he should recognize them as the influence of the "obstructive
363 B forces" and should counteract by intensifying his devotion to the noble practice. Moreover, everything that impedes the meditation is to be treated as the influence of the "obstructive forces."

Je Gampopa urges meditators to intensify the understanding of one flavor:

> The vital importance in mastering the one flavor through diverse realities lies in concentrating on its inner experience without getting entangled with the general comprehension.

And Je Gyare explains:

> When commanding the yoga of one flavor,
> One sows the seeds of fulfillment for others.
> Even when one does not have to account for one's karma,
> One establishes good causes [in order to produce good results].

Je Yanggönpa elaborates:

> Any appearance emerging through the five senses
> Is the luster of an unceasing flux.
> That which arises from the sense objects without any mental clinging
> Is the nature of nonarising [emptiness].
> Even when attachment to appearance has not ceased,
> It is sublimated to natural meditation.
> Perceiving emptiness through appearance without discrimination
> Is the inner process of elevation.
> Do not view appearances as being deficient,
> But abandon your attachment to them.
> You will penetrate the expanse of the meditation of one flavor.

The meditator should know this elucidation on the need to detach himself from any clinging to thoughts or appearances. By maintaining [the yoga of one flavor], he will realize the state of nonmeditation, which consists of the union of absorption and postabsorption as well as distraction and mindfulness. This is the result of his having abandoned the stain of inner sensations and having achieved the blend of realization on the path with realization of the mind's abiding nature.

Differentiating the Levels of Each Stage Separately: The Yoga of Nonmeditation

This consists of three points:

1. The differentiation of the yoga of nonmeditation
2. How inner sensation and experience will dawn
3. How this yoga is maintained

The Differentiation of the Yoga of Nonmeditation

The term "nonmeditation" generally means that the meditation cannot be conceived of as having any substance or innate self-nature. Both the *Kālacakra* and the *Guhyasamāja* define it thus:

> Because it is devoid of any innate substance,
> Meditation does not exist.
> The act of meditation is not meditation;
> Because it is neither substance nor nothingness,
> Meditation cannot be a conceivable reality.

Referring to the meaning of nonmeditation as being without the duality of meditation and meditator, Saraha comments:

O, do not claim to meditate
On that which is empty of any self-nature,
For by conceiving the duality of meditation and meditator
364 B And by clinging to it
You will abandon enlightenment.

Based on these sayings, some people asserted that these two [nonsubstance or no self-nature and no duality] are the yoga of nonmeditation. This is not correct. The former [nonsubstance] would mean that the meditative states from the yoga of nondiscrimination upward are the yoga of nonmeditation. The latter [nondual meditation] would turn even the yoga of one flavor into the yoga of nonmeditation. If one wonders what this nonmeditation actually is, it is a state that clears even the subtle attachment to the duality of meditation and meditator, which existed earlier on in the yoga of one flavor. Being a fully awakened state, it neither requires any effort at meditation nor is it divided into the duality of mindfulness and unmindfulness, absorption and postabsorption. Hence the designation of "nonmeditation."

Śavari comments:

A realized mind does not conceive the duality of meditation and meditator;
Just as space does not conceive space,
So emptiness does not meditate on emptiness.
Just as water and milk blend naturally,
So nondual awareness and diverse cognitions blend harmoniously
Into the one flavor of the unceasing stream of bliss.

Je Shang concludes:

When the state of nonmeditation dawns,
Inmost awareness is separated from its support.
The yogin will gain freedom from the acts of meditation,
365 F Will eliminate the meditator in himself,
And will realize the expanse of reality.

The yoga of nonmeditation has three levels. The meditator on the lower level will experience all appearances, which dawn in him, as the meditational state. Once he has realized this nonmeditational state, unstained by the duality of meditation and meditator, he needs neither to maintain it with the support of mindfulness nor to seek absorption through meditation. However, on this lower level he will still have a very subtle clinging, like an ephemeral illusion, to the sublime sensations. On the average level the meditator will achieve the ground of spontaneous perfection, having freed himself from the subtle clinging [that existed at the lower level] and having realized the state of nonmeditation, which lasts through an entire cycle of day and night. However, he will, during postabsorption, perceive the subtle consciousness as crystallizing itself. The meditator on the great level will achieve the transformation of that subtle consciousness into transcending awareness and will thereby blend the meditational luminous awareness with that which emerged spontaneously. Hence he will continuously experience the infinite expanse of awareness.

The differentiation between the realization and nonrealization of the union of the two luminous awarenesses is as follows. The meditator has gained true insight into the essential nature of nonmeditation if his awakened state no longer needs to apply mindfulness or to master the yoga of nonmeditation. On the other hand, he has not yet gained the ultimate insight if his realization is still in need of a little more perfection or clarity.

5 B The meditator has achieved the consummate power of nonmeditation if he has eliminated not only the subtlest perception of duality and the slightest nonawareness of the mind's intrinsic nature [emptiness], but has also achieved its union with transcending awareness. On the other hand, he has not realized that consummate power if he still perceives the subtlest duality and is still slightly unaware of the mind's nondiscriminatory state.

The meditator has experienced the dawning of all dualistic thoughts as the meditational state when he has transformed all levels of his source consciousness—instead of eliminating them—into the awareness of infinite reality. He has not experienced the dawning of thoughts as the meditational state if he still has the slightest latent clinging to his body, mind, and appearances and a subtle stain of inner sensation.

The transcendent qualities of the nonmeditation yoga have blossomed in the meditator when he has achieved the rainbowlike physical transformation of his mortal body into the illusory form of awareness [jñāna-rūpakāya], when his mind has transformed itself into lucid awareness [dharmakāya], and when he perceives the countless buddha realms. No such transcendent qualities have blossomed in him if he continues to perceive his body and mind, the external worlds, and all sentient beings as impure and if he still has a slight mental clinging [to his realization].

The meditator has perfected and dominated his perception of apparent reality when he has attained all the perfect qualities of enlightenment such as the [ten] transcendent powers and the [four] states of fearlessness.[198] On the other hand, he has failed to perfect and dominate his perception of apparent reality if the qualities of enlightenment have not blossomed fully. This is because they are being clouded by the three kinds of mundane imprints [trimudrā]—the imprints of the body [which still remain as germinators of karma], the imprints of the inmost psyche [which still manifest themselves], and the imprints of his mental consciousness [which still remains partly imperfect].

366 F The meditator has completely germinated the seed of the transcending body when he has attained the enlightenment of dharmakāya, which consists of the inseparable union of infinite emptiness and his transcending awareness, and when he is able through inexhaustible cycles of his enlightened body, speech, and mind to give sentient beings the never ending spiritual benefits. If he still has to rely on his efforts to attain the cosmic realms of the buddhas, then the meditator has not germinated completely the seed of the transcending body.

The perfect realization of the nonmeditation yoga and the attainment of complete enlightenment take place at the same time. For this reason one does not attain the ultimate state of nonmeditation in this lifetime. That which is usually achieved in this life is only an approximate adaptation of nonmeditation. Je Gyare clarifies this:

> Nonmeditation being the seat of dharmakāya,
> It is but an appropriate adaptation for most meditators.

Je Gomtsül elucidates the distinction of the four yogas in answering the question of Lengom:

> The one-pointed yoga brings about the understanding of the intrinsic
> 366 B nature of one's own mind. The nondiscriminatory yoga brings about the understanding of the inherent nature of emptiness. The yoga of one flavor brings about the understanding of the inherent nature of appearances. As for what is known as the yoga of nonmeditation, I am unable to evaluate it.

Thus he has refused to accept the yoga of nonmeditation. The disciples of Je Phagmo Trupa say that three quarters of them have realized the yoga of one flavor. Even Je Götsangpa and the great saint Ugyenpa admitted to having realized nothing higher than the yoga of one flavor. Nowadays there are those who claim to have realized one-flavor and also to have realized the yoga of nonmeditation. They cannot be trusted, because these assertions were made out of sheer arrogance and ignorance, without thorough knowledge of the four yoga stages.

How Inner Sensation and Experience Will Dawn

On the lower level of nonmeditation, the meditator will clear most of the perceptive dualities. He will experience the dawning of appearances as the meditational state, without having to make a special effort to meditate or to apply mindfulness. He will remain imperturbable and immobile [for a long time] in this state of nonmeditation. During the period of postabsorption, when the meditator perceives sensory appearances, he will experience a state of mind that is neutral in its function. This is a noncognitive aspect of his source consciousness, which is a residual nonawareness or ignorance. Hence the designation as the indeterminate nondual state. This subtle mind is considered to be the one that contains a stain of a subconscious befuddlement. While in his postabsorptive consciousness, he will not accumulate any more karma, but a subtle clinging to his transcending awareness will continue to flicker, like an illusion. This clinging to reality will also manifest itself in his dreams.

On the average level of nonmeditation, the meditator will be able to clear even those illusionlike subtle appearances of duality and thus remain in the realized state throughout entire cycles of days and nights. During the postabsorptive perception the meditator will experience the subtlest indeterminate nondual mind. This state manifests itself in what is termed as "self-clarity," which means that it is in harmony with its intrinsic form. Yet it is the subtlest stain of a nonvirtuous mind. A little of that indeterminate nondual mind will manifest itself in sleep as well.

On the great level of nonmeditation, the subtlest indeterminate nondual mind is completely transformed into transcending awareness. The meditator will achieve a harmonious blend of the two kinds of luminous awareness, the one that has been mastered through meditation and the one that dawns naturally in his realized state. As a result of this he will realize the infinite expanse of transcendental awareness, which is simply designated as enlightenment in dharmakāya, thus fulfilling his ultimate personal aim.
B He will simultaneously realize the transcending form of enlightenment [rūpakāya], thus realizing his aim for fulfilling the wishes of other sentient beings for as long as the cycle of existence remains. The achievement of the latter will come about as a result of the combined interaction between the meditator's unimpeded mastery of power through luminous awareness and the attitudes of his future disciples through which they look upon him as the embodiment of spiritual perfection.

How This Yoga Is Maintained

The dawning of the three levels of nonmeditation has thus been explained. Admittedly, the level of this ultimate state that is attainable in this life is nothing more and nothing less than an all-encompassing awareness of certainty, which will dawn in the meditator vividly and spontaneously. It is a transcending awareness without any division between absorption and postabsorption, an awareness that looks upon the mind as natural enlightenment and as such is detached from the purificatory process and purifying mind. The intrinsic nature of this mind is such that there is nothing that needs to be abandoned or remedied through spiritual countermeasures. The understanding immanent in this state is that it is not conditioned by the cycle of rebirth and death.

Concerning the method for maintaining the experience of nonmeditation, Gampopa comments:

> It is important for the meditator in this state not to be attached to the luster of sublime sensations and experiences, but to remain detached from such an experience.

Thus the meditator on the stage of nonmeditation is urged to be cautious of attachment to the sublime sensations and experiences. So it is vitally important for him to remain free not only from attachment to these experiences, but also from volatile feelings of pleasure through good experiences or dismay
368 F through bad ones. Every aspect of the undermined latent consciousness should now be brought to the level of the determined awareness through perfect mindfulness or supraconscious awareness. Thus undistracted mindfulness constitutes the foundation of meditation. Hence the need to fully realize ordinary awareness, characterized as undistracted and nonmeditating, while devoting oneself relentlessly to raising the banner of meditation.

The manner of maintaining absorption on the lower and average levels of nonmeditation is stated to be the same as that of one flavor. Je Gyare states:

> The lower level of the nonmeditation yoga
> Is the same as that of one flavor,
> For their methods of meditation are identical.
> The highest level of nonmeditation
> Constitutes the ground of enlightenment,
> For it is detached from seeking and striving.

Je Yanggönpa instructs:

> Look at the state of your awareness
> And find out if the duality of meditation and meditator exists.
> Detach this nondual awareness from its inbred base
> And maintain nondualistic awareness.
> You will then achieve all-encompassing absorption
> Throughout the cycles of days and nights.

368 B Thus the meditator is urged to maintain the awareness that is devoid of the duality of meditation and meditator. He is to cease his clinging to and directing of this awareness of "no mindfulness" and "no discrimination." The meaning of these two aspects has been explained earlier. Generally speaking, the prolonged inner sensation arising from absorption of one-pointed yoga seems to be similar to that of nonmeditation. A simple nondual meditation which is devoid of the duality of meditation and meditator is achieved even at the stage of nondiscriminatory yoga. The absorption in

which all sensory appearances emerge as the meditational state and which is a simple nonmeditation, detached from the duality of tranquil absorption and postabsorption, might also dawn at the stage of one flavor. The meditator should be able to discern for himself that all these are mere aspects of the inner sensations arising from meditation and that they are not the exact stage of nonmeditation.

The distinctive features of the four yoga stages in general have to be elucidated according to one's personal experience. They are far more difficult to explain than other doctrinal treatises. The most difficult of all is how to explain the higher levels of these yogas without [the teacher himself] having experienced the dawning of these states. However, I have explained
F them in great detail, using the oral instructions of the senior and junior noble Gampopas and the works of the undisputed ancient saints as the basis.

Differentiating the Levels of Each Stage Separately: The Summary of Their Vital Significance

The root of saṃsāra is the mind's inbred clinging to the duality of self and others. This is illustrated in the *Ratnāvalī*:

> As long as there is any mental clinging to one's psychophysical aggregates. . . .[199]

The *Pramāṇavarttikā* comments:

> One cognizes others if one perceives the self.

The *Bodhicaryāvatāra* states:

> As much violence as there exists in this transient world,
> Just that much fear and misery abounds in it.
> All these originate from man's clinging to a self.
> What should I do with this great devil?

By intensifying the clinging to a self instead of purging it, one will not only perpetuate such clinging but will, as a consequence, wander like a wheel in motion throughout the existential realms without achieving liberation. Some seekers of liberation fail to recognize the clinging to a self as the root of their karma and mental defilements. Without knowing how to eliminate the self [they will not achieve liberation], no matter how much they may try to abandon harmful deeds and practice virtue of a composed nature, such as listening to dharma discourses and contemplating them. This they do out of the desire to eliminate the miseries of existential life, which are the result of their deluded mind and evil karma. Even as they devote themselves to virtuous deeds, they cannot be certain of the result if these are not based on

wholesome or magnanimous attitudes. Given a wholesome attitude, their
369 B virtuous practices cannot directly ensure the elimination of their clinging to the self. This kind of virtuous practice can help them only indirectly [by enriching their spiritual devotion].

On the other hand, there are some meditators and seekers who state [rightly] that the meditation on nonselfhood is essential for eliminating the clinging to the self. They abandon clinging to the perceived reality of the self while strengthening their conscious certainty of emptiness. This causes their clinging to expand so much that they fall victim to the great vision of nihilism. Even those who are particular about true meditation and realization succumb to their attachment and clinging to the inner sensation arising from their meditation, so that they drift toward the fallacious courses known as the four aberrations and the three deviations. If one lets one's mind cling to absorption, this will lead one toward a fundamental error and deviation. And if one clings to the consciousness of postabsorption, this will lead one toward wandering in saṃsāra. All afflictions and deficiencies of life originate from the mind's attachment and clinging. It is therefore vitally important for a meditator not to be overcome by attachment and clinging.

370 F Saraha explains with:

> He who is enchanted with something delightful
> And who pursues it passionately
> Will indeed be afflicted by miseries,
> Even by one as small as the husk of a sesame seed.

And:

> He who views substantial existence is like a cow;
> He who views nothingness is even more ignorant.

And again:

> He should abandon his attachment in all its forms.

For this reason it has been stated that the highest path for a yogin consists of sustaining the mind and of not letting it cling to anything, ranging from inner sensations, which arise from visualized meditation or formless meditation, to normal appearances, which arise from their latent psychic imprints. Je Gampopa emphasizes:

> Remaining free from clinging to everything that arises in the mind
> Represents the highest path, leaving nothing higher to aspire to.

If the meditator achieves the propensity for maintaining a mental state devoid of any clinging, he will acquire many great qualities. He will clear the sensory appearances that arise from the latent karmic imprints in his inmost
370 B consciousness. He will also achieve the instantaneous release of every

thought as it emerges. His stream consciousness will be cleansed of any stains. He will experience all sensory appearances as manifestations of dharmakāya.

Je Gampopa points out:

All this diversity of appearances
Is the solid manifestation of one's latent consciousness.
It will all clear by itself without having to be abandoned
If only one masters nonattachment and nonclinging.
All that the mind clings to
Becomes the seed of perceptive duality.
For the mind that does not cling to any [thought or appearance]
Its arising and release occur simultaneously.

He continues with:

When the mind does not cling to every emerging appearance,
The stream of this mind becomes free
From any stain of deluded discrimination.

And:

Even if the stain of clinging to duality
Has not been removed even for a moment,
The very nature of this duality
Is immanent with the power of dharmakāya.

And finally:

Where there is no evaluation, any discriminating thought
Will achieve a simultaneous arising and release;
Where there is no deep attachment,
Everything remains in even harmony.
If one realizes this,
The stream of meditation will not cease;
One will become a sovereign
Dominating the cycle of birth and death
And will be free from any clinging to duality.
Luminous awareness will prevail throughout the cycle of time.

371 F Concerning the question of how liberation may be achieved by eliminating the mind's clinging, the elimination of the mind's clinging to the internalized "I" and the externalized "mine" will terminate one's entanglement with the process of "composing" a new psychophysical form in the womb of a [future] mother. The termination of such a process will put an end to rebirth. This will, in turn, eliminate one's karma and inner defile-

ment, so that the meditator will inevitably achieve liberation. The *Mūlamadhyamaka-kārikā* states:

> Upon the simultaneous elimination of the subjectified "I" and the objectified "mine"
> The clinging to the self will come to an end.
> Upon the elimination of this, rebirth will come to an end.
> Upon the elimination of karma and mental defilement, one will achieve liberation.

The elimination of one's attachment to everything is embodied in the following terms, [which are widely used in this text]. They are: no clinging, no attachment, no mental image, no perceptive mark, no direction, no affirmation and no rejection, no acceptance and no abandonment, no desire, no doubt, and no craving. They have the same vital significance. The meditator should know that it is always essential to remember all these methods in their minute details. It is equally essential not to cling to anything but to remain undistracted from the actuality of absorption at each
371 B and every level of the four yogas and other related practices.

HOW THE VARIOUS GROUNDS AND PATHS [OF ENLIGHTENMENT] ARE REACHED THROUGH THE FOUR YOGAS

I found no comments by either Gampopa or his nephew [Gomtsül] on adapting the different grounds and stages of the realization, as established in the scriptures of the vehicle of logical definition [i.e., Hīnayāna and Mahāyāna] to the four yogas of mahāmudrā. However, the great saint Shang, who was the disciple of Je Gomtsül, commented as follows:

> The great seal is attainable in one stride.
> It is deluded ignorance to divide it
> Into grounds and paths.
> However, if only to delight the hearts of the confused,
> I shall divide it into grounds and paths,
> Adapting it to the system of logical definition.

The great seal [mahāmudrā] is the very essence of reality and the all-in-one path [chikchö]. The essence of reality being nondifferentiable, its division into the grounds and paths cannot be acceptable from the ultimate standpoint. The commentary on the *Madhyamakāvatāra* says this is so:

> Because it is the intrinsic nature of consciousness, and because, from the standpoint of its essence, it cannot be differentiated.

And it continues:

> Just as no skillful person can either see or describe a bird's path across the trackless sky, so no person can either describe or listen to [accounts of] the grounds trodden by the sons of the victorious Buddha.

The *Sphuṭārthā* supports this:

> Because of the direct perception of that which is inseparable from the abiding nature of reality, there exists no separation of the paths into the paths of insight and of true meditation. Therefore, a distinct path of meditation has not been described.

However, it has been considered that the spiritual ground and path of the vehicle of the logical definition should be adapted to the four yoga stages, if only for the benefit of those ignorant ones who might wonder how they may determine their meditatve attainment in terms of the spiritual grounds and paths.

The *Drelpa Dönsal* (*Sphuṭārthā*) comments:

> The clear illumination of realization
> Is the joyous ground, the path of insight;[200]
> The perfect mastery of the realized state of one flavor
> Is the path of true meditation.
> Since the latter requires no meditation,
> It is the ultimate path.

372 B As is explicit in this quotation, the first ground, the path of insight,[201] is the illumination of nondual awareness or the union of awareness and its intrinsic emptiness. The expansion of that insight is the path of true meditation, which incorporates the grounds from the second up to the tenth ground. The nonmeditation yoga is described as the ultimate path and the ground of buddhahood. Thus it contains no explicit reference to the yoga of nondiscrimination. I would imagine that this state may have been regarded as the [supramundane] path of insight and the first ground. Thus, by implication, the one-pointed yoga is shifted to the [mundane] path of virtuous absorption.

Je Gyare describes the five paths of enlightenment thus:

> Even though the grounds and paths are not essential,
> I consider them to be as follows:
> Making a symbolic offering of the universe
> Represents the [mundane] path of spiritual merits;
> Gaining experience represents
> The [mundane] path of virtuous absorption;
> Realizing nondiscriminatory awareness

Represents the [supramundane] path of insight;
Perfecting that realization
Represents the path of true meditation;
Realizing the yoga of one flavor
Represents the eighth ground [i.e., the path of true meditation];
Reaching the yoga of nonmeditation
Represents the eleventh ground on the ultimate path.

Accordingly all practices of accumulating spiritual merits and clearing mental defilements, beginning with the preparatory exercises, represent the path of spiritual merit. The one-pointed yoga represents the path of virtuous absorption. The yoga of nondiscrimination represents the path of insight. The experiences of one flavor, which begin with the illuminating insight into
373 F the union [of appearance and emptiness], represent the path of true meditation. The lower and average levels of nonmeditation represent the ninth and tenth grounds, while its great level represents the ultimate path, the eleventh ground. Je Götsangpa describes them:

> The accumulation of spiritual merits is the path of spiritual merits and the ground of the beginners. The experience of the one-pointed yoga is the path of virtuous absorption and the ground of joy. The experience of nondiscrimination is the path of insight and the first ground. The experience of one flavor is the second up to the seventh ground. The lower and average levels of nonmeditation are the last three grounds [i.e., the eighth to the tenth] and the path of true meditation. The great level of nonmeditation is the ultimate path and the ground of buddhahood.

Some texts refer to a subdividing of the four yogas into twelve and then into twenty-four, according to the levels of inner sensations and experiences. The twelve inner sensations and experiences represent the four levels of the path of virtuous absorption. Out of the twelve levels of realization the three levels of the one-pointed yoga represent the first, second, and third grounds. The three levels of the nondiscriminatory yoga represent the fourth, fifth, and sixth grounds. The three levels of the one flavor yoga represent the seventh, eighth, and ninth grounds. The three levels of the nonmeditation yoga represent the tenth, eleventh, and twelfth grounds.

373 B My own idea is that the progressive attainment of the path described in the treatises of the vehicle of logical definition is based on the great qualities meditators can achieve. According to the mahāmudrā tradition the same self-realization can be achieved instantaneously through "the path of primordial evenness and all-in-oneness,"[202] since this is based on the nature or self-realization. The two systems ultimately must be identical, even though they are contradictory from the conventional standpoint. The former con-

siders the possibility of cosmic eons, while the latter does not require many lifetimes, providing the requisite conditions are present. Thus the difference between the effectiveness of the two systems is like that between a long and a short road.

I shall make a superficial comparison between the grounds and the paths of these two systems. The three levels of the one-pointed yoga, including the preparatory practices, represent the [mundane] path of the spiritual merits and the first ground. The three levels of the nondiscriminatory yoga represent the [mundane] path of virtuous absorption and the ground of joy. The three levels of one flavor and the lower and average levels of nonmeditation
F represent the [supramundane] path of insight and the path of true meditation, as well as the first through the tenth grounds. The great level of nonmeditation represents the ultimate path, the ground of buddhahood.

These attributions of the paths and the grounds seem an excellent idea. However, it is difficult to differentiate the levels of realization between the great level of nondiscrimination and the lower level of the one flavor and those between the great level of one flavor and the lower level of nonmeditation. Following the order of the twelve levels of the four yogas that are being taught nowadays, I shall give a description. The great level of nondiscrimination is not the exact insight into the one even flavor of appearances and emptiness. Without this intrinsic reality cannot be realized. Having considered this designation of the first ground and the path of insight for the yoga of nondiscrimination as somewhat inappropriate, I implore the learned teachers to reexamine this matter. Although some people consider that this attribution [of the first ground] to nondiscrimination agrees with that by Je Gyare and Je Götsangpa, these two masters were thinking of the perfect level of nondiscrimination as the basis for the first ground and the path of insight. That level is unstained by any inner sensations and attachment to
374 B the concept of emptiness, for it is a transcendent awareness of the one even flavor [of appearances and emptiness]. Therefore this must be recognized as the yoga of one flavor. I consider it irrelevant to attribute the first ground to the lower and average levels of the nondiscriminatory yoga in light of their present descriptions and of the incompatibility between the ground thus assigned and the level of inner sensations and experiences associated with that state.

Some people have refuted these correlations [of the grounds and the paths] to the four yogas of mahāmudrā as contradictory with all the sacred sūtras and tantras by referring to them as follows:

> One-pointed, nondiscrimination,
> One flavor, and nonmeditation
> Are the four yogas.
> The yoga of one-pointedness

Is the path of insight;
The yoga of nondiscrimination is the grounds
From the first up to the seventh;
The yoga of one flavor
Is the three higher grounds;
And the yoga of nonmeditation
Is the ground of buddhahood.

I myself have not seen such words of the renowned ancient saints of the Meditation Lineage. Maybe they do exist. Even so, I see no contradiction with the sūtras and tantras in attributing the grounds and the paths to the four yogas of emptiness, let alone the other sets of four yogas. Moreover, the sūtras and tantras do not contain passages prohibiting the use of such
375 F designations. This way of expressing their opinion does not go well with present-day terminology, because there are no [four yogas that represent all the] sūtras and tantras at the same time.

Some have offered the following comment:

Only an ignorant person can make the false statement
That he who has realized the path of insight in this life
Will achieve the great qualities in the next.

They commented for the sake of criticizing. Without any definite knowledge they said that it is the lie of an ignorant person to say that he who has realized the path of insight in this life will attain the twelve-hundred great qualities in the next. No scriptural passage specifically states that one who has realized the path of insight will instantly gain all the sublime qualities while not being deceased. However, a passage saying that such a realized one will be reborn as a universal monarch, dominating the world through the wheel of mystical power, refers to the next but not to this life. For example, a female yogin who realized the path of insight will not physically transform herself into a universal monarch without departing from this life. Moreover, if someone who has attained this path of insight must literally demonstrate all the great qualities that represent his first ground of enlightenment, so
375 B clearly described in the treatises, he would be impelled to deny the achievements of not only the scholars and saints of Tibet and ancient India but even of the bodhisattvas, the disciples of the Buddha. This would contradict the historical events. Apparently these critics have failed to examine the sūtra expositions.

The *Daśabhūmika-sūtra* states:

He who has attained the first ground is likely to be reborn as a universal monarch. If he [in his next life] dwells in the solitude of a forest, having renounced his worldly life, he is likely to achieve the twelve-hundred great qualities, including a hundred different forms of absorption.

The term "likely" indicates that there is no absolute certainty with regard to all these possibilities. To imply that the *Daśabhūmika-sūtra* is the source of what they referred to as "the false statement" is a great shame.

Some treatises state that even though one may have fully realized the mind as being the aspect of ultimate reality [dharmakāya], one might not
F have acquired the great qualities of enlightenment in this life, because one has not achieved the release from the threefold bondage, such as the body. This physical hindrance is compared to the eggshell of an eagle, which entraps the infant eagle. However, such an aspirant will, during the stages of his death, rise in an illusory form of consummate bliss [sambhogakāya], having just experienced the luminous awareness.

Referring to the belated realization of the great qualities, other people have criticized by saying that it is astonishing for the sunlight to appear tomorrow when the sun has already risen today. This is absolutely wrong. Because they ignored the treatises of mysticism [mantrayāna], which proclaim that mystics will realize the enlightenment of dharmakāya through the process of dying and of sambhogakāya through the intermediate state [bardo]. The treatise entitled the *Caturdevīparipṛcchā* proclaims:

> When one's physical vehicle of karma disintegrates,
> Then, through one's spiritual power,
> One will achieve such a body as one has aspired to.
> This body will permeate all static and dynamic phenomena,
> The way space encompasses everything.
> Understand that it remains so.

The *Sampuṭa* affirms:

> When one's physical vehicle of karma disintegrates,
> One will attain a supreme form.

Keeping in view this matter [of attaining some of the great qualities long after one has realized the spiritual path], Je Shang states:

376 B
> Misery may not completely disappear
> Immediately upon realizing the [truth of] nonduality.
> Who can deny that someone has attained the path of insight,
> Even though he has yet to realize the complete qualities?
> The early morning sun can neither melt frozen water
> Nor heat the ground and stones at once.
> Yet, who can deny the existence of the sun?

Such sayings are consistent with the fact of human experience. For instance, the new moon may be incomplete in its form, yet it is still the moon. A child may not be fully grown, yet it is still a human being. However undeveloped a lion's cub, it is still a lion. In this respect Je Gyare comments:

Even among the arhats
There are two kinds:
Adorned and unadorned ones.[203]
Even among bodhisattvas
There are two kinds:
Renowned and unrenowned ones.
Even in the mystic tradition
There are two kinds of mystics:
The ones practicing secretly and the ones doing it amidst an assembly.
Even in knowledge
There are two kinds:
The describable one and the demonstrable one.
Even as the great qualities are attributed on purpose
To the grounds and paths of realization,
Some great meditators achieve the power of supertransformation,
While others fail to achieve it;
Some of them fulfill the needs of sentient beings,
While others fail to fulfill them.
These are due to the difference of quality in their practices.

377 F I shall now sum up these sayings. The great qualities associated with the grounds and the paths according to the treatises of the vehicle of dialectics are revealed skillfully out of some higher motivation. The paths [of the four yogas] are not the same as these. Even the inner signs of realization on these paths are different. Just as there existed adorned and unadorned arhats and renowned and unrenowned bodhisattvas, there are different types of great meditators, some possessing the sublime power of transformation and others lacking this power, due mainly to the difference in the quality of their practices. It has been said that in order to achieve the sublime power of transformation and other great qualities, one must strive hard on the path of the transient world and the higher path of Mantrayāna.

With this I have completed the elucidation of the meditation on the mahāmudrā of ultimate certainty, especially the differentiation of each of the four yogas and the methods for crossing the grounds and the paths of enlightenment.

Dedication

The author, the great Tashi Namgyal of the Takpo Kagyü order, solemnly dedicates the spiritual merits arising from his exhaustive elucidation of the metaphysics and the meditation of mahāmudrā to the well-being and enlightenment of all sentient beings.

Fortunate seekers with a yearning for liberation
Will find the entrance to the teachings of Buddha
Through the application of the principles of the sacred law,
Through hearing, examining, and meditating on the dharma
In the ways known to learned teachers.
But the perfect way of cutting the root of cyclic existence
Is the meditation on ultimate reality,
Which has been so acclaimed.

The glorious *Kālacakra* has rejected
Some methods of meditation on the emptiness of reality.
Among those are the meditation on complete emptiness,
As determined through the deductive logic known as complete
negation [megak],
And the meditation on conceptualized emptiness
377 B Is simply an absence of an ultimate inert matter.
Certain other concepts of emptiness contradict
The treatise of the Quintessential Realization [drubnying].

The method of meditating on the supreme emptiness of all forms
Was known to the followers of the great Saraha in ancient India
And to the lineage of the Takpo Kagyü in this land of snow
mountains.
It was hailed by fair-minded scholars and saints.

The true meaning of that system
Is the mahāmudrā of ultimate certainty.
Both the name and the meaning have been widely known
To the sūtras, tantras, and Sanskrit treatises
As well as to this Meditational Order.

Many elaborate and concise treatises on mahāmudrā
Are spread far and wide throughout this land.
However, knowing the rarity of any definite treatises,
I have, in all humility, resolved to compose such an exegetical treatise
In order to remove any misconceptions, doubts, and skepticism on the subject.

In this present age most scholars are confused
About the vital import of inner sensations and experiences.
Some of the realized ones are ignorant
Of the sūtras and tantras.
Those who have combined the two achievements
Are lacking in kindness and concern for others.

I myself have neither the perfect knowledge of the treatises,
378 F Nor have I gained the sublime experiences.
Even so, I have thoroughly acquainted myself
With the teachings of the precious Kagyü lineage
And have composed this text
Through my loving concern for others.

I ask the holy ones for forgiveness
If my work contains matters I myself have not understood,
Have misunderstood, or have had doubts about.
I entreat them to purge any wrong elucidations
By employing unsatined exposition and inferential logic,
So that the purity of Buddha's teachings may endure.

If ever one is aroused by the evil power of prejudice,
Condemns the good by thought and deed,
Or turns the positive into negative and truth into falsity,
One will indeed be scorned by wise and impartial minds.

If this text contains many excellent qualities,
It deserves the favorable comment of other scholars and saints,
Particularly those of the Takpo Kagyü order.
It deserves to be studied and examined by discriminating minds.

May the ever brightening sunlight of the virtuous thoughts and deeds
Devoted to this treatise
Illuminate the dark ignorance of sentient beings.
May the luminosity of their self-comprehending awareness increase.

May I, too, gain the unobstructed good opportunity
Of associating myself with this supreme path
Throughout all future lives.
May I realize the dharmakāya directly and before long
And fulfill the wishes of innumerable sentient beings.

Concerned by the rarity of any definitive treatise of the stages of meditation on the mahāmudrā of ultimate certainty, moved by a genuine concern for clearing the misconceptions affecting people, and desirous to ensure a dawning of conscious certainty in those having faith in this Meditational Order, I, Gampopa Tashi Namgyal, started composing this text at an auspicious time and completed it on an auspicious day of the third month of the Ox year,[204] at the *Nāgakoṭa* retreat, below the glorious monastery of Taklha Gampo. The founding of this monastery was prophesied by the Buddha. The scribe was Thupden Palbar, who is himself a dedicated master of the Mantrayāna system. May his service enrich all sentient beings with virtue and excellence.

Colophon

By Lama Ngawang Pema Chögyal of Ladakh who commissioned the carving of the woodblocks.

May peace and perfection prevail!

379 F His all-knowing mind is the jewel mountain Sumeru;
His discourse, debate, and writing represents its resplendent terrace;
He stands majestically amidst the eminent scholars,
Who are like the chain of gold mountains.
The sun of his realization radiates the twin wisdoms,
While riding the seven horses[205] of the Meditation Lineage;
His wonderful compassion is like a sandalwood tree;
His magnanimous actions spread out like its flourishing leaves and branches;
The benefits and welfare he brings about widely are like its scent;
He is revered by scholars and saints
The way the nāgarājas [the serpent gods] revere their crown jewel.
I pay homage to this supreme master!

The incomparable Takpopa [Gampopa],
Who is otherwise known as the monk-physician,
Fulfilled the prophesy of the Great Sage [Buddha].
Through his reverberating voice of the ultimate dharma at Mount Śānti,
The quintessence of the teachings shone like the sun.

When in this present age the scholars were concerned
With the only conventional knowledge.
When true knowledge was rare, even among those known for their realization,
There came the learned and realized guru,
Who established anew this ultimate doctrine and meditation.
This was due to the glorious merits of sentient beings.

Moving across the infinite space of his wisdom
Are the green celestial horses symbolizing his vision of ultimate
reality.
By the moonlight of his elegant sayings
May the lilylike young minds open up!

This definitive elucidation is the golden key,
Which will open the vast treasures of the teachings.
With this excellent ship of the sūtras and tantras
One may collect the precious gems of ultimate certainty.

With this unstained doctrine and logical reasoning
One may destroy the confidence of learned heretics;
With this jewel light of the perfect viewpoint
One may illuminate the looming darkness of wrong views.

With this sharp sword of the perfect mind
One may cut the entangled creepers of doubts about reality and
unreality;
In this silver mirror of deep meaning
One may see the beautiful face of true reality.

May this excellent treatise also spread far and wide
And may it remain firmly established
As long as the meditational teachings
Of the Great Sage remain!

Having felt that this elegant literary composition will be
Like a path to walk on or the eyes to see with
For those who seek liberation,
I, Ngawang Pema Chögyal of Ladakh,
Endowed with the three kinds of faith,[206]
Have commissioned the carving of the xylographs
In order to make an inexhaustable gift of the dharma
For the benefit of sentient beings and the teachings of the Buddha,
80 F Like a generous master of coral divers,
Who makes a gift of the precious sapphire [yik or yikngön].

May the merits arising from this deed
Help enrich those who lack
Knowledge, skill in debate, and meditation!
May many realized ascetics dwell on this earth
Like Marpa, Milarepa, Gampopa,
Tsangpa Gyare, Lorepa, and Götsangpa!
May I also perfectly realize the dharmakāya,
The exact nature of all things!

May I fulfill the wishes of all other sentient beings
By realizing all the diverse aspects of all that exists!

May the three planes [of the universe]
Become pure by the power of this attainment;
May they be free from diseases, famines, wars, and quarrels!
May the sunlight of fulfillment shine upon all
At the moment of their wishing!
May the lotus of their sublime bliss bloom!

May all the scribes, carvers of xylographs, and editors
Who have associated themselves with this work
Through their body, speech, and mind
And all other sentient beings
Throughout the vast expanse of space
Clear the cloud of their duality!
May they realize the expanse of the unborn dharmakāya!
May their virtue prevail!

The woodblocks of this text were at Śrī Neuteng of Gyel [in the Dingri district of Western Tibet].

Translator's Notes

AUTHOR'S INTRODUCTION

1. "Indestructible mind" (Skt. vajracitta, Tib. semkyi dorje) refers to the mind's original nature. This term, found only in the Vajrayāna treatises, reveals two meanings, the apparent and the ultimate. The apparent meaning points to the concrete perceptible form of the dorje as diamond. The ultimate meaning, relevant here, points to the abstract, imperceptible characteristics of the diamond, namely, its indivisibility and indestructibility. This in turn implies the mind's ultimate state, i.e., the indestructibility of the void. Even though observation and investigation in Buddhist meditation are centered on the mind and the mind is considered the source of creativity, the significance of the dorje extends to material phenomena, because the intrinsicality of the void is universal. The intrinsic void symbolized by the dorje is not merely an absence of the inner essence, the self-nature (svabhāva), in the phenomena of mind and matter, but as inner space it provides the substratum for these realities and is the unifier of all things.

The Vajrayāna tradition describes the unity of mind and its intrinsic void as the indivisibility of awareness and its void. Similarly the unity of matter and its intrinsic void is referred to as the indivisibility of perceptive reality and its void. The intrinsic unity of external and internal realities remains unknown and imperceptible until one has been awakened by means of initiatory and meditational processes. This process of awakening to the indivisible union of blissful awareness and its inner space consists of a self-transformation according to the Vajrayāna practice and self-observation according to the mahāmudrā meditation. The fundamental basis has been provided by Mahāyāna sūtras in the form of its "indivisible wisdom and compassion." The function of an ever-deepening wisdom is the penetration into the unknown imperceptible state of the void, while the dimension of compassion embraces all sentient beings. These supreme qualities are to be developed and realized through one single means, the enlightenment spirit (bodhicitta), wherein the two qualities are merged into one indivisible whole.

2. "Vajradhara" (Tib. Dorjechang) refers to the fully enlightened one. From the Vajrayāna standpoint the term means literally "holder of the scepter," i.e., the mystical form of Buddha. Its true meaning is "the essence of an enlightened state," which is the indivisible union of blissful awareness and its intrinsic void. This is signified by the indivisible quality of the vajra. In the common rationale of Buddhism this state is described as "the indivisible state of wisdom and compassion." As the metacosmic Buddha, Dorjechang embodies the ultimate simplicity (dharmakāya). Vajrayāna metaphysics perceives him as the master of universal excellence and the source of spiritual transmission and functions. As such, he is depicted in the mystic

pantheon and the conclaves of the maṇḍala as the sovereign sixth order who unifies the five aspects of transcendental wisdom and the five orders of the mystic buddhas in sambhogakāya form (known as pañcajñāna and pañcakula dhyānībuddha).

These two different meanings are part of the intricate elucidating system known as the six modes and the four systems. This refers to the four methods of explanation and the six modes of elucidating the Buddhist tantric doctrine. The four are (1) the literal meaning, including that of symbolism and mantra, (2) the general meaning, (3) the hidden meaning (allusions to certain omitted crucial explanations, and (4) the ultimate meaning. The six modes are teachings given (1) with or (2) without concealed intention or insight; those that have (3) apparent or (4) ultimate meanings; and (5) those that have literal etymological meanings and (6) those that have a meaning different from the literal. These extraordinarily cautious approaches were necessitated by the possibility of unscrupulous individuals misleading and exploiting innocent seekers.

3. "Triyāna" refers to (1) the three types of Buddha's teachings (according to the Mahāyāna sūtras, notably the prajñāpāramitā series, there are three vehicles of enlightenment, namely śrāvaka-yāna, pratyekabuddha-yāna and bodhisattva-yāna) and (2) the three vehicles of Buddhist doctrine, which constitute a completely integrated Buddhism (the Primary Vehicle, or Hīnayāna, now represented generally by the Theravāda school; the Great Vehicle, or Mahāyāna; and the Indivisible Vehicle of Mysticism, or Mantrayāna).

4. The "three mystical qualities" (Tib. sangwa sum, Skt. triguhya) refers to the mystical powers of body, speech, and mind of the fully enlightened one. The first is the mystical power of manifestation, which is believed to emanate from the ultimate simplicity (dharmakāya) in diverse forms and at various levels of sentient beings to help guide them toward eventual liberation and enlightenment. The second is the mystical power of speech, which refers to (1) the unique ability to convey the noble doctrine in ways and forms that individuals of diverse levels and temperaments can understand, and (2) the supramundane communication based on the symbols of mystical transformation, as in the case of that which happens between the metacosmic buddhas and the attending bodhisattvas in the higher order. The third is the mystical power of all-knowing awareness, which commands the infinite diversity of knowledge and the awareness that merges with ultimate reality, the suchness of the all-encompassing expanse of the void (chöying tongpa teshinnyi), so that its unceasing active power of wisdom and compassion makes every process of self-realization possible for practitioners.

5. "Apparent meaning" (Skt. neyārtha, Tib. trangdön) refers to the Buddha's words intended generally to show the transitional path as opposed to the ultimate path. The Tibetan term "trang" denotes "a means of attracting to" or "leading toward" the ultimate path or the real meaning (which the second syllable "don" signifies). The transitional path reveals (1) the ordinary doctrine with moral and rational overtones and (2) the selective concepts imbued with deliberately contrived meanings. The ordinary doctrine, expounded as only a psychological and moral foundation, ranges from the recognition of life's misery, of deluded mind as the cause of misery, of the potential for permanent freedom, and of the moral and psychological means of

perfection to the partial revelation of truth, i.e., the nonselfhood of personality (pudgala-nairātmya). As for the selective concepts imbued with those deliberately contrived meanings, they were given as a psychological means for alluring misguided minds toward the eventual realization of the ultimate truth. For example, it has been taught that "the reality of the six senses exists" or that "the self of personality exists." From the standpoint of the true doctrine, the self as a distinct solitary entity is nonexistent, and the senses are transitory realities whose emergence depends upon the interaction between senses and objects, supported by the psychophysical elements and spatiotemporal dimension, all of which—as a flux of events—are said to have been caused by the inner delusion or the normal consciousness of an individual.

When Buddha expounded the sūtras or sermons designed to meet the needs and temperaments of individuals or groups, he laid down guidelines based on doctrinal exposition and rational appreciation for differentiating the meanings as apparent or real, fabricated or alluded to and for understanding them in the light of his intended purpose and his personal realization. The original guidelines bearing the principles and the methods of differentiation are found in such important sūtras as the *Akṣayamatiparipṛcchā-sūtra* (*Lodrö Misepe Shüpe Do*) and the *Saṃdhinirmocana-sūtra* (*Do Gongpa Ngedrel*).

The two great teachers Nāgārjuna (2nd century C.E.) and Asaṅga (4th century C.E.) elucidated the principles and methods of interpretation. Nāgārjuna did this in terms of the Buddha's central philosophy (Madhyamaka) and by dealing with the subject in his works *The Collected Teachings of the Sūtras* (*Sūtrasamuccaya*) and *The Six Treatises of the Central Philosophy* (*Ṣaṣṭhakula-madhyamakaśāstra*). Asaṅga elucidated them in terms of the idealist view of reality (Vijñānavāda) through his *Five Treatises on the Grounds* (of Enlightenment)" (*Pañcasenabhūmi*).

The importance attached to proper interpretation can be deduced from the innumerable comments and works of the Tibetan teachers. To mention just a few, there is Sakya Pandita's (1181–1251) *Shungluk Lekpar Shepa*, Gyalwa Longchenpa's (1308–1363) *Trupthadzö*, Incomparable Tsongkhapa's (1357–1419) *Trangnge Lekshe Nyingpo*, and Khedrubje's (1385–1438) *Gyüde Cinam*. These complex and even contradictory teachings were the result of the deliberate approach to satisfy and guide seekers, which extended over a forty-year period of Buddha's ministrations. The sūtras containing these teachings are differentiated in terms of the meanings that are either apparent or real, fabricated or alluded to, according to the main school of Madhyamaka. Each of the three other schools, Vaibhāṣika, Sautrāntika, and Vijñānavādin, adopted a different system of identifying the sūtras, none of which share the Madhyamaka system.

Differentiating the meaning of the sūtras in terms of apparent and real, fabricated and alluded to, is done by categorizing the sūtras as belonging to one of the three phases of Buddha's turning the wheel of law. The sūtras of the first phase contain the doctrine with apparent and fabricated meanings. To the apparent meaning belong the teachings on the cyclic existence, the miseries of life, the cause and remedy, including the important segments that reveal the truth in a limited way, namely the nonselfhood of the stream consciousness and the state of sublime peace (nirvāṇa). These are designed eventually to lead individuals toward the valid view of reality and a wholesome attitude toward life. The discourses with fabricated meaning contain the teachings on the reality of the senses and the self of personality. Among the sūtras containing such teachings are the *Vinaya-sūtras*, the *Lalitavistara*, the *Karmaśataka*, and the *Smṛtyupasthāna*.

The sūtra teachings of the middle phase are regarded by the main Madhyamaka school as representing the real or ultimate truth, which is centered on the concept of the absolute unreality of dualistic phenomena (sarvadharma-śūnyatā). This śūnyatā (encompassing inner space) is considered to be identical with the dynamic flux of conditioned reality, which Buddhism's central philosophy describes as being the interdependent chain of events (pratītyasamutpāda). The extraordinary concept of reality revealed in the *Prajñāpāramitā-sūtras* (teachings of transcendental wisdom) was deliberately couched in cryptic terms from which only trained and devout seekers could derive benefit, even though these sūtras conceal the clear definition of the absolute unreality and the differentiation between the nonexistence of the absolute and the conditionality of phenomena. A case in point are the passages in the *Heart Sūtra* (*Prajñāpāramitā-hṛdaya-sūtra*), which literally negate all realities from the senses up to the psychophysical aggregates and indeed negate the reality of mind and matter. Absolute unreality shown in this way could easily create the misunderstanding of seeing it as the total negation of everything. The literary form in which it was described was intentionally unequivocal and even sweeping. Yet it was meant, not to be read literally, but to be examined in the light of broader guidelines, which precisely means incorporating the qualifying terms and fuller definitions.

The key to the proper understanding of absolute unreality lies in the fact that it is naturally linked and inseparably intertwined with conditioned phenomena. What is valid is this transient illusory reality, which provides the basis for conceptual designation, which in turn facilitates the unobstructed function of the human intellect. Far from being absolute nihility—which is an unmasked form of materialism—absolute unreality held by Mahāyāna Buddhism shows that absolute unreality is nothing other than the innate void (sahaja-śūnyatā) and that this void, being the unconditioned state of all things, cannot be bifurcated from the conditioned realities. Buddha affirms the all-pervading unity of the diverse realities thus: the void is not different from matter and matter is not different from the void. As a spiritual way of life, absolute unreality upholds the principle of the stream consciousness and its innate potential for supreme elevation.

The ultimate reality of things can be fully realized by the joint development of discerning wisdom and infinite compassion. Among the notable sūtras of this phase are *The Heart Sutra* (*Prajñāpāramitā-hṛdaya-sūtra*), *The Sovereign of Contemplative Absorption* (*Samādhirāja*), *The Great Jewel Mansion* (*Mahāratnakūṭa*), and *The Great Multitude of Buddhas* (*Buddha-avataṃsaka*).

Of the sūtras identified with the Buddha's third phase of turning the wheel of law, some contain the discourses bearing apparent meanings, which cannot be read literally, but others contain the doctrine that reveals the ultimate truth. The sūtras therefore provide the clear definitions of all things. (For further information on these methods of interpretation, consult a learned Geshe or, better still, study such treatises as the *Trangnge lekshe nyingpo* of Tsongkhapa and the *Truptha thupten lhünpö dzegyen* of Changkya Rölpe Dorje.)

These sūtras are differentiated in terms of the three characteristic marks, of which the first two represent the aspects of apparent reality (saṃvṛtisatya) and the third that of the ultimate reality (paramārthasatya). The first characteristic marks appertaining to "all conceptually designated things" (parikalpita) have only a nominal and symbolic identity, for they are devoid of an intrinsic essence. Even though all conditioned and unconditioned things provide the basis for the conceptual designation upon which the dynamic function of life rests, the conceptualized self-entity of an individual and that of phenomena lack any validity whatsoever, since these dual essences are totally false and nonexistent.

The second principle, that of dependent relativity or modulated perceptive phenomena (paratantra), is defined as being devoid of intrinsic essence and is therefore unreal. Emergence, existence, and cessation of every modulated perception (in the realm of dependent relativity) is dependent upon or conditioned by the interaction of appropriate factors and intervening circumstances. The ordinary mind perceives duality as being real with the attributes of an inborn essence or innate characteristics that stand apart from a perceived reality, for the normal vision of reality is basically distorted or modulated by the inbred stain of mental defilement. Dualistic perceptions, in general, and attachment to the notion of true personality and phenomena, in particular, are stated to be the incessant projection of one's mind. The only positive validity and the basis of function can be deduced from the simile that equates all perceived realities with magical scenes conjured up through a combination of factors that are unreal. The principle of modulated perceptive phenomena includes the perfectly altered mental state, i.e., the supremely enlightened awareness, and this cannot be identified with the former.

The third principle, namely the perfect state or ultimate reality of things (parinişpanna), is defined as being all-pervading space (dharmadhātu-śūnya), known as the suchness of void (tathatā-śūnya). It is the inconceivable aspect of all realities—conditioned and unconditioned—and the unifier of them into one flavor and one expanse. The unconditioned (ultimate reality) can be differentiated from apparent reality, even though the former remains impervious to the senses and unknown to an ordinary intellect, while the latter is perceived as real by an ordinary mind. This is because apparent reality is nothing more than a fanciful notion, just like the form of a horse conjured up by a magician. The conditioned and unconditioned, the apparent and ultimate, cannot be two complete realities, but have to be two aspects of one, for the inconceivable void remains the intrinsic state of apparent reality. Analyzed deductively, the apparent lacks the intrinsic marks (essence) and thus excludes the possibility of any true dualism. However, it is important for one who follows the middle-path (madhyamaka) vision of reality to note that the unreality of the apparent does not mean its total negation, as in the case of a nihilistic standpoint. A nonerroneous inference and contemplative analysis can show that the apparent has only relative validity, since it arises from the natural contrivance brought about by the incessant interaction of causes and conditions.

What is the ultimate state in terms of the human mind? The suchness of the void in the final analysis means nondual simplicity, which is the object of realization. The term "perfect state" (parinişpanna) denotes the ultimate, immutable, all-pervading space which is "the suchness of the void." When perceived inferentially in a higher contemplation, the suchness of the void has to be understood as being not merely the natural emptiness of true essence or "dual entities," but also as all-pervading space that encompasses everything from perceived matter to supreme enlightenment. This represents the perfect self-realization process as true insight and supreme virtue.

"Ultimate meaning" (Skt. nītārtha, Tib. ngedön) refers to those teachings that can be read literally and that deal with the ultimate truth, the doctrine of emptiness (śūnyatā) and transcending awareness (jñāna). In short, all teachings that deal with the existential state (saṃsāra) contain the apparent meaning, whereas the teachings that deal with enlightenment (sambodhi or nirvāṇa) contain the ultimate meaning. The *Akṣayamatiparipṛcchā-sūtra* contains a complex differentiation of the apparent and ultimate meanings.

6. Lhachok Tumpo, usually known as Trowo Miyowa (Skt. Krodha-acala), is a wrathful meditation deity, white in color. Through devotion to and meditation on him, devotees will enhance the power of their intellectual faculties.

7. The list refers to the early masters of the quintessential self-realization. Saraha probably lived during the first and second century B.C.E. (See *The Royal Song of Saraha* in English translation with elucidating comments by Dr. Herbert V. Guenther, Seattle and London: Univ. of Washington Press, 1969.) Besides Saraha, the following are the early teachers of the self-realization tradition:

Nāgārjuna	2nd century B.C.E.
Śavari	2nd century B.C.E.
Tilopa	988–1069
Nāropa	1016–1100 (see *The Life and Teaching of Naropa*, translated by H. V. Guenther)
Maitrīpa	1012–1097
Marpa	1012–1099
Milarepa	1040–1123

8. This refers to Gampopa (1079–1153).

9. The Buddha's prophecy is found in the *Samādhirāja-sūtra*.

10. The "three spheres of the universe" are the form world (kāmarūpa), the superior form (rūpadhātu), and the formless state (ārūpadhātu).

11. The "dharma of the ultimate reality" refers to mahāmudrā.

12. "Mysticism" or Mantrayāna refers to the doctrine and meditation of the mystic yoga of Vajrayāna, the adamantine vehicle.

13. The Kagyü order of Takpo was founded by Gampopa and gave rise to most of the other branches of the Kagyü order. Its only religious institution was the monastery of Taklha Gampo in South Tibet, which is now in ruins, one of the monasteries destroyed by Maoist radicals in the 1960s.

14. This refers to the original Buddhist scriptures, the sūtras and tantras combined to form the Kagyur (in 104 or 106 volumes). In Theravāda tradition, the epithet is tripiṭaka (the three containers), namely vinaya-, abhidharma-, and sūtra-piṭaka.

15. "Intrinsic reality" (Skt. samārtha, Tib. yangdak tön).

16. "The rabbit in the moon" refers to an ancient fable about the visible shadow in the moon.

17. The ten dharma practices (Tib. chöchöchu, spelled chos-spyod bcu; Skt. daśacārya-dharma) are (1) writing down (the dharma), (2) reading, (3) reciting, (4) listening, (5) examination, (6) contemplation, (7) meditation, (8) worship of the three jewels, (9) the shunning of possessions, and (10) teaching.

18. Guru Śabareśvara is identical with Śavari, who was mentioned among the early masters of the self-realization tradition.

19. "Sediment of impressions" (Tib. pakchak, spelled bag-chags; Skt. vāsana) refers here specifically to a negative psychic imprint. The term "pakchak" generally means a psychic imprint latent in the store-consciousness (ālayavijñāna) of every individual and also connotes the seed, the generative force, or the potential. According to the idealist school of Buddhism (cittamātravādin or vijñānavādin, the exponents of consciousness only) pakchak means the generative force of good, bad, or neutral imprinted upon an individual's store-consciousness through the imputed senses and particularly through the all-pervading notion of a self. Such a psychic imprint is described as being a steady stream. When not consciously activated through negative or positive will and action, it remains dormant, like a seed detached from soil, moisture, and air, manifesting neither good nor bad. Hence it is regarded as a neutral subtle consciousness. Of the numerous kinds of psychic imprints there are three worth mentioning: (1) the conceptualized psychic imprint of the store-consciousness, from which arise conceptually designated phenomena such as form, sound, etc.; (2) the dualistic psychic imprint, from which arises the appearance of self and others; and (3) the positive or negative psychic imprint, which is the cause of existential life and from which the cycle of rebirth and death arises.

The following short description of the psychic imprints is intended to illustrate the diverse views of sister schools on the aspects of mind and reality. They should in a sequential order lead a student toward an ever higher doctrine and an eventual resolution through more refined investigation and contemplation. To begin with, the idealist school holds that the store-consciousness, which accumulates psychic imprints, is the causal consciousness. When the dualistic consciousness arises from the store-consciousness, this is considered to be the resultant consciousness. Thus, the two are interrelated as cause and effect. The exponents of independent reality (svātantrika-mādhyamika) hold that only the stream-consciousness—not the store-consciousness—fulfills the two phases of the psychic imprint and projection. Hence the identity of cause and effect. The exponents of critical reductionism (prāsaṅgika-mādhyamika)—while rejecting both the store-consciousness and the stream-consciousness as an established reality in terms of an independent or intrinsic entity—hold the "mere self" to be a conceptual stream that serves as the basis of a psychic imprint and subsequent projection.

20. This passage explicitly shows the idealistic position of the pure mind school of Buddhism (vijñānavāda), whose chief exponent was Asaṅga (4th century C.E.). He received the doctrine from Maitreya.

21. This text is written by Nāgārjuna.

22. "Thatness" (tattva) here means meditation in the highest sense. Such a meditation is a harmonious blend of tranquil absorption and awareness of tattva or "that very essencelessness" of all things.

23. The three kinds of enlightenment (tribodhi). The first level of enlightenment is attained by the śrāvakas (awakened listeners); the higher enlightenment is attained by bodhisattvas; the highest enlightenment is attained by buddhas, according to *Abhisamayālaṃkāra*, a treatise which condenses the Mahāyāna teachings of the Prajñāpāramitā series.

BOOK ONE

1. The five treatises of Maitreya are:

The *Dodegyen* (*Sūtrālaṃkāra*)
The *Ngöntokgyen* (*Abhisamayālaṃkāra*)
The Üthanamje (*Madhyānta-vibhaṅga*)
The *Chödang Chönyi Namje* (*Dharmadharmatā-vibhaṅga*)
The *Gyülama* (*Uttara-tantra-śāstra*)

The treatises of *Sade* by Asaṅga are:

The *Sa'i ngöshi* (This is the collective title of four other texts such as the *Bodhisattvabhūmi*, etc.)
The *Shiduwa* (*Vastusaṃgraha*)
The *Namdrang Duwa* (*Paryāyasaṃgraha*)
The *Nampar Shepa'i goduwa* (*Vivarṇasaṃgraha*)
The *Nampartenla Uppaduwa* (*Viniścaya saṃgraha*)

Added to these ten titles are ten more treatises which form what is known as "The Twenty Treatises on Maitreya's Teachings." They were written down or composed by his disciple Asaṅga. Most of these treatises deal with the idealistic philosophy (vijñānavādin), while some are mixed with the middle path philosophy (madhyamaka). The *Ngöntokgyen* contains the madhyamaka doctrine known specifically as "wisdom-gone-beyond" or transcendental wisdom (prajñāpāramitā).

2. Tathāgata (Tib. deshin shekpa) is one of the epithets that indicate the rank of all buddhas and their supreme attainments. The word "tathā" is derived from a metaphysical term, "tathatā" (Tib. deshinnyi), which means "that very suchness" or "the suchness of the void." This implies the ultimate reality of all things. While the suchness of the void perceived by the buddhas negates the existence of an absolute essence, it is regarded as being the natural simplicity and primal ground of both ordinary and enlightened minds, the realization of which is signified by the second word, "gata," meaning "having realized" or "reached" by means of transcendental wisdom. This epithet epitomizes the mystic letters of wisdom-gone-beyond (dhāraṇī of prajñāpāramitā). The full rationale and metaphysical background is available in the *Prajñāpāramitā-sūtras* and the commentaries generally known as *abhisamayālaṃkāra-ṭika* by great lamas of the various orders of Tibetan Buddhism.

3. Mental image: Tib.: mikpa, spelled dmigs-pa; Skt. vikalpa.

4. Sensual incitement: Tib. göpa, spelled rgod-pa; Skt. auddhatya. The term "göpa" has been defined by Tsongkhapa in his *Changchup Lamrim Chenmo* (Tibetan folio 338 back, line 6) as "an outflowing thought attracted toward sense objects." Hence the term has been rendered as "sensual incitement." Some recent publications rendered it as "excitement," which usually means a stirred-up feeling or a sensation arising from any extraordinary event, including a violent situation. "Excitement" here is inaccurate, as it lacks that specific quality. It may be noted, however, that all

outflowing thoughts, including excitement, are covered by another Tibetan term, "trowa" (spelled 'phro-ba).

5. Resentment: Tib. gyöpa, spelled 'gyod-pa; Skt. upanāha.

6. Sluggishness: Tib. mukpa, spelled rmugs-pa; Skt. styāna. This term has sometimes been rendered as "lethargy."

7. Perfect ease: Tib. shinjang, spelled shin-sbyangs; Skt. suvinit or prapraddhi.

8. Sthiramati was a disciple of Vasumitra.

9. Memory: Tib. trenpa, spelled dran-pa; Skt. smṛti. Though in this case the term "memory" is used, its definition is applicable to the popular "mindfulness." The latter is preferred by most teachers and scholars, since it indicates a continued mental focus on any chosen object (either concrete, abstract, or formless), and on the precepts as well as on the enlightened qualities.

10. Vigilance (Tib. sheshin, spelled shes-bzhin; Skt. nvadhantā) refers to the mind's ever-present concentration on a perceived image in tranquil meditation. Its specific function is to instantly detect either the emergence of a distraction in the form of a discursive thought or a fading of concentrative focus.

11. Mental exertion or thought formation: Tib. duje, spelled 'du-byed; Skt. saṃskāra.

12. Equanimity: Tib. tang-nyom, spelled btang-snyom; Skt. upekṣa.

13. Impermanence: Tib. mitakpa, spelled mi-rtag-pa; Skt. anitya.

14. Tranquility: Tib. shine, spelled zhi-gnas; Skt. śamatha. Insight: Tib. Lhakthong, spelled lhag-mthong; Skt. vipaśyanā.

15. Nonconceptual: Tib. nampar mitokpa, spelled rnam-par mi-rtog-pa; Skt. avikalpa or nirvikalpa.

16. Illuminated Conqueror: Tib chomdende, spelled bcom-ldan-'das; Skt. bhagavan. This term has sometimes been rendered as "Illuminated Subduer."

The Tibetan equivalent of the Sanskrit "bhagavan" is "chomden." The ancient dharma translators of Tibet added one definitive term, "de." The purpose of doing so was to confine this modified term uniquely to Buddha and to distinguish it from its common application to Hindu gods and teachers. The Tibetan descriptive terms usually abound in meanings originating from the doctrinal treatises or the qualities embodied in each subject, as is this term, "chomdende." The syllable "chom" means the conquest of the four negative forces (caturmāra). That is, one conquers (1) the inner affliction and eliminates (2) the human inclination to deviate onto a false course, from a higher to a lower level; then one's immaculate attainment obviates (3) the force of death, and this breaking of the chain of rebirth brings about permanent freedom from (4) the force of the psychophysical burdens.

The second syllable, "den," means "being in possession of" (or realizing) enlightenment with all its transcendental qualities, of which the six principal ones are described here:

The power of spontaneous fulfillment
The perfection of the Buddha body
The suprasensory objects of the Buddha realm
The renown of the Buddha in this world
The transcendental awareness that perceives things in their diverse forms and as they truly are
Perfect assiduity in serving sentient beings

These qualities are described as being the natural result of Buddha's having perfected the six principles of transcending wisdom while still striving as a bodhisattva, which in turn brought forth the blossoming of the above six qualities in corresponding order.

The last syllable, "de," means "transcendental" and denotes that the qualities of Buddha are supreme and surpassing all that is worldly.

17. The nine steps of stabilizing the mind: Tib. semnegu, spelled sems-gnas-dgu.

18. The six principles of gone-beyond are limitless generosity, morality, tolerance, striving, tranquility, and wisdom.

19. Transformation (Tib. kyerim, spelled bskyed-rim; Skt. utpattikrama) and perfection (Tib. dzogrim, spelled rdzogs-rim; Skt. sampannakrama) refer to the higher esoteric meditations.

20. A yogin (Tib. naljorpa) is "one who devotes himself to the path of true yoga or who has reached the mind's primal purity."

21. A bodhisattva is a highly attained person who choses to reincarnate again and again in order to guide humanity toward liberation. The epithet is also applicable to any potential bodhisattva from the moment he or she accepts the vow of an enlightened mind (bodhicitta) and practices the precepts and teachings on the path and goal of a bodhisattva. An arhat is a highly attained monk who sought and realized the personal liberation from inner bondage of self and defilement.

22. The six spheres of sentient beings are:

The sphere of celestial beings
The sphere of subcelestial beings (often referred to as demigods)
The sphere of human beings
The sphere of animals
The sphere of spirits (often referred to as hungry ghosts)
The sphere of afflicted beings (of the lower realm)

23. Psychophysical aggregates: Tib. phungpo, spelled phung-po; Skt. skandha.

24. Insight without mental activity: Tib miyowai lhakthong, spelled mi-gyo-ba'i lhag-mthong; Skt. acalavipaśyanā.

25. Conceptual perception: Tib. tshenmai chingwa, spelled mtshan-ma'i 'ching-ba.

26. Harmful psychophysical tendencies: Tib. nengen lengyi chingwa, spelled gnasngan len-gyi 'ching-ba.

27. The four levels of contemplation. The contemplative attainment on these levels is said to be similar to those attained on the four higher celestial realms on the plane of form (rūpadhātu). They are brahmaloka, prabhāsvara, kuśalapuṣati, and mahāphala devaloka, respectively. With the attainment of insight into the four aspects of the truth (catursatya), these four contemplative levels can achieve the transcending state. The four levels devoid of such insight are on the mundane state, which is typical of the higher celestial realms. The four contemplative levels with insight will lead to still higher contemplation, namely the four absorptive states and the final absorption (samāpatti). Thus, these nine levels constitute the fundamental sutric meditation. These four levels of contemplation correspond to the four heavens of the rūpadhātu (see next note).

28. The four heavens of rūpadhātu (the plane of higher form) are:

Tsangpa, spelled tshangs-pa
Ösel, spelled 'od-gsal
Gegye, spelled dge-rgyas
Drebu chelha, spelled 'bras-bu che-lha

29. "Their sons, the awakened hearers, and the lonely buddhas" (also rendered as solitary or silent buddhas) are equivalent in Sanskrit to the bodhisattvas, śrāvakas, and pratyekabuddhas.

30. The term "dharmakāya," literally "the body of all things," refers to the ultimate state of enlightenment. This highest level of enlightenment is thought of as unfolding, radiating, expressing itself (in roughly equivalent Western terms, as "emanating") throughout all levels of cosmic reality, including both the material world and the realms of subtle reality. In its latter manifestation it is the sambhogakāya; in the former, as an earthly incarnation of supreme reality, it is the nirmāṇakāya—Buddha present as a human body.

In the idea of dharmakāya one finds an expression of the Mahāyāna equation of consciousness (in its highest sense) and reality. Analytically speaking, dharmakāya is essentially composed of transcendent awareness and its inmost nature of emptiness. It is all-encompassing space, by no means perceivable or even thinkable by the ordinary, egoistically conditioned human mind. Dharmakāya is the substratum of all things and the source of all possibilities from immediate inner peace to the highest level of illumination. Dharmakāya's innate character of total simplicity and purity of awareness is what is ordinarily regarded as the state of nirvāṇa, the state in which the mind has wiped out transient "stains" of delusion and distortion. However, here it is not only a "subjective" state (as in Hīnayāna Buddhism), but the ontological reality. Being unconditioned, it is described as unborn, unlocalized, and indissoluble. Its character is such that it transcends discursive thought and can be neither designated nor discriminated against.

31. The "seven aspects" (Skt. saptadharma-Vairocana) refers to the ideal posture of the Dhyāni Buddha Vairocana. Depicted as the Supreme Illuminator, his form represents the most perfect of all forms. Its adaptation—after the initial hardship—will be beneficial to meditators. One should sit as follows:

1. Straighten the upper body and the spinal column.
2. Look slightly downward into the space straight across from the tip of the nose (while keeping the chin and the neck straight).
3. Straighten the shoulder blades evenly in the manner of a vulture flexing its wings.
4. Keep the lips touching gently.
5. Let the tip of the tongue touch the upper palate.
6. Form the legs into either the vajrāsana or padmāsana posture (the sacred scepter or lotus posture).
7. Keep the back of the right hand flat on the left open palm (just like two planks placed one upon another) with the inside of the tips of the thumbs gently touching.

32. The comprehensive visualization: Tib. khyappai mikpa, spelled khyab-pa'i dmigs-pa. The analytical meditation: Tib. cheypa namjong-gyi mikpa, spelled spyad-pa rnam-sbyong-gyi dmigs-pa. Skillful investigation: Tib. khepai mikpa; spelled mkhas-pa'i dmigs-pa. Meditation on the elimination of mental defilements: Tib. nyönmong namjong-gyi mikpa, spelled: nyon-mong rnam-sbyong-gyi dmigs-pa.

33. The twelve links (Tib.: tendrel chunyi, spelled: rten-'brel bcu-gnyis; Skt.: dvadaśa-pratityasamutpāda) are the following:

Ignorance (Tib. marigpa, spelled ma rig-pa; Skt. avijñāna or avidyā) about one's own identity gives rise to:
Karma formation or psychic generation (Tib. dhuje, spelled 'du-byed; Skt. saṃskāra), which activates:
Consciousness (Tib. namshe, spelled rnam-shes; Skt. vijñāna), which brings forth:
Psychosomatic form or embryo of life (Tib. mingzuk, spelled ming-gzugs; Skt. nāma-rūpa), which in turn leads to:
Six sense fields or impressions (Tib. kyeche druk, spelled skye-mched drug; Skt. ṣaḍāyatana), which arouse:
Feeling or contact with sense impressions (Tib. rekpa, spelled reg-pa; Skt. sparśa), causing:
Sensory stimuli (Tib. tsorwa, spelled 'tshor-ba; Skt. vedanā) to arise, resulting in:
Craving for sensory or sensual enjoyments (Tib. sepa, spelled sred-pa; Skt. tṛṣṇā) which inevitably turns into:
Clinging to life (Tib. lenpa, spelled lenpa; Skt. upādāna or prayavasthāna), completing the process of:
Coming into being (Tib. sipa, spelled srid-pa; Skt. bhava), which is:
Rebirth (Tib. kyewa; spelled skye-ba; Skt. jāti) of the psychophysical form, which inevitably leads to:
Decay and death, maturity and destruction (Tib. gawa chiwa, spelled rga-ba chi-ba; Skt. jarā-maraṇa).

The Tibetan wheel of existence depicts how individuals fare in steering the destiny of their lives through the cycle of existence. Reflecting the Buddhist concept of cosmic flux, the chart shows the uninterrupted continuity of an individual's stream consciousness and the evolutionary process of the cosmos. The first to the third link in the chain refer to the past life, the fourth to the eleventh appertain to the present, while the twelfth—death—is linked to the next life. The reversal of this process is the mastering of the path of liberation.

There is a direct corelationship between the chain of the twelve links and the four noble truths representing the basic doctrine of Buddha. The first and second noble truths, i.e., the noble truths of suffering and of the cause of suffering, are embodied in the twelve links of the wheel, whereas the third noble truth—the noble truth of eliminating suffering and its cause—means achieving nirvāṇa or permanent peace. The fourth noble truth—the noble truth of the path of the dharma—is inherent in the reversal of the chain.

34. The personal self (Tib. gangzaki dak, spelled gang-zag-gi bdag; Skt. pudagalātman) refers to the individual's intrinsic self. According to the basic doctrine of Buddha, the notion of and attachment to "self," which arises from inbred delusion, forms the root cause of an individual's cyclic existence (Tib. khorwa, spelled 'khor-ba; Skt. saṃsāra). Only by realizing the "nonselfhood" of the individual (Tib. gangzaki dakme, spelled gang-zag-gi bdag-med; Skt. pudgala-nairātmya) can meditators achieve liberation (Tib. tharpa; Skt. mokṣa). Such an insight into one's self will dawn through the development of superior discrimination, since it alone can eliminate the veil of self-delusion and all its attendant defilements, such as lust and hate.

Identification of the misconceived self is crucial to the meditational inquiry and the resultant awakening. Mahāyāna Buddhism, having refuted the concept of an independent eternal self (Tib. dak, spelled bdag; Skt. ātman) rejects two other notions of self: (1) existing upon the conjunction of an individual's psychophysical aggregates and (2) existing as an entity distinct from or nondependent on his psychophysical aggregates. The latter is a "normal" view held by every human being. Also, it should be noted that Buddha rejected the materialistic abnegation of a consciousness, a fundamental misconception that debases man to the level of inanimate matter.

Furthermore, Buddha, in his more advanced view known as the unreality of intrinsic phenomena (Tib. chökyi dakme, spelled chos-kyi bdag-med; Skt. dharma-nairātmya), rejected any substantive essence of the material phenomena. Thus the unreality of a dualistic essence (Tib. nyisu mepa, spelled gnyis-su med-pa; Skt. advaita) brought about an advancement of the Buddhist ontology and epistemology and far-reaching ramifications in the experience of the enlightenment spirit (Tib. changchupsem, spelled byang-chub-sems; Skt. bodhicitta).

35. The eighteen psychophysical elements (Tib. kham, spelled khams; Skt. dhātu) are the inherent elements of the body-mind aggregates which constitute a man. The term "kham" denotes the substratum or source, i.e., the sensory and psychical perceptions. The eighteen elements are (a) the six elements of the sense organs (eye, ear, nose, tongue, body, and mind), (b) the six elements of the sense objects (form, sound, smell, taste, touch, and the phenomena of composite and noncomposite things), and (c) the six elements of consciousness (eye consciousness, ear consciousness, nose consciousness, tongue consciousness, tactile consciousness, and mental consciousness). The eighteen elements are usually incorporated into or represented

by the twelve sense formations (Tib. kyeche, spelled skye-mched; Skt. āyatana), i.e., the senses are formed through the interaction of the six sense organs and six sense objects. The Abhidharma treatise (representing the Hīnayāna tradition) holds these elements to be essential realities, while the Prajñapāramitā (representing the Mahāyāna tradition) holds them to be unrealities being devoid of any intrinsic essence.

36. The sixteen subdivisions of the four noble truths deal with the right and wrong view of cyclic existence. Each truth is described in terms of four principles. The first truth, "all life is suffering," is further elucidated by four aspects. Life is:

1. impermanent,
2. the outcome of an individual's own karma and mental defilement,
3. yet is neither dependent upon nor controlled by suprapersonal power,
4. nor is endowed with a distinct self-essence.

The second Truth that "sufferings are generated by causes" is elucidated by four principles. The causes are:

1. a craving for sensory gratifications (according to Hīnayāna) and self-delusion (according to Mahāyāna), which brings forth:
2. the cycle of rebirth and death.
3. Such rebirth takes the level of a celestial, human, animal, spirit, or "afflicted" being, and
4. the immediate condition for every rebirth is the vigorous yearning for sensory pleasures.

The first and second truths reveal the wrong view of life. The next two truths with their descriptive principles will show the right view and the path to happiness. The third truth, "the elimination of suffering and its cause," is permanent peace (nirvāṇa). It is further elucidated by these four principles:

Nirvanic peace is the transcendental state detached from suffering.
Such peace is the result of one's having eliminated mental defilements.
It is completely virtuous and enduring purity.
It is a state of freedom through a nondegrading liberation.

The fourth truth, "the realization of the path," consists of four aspects:

It is the process of developing wisdom (Tib. sherap, spelled shes-rab; Skt. prajñā).
As a higher awareness it eliminates the clinging to self (Tib. dakdzin, spelled bdag-'dzin; Skt. ātmagraha).
It is a process of widening insight into the true reality.
It is the spiritual elevation to the nondegrading liberation.

The four noble truths also reveal the misconceptions regarding (1) the nature of existential life and (2) its cause, elimination, and process. The first noble truth shows the fourfold misconceptions that life is by nature (1) pure, (2) peaceful, (3) enduring, and (4) endowed with an independent, eternal self or soul. The second truth shows the four misconceptions, (1) that cyclic existence emerges without appropriate cause, (2) that it emerges due to a unitary cause such as an eternal reality, (3) that it is due to an immutable cause which manifests itself through mutable conditions, and (4) that it is created by a supreme creator. The third noble truth shows the four misconceptions (1) that spiritual liberation is nonexistent, (2) that it is perceived to be a stable substantive realm, (3) that the liberation sought by an individual, eternal soul is perceived to be the absolute reality, which remains the source of the illusory world, and (4) that there is only a temporary liberation and no permanant one. The fourth noble truth shows the four misconceptions: (1) that the process of liberation is perceived to be nonexistent, (2) that the perfect wisdom, which realizes true reality as devoid of self-essence, is thought of as a wrong path, (3) that there exists a path that is superior to the path of liberation, and (4) that the noble path of Buddha is incapable of eliminating the miseries of life.

37. This refers to the interaction between the six sense organs and six objects, namely the eye, ear, nose, tongue, body, and mind, and form, sound, smell, taste, touch, and all composite and noncomposite things.

38. Āryaśura is also known as Tayang (spelled rta-dbyangs; Skt. Aśvaghoṣa). Born in Kashmir, he was a learned teacher of Vedānta and was a realized devotee of Śīva. He defeated many Buddhist teachers of Kashmir and was himself finally defeated by the incomparable Āryadeva, the foremost disciple of Nāgārjuna. Having fallen into a limbo—not being able to abandon his own faith and embrace that of his conqueror, as was originally agreed upon by both contending parties—he took his own time. It was during this period of contemplation and study that a sudden awakening overwhelmed him so that he embraced Buddhism as one who truly understood it. Soon he mastered the great Buddhist treatises and became no less revered and realized a teacher than his conqueror. Among his numerous works were the most popular poetic composition *Kyerap Soshipa* (spelled skyes-rabs so-bzhi-pa; Skt. *Caturtriṃsat Jātaka*) and the *Sangyekyi Chöpa* (spelled sangs-rgyas-kyi spyod-pa; Skt. *Buddhacarita*).

39. Bodhibhadra (Tib. Changchup Zangpo). It is rather difficult to identify this teacher since there were many by the same name. The author in this case could well be the lay Buddhist (upāsaka) who not only mastered the sūtras and tantras but also became a realized teacher (according to *The History of Buddhism in India* by Tāranātha). The quote here comes from the *Samādhisambhavā-parivarta* (Tib. *Tingdzin Tsokkyi Leu*, spelled ting-'dzin tshogs-kyi le'u).

40. "Khaṭvāṅga" refers to a mystic's staff, symbolizing the highest aspects of the rapid path and living enlightenment, according to the unsurpassed stream of Buddhist tantra (Tib.: sangngak lame; Skt.: anuttara tantra). In its quintessential form the mystic staff symbolizes the efficient methods for integrative transformation of an individual's psychophysical form into the indivisible state of "illusory form" and luminous awareness (Skt. māya-kāya; prakaśa-jñāna).

41. "A tiny imaginary symbol" refers to the visualized radiant body of Buddha or a luminescent syllable of a tiny size.

42. Candragomin was an upāsaka (lay teacher) of unmatched learning and attainment. A child prodigy born in South India, he was stated to have composed at the early age of seven an answer to an enigmatic poem composed by a formidable critic of Buddhism in order to challenge the Buddhist teachers to open debate, when even his learned father could not understand it. In the debate the child emerged triumphant and his reputation spread by leaps and bounds. He understood and absorbed the meanings of every doctrinal treatise by going though it once. Of the numerous treatises he himself composed, the concise Sanskrit grammar *Candravyākaraṇa* proved to be a clear elucidation of the well-known Sanskrit grammar *Pāṇnivyākaraṇa*.

43. The three forms of laziness are laziness, idleness, and indifference.

44. "Coarse defilements" usually refers to strong emotions such as the five poisons: delusion, lust, hate, conceit, and jealousy. "Subtle defilements" refers to secondary mental events. The Abhidharma lists some forty-eight of these, while the *Abhidharmasamuccaya* lists fifty-three.

45. This refers to the mind's intrinsic simplicity, i.e., the primal awareness that transcends dualism.

46. Vasubandhu was great Buddhist teacher of the fourth century. He was the younger (half) brother of Asaṅga and was born at Purusapura (present-day Peshawar) in Gandhara, capital of Kanishka's kingdom. As the teacher of the Sarvāstivāda school of the Hīnayāna tradition, he composed the treatise *Abhidharmakośa*. Inspired by Asaṅga, one of the great teachers of Mahāyāna and an exponent of the idealistic school (Vijñānavāda), Vasubandhu later embraced Mahāyāna Buddhism.

47. Atīśa (Dīpaṃkara Śrījñāna) was a great eclectic teacher (born at Vikramaśīla in 982) known for his incomparable learning, moral purity, and boundless compassion. At the persistent invitation of the princes of western Tibet's Guge Kingdom, Atīśa visited Tibet and died at Nyethang, near Lhasa, in 1054, after seventeen years of service in the revival of Buddhism in Tibet. He propagated mainly the most important sutric teachings, known as the systematic paths to enlightenment. A vast body of moral and metaphysical teachings of the Hīnayāna and Mahāyāna traditions was systematized, summarized, and condensed clearly in his Sanskrit composition called the *Changchup Lamdrön* (spelled byang-chub lam-sgron; Skt. *Bodhipathapradīpa*), which was translated into Tibetan by Gewai Lodrö.

These sutric teachings, along with those of specific tantras such as *Thigle Cudruk* (spelled thig-le bcu-drug; Skt. *Ṣoḍaśabindu*), were popularized by his Tibetan disciples led by Domtönpa (1004–1064). Thus the new order of Buddhism known as Khadampa (comprehender of the Buddha's words) came into being. The sutric teachings—commonly known as lamrim (paths to enlightenment)—were soon embraced by the older and newer orders of Tibetan Buddhism, including the Kagyüpa order. Great Tibetan teachers provided elaborate commentaries with the same name as the subject, "the systematic paths to enlightenment." For historical information, see "Buddhism in Tibet" by Lobsang Lhalungpa in *Path of Buddha*, edited by Kenneth Morgan (New York: Ronald Press, 1954).

48. Maitreya is the future Buddha, who according to tradition resides in the celestial Gaden (spelled dga-ldan; Skt. Tuṣita). He is said to have appeared before Asaṅga after the latter's nine years of contemplative quest and to have transmitted to him a series of Mahāyāna teachings. Asaṅga, the best-known Mahāyāna teacher after Nāgārjuna, lived in the fourth century. As a result of his undaunted efforts in the transmutation of knowledge into supreme realization, he is said to have had a mystical encounter with Maitreya. Thus completely awakened, Asaṅga composed what is known as the twenty-five treatises on the teachings of Maitreya. These masterpieces of Mahāyāna philosophy have immensely enriched the Buddha's teachings. The tradition hails Asaṅga not only as the great "charioteer" of Buddhist idealism and self-realization, but also as the great elucidator of the middle doctrine of Mahāyāna in the treatise based on the words of Maitreya and entitled *Sherchin Ngöntok Gyen* (spelled sher-phyin mgon-rtogs rgyan; Skt *Abhisamayālaṃkāra*). This represents the heart of Mahāyāna, enunciating directly the metaphysical doctrine of the all-encompassing void (Tib. chökün tongpanyi, spelled chos-kun stong-pa-nyid; Skt. sarva-dharma-śūnyatā), while indirectly showing the elaborate practice of universal compassion and the spirit of enlightenment (Tib. Changsem, spelled byang-sems; Skt. bodhicitta).

Maitreya and Asaṅga were the most revered teachers whose lineage of expanding application was one of the three enlightened lineages of lamrim. The other two are (1) the lineage of profound vision (arising from transcendental wisdom), whose principal inspirers and exponents were Mañjuśrī and Nāgārjuna, and (2) the lineage of inspirational blessings for self-realization, whose chief expounder was the mystical Buddha Vajradhara and whose chief propagators were Tilopa and Nāropa, among others.

49. "Madhyamaka" (Tib. umai tawa, spelled dbu-ma'i lta-ba) refers to the Buddha's ultimate view of reality (and not to the middle path approach to personal morality). The middle doctrine, while denying the conflicting concept of dualism—the absolute individual soul and the materialistic abnegation of stream-consciousness—holds as mutually compatible and nondual the complete unreality of all things and the appearance of reality which arises from the interactions of causes and conditions. The Madhyamaka doctrine of Buddha is enshrined in the Prajñāpāramitā sūtras. Its extracanonical literature, consisting of root texts, commentaries, critical elucidations, etc., by numerous Indian and Tibetan teachers, is quite extensive.

50. Candrakīrti (Tib. Dawa Drakpa, spelled zla-ba grags-pa) was a preeminent disciple of Nāgārjuna. While a monk at Nālandā monastery, he not only surpassed the others in mastering the complex doctrines of Buddhism and Brahmanism but became totally absorbed in his meditation. A formidable dialectician and metaphysician, Candrakīrti defeated many formidable dialecticians who were critics of Buddhism in open debates and composed many authoritative commentaries such as the *Umajukpa* (spelled dbu-ma 'jug-pa; Skt. *Madhyamakāvatāra*), the *Umatsiksal* (spelled dbu-ma tshig-gsal; Skt. *Madhyamaka-prasannapadā*) and others, which are masterpieces of Buddhist philosophy.

51. "The two 'selves' engender karma" refers to the way in which an individual

creates karmic causes for his cyclic existence. The primal cause is the individual's notion of true duality: the real self of personality and that of the phenomena. From a confused discrimination arises self-love (ego) which gives rise to craving for enjoyable sensory experiences and to displeasure or hatred for unpleasant sensory objects, as well as to pain brought about by the transitory changes in life and its environments. In short, karma is committed consciously in seeking to satisfy one's earthly desires and to fulfill egoistic designs, which includes employing diverse means of destroying anything standing in the way.

52. "Skillful means" refers to a bodhisattva's performance of the six principles of gone-beyond: generosity, morality, tolerance, striving, contemplation, and wisdom. Of these, the first five are devised skillfully as the practical application of love and compassion, while the last, discriminating wisdom, provides insight into the true nature of man and his world. These six principles are usually condensed into an indivisible path of compassion and wisdom. Thus, the joint mastery of the two represents the heart of Mahāyāna Buddhism.

53. Vision of reality: Tib. nelukky tawa, spelled gnas-lugs-kyi lta-ba; Skt. prakṛti-dṛṣṭi.

54. The innate nature of all things (Tib. chonyi, spelled chos-nyid; Skt. dharmatā) refers to the imperceptible all-encompassing void (Tib. chökün tongpanyi, spelled chos-kun stong-pa nyid; Skt. sarvadharma-śūnyatā). The void being the inseparable aspect of all appearances appertains to the intrinsic state that is empty of any true substantiality or essence and hence transcends all discrimination (Tib. trödrel, spelled spros-bral; Skt. sarvakalpanā-virahitam).

55. Nonarising: Tib. makyepa, spelled ma-skyes-pa; Skt. ajāla.

56. Liberation: Tib. tharpa; Skt. mokṣa.

57. The innate nature of the all-embracing expanse of reality: Tib. chöyinggyi rangshin, spelled chos-dbyings-kyi rang-bzhin; Skt. dharmadhātu-svabhāva.

58. Je Götsangpa (1180–1258) was one of the Tibetan mahāsiddhas. He founded the Tödruk subschool of the Drukpa Kagyüpa order.

59. Exhaustive analysis: Tib. chepa namjong, spelled dpyad-pa rnam-sbyong.

60. Defilement: Tib. nyönmong, spelled nyon-mongs; Skt. kleśa.

61. Analytical investigation: Tib. chegom, spelled dpyad-sgom.

62. Inner diversion: also rendered as sensual incitement; Tib. göpa, spelled rgod-pa; Skt. auddhatya.

63. Master Jñānagarbha composed the root text and the commentary of the *Dennyi Namje* (spelled bden-gnyis rnam-'byed; Skt.: *Satyadvaya-vibhaṅga*). He seems to have lived in the period after Ācārya Bhavya and before Śāntarakṣita.

64. Nonsubstantiality of dualism: Tib. dentong.

65. Nonconceptual awareness: Tib. mitok yeshe, spelled mi-rtog ye-shes; Skt. avikalpajñāna.

66. Determinate awareness: Tib. ngeshe, spelled nges-shes; Skt. nirūpana.

67. Inferential judgement: Tib. jepak; spelled rje-dpag; Skt. anumāna.

68. The stream of nondiscriminating mindfulness: Tib. mitokpai drengyun, spelled mi-rtog-pa'i dran-rgyun; Skt. nirvikalpa-smṛti-tantra.

69. Visualized image: Tib. mikpa, spelled dmigs-pa; Skt. pratilambha.

70. Discerning Wisdom: Tib. sosor tokpai sherap, spelled so-sor rtogs-pa'i shes-rab; Skt. pratisamaya-prajñā.

71. Meditational equipoise: Tib. nyamshak, spelled mnyam-gzhag; Skt. samāhita.

72. A complete rendering of this passage has not been made since it appears in the extract above.

73. The Hwashang school was a purely contemplative branch of Chinese Ch'an Buddhism, taught by Master Hwashang Mahāyāna at Samye, Tibet's first eclectic monastery, built in the eighth century under the patronage of King Trisong Detsen. It was during this critical formative period of Tibetan Buddhism, when the two founders of Samye Monastery were no more—Śāntarakṣita having died and Padmasambhava having departed from Tibet—that the Chinese Master Hwashang Mahāyāna attracted a growing number of Tibet's elite and ordinary people to his system of Buddhism. The adherents of Indian Buddhism charged that the Chinese system completely ignored the requisite moral foundation, intellectual preparation, and practical applications.

In an atmosphere of rivalry and even hostility between the two sister schools of Buddhism, the Tibetan king ordered a public debate between the Chinese master and the newly invited Indian teacher Kamalaśīla (to whom his teacher, the late Śāntarakṣita, had assigned this task in his prophetic testimony). The Tibetan historical records of the event state that the Chinese master, who specialized in pure contemplation, was defeated by the great eclectic Kamalaśīla with his proven skill in debate. The defeat was gracefully acknowledged when Hwashang offered a flower garland to the Indian teacher. However, Kamalaśīla was later assassinated and the culprit escaped. As a corollary to this tragic event in an otherwise civilized contest of knowledge, the Chinese side subsequently seems to have produced some controversial written material depicting the outcome of this historical saga in their favor.

The immediate result of the debate was the royal decree banning the propagation of the purely contemplative system in Tibet. Indian Buddhism with its Madhyamaka was proclaimed the state religion. However, centuries after the disappearance of the Hwashang system, the problem of his influence persisted. Great Tibetan teachers of various historical times charged other Tibetan religious orders with following the Hwashang system, especially the pure contemplation, which they contended was nothing more than a suppression of the senses and thoughts while focusing on the dark realm of consciousness. Sakya Paṇḍita (1181–1251) was perhaps the first of such open critics of that system. Reading his *Three Distinctive Commit-*

ments to the Precepts (Tib. *Domsum Rabye*), one gets the feeling that he was criticizing certain trends in the Kagyüpa and Nyingmapa meditation rather than the Mahāmudrā and Mahāsampanna (Chakchen Dzokchen). He says, "Ignorant ones who meditate on mahāmudrā may well be creating a cause to be reborn as animals."

74. The three marks of syllogism are:

1. A subject matter or topic of debate
2. An irrefutable conclusion
3. An inferential logic on which the conclusion is based

This is one of the dialectical methods used in meditational training in order to gain true knowledge about mind and material phenomena. The pronouncement of a topic is immediately followed by a statement of the conclusion. A straightforward inference ensues to show how a flawless logic arrived at that conclusion. For instance, the topic "the selves (entities) of individual and the phenomena are unreal because they are devoid of any intrinsic or real entities whatsoever."

75. The path of dialectics: Tib. toggai lam, spelled rtog-ga'i lam: Skt. tarkka-mārga.

76. Primal cognition: Tib. ngönsum, spelled mngon-sum; Skt. pratyakṣa-pramāṇa.

77. Confused by duality: Tib. tsurthong, spelled mtshur-mthong.

78. The void of supreme form refers specifically to a higher meditational state in which a meditator simultaneously achieves the elevation of his ordinary mind to a luminous awareness (Tib.: ösel, spelled 'od-gsal; Skt.: prabhāsvara) and of his inmost vision of the body to a supreme illusory form (Tib.: gyulü, spelled sgyu-lus; Skt.: māyā-kāya). The perfect example of this state is an enlightened master and is described by such nondualistic terms as "the union of sublime form and mind" and "the nondual state of luminous awareness and the illusory body" (Tib.: gyulü ösel zungjuk, spelled sgyu-lus 'od-gsal zung-'jug; Skt.: māyā-kāya-prabhāsvara-yoga). (The Sanskrit term was composed by the translator.)

79. The complex neuropsychical system, according to the Vajrayāna tradition, is a microcosmic power center consisting of lower and higher levels or active and passive, worldly and supramundane levels. To the former belong the dynamic nervous system, the energies, and the creative elements (known collectively as tsa-lung-thigle), which play a vital role in the body-mind function. The higher level consists of the central neuropsychic power source with six centers (known as tsa-uma and tsakhor druk). They remain inactive until awakened by a prolonged meditation of a special kind, such as the six yogas of the supreme tantra. Detailed information and secret instructions are given to practicing initiates.

80. This passage refers to the Gelukpa vision and meditation system established by its founder, the incomparable Tsongkhapa. This specific stanza is to be found in his *Songs of Enlightenment by Stages* (Tib. *Lamrim Nyamgur*, spelled lam-rim nyams-mgur).

81. Realm of peace: Tib. dedro, spelled bde-'gro. Realm of affliction: Tib. ngendro, spelled ngan-'gro.

82. The *Dharmadhātu-stava* was composed by Nāgārjuna.

83. Conceptual reality: Tib. tshenma, spelled mtshan-ma; Skt. lakṣaṇa or liṅga.

84. This refers to the texts containing the teachings of Maitreya, as recorded in writing by his disciple Asaṅga.

85. The "Two Great Chariots" refers to Nāgārjuna and Asaṅga as founders of the central philosophy (madhyamaka) and the mind-only-school (vijñānavāda).

BOOK TWO

1. The vehicle of metaphysical dialectics: Tib. tsennyi thekpa, spelled mtshan-nyid theg-pa; Skt. lakṣaṇa-yāna.

2. The esoteric vehicles of external performance and of physical and mental performance: Tib. chagyü, spelled bya-rgyud; Skt. kriyā tantra; and Tib. chögyü, spelled spyod-rgyud; Skt. caryā tantra.

3. Devoid of [self-nature], i.e., absolute emergence, endurance, and extinction: Tib. kyewa mepa, spelled skye-ba med-pa; Skt. anupati or ajanna; and Tib. nepa mepa, spelled gnas-pa med-pa; Skt. apratiṣṭhita; and Tib. gakpa mepa, spelled 'gag-pa med-pa; Skt. aniruddha.

4. Listening, examination, and meditation: Tib. thö-sam-gom-sum.

5. The twin purities: Tib. dakpa nyiden, spelled dag-pa gnyis-ldan; Skt. dviviśuddhi. This refers to the nature of enlightened mind. It is differentiated for intellectual understanding into two aspects (and not into two separate states):

> Its original nature of simplicity, usually referred to as the buddha nature (Tib. rangshin namdak, spelled rang-bzhin rnam-dag; Skt. prakṛti-viśuddhi)
>
> The purified state whose transitory defilements have been eliminated through the self-realization process

6. The quote apparently refers to the four spiritual levels: impure, impure, pure, and supremely pure. The first "impure" is often qualified as "very impure" (shin-tu ma dak), since it refers to saṃsāra. The second "impure" refers to the partially impure level of arhats. The third level, "pure," refers to the spiritual level of bodhisattvas. "Supremely pure" refers to the fourth level, that of the Buddhas.

However, the next two lines in the same quote clearly specifies three levels, omitting that of the arhats. There is really no contradiction, since in the Buddhist tradition arhats and bodhisattvas are usually categorized together into the broad rank of the enlightened lineage.

7. The four parts of mahāmudrā are:

> The mystical performance: Tib. lekyi chakgya, spelled las-kyi phyag-rgya; Skt. karmamudrā
>
> The spiritual bond or commitment: Tib.: Damtsikki chakgya, spelled dam-tshig-gi phyag-rgya; Skt. samayamudrā
>
> Awareness: Tib. yeshekyi chakgya, spelled ye-shes-kyi phyag-rgya; Skt. jñānamudrā
>
> Phenomena: Tib. chökyi chakgya, spelled chos-kyi phyag-rgya; Skt. dharmamudrā

8. "The seal of the great mother" is the literal rendition of a rarely used Tibetan term in which the masculine particle at the end of the word of "mahāmudrā" is changed to the feminine particle "mo." Thus the term is "chakya chenmo" (phyag rgya chen mo). The traditional designation of "mother" is appropriate for a treatise

or a doctrine on ultimate reality, emptiness. In the same way, the term "great mother" is applied to the doctrine of wisdom gone-beyond (Skt. prajñāpāramitā) and also to the notion "expansive emptiness" (Tib. chöying; Skt. dharmadhātu).

Readers may wonder why this quotation contradicts the content of other quotations immediately before and after it. The author, Tashi Namgyal, through these quotations, shows the mahāmudrā to be superior to and purer than other tantric methods that allow the initiate to engage in sexual union with a female consort with the express purpose of sublimating his sensual experience to nondual awareness. Review of the quotation (which is translated exactly and literally from the original) shows this tantric tendency as being in direct contradiction with the simpler and purer approach of mahāmudrā.

9. "The inner consort of manifest awareness" (Tib. lekyi chakgya; Skt. karmamudrā) in this case refers to a female counterpart in the mystic performance of the tantra, according to the supreme tantra (Skt. anuttara tantra). This particular practice was employed by some great mystics (mahāsiddhas) in the past. In Tibet it was generally discouraged, and in any case no celibate monk or lama was allowed to practice it. Many great teachers opposed it on the ground that it could not be interpreted literally, since the higher tantric texts are purposely written in a peculiar language that must be deciphered through the six modes and four methods. The true meaning of the concept appertains to the integration of higher psychophysical elements, energies, and creative forces inside and around an individual human body. The term "karmamudrā" in the lower tantras, such as kriyā, caryā, and yoga tantra, means a ritual hand gesture.

10. The order to these practices in Tibetan Buddhism is the other way around, i.e., the mudrā of visualized transformation comes last.

11. This "certain teacher" refers to Sakya Paṇḍita (1181–1251). The quotation comes from his *Differentiating the Three Precepts* (Tib. *Domsum Rabye*, spelled sdom-gsum rab-dbye).

12. The great Saraha is the celebrated mahāsiddha Saraha; the lesser Saraha is perhaps Śavari.

13. "Indivisible mind" refers to the enlightened mind, a perfect state whose innate void and immutable bliss are indivisible.

14. The two stages of esoteric meditation: Tib. kyerim and dzokrim, spelled bskyed-rim and rdzogs-rim; Skt. utpattikrama and sampannakrama. The reference to avoiding the two stages of esoteric meditation and also the incantation of sacred syllables can be taken literally to mean what the passage says. The valid reason for avoiding them lies in the fact that one is already being trained in the more simple but effective mahāmudrā meditation.

15. "Devī" is synonymous with "Ḍākinī."

16. The inner fire: Tib. tummo; Skt. caṇḍālī.

17. *Kālacakra*, *The Cycle of Time*, belongs to the nondual class of the supreme tantra

(anuttara tantra). The original tantra was revealed by Buddha to King Sucandra of Shambhala. The *Kālacakra* literature is to be found in the Tibetan Kagyur and Tengyur, as well as in the collected works of great lamas such as Jonangpa Tāranātha, Butön, Tsongkhapa, Khedrupje, some of the Panchen Lamas, etc. The salient features of the *Kālacakra* doctrine are the tricentric realms (Tib. chinang shensum, spelled phyi-nang gzhan-gsum). The external and internal cycles of time (Tib. chidükyi khorlo, spelled phyi-dus-kyi khor-lo; Skt. antara-kālacakra) refer to the material and psychophysical cosmos, which are the manifestations of the physical and psychical energies. The *Kālacakra* astronomy and astrology deal with the role and function of both the macrocosm and microcosm. The constant interplay and interaction of these cosmic energies not only sets in motion the process of evolution and determines its form and course, but also continually influences their functions. The microcosm, e.g., the psychophysical realm of humans, remains prone to the influence of the interplanetary conjunctions and macrocosmic energies, which strengthen the negative energies within man's psychophysical system. Thus the power of self-delusion, ego, and hatred is strengthened.

The doctrine and practice of *Kālacakra* is the third cycle of time, a countervailing force against or a positive alternative to the twin cosmic cycles of time referred to earlier. The essence of the *Kālacakra* centers on the inward transformation of energies—the cosmic and psychoneurotic kinds. The transcendental *Kālacakra* is supreme purity and simplicity. In other words, this enlightened state unifies all perfect attributes, such as tranquility and insight, bliss and void, wisdom and compassion. Thus this essentially psychological doctrine and science of cross-cosmic and psychoneurotic energies is considered both relevant and effective for this age of crises and conflicts.

The *Kālacakra-tantra* was introduced into Tibet in 1033. During the first four centuries the *Kālacakra* was subjected to critical examination, both in its doctrinal and meditational aspects. Its gradual popularity was due largely to great lamas like Butön, Tsongkhapa, and Jonangpa. Successive Dalai Lamas and Panchen Lamas contributed to its universal acceptance and reverence throughout Tibet, Mongolia, and the Himalayan Buddhist regions.

18. This refers to Sakya Paṇḍita, and the quotation comes from his *Differentiating the Three Precepts* (Tib. *Domsum Rabye*, spelled sdom-gsum rab-dbye).

19. Even though half the passage, written in an equivocal form, reads, "The only change made was from its original designation 'the swooping down path' and 'the climbing up path' [Tib. yebab, spelled yas-bab; and medzek, spelled mas-'dzegs] to 'the path of sudden realization' and 'the gradual realization' [Tib. chikcharwa, spelled gchig-char-ba; and rimgyipa, spelled rim-gyis-pa]," my translation is based on the clearly stated passage in the commentary of the *Domsum*. According to this text, the Chinese Master Hwashang Mahāyāna, during the crucial debate with the Indian teacher Kamalaśīla at Samye monastery in the eighth century, used such descriptive terms for his system as "swooping down like an eagle" and "the omnipotent white path" (Tib. karpo chikthup). This means that this path is capable of bringing about a swift and sudden illumination. His description for the gradual path of the Indian system was the simile "climbing up like a monkey." (See the *Domsum Rabye* of Sakya Paṇḍita, ff. 75, l. 5).

It must be pointed out, however, that the Kagyüpa and the Dzogchenpa traditions contain the doctrines and the practices of both sudden and gradual realization. The two other traditions, Sakyapa and Gelukpa, generally do not accept the claim of sudden enlightenment by means of a simple nonconceptual meditation (which they characterize as being the meditation on a plain negation and suppression of the thoughts and senses). However, they do not exclude the possibility of sudden enlightenment for extraordinarily sensitive minds. The emphasis on gradual enlightenment is—they hold—not only logical and practical but natural. This is because the enlightening process is gradual. Purification of an individual's mental defilements and a joint development of compassion and wisdom are the gradual process, like the "waxing of the moon."

20. Interdependent arising: Skt. pratītyasamutpāda.

21. "The highest manifestation" generally refers to the supreme illusory form of the enlightened ones (Skt. rūpakāya) and specifically to the nirmāṇakāya and sambhogakāya (the earthly and mystical manifestations).

22. The author equates nonconceptual quietude with "nonconscious inertia, devoid of mindfulness and awareness"; but here the author is refuting himself, for one of the avenues to wisdom is mindfulness and awareness.

23. "By means of the third empowerment" refers to Sakya Paṇḍita's statement contained in his *Domsum* that a truly transcending awareness of mahāmudrā experience is attainable through the higher initiatory process involving yogic sexual union. The venerable Tashi Namgyal, in this passage, seems to refute the former, while claiming that such experience can only be realized through meditation on the mahāmudrā system. It is not presumptuous to state that these two conflicting systems are capable of leading to self-realization. To many, like Tashi Namgyal, the mahāmudrā system represents the best and simplest way to self-realization. Concerning the controversial topic of yogic sexual practice, there has been a good deal of misrepresentation and misuse in the Western world of this highly specialized method. It is a gross deception to believe that, with a little experience in basic meditation and bountiful energy, anyone can engage in a yogic sexual performance to heighten the ecstasy. This misguided self-indulgence not only profanes the sacred tradition but also defeats its real purpose.

Vajrayāna mysticism offers many proven choices to earnest initiates to actualize here and now an enlightened state manifesting as limitless compassion and transcending wisdom. The yogic sexual performance is—in theory—one of many choices before serious initiates. The tradition forbids it on moral grounds and also from a practical standpoint. This is not to say that it does not exist in practice. It remains a part—though not an indispensable one, and certainly not a regular practice—of the Dzogchen training. This tantric order, and perhaps a few mystics, uphold as valid both the symbolic and practical significance of sexual yoga. This is understandable since many of the Dzogchen teachers were and are married men and women or noncelibate mystics. The plausible reason for such exceptional nonconformity to the mainline tradition is that instantaneous self-realization must encompass an all-around transformation of one's stream consciousness, from the senses and thoughts to a subtle, psychic dream state, from psychoneurosis to the neuroenergy systems, from a notion of self-entity and deluded source consciousness to wild passions, lust, and hatred. The traditional description of turning poison into ambrosia signifies the metaphysical reorientation and the psychological sublimation of life. However, a word of caution is in order here: a great risk to health and mental stability is unavoidable, if half-trained initiates dare to venture into sexual yoga. The full benefits may be realized only by those who complete the advanced study of the supreme tantra (anuttara tantra) and years of rigorous training in the six branches of the higher yoga.

24. "Tathāgata" is one of the many epithets of the buddhas.

25. "Śāstra" (Tib. tenchö, spelled bstan-bcos) refers to the works of the Buddhist teachers other than the Buddha. The tradition defines a śāstra as embodying the doctrine that is capable of bringing about an inward transformation in every seeker from his deluded consciousness to an enlightened awareness.

26. "The three subtle cognitions" (Tib. nang-che-thop-sum, spelled snang-mched-thob-gsum) refers to the suprasensory manifestations of the psyche arising from three basic defilements: ignorance, lust, and hatred. Being deluded psychic energies, they arise in a sequential order as lights of white, red, and dark hues. The moment the dark hue dissolves, there emerges the individual's primal state or higher consciousness, metaphorically termed "luminous clarity," or specifically "an all-encompassing void with luminous clarity" (Tib. chöying ösel tongpa, spelled chos-dbyings 'od-gsal stong-pa; Skt. śūnya-dharmadhātu-prabhāsvara). It has been stated that an untrained or unenlightened mind fails to understand when these subtle psychic phenomena occur, either during an undisturbed natural dying process or during a certain (rare) moment while achieving an extraordinary sexual ecstasy. Only those who are perfectly trained in controlling the entire psychoneurotic energy system of their body can actualize these subtle psychic phenomena. Highly attained minds, however, are said to advance rapidly by harmonizing their attained state with the naturally luminous clarity during the period of their death, so that they either remain in a pure enlightened realm or are reborn at will, as a reincarnation, in order to carry on the spiritual ministration of humanity.

27. The four kinds of joy (Tib. gawashi, spelled dga-ba bzhi; Skt. caturānanda) are experienced during an uninterrupted meditative transformation of the neuropsychical energies into their purer forms, thus bringing about an illuminated awareness. This state is considered to be a model luminous clarity, which precedes true realization and which spontaneously unifies its great bliss and insight with its innate void. The four joys are joy, perfect joy, special joy, and spontaneously coemerging joy (Tib. gawa, chokga, khyepargyi gawa, lhenkye gawa).

28. "The secret enactment of the self-realization process" (Tib. tülshuk chöpa, spelled brtul-zhugs spyod-pa; Skt. parākācarya) generally refers to a kind of daring practice done with an irrational overtone in a wilderness area where a practitioner plunges himself into or encounters conditions of discomfort, distress, fear, and danger of various kinds. Such practitioners were yoga mystics who had lived for years in mountain solitude or caves and who were now in need of a rapid, powerful

impetus. With the approval and guidance of their initiatory master the mystics, having renounced their habitat, friends, and possessions, would wander around aimlessly as mendicants for a period of time, traveling into wilderness areas, valleys, villages, or towns. While inwardly awakened and peaceful, the yoga mystics would deliberately behave like crazy people—short of committing any crimes—in their manner of movement, speaking, eating, etc., so that they could inwardly purify all their residual fear, desires, selfishness, and dualistic delusions, accentuated by the ghastly and dreadful conditions they had encountered, and thus provide a rapid and powerful self-transformation. There are a few specific kinds of performances like this which need not be described here, since they do not concern mahāmudrā meditation.

29. The deductive formula that negates one or many self-entities of individuals (Tib. chigdu dralgyi rikpa, spelled gcig-du bral-gyi rigs-pa) is a method of investigating the notion of self-entity and is commonly used by every school of Buddhism as the principal among many investigative procedures in the analytical phase of insight meditation. All Buddhist schools are in agreement in their rejection of what Buddha himself called "extreme dualism," i.e., that of an eternal independent self (including the supreme creator postulated by some dogmas) and that of materialistic nihilism. The Buddhists are also agreed on the complete nonexistence of a "nondependent self-entity" perceived by the ordinary mind. It may be noted that for the advanced school of absolute reductionism (Tib. uma thalgyurwa, spelled dbu-ma thal-'gyur-ba; Skt. prāṣaṅgika-mādhyamika) this definition of self is inadequate, as it lacks the subtle notion of self. It is the form and manner in which man's inmost consciousness perceives it as being self-existing in its own essence or in its perceptive mark. The reductionists therefore analyze every inbred notion of self systematically, using authentic logical formulae and doctrinal aphorisms. Such intellectual determination provides a strong basis for a deeper quest through contemplation with its direct observation and determination of one's inmost stream consciousness. Only then can a serious meditator begin to understand the fanciful notion of self, which is without any reality whatsoever, either as one or as multiple entities. Once the object of rejection is so explored and understood, the meditator has taken a crucial step in understanding the mind.

30. "Thatness" (Tib. dekhonanyi, spelled de-kho-na-nyid; Skt. tattva) stands for "truth," which is interchangable with "void." Both concepts signify the unreality of all phenomena. Thatness of the truth or the void means the ultimate state of things, which is the unifying factor and the base of all possibilities arising from the interactions of causes and conditions. The void should in no way be confused with nonexistence as opposed to existence. These two stand as conflicting opposites or an unconnected duality.

31. "The entire eighty-four thousand forms of the dharma" refers figuratively or theoretically to the entire body of the Buddha's teachings, as enshrined in the collected sūtras and tantras. These large enumerations of dharma are stated to have been given as the antidotes for mental defilements. In practical application, the three essential doctrines on moral purity, contemplative quietude, and transcending

wisdom are collectively and separately antidotes for or countermeasures against the three mental poisons: ignorance (deluded consciousness), lust, and hatred.

32. Nivaraṇaviṣkambhi (Tib. Drippa Namsel, spelled sgrib-pa rnam-sel) is one of the eight bodhisattvas who received teachings from Buddha himself.

33. "Eating food that is natural and unmodified" refers to meditative absorption in the mind's natural and unaltered state.

34. "Liberation and enlightenment" indicates the attainment of arhathood and buddhahood (or sublime awareness and supreme awareness, respectively).

35. "Three years and three months" refers to a long tantric meditational retreat which actually extends to a period of three years, three months, and three days.

36. The city of Vidarbha is near modern-day Amraoti or Amaravati in South India, the birthplace of Nāgārjuna.

37. The Tibetan text refers to the five perfectly accomplished ones in the summation of the early hagiography without listing them individually. An earlier passage in the same text provides the names of individual teachers through whom the doctrine was handed down. Thus this collective designation seems to have been applied to the five preeminent teachers of the early lineage: King Visukalpa, Mañjughoṣa, Avalokiteś-vara, Saraha, and Nāgārjuna.

38. "The illusory form or the spacelike mystical form" generally refers to the "rainbow form" (Tib. jalü, spelled 'ja'-lus; Skt. indracapa). According to the Vaj-rayāna tradition, enlightenment consists of the dual aspects of the perfect illusory form and ultimate awareness. Terms such as "the illusory form" should not be conceived as consisting of a resplendent substance or a radiant form. Higher mani-festations are said to arise from a perfect transsubstantiation of a mystic's mortal body. The hagiography of every Tibetan Vajrayāna order provides the biographies of great mystics who had attained such a form of enlightenment. The highest of such manifestations is "a supercosmic illusory form" (Tib. longku, spelled longs-sku; Skt. sambhogakāya). The highest means of communication, it arises from the enlightened state of ultimate simplicity (Tib. chöku, spelled chos-sku; Skt. dharmakāya).

39. Śrīparvata refers to the sacred hill in South India (in the modern Indian state of Andhra Pradesh) were Nāgārjuna's monastery was located. Along with the foothill, the area, known as Nāgārjunakonda, is one of the holy places. The great Chinese monk-pilgrim Hiuen Tsiang visited it in the seventh century. The ruins of the Buddhist monastery and the stone sculptures were removed from this valley up to the hill, where they were installed in a modern museum in the late 1950s. The valley was then turned into a great modern reservoir for a hydroelectric project.

40. Cittavajra (Tib. thugkyi dorje, spelled thugs-kyi rdo-rje; Indivisible Mind) should not be confused with the name of one of the five dhyāni buddhas, Vajrasattva.

41. "The realm of ḍākinīs" refers to the tradition that these devotees attained

enlightenment through the rainbow forms (leaving virtually nothing of their earthly bodies behind).

42. The four mystic transmissions are the transmissions of:

The teachings and secret instructions of mahāmudrā meditation
The yoga of inner heat
The dream yoga
The yoga of illusory form.

In ancient times each transmission was handed down from one master to one disciple. Thus their separate lineages came into being and the great masters, then as now, inherited the secret transmissions.

43. A Repa is a cotton-clad mystic.

44. "Lucid awareness" refers to an individual's pure consciousness, which is detached from any dualistic discrimination. A perfect insight into the intrinsic void of reality, it is wisdom with clarity. This is one of those important points which have been misinterpreted in the West. The literal rendering of the original Tibetan term "ösel" (spelled 'od-gsal) as "clear light" seems to be the case. It is a metaphor, signifying an inbred clarity.

The Tibetan text (f. 204 B, l. 4) gives the following description:

> The meaning of ösel (clear light) consists of its being a natural state—detached from any absolute emergence or cessation and from any substance or element—and being unstained and immutable like spaces or nondifferentiable from it.

Furthermore, the common description "the void of clear light" (Tib. ösel tongpanyi, spelled 'od-gsal stong-pa-nyid; Skt. pratibhāsa śūnyatā) makes my point eminently clear.

45. "Kuberas" refer to a class of semicelestial beings. According to ancient mythology, they are gods of wealth who reside at the base of Mount Sumeru. Their chief is Vaiśravaṇa, one of the guardians of the Buddhist faith. He is usually depicted as yellow in color, seated on a lion in the northern realm of the world, and wearing a warrior's armor.

46. The three seekers are three types of devotees on the three levels of training and inner development. They are the lesser, average, and great seekers. The whole teaching of gradual enlightenment (lamrim) centers on these ideas.

47. *The Means of Realizing Coemergent Awareness* is a text called in Tibetan *Lhenchik kyejor* (spelled lhan-cig skye-sbyor; Skt. sahāja-yoga).

48. Pal Phagmo Drupa (1110–1170) was among the foremost disciples of the incomparable Gampopa and was the founder of the Phakdru Kagyü order. This order has no separate establishment anymore.

49. Je Tüsum Khyenpa (1110–1193) was the first Karmapa (the founder of the black hat Karmapa lineage). His reincarnation, Karma Pakshi (1206–1283), was the first

reincarnate lama with whom began the institution of incarnate lamas in Tibet. Before long, the tradition spread to all the other Buddhist orders. The successive Karmapas (up to and including the 16th, Rikpai Dorje, 1924–1981) played a vital role in spreading Tibetan Buddhism in Tibet, Mongolia, China, and in recent years the Western countries.

50. Mahāmudrā in five sections: Tib. chakchen ngaden; Skt. pañcavāti mahāmudrā.

51. In this passage the term "basis" (for meditation) was chosen since the Tibetan word "kangpa" (spelled rkang-pa) implies "basis" when used in an abstract sense.

52. Buddha, dharma, and saṅgha are commonly called "the three jewels." These are the three supreme refuges in Tibetan Buddhism.

53. "Skillful means" refers to practical humanistic principles, namely the perfection of generosity, morality, tolerance, and striving—all of which must be based on limitless compassion and transcending wisdom.

54. The Primary Vehicle is also called the Lesser Vehicle (Hīnayāna Buddhism).

55. Brahmaloka is the summit of heaven in Hindu mythology. Buddhism, while regarding it as being the highest celestial realm, does not equate it with liberation and enlightenment.

56. "Rūpakāya" refers to the earthly and the supramundane manifestations of the Enlightened Ones known as nirmāṇakāya and sambhogakāya respectively.

57. "The ten virtues of dharma" are also rendered as "the ten dharma practices" (see note 17 for "The Resolution to Compose This Work" in the Introduction).

58. The four ways of winning devotees (Tib. duwai ngöpo-shi, spelled bsdu-ba'i dngos-po-bzhi) are (1) to give gifts to devotees, (2) to speak delightfully, (3) to guide them in the practice of the six principles of gone-beyond, and (4) to set an example by practicing these principles oneself.

59. Bhavilha: Skt. Bhavi Deva.

60. "Realization deity" is the same as "meditation deity."

61. "Outer, inner, and inmost offerings" refers to kinds of offerings which consist of material, symbolic, and contemplative offerings. The outer ones consist of material offerings like juice, ablution of feet, flowers, incense, butter lamps, scent, cake, and music. In addition there are the offerings of the five sensory enjoyments: form, sound, scent, flavor, and touch. The inner offerings refers to a symbolic and contemplative "drink of ambrosia." Its material form is tea water or wine in a real or replica human skull. The content symbolizes the ten products of five sentient beings (animals and human beings). They are meditationally transsubstantiated into celestial ambrosia by the meditator's utterance of and meditation on the seed syllables of the five mystic buddhas and five enlightened female mystics (ḍākinīs). The inmost offering refers to a higher contemplative offering. This takes the form of an imagined or actualized state which embodies perfect bliss and transcending aware-

ness, arising from a contemplative transformation of the meditator's psychoneurotic energies and forces.

62. Yangönpa was a Kagyüpa eclectic mystic (1213–1258). A child prodigy, he stunned people in his native Latö (Tsang Province) by his spontaneous utterances of religious invocations and his ability to foretell unknown events. He became a disciple of Gyalwa Götsangpa. He also studied under eminent gurus of other orders such as Sakya Paṇḍita and Sangye Mikyö Dorje of the Nyingmapa order. Among his writings are the *Three Part Teachings in Mountain Retreat* and *The Six Mothers*.

63. The eight worldly emotions or reactions are grouped into two parts—positive and negative. The four positive emotions are to be pleased by pleasure, praise, gain, and delightful words; the four negative emotions are to be disturbed by displeasure, criticism, loss, and dreadful words. These emotions invariably arise from a deeper source—the mind's clinging to self.

64. The ordinations for lay devotees are what is in Tibetan called genyen (spelled dge-bsnyen; Skt upāsaka). The female devotee is a genyenma (spelled dge-bsnyen-ma; Skt. upāsika). One becomes a lay devotee once one has received, on one's own initiative, the fundamental precept of seeking refuge in the three jewels (the Buddha, the dharma, and the saṅgha or communities of enlightened and ordinary practitioners). Each devotee also accepts one or more precepts. The five basic precepts are (1) not to take life, (2) not to take anything that has not been given, (3) to abstain from any sexual misconduct, (4) to abstain from indulging in intoxicating drinks, and (5) not to lie. A person wishing to be a celibate lay devotee accepts the vow of celibacy in addition to the five basic precepts. Based on the number of precepts accepted, there are six categories of lay devotees.

65. The quintessence of reality: Tib. nyingpoi dön, spelled snying-po'i don; Skt. hṛdayārtha.

66. Ḍombipa is also known as Ḍombi Heruka. One of the great Buddhist mahāsiddhas, he was a contemporary of the great Candrakīrti.

67. The three spiritual brothers are Potowa, Phuchungwa, and Chenngawa, who lived in the eleventh century.

68. "The meditational stages of the sūtra" refers to the theory and practice of tranquility and insight, which originate from the sūtras.

69. "The natural foundation of existence" refers to the fundamental nature of mind, which is the indivisible state of awareness and its intrinsic void (Tib. riktong yerme).

70. The vajra posture is the way Buddha images are seated.

71. The bodhisattva posture is the way the bodhisattva Siṃhanāda Avalokiteśvara is depicted, with the right leg slightly outstretched and the left curved inward toward the right knee. This is often referred to as "the royal rejoicing posture."

72. Contemplative hand postures are the same as mudrās.

73. Thermal energy: Tib. menyam, spelled me-myam; Skt. samāna. Diffusive energy: Tib. khyabje, spelled: khyab-byed; Skt. byāna. Vital life energy: Tib. sokzin, spelled srog-'dzin; Skt. prāṇa-graha. Ascending energy: Tib. gyengyu, spelled gyen-rgyu; Skt. udāna.

74. The "enlightening spirit" refers to the creative elements or sexual energies (Tib. changchup kyisem, spelled byang-chub-kyi sems; Skt. bodhicitta). Its full description is "the white enlightening spirit" (Tib. changsem karpo, spelled byang-sems dkar-po; Skt. sita-bodhicitta).

75. The "dogmatists or hostile critics" refers to different orders within the Indian Brahmanic system. Buddhist texts refer to them as "dogmatists" (Skt. tīrthika).

76. Supranormal cognition: Tib. ngönshe, spelled mngon-shes; Skt. abhijñā.

77. See note 38 for Part One.

78. The life breath is the same as the vital life energy mentioned earlier.

79. Subtle dullness: Tib. chingwa tramo, spelled bying-ba phra-mo.

80. *Tüshi Nyamjor*, spelled du-bzhi myam-sbyor; Skt. Catuḥ-samata-yukti.

81. "Sensual incitement" is sometimes rendered as "thought flow."

82. Approximate tranquility: Tib. shine jethünpa, spelled zhi-gnas rjes-mthun-pa; Skt. anuloma śamatha.

83. Mundane and supramundane: Tib. jikten and jiktenle depa, spelled 'jig-rten and 'jig-rten-las 'das-pa; Skt. loka and pratālloka.

84. The four feet of miraculous power (Tib. dzutrülgyi kangpa shi, spelled rdzu-'phrul-gyi rkang-pa bzhi; Skt. catur-ṛddhi-pāda) are the specific methods of achieving a perfect absorption. They are:

The feet of miraculous enthusiasm
The feet of miraculous endeavour
The feet of miraculous concentration
The feet of miraculous discernment

85. The eight levels of absorption on the plane of sublime form and the formless plane: Tib. samten gye, spelled bsam-gtan brgyad; Skt. aṣṭa samāpatti. This means that each plane consists of four levels. All those on the mundane level collectively constitute a tranquil consciousness or contemplation. Of the eight levels of absorption the first four are on the plane of sublime form and the next four on the plane of formlessness. The mastery of the first four brings about an absorptive state accompanied by a sense of equanimity, a good memory (mindfulness), and a stable mental evenness. In mastering them one eliminates the intellectual process of examination, the flow of normal thought and breath. One then attends to the next four levels on the formless plane: (1) by separating the mind from the perception of form one focuses on the infiniteness of form, (2) by going beyond the infinite space one concentrates on the infinitude of consciousness, (3) by transcending even the realm of consciousness

one perceives pure nonexistence, (4) by extending the third level one reaches an unidentified absorption characterized as being neither perceptive nor nonperceptive. These states are obtainable not only on the higher planes of form and formlessness but also on the plane of desire.

When not integrated with the understanding of the four noble truths, these concentrated levels remain in the mundane realm characterized as that which is associated with sensory outflow. When all contemplative levels—barring the last one—form the support for meditation on the four noble truths, and when insight into them has dawned, they attain to the supramundane state. The last absorptive state, though designated as the summit of the existential realm, cannot be used as the support for higher meditation, since the mind is deeply engrossed in the ecstasy of absorption to such an extent that it lacks clarity and sensitivity. This imperfect contemplation is the result of a faulty meditation done by such a meditator in his past life. On the other hand, humans on the plane of desire become arhats (exalted ones) by breaking the subtle bondage of ecstatic absorption and thus achieve nirvāṇa.

86. The eight processes of liberation (Tib. nampar tharpagye, spelled rnam-par thar-pa brgyad; Skt. aṣṭa-vimokṣa) are aimed at eliminating any residual sensual imprints. They cognize (1) the existence and (2) the nonexistence of one's form aggregate (Tib. zuk, spelled gzugs; Skt. rūpaskandha) and then perceive every external form as devoid of beauty. (3) They cognize every form as beautiful and then produce forms of beauty by means of contemplative power. These must lead to an understanding that all forms of beauty and ugliness are but mental designations. The remaining processes of liberation (from 4 to 7) refer to the effect of four contemplative cognitions on the formless plane, which clear any residual sensual attachment that originated from previous association with the planes of form and desire. (8) This process, known as the "liberated state of cessation," consists of such a deep absorption that all outflows arising from the psychoneurotic and sensory activities cease completely. Being the supramundane path, this is sought and achieved only by realized meditators, namely arhats. This exalted state can reach its ultimate perfection as a fully enlightened awareness (buddhahood).

87. The eight overpowering contemplative manifestations (Tib. zilnön gye, spelled zil-gnon brgyad; Skt. aṣṭau abhibhvāyatanāni) are the exercises of contemplative power attained by arhats. The first two consist of performances overpowering small and large forms (microcosm and macrocosm) by inwardly cognizing the forms of sentient beings and the material world. The third and fourth refer to the overpowering of these two forms in their diverse shapes by contemplating the nonexistence of the forms. The next four cognitive transmutations refer to the overpowering of lights in four colors: blue, yellow, white, and red. Thus the power of contemplation can cause forms and lights to emerge before others, while the realized performer remains free from any attachment to forms and lights. Arhats, during the various periods of Buddhist history, were said to have performed these powers.

88. The ten all-encompassing contemplative transformations (Tib. zepar chu, spelled zad-par bcu; Skt. daśa kṛtṣṇāyatanāni) are the outward projection of any perceived appearances (i.e., forms and lights) by visualizing a specific phenomenon. Such a meditator may cause any chosen form or color to emerge in front of others.

The objects of the projections are the five elements (earth, water, fire, air, and space) and the four colors of light (blue, yellow, white, and red), and one's consciousness is the projector.

All these three categories of contemplative achievement and power are referred to as the way of practicing contemplative transformation and manifestation.

89. Udraka (Tib. Lhakchö, spelled lhag-spyod) was one of the six Brahmanic ascetics who were contemporaries of the Buddha. Buddhist tradition has it that there was a fundamental flaw in his view of reality and meditational practice. By holding fast to the belief in a universal creator and the existence of an independent eternal soul, he failed to achieve liberation from the miseries of life. Having earnestly explored the meditative systems of Udraka and others and found them to be flawed, Buddha then proclaimed in his new revolutionary doctrine that the root cause of all miseries is self-delusion, attachment, and hatred. Man is, in principle, the master of his own destiny and a creature of his own will and action.

90. Root and attendant defilements: Tib. tsawai nyönmong and nyewai nyönmong, spelled rtsa-ba'i nyon-mongs and nye-ba'i nyon-mongs; Skt. mūlakleśa and upakleśa.

91. "The conceptual doctrine with its assigned meanings" (Tib. trangdön thanye, spelled drang-don tha-snyad) refers to those teachings of the Buddha that concern themselves with the knowledge of dualism and to those teachings with their assigned meanings for the sake of dull minds that can eventually be led to the true doctrine.

92. "Bearer of karma" (Tib. shelekye, spelled shed-las skyes; Skt. manuja [born of Manu]) and "product of karma" (Tib. shebu, spelled shed-bu; Skt. manuva [offspring of Manu]) are synonyms for "the true self" (ātman) in the Brahmanic lexicon. As for the Sanskrit name Manu, the *Sanskrit-English Dictionary* of Sir Monier-Williams (p. 784, col. 2) mentions him as being "the representative man and father of the human race" and states that the name Manu "is especially applied to the fourteen successive mythical progenitors and sovereigns of the earth."

93. Spontaneous coemergence: Tib. lhenkye, spelled lhan-skyes; Skt. sahaja.

94. Its full title is *Raptu Nepa Dordupa Gyü*, spelled rab-tu gnas-pa mdor-bsdus-pa'i rgyud; Skt. *Supratiṣṭha-tantrasaṃgraha*.

95. The relative mind of enlightenment: Tib. kundzop changchup sem, spelled kun-rdzob byang-chub-sems; Skt. saṃvṛtya bodhicitta.

96. The ultimate mind of enlightenment: Tib. döndam changchup sem, spelled don-dam byang-chub-sems; Skt. paramārtha bodhicitta.

97. The conceptually designated: Tib. küntak, spelled kun-brtag; Skt. parikalpita. Dependent conditionality: Tib. shenwang, spelled gzhan-dbang; Skt. paratantra. Established reality: Tib. yongdrup, spelled yongs-grub; Skt. pariniṣpanna.

98. Nondiscriminating absorption: Tib. nampar mitokpai tingnge-dzin, spelled: rnam-par mi-rtog-pa'i ting-nge-'dzin.

99. "Vajra eyes" refer to penetrating insight into the vajralike (diamondlike) indi-

visible union of great bliss and awareness of the void, according to the Vajrayāna teachings of Buddhism.

100. Lucid awareness: Tib. rang-rik rangsel, spelled rang-rig rang-gsal.

101. Kinnaras are a class of subcelestial beings, according to ancient Indian mythology.

102. This expression specifically refers to the elimination of the mind's dualistic clinging, speculation, and skepticism.

103. Sudden illumination of awareness: Tib. drenrik lobur, spelled dran-rig glo-bur.

104. "Psychic sediment" (Tib. bakchak or namtok bakchak) refers also to an inbred accumulation of delusion.

105. Sediment of delusion: Tib. trülpai bakchak, spelled 'khrul-pa'i bag-chags.

106. Psychic imprint of dualism: Tib nyinang bakchak, spelled gnyis-snang bag-chags; Skt. dvaitoloka-vasanā.

107. The six consciousnesses are those arising from visual sensation, sound sensation, smell sensation, flavor sensation, tactile sensation, and mental perçeption.

108. "Valid cognition" (Tib. ngönsum tsema, spelled mngon-sum tshad-ma; Skt. pratyakṣa) refers to five direct perceptions plus a direct mental cognition.

109. Absolute mode of emerging, dwelling, or destination: Tib. jung-ne-dro-sum, spelled 'byung-gnas-'gro-gsum.

110. "Psychoneurotic energy" (Tib. lung, spelled rlung; Skt. vāyu or prāṇa) implies a current of energy arising from the archetypal mind or the matrix of mind (Tib. tsosem, spelled gtso-sems; Skt. anuttara-manas).

111. "Archer" refers to Saraha.

112. "The adherents of the dogma" refers to all those who hold the view of eternal reality, on the one hand, and materialistic nihilism, on the other.

113. Infallible insight: Tib. lhakthong chinchi malokpa, spelled lhag-mthong phyin-ci-ma-log-pa; Skt. abhiprayasavipaśyanā.

114. "Unobstructed lucidity" refers to the mind's primal clarity, which perceives or reflects phenomena spontaneously and unobstructedly.

115. Je Drikhungpa Jikten Gönpo (1143–1217) was one of the foremost disciples of Phagmo Trupa. He founded the Drikhung Kagyü order.

116. Coemergent awareness: Tib. lhenkye yeshe, spelled lhan-skyes ye-shes; Skt. sahaja-jñāna.

117. *Yumla Töpa*, spelled yum-la-bstod-pa; Skt. *Matta-stotra*.

118. Wisdom-gone-beyond: Tib. sherap pharchin, spelled shes-rab phar-phyin; Skt. prajñāpāramitā.

119. The three poisons are ignorance, lust, and hatred.

120. Nondwelling nirvāna: Tib. minepai nyangde, spelled mi-gnas-pa'i myang-'das; Skt. apratiṣṭha nirvāṇa.

121. This unnamed critic is Sakya Paṇḍita, who held as the principal doctrine the nondifferentiability of the mind's innate clarity and void. This corresponds to "the nondifferentiability of saṃsāra and nirvāṇa."

122. "All appearances being the mere manifestations of individual minds" refers to the unique view of omnidimensional mental reality as posited by the Buddhist idealists (vijñānavādins). They reject the notion of external reality as consisting of conglomerated particles. Our text will show this view of reality to be a stepping stone to the higher, nondualistic view held by the Madhyamaka school of Mahāyāna in general, and that of the Kagyupa mahāmudrā and the Nyingmapa mahāsampanna in particular.

123. Psychic imprints of the past: Tib. ngöngyi bakchak, spelled sngon-gyi bag-chags.

124. Coemergent appearance: Tib. nangwa lhenkye, spelled snang-ba lhan-skyes; Skt. āloka sahaja.

125. Coemergent mind: Tib. semnyi lhenkye, spelled sems-nyid lhan-skyes; Skt. sahajamanas.

126. Je Lingrepa Pema Dorje (1128–1188) was a Tibetan mahāsiddha who was the teacher of Drogön Tsangpa Gyare. The latter founded the Namdruk monastery in South Tibet.

127. Great one flavor: Tib. ronyom chenpo, spelled ro-snyom chen-po.

128. Undetermined appearance: Tib. Nangla mangepa, spelled snang-la ma-nges-pa.

129. "A certain meditation system" refers to the distinct view of and approach to insight meditation as enunciated by Tsongkhapa (1357–1419), the founder of the Gelukpa order, to which the Dalai Lama and the Panchen Lama officially belong.

130. "A certain critic" refers to Sakya Paṇḍita, who made this statement in his *Domsum Rabye*. It may be noted that most great Kagyüpa masters chose not to counterrefute him, on the ground that he directed his criticism mainly toward "ignorants" or "uninformed meditators."

131. Koṭali (Tib. Toktsepa) was one of the Buddhist mahāsiddhas.

132. Ordinary mind: Tib. thamel shepa.

133. This position of identifying "the ordinary awareness of an untutored lay

person" with that of all-seeing awareness is a unique view maintained by both the mahāmudrā (Chakgya Chenpo) and the mahāsampanna (Dzokpa Chenpo), i.e., the Kagyüpa and the Nyingmapa orders.

134. The vision of nondiscriminating simplicity (Tib. trömegyi tawa) is the primal awareness that transcends all conceptual or perceptive discrimination and notion of duality in all its forms.

135. The eight worldly principles are said to arise from the mind that clings to the notion of self. They are grouped into two parts, positive and negative. The four positive reactions are to be pleased by pleasure, praise, gain, and delightful words. The four negative reactions are to be disturbed by displeasure, criticism, loss, and bad words.

136. This is the first part of a quotation from the *Deshin Shekpai Sangwai Do*. It would continue as follows: "Self-restraint is defined as having no flow of sensual thoughts, of malignance, of violent motivation, and of lust, hatred, and ignorance—which are the root of all vicious deeds. Self-restraint is defined as being devoid of any physical, vocal, and mental misdeeds." The author, Tashi Namgyal, left out this portion but then continued the quotation.

137. He who attained inner tranquility: Tib. dewar shekpa; Skt. sugata.

138. The four evil robbers are: (1) inner delusion, (2) the five aggregates of psychophysical existence, which imprison man in the turning wheel of birth and death, (3) the unfailing force of death, and (4) the external and internal forces that seek to seduce man into harmful action.

139. Vigorous mindfulness: Tib. jurdren, spelled 'jur-dran.

140. Retentive mindfulness: Tib. zungdren, spelled gzung-dran.

141. No memory: Tib. drenpa mepa, spelled: dran-pa med-pa.

142. No mental activity: Tib. yila mijepa, spelled yid-la mi-byed-pa.

143. The stream of nondiscriminatory awareness: Tib. nampar mitokpai drengyün, spelled rnam-par mi-rtog-pa'i dran-rgyun; Skt. avikalpa smṛti śrota.

144. Absorption: Tib. nyamshak, spelled mnyam-gzhak; Skt. samāhita. Postabsorption: Tib. jethop, spelled rjes-thob; Skt. pṛṣṭhalabdha.

145. Postcontemplative thought: Tib. jeshe, spelled rjes-shes; Skt. anujñāna. Postcontemplative appearance (also rendered as "postabsorptive perception"): Tib. jenang, spelled rjes-snang; Skt. anu-abhi or anubhanu.

146. Postabsorptive perception: see preceding footnote.

147. Reality and unreality: Tib. denpar druppa yin-min, spelled bden-par grub-pa yin-min.

148. *Semnyi Ngalso*, spelled sems-nyid ngal-gso; Skt. *Manas-virama*.

149. *Chakgya Chenpo Yige Shipa*, spelled phyag-rgya chen-po yige bzhi-pa; Skt. Caturākṣa Mahāmudrā.

150. Khedrup Chegompa was a Kagyüpa master.

151. "Sensory incitement" is used here to indicate all thought flow in general. Another term used earlier is "thought flow."

152. The fourfold daily conduct refers to the four physical conducts: walking, moving around, sitting, and sleeping.

153. Gandharvas (Tib. driza) are mythological celestial maidens who were said to be enchanting musicians and singers and whose chief was horse-headed, according to Indian folklore.

154. "Absorptive evenness" has also been rendered as "absorption," "absorptive equipoise," or "contemplative absorption."

155. The supreme emptiness of all forms: Tib. namkün chokden tongnyi, spelled rnam-kun mchog-ldan stong-nyid; Skt. sarvākāravaropetā śūnyātā.

156. The "no essence mantra" means the sacred syllables that signify the emptiness of essence of all things. They are intimately linked to the tantric meditation on the ultimate nature of reality. This meditation begins by mentally dissolving duality into the total void, ultimate simplicity. The specific sacred syllables (mantra) read: "Let all things dissolve into the void detached from any intrinsic essence" (Skt. Oṃ svabhāva-śuddhāḥ sarvadharmāḥ svabhāva-śuddho 'ham).

157. "One substance" refers to the universal substratum of phenomena, i.e., the void (or emptiness).

158. The first inmost perception of a "mirage" dawns in the meditative absorption as a result of the body's earth element having integrated with the water element. The second inmost perception of "smoke" emerges as a result of the water element having transmutated with the fire element. The third inmost perception of "blinking lights," like those of fireflies, comes about as a result of the fire element having transmutated with the air element. The fourth inmost perception of "flames," like those of butter lamps, arises as a result of the air element having transmutated with the appearance of the phenomena. The fifth inmost perception of a "clear sky" dawns as a result of one's consciousness having transmutated with awareness, in which there is no duality of its insight and clarity.

159. Regarding the eight beneficial results, the author has not explained or enumerated every such set of ideas or principles. The description of these is found in the *Commentary on the Inner Meaning of Mysticism* (Tib. *Zabmo Nangdön*) by that great eclectic Kagyüpa master Lodrö Thaye (Jamgön Kongtrül, 1813–1899). The eight beneficial results are stated to be realized by perfecting the integrated yoga meditation on the control and retention of the body's air energy flowing inside the central nervous system, and on the "indivisible soundless utterance" (Tib. dorjai depa; Skt. vajrajāpa) by means of a rhythmic inward and outward flow. The same benefits are obtainable through the very direct and simple mahāmudrā meditation.

The first three benefits are obtained through the elimination of the three psychic poisons (delusion, lust, and hatred) and through the realization of certain qualities, namely the sublime manifestation, speech, and mind of the enlightened. The other five benefits are obtained through the mastery of the five sensory perceptions, which, in its wake, brings about the realization of the five transcending states of awareness. In the process of self-realization, the first three benefits arise from the efficient control of the body's ascending air-energy, which has thermal power like the sun. The next five benefits are realized through the mastery of the descending air energy, which has a cooling power like that of the moon.

160. "Incessant misery" (Tib. nyalwa, spelled dmyal-ba) means the realm of the hells.

161. "A lack of compassion and love" refers to the Hīnayāna doctrine. The Hīnayāna tradition does teach the principle and practice of compassion and love but does not make it an essential condition for realizing simple nirvāṇa. In the Mahāyāna tradition these two principles form the requisite condition for realizing the supreme nirvāṇa, full enlightenment. The joint development of wisdom and compassion is therefore an indispensable requirement for Mahāyāna adherents. However, the Hīnayāna doctrine contains a set of great humanistic principles known as the four boundless thoughts (joy, compassion, love, and equanimity), which clearly embody love and compassion. They constitute a higher contemplative state leading to the summit of the three planes known as the Brahmaloka. The four boundless thoughts are expressed in the form of this solemn wish:

May sentient beings be blessed with boundless joy!
May sentient beings be blessed with a well-being free from suffering!
May sentient beings be blessed with peace!
May sentient beings be blessed with inner equanimity!

By actualizing a perfect insight, arising from wisdom, into the nonselfhood of their stream consciousness and that of the natural elements Hīnayānists may realize the supramundane levels of arhathood (the exalted state) and may thus achieve nirvāṇa—the state of timeless quiescence—for themselves.

162. The unimpeded path: Tib. barche melam, spelled bar-chad med-lam.

163. The "rumor about a monster" refers to a parable on the consequence of being too credulous. The story begins with a rabbit who heard a loud splash in a lake sounding like "chel" and saw a dark image amid the widening ripples. Scared stiff, he took it to be a monster and began to run away into the forest. On the way he shouted "Monster!" to every animal and ran until he finally met the king of beasts. The lion heard the scary story and said: "Wait a moment and let us all examine this!" They discovered that all that had happened was that a tree branch had fallen into the water.

164. "This critic" refers to Sakya Paṇḍita.

165. The one intent system: Tib. damchö gongcigma, spelled dam-chos dgongs-gcig-ma; Skt. saddharma ekacitta). This holy doctrine of one intent represents the integrated Buddhist teachings comprehensively presented along with interpreta-

tions in the well-known treatise bearing this title. The text was composed by the founder of the Drikhung Kagyüpa order, Kyoppa Jikten Sumgön (1143–1217). The text, with its many commentaries, has been the principal teaching manual for the Drikhungpa order. This text not only serves as the introduction to the treasure of Buddhist doctrines but also reveals through its complex form the "one intent of the Buddha," namely "to awaken every deluded mind to the one natural state of all things," i.e., the inconceivable and imperceptible void. Kyoppa Jikten Sumgön, the great master of the Drikhungpa order, showed even a distinctly uncommon approach to explaining and interpreting the Buddhist doctrines by differing from a generally accepted meaning. He went so far as to state that all of the Buddha's teachings were given in one common form to be read literally. The different meanings such as the contrived and real meaning, etc. were evolved, according to the author, by individuals who understood them differently. To him "one common form" is the natural corollary to "the doctrine of one intent."

166. The four concentrated states and the four higher sense faculties are also called "the eight levels of absorption on the plane of sublime form and the formless plane." See note 85 for Book Two.

167. The nonreturning state: Tib. drachom chirmiwong, spelled dgra-bcom phyir-mi-'ong; Skt. anāgami.

168. "The two inbred obstacles" refers to (1) a deluded mind and (2) the nonawareness of incognitive absorption. The deluded mind means the perception that misconceives the appearance of dualism as the true reality and thereby misconceives the personality of self and that of others. This attachment to the ego gives rise to selfishness, lust, and hatred. Nonawareness of incognitive absorption means an absorptive obstacle. It means that the incognitive absorption, by nature, is so deep and so totally detached from any awareness that it becomes completely oblivious to the highest illumination. It must, however, be made clear that these two kinds of arhats might not—as a rule—enter the incognitive absorption but would advance further toward the fourth and final level of arhathood. Only at this stage could they become true arhats. Both the Abhidharma and Prajñāpāramitā treatises describe the successive levels of arhathood as the four preparatory applications and the four attainments.

169. The four enlightened aspects are:

The earthly manifestation (Skt. nirmāṇakāya)
The supreme manifestation (Skt. sambhogakāya)
The ultimate state of enlightenment (Skt. dharmakāya) (see note 62 for Part One)
The essence of enlightenment (Skt. svabhāvikakāya)

170. "Tranquil inertia" (Tib. shine tengpo, spelled zhi-gnas stengs-po) refers to a kind of tranquility that lacks focus on stability and clarity due to an excessive suppression of mindfulness.

171. The Tripiṭaka, the three containers of the Buddha's teachings or the three collections of scriptures, are:

Dülwa (Skt. vinaya piṭaka), the canon of moral and monastic law
Dode (Skt. sūtra piṭaka), the concise teachings on the Buddhist practices
Ngönpa (Skt. abhidharma piṭaka), the sublime psychology and metaphysics

172. All-encompassing meditation: Tib. gom khoryuk, spelled sgom 'khor-yug.

173. Discrimination: Tib. tröche, spelled spros-bcas. Nondiscrimination: Tib. tröme, spelled spros-med. Complete nondiscrimination: Tib. shintu trome, spelled shin-tu spros-med.

174. These three kinds are:

The secret practice (Tib. sangchö, spelled gsang-spyod; Skt. guhya-carya)
The uninhibited practice (Tib. tülshuk chöpa, spelled brtul-zhugs spyod-pa; Skt. prakacarya)
The practice of triumph over all adverse circumstances (Tib. chokle namgyalgyi chöpa, spelled phyogs-las rnam-rgyal-gyi spyod-pa; Skt. digvijaya-carya)

"The secret practice" refers to a meditation on a secret sensual performance with a chosen female mystic; "the uninhibited practice" refers to a public association with a female mystic; and "the practice of triumph" refers to a mystic's demonstration of his attained power over adverse conditions and evil forces.

175. Kusului tsok (spelled ku-su-lu'i tshogs; Skt.: kusala ciṣati (?) kusāli punya gaṇa) refers to a mystical contemplation on the visualized self-sacrifice to the "assembly of refuge" (the three jewels: Buddha, dharma, and saṅgha). In this visualized meditation the mystic "turns his body into an ambrosia, having prepared himself well through the secret empowerment, the oral instructions, and the practice known as "chö," which means "cutting the root of self-delusion." The mystic performs this meditation with the ritual at night, in a desolate area, in mountain solitude, or among isolated cremation rocks. Both before and after the mastery of the practice in this kind of wilderness, it can be done at one's own home, if the conditions are favorable. The purpose of this meditation is to gain true insight into one's mind, particularly into the unknown aspects and forces that are agitated and challenged by difficult conditions and terrifying circumstances.

176. "The vision of abiding reality" refers to the way the mental and material phenomena exist in their natural state. Being conditioned by the interaction of causes and effects they are devoid of any intrinsic substance. Only the void is omnipresent as the infinite space, which encompasses the whole cosmic universe, while constituting the inner expanse of every moment of stream consciousness and every particle.

177. The four demonic forces (Tib. dreshi, spelled 'dre-bzhi) are not specified by the author. Names found later in this chapter seem to fit these four forces. They are:

The serpent gods (Tib. lu, spelled klu; Skt. nāga)
The earth protectors (Tib. sadak, spelled sa-bdag; Skt. bhūmi-ātman)
The vicious tsen (spelled btsan)
The demonesses (Tib. srinmo, spelled srin-mo; Skt. rākṣasa)

178. Ronyom, spelled ro-snyom; Skt. rasāsama or rasākāya.

179. The vicious *tsen* are a class of male spirits in the Tibetan animistic tradition.

180. The three kinds of miseries are:

Mutable suffering (Tib. khyappa dujeygyi dukngel, spelled khyab-pa 'du-byed-gyi sdug-bsngal; Skt. saṃskāra duḥkhatā)
Inherent conditions for suffering (Tib. gyurwai dukngel, spelled 'gyur-ba'i sdug-bsngal; Skt. viparināma duḥkhatā)
Suffering of suffering (Tib. dukngel-gyi dukngel, spelled sdug-bsngal-gyi sdug-bsngal; Skt. duḥkha-duḥkhatā)

"Mutable suffering" refers to suffering brought forth by such changes in the psychophysical conditions as (a) young to old and infirm, strong to weak, higher existence to lower existence, (b) a feeling of pleasure to pain, desire to despair, hope to resignation, and (c) an adverse turn of climate or environment.

"Inherent conditions for suffering" refers to the potential for miseries being ever-present in every psychosomatic being, like a store of karmic seeds. A person therefore remains largely susceptible to sufferings arising from a sudden illness, an emotional disturbance, an excess of heat or cold, or an accident.

"Suffering of suffering" refers mainly to sentient beings of the three lower realms: the animal world, the hungry spirits, and the spiritual beings in hell. It also applies to human beings who are indiscriminately afflicted by acute miseries. Just as the ignorant, poor, deformed, old, and infirm suffer from hunger, disease, and deprivation, so the educated and wealthy people are afflicted by acute physical or mental misery, or both.

181. This remark concerning nirvāṇa stems from the idea that the nirvāṇa achieved by the arhats and pratyekabuddhas is not of the highest order, as that attained by buddhas. The tradition often describes the former as being like the crescent moon and the latter as the full moon.

182. "Primal ignorance" refers to the fundamental flaw immanent in the ordinary mind, i.e., its lack of understanding of and insight into the true state of reality designated as "that very void of reality" (Tib. chönyi tongpa, spelled chos-nyid stong-pa; Skt. dharmatā-śūnyatā). Implicit in the void is the nonexistence of a substance or self-essence with respect to the phenomena of mind and matter. Originating from this primary ignorance is the confusion about the workings of the natural law of cause and effect.

183. White illumination: Tib. nangwa, spelled snang-ba. Red diffusive glow: Tib. chepa, spelled mched-pa. Descending darkness: Tib. nyerthop, spelled nyer-thob.

184. "Training of the mind" refers in this case to the advanced training methods designed especially to help guide individuals toward self-purification and self-development. The prerequisite for this training is that religious adherents must master—either completely or sufficiently—the general understanding and practice of the integrated path of enlightenment (Tib. changchup lamrim).

The principle and practice of mind training, initiated by Buddha, is clearly illustrated, apart from the well-established tradition, in his key instructions, such as:

O mendicant monks,
To abstain from any harmful actions,
To practice all that is perfect,
To conquer your mind completely—
This is the teaching of the Buddha!

The advanced mind training draws, on the one hand, from the Buddha's profound doctrine on the ultimate reality and from its elucidation by the greatest of the Mahāyāna masters, Nāgārjuna (second century B.C.E.) and, on the other hand, from the instructions on the elaborate practice of compassion and the thought of enlightenment. The latter originated from two separate but interrelated sources: (1) Maitreya and his disciple Asaṅga and (2) Mañjuśrī and Prince Śāntideva. The practice elucidated by Maitreya is called "the sevenfold instructions on the cause and effect development of the compassionate enlightenment mind." The other method, called "loving others more than oneself," was elucidated by Śāntideva to whom it was revealed by Mañjuśrī. The general study of the integrated path of enlightenment and the advanced training methods, along with the vital instructions, were introduced in Tibet in the eleventh century by the great teacher Dīpaṅkara Atīśa and his Tibetan disciples, who established the Khadampa order (the order of "Seekers of Awakening through Every Word of the Buddha"). The twofold training system became the essential aspect of religious studies for the sister schools of Tibetan Buddhism.

The advanced training is especially designed to rapidly enhance in each seeker profound compassion and insight into true reality. The nature of such training consists of an instantaneous transformation of every deluded thought into transcending wisdom, every selfish idea into compassion and the thought of universal enlightenment. The scope of this self-transformation is extended to every conscious or subconscious thought, especially to deluded, depressed, or distressed minds.

The thought of enlightenment (bodhicitta) is rooted in universal love and compassion. In other words, the thought of enlightenment for all other beings and the pledge to work toward that end is the highest manifestation of such love and compassion. Bodhicitta in fact has many levels of meaning. At the level of an aspiring bodhisattva, it must take the form of an intense yearning for and relentless effort at attaining immediate liberation and eventual enlightenment for all sentient beings. On the level of the realized state, bodhicitta means a perfect awareness of the ultimate reality, an awareness that is completely free from any substance or essence, wherein compassion and wisdom become an indivisible whole. Yet, this wisdom is defined as the intellectual faculty that perceives all things as they truly are, as opposed to the way a deluded intellect perceives them. Often described as transcending awareness, this wisdom differentiates the aspect of apparent from ultimate reality, while perceiving the interrelationship of all things.

185. The one-pointed stage: Tib. tsechik, spelled rtse-gcig; Skt. ekāgra. The nondiscriminatory stage: Tib. trödrel, spelled spros-bral; Skt. niṣprapañca. The stage of one flavor: Tib. ronyom, spelled ro-snyom; Skt. rasāsama. The stage of nonmeditation: Tib. gomme, spelled sgom-med; Skt. abhavanam.

186. Evanescent realization: Tib. thögel, spelled thod-rgal.

187. Comprehension: Tib. go, spelled go; Skt. jña. Experience: Tib. nyong, spelled myong; Skt. vetanā. Understanding: Tib. tok, spelled rtogs; Skt. buddhaka.

188. Inner sensation: Tib. nyam, spelled nyams; Skt. ābhāsa.

189. The fusion of the dynamic and stable aspects of the mind: Tib. negyu drepa, spelled gnas-'gyu 'dres-pa.

190. The three transcending forms are:

1. The earthly manifestation (Tib. trülku, spelled sprul-sku; Skt. nirmāṇakāya)
2. The supreme mystical manifestation (Tib. longku, spelled longs-sku; Skt. sambhogakāya)
3. The state of ultimate simplicity (Tib. chöku, spelled chos-sku; Skt. dharmakāya)

These are part of the four enlightened aspects. (See note 164 for Part Two.)

191. The five aspects of awareness are:

Mirrorlike awareness (Tib. melong yeshe, spelled me-long ye-shes; Skt. adarśajñāna),
Even awareness (Tib. nyamnyi yeshe, spelled mnyam-nyid ye-shes; Skt. samatājñāna),
Discerning awareness (Tib. sortok yeshe; spelled sor-rtogs ye-shes; Skt. pratyavekṣanajñāna)
Spontaneously fulfilling awareness (Tib. chadrup yeshe, spelled bya-grub ye-shes; Skt. kṛtyānuṣṭhānajñāna)
All-encompassing expanse of awareness (Tib. chöying yeshe, spelled chos-dbyings ye-shes; Skt. dharmadhātujñāna)

192. Luminous awareness: Tib. ösel yeshe, spelled 'od-gsal ye-shes; Skt. prabhās-varajñāna). Supreme illusory form: Tib. namdak gyumaiku, spelled rnam-dag sgyu-ma'i sku; Skt. viśuddhi-māyā-kāya). The path of noncultivation: Tib. miloblam, spelled mi-slob lam; Skt. aśaikṣa-mārga.

193. "The eightfold consciousness" (Tib. namshe gye, spelled rnam-shes brgyad; Skt. aṣṭa vijñāna) refers to consciousness as conceived by the idealistic school (vijñānavādins). The eight consciousnesses are the six forms of consciousness arising from the sense organs (eyes, ears, nose, tongue, body, and mind), the pervasive delusion, and the source consciousness.

194. Torma offerings generally refer to the offerings made from roasted barley flour in a stūpalike shape, often colored and decorated with butter designs by the skillful hands of butter sculptors. Such offerings are reverentially called shelze (spelled zhal-zas) or offerings of edibles. Tormas come in different shapes, colors, and flavors. Some will later be eaten like sacramental cakes.

195. This kind of complete solitude, in a cell or a mountain cave, was carried out for years, sometimes even for life, by mystics, especially those of the contemplative orders like the Kagyüpa and Nyingmapa schools. However, those mystics who followed in the footsteps of the great masters eventually left their caves in order to

undertake the spiritual ministration and teaching of people. All four orders of Tibetan Buddhism still today maintain the tradition of solitary meditation retreats of varying length. The three-year, three-month, three-day retreat is the most commonly practiced retreat. A number of serious Western Buddhists in recent years have undertaken such retreats under the guidance of their gurus in India, Europe, and America.

196. A meditator who achieves great psychic power is said to be able to help or harm others. By virtue of his knowledge of the Buddhist doctrine, his insight into the true reality, his compassion and concern for all sentient beings, and his special mind power, he is destined to help others through relieving their miseries, guiding them in their spiritual endeavor, and even healing those afflicted with diseases. However, if anyone deviates from the noble path and misuses the powerful methods of yoga for his selfish, materialistic ends, he is likely to harm others. Such a profanization of the sacred tradition inevitably brings consequences absolutely detrimental to his physical well-being and mental stability.

197. "Prophetic directions from the ḍākinīs" refers to the protective role of the ḍākinīs. Regarded as the custodians of the secret Supreme Yoga, the ḍākinīs have been looked upon by Buddhist mystics as the protectors from forces of destruction and unscrupulous profanization. One might wonder whether the concept of supernatural powers fits with Buddhism, since the latter does not believe in monotheism or polytheism. As the path of universalization and elevation of all sentient beings to the "order of enlightened ones," Tibetan Buddhism treats the ḍākinīs as advanced practitioners, and the highest order of ḍākinīs is looked upon as a manifestation of the enlightened ones. They are considered the custodians and repository of the inexhaustible treasure of the highest yoga doctrine. See also *The Life of Milarepa*, trans. Lobsang Lhalungpa (New York: E. P. Dutton, 1977; and Boulder: Prajñā Press, 1982), p. 206, note 14, on ḍākas and ḍākinīs.

198. "The four states of fearlessness" refers to the Buddha's undaunted courage in proclaiming to the world (1) that he has attained the transcendental wisdom that directly perceives and penetrates into all the diverse levels of knowledge, (2) that he has completely eliminated the mind's affliction and intellectual confusion, (3) that the joint development of wisdom and compassion is the surest way to liberation, and (4) that inner delusion, lust, and hatred are the obstacles to liberation. The first two represent the supreme fulfillment of his personal aspiration, and the last two represent the fulfillment of his universal aspiration for the permanent good of all sentient beings.

199. This quotation would convey the intended meaning only if the next line had also been quoted in the Tibetan text. It reads, "... there will exist self-clinging to them."

200. "The joyous ground, the path of insight" refers to the first awakening into true reality, or the first of the ten grounds of the bodhisattva. (See next note.)

201. "The first ground, the path of insight" (Tib. thonglam rabtu gawai sa, spelled mthong-lam rab-tu dga-ba'i sa; Skt. darśana-mārga pramuditā-bhūmi) refers to the first awakening into true reality, which is deepened progressively until its com-

pletion, designated as the tenth ground of the bodhisattva (Tib. changchup sempai sachu, spelled byang-chub sems-dpa'i sa-bcu; Skt. bodhisattva-daśa-bhūmayaḥ).

202. The path of primordial evenness and all-in-oneness: Tib. gom nyamnyi nyukmai lam chikchö, spelled sgom mnyam-nyid gnyug-ma'i lam gcig-chod).

203. "Adorned ones" refers to those arhats who, having overcome the mental defilements and the incognitive absorption, attained liberation with its eight qualities. Unadorned ones are those arhats who attained liberation through the power of discerning wisdom.

204. "The Ox year" refers to the date of the completion of this text. The Ox year could be either the Wood Ox year, 1566 C.E., or the Fire Ox year, 1578 C.E.

205. The seven horses are the mounts of the sun, according to ancient Hindu mythology.

206. The three kinds of faith are:

Trust born of faith
Trust born of admiration
A yearning for the same attainment as that of the Buddha and his enlightened disciples

Bibliography

Tibetan folio	*Tibetan (phon. and trans.)*	*Sanskrit*
4 B	Sachupe Dho (Sa-bcu-pa'i mdo)	Daśabhūmika-sūtra
4 B	Dorje Gur (Rdo-rje gur)	Vajrapañjara-tantra
4 B	Sambuti Samti (Sambuti sam-ti)	Sampuṭa-tantra
5 F	Langkar Shekpai Dho (Lang-kar gshegs-pa'i mdo)	Laṅkāvatāra-sūtra
5 B	Gyü Taknyi (Rgyud-brtags-gnyis)	Hevajra-tantra
6 F	Phelpoche (Phal-po-che)	Avataṃsaka-sūtra
6 F	Könchoktrin (Dkon-mchog-sprin)	Ratnamegha-sūtra
7 F	Dongpo Köpa (Sdong-po bkod-pa)	Gaṇḍhavyūha-sūtra
7 B	(Jampal) Nampar Rölpe Dho ('Jam-dpal rnam-par-rol-pa'i mdo)	Mañjuśrivīkrīditā-sūtra
7 B	Chöjuk (Spyod-'jug)	Bodhicaryāvatāra
8 F	Shetring (Bshes-spring)	Suhṛllekha
8 F	Tekhonanyi Tenpe Dho (De-kho-na-nyid bstan-pa'i mdo)	Tattvaprakaśa-sūtra
8 F	Tsuktor Chenpö Dho (Gtsug-tor chen-po'i mdo)	Mahoṣṇīṣa-sūtra
8 B	Tokpa Gye Dho (Rtogs-pa rgyas-pa'i mdo)	
8 B	Dhodüpa (Mdo-sdud-pa)	Prajñāpāramitā-saṃcayagāthā

Tibetan folio	*Tibetan (phon. and trans.)*	*Sanskrit*
8 B	Se Nyingpo Khorlo Chupe-do (Sa'i-snying-po 'khor-lo bcu-pa'i mdo)	Dasácakra-kṣitigarbha-sūtra
9 F	Chö Yangdakpar-düpa (Chos yang-dag-par-sdud-pa)	Dharmasagīti-sūtra
9 F	Dhode-gyen (Mdo-sde-rgyan)	Sūtrālaṃkāra
9 B	Gongpa Ngedrel (Dgongs-pa nges-'grel)	Saṃdhinirmocana-sūtra
9 B	Sade (Sa-sde)	
9 B	Ngönpa Küntü (Mngon-pa kun-btus)	Abhidharmasamuccaya
9 B	Gomrim (Second) (Sgom-rim bar-pa)	Bhāvanākrama
10 F	Thekchenla Tepa Gompe-Dho (Theg-chen-la dad-pa sgom-pa'i mdo)	Mahāyanaprasādaprabhāvana-sūtra
10 B	Gomrim (Third) (Sgom-rim tha-ma)	Bhāvanākrama
11 B		Prātimokṣa-sūtra
13 B	Ngönpa Dzö (Mngon-pa mdzod)	Abhidharma-kośa
15 F	Ütha Namje (Dbus-mtha rnam-'byed)	Madhyāntavibhāga
17 F	Üthe Drelshe (Dbus-mtha'i 'grel-bṣhad)	Madhyāntavibhāga-vṛtti
18 F	Nyensa (Nyan-sa)	Śrāvakabhūmi
19 F	Se Ngöshi (Sa-yi dngos-gzhi)	
20 F	Gomrim (First) (Sgom-rim dang-po)	Bhāvanākrama
20 F	Uma Nyingpo (Dbu-ma snying-po)	Madhyamakahṛdaya
20 B	Pharchin Düpa (Phar-phyin bsdus-pa)	Prajñāpāramitā-saṃcayagāthā

Tibetan folio	*Tibetan (phon. and trans.)*	*Sanskrit*
22 B	Jangsa (Byang-sa)	Bodhisattvabhūmi
23 B	Sherchin Menngak (Sher-phyin man-ngag)	Prajñāpāramitopadeśa
30 B	Jangchup Sempe Ḍenö (Byang-chub sems-pa'i sde-snod)	Bodhisattvapiṭaka
30 B	Dawa Drönme Do (Zla-ba sgron-ma'i mdo)	Candrapradīpa-sūtra
34 B	Jangchup Lamdrön (Byang-chub lam-sgron)	Bodhipathapradīpa
34 B	Dodüpa (Mdo-bsdus-pa)	Prajñāpāramitā-saṃcayagāthā
35 F	Sherchin Düngyapa (Sher-phyin bdun-brgya-pa)	Saptaśatikā-prajñāpāramitā-sūtra
39 B	Namdrü Shüpe Dho (Nam-grus zhus-pa'i mdo)	
41 F	Tingdzin Gyalpo (Ting-'dzin rgyal-po)	Samādhirāja-sūtra
42 F	Shaktö (Bshags-bstod)	Deśanastava
50 F	Shigyapa (Bzhi-brgya-pa)	Ćatuḥśataka
50 B	Do Silbu (Mdo sil-bu)	
50 B	Rinchen Trengwa (Rin-chen phreng-ba)	Ratnāvalī
51 F	Uma Jukpa (Dbu-ma 'jug-pa)	Madhyamakāvatāra
51 F	(Uma) Tsashe (Dbu-ma rtsa-shes)	Mūlamadhyamaka-kārikā
53 B	Jangchup Semdrel (Byang-chub sems-'grel)	Bodhicittavivaraṇa
55 F	Köntsek (Dkon-brtsegs)	Mahāratnakuṭa-sūtra
55 B	Dennyi Drelpa (Bden-gnyis 'grel-pa)	Satyadvayavibhaṅga-vṛtti
58 B	Chönyi Miyowe Do (Chos-nyid mi-g.yo-ba'i mdo)	Dharmatāćala-sūtra

Tibetan folio	*Tibetan (phon. and trans.)*	*Sanskrit*
	(Full title of above) Chönyi Ranggi Ngowo Töngpanyile Miyowar-thadepar Thamchela Nangwe Do (Chos-nyid rang-gi-ngo-bo stong-pa-nyid-las mi-g.yo-bar tha-dad-par tham-cad-la snang-ba'i mdo)	Dharmatāsvabhāva-śūnyatācala-pratisarvāloka-sūtra
58 B	Chökyi Yingkyi Rangshin Yer-mepar Tenpe Do (Chos-kyi dbyings-kyi rang-bzhin dbyer-med-par bstan-pa'i mdo)	Dharmadhātu-prakṛtyasambhedanirdeśa-sūtra
59 F	Yumla Töpa (Yum-la bstod-pa)	
59 B	Namkha Tabü Tingnge-dzingyi Dho (Nam-mkha' lta-bu'i ting-nge-'dzin-gyi mdo)	
59 B	Tingdzin Tampe Dho (Ting-'dzin dam-pa'i mdo)	
60 F	Gyetongpa (Brgyad-stong-pa)	Aṣṭasāhasrikā-prajñāpāramitā
60 F	Namkha Rinpoche Dho (Nam-mkha' rin-po-che'i mdo)	
66 F	Ösungkyi Shüpe Dho ('Od-srungs kyis zhus-pa'i mdo)	Kāśyapaparivarta-sūtra
70 B	Tsema Künletü (Tshad-ma kun-las btus)	Pramāṇasamuccaya
74 B	Uma Tsiksel (Uma Tsawe Drelpa Tsiksel) (Dbu-ma tshig-gsal) (Dbu-ma tsa-ba'i 'grel-pa tshig-gsal)	Mūlamadhyamaka-vṛtti Prasannapadā
75 F	Chöying Töpa (Chos-dbyings bstod-pa)	Dharmadhātustava
77 F	Tawa Dordü (Lta-ba mdor-bsdus)	Dṛṣṭisaṃkṣepta
77 B	Sangwa Düpa (Gsang-ba 'dus-pa)	Guhyasamāja-tantra
79 B	Ume Menngak (Dbu-ma'i man-ngag)	Madhyamakopadeśa

Tibetan folio	*Tibetan (phon. and trans.)*	*Sanskrit*
81 B	Nampar Mitokpar Jokpe Zung (Rnam-par mi-rtog-par 'jug-pa'i gzungs)	Avikalpapraveśa-dhāraṇī
82 B	Namkha Dzökyi Shüpe Dho (Nam-mkha'-mdzod-kyis zhus-pa'i mdo)	Gaganagañjaparipṛcchā-sūtra
83 F	Sangwa Truppa (Gsang-ba-grub-pa)	Guhyasiddhi
83 F	Chakchen Thigle (Phyag-chen thig-le)	Mahāmudrātilaka
83 B	Rimnga (Rim-lnga)	Pañcakrama
83 B	Tekhonanyi Chupa (De-kho-na-nyid bcu-pa)	Daśatattva
83 B	Tükhor (Dus-'khor)	Kālacakra-tantra
84 F	Thektrön (Theg-sgron)	
84 B	Yeshe Truppe Drupthap (Yes-shes grub-pa'i sgrub-thabs)	Jñanasiddhi-sādhana
84 B	Jorwa Dünpa (Sbyor-ba bdun-pa)	Yogasapta
85 B	Gyü Lama (Rgyud bla-ma)	Uttaratantra
85 B	Dechok Jungwa (Bde-mchog 'byung-ba)	Saṃvarodaya-tantra
85 B	Yeshe Nyingpo Gyü (Ye-shes snying-po rgyud)	Jñānagarbha-tantra
86 B	Lodrö Gyatso Shüpe Dho (Blo-gros rgya-mtsho zhus-pa'i mdo)	Sāgaramatiparipṛcchā-sūtra
87 F	Jampal Jukpe Dho ('Jam-dpal 'jug-pa'i mdo)	Maitreyaprasthāna-sūtra
87 F	Bumo Rinchengyi Shüpa (Bu-mo rin-chen-gyis zhus-pa)	
87 B	Kocha Köpar Tenpa (Go-cha bkod-par bstan-pa)	Varmavyūhanirdeśa-sūtra
87 B	Jampel Tsagyü ('Jam-dpal rtsa-rgyud)	Mañjuśrī-mūlatantra

Tibetan folio	*Tibetan (phon. and trans.)*	*Sanskrit*
87 B	Namnang Ngönjang (Rnam-snang mngon-byang)	Vairocanābhisaṃbodhi
87 B	Kezang (Skal-bzang)	Bhadrakalpika
88 B	Tawe Döpa Dortenpa (Lta-ba'i 'dod-pa mdor-bstan-pa)	
88 B	Drönsel (Sgron-gsal)	Pradīpoddyotana
88 B	Shegyü Dortreng (Bshad-rgyud-rdor-'phreng)	Vajramāla-ākhyāta-tantra
88 B	Dasang Thigle (Zla-gsang thig-le)	Candraguhyatilaka
89 F	Sanggye Nyamjor (Sangs-rgyas mnyam-sbyor)	Buddhasamāyoga
89 F	Sanggye Thöpa (Sangs-rgyas thod-pa)	Buddhakapāla-tantra
89 F	Chakgyashi Tenla Wappa (Phyag-rgya bzhi gtan-la dbab-pa)	Caturmudrāniścaya
90 F	Chakchen Tsikdü (Phyag-chen tshig-bsdus)	
90 F	Yeshe Selje (Ye-shes gsal-byed)	
90 F	Chakchen Gangama (Phyag-chen gang-gā-ma)	Mahāmudropadeśa
91 F	Dortreng (Rdor-'phreng)	Vajramālā
92 F	Yeshe Thigle (Ye-shes thig-le)	Jñānatilaka
92 F	Sangwe Tekhonanyi (Gsang-ba'i de-kho-na-nyid)	Guhyatattva
92 B	Pemachen (Pad-ma can)	Padminī
92 B	Wangkur Ngeten (Dbang-skur nges-bstan)	Sekanirdeśa
93 F	Domjung (Sdom-'byung)	Saṃvarodaya
93 F	Truppa Dedün (Grub-pa sde-bdun)	

Tibetan folio	*Tibetan (phon. and trans.)*	*Sanskrit*
94 F	Doha Korsum (Do-ha skor-gsum)	
94 F	Tochung Dzögye (Do-chung mdzod-brgyad)	
94 F	Trupnying (Grub-snying)	
94 F	Amanasi (A-ma-na-si)	Amanasi
98 B	Thupgong (Thub-dgongs)	
102 F	Khyepar Semkyi Zhüpai Dho (Khyad-par sems-kyis zhus-pa'i mdo)	
102 F	Dorje Tingnge Dzingyi Dho (Rdo-rje ting-nge-'dzin-gyi mdo)	Vajrasamādhi-sūtra
102 B	Raptu Minepe Gyü (Rab-tu mi-gnas-pa'i rgyud)	
102 B	Dorje Khado Gyü (Rdo-rje mkha'-'gro rgyud)	Vajraḍākinī-tantra
103 F	Dorje Nyingdrel (Rdo-rje snying-'grel)	Hevajra-piṇḍārtha
103 F	Sangwa Dütsi Gyelpö Gyü (Gsang-ba bdud-rtsi rgyal-po'i rgyud)	Amṛtaguhya-tantrarāja
104 F	Abhidhane Gyü (A-bhi-dha-na'i rgyud)	Abhidhāna-tantra
104 F	Nyida Truppa (Nyi-zla grub-pa)	Sūrya-candra-sādhana
104 B	Pel Nyokpa Mepa (Dpal rnyogs-pa med-pa)	Śrī-anāvila-tantra
104 B	Datsa (Brda-rtsa)	
104 B	Gyagar Sangchö (Rgya-gar gsang-spyod)	
106 F	Nyingpo Kordruk (Snying-po skor-drug)	
106 B	Sangchö (see above) (Gsang-spyod)	

Tibetan folio	*Tibetan (phon. and trans.)*	*Sanskrit*
109 B	Nyingje Pema Karpo (Snying-rje pad-ma dkar-po)	Mahākaruṇāpuṇḍarīka-sūtra
112 B	Chödü (Spyod-bsdus)	Caryāsaṃgraha
112 B	Kapey (Ka-dpe)	Āhapramāṇasamyak
113 B	Lhenchik Kyejor (Lhan-cig skyes-sbyor)	
113 B	Yige Shipa (Yi-ge bzhi-pa)	
117 B	Pajingyi Zhüpai Dho (Dpa'-sbyin-gyi-zhus-pa'i mdo)	Vīradatta-gṛhapatiparipṛcchā-sūtra
118 B	Sangwa Samgyi Mikhyabpai Dho (Gsang-ba bsam-gyi mi-khyab-pa'i mdo)	Acintyaguhya-sūtra
120 F	Chözhi Tanpa'i Dho (Chos-bzhi bstan-pa'i mdo)	Caturdharmanirdeśa-sūtra
120 B	Pungzangyi Zhüpai Dho (Dpung-bzang-gi zhus-pa'i mdo)	Subāhuparipṛccha-sūtra
121 F	Tsom (Tshom)	Udānavarga
121 F	Lekdrup (Legs-grub)	Susiddhi
121 B	Jampel Tsenjö ('Jam-dpal mtshan-brjod)	Mañjuśrīnāma-saṃgīti
123 F	Chokchupe Dho (Phyogs-bcu-pa'i mdo)	Daśadharmaka-sūtra
123 F	Dorje Nyingpo Gyen (Rdo-rje snying-po rgyan)	Vajrahṛdayyālaṃkāra
123 B	Könchok Tale Zung (Dkon-mchong ta-la'i gzungs)	Ratnolkā-dhāraṇī
126 F	Jangchup Sempe Chöjuk (Byang-chub-sems-dpa'i spyod-'jug)	Bodhicaryāvatāra
127 F	Tshultrim Tang Denpai Dho (Tshul-khrims dang ldan-pa'i mdo)	Śīlasaṃyukta-sūtra
132 F	Jangchup Lamrim (Byang-chub Lam-rim)	

Tibetan folio	*Tibetan (phon. and trans.)*	*Sanskrit*
132 B	Sangjor (Gsang-sbyor)	
139 B	Zangkyonggi Shüpe Dho (Bzang-skyong-gi zhus-pa'i mdo)	Bhadrapālaparipṛcchā-sūtra
143 B	Dorje Khadrö Gyü (Rdo-rje mkha'-'gro'i rgyud)	Vajraḍākinī-tantra
152 F	Tüshi Nyamjor (Dus-bzhi mnyam-sbyor)	
163 F	Ngakwö Ngaktö (Bsngags-'os bsngags-bstod)	
165 F	Lodrö Mizepae Tenpa (Blo-gros mi-zad-pas bstan-pa)	Akṣayamatinirdeśa-sūtra
168 F	Düpe Dho (Chos-yang-dag-par-bsdus-pa'i mdo)	Dharmasaṃgīti-sūtra
168 F	Daka Yeshe (Da'-ka ye-shes)	Atyayajñāna-sūtra
169 B	Dügyü (Bsdus-rgyud)	Saṃcaya-tantra
169 B	Jampal Zheylung ('Jam-dpal zhal-lung)	Dvikramatattvabhāvanā-nāma mukhāgama
169 B	Yulkhor Khyongyi Zhupai Dho (Yul-'khor-skyong-gi zhus-pa'i mdo)	Rāṣṭrapālaparipṛcchā-sūtra
174 F	Sumchu Tsasumpai Liu (Sum-cu-rtsa-gsum-pa-'i le'u)	Trayastriṃśat-parivarta
176 F	Tsugna Rinpoche Dho (Gtsug-na rin-po-che'i mdo)	Ratnakūṭaparipṛcchā-sūtra
178 F	Chödü (Spyod-bsdus)	Śikṣāsamuccaya
178 F	Teshin Shekpa Tamchekyi Menngak Yangdakpar Drowa (De-bzhin-gshegs-pa tham-cad-kyi man-ngag yang-dag-par 'gro-ba)	Caryamelaka
178 B	Nyingje Chenpo Tenpe Dho (Snying-rje chen-po bstan-pa'i mdo)	Mahākaruṇānirdeśa-sūtra
178 B	Jam Shükyi Dho (Byams zhus-kyi mdo)	Maitreyaparipṛcchā-sūtra
180 F	Gongpa Lungtangyi Dho (Dgongs-pa lung-bstan-gyi mdo)	Saṃdhivyākaraṇa-sūtra

Tibetan folio	*Tibetan (phon. and trans.)*	*Sanskrit*
182 F	Tingdzin Tampe Dho (Ting-'dzin dam-pa'i mdo)	
196 B	Chökyi Gyalpö Dho (Chos-kyi rgyal-po'i mdo)	Dharmarāja-sūtra
196 B	Dampaichö Yongsuzinpai Dho (Dam-pa'i chos yongs-su-'dzin-pa'i mdo)	Saddharmaparigraha-sūtra
203 F	Mennye (Man-snye)	Āmnāyamañjarī
204 F	Dennyi (bden-gnyis)	Satyadvaya
204 B	Nyewar Khorgyi Shüpa (Nye-bar 'khor-gyis zhus-pa)	Upāliparipṛcchā
205 F	Yeshey Nangwa Gyan (Ye-shes snang-ba rgyan)	Jñānālokālaṃkāra-sūtra
206 B	Dükhor Drelchen (Dus-'khor 'grel-chen)	Vimalaprabhā
207 F	Sangwa Samgyi Mikhyabpai Gyü (Gsang-ba bsam-gyis mi-khyab-pa'i rgyud)	Guhyācintya-tantra
210 F	Lhanchik Kyedrup (Lhan-cig skyes-grub)	Sahajasiddhi
214 B	Yeshe Chakgye Dho (Ye-shes phyag-rgya'i mdo)	Jñānamudrā-sūtra
215 F	Namkha Tabui Tingnge Dzingyi Dho (Nam-mkha' lta-bu'i ting-nge 'dzin-gyi mdo)	
215 B	Gyacher Rolpe Dho (Rgya-cher-rol-pa'i-mdo)	Lalitavistara-sūtra
217 F	Chakgya Chenpo Rabtu Mineypai Gyü (Phyag-rgya chen-po rab-tu mi-gnas-pa'i rgyud)	
218 F	Lodrö Gyatsö Zhüpa (Blo-gros rgya-mtshos zhus-pa)	Sāgaramatiparipṛcchā-sūtra
218 B	Chöthamche Jungwa Meypar Tenpa (Chos thams-cad 'byung-ba med-par bstan-pa)	Sarvadharmapravṛttinirdeśa

Tibetan folio	*Tibetan (phon. and trans.)*	*Sanskrit*
219 F	Mitokpe Rabjey (Mi-rtog-pa'i rab-byed)	Nirvikalpaprakaraṇa
219 B	Tsigdü (Tshig-bsdus)	
222 B	Chö Thamchekyi Nampartröpe Tingnge Dzingyi Gyalpo (Chos thams-cad-kyi rnam-par spros-pa'i ting-nge-'dzin-gyi rgyal-po)	Sarvadharmasvabhāvasamatāvipañcita-samādhirāja
223 B	Lhanchik Kyepa Samgyi Mikhyabpai Gyü (Lhan-cig skyes-pa bsam-gyis mi-khyab-pa'i rgyud)	
232 B	Dekhonanyi Raptu Mineypai Gyü (De-kho-na-nyid rab-tu mi-nges-pa'i rgyud)	
233 F	Tsokchö Chenmo (Tshogs-chos chen-mo)	
237 F	Gomdön Drubpa (Sgom-don grub-pa)	Bhāvanārthasiddhi (Dhvanārtha)
241 F	Tsukna Rinchengyi Zhüpa (cf. 336)	
243 F	Dezhin Shekpai Sangwai Dho (De-bzhin-gshegs-pa'i gsang-ba'i mdo)	Tathāgatācintyaguhyanirdeśa-sūtra
243 B	Dawa Dönmai Dho (Zla-ba sgron-ma'i mdo)	Candrapradīpa-sūtra
246 F	Phakpa Sangye Drowa ('Phags-pa sangs-rgyas 'gro-ba)	Ārya-buddhasaṃgīti
246 F	Drenpa Nyerzhak (Dran-pa nyer-bzhag)	Smṛtyupasthāna
246 F	Jedren (Rjes-dran)	Anusmṛti
246 B	Nampar Mitogpala Jukpai Zung (Rnam-par mi-rtog-pa-la 'jug-pa'i gzungs)	Avikalpapraveśa-dhāraṇī
257 F	Chakgya Chenpo Yigeshipa (Phyag-rgya chen-po yi-ge bzhi-pa)	
287 B	Tsokchö Tashi Phüntsok (Tshogs-chos bkra-shis phun-tshogs)	

Tibetan folio	*Tibetan (phon. and trans.)*	*Sanskrit*
288 F	Ngönpa Dzö Rangdrel (Mngon-pa mdzod rang-'grel)	Abhidharmakośa-bhāṣya
307 F	Ghappa Ngönchung (Gab-pa mngon-phyung)	
308 F	Shülen (Zhus-lan)	
311 B	Trubnying (Grub-snying)	
315 F	Zer Nampa Ngai Menngak (Gzer rnam-pa lnga'i man-ngag)	
369 F	Namdrel (Rnam-'grel)	Pramāṇavarttikā
372 F	Drelpa Tönsel ('Grel-pa don-gsal)	Sphuṭārthā
376 F	Sangdü Lhamo Shishü (Gsang-'dus lha-mo bzhis-zhus)	Guhyamsamāja Caturdevīparipṛcchā

Index of Quotations

DIFFERENT EDITIONS USED

	Abbrev. Used	Edition
1.	KNE	Kagyur Narthang Edition
2.	TNE	Tangyur Narthang Edition
3.	KJE	Kagyur Japanese Edition
4.	TJE	Tangyur Japanese Edition
5.	KPE	Kagyur Peking Edition
6.	TPE	Tangyur Peking Edition
7.	KLE	Kagyur Lhasa Edition
8.	GM	Gampagar Monastery (Tashijong)
9.	NBE	New Bilingual Edition
10.	LE	Lhalungpa Edition
11.	RE	Rumtek Edition of *Madhyamakamūla-śāstra*
12.	DE	Delhi Edition
13.	KZ	Annotated Commentary by Khenpo Zhanga, Derge Edition
14.	LEM	Lhalungpa Edition of *Six Yukt Śāstra of Madhyamaka*

Sūtra or Tantra within the editions is designated by (S) or (T)

Index to Kagyur and Tangyur of Quotations in Mahāmudrā Text

Tib. Folio	*Quotation*	*Source*
4 B	Sachupai-dho	Dho-phel-po-che (Avataṃsaka-sūtra) (S) KJE, V. Li, F. 103, l. 8
4 B	Dorje Gur	(T) KNE, V. KA, F. 375B, l. 7
4 B	Sambuti	(T) TNE, V. GA, F. 309, l. 3
4 B	Lama Ritro Aungchuk	Doha-dzogye (Aśata-dohākośa) GM, F. 2, l. 1
5 F	Langkar Shekpai Dho	
5 F	Sambuti	(T) TNE, V. GA, F. 309, l. 4
5 B	Saraha	TPE, V. TSI, F. 32B, l. 3
5 B	Gyu-taknyi	(T) TNE, V. KA, F. 336, l. 5
5 B	Sambuti	(T) KNE, V. GA, F. 374, l. 7
6 F	Nāgārjuna	
6 F	Langkar Shekpai Dho	(S) KNE, V. DU, F. 285B, l. 5
6 F	Phal-po-che	(S) KJE, V. YI, F. 152B, l. 1
6 F	Könchoktrin	
6 B	Dorje Gur	(T) TNE, V. KA, F. 396, l. 3; F. 395B, l. 7
7 F	Dongpo Köpa	
7 B	Jampal Nampar Rolpai Dho	
7 B	Chojuk	
8 F	Sheytring	
8 F	Dekhonanyi Tenpe Dho	
8 F	Tsuktor Chenpö Dho	
8 B	Tokpa Gyepe Dho	
8 B	Dhodüpa	
8 B	Senyingpo Khorlo Chupai Dho	
9 F	Dhode-gyen	KZ, F. 64B
9 B	Gongpa Ngedrel	(S) KLE, V. DU, F. 37B, l. 7
9 B	Gomrim Barpa	(Śāstra) TNE, V. A, F. 46B, l. 4
10 F	Thekchen-la Depa Gompai Dho	(S) KLE, V. DA, F. 36, l. 6

Tib. Folio	*Quotation*	*Source*
10 B	Gomrim Thama	(Śāstra) TNE, V. DO, F. 59B, l. 1
11 F	Dho Gongpa Ngedrel	(S) KLE, V. DU, F. 37B, l. 8
11 B	Second Gomrim	(Śāstra) TNE, V. A, F. 48, l. 2
11 B	Dhodegyen	(Śāstra) KZ, F. 50, l. 1
12 B	Dho Gongpa Ngedrel	(S) KLE, V. DU, F. 38, l. 8
13 B	Second Gomrim	(Śāstra) TNE, V. A, F. 50B, l. 3
14 B	Dho Gongpa Ngedrel	(S) KLE, V. DU, F. 38B, l. 3
15 F	Ütha Namje	(Śāstra) TPE, V. PHI, F. 46B, l. 1
16 F	Ütha Namje	(Śāstra) TPE, V. PHI, F. 46B, l. 8
16 B	Ngönpa Küntu	(Śāstra) KZ, F. 12, l. 1
17 F	Ngönpa Küntu	(Śāstra) KZ, F. 11, l. 3
17 B	Bodhicaryāvatāra	(Śāstra) NBE, F. 60
18 F	Ngönpa Küntu	(Śāstra) KZ, F. 4B, l.5
18 F	Nyensa	(Śāstra) TPE, V. WI, F. 174, l. 4
18 B	Nyensa	(Śāstra) TPE, V. WI, F. 174, l. 6
19 F	Se Ngöshi	(Śāstra) TPE, V. WI, F. 153, l. 6
20 F	Gomrim Dangpo	(Śāstra) TNE, V. A, F. 33, l. 5
20 F	Uma Nyingpa	(Śāstra)TPE, V. DZA, F. 4, l. 8
20 B	First Gomrim	(Śāstra)TNE, V. A, F. 33, l. 6
20 B	Madhyamika Hṛdaya	(S) TPE, V. DZA, F. 4B, l. 8
21 F	Dho Gongpa Ngedrel	(S) KLE, V. DU, F. 28B, l. 5
21 B	Könchog-trin	(S) KLE, V. TSHA, F. 146, l. 7
21 B	Sūtrālaṃkāra	(Śāstra) KZ, Peypung Mon., F. 54, l. 1
23 F	Dho Gongdrel	(S) KLE, V. DU, F. 28, l. 7
23 B	Second Gomrim	(Śāstra) TNE, V. A, F. 49, l. 3
25 F	Dho Gongdrel	(S) KLE, V. DU, F. 38B, l. 2
25 F	Dhode-gyen	(Śāstra) KZ, Peypung Mon., F. 54, l. 4
25 B	Ngönpa Küntu	(Śāstra) KZ, Peypung Mon., F. 118B, l. 6
25 B	Dho Gongdrel	(S) KLE, V. DU, F. 30, l. 3
25 B	Ngönpa Küntu	(Śāstra) KZ, Peypung Mon., F. 112, l. 4
26 B	Nyensa	(Śāstra) TPE, V. WI, F. 162, l. 6
27 F	Nyensa	(Śāstra) TPE, V. WI, F. 163B, l. 2
27 B	Dhode-gyen	(Śāstra) KZ, Peypung Mon., F. 60B, l. 3
27 B	Sheytring	(Śāstra) TPE, V. NGE, F. 289, l. 2
27 B	Bodhicaryāvatāra	(Śāstra) NBE, F. 136
28 B	Ngönpa Küntu	(Śāstra) KZ, Peypung Mon., F. 119B, l. 4
29 B	First Gomrim	(Śāstra) TNE, V. A, F. 31B, l. 5
29 B	Middle Gomrim	(Śāstra) TNE, V. A, F. 47B, l. 3
30 F	Second Gomrim	(Śāstra) TNE, V. A, F. 46B, l. 6
30 F	Dho Gongpa Ngedrel	(S) KLE, V. DU, F. 47, l. 3

Tib. Folio	*Quotation*	*Source*
31 B	Nyensa	(Śāstra) TPE, V. WI, F. 179, l. 2
31 B	Third Gomrim	(Śāstra) TNE, V. A, F. 63B, l. 2
33 B	Dho Gongpa Ngedrel	(S) KLE, V. DU, F. 38, l. 2
34 F	Dho Gongpa Ngedrel	(S)KLE, V. DU, F. 38, l. 4
34 B	Sherchin Düpa	
34 B	Sheytring	(Śāstra) TPE, V. NGE, F. 285, l. 6
34 B	Jangchub Lamdrön	(Śāstra) TPE, V. KI, F. 276, l. 8
34 B	Dhodüpa	(S) KNE, V. KA, F. 217B, l. 1
34 B	Dhodüpa	(S) KNE, V. KA, F. 222, l. 1
35 F	Sherchin Düngyapa	(S) KNE, V. KA, F. 161, l. 3
36 F	First Gomrim	(Śāstra) TNE, V. A, F. 31B, l. 6
38 B	Nyansa	(Śāstra) TPE, V. WI, F. 93, l. 3
39 F	Nyansa	(Śāstra) TPE, V. WI, F. 93, l. 7
39 B	Namdrü Shüpe Dho	(S) TPE, V. WI, F. 93, l. 3
41 F	Tingdzin Gyalpo	(S) KNE, V. TA, F. 22B, l. 3
41 F	Third Gomrim	(Śāstra) TNE, V. A, F. 60B, l. 7
41 F	First Gomrim	(Śāstra) TNE, V. A, F. 32B, l. 7
41 B	Uma Nyingpo	(Śāstra) TPE, V. DZA, F. 4B, l. 7
42 B	Ütha Namje	(Śāstra) TPE, V. PHIP, F. 46, l. 8
43 B	Dhode-gyen	(Śāstra) KZ, Peypung, F. 54, l. 4–F. 54B, l. 2
45 F	Nyensa	(Śāstra) TPE, V. WI, F. 162, l. 2
46 F	Nyensa	(Śāstra) TPE, V. WI, F. 162, l. 2
50 B	Rinchen Trengwa	(Śāstra) V. LE, F. 61, l. 16
50 B	Zhigyapa	(Śāstra)TPE, V. TSHA, F. 18, l. 1
51 F	Uma Jukpa	(Śāstra) TPE, V. 'A, F. 254B, l. 3
51 F	Tsashe	(Śāstra) RE, F. 18B, l. 6
51 F	Tsashe	(Śāstra) RE, F. 19, l. 2
51 B	Tsashe	(Śāstra) RE, F. 31B, l. 5
51 B	Tsashe	(Śāstra) RE, F. 18B, l. 4
52 F	Tsashe	(Śāstra) RE, F. 32, l. 1
52 F	Uma Jukpa	(Śāstra) TPE, V. 'A, F. 254B, l. 7
52 F	Tsashe	(Śāstra) V. RE, F. 18B, l. 5
52 F	Uma Jukpa	(Śāstra) TPE, V. 'A, F. 257, l. 2
52 B	First Gomrim	(Śāstra) TNE, V. A, f. 51, l. 7
52 B	Tsashe	(Śāstra) RE, F. 2, l. 1
53 F	Tsashe	(Śāstra) RE, F. 21, l. 6
53 F	Uma Jukpa	(Śāstra) TPE, V. 'A, F. 253B, l. 4
53 F	Tsashe	(Śāstra) RE, F. 15, l. 1
53 B	Jangchub Semdrel	(Śāstra) TPE, V. GI, F. 43B, l. 7
53 B	Jangchub Semdrel	(Śāstra) TPE, V. GI, F. 43B, l. 8
54 F	Langshek	(S) KLE, V. DU, F. 180B, l. 1
54 F	Tingdzin Gyalpo	(S) KLE, V. TA, F. 43, l. 2
54 F	First Gomrim	(Śāstra) TNE, V. A, F. 51B, l. 2

Tib. Folio	*Quotation*	*Source*
54 B	Tsashe	(Śāstra) RE, F. 14, l. 4
55 F	Köntsek	(S) KJE, V. 'i, F. 115, l. 6
55 F	Jangchub Semdrel	(Śāstra) TPE, V. GI, F. 45, l. 4
55 F	Tsashe	(Śāstra) RE, F. 27, l. 6
55 B	Tsashe	(Śāstra) RE, F. 23B, l. 6
55 B	Tsashe	(Śāstra) RE, F. 24, l. 1
55 B	Tsashe	(Śāstra) RE, F. 15B, l. 2
56 F	Langshek	(S) TPE, V. DU, F. 149, l. 5
56 F	Chöjuk	(Śāstra) NBE, F. 190–191
56 F	First Gomrim	(Śāstra) TNE, V. A, F. 51B, l. 5
58 B	Chönyi Miyowai Dho	(S) KLE, V. TA, F. 272, l. 5
58 B	Dhüpa	(S) KNE, V. KA, F. 202, l. 4
59 F	Tsashe	(Śāstra) RE, F. 29, l. 2
59 B	Sherchin Düngyapa	(S) Kagyur, Mahāratnakūṭa, V. 'i, F. 177, l. 2
60 B	Jangchub Semdrel	(Śāstra) KZ, Derge, Peypung, F. 18, l. 4
61 F	Tingdzin Gyalpo	(S) KNE, V. JA, F. 43B, l. 2
61 F	Tingdzin Gyalpo	(S) KNE, V. TA, F. 43B, l. 7
65 B	First Gomrim	(Śāstra) TNE, V. A, F. 32, l. 4
66 F	Osungkyi Shüpa	(S) KLE, V. 'i, Mahāratnakūṭa, F. 116B, l. 7
66 F	Uma Jukpa	(Śāstra) TPE, V. 'A, F. 254, l. 8
67 F	Dho Gondrel	(S) KPE, V. DU, F. 29B, l. 8
69 B–70 F	First Gomrim	(Śāstra) TNE, V. A, F. 54B, l. 7
74 B	Tsashe	(Śāstra) RE, F. 14, l. 4
74 B	Tsashe	(Śāstra) RE, F. 26B, l. 5
75 B	Dramze Chenpo	(Śāstra) TPE, V. TSI, F. 34, l. 6
75 B	Bodhicaryāvatāra	(Śāstra) NBE, F. 185
75 B	Dhodüpa	(S) KNE, V. KA, F. 197B, l. 5
76 F	Saraha (from Damngadzö)	DE, V. NGA, F. 9, l. 3
76 F	Jangchub Semdrel	(Śāstra) TPE, V. GI, F. 45, l. 1
76 F	Uma Jukpa	(Śāstra) TPE, V. 'A, F. 254B, l. 1
77 F	Jangchub Semdrel	(Śāstra) TPE, V. GI, F. 46, l. 3
77 F	Tawa Dhodü (from Doha Dzogye)	(Śāstra) GM, F. 20, l. 5
77 B	Dorje Gur	(T) KNE, V. KA, F. 375B, l. 6
77 B	Langkar Shekpai Dho	(S) KPE, V. DU, F. 184, l. 3
78 B	Osungkyi Shüpa	(S) KLE, V. 'i Mahāratnakūṭa, F. 116B, l. 7
78 B	Second Gomrim	(Śāstra) TNE, V. A, F. 32B, l. 5
79 F	Gomrim Dangpo	(Śāstra) TNE, V. A, F. 35B, l. 6
79 F	Gomrim Dangpo	(Śāstra) TNE, V. A, F. 34B, l. 7

Tib. Folio	*Quotation*	*Source*
79 B	Umai Menngak	(Śāstra) TPE, V. GI, F. 8B, l. 5
80 B	Gomrim	(Śāstra) TNE, V. A, F. 75B, l. 1
	(This quote was found in Kamalashila's *Naljorla Jugpa* and not in any of the three Gomrims.)	
81 F	Tingdzin Gyalpo	(S) KNE, V. TA, F. 22B, l. 4
81 F	Second Gomrim	TNE, V. A, F. 52B, l. 7
81 B	Second Gomrim	TNE, V. A, F. 52B, l. 9
81 B	Jangchub Lamdrön	TPE, V. KI, F. 277, l. 5
82 B	Namkha Dzökyi Shüpai Dho	KLE (S), V. DA, F. 363B, l. 4
83 B	Rimnga	TPE (T), V. GI, F. 54, l. 3
83 B	Sangdü	
84 B	Maitrēpa	GM, F. 15B, l. 4
85 B	Gyü Lama	KZ, Peypung, F. 12, l. 3
86 B	Maitrīpa	GM, F. 21, l. 1
86 B	Lodrö Gyatso Shüpai Dho	KLE (S), V. NA, F. 118B, l. 5
86 B	Lodrö Gyatso Shüpai Dho	KLE (S), V. NA, F. 120, l. 7
86 B	Lodrö Gyatso Shüpai Dho	KLE (S), V. NA, F. 39, l. 1
87 F	Bumo Rinchengyi Shüpai Dho	KLE (S), V. PA, F. 438B, l. 7
88 B	Dasang Thigle	KNE (T), V. KA, F. 453B, l. 6
95 F	Third Gomrim	TNE (S), V. A, F. 65B, l. 5
100 F	Gampopa	Coll. Works 1st part, V. CHA, F. 141, l. 5
101 B	Second Gomrim	TNE (S), V. A, F. 51, l. 1
102 F	Rimnga	TPE (T), V. GI, F. 57, l. 3
102 F	Khyepar Semkyi Shüpai Dho	KLE (S), V. PA, F. 41, l. 1
102 B	Saraha	DE, V. NGA, F. 5, l. 5
102 B	Dorje Khado	KNE (T), V. KA, F. 512, l. 7
103 F	Taknyi	KNE (T), V. KA, F. 313B, l. 5
103 B	Saraha	DE, V. NGA, F. 40B, l. 7
103 B	Tilopa	DE, V. NGA, F. 17B, l. 3
104 F	Nyida Truppa	TPE (T), V. NGA, F. 244B, l. 4
111 B	Dzö	Root Text of Abhidharma-kośa (in Xylograph)
111 B	Gomrim Dangpo	TNE (S), V. A, F. 28B, l. 4
112 F	Taknyi	KNE (T), V. KA (T), F. 347, l. 6
114 F	Chakdan Thigle	KNE, V. KA (T), F. 414. l. 4
114 F	Sangye Thöpa	KPE (T), V. NGA, F. 134, l. 7
115 F	Tilopa	DE, V. NGA, F. 18, l. 2
116 B	Dongpo Köpai Dho	KLE (S), V. HI, F. 203, l. 6
116 B	Rinchen Trengwa	LEM, P. 80, l. 21
117 B	Pajingyi Shupai Dho	KLE (S), V. ZI, (Mahāratnakūṭa), F. 210, l. 1
118 B	Dhodüpa	KNE (S), V. KA, F. 211B, l. 4

Tib. Folio	*Quotation*	*Source*
118 B	Sangwa Samgyi Mikhyabpai	KLE (S), V. Tshi, Mahāratnakūṭa, F. 116, l. 3
119 B	Tsom	KNE (S), V. LA, F. 375B, l. 5
121 F	Tsom	KNE (S), V. LA, F. 355B, l. 1
122 F	Bhavilha	TPE (T), V. NU, F. 244B, l. 7 & 242B, l. 8
122 F	Dorje Nyingpo Gyen	KPE, V. CHA (T), F. 316, l. 4
122 F	Dorje Gur	KNE (T), V. KA, F. 411B, l. 6
122 F	Bhavilha	TPE, V. NU (T), F. 242B, l. 7
122 B	Dorje Khado	KNE, V. KHA (T), F. 425, l. 2
122 B	Rimnga	TPE, V. GI (T), F. 60, l. 4
123 F	Dorje Nyingpo Gyen	KPE, V. CHA (T), F. 316B, l. 5
123 F	Bhavilha	TPE, V. NU (T), F. 243B, l. 6
123 F	Chochupai Dho	KLE, V. DZI, Mahāratnakūṭa, F. 185, l. 4
124 B	Gampopa	Coll. Works, 2nd Part, V. BA, F. 251, l. 1
124 B	Gampopa	Coll. Works, 2nd part, F. 252B, l. 3
125 B	Yanggönpa	Coll. Works of Yanggönpa, E., F. 21F, l. 5
126 B	Tshultrim Denpai Dho	KPE (S), V. SHU, F. 133, l. 2
127 B	Jangchub Sempai Chöjuk	NBE, Pg. 79
127 B	Dhodüpa	KNE (S), V. KA, F. 209, l. 5
128 B	Sheyting	TPE, V. NGE (Tam-tshog), F. 285, l. 4
132 B	Kapay	DE, V. NGA, P. 35, l. 3
135 F	Dorje Trengwa	KNE (T), V. CHA, F. 183F, l. 1
135 B	Nāropa	DE, V. NGA, p. 35B, l. 6
136 B	Dhodüpa	NBE, V. KA (S), F. 222
137 F	Utha	TPE, V. PHI, F. 46B, l. 1
137 B	Tilopa	GM, F. 17B, l. 1
139 B	Zangkyonggyi Shüpai Dho	KLE, V. THA (S) (has somewhat similar passage)
140 B	Tilopa	GM, F. 14, l. 4
144 F	Nāropa	DE, V. NGA, F. 35, l. 2
145 B	Dohā	DE, V. NGA, F. 8, l. 2
145 B	Dohā	DE, V. NGA, F. 6, l. 4
146 F	Dohā	DE, V. NGA, F. 8, l. 4
148 F	Ǖtha Namje	TPE, V. PHI, F. 46B, l. 2
148 F	Middle & Last Gomrim	TNE, V. A, F. 63F, l. 5
150 F	Dohā	DE, V. NGA, F. 71, l. 2
150 B	Saraha	DE, V. NGA, F. 71, l. 3
150 B	Maitrīpa	GM, F. 14, l. 3
150 B	Tilopa	GM, F. 15, l. 3
152 B	Utha Commentary	TPE, V. WI, F. 20B, l. 2

Tib. Folio	*Quotation*	*Source*
153 F	Second Gomrim	TNE, V. A, F. 50B, l. 1
153 B	Nyensa	TPE, V. WI, F. 160B, l. 6
154 F	Nyensa	TPE, V. WI, F. 160B, l. 7
155 F	Utha	TPE, V. PHI, F. 46B, l. 1
156 B	Second & Third Gomrim	TNE, V. A, F. 54B, l. 4
156 B	Second Gomrim	TNE, V. A, F. 50B, l. 6
157 F	Tilopa	GM, F. 17F, l. 6
160 F	First Gomrim	TNE, V. A, F. 33B, l. 3
162 F	First Gomrim	TNE, V. A, F. 33B, l. 1
162 B	First Gomrim	TNE, V. A, F. 31B, l. 5
163 B	Second Gomrim	TNE, V. A, F. 46B, l. 6
164 F	Tingdzin Gyalpo	KLE, V. TA, F. 44, l. 7
164 B	Second Gomrim	TNE, V. A, F. 48B, l. 5
165 F	Lodrö Mizepae Tenpa	KLE, V. PHA, F. 231, l. 6
165 F	Lodrö Mizepae Tenpa	KLE, V. PHA, F. 232, l. 4
166 B	Taknyi	KLE, V. KA (T), F. 320B, l. 1
168 B	Saraha	DE, V. NGA, F. 6B, l. 3
168 B	Tilopa	GM, F. 16B, l. 5
168 B	Chojuk	NBE, F. 56
169 B	Dorje Khadro	KLE, V. NGA, F. 40F, l. 6
169 B	Taknyi	KNE, V. KA (T), F. 339, l. 5
170 F	Dorje Gur	KNE, V. KA (T), F. 375B, l. 6
170 B	Jangchup Semdrel	TPE, V. GI (T), F. 44, l. 5
170 B	First Gomrim	TNE, V. A (S), F. 51B, l. 5
171 B	Saraha	TPE, V. TSI (T), F. 36, l. 3
173 B	Saraha	TPE (T), V. TSI, F. 34B, l. 6
174 F	Köntsek	KLE (Mahāratnakūṭa Sūtra), V. 'i, F. 123, l. 2
174 F	Köntsek	KLE (Mahāratnakūṭa Sūtra), V. 'i, F. 224, l. 3
174 F	Sumchu Tsasumpai Liu	KLE (S), V. TSA, F. 215, l. 7
174 B	Chökyi Yingki Rangzhin Yermeypar Tenpa (Köntsek)	KLE, Mahāratnakūṭa) V. DZI, F. 161, l. 1
175 B	Köntsek	KLE, Mahāratnakūṭa, V. 'i, F. 123, l. 2
176 F	Tsugna Rinpoche Dho	KLE, Mahāratnakūṭa, V. 'i, F. 224, l. 2
177 B	Jangchup Semdrel	TPE (T), V. GI, F. 44B, l. 6
179 F	Saraha	DE, V. NGA, F. 6B, l. 4
179 F	Saraha	DE, V. NGA, F. 15B, l. 6
179 B	Tilopa	GM, F. 15, l. 3
179 B	Śavari	DE, V. NGA, F. 15B, l. 4
180 F	Osungkyi Shüpa	KLE, Mahāratnakūṭa, V. 'i, F. 116B, l. 8
180 F	Gongdrel	KLE (S), V. CHA, F. 10, l. 1
180 B	Gongpa Lungtangyi Dho	KNE (S), V. CHA, F. 284B, l. 4
180 B	Taknyi	KNE (T), V. KA, F. 320B, l. 1

Tib. Folio	*Quotation*	*Source*
180 B	Taknyi	KNE (T), V. KA, F. 320, l. 4
181 B	Saraha	DE, V. NGA, F. 6B, l. 4
181 B	Śavari	DE, V. NGA, F. 14B, l. 6
182 F	Maitrīpa	GM, F. 20B, l. 6
182 B	Langshek	KPE (S), V. DU, F. 128B, l. 1
182 B	Dorje Gur	KNE (T), V. KA, F. 376, l. 2
183 F	Langshek	KPE (S), V. DU, F. 180B
183 F	Dorje Gur	KNE (T), V. KA, F. 396, l. 3
183 B	Virūpa	GM, F. 9, l. 6
184 F	Dorje Gur	KNE (T), V. KA, F. 395B, l. 7
184 F	Jangchub Semdrel	TPE (T), V. GI, F. 44, l. 6
184 F	Saraha	DE, V. NGA, F. 6B, l. 2
184 B	Zhiyapa	TPE, V. TSHA, F. 10B, l. 3
184 B	Dennyi	TPE (Madhyamaka), V. GI, F. 7, l. 3
185 B	Jangchup Semdrel	TPE (T), V. GI, F. 45B, l. 1
193 F	Jangchup Semdrel	TPE (T), V. GI, F. 44B, l. 3
194 F	Saraha	TPE (T), V. TSI, F. 31B, l. 5
195 B	Second Gomrim	TNE (S), V. A, F. 52F, l. 2
200 F	Nyensa	TPE, V. WI, F. 162, l. 6
203 F	Gampopa	Coll. Works, 2nd part, V. DZA, F. 24, l. 4
203 B	Sangdü	KNE (T), V. CHA, F. 71B, l. 4
204 F	Jangchup Semdrel	TPE (T), V. GI, F. 43F, l. 6
204 F	Dennyi	TPE (Madhyamaka), V. GI, F. 7B, l. 8
204 B	Zhigyapa	TPE (Madhyamaka), V. TSHA, F. 10B, l. 3
205 F	Gyü Lama	KZ, F. 13B, l. 2
205 F	Sangdü	KNE (T), V. CHA, F. 72, l. 7
206 F	Nāropai Tawa Dhordü	GM, F. 18, l. 3
207 F	Nāropai Tawa Dhordü	GM, F. 19B, l. 3
207 B	Sambhuti	KNE (T), V. GA, F. 294B, l. 5
208 F	Sambhuti	KZ, F. 17B, l. 1
208 B	Taknyi	TNE (T), V. KA, F. 338B, l. 7
209 B	Taknyi	TNE (T), V. KA, F. 331B, l. 2
210 F	Taknyi	TNE (T), V. KA, F. 319B, l. 2
212 F	Gampopa	Coll. Works, V. SA, F. 5B, l. 4
212 B	Saraha	TPE (T), V. TSI, F. 31B, l. 6
212 B	Śavari	DE, V. NGA, F. 15, l. 1
212 B	Virūpa	GM, F. 7B, l. 1
215 B	Sambhuti	KLE (T), V. GA, F. 397, l. 3
216 F	Tawa Dhordü	F. 10B, l.4
	Lodrö Mezepe	KLE, V. PHA, F. 247, l. 6
218 B	Chöthamche Jungwa Meypar Tenpa	KLE, V. PHA, F. 463, l. 4
218 B	Taknyi	KNE, V. KA, F. 336B, l. 3

Tib. Folio	*Quotation*	*Source*
219 F	Saraha	TPE (T), V. TSI, F. 37B, l. 7
219 F	Virūpa	GM, F. 8B, l. 1
219 B	Nāropa & Maitrīpa	GM, F. 21, l. 2
219 B	Songs of Milarepa	Chitari Monastery, F. 142, l. 5
219 B	Gampopa	Coll. Works, V. GA, F. 55, l. 3
222 B	Sherab Nyingpo	KNE (S), V. KA, F. 263, l. 2
222 B	Nyampanyi Nampartröpa	KNE (S), V. TA, F. 135, l. 5
223 F	Taknyi	KNE (T), V. KA, F. 320, l. 3
223 F	Dorje Gur	KNE (T), V. KA, F. 376, l. 3
223 B	Sambhuti	KNE (T), V. GA, F. 294, l. 6
223 B	Saraha	TPE (T), V. TSI, F. 34B, l. 5
224 F	Śavari	DE, V. NGA, F. 15B, l. 2
224 F	Nāropa	GM, F. 18, l. 3
224 B	Gampopa's Life (The Jewel of Liberation)	Namthar Thargyen, F. 55, l. 3
227 F	Bodhicaryāvatāra (Chöjuk)	NBE, F. 197
227 B	Gampopa	Coll. Works, V. SA, F. 499, l. 4
228 F	Gampopa	Coll. Works, V. 'A, F. 358B, l. 2
229 F	Taknyi	KNE (T), V. KA, F. 327, l. 4
232 B	Pal Śavari	DE, V. NGA, F. 15B, l. 7
233 F	Gampopa	Coll. Works, V. PHA, F. 65, l. 3
233 F	Gampopa	RE, F. 13B, l. 4
234 F	Yanggönpa	Coll. Works of Yanggönpa, F. 125B, l. 3
234 B	Gampopa	Coll. Works, V. THA, F. 218, l. 5
235 F	Yanggönpa	Coll. Works of Yanggönpa, F. 4B, l. 5
235 B	Yanggönpa	Coll. Works of Yanggönpa, F. 126, l. 2
236 F	Gampopa	Coll. Works, V. PHA, F. 63 B, l. 1
236 F	Gomchung	Coll. Works of Gampopa, 1st part, V. GA, F. 50, l. 2
236 B	Sangwa Dütsi Gyalpoi Gyü	KPE (T), V. NGA, F. 52B, l. 6
238 B	Gampopa	Coll. Works, 2nd part, V. YA, F. 363, l. 5
240 F	Tilopa	GM, F. 17, l. 2
240 F	Songs of Milarepa	Chitari E, F. 241, l. 2
240 B	Ngöntok-gyen	Xylograph of Sikkim, E, F. 11, l. 5
240 B	Chöjuk	NBE, F. 58
241 F	Tsugna Rinchengyi Shüpa	KLE (Mahāratnakūṭa), V. 'i, F. 239B, l. 6
243 F	Chöjuk	NBE, F. 59
243 F	Dezhin Shekpai Sangwai Dho	KLE (Mahāratnakūṭa), V. TSHI, F. 205, l. 1
243 B	Sheytring	TPE (Tamtshog Section), V. NGEY, F. 283, l. 3

Tib. Folio	*Quotation*	*Source*
244 F	Sheytring	TPE (Tamtshog Section), V. NGEY, F. 286, l. 2
244 B	Gampopa	Coll. Works, V. TA, F. 185B, l. 4
246 B	Nampar Mitogpala Jukpai Zung	V. A, F. 35, l. 3
247 F	Śavari	DE, V. NGA, F. 15, l. 5
247 F	Third Gomrim	TNE (S), V. A, F. 66B, l. 2
248 F	Third Gomrim	TNE (S), V. A, F. 67, l. 5
248 B	Umai Menngak	TNE (Madhyamaka), V. GI, F. 9F, l. 2
250 F	Gampopa	Coll. Works, 2nd part, V. RA, F. 371B, l. 4
251 F	Gampopa	Coll. Works, 1st part, V. DA, F. 40B, l. 5
252 F	Śavari	DE, V. NGA, F. 16, l. 2
252 B	Damngakdzö	DE, V. NGA, F. 15B, l. 7
252 B	Virūpa	GM, F. 9, l. 2
253 F	Śavari	DE, V. NGA, F. 15, l. 2
253 F	Virūpa	GM, F. 7, l. 3
253 B	Śavari	DE, V. NGA, F. 15, l. 7
253 B	Virūpa	GM, F. 9B, l. 5
254 F	Tsokchö	Coll. Works of Gampopa, 1st part, V. CHA, F. 139, l. 1
254 B	Saraha	DE, V. NGA, F. 7, l. 2
255 F	Virūpa	GM, F. 7B, l. 2
256 B	Gampopa	Coll. Works, 2nd part, V. DZA, F. 325B, l. 7
256 B	Śavari	DE, F. 15B, l. 7
256 B	Gampopa	Coll. Works, 2nd part, V. DZA, F. 318, l. 6
257 B	Gampopa	Coll. Works, 2nd part, V. 'A, F. 54, l. 1
259 B	Virūpa	GM, F. 9B, l. 2
260 F	Śavari	DE, V. NGA, F. 15, l. 7
260 F	Virūpa	GM, F. 9, l. 3
261 F	Dohādzogye	GM, F. 8B, l. 6
262 F	Dhūpa	KNE (S), V. KA, F. 206B, l. 6
262 F	Jangchup Semdrel	TPE (T), V. GI, F. 45, l. 5
262 B	Chöjuk	NBE, F. 193
263 F	Gampopa	Coll. Works, 1st part, V. GA, F. 53, l. 3
264 B	Chöjuk	NBE, F. 191
266 B	Śavari	DE, V. NGA, F. 15B, l. 3
266 B	Virūpa	GM, F. 7B, l. 1
266 B	Gampopa	Coll. Works, 2nd part, V. 'a, F. 379, l. 4

Tib. Folio	*Quotation*	*Source*
267 F	Saraha	DE, V. NGA, F. 15B, l. 5
267 B	Saraha	DE, V. NGA, F. 9, l. 3
269 B	Dhodupa	KNE (S), V. KA, F. 198, l. 4
270 B	Śavari	DE, V. NGA, F. 16B, l. 1
271 B	Jangchub Semdrel	TPE (T), V. GI, F, 46B, l. 6
273 B	Gampopa	Coll. Works, 2nd part, V. PHA, F. 266, l. 5
273 B	Gampopa	Coll. Works, 1st part, V. THA, F. 221B, l. 7
274 B	Gomtsül	Coll. Works of Gampopa, 1st part, V. NYA, F. 119, l. 3
275 F	Dhüpa	KNE, V. KA, F. 197B, l. 7
275 F	Śavari	DE, V. NGA, F. 15, l. 7
278 F	Gampopa	Coll. Works, 1st part, V. GA, F. 54, l. 3
278 B	Tsashe	RE (Madhyamakamūla-prajñā) F. 27, l. 6
278 B	Jangchup Semdrel	TPE (T), V. GI, F. 45B, l. 8
299 F	Gampopa	Coll. Works, 1st Part, V. GA, F. 50, l. 3
299 B	Taknyi	KNE (T), V. KA, F. 323B, l. 6
280 F	Virūpa	GM, F. 7B, l. 5
280 F	Śavari	DE, V. NGA, F. 14B, l. 7
280 F	Gampopa	Coll. Works, 2nd part, V. ZHA, F. 340, l. 2
281 F	Dhode-gyen	KZ, F. 18, l. 2
281 F	Chöjuk	NBE, F. 199
283 B	Gampopa	Coll. Works, 2nd Part, V. A, F. 17, l. 7 & V. SA, F. 407, l. 4
285 F	Gampopa	Coll. Works 1st Part, V. NYA, F. 175B, l. 5
287 F	Yanggönpa	Coll. Works of Yanggönpa. F. 6B
287 B	Gampopa	Coll. Works, 2nd part, V. SA, F. 407, l. 7 & 1st part, V. NGA, F. 80, l. 3
288 F	Ngönpa-dzö	Xylograph E. at Inst. of Tibetology, Sikkim, F. 2, l. 2
288 F	Chöjuk	NBE, F. 197
288 F	Dho	KNE (S), V. TA, F. 45, l. 7
290 F	Gampopa	Coll. Works, 1st part, V. GA, F. 54, l. 3
290 B	Gampopa	Coll. Works, 2nd part, V. ZHA, F. 340, l. 6
291 F	Gampopa	Coll. Works, 1st part, V. NGA, F. 80, l. 5
291 B	Gampopa	Coll. Works, 2nd part, V. KI, F. 449B, l. 1

Tib. Folio	*Quotation*	*Source*
292 F	Gampopa	Coll. Works, 1st part, V. NYA, F. 172, l. 7
294	Songs of Milarepa	Xylograph at Chitari Mon. in Kulu, F. 231
298 F	Śavari	DE, V. NGA, F. 14B, l. 2
298 F	Virūpa	DE, V. NGA, F. 14B, l. 6
301 F	Śavari	DE, V. NGA, F. 15B, l. 3
301 F	Virūpa	GM, F. 7B, l. 4
303 F	Śavari	DE, V. NGA, F. 16, l. 1
303 F	Virūpa	GM, F. 9, l. 2 & F. 10B, l. 1
305 B	Virūpa	GM, F. 8, l. 4
306 B	Gampopa	Coll. Works, V. PHA, F. 64, l. 2
307 F	Śavari	DE, V. NGA, F. 14B, l. 16
310 B	Taknyi	KNE (T), V. KA, F. 314B, l. 5
311 F	Taknyi	KNE (T), V. KA, F. 327B, l. 4
313 F	Gampopa	Coll. Works, V. CH'A, F. 18, l. 6
314 F	Taknyi	KNE (T), V. KA, F. 329, l. 5
316 B	Taknyi	KNE (T), V. KA, F. 329, l. 5
317 F	Gampopa	Coll. Works, V. CH'A, F. 5B, l. 2
318 B	Taknyi	KNE (T), V. KA, F. 319, l. 6
318 B	Sambhuti	KNE (T), V. GA, F. 285B, l. 2
319 F	Taknyi	KNE (T), V. KA, F. 329, l. 7
319 F	Saraha	DE, V. NGA, F. 8, l. 7
320 B	Jetsün Chenpo (Milarepa)	Songs of Milarepa, Chitari Mon. E, F. 26B, l. 1
320 B	Jetsün Chenpo (Milarepa)	Songs of Milarepa, Chitari Mon. E, F.22, l.1
323 F	Dorje Gur	KNE (T), V. KA, F. 394F, l. 2
329 B	Gampopa	Coll. Works, V. KI, F. 49B, l. 4
331 F	Laṅkāvatāra	KPE (S), V. DU, F. 95B, l. 1
331 B	Laṅkāvatāra	KPE (S), V. DU, F. 95B, l. 3
332 F	Laṅkāvatāra	KPE (S), V. DU, F. 95B, l. 6
332 B	Laṅkāvatāra	KPE (S), V. DU, F. 96, l. 7
333 F	Laṅkāvatāra	KPE (S), V. DU, F. 96, l. 2
333 F	Laṅkāvatāra	KPE (S), V. DU, F. 194, l. 5
334 F	Taknyi	KNE (T), V. KA, F. 320B, l. 4
334 F	Taknyi	KNE (T), V. KA, F. 313F, l. 3
334 B	Yanggönpa	Coll. Works of Yanggönpa, F. 123, l. 4
335 B	Gampopa	Coll. Works, 2nd Part, V. 'A, F. 54F, l. 3
340 F	Dhodüpa	KNE (S), V. KA, F. 210B, l. 7
343 B	Gampopa	Coll. Works, 2nd part, V. DZE, F. 324F, l. 2
345 F	Rinchen Trengwa	LEM, Pg. 61, l. 16
345 B	Gampopa	Coll. Works, V. PHA, F. 66F, l. 5

Tib. Folio	*Quotation*	*Source*
346 F	Bodhicaryāvatāra	NBE, Pg. 193
349 F	Yanggönpa	Coll. Works of Yanggönpa, F. 312B, l. 1
353 B	Gampopa	Coll. Works, V. 'A, F. 54, l. 5
353 B	Gampopa	Coll. Works, V. GA, F. 54, l. 3
353 B	Tsashe	RE, F. 1, l. 3
358 F	Gampopa	Coll. Works of Gampopa, V. DA, F. 241B, l. 7
358 F	Yanggönpa	Songs of Yanggönpa, F. 55, l. 6
363 B	Gomtsül	Coll. Works of Gampopa, V. WA, F. 31B, l. 3
363 B	Gampopa	Coll. Works of Gampopa, V. DA, F. 242F, l. 1
363 B	Yanggönpa	Songs of Yanggönpa, F. 56, l. 2
364 F	Dükhor & Sangdü	KNE (T), V. KA, F. 71B, l. 1
367 B	Gampopa	Coll. Works, V. DA, F, 242F, l. 1
368 F	Yanggönpa	Songs of Yanggönpa, F. 56, l. 4
369 B	Rinchen Trengwa	LEM, Pg. 61, l. 16
369 F	Chöjuk	NBE, F. 171
370 F	Gampopa	Coll. Works, V. PHA, F. 65B, l. 3
370 B	Gampopa	Coll. Works, V. PHA, F. 65B, l. 3
376 F	Lhamo Shishü	KNE (T), V. GA, F. 277F, l. 3